Reading to Learn in the Content Areas

SIXTH EDITION

Reading to Learn in the Content Areas

Judy S. Richardson
Virginia Commonwealth University

Raymond F. Morgan
Old Dominion University

Charlene E. Fleener
Old Dominion University

THOMSON

WADSWORTH

Australia • Brazil • Canada • Mexico • Singapore • Spain • United Kingdom • United States

Reading to Learn in the Content Areas, Sixth Edition

Judy S. Richardson, Raymond F. Morgan, Charlene E. Fleener

Publisher: Vicki Knight
Acquisitions Editor: Dan Alpert
Development Editor: Tangelique Williams
Assistant Editor: Jennifer Keever
Editorial Assistant: Larkin Page-Jacobs
Technology Project Manager: Barry Connolly
Marketing Manager: Terra Schulz
Marketing Assistant: Rebecca Weisman
Marketing Communications Manager: Tami Strang
Project Manager, Editorial Production: Paul Wells

Creative Director: Rob Hugel
Art Director: Maria Epes
Print Buyer: Lisa Claudeanos
Permissions Editor: Joohee Lee
Production Service: The Cooper Company
Copy Editor: Meg McDonald
Cover Designer: Yvo Riezebos
Cover Image: M. Thomsen / Masterfile
Compositor: Stratford Publishing Services
Printer: R.R.Donnelley/Crawfordsville

Thomson Higher Education
10 Davis Drive
Belmont, CA 94002-3098
USA

For more information about our products, contact us at:
Thomson Learning Academic Resource Center
1-800-423-0563

For permission to use material from this text or product, submit a request online
at **http://www.thomsonrights.com.**
Any additional questions about permissions can be submitted by e-mail to **thomsonrights@thomson.com.**

Library of Congress Control Number: 2005926411

Student Edition: ISBN 0-534-55338-9

To teachers who have inspired the readers and learners of the world. You have given a cherished gift.

Judy S. Richardson

This work is dedicated to Sue . . . companion, best friend, and loving wife.

Raymond F. Morgan

To my parents, Doyle and LaVerne
who lived and gave to me a spirit of joy, humor, excellence, and love for the people in my life and in the work that I do.

To Steve and our two children, Kirk and Paula, for providing unwavering support, patience, and love and to my grandson, Travis, a true source of inspiration and joy.

Charlene E. Fleener

Contents

CHAPTER 3

A Guide to Evaluation and Assessment for Content Teachers   69

CHAPTER 4

Technology in Today's Content Classrooms   103

CHAPTER 5

Moving Beyond the Traditional Textbook   122

Preparing Learners   164

CHAPTER 7

Assisting Comprehension and Reflecting on Learning   190

Study Skills   240

CHAPTER 9

Teaching Vocabulary   278

Writing to Learn in the Content Areas   328

CHAPTER 11

Cooperative Learning and Reading   374

CHAPTER 12

Engaging Students through Teaching in the Affective Domain   407

Preface

REFLECTIONS ON THE SIXTH EDITION

As we reflect on the launching of our sixth edition, we realize how proud we are to have written a text that has weathered five previous editions. We are pleased to have provided what many instructors, teachers, and prospective teachers found useful. Our basic approach to content reading instruction has remained unchanged but our knowledge of the field grows with each edition. We thank those of you who have weathered these editions with us, and welcome those of you new to our text. We hope you will find it to be just what you needed.

WHO SHOULD READ THIS BOOK?

This textbook is meant for anyone who wants to teach students to learn and think about subject matter. This book is for readers who have never studied about reading, as well as for those who have studied how students learn to read, but not how they read to learn and think in subject areas. This book demonstrates how teachers can use reading and writing as a vehicle for learning in any discipline.

WHY DID WE WRITE THIS BOOK?

As authors, we enjoy reading about new topics and ideas. Learning is a pleasure for us and we like to increase our knowledge. But we recognize that many do not think they enjoy reading and learning. This is often because their instruction in content areas was ineffective and the task of learning created a lasting, negative impression. We don't want learning to be dull or uncomfortable. We want to encourage curiosity, inquiry and investigation, the confidence to read and discover, and ultimately lifelong learning.

This is why we have been teachers and college professors for more than 30 years. We believe in what we teach. We realize that all serious learning must be put in perspective. We have ideas about how to share the joy of reading, thinking, and learning with students of all ages. We have ideas to share with you.

Teacher preparation has been criticized. Some say teachers are not able to teach their students to think critically or to teach students to complete complex tasks required to advance in college or the workplace. Some critics say teachers learn too much content, not enough methodology. Others critics say the opposite. Many critics say teachers have learned to teach content rather than to teach students the content.

This textbook represents an ongoing effort to find positive solutions to the criticisms just cited. We believe that, if teachers learn to follow a simple instructional framework and teach strategically by using activities that demonstrate how reading can be a tool for learning, many of our classroom problems can be alleviated.

SPECIAL FEATURES OF THIS TEXTBOOK

1. Reader involvement is important in this textbook. We believe that readers need to be prepared to read, need some assistance to understand, and need to be guided to reflect on their reading. So we ask readers to engage in all three stages as they read each chapter of this textbook. We are reader friendly: we introduce new terms first with a checklist, then within the text in boldface with explanation; we maintain informality to keep our readers comfortable and interested.

2. We take a balanced approach, a realistic and practical treatment of reading and methodology issues, theory, research, and historical perspective. We emphasize the effect of the past on the present.

3. We address teachers of primary through secondary grades. We look at reading in the classroom as a natural tool for learning, no matter what the grade level or content area. We provide examples that show how an activity can work at different levels and in different content areas.

4. We select one instructional framework, one that reflects current thought but is uniquely ours: PAR (Preparation / Assistance / Reflection). We explain it, compare it, and apply it throughout the book, and it is presented on the front endsheets as well. Readers will appreciate this consistency and our constant reference to the framework.

5. Our organization is considerate of our readers. You can expect to find a graphic organizer at the beginning—and sometimes at the end—of each chapter; the Prepare to Read section that starts each chapter builds reader background and provides objectives; a one-minute summary (for the streamlined reader) is always provided; and Assistance as well as Reflection activities provide chapter closure.

6. Visual literacy is featured in this textbook. We use many visuals because visual literacy is the first literacy. One important visual is the PAR Cross-Reference Guide on the endsheets at the back of the book, which identifies specific activities for different content areas and grade levels.

7. Our philosophy is that of reading and the other language arts working together. Just as students listen and discuss to learn, so do they read and write to learn. We integrate the communicative arts. When an activity is presented, we explore

with the reader how that activity facilitates/encourages discussion, reading, and writing.

8. Ours is a strategy-based approach. When readers learn about a new activity, they should understand that activity as a strategic means to aid learning. We present the activity as a way to enhance instruction and help teachers see how this activity can be both an instructional strategy and a learner strategy.

9. Ours is a theory-based approach. When readers learn about a new activity, they should understand how it reflects sound instruction and why that is so.

10. This textbook contains several unique chapters. Chapter 2 demonstrates how to support diverse learners in the classroom, including at-risk, struggling and English Second Language learners. Chapter 3 helps teachers understand assessment and evaluation issues. Chapter 4 considers the import of electronic literacy in today's content classrooms. Chapter 8 on study skills and Chapter 11 on cooperative study provide more attention to study techniques than many content textbooks do. Chapter 12 discusses the affective domain of teaching, a topic crucial to learning but so often neglected. All chapters cover information on the cutting edge of content area instruction.

New to this Edition

We are glad to welcome Dr. Charlene Fleener to this edition. She has added a new perspective to our text. She has extensively revised Chapters 9 and 10, as well as provided excellent insight about other chapters, the Instructor's Manual, and activities.

This edition reflects the influence of technology on reading to learn and think through the accompanying CD-ROM, which includes many links to websites, examples of teachers using technology as they teach their content, suggestions for software, and much more. This edition emphasizes the use of technology throughout the text and in a new chapter devoted to electronic literacy. Both the CD and the text chapters describe the effective use of the Internet and computer technology in content teaching.

In this edition, we have updated all of the chapters from the fifth edition and added two new chapters. Chapter 1 presents three examples of the PAR Lesson Framework, from primary through secondary level, showing how technology and literature can be part of good content lessons. Chapter 5 presents the use of multiple resources for teaching that encourage teachers to move beyond the standard textbook. In this edition, Chapters 9 (vocabulary) and 10 (writing) have been extensively revised. The PAR framework is presented in Chapters 6 and 7 and demonstrated throughout the rest of the chapters.

Current research and professional resources have been incorporated in the revision. We have endeavored to maintain a theory-to-practice balance. Visuals continue to play an important part in expressing our ideas: cartoons, diagrams, and examples are provided throughout. All chapters have been revised to include new ideas, activities, and references.

ORGANIZATION OF THIS BOOK

The first four chapters are foundational. Chapter 1 discusses research and principles of content area instruction. In it you will discover our philosophy of teaching. It also presents a capsule view of the PAR framework for instruction and how it works in three different types of classrooms. Chapter 2 explains how to provide for diverse learners. Chapter 3 considers the role of assessment and evaluation as it influences classroom teachers. Chapter 4 leads teachers into ways to use technology in their content teaching. Chapter 5 presents the importance of learning with multiple resources rather than reliance on only a textbook.

Chapters 6 and 7 are PAR Lesson Framework chapters. Chapter 6 demonstrates how to determine reader background and prepare readers to study content material. Chapter 7 is an assistance chapter, demonstrating why and how to provide an appropriate instructional context to develop comprehension and also considers the role of reflection that stresses how to help readers think critically about, extend, and demonstrate their knowledge of their reading.

Chapters 8 through 11 demonstrate how PAR works. We show how vocabulary, writing, study skills, and cooperative learning can be used at all phases of the PAR framework. Chapter 12 discusses the affective domain of teaching, a topic crucial to learning but so often neglected.

INSTRUCTOR'S MANUAL

The Instructor's Manual summarizes each chapter's main points, theories, and strategies, and also provides test questions. With it, instructors will be able to assign group activities for their classes; assign individual activities to students for homework; guide their students in analyzing content area reading material; select test items for multiple choice, true/false, and essay tests; and display the authors' graphic organizers and vocabulary inventories for each chapter.

Section I explains the features of the Instructor's Manual. Section II contains recommendations about grouping. Section III contains preparation, assistance, and reflection activities; teaching tips on how to use the activities; and other resources that may be used in class, such as quotes, suggestions for further reading, book lists, graphic organizers, vocabulary inventories for each chapter, and test items.

In Section IV the authors provide possible assignments for the course, such as guides to analyze a chapter in a content area textbook.

CD-ROM

Our sixth edition includes a CD-ROM for the second time. We reflect the influence of technology on reading to learn and think through this CD, which includes many links to sites, examples of teachers using technology as they teach their content, suggestions for software, video that demonstrates content reading in action, and exercises that can be completed using Wadsworth's free subscription (included with the textbook) to InfoTrac® College Edition. The entire edition emphasizes the use of technology in content teaching. At the end of each chapter, and within the Instructor's Manual, suggested electronic literacy activities are provided.

ACKNOWLEDGMENTS

We extend thanks to the colleagues who encouraged us, and aided and abetted us, in this endeavor. We appreciate the comments of our students who used the fifth edition of the textbook and provided useful suggestions.

We acknowledge gratefully the contributions of the reviewers, who gave us such excellent suggestions throughout the writing of this textbook: Rosa Casarez-Levison, San Francisco State University; Jacquelyn Culpepper, Mercer University; Nancy Hadaway, University of Texas at Arlington; James Johnston, Central Connecticut State University; Andrea Smith, Western Michigan University; Gary Smithey, Henderson State University.

Our writing was a more pleasant experience because of the support and kind assistance of our editor, Dan Alpert, and editorial assistant, Larkin Page-Jacobs. We also thank Paul Wells and our production managers, Barry Connolly, Technology Project Manager, and Marketing Managers Dory Schaeffer and Terra Schultz for their thoughtful guidance and hard work: it makes a difference!

CHAPTER 1

If the only tool you have is a hammer, you tend to treat everything as if it were a nail.

A. MASLOW

Content Teachers and Content Literacy

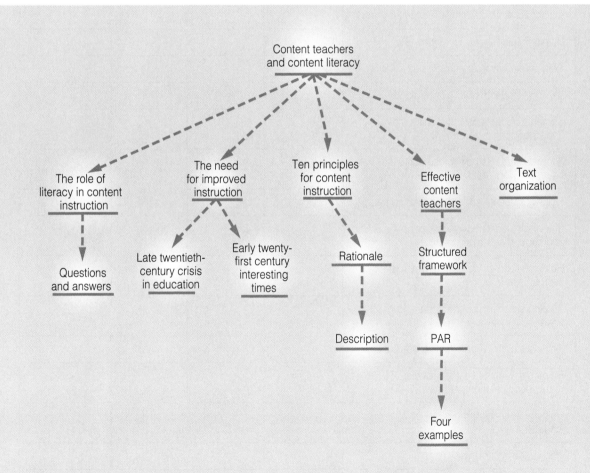

PREPARING TO READ

1. How do you currently help your students discuss, read, and write about the content they study for deep understanding? First, make a list of all the ways you guide your students. Now consider the following list of several research-based strategies and activities; select the ones you already use and how effectively you think you use each one.

   Rate yourself as *highly effective, moderately effective, ineffective,* or *don't know this strategy.*

Strategy	Highly Effective	Moderately Effective	Ineffective	Don't Know This Strategy
Using writing to learn				
Using discussion to learn				
Asking students to think about what they already know about a topic before they learn				
Helping students preview before they read				
Helping students set purposes for reading				
Showing students how to think aloud				
Showing students how to monitor their understanding				
Showing students how to use context to figure out word meanings				
Helping students adjust their reading pace				
Showing students how to find main ideas and supporting details				
Helping students identify the way material is organized				
Helping students use the visual and graphic clues in material				
Helping students find effective ways to study				
Helping students find effective ways to remember what they read				
Helping students demonstrate what they learned				
Add your own strategy:				
Add your own strategy:				

By engaging learners using research-based strategies, teachers give students the support they need to try out, practice, and become strategic and proficient in learning.

2. Following is a list of terms used in this chapter. Some may be familiar to you in a general context, but in this chapter they may be used in unfamiliar ways. Rate your knowledge by placing a plus sign (+) in front of those you are certain you know, a check mark (✓) in front of those you have some knowledge about, and a zero (0) in front of those you don't know. Be ready to locate them in the chapter, and pay special attention to their meanings.

_____ assumptive teaching
_____ communicative arts (language arts)
_____ visual literacy
_____ technological literacy
_____ dependent learners
_____ fading
_____ autonomous learners
_____ strategic learning
_____ incomplete thinking
_____ fix-up strategies
_____ PAR Lesson Framework
_____ preparation step
_____ assistance step
_____ reflection step

OBJECTIVES

As you read this chapter, focus your attention on the following purposes. You will

1. learn some recent history about research and views of education.

2. understand why there is a need to improve instruction in schools today.

3. become acquainted with 10 principles for content reading instruction and understand the importance of each.

4. understand the use of the PAR Lesson Framework.

5. learn the characteristics of an effective teacher.

6. learn why it is important to use a lesson framework when teaching.

7. become acquainted with the steps in the PAR Lesson Framework.

8. read examples of the PAR Framework used at the primary, elementary, middle, and high school levels.

9. learn how this textbook is organized.

WHAT IS THE ROLE OF LITERACY IN CONTENT CLASSROOMS?

 Many teachers wonder why they should complete a course in content reading instruction. After all, when teaching content, they are not teaching reading—or are they? Consider the following questions and answers, and then read more about the role of literacy in content classrooms.

Question:

Why should teachers of subjects such as mathematics, social studies, science, English, foreign language, vocational education, art, music, or physical education even think about using reading and writing as a means to learning? Isn't that the job of the language arts or reading teacher?

Response:

Reading and writing are the main tools for learning any subject. They help us learn how to learn. So these tools must be used in every classroom, at every grade level, and in every school to provide the application and practice necessary for students to become effective learners.

Question:

What exactly is reading to learn? Is that like teaching students how to read with phonics and decoding?

Response:

No, we recognize that content teachers teach a subject, not how to read. But within your subject, students will encounter many new words, or words used in new ways in your subject area. They will have to read with understanding and study effectively to learn your subject. Those skills—vocabulary, comprehension, and study skills—are the ones we introduce in this textbook.

Question:

Why should content teachers change their instructional practices?

Response:

In the past several years, public comment, research, and assessment results have led to concern over and criticism of our educational system. Some criticism states that students are not learning important factual information, are unable to think critically, and cannot apply skills in the real world of work and college. This textbook helps teachers and administrators find positive, effective solutions to these criticisms.

Question:

How difficult is it to implement the content of this textbook in my instruction?

Response:

We present a simple instructional framework in this first chapter, then guide you in applying it as you learn about practical strategies you can use in your classroom almost immediately.

NEED FOR IMPROVED INSTRUCTION

During the twentieth century, many politicians and educators wrote about a crisis in education. They cited evidence that achievement levels were declining in our nation's schools. Test results on the National Assessment of Educational Progress (NAEP) had fluctuated only slightly; this is still true, although some gains are being made as the twenty-first century begins. Over the past 35 years, national results (National Center for Educational Statistics, 2003) for fourth and eighth graders have shown a decline (although this decline was slight from 2002 to 2003); however, higher percentages of fourth and eighth graders have performed at or above proficient levels compared with 1992 scores. But only 31 percent of fourth graders and only 32 percent of eighth graders attained a "proficient" level—a standard that test officials say all students should reach. Thirty-seven percent of fourth graders and 26 percent of eighth graders did not achieve a basic level of reading proficiency, according to the NAEP 2003 report. Although NAEP results show schools are performing well in teaching fundamental language arts, problems continue in teaching advanced reading and writing skills.

A number of reports and books have portrayed U.S. schools as being in crisis, questioning the practices and core beliefs of our entire educational system (Bloom, 1987; Hirsch, 1987). Several of these reports (Kirsch & Jungeblut, 1986; Miklos, 1982), published within a few years of one another, indicate that students experience difficulty with higher-level reading and writing skills such as critical thinking, drawing inferences, and applying what is read. Applebee, Langer, and Mullis, in *Learning to Be Literate in America* (1987) maintain that students have difficulty because schools are not teaching students to learn how to learn. Hynd (1999) recommends, as a result of her study of adolescent reading behaviors when using multiple texts in history, that "students should be taught that texts are to be read critically" (p. 435). Some researchers (Ralph, Keller, & Crouse, 1994) say that until schools emphasize problem solving, critical thinking, and language development, achievement levels probably will not climb appreciably.

Many educators and policymakers are now moving to a more positive stance, trying to identify how we can improve. David Berliner (2001), a prominent psychologist interested in education, maintains that posturing about poor schools and instruction has wasted money, harmed already effective school programs, and added to the declining morale among teachers. Berliner challenges many widely held beliefs about schools. He says that schools are not nearly as bad as many reports claim and further asserts that schools are doing as good a job of educating our youth as has ever been done in our history. He feels the educational system produces good results in most instances. According to Berliner, problems that exist result from poverty, dysfunctional families, and poor health care. A growing number of researchers (Bracey, 1997; McQuillan, 1998; Whittington, 1991) agree with Berliner that children in the United States are reading as well now as they did in past generations, and maybe even better. Godwin and Sheard (2001) provide a history of some of the policymaking interventions, such as vouchers and national testing, and speculations as to what may come from these initiatives. Glickman (2004) describes several ways we can move forward with best educational practices such as championing public education; providing policymakers with concrete focus; encouraging and empowering communities and schools; redefining education acts at the federal level; and regaining confidence in pedagogy. Chi (2004), as editor of *Spectrum,* a publication of the Council of State Governments, presents three different perspectives of the recent federal No Child Left Behind Act, to encourage forward movement with the best suggestions for educational initiatives.

The twenty-first century has been called the "Information Age" (Frand, 2000). Pedagogy has subsequently undergone radical change in the past several years. We are in an age of technological innovation (Kleiner & Lewis, 2003), accountability (Johnson & Johnson, 2002; Stewart, 2004), high-stakes testing (Afflerbach, 2002; Worthy & Hoffman, 2000), and standards for learning (Valencia & Wixson, 1999). These innovations and issues cross school divisions, states, and nations. Literacy has gained a level of attention far greater than in past generations. It is no longer enough to focus on literacy at only the beginning reader level or in just the elementary school. Educators recognize that literacy permeates learning at all ages and in every classroom.

Questions and concerns remain, though, as we forge ahead. The adoption of state and national standards may create too much emphasis on testing and not enough on learning content (Berube, 2004). Emphasis on the "new" literacy, specifically technology, may alter teacher training for better or worse (Henderson & Scheffler, 2004). As Boyd (2004, p. 105) expresses this new direction, "we are living in what the Chinese call 'interesting times.' Already facing difficult times, public education—and the arts as well—are in real danger of a confluence of forces that could form a 'perfect storm.'"

The bottom line resulting from these many concerns is that teachers need more exposure to information and training that will enable them to teach higher levels of language and literacy. But often teachers do not have this exposure, even though they expect students in their classes to be fluent in processing reading material, making inferences, and reading critically. They assume that students will be able to express their understanding of the material orally and on tests. They expect that students possess a certain amount of knowledge and have a desire to read to learn. This is **assumptive teaching,** described later in this chapter as Principle 7. Such assumptive teaching creates a difficult instructional dilemma.

TEN PRINCIPLES FOR CONTENT READING INSTRUCTION

An obvious first step in these new expectations is to encourage teachers to teach language and literacy in content area instruction. To accomplish this, teachers must have principles to follow. In this section we present 10 guiding principles for facilitating reading to learn. Teachers who can articulate their beliefs about teaching are in a good position to improve their instruction. Like all learners, teachers will alter their approaches if they see a need to do so. We altered our own instruction based on current research; to clarify our thinking, we encapsulated our approach in 10 principles. By sharing these principles with teachers and demonstrating how they relate to content area teaching, we hope to influence teachers to consider instructional changes in their own classrooms.

These principles are grounded in theory and supported by research. Many teachers think that theory has nothing to do with the classroom, perhaps because theory has been presented to them in isolation from its application. But we believe that when teachers ask for "what works," they are also asking why a particular technique works, so they can replicate it in optimal circumstances. Teachers know that imposing an activity on students in the wrong circumstances can produce a teaching disaster. No activity has much merit aside from the construct underlying it (Hayes, Stahl, & Simpson, 1991). Teachers want theory that makes sense because it explains why some activities work well at a particular time in the course of instruction. The 10 principles presented here link the theoretical with good practice in content area instruction.

1. Reading is influenced by the reader's personal store of experience and knowledge.   Successful reading depends on numerous factors. The reader's store of knowledge and experience certainly contributes, as well as the reader's attitude toward reading. Even though many people may share the same experience, read the same book, or hear the same lecture, the thinking and learning that occur differ from individual to individual because of what each person brings to the experience. People relate to a common body of knowledge in different ways because of what they already know—or don't know. Thus, for example, converting to the metric system will probably be especially difficult for learners who were taught measurements in inches, feet, and miles. Understanding conflicts in another nation can be difficult when learners do not know the life, climate, geography, and history of that nation. If learners cannot find relevance in a subject, they are likely to ignore it. Teachers, then, must become aware of what previous knowledge and experiences their students possess about a particular concept in content subjects.

2. The communicative arts foster thinking and learning in content subjects. The traditional **communicative arts,** or **language arts,** are listening, speaking, reading, writing, and visual literacy. Kellogg (1972) describes the communicative arts as blocks that build on one another. One cannot use one communicative art without also using another. This integration occurs with greater facility as children practice each literacy skill. Yet school environments are often artificial rather than natural in their application of informative communication. Usually, teachers talk and students listen so much of the time that little response and interaction can take place. In reviewing the 51 articles on content reading published in *The Reading Teacher* from 1969 to 1991, Armbruster (1992) noted the "emphasis on the importance of integrating writing and reading in content instruction." It is our premise that students can learn better if they spend more time practicing all the language arts in their content subjects. Subject matter and language are inextricably bound.

But the main concern for the subject-matter teacher is teaching content. In 1965, Nila Banton Smith reminded readers that the term *primer* did not originally mean "first book to read," as it does today, but referred to the contents of a book as being primary, or foremost. Today the content of a subject is still primary for teachers, as it should be. But using the communicative arts as a learning tool creates a positive combination for enhancing critical thinking and learning. For example, Richardson (2004) describes several successful content lessons designed by content teachers that incorporate language arts and technology. The communicative arts are essential to teaching content area subjects, and teachers want to encourage students' use of all the communicative arts as effective thinking and learning tools. As we present activities in this book, we often identify how they facilitate the use of language to enhance content learning. The role of writing, in particular, is discussed in Chapter 10.

3. Literacy includes not only the traditional communicative arts but also visual literacy.   Sometimes communication occurs most easily through nonverbal, visual literacy. For instance, a picture of a pie divided into pieces may convey the concept of fractions more effectively than a page of explanation. Sinatra (1986) calls **visual literacy** the first and most pervasive literacy. Sinatra's model of literacy development suggests the interactive relationship of visual literacy with the oral and written literacies (see Figure 1.1).

Visual literacy conveys emotion through such means as illustration and art. Visual literary precedes listening and helps build experiences necessary to thinking and learning. It is action oriented; the scribbles that young children call writing are a manifestation of visual literacy. Teachers know that when they use visual aids such as graphs, charts, and pictures, they ensure and reinforce learning for many students. An alternative approach is offered for those who excel in visual but not traditional literacy. Because visual literacy has implications for the affective aspects of instruction, it is discussed further in Chapter 12. Many activities presented in this book capitalize on visual literacy.

4. Reading should be a rewarding experience.   Reading in content subjects should be satisfying. People avoid doing what is not interesting or rewarding in some personal way. Students avoid reading in content subjects they find boring. When left to their own devices, children often select content (nonfiction) books to read just as readily as fiction. We have noticed that younger children are even more likely to read for information than are older ones. If teachers can help by providing a beneficial reading environment in content subjects, learning will improve. Because this principle is so important, we devote an entire chapter (Chapter 12) to the affective dimension of reading in the content areas.

Pleasurable feelings about reading will lead to successful reading and to more reading. Taylor, Frye, and Maruyama (1990) documented that the amount of time students spend reading at school contributes significantly to their level of achievement. The more students observe teachers and parents reading, the more they will want to try it. The more students hear parents and teachers read to them, the more they will want to try it. Teachers would like to teach students who have good reading habits. This does not happen just because teachers tell, or even implore, students to read. However, it does happen through modeling. Morrison, Jacobs, and Swinyard

FIGURE 1.1

Stage Three of Literacy Development: Visual Literacy and Its Interactive Relationship with the Oral and Written Languages

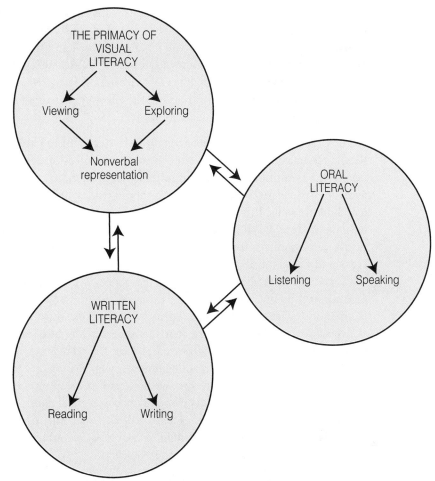

From R. Sinatra, *Visual Literacy Connections to Thinking, Reading, and Writing,* 1986. Courtesy of Charles C. Thomas, Publisher, Springfield, Illinois.

(1999) documented that teachers who read are better able to motivate students to read. Modeling takes place when teachers share a newspaper article on the content subject or a book they have read that relates to the topic at hand. Modeling is a form of visual literacy. When teachers model reading visually, they are using one communicative art to promote another. We believe that teachers need to model use of all the strategies we describe in this textbook. Morrison and colleagues (1999) found that teachers who read for personal pleasure report using recommended literacy practices in their classrooms significantly more often than do teachers who report less personal reading.

Good readers read because it gives them pleasure and they do it well; consequently, they get practice in reading and become better at it. In a series of questionnaires we administered for four years to incoming college students, we found a consistent correlation between those who chose not to read and those who perceived that they had poor reading and study habits. This confirms the notion that readers tend to avoid reading if it is not easy, pleasurable, or satisfying. Many poor readers get so discouraged that they lose the will or desire to read and thus to succeed. In these cases, teachers need to give more attention to bolstering students' will to learn (Fleener et al., 2000). Improving the will to learn is called *conation* and is discussed in Chapter 12. It is an important variable in the affective domain of learning, along with attitude, self-concept, feelings, and emotions.

5. The practice of critical reading enables better thinking and learning to occur.
Reading is an active, thinking-related process. As soon as readers can pay more attention to the meaning of words than to their recognition, they can begin to think and learn about the material itself rather than about reading it. Yet students often lack critical thinking skills. It is not that students are incapable of critical thinking; they just have not had the practice. In the earlier section about the need for improved instruction, several studies were mentioned that support this principle. By using tools of literacy and being immersed in a thinking climate, students can practice these skills. Raths and associates (1986) believe that teachers who provide students with extensive practice in thinking will train better thinkers. When exercises ask students only for factual comprehension, thinking deficits will occur (Wassermann, 1987).

Special note: We recognize that literal reading is often a necessary first step toward critical reading. Although we emphasize critical reading, we are not disregarding the importance of factual reading. A reader who already understands material at a factual level and is able to interpret what is read can respond critically with greater success. However, many students who are unable to recall names or dates can predict and infer. It is probably because teachers realize the necessity of literal reading that so much classroom time is spent on literal recall of reading material, to the detriment of higher-level thinking and reading comprehension.

6. Meaningful reading should start early and continue throughout life.　From the first grade on, learning content material is part of most school curricula. Some schools even introduce science, math, and social studies material in kindergarten. The *Weekly Reader,* that ubiquitous early-grades newspaper, contains content material. Because most children are still learning to read in the early grades, reading to learn may not be employed as often as visualizing, listening, and speaking to learn. However, both reading and writing to learn are being advocated more frequently for children in the early grades. By the same reasoning, learning about content subjects continues far beyond high school. Content information bombards learners daily as they listen to radio and watch television, read the newspaper, and surf the Internet on their computers. The basic difference here is that the learner can structure the environment and choose what to learn and what to avoid. The adults whom teachers meet daily will attest that they continue to enjoy and learn about topics that interested them in school. Sturtevant and Linek (2003) found that nine outstanding teachers who successfully blend literacy and content have the following attributes in common: strong beliefs in meeting students' needs, value for interpersonal relationships, and commitment to lifelong learning. We develop lifelong learners by introducing them to reading for learning at an early age.

7. Teachers need to refrain from assumptive teaching.   Herber (1978) used the term *assumptive teaching* to describe what teachers do when they unconsciously take for granted that students know how to read and to learn and have the motivation and interest to do so. Teachers may picture all students as having plenty of reading resources and supportive home environments. Unfortunately, these assumptions are not always true. Some assumptive teaching is necessary. Teachers cannot "start all over again" every year in a content subject. They may need to assume that a particular skill or concept was covered the year before. Yet if a teacher assumes too much about a student's knowledge or frame of mind, the teacher can act as if what is being taught is already known. Finding the point of familiarity with a concept and guiding the students forward is crucial. Content area teachers should be certain about what they are assuming their students already know. By learning to determine and build students' background, teachers can avoid assumptive teaching.

8. All students, no matter at what level of literacy or learning challenges, deserve instruction in content subjects that enables them to learn.   The "average" student is an elusive creature. Teachers teach students who are gifted, learning disabled, or physically disabled; who speak English as a second language, struggle with reading, or are at risk of failure, to list just a few heterogeneous students. All students in content classrooms deserve instruction that helps them to learn. Chapter 2 describes many of these students and suggests how to instruct them in meaningful ways within the content classroom.

9. Teachers should use the literacy "tools" that enable students to learn content material strategically.   Teachers need knowledge and skills—new tools, according to Maslow—that match this new age. Yet some teachers have only one tool: the lecture. That is simply not adequate. Teachers must incorporate the full spectrum of the language arts into their instruction: discussion, which combines listening and speaking; reading; and writing. Research in the past two decades shows us that the most effective, long-lasting learning occurs when learners of any age are active in the process and think and evaluate their learning. Therefore, teachers need to know how to engage their students in literacy activities that motivate them to learn (Gambrell 1996; Guthrie 2000, 2004.) While many of *us* sat through classes in elementary, middle, and high school and college in which the teacher only had one tool—the lecture—students today expect more.

For instance, **technological literacy**—that is, learning to become more proficient in using emerging technology—is one new tool. Ample evidence indicates that technology is changing how people function in society (Anderson & Lee, 1995). Emerging and increasingly sophisticated technologies have become so interwoven with every aspect of our daily lives that we do not always comprehend their pervasiveness. Computers are common in the workplace, and their use in homes is growing. A strong argument can be made to increase the use of computer technology in the schools to ensure that students are adequately prepared for the future (Reinking, 1997). Although computers are one of the greatest technological innovations, fax machines, cellular phones, ATM machines, voice mail, CDs/DVDs, and satellite dishes are other relatively new tools that we now take for granted. In this text, whenever possible we show technological applications in content area instruction activities. Technological literacy is an important, pervasive form of literacy that teachers need to emphasize to students; it is discussed further in Chapter 4.

10. Content reading instruction enables students to become autonomous learners. **Dependent learners** wait for the teacher to tell them what a word is, what the right answer is, and what to do next. Such learners are crippled intellectually. When they need to function independently, they will not know how. Teachers who abandon the textbook because it seems too hard for their students do their students no favor. Teachers who give students all the answers or hand out the notes already organized in the teacher's style bypass opportunities for students to learn how to find answers or take notes. High school can become a place where students avoid responsibility, and schools can perpetuate an environment in which students are excused from learning. The goal of teaching is to take students from depending on the teacher to being independent in their learning habits. We call this "making students autonomous learners." But it is not fair to expect that students can become autonomous in thinking and learning without the benefit of instruction. No matter what the grade level or subject area, teachers can assist students in this transfer of responsibility when they balance the students' level of proficiency and the content to be studied.

One way to describe this change from dependence to independence is **fading** (Moore et al., 1998). Singer and Donlan (1985) have called it "phasing out the teacher and phasing in the student." Armbruster (1992) identified as a trend in content reading the "need to foster independent learners" (p. 166). To become independent learners, students need to practice a study system to make learning easier. The PAR Lesson Framework, explained in this chapter and used as the basis for this textbook, is a system that enables the teacher to show students how to become autonomous learners. The teacher first models PAR, then gradually weans students to independent use of PAR. The four examples presented later in this chapter illustrate such independent learning.

EFFECTIVE CONTENT TEACHERS

Students at all levels need excellent teachers to guide and facilitate their learning. Because the learning process is complex and subtle, students can lack competence and confidence to learn. At such times students need a teacher who is able to impart both content and the desire and willingness to learn. What constitutes effective teaching? And will principals, supervisors, and, especially, students value and appreciate the instruction? Good teachers continually explore and learn in an ongoing effort to facilitate student learning. They make their classes relevant by keeping current through their own reading. They provide discussions and activities that link students to the larger outside world. And although they might not be appreciated to the fullest in the short term, they obtain great satisfaction in knowing that their students were challenged to think in an atmosphere conducive to learning.

Effective teachers never just tell students what they need to know to succeed in a course. Telling is not enough. They do not view students as "empty vessels" to fill with knowledge bit by bit each day. Also, effective teachers do not simply assign new chapters or other lengthy readings for homework and expect students to be able to discuss them in class the next day. Good teachers use appropriate and effective tools to teach, including strategic instruction, relevant activities, and literacy engagement.

Good teachers often inspire students to think for themselves in deciding how to solve problems, attack reading selections, and evaluate what they are reading. Inspired instruction helps students to become **autonomous learners**—individuals who are independent in their learning habits. Rosemary Altea in *The Eagle and the Rose* (1995) best captured the role of a teacher when she spoke affectionately of her mentor:

> Part of his role as my guide is to teach me to teach myself, so when I ask my question of him, his answer is usually, "What do you think?" He can, and often does, help me to discover answers, like all good teachers; and like all good teachers, he is always there to listen, to encourage, and to steer me gently along my path (p. 74).

Teachers provide inspired instruction when they guide students by showing them how to learn **strategically**—that is, by using the most efficient and effective ways to suit the learning situation.

Despite the best efforts of teachers, students sometimes misinterpret text in reading. When they do so, they are demonstrating **incomplete thinking.** Students manifest this behavior in a number of ways, such as when they skip important steps in the lesson. The student who has trouble identifying all the steps and who tends to skip steps will have to slow down and rediscover them, or else study will grind to a halt. Such students have no **fix-up strategies** (explained further in Chapter 2)—special intervention strategies that good readers have to aid in comprehension when they are confused by the reading material.

Edward de Bono (1976) has called this shortcutting of steps *two-finger thinking.* According to de Bono, two-finger thinking is analogous to two-finger piano playing. A person who plays the piano with only two fingers uses fewer resources than could be used, which is fine for playing "Chopsticks" but not suitable for Chopin! In the same way, two-finger thinking uses only part of the brain to perceive and comprehend important reading material. Inadequate use of resources can cause trouble when complex learning skills are required. For instance, two-finger thinking may work on an easy math word problem, but a difficult one will stump the same reader.

Effective teachers give students both the content of instruction and, at the same time, all the steps students need for effective thinking and study. Such teachers realize that there is no shortcut to learning and understand the need to provide students reading and writing strategies to help them overcome incomplete thinking. In this text we describe many strategies for training students in reading and thinking. However, the initial step for any teacher is acceptance and use of a framework of instruction as a way to improve learning.

The Importance of Structure through a Lesson Framework

 Many mental operations are necessary in reading. For instance, one must sort out relevant from irrelevant information. In addition, readers must be able to summarize information, draw inferences from the text, generate their own questions to be answered in the reading, and monitor their comprehension as they read (Dole et al., 1991; Guthrie, 2004). Students who do not think well—that is, do not adequately perform these mental operations in reading—get great benefit from a well-prepared teacher's structured guidance in learning to better "think through" a lesson. Conversely, students who are poor thinkers cannot afford to be in unstructured classrooms with haphazard teaching. Poor readers, then, need repetition and structure to learn better habits of thinking and reading. This is what a lesson framework provides.

A *framework* is the structure around which anything is stretched. It is the systematic arrangement of the basic parts of something. Further, it can represent an organized plan condensed to a series of steps, usually represented by key words. Such a framework becomes a model for finishing a task. It must be complete and clearly explain all parts of the task.

The framework becomes an aid to learning and a way to activate students to learn. An instructional framework that identifies successful components of a content lesson facilitates the relationship among reading, thinking, and learning. Frameworks for content reading instruction are historically grounded (Herber, 1978; Singer & Donlan, 1985; Vaughan & Estes, 1986) and formulate instruction in a complete and structured way. The most popular content reading frameworks include three basic assumptions:

1. The learner must be ready to learn—thus the teacher must prepare the learner beforehand.

2. The learner must be guided through the learning so that comprehension can be developed during the lesson.

3. The learner should review what has been learned. As part of this third step, the teacher must provide after-reading opportunities to help students retain the learning.

If these basic steps are repeated consistently in the instructional sequence, the learner begins to use them independently. It does not matter what key words are used in a framework, as long as they stimulate recall of the steps incorporated in the framework and help teachers adhere to the framework's structure.

PAR: A Lesson Framework for Instruction

 PAR stands for "preparation, assistance, and reflection." The **PAR Lesson Framework** is a framework for content reading instruction (see Figure 1.2). PAR is similar to other content instructional frameworks. We coined the acronym *PAR* to develop an associa-

FIGURE 1.2

The PAR
Lesson
Framework

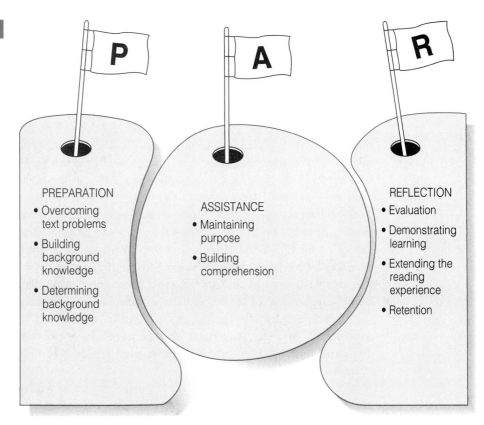

PREPARATION
- Overcoming text problems
- Building background knowledge
- Determining background knowledge

ASSISTANCE
- Maintaining purpose
- Building comprehension

REFLECTION
- Evaluation
- Demonstrating learning
- Extending the reading experience
- Retention

Developed by Dawn Watson and Walter Richards.

tion with the golf term *par,* which refers to the completion of a hole or holes by taking only the allotted number of strokes—not exceeding the limit. Golfers usually feel pleased when they achieve par for a course. Likewise, teachers who consistently use PAR as the underpinning of their instruction will be pleased because students will be more meaningfully engaged in their learning. As a by-product, discipline problems that grow from inattention and boredom will be greatly reduced. (Discipline problems cause most teacher burnout.)

In the **preparation step,** as noted in Figure 1.2, teachers need to consider text problems and student background of knowledge. Sometimes students have incorrect or insufficient background knowledge, which makes it difficult to begin reading. The teacher needs to choose preparation activities that will build a conceptual base of understanding for students and thereby enable them to be more successful in the reading. The preparation step helps motivate students to want to read. Put another way, the more preparation a teacher does with students, the more motivated they are going to be to study the topic.

Once motivation is heightened in the preparation step, the teacher moves to the **assistance step,** where an instructional context for the lesson is provided. This is the crucial step to help students better comprehend the passage. Often teachers prepare and motivate students but then tell them to read the passage on their own in class or for homework. Teachers fail to realize that students who think poorly do not have adequate study skills or do not think critically and need assistance as they read to maintain purpose and build comprehension. Comprehension will be improved if strategies are chosen for students to react to as they read. The strategies also help provide a concrete, clear purpose for completing the reading.

In the **reflection step,** teachers use the material that was read to provide extension, enrichment, and critical thinking opportunities. Careful reflection by students is not the same as answering questions either posed by the teacher or listed at the end of the chapter. True reflection occurs when students ask themselves tough questions such as "What did I learn from this reading?" "Was it appropriate for me?" "Do I believe what the author said?" "Is this reading material worth retaining?" When students truly reflect on a reading, they retain the material longer and at greater depth.

Using the PAR Lesson Framework improves a teacher's ability to both teach and monitor the reading comprehension of the student; however, each phase of PAR is also notable for distinct contributions to the learning environment. As we mentioned, careful preparation for reading enhances students' desire and motivation to learn. In the preparation phase the teacher gets students to *want* to read by awakening natural curiosity. We have seen students in classrooms become very interested in a topic that they cared nothing about before a teacher prepared them through the use of one or more strategies.

The assistance phase of PAR is the key area for teachers who need to improve students' reading comprehension. When a student is assisted while reading, purpose for the reading is established. It follows that comprehension is usually improved when students have a purpose for reading. Finally, using the reflection phase of PAR reinforces students' retention of concepts.

Although we recommend following all the phases of PAR to completion, teachers can emphasize the phase of PAR where their students are having the most difficulty. If students are not motivated, teachers need to prepare more for the lesson. If students are motivated but not comprehending, teachers need to emphasize the assistance phase. And if students are motivated and seem to comprehend the reading but fail to retain the material, then, of course, more emphasis needs to be placed on the reflection phase. Whichever phase is emphasized, the key for the teacher is to consistently model all the PAR steps with the understanding that students will, through such guided practice, significantly improve their reading.

The following sections present four examples of content-specific lessons that illustrate use of the PAR Framework. They provide a sense of how this simple structure can be used to improve any teacher's delivery of content. The PAR Framework can help both the novice teacher and the experienced teacher become more effective in the classroom.

FOUR LESSONS OF PAR USED IN TEACHING CONTENT

 To show that PAR easily accommodates any content area of instruction at any grade level, we chose four lessons—primary, elementary, middle, and high school—to illustrate its adaptable nature. All four teachers in these examples use the same framework to lead their learners in a structured and well-paced lesson before, during, and after reading about the assigned subject. These examples provide only an overview; directions for constructing their activities are given in succeeding chapters, where the activities are presented in a larger context. The examples demonstrate how literature, technology, and language arts can be incorporated into content lessons. They help address the recent concerns in our country about the reading achievement levels of students at all ages and grade levels.

Example from a Primary Social Studies Lesson

Alex Seely, a first grade teacher, incorporated literature into her lesson about school and classroom rules. The lesson would be taught at the beginning of the school year, when first graders are beginning to understand school and classroom expectations, as well as how to be good citizens. She chose the book *David Goes to School* (David Shannon, Blue Sky Press, New York, 1999). It is about a boy who is in school but does not seem to understand the rules. The book is funny and silly, but at the same time it makes the students think about the poor choices David is making and how his choices impact everyone around him, as well as himself. The lesson is intended to coordinate with Virginia Standards of Learning (SOLs) for first grade civics:

The student will apply the traits of a good citizen by

- focusing on fair play, exhibiting good sportsmanship, helping others, and treating others with respect.
- recognizing the purpose of rules and practicing self-control.
- working hard in school.
- taking responsibility for one's own actions; valuing honesty and truthfulness in oneself and others.

It also coordinates with the Virginia SOLs for first grade English:

- The student will continue to expand and use listening and speaking vocabularies.
- The student will use meaning clues and language structure to expand vocabulary when reading.

To *prepare* her students, she would present this lesson after several days of discussing the rules. In order to highlight literacy, she would read the title and author of the book and show children the cover art. Asking students to predict what the book might be about would promote discussion and engagement in the reading experience.

The children would look at the pictures in the book (*picture walk*) to further predict David's school experience. During this prereading strategy, the children would be demonstrating their prior knowledge of rules.

To *assist* her students, the teacher would read the story. She would construct a cause–effect chart on the board to note what David does and how it affects him and the other children (see Activity 1.1). Then the class would discuss what would happen if David were in their class, and how his behaviors would make the children feel. Also, they would comment on how David should act.

Next the teacher would write (on a chart, chalkboard, or computer screen) the rule that goes along with what David did wrong. Then she would ask the children to present other rules that would benefit the class. With each rule they would be asked to explain why it is necessary. The children might even role-play some of these good and bad behaviors.

To help children *reflect,* she would give the children pieces of drawing paper, folded in half. On one side they would draw a sad face at the top, and underneath a picture of David breaking a school rule. On the other side of the paper, they would draw a happy face and a picture of David following the rule he was breaking. Under each picture drawn they would write a sentence about the picture. (If a software program such as *Inspiration* and computers were available, the lesson could incorporate technology as another learning tool.) Afterward they would share their pictures and make a class book to take home and share with their families. The teacher would include in the book a letter to the parents about the making of the book, and the direction to please read the book carefully with their children to review the rules.

This lesson for young children is about a content subject and uses material that meets state standards for instruction. It also includes several literacy/reading-to-learn objectives and activities such as predicting, determining cause and effect, and using graphic organizers as it follows the PAR format.

Example from a Fourth Grade Science Class

Elisabeth Groninger designed a science lesson to help her fourth grade students understand scientific investigations and ecosystems. The class had just finished a unit on botany, so some of the groundwork for the concepts of food chains and food webs had been established. As a result, the students' vocabulary included words to be used within this lesson, such as *producer, photosynthesis, energy,* and *reproduction.* The lesson would fulfill the following standards of learning (SOLs) for Virginia schools:

INVESTIGATING SKILLS

These skills include, but are not limited to, "differentiate among simple observations, conclusions, and predictions, and concretely apply the terminology in oral and written work," "classify into basic categories to organize the data."

This subset also requires that students learn to "create a plausible hypothesis from a set of basic observations, stated in terms of cause and effect that can be tested."

INVESTIGATING ECOSYSTEMS

"Illustrate food webs in local area."

Cause	Effect	Rule
David did not wait his turn.	Other children had to wait longer.	Everyone gets a turn when we all wait for our turn.
David pushed another child.	Someone got hurt.	No pushing—respect each other.

"Differentiate between positive and negative influences of human activity on the ecosystem."

"Distinguish between structural and behavioral adaptations."

The lesson would also satisfy language arts objectives for oral presentations, vocabulary, and composition; study of nonfiction material; and usage mechanics.

The lesson used two sources of writing. The first selection, "Leopard, Goat, and Yam," is an African folktale found in the anthology *Favorite Folktales from Around the World* (Jane Yolen, ed. Pantheon Books, New York, 1986). The story is a riddle involving a man, two animals, and a vegetable. The riddle and its solution address the question of hierarchy on the food chain. Riddles are fun for all ages; although the answer to the riddle requires some advanced reasoning skills, with collaborative brainstorming and use of drawings to visually depict the possible solutions, the class could attempt the answer. Another appeal of this particular folktale was its African origin: a reminder that food chains are everywhere, each specific to its ecosystem.

The second selection was the book *Who Eats What? Food Chains and Food Webs* (Patricia Lauber, HarperCollins, New York, 1995). This text is bright, engaging, and to the point. It addresses the concept of food chains, food webs, and how animals, plants, and humans are linked ecologically. Although the selection is written more simply than a fourth grade text, the teacher saw that as an advantage. The book supplies basic information while capturing attention with bright colors, attractive illustrations, and information about different ecosystems. The text opens with a picture of a caterpillar munching a leaf from an apple tree—a beginning step on the food chain continuum. From there, the book continues along the food chain, ending with a boy having his meal.

For *preparation,* the teacher read the folktale "Leopard, Goat, and Yam" aloud. With the teacher's assistance, the class brainstormed about possible answers to this riddle. Because the story tells of the possibilities of the farmer's possessions being eaten if not supervised, the class could consider the components of a food chain and, as the second literature selection so succinctly says, "who eats what."

Once the riddle was solved (or the solution given and responses taken), the teacher *assisted* students by reading aloud the second selection, *Who Eats What? Food Chains and Food Webs.* After this was read, the teacher put large cards with the words for the unit on the front board. The concepts for these words had been introduced in the reading: *producer, prey, predator, herbivore, carnivore, omnivore, decompose, food chain,* and *food web.* The definitions of these words were discussed, with the aid of pictures to represent the various terms (such as a picture of a cow for *herbivore*), with the students contributing answers based on the information in the read-aloud and the clues from the pictures. The students were then given charts to fill out with the terms in the first column, definitions in the second column, and examples of each term in the third (see Activity 1.2). The terms were already listed for the students; the class completed the second column. The teacher asked for definitions from students as they filled out the second column, assisting when there was a question or confusion. The students filled out the third column (examples of each term) working in small groups of three or four. Once the charts were completed, the students participated in sharing and discussing their ideas for examples of each of the terms; this discussion also reviewed the meanings of each component of the food chain and food web.

The teacher gave each group a bag containing small cards with the lesson words on half of the cards and the definitions on the other half. The groups turned the cards face down and collaborated in playing "memory," helping each other to remember which explanations went with each word. This provided not only a fun way to review the words and collaborate about the meanings while playing a game, but also an opportunity for the teacher to evaluate how well the students grasped the vocabulary.

For *reflection*, a large piece of drawing paper was given to each student. The students were asked to choose a favorite meal, showing the parts of that meal across the top of the paper. They then drew and labeled the food chain leading to each final component. The teacher was available for advice and guidance; the students also consulted with each other as they thought about their projects. Copies of *Who Eats What?* were also available as reinforcement and for examples of food chain pictures. The teacher could evaluate how well the students understood the concepts in the lesson and could plan additional teaching and review, if necessary. The students then shared their drawings and conclusions for the food chains creating their meals. The papers were displayed around the room.

For additional reflection, the students were given the following questions to answer in writing for homework:

1. List some of the animals and plants that live in your neighborhood. Are the animals herbivores, carnivores, or omnivores?
2. What would happen if the sun were taken out of the food chain?
3. What would happen if the food chain lost a part of the chain (for instance, if all the plants died)?
4. What is the role of a producer in the food chain? Name one.
5. Why are carnivores important in the food chain?
6. Why are herbivores important in the food chain?
7. A hawk is bigger than a robin. Which do you think needs more energy to live?

Term	Definition	Example
Habitat	The environment in which an organism lives	A park, a field, a stream
Herbivore	An animal that eats only plants (producers)	A horse, a cow, a giraffe
Carnivore	An animal that eats only meat	A hawk, a wolf, a crocodile
Omnivore	An animal that eats both plants and meat	Humans, a raccoon
Predator	Eats prey	A hawk, a tiger

8. Make a list of everything you eat in one day. What other animals might eat each of these foods if they had a chance?

The teacher also supplied some interactive websites for the students to visit for fun.

Example from a Middle School Mathematics Lesson

Michael Tewksbury, a middle school mathematics teacher, designed a lesson to teach the difference between ratios and fractions. He had found that many students could not differentiate between what they had learned about fractions and ratios. However, from a practical and conceptual standpoint the two are quite different. In short, all ratios are fractions, but not all fractions are ratios. A ratio is a comparison between two quantities. A key developmental milestone is the ability of a student to begin to think of a ratio as a distinct entity, different from the two measures that make it up. Recalling a book he had read to his own five-year-old son, he selected it as the basis for this lesson (*If You Hopped Like a Frog,* David M. Schwartz, Scholastic Press, New York, 1999). This picture book highlights the amazing abilities of animals by showing what children could accomplish if they were capable of the speed, strength, and size of certain animals. Following the story, the book provides detailed proof of the outlandish claims found in the first 24 pages. These two aspects of the book make it an attractive preliminary instructional activity on ratios. For instance, "If you hopped like a frog . . . you could jump from home plate to first base in one mighty leap!"

The teacher *prepared* his students with a brief overview about ratios and the course of study for the unit, using a What-I-Know Activity (WIKA) about ratios. Students were asked to list what they already knew about ratios and what they needed to know. Their lists might be short, but could be reviewed later for follow-up and additions at the end of the lesson. The teacher also used this *preparation* to assess and build background knowledge. As the ratio lessons continued, the WIKA could be reviewed and updated.

After the WIKA activity, the teacher read *If You Hopped Like a Frog,* with student interaction as the story progressed. This helped to introduce important mathematical concepts, consistent with the following Virginia Standards of Learning (SOLs):

> The student will identify representations of a given percent and describe orally and in writing the equivalence relationships among fractions, decimals, and percents.

> The student will describe and compare two sets of data, using ratios, and will use appropriate notations, such as *a/b, a to b,* and *a:b.*

> The student will compare and order whole numbers, fractions, and decimals, using concrete materials, drawings or pictures, and mathematical symbols.

For *assistance,* students selected one of the comparisons made in the book and fact-stormed a number of ideas about how this comparison could be visually represented (numerically, graphically, or any way they chose). After this discussion, the teacher shared all 12 sets of actual ratio information detailed at the end of the book. Students incorporated this information into charts. Next students worked in groups of three to find and develop an original animal–personal comparison. To determine specific examples, students researched statistics and facts from one of several Internet sites (see Activity 1.3).

After their comparison and facts were identified, students designed visuals to represent their ratios and wrote an explanation of their representation and why they selected a particular representation method. When students had completed the written portion of this task, each group was asked to share their findings, explanations, and justifications as part of a class discussion. The teacher's primary objectives during this assistance activity were to assess student understanding, clarify misunderstandings, and maintain a focus of relevant discussion and build comprehension around the concepts of relationships and ratios. The process of focusing discussion and building comprehension was largely accomplished by providing divergent questions aimed at helping students develop a conceptual understanding of ratios.

For *reflection,* students returned the What-I-Know Activity as a review and preparation for the next lesson on ratios. The specific items reviewed included what they knew now, what they'd still like to know, and interesting and important concepts. This lesson is meant to help students independently formulate their own working conceptual framework and connections for ratios. The hope is that much of this will occur as a direct result of opportunities created for listening, reading, writing, and speaking.

Example from a High School Health/Physical Education Class

A ninth grade health and physical education class co-taught by James J. DiNardo III and Yogi Hightower Boothe began with students sitting in groups. The teachers frequently regrouped the students heterogeneously based on their reading ability. (The students were told only that the grouping was "randomly assigned," and they had no reason to question this because they could see no pattern to the groups.)

The *preparation* phase began immediately as the students entered the room. Students began the class even before the teachers told them to, by copying into two-

http://www.pbs.org/wnet/nature/critter.html	Fabulous site with a plethora of information specific to this lesson and other math activities
http://www.woburnsafari.co.uk/animalfacts.asp	Interesting and fun facts about 20 or so animals
http://nationalzoo.si.edu/default.cfm	A great source of information for this study of ratios and proportions

* For a direct link to updated sites, click on the web links option of Chapter 1 resources on our companion website.

column notes the three objectives for the day, written on the chalkboard. They were accustomed to starting each class this way, with no communication necessary from the teachers. Once this was done, students were instructed to take a few moments to preview the passage they would read. Each student perused the reading, noting features such as the title, subtitles, boldface and italicized words, pictures and captions, review questions at the end of the reading, and any other clues that might help them make sense of the text when they later read it.

The teachers then asked the students to close their books. They distributed a single sheet of paper, which they called an anticipation guide (see Activity 1.4), to each student. DiNardo explained to the students, "What good readers do when they read text such as this is that they predict what the text will say. They make such predictions based on prior knowledge. Then when they go into the text, it really does not matter whether they find out that their predictions are true. Just having made the predictions helps them to stay engaged in the text. Today, we help you in this process because *we* have made some predictions for you on this anticipation guide. All you need to do is, before you read, place a check mark next to the ones you think to be true. Don't worry about whether you are correct. Remember that you are just practicing the habit of predicting before reading. In fact, some of these statements you will later find to be correct, some will be incorrect, and some will be arguable. That is, some of you may interpret them to be true and have evidence to prove this while others in the room will have evidence that disproves the same statements. We will have to resolve those issues at that time."

Students were then given a few minutes to check the statements on the anticipation guide. However, they were told not to open their textbooks; instead, students worked in groups to discuss what they checked and to try to come to consensus on their understanding of the statements on the guide. In fact, when Boothe and DiNardo worked with the school's communication skills teacher to construct this anticipation guide, they kept in mind four characteristics that make anticipation guides work well to help students interpret difficult text material:

- Rephrase important concepts in the language of students.
- Include a few statements that are intuitively appealing to students but will prove to be inaccurate through a reading of the text.
- Write in such a way as to force students to interpret large segments of text, such as a paragraph or two. This prevents the reading experience from

NAME _____ DATE _____

ANTICIPATION GUIDE: THE DIGESTIVE SYSTEM

Instructions: Before reading pages 172 through 176 in your textbook, place a check mark (✓) in the space to the left of each of the statements with which you agree. Then, during or after the reading, cross through statements you wish to change, and check any new ones you find to be true. *Be sure you are able to refer back to the text to provide evidence for or against each statement.*

_____ 1. Saliva is important to digestion.

_____ 2. If you ate standing on your head, it would be more difficult for you to swallow and for the digestive system to function properly.

_____ 3. You digest food in your mouth.

_____ 4. Your digestive system could still function properly if the middle 10 feet of your small intestine were removed.

_____ 5. A combination of hydrochloric acid, enzymes, and mucus turns food in your stomach into a thick gooey mush called *chyme*.

_____ 6. If you are preparing to participate in an aerobic sport such as distance running or biking, you should eat a big meal (such as a hamburger, fries,

and shake) at least one hour before you do it.

_____ 7. Both the pancreas and the liver produce digestive juices that are stored in the gallbladder.

_____ 8. Capillaries and villi play a major role in the digestive process.

_____ 9. All remaining undigested food passes through the large intestine, which separates fecal waste from water and prepares it for elimination through the rectum.

_____ 10. Diarrhea and constipation are problems of the large intestine.

_____ 11. You could die from diarrhea.

_____ 12. Ulcers, ulcerative colitis, and heartburn are all caused by the same things.

By Mark A. Forget, Yolanda Hightower Boothe, and James J. DiNardo III.

_____

turning into a simple "decoding exercise," which is what many textbook worksheets are.

• Word the guide to provoke critical thinking about the key concepts. Make statements somewhat vague or subject to interpretation, rather than just true/false statements. Based on their prior knowledge or on the material being presented, students might disagree and provide valid evidence for either side of arguments, both before and after the reading.

Next the *assistance* phase began. The teachers reminded students to begin silent reading without distracting either themselves or others while reading the chapter on nutrition. Students were reminded to note the page, column, and paragraph that they were using to interpret whether a statement was provable.

The room became quiet as students read to find out whether their predictions were correct. Boothe and DiNardo either read at the same time or quietly moved around the room to monitor student work with the anticipation guides. One or the other occasionally whispered encouragement to a student, but they were cautious to avoid causing distractions during the reading time.

After about 20 minutes, many of the students were stirring, anticipating the next step: meeting in their groups to attempt to come to a consensus. The teachers instructed them to do just that, reminding the students that coming to consensus is different from attempting to find a majority: all voices are heard and all students participate. Once again, the teachers moved around the room to monitor and assist. In addition, they reminded students that they must act like "attorneys presenting evidence to support their claims."

This was the *reflection* phase of the lesson. The room was loud as students argued vociferously over statements such as "You digest food in your mouth." Although few checked that statement before or during the reading, some students thought that because saliva and mastication are important to digestion, it could be said that digestion occurs in the mouth. Many such arguments occurred in the small groups. The teachers identified the first group to achieve consensus, and they noted the statements that group members believed should be checked now that they had read and discussed them. The teachers placed a check mark next to those statements on a transparency of the anticipation guide on an overhead projector.

The final phase of the discussion occurred when the teachers turned on the overhead projector and asked for the attention of all the students to try for a classroom consensus. Now the students, after their practice in small group discussions, could sort out their differences over the few statements about which the class had not yet achieved consensus. This process took a few more minutes, and students obviously relished their abilities to present their interpretations of the evidence they found in their textbooks. The discussion was orderly and mature, and all students seemed interested in the outcome. After achieving consensus, the teachers asked the students to report by a show of hands how many felt that using the anticipation guide to make predictions about the reading beforehand had made the passage interesting and desirable to read. All the students raised their hands. In this way the teachers reminded the students of the skills they used to engage themselves in the reading.

The class was nearly over. The teachers reminded students that they must go back through the reading as a homework assignment to complete their notes based on the objectives that were on the chalkboard at the start of the class, which each student had copied into his or her notebook.

Students usually like the health and physical education classes of Boothe and DiNardo. They say, "We always get to *think* in their class. It's more interesting." The teachers are used to letting the students learn through techniques that encourage them to set their own purposes for reading and then pursue knowledge from the text and reflect on it through discussion or writing. They can see the students develop their own understanding of the text. At the same time they know that active pursuit of understanding will help the students retain the information and apply it in their own lives. They also know that their students have practiced a learning skill that they will be able to use in any class. Boothe and DiNardo are happy to be reading-to-learn teachers.

The Organization of This Text

The 10 principles presented in this chapter are an integral part of the discussion in every chapter. The first four chapters are foundation chapters; they present the basic theory and rationale for the approach used in this text. Chapter 2 describes the many different types of learners in content classrooms and ways to help them. Specific strategies and activities are provided. Chapter 3 presents information about the trend for accountability and evaluation for students in content classrooms, through standardized testing. Chapter 4 introduces technological literacy and how to use it in content classrooms. Chapter 5 presents ways to teach with multiple resources, beyond the traditional textbook. Chapter 6 focuses on preparing students to learn and Chapter 7 on assistance and reflection. Applications for teachers are provided, as well as examples from several content areas and grade levels. Chapters 8 through 11 discuss how PAR works with study skills, vocabulary, writing, and cooperative learning. Chapter 12 describes how to create an affective learning climate.

In each chapter we employ the PAR steps by asking readers to prepare themselves to read, to assist themselves in their reading, and to reflect on their comprehension. We recommend that you, the reader, now select a subject topic to aid you in creating practice activities. The topic should be one that you are currently teaching or may use in the future as you teach. The books you select will be resources for completing some of the assignments given at the end of each chapter. On completion of this textbook, you should be able to analyze any resource or textbook for its suitability for learners, its effective qualities, whether it is amenable to the PAR Lesson Framework, its study skills and vocabulary aids, and its attention to different learners. In addition, you should be able to construct activities that help you teach content through a reading-to-learn approach. When teachers use the PAR Lesson Framework they facilitate improvement in students' thinking ability. This type of teacher intervention and guidance is a necessary step in improving cognitive ability. In 1983 Pearson and Tierney assessed the instructional paradigm most used by teachers. They found that the key elements of instruction featured the use of many practice materials, little explanation of cognitive tasks, little interaction with students about the nature of specific tasks, and strong emphasis on one correct answer, with teachers supplying answers when confusion remained. Not surprisingly, Pearson and Tierney concluded that such a paradigm was ineffective. We have had much experience since that time observing the type of teaching occurring in schools. We find the same practices prevalent today that they observed. Applying the PAR Lesson Framework to teach specific strategies and skills will help change instruction for the better. Use of this framework will make teachers more effective in content area classrooms.

One-Minute Summary

This chapter has provided a short historical overview of the status of education and reading in the late twentieth and early twenty-first centuries. Ways that teachers can effectively teach reading, writing, and thinking in their content area classrooms were introduced briefly to launch the book focus. Next the chapter summarized the authors' beliefs about reading to learn and provided the foundation for this textbook by describing 10 core principles for content reading instruction. The goal of good content reading instruction is to aid students in becoming autonomous learners in the classroom. Well-planned reading instruction can help alleviate incomplete thinking on the part of students, when, out of frustration, they sometimes skip important parts of the lesson. The PAR Lesson Framework provides a way to overcome incomplete thinking and poor student learning by offering a structured plan for teachers to deliver content in an effective and organized manner. This chapter provided four examples of the use of the PAR Lesson Framework and documented the need for improved reading instruction as evidenced by failures in reading achievement at all levels of education from kindergarten through adulthood. It also cited studies of researchers who document the many achievements of our educational system. Finally, a plan for how we apply these 10 principles and the PAR Lesson Framework throughout this textbook was provided.

PAR Online

Visit *Reading Online* and read Guthrie's article on engagement and motivation in reading. (The URL is located in the references for this book.)

While at *Reading Online*, read the article by Richardson (the URL is located in the references for this book), from which the PAR examples in this chapter are drawn.

Go to the National Center for Educational Statistics site and read some of the statistics about literacy in the United States. (The URL is located in the references for this book.)

Participate in a threaded discussion in which you share your thoughts about the principle with which you most agree and why.

END-OF-CHAPTER ACTIVITIES

Assisting Comprehension

1. Return to the table of effective instructional strategies introduced at the beginning of this chapter. Now add, on the basis of what you have read, a reason why each of these strategies might be important in teaching reading in the content areas. Indicate if there are strategies you have not used before, but might now adopt.

2. Is the PAR Lesson Framework similar to, or different from, any way of teaching that you have used in the past? What associations with other frameworks or other forms of teaching can you make? How do you think you will be able to apply this framework to your teaching?

Reflecting on the Reading

The International Reading Association (2003) has developed a set of standards that identify the performance criteria relevant to classroom teachers.

Standard One delineates four elements of foundational knowledge that a classroom teacher should possess. Two of these are addressed in this chapter. Teachers should

- know foundational theories related to practices and materials used in the classroom.
- recognize historical antecedents to contemporary reading methods and materials, and articulate how their teaching practices relate to reading research.

How were these two elements addressed in this chapter? How does being informed about these elements aid in content instruction?

There will never be a single solution that will be a perfect fit for our diverse society. Don't wish for a unilateral answer to our educational dilemmas. Instead, we should work toward partnerships of families, communities, and educators who will enjoy the process of problem-solving.

ELAINE GRIFFIN, 1995
UNITED STATES TEACHER
OF THE YEAR

Supporting Diverse Learners in Content Classrooms

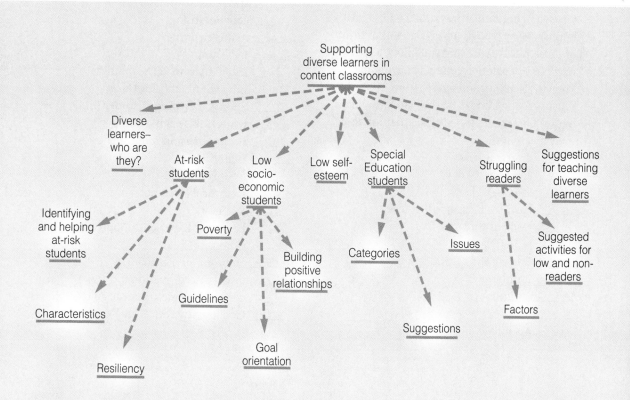

PREPARING TO READ

1. Respond to the following statements carefully and be ready to discuss your instruction for diverse students:

   I do not (or expect I will not) encounter students with cultural or language diversity in my classroom.

   I know how to accommodate instructional practices in my classroom—or future classroom—for learners with a wide range of needs.

   I can use student interests, reading abilities, and backgrounds to plan highly successful content lessons, no matter how diverse the students might be compared to the "average" student.

2. Following is a list of terms used in this chapter. Some may be familiar to you in a general context, but in this chapter they may be used in unfamiliar ways. Rate your knowledge by placing a plus sign (+) in front of those you are sure that you know, a check mark (✓) in front of those you have some knowledge about, and a zero (0) in front of those you don't know. Be ready to locate them in the chapter, and pay special attention to their meanings.

   _____ diverse learners
   _____ equity pedagogy
   _____ at-risk students
   _____ hard-to-reach/hard-to-teach
   _____ resilient students
   _____ self-efficacy
   _____ English as a second language (ESL)
   _____ immigrants
   _____ refugees
   _____ acculturate
   _____ assimilate

   _____ $i + 1$
   _____ affective filter hypothesis
   _____ Basic Interpersonal Communication Skills (BICS)
   _____ Cognitive Academic Language Proficiency (CALP)
   _____ English for Academic Purposes (EAP)
   _____ cultural discontinuity
   _____ culture shock
   _____ survivor guilt
   _____ English Language Learner (ELL)
   _____ Teaching English to Speakers of Other Languages (TESOL)
   _____ Cognitive Academic Language-Learning Approach (CALLA)
   _____ bilingual education
   _____ sheltered content instruction
   _____ group frame
   _____ special education
   _____ collaboration
   _____ mainstreaming
   _____ inclusion
   _____ Individuals with Disabilities Education Act (IDEA)
   _____ Specific Learning Disorder (SLD)
   _____ Universal Design
   _____ comprehension monitoring
   _____ PLEASE
   _____ fix-up strategies
   _____ reciprocal teaching
   _____ ReQuest
   _____ Language Experience Approach (LEA)
   _____ auditory discrimination
   _____ visual discrimination
   _____ concept-formation study guides
   _____ Collaborative Strategic Reading (CSR)

As you read this chapter, focus your attention on the following purposes. You will

1. understand and identify characteristics of at-risk students.

2. understand why teachers have to discourage passive approaches to reading.

3. identify teacher-directed reading strategies for aiding at-risk, low-socioeconomic, and low-self-esteem learners.

4. identify teacher-directed reading strategies for aiding English language learners.

5. identify teacher-directed reading strategies for aiding special-education students.

6. identify teacher-directed reading strategies for aiding struggling readers.

DIVERSE LEARNERS

Who are diverse learners? When we take the time to get to know each student in our classrooms, we begin to realize that all learners are actually diverse. Even in classrooms that may be designated as homogeneous—that is, where all learners are supposed to be grouped on a like factor such as giftedness or advanced or deficient academic ability—we discover a great range of diversity.

Diverse learners defined

Equity pedagogy stresses instructional opportunity for all learners.

Within every classroom teachers find students who are diverse in intellectual ability, social and emotional background, language proficiency, racial background, cultural background, and physical attributes. Teachers must be prepared to deal effectively with these individual differences (Au, 1992; Heilman, Blair, & Rupley, 1994; Wassermann, 1999; Hammerberg, 2004). Educators often define **diverse learners** as those who might be at risk for academic failure and need special understanding and attention. The current trends in the United States indicate that our population will continue to diversify. Content area teachers must practice **equity pedagogy** (Banks, 1995; Au, 2001), striving to educate every student, no matter what their heterogeneous or diverse qualities. All students must be able to take their rightful place in a workforce that is "ready with the technical and communication skills to compete in a global economy" (Brotherton, 2000, p. 21).

AT-RISK STUDENTS

At-risk learners may have characteristics that are diverse. Some learners who come from low socioeconomic backgrounds find learning and the demands of literacy more difficult because they have had limited experience with reading; others have low self-esteem. Some are new to the English-speaking world. Some learners have special education needs; some struggle with reading. And some learners may have a combination of these characteristics. Such students are not able to keep up with the majority in a content classroom. In this chapter we explore some of the characteristics of each of these groups of diverse learners and some strategies that can help content teachers teach them effectively. All students will benefit from the information in this chapter, but diverse students in particular need these strategies and suggestions.

Characteristics of At-Risk Students

At-risk students are students who are in danger of dropping out of school, usually because of educational disadvantages, low socioeconomic status, or underachievement. Although poor minority children may be at greatest risk, many other students in our classrooms also are at risk of school failure. The reasons are varied: poverty, drug and alcohol abuse, crime, teen pregnancy, low self-esteem, ill health, poor school attendance, and welfare dependence.

The National Assessment of Educational Progress (NAEP) *Reading Report Card* (2003) indicates that only 31 percent of fourth graders and 32 percent of eighth graders attained a "proficient" level—a standard that test officials say all students should reach. Thirty-seven percent of fourth graders and 26 percent of eighth graders did not achieve a basic level of reading proficiency. Furthermore, children in families living below the poverty line do not have opportunities to participate in preschools where they might receive early help to overcome at-risk factors; this situation applies to as many as 47 percent of our children. Such statistics should give us pause: Real wages are down, the incidence of poverty is up, the youthful population is declining, and the proportion of minorities and those for whom English is not the first language is growing. In addition, minorities and those with limited English proficiency are disproportionately represented among the poor and among those who fail in our school system. Many of these students, challenged in many ways by society, will face a lifetime of debilitating poverty unless we, as educators, generate the imagination, will, and resources necessary to educate these at-risk students for independent, productive, and effective lives (Hornbeck, 1988).

In 1987 David W. Hornbeck, as president of the Council of Chief State School Officers, declared that the focus of the council would be on the "children and youth of the nation with whom we have historically failed." As a result of the council's work, an important volume was published that drew national attention to the plight of at-risk youth: *School Success for At-Risk Youth*. In the introduction to this volume, Hornbeck writes,

> In our grand experiment in universal free public education in America, we have
> fashioned a system that works relatively well, especially for those who are white, well

At-risk students defined

NAEP statistics demonstrate the numbers of at-risk students teachers instruct.

motivated, and from stable middle- to upper-middle-class families. But as students have deviated more and more from that norm, the system has served them less and less well. We sometimes seem to say to them, "We've provided the system. It's not our fault if you don't succeed." Whether that attitude is right or wrong, the critical mass of at-risk youth has grown proportionately so large that we are in some danger of being toppled by our sense of rightness and righteousness. Instead of blaming the students for failing to fit the system, we must design and implement a new structure that provides appropriate educational and related services to those most at risk. (Hornbeck, 1988, 5)

Four affective needs of at-risk learners

At-risk learners are desperate yet unfulfilled, trying to meet these four important affective needs: power, love, freedom, and fun (Glasser, 1986). Often their lives are governed by fear, threat, and negative thinking. They feel helpless and powerless and exhibit an external locus of control (discussed in Chapter 12), feeling that they lack control of their own destiny. Pellicano (1987) defines at-risk students as "uncommitted to deferred gratification and to school training that correlates with competition, and its reward, achieved status" (p. 47). Pellicano sees at-risk students as "becoming unproductive, underdeveloped, and noncompetitive" (p. 47) in our technological and complex world. He sees at-risk youngsters as not so much "socially disadvantaged" (the label of the 1960s) but rather as economically disadvantaged. Pellicano cites a litany of dropouts, school failures, alcohol and drug abusers, and handicapped and poverty-stricken children—all putting the United States "at risk" of becoming a third-rate world power unable to respond to economic world market forces. He calls for a national policy agenda that "legitimates the school as a mediating structure for those who are powerless to develop their own potential" (p. 49).

Further characteristics of at-risk learners

Zaragoza (1987) describes at-risk first graders as children from a low socioeconomic background who often do not speak English, have poor standardized test scores, and perform unsatisfactorily on reading and writing exercises. Many of these students come from the inner city. The students to whom Pellicano and Zaragoza allude manifest the poorest reading behaviors and are so fearful and negative that they often cannot be motivated, especially by threats (see Chapter 12). Psychologists tell us that when an organism is threatened, its perception narrows to the source of the threat. This may be why so many poor students "take it out" on the teacher. Feeling threatened, they don't pay attention to coursework, to commands, or to anything but how to repay the teacher for all the failure and frustration they feel. Like children who have not matured, at-risk students tend to focus entirely too much on the teacher, thus developing an external locus of control. Therefore, a teacher's attitude toward students and learning can be powerful; in fact, it appears to be a major factor in promoting interested readers (Wigfield & Asher, 1984).

Identifying and Helping At-Risk Students

Some at-risk learners become successful learners.

The current attention on at-risk students can serve a useful purpose by helping educators focus on the importance of identifying and helping these students so that they become successful learners. Care must be taken, however, that the label *at risk* is not used as a prediction of failure, perpetuating a self-fulfilling prophecy (Gambrell,

1990). In fact, studies have demonstrated that with careful attention and instruction, many students labeled as being at risk overcome this label to graduate from high school and attend college (Ferguson, 2000).

Some terms are more positive than others.

Of the many terms used to describe at-risk students, a less desirable term is **hard-to-reach/hard-to-teach,** which resounds negatively and also seems to place responsibility on the students. The designation "students who present special challenges" may come closer to expressing the challenge to teachers rather than the deficiencies of students; for the present, the term *at risk* seems to be the accepted terminology.

How do we develop the potential of this type of student? First, teachers need to be positive and caring enough to realize that behaviors that put these students at risk cannot be changed quickly. At-risk students have acquired bad study habits and negative thinking over an entire lifetime. As Mark Twain once said, "A habit cannot be tossed out the window. It must be coaxed down the stairs a step at a time." Hilliard (1988) contends that we already have the knowledge we need to help at-risk students. Hilliard draws the following conclusions from research on programs for these students:

Conclusions from research

- At-risk students can be taught to perform successfully at demanding academic levels.
- Dramatic positive changes in the academic achievement of at-risk students are possible within a short time.
- There is no one way to achieve success with at-risk students.
- There are no absolute critical periods with human beings; it is never too late to learn.
- At-risk students thrive on intellectual challenge, not on low-level remedial work.
- There is no special pedagogy for at-risk students; the pedagogy that works for them is good for all students.

Resilient Students

Unless students can be resilient to challenges such as difficult environmental and academic challenges, as well as stress and setbacks in education, they will face great difficulty in school (Martin, 2002). Students who are resilient can adapt successfully to such challenges despite the difficult circumstances they may face (Borman & Overman, 2004). **Resilient students** are those who, despite hardships and risk factors, bounce back and succeed in school (Howard & Johnson, 2000; Patterson, 2001). McMillan and Reed (1994), after an exhaustive analysis of the literature concerning at-risk students, interviewed 62 students (27 elementary, 16 middle, 19 high school) who had been identified as at risk but "resilient." The research findings indicate six characteristics of resilient students:

What are some of the characteristics of resilient students?

1. They use their time well.
2. They have clear, long-term goals.
3. They possess an internal locus of control.

4. They have been positively influenced by teachers or by school expectations, believing they can succeed.

5. They came from dysfunctional homes but did not attribute failure to them.

6. One person, usually a teacher or a mother, was significant in helping them.

Figure 2.1 depicts a model of these factors and their influence on resilient at-risk students. In a related article, Reed, McMillan, and McBee (1995) recommend the following:

- Use instructional strategies that promote an internal locus of control.
- Help students set long-term goals so they can focus forward rather than on immediate gratification.
- Ensure a positive, supportive school environment with high expectations but not impossible standards.
- Encourage extracurricular activities and required helpfulness, such as volunteer work.
- Use cooperative grouping.
- Develop strong, positive relationships with these students.

What factors influence resiliency?

All the characteristics and problems associated with at-risk youth cannot be adequately addressed in one chapter. Physical and mental disabilities, substance abuse, and many other issues are beyond the scope of this chapter. What we cover are some of the characteristics associated with at-risk youth and school failure that are critically linked to reading achievement: low socioeconomic environments, low self-esteem, English language learners (ELL), special-education needs, and struggles with reading. These characteristics are not necessarily independent. An at-risk student with English second language needs may come from a low socioeconomic environment or suffer from low self-esteem. Rarely does a student fail school as a result of only one of these characteristics.

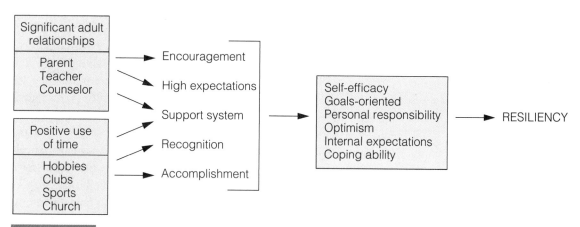

FIGURE 2.1 A Conceptual Model of Factors Influencing Resilient Students at Risk

From *The Journal of At-Risk Issues*, Vol. 1, No. 2 (Fall 1994), Fig 1, p. 32. Used with permission.

We do not claim that simply using the techniques and strategies described in this chapter will solve our nation's problem with at-risk students. The task is arduous and often frustrating for teachers, and no one set of strategies will solve such an overwhelming problem. We do suggest, however, that using the PAR Lesson Framework and the techniques explained in this text, along with much attention to the affective domain of teaching, is a step in the right direction. Certainly, studies such as Borman and Overman's of mathematics students who "beat the odds" (2004) and of McMillan and Reed's (1994) indicate this is true. We must now enable this sizable group of failing students to become successful participants in the educational process.

STUDENTS FROM LOW SOCIOECONOMIC ENVIRONMENTS

Who are these students? They usually come from impoverished neighborhoods and often score in the low range on standardized tests. There is not much extra money for anything beyond food and basic clothing. Most such students are interested in school and eager to learn, but many of them do not get the necessary educational or cultural exposure outside the classroom.

By all accounts far too many students in classrooms today suffer from the effects of living in poverty. The impact of poverty on students' lives is profound, and the consequences are complex. Hornbeck (1988) contends that schools have persistently failed to serve poor students adequately.

Poverty and School Achievement

NCES provides an excellent website where one can view study reports and charts that summarize data.

The conditions that exist in these students' environment put them at serious risk of school failure. A study reported by the National Center for Educational Statistics (NCES) (2001) indicates that impoverished kindergarten children perform markedly less well on home educational and literacy experiences than do children from homes above the poverty index. Such low performance, seemingly influenced by poverty, contributes to continuing literacy struggles for adolescents (Hinchman et al., 2004). The differences between low-income and middle-income homes indicate that poverty leads to many fewer literacy resources for children (Neuman & Celano, 2001). The NCES study was conducted in homes, but what about homeless children? They are often not available for such studies because they live in shelters, motels, or campgrounds. Without adequate shelter, they often go hungry and attend school sporadically. Their literacy is at peril (Noll & Watkins, 2003).

The effect of enriched language activities in the home

Adams (1990) notes that children raised in high-literacy homes may have experienced more than 1,000 hours of reading and writing activities before they even arrive at school. Many students from low-socioeconomic families come from homes characterized by oral literacy rather than books, magazines, and adults who read. In an oral environment, children are socialized through the use of stories, parables, proverbs, and legends that are committed to memory (Egan, 1987). Although these are rich language experiences, they are not the ones many teachers assume children possess. According to Reyhner and Garcia (1989), schools often fail to recognize the cultural and linguistic strengths of students from an oral-literacy environment.

Impact of poverty on literacy

Poverty is particularly associated with low achievement and dropping out of school, for reasons that include the following factors (Neckerman & Wilson, 1988):

- Poorly educated parents spend less time reading to their children.
- Class or ethnic differences in patterns of language acquisition contribute to difficulties in the early years of schooling.
- As poor children get older, they are much more likely to become teenage parents.
- As poor children get older, they are much more likely to get into trouble with the law or have disciplinary problems in school.

Also, the preconceived notions that some teachers hold about poor students' capacity to learn may result in less effective instruction for them.

Goal Orientation and Low Socioeconomic Environments

Students who seem lazy may instead be influenced by low socio-economic environments.

Many students come to school with a future orientation: they can set goals and set smaller subgoals to reach the larger goals. Some students from low socioeconomic environments, however, have not been exposed to and have not developed the traditional goal orientation associated with school achievement. These students have had little experience with the type of success in which most teachers believe. According to May (1990), teachers should be aware that lack of goal orientation does not necessarily mean that these students are lazy. It may simply mean that the teacher must try a variety of ways to motivate them. Behavior management techniques that require the teacher and student to establish short-range goals may help these students develop the skills necessary for successful school learning.

Instructional Guidelines for Working with Students from Low Socioeconomic Environments

Surveys show that even those at the poverty level in American society see education as the key to a better life (Orfield, 1988). Keep in mind the following guidelines for working with students from low socioeconomic environments:

1. Be sensitive to the environmental conditions of the home and community that may influence the students' behavior and achievement. Students from deprived environments tend to have a poor self-concept and low aspirational levels, to be tardy and absent frequently, to be poorly oriented to school tasks, to display hostility toward school and authorities, and to resist or reject values that are foreign to them (Heilman, Blair, & Rupley, 1986). Examine your background knowledge and find resources (Noll & Watkins, 2003).

2. Be aware of the effect of poor nutrition and health on learning. The capacity to learn is obviously influenced by nutrition and health. Students without sound diets and with health problems are not likely to be able to concentrate and will

lack the feeling of well-being that is essential to learning. Teachers must work with families and social service agencies in the community to diagnose and address the diet and health care needs of students to improve their capacity to learn (Levin, 1988).

3. Take action to change students' lives for the better. Rhodes's (1990) admonition, "Don't be a bystander," should be taken to heart by every teacher who works with students who live in a culture of poverty. Richard Rhodes, recipient of the Pulitzer Prize and the National Book Award for his 1987 book *The Making of the Atomic Bomb,* suffered the effects of physical abuse and poverty during early adolescence. In contemplating why he survived with his capacity to love intact, Rhodes concludes that he did so because others not only cared but acted. He cites several teachers who helped him—in particular, one teacher who saw that he was undernourished and managed to supplement his meager lunch and another who saw that he was poorly clothed and provided clothing.

Do *not* stand by—help these students whenever you can; this is every teacher's responsibility!

Teachers should act when they see students who suffer from the consequences of poverty. Many resources are available to the teacher to help these students: social service agencies that can address the basic needs of families, including health care, shelter, nutrition, and counseling; youth agencies, such as Big Brothers and Big Sisters, that can offer enrichment programs after school, on weekends, and during summers; adult tutors, particularly senior citizens, who can work with individual students. Teachers should not be passive bystanders in the lives of children of poverty; timely intervention can make a decisive difference.

STUDENTS WITH LOW SELF-ESTEEM

The relationship between self-esteem and learning is stressed continually throughout the current literature on at-risk students (Patterson, 2001). According to Coopersmith (1967), the four basic components of self-esteem are significance, competence, power, and virtue.

Four basic components of self-esteem

- *Significance* is found in the acceptance, attention, and affection of others, particularly significant others. At-risk students may feel rejected and ignored and believe that they do not belong.

- *Competence* is developed as a person masters his or her environment. For the student, the school environment is of particular concern. Success in school tasks generates feelings of competence. The at-risk student may experience failure in school tasks, which in turn stifles motivation and promotes feelings of incompetence.

- *Power* resides in the ability to control one's behavior and gain the respect of others. At-risk students may feel helpless and powerless, particularly with respect to school learning, and may feel that their failure cannot be overcome (Dweck, 1975; Martin, 2002).

- *Virtue* is worthiness, as judged by the values of one's culture and of significant others. Feelings of being worthy and valued are necessary for life to be fulfilling. The at-risk student may feel worthless and valueless as a result of school failure. Appearing and behaving somewhat differently from their peers may also make some students feel less worthy or acceptable (Harris & Smith, 1986).

Lack of self-esteem manifests itself most obviously during adolescence, when students are in a state of flux, constantly searching, focusing, and reevaluating themselves. During adolescence students are trying to find a stable image of themselves (Kerr, Nelson, & Lambert, 1987). Unfortunately, by the time some students enter middle school, they have a negative self-image, viewing themselves as helpless and without control over their level of achievement. They behave in ways that cause teachers to label them as unmotivated, immature, uncooperative, and even hostile. Although the behavior of these students may be inappropriate, it most likely reflects their distress at facing failure in the classroom day after day (Hinchman et al., 2004).

Motivation and Self-Esteem

What is self-efficacy?

Motivation has been defined as the process of initiating, directing, and sustaining behavior. Motivation is viewed as a drive toward competence that is sustained and augmented by the feelings of efficacy that accompany competent interaction with the environment (Connell & Ryan, 1984). Bandura (1977) popularized the term **self-efficacy**—an individual's belief in her or his own effectiveness to cope with given situations. Self-efficacy determines the degree and quality of effort and the limits of persistence of which an individual is capable.

Self-efficacy is related to a more specific form of motivation: achievement motivation. *Achievement motivation* is the need to try to reach a goal that is determined by expecting and valuing the successful completion of a task (Wigfield & Asher, 1986). According to Dweck (1985), two kinds of goals are important to achievement motivation: learning goals and performance goals. Learning goals help students strive toward increased competence; performance goals lead students to gain positive and avoid negative judgment.

BUILDING POSITIVE RELATIONSHIPS

The importance of teachers' building positive relationships with at-risk students cannot be stressed too strongly. Brendtro, Brokenleg, and Bockern (1990) offer guidelines for building relationships that promote self-esteem; the following suggestions are adapted from their work (pp. 62–63).

Building a positive relationship is a process of giving that is typified by caring, knowledge, respect, and responsibility (Fromm, 1956). Caring is real concern for the life and growth of the student. Knowledge is genuine understanding of students' feelings, even if they are not readily apparent. Respect is the ability to see and appreciate students as they are. Responsibility means being ready to act to meet student needs.

Tracy Kidder (1989) writes in *Among Schoolchildren* about a boy who typifies low self-esteem and an impoverished environment. This fifth grader attempted to create a science project after much encouragement from his teacher. On the day the projects were due, he "forgot" his, and Chris, his teacher, was furious. She sent him home for it and when he returned, she started to scold him. When she saw that his project was an utter failure, she realized that he had tried but failed because of his lack of resources and low self-image. The teacher then demonstrated respect and responsibility for this troubled student.

Crisis as Opportunity

The struggling students who are most difficult to work with are those who create trouble rather than friendships. These students are often labeled "hard to reach": if one were to wait for them to warm up to the adult, one might wait forever. Many effective teachers have long recognized the great hidden potential of turning crisis into opportunity, as in the following story shared by a high school teacher:

> Rob entered first period class 10 minutes after the bell, looking disheveled and agitated. I asked for his late pass and he swore and stormed from the room. I stepped into the hall to confront him about his behavior but recalled our discussion of "crisis as opportunity." I called him back and asked simply, "What's wrong, Rob?" "What's wrong!" he exclaimed. "I'm driving to school and my car gets hit. After I get through with the police, I'm late into the building and get stopped by the principal. When I tell him what happened he tells me to get to class. Now you send me out of class!" He whirled around starting down to the office. "Where are you going?" I asked. "To get a pass!" he replied. "That's OK, Rob, enough has gone wrong for one day; you're welcome in class." His hostility melted in tears. After a moment he regained his composure and thanked me, and we went back in the room. (Brendtro, Brokenleg, & Bockern, 1990, p. 62)

The teacher in this example could easily have responded in a manner that would have alienated this student. Instead, the teacher used this crisis situation as an opportunity for relationship building. When a teacher manages a crisis with sensitivity, the relationship bonds become more secure.

Caring for All Students

Struggling students—students who suffer from low self-esteem, those who are withdrawn, or those from a different economic or cultural background—may not find others lining up to build relationships with them. These are the students who are sometimes ignored or rejected. These students often believe that teachers are uncaring, unfair, and ineffective (Wehlange & Rutter, 1986). Teachers need to take affirmative action to enhance the standing of these students with their peers. Doing this will require that teachers actively focus on identifying the strengths of these at-risk students. Lipsitz (1995) points out that "we are not being respectful or caring when we fail to teach children to read, compute, and write; nor are we respectful or caring when we hold different expectations for children because of their race, gender, or economic status" (p. 666). Bosworth's (1996) observations indicate that teachers tend to engage in neutral rather than caring interactions with students. Yet, "for many nonwhite students, caring is more concrete and is translated through such activities as 'spending time with someone,' 'sharing,' and 'listening when someone has a problem'" (p. 689).

Earning Trust

Perhaps the central ingredient in building positive and effective relationships is trust. According to Brendtro, Brokenleg, and Bockern (1990), trust between the student and the teacher develops over time in three predictable stages.

Three stages of building relationships

Casing   In this stage, the student needs to "check out" the teacher. The student is observing how the teacher behaves, how much power the teacher wields, and how others respond to this adult. All these observations are crucial data to students who may view virtually all teachers and adults as threatening.

Limit Testing   During this stage, the student "tests out" interactions with the teacher. A student who distrusts a teacher's friendly manner may misbehave or provoke the teacher to determine whether this person is really different. In this situation, the teacher should take a calm but firm approach to avoid either "giving in" or confirming the student's view that this adult is really just like all the others who cannot be trusted.

Predictability   The previous two stages, casing and limit testing, provide a foundation for developing a more secure relationship between the student and the teacher. Consistency is important to building a trusting relationship. In such a relationship, each party—the student and the teacher—knows what to expect from the other. In some situations where trust building is difficult, it may be better for the teacher to simply acknowledge, "I know you don't feel you can trust me yet, and that's all right." It takes patience and persistence to build trust, and it is important to remember that trust begets trust.

Guidelines for Working with Students with Low Self-Esteem

Intuition tells us that when students feel better about themselves, they do better in school. Improving the self-esteem of students is a major concern of most teachers but especially for teachers of at-risk students.

1. Focus on the strengths of students with low self-esteem.   At-risk students typically have low self-esteem because they have not succeeded in school. These students, however, may have had many successful experiences outside the classroom. With some discussion and probing, students often identify successful aspects of their lives that they have not recognized before. Spend time having students recall, write about, draw, and share their past achievements. Teachers must plan instruction that allows students with low self-esteem to demonstrate their strengths.

2. Make sure these students are given opportunities to read from materials that are within their reading proficiency level.   Students need to be successful in their reading in order to build positive self-concepts as readers. This means that the material should be familiar enough so that the student can use sense-making strategies. When readers continually have to deal with text that is too difficult, they expend their energy constructing a hazy model of meaning and do not have the opportunity to elaborate on the content or strategies needed to enhance comprehension (Walker, 1990).

3. Provide opportunities for students to engage in cooperative learning. Research conducted by Johnson and Johnson (1987) and Slavin (1983) and his associates provides evidence that cooperative learning promotes higher self-esteem, greater social acceptance, more friendships, and higher achievement than competitive or individual learning activities. For instance, Forget and Morgan (1995) found that when reading to learn was emphasized in a school-within-a-school setting in working with at-risk youngsters in cooperative situations, attitudes and school attendance improved significantly. Cooperative learning experiences such as those we describe in Chapter 11 are beneficial for all students but especially for those with low self-esteem. Students can be organized into small groups that are monitored and rewarded for both individual and group accomplishments. Cooperative learning can be used in any content area, as well as for reading and writing lessons and activities. The major principle of cooperative learning is that members of a team can succeed only if all members of the group are successful. Students have a vested interest in ensuring that the other group members learn.

ENGLISH SECOND LANGUAGE STUDENTS

At the turn of this century, increasing numbers of students whose first language is not English arrive in classrooms daily (National Clearinghouse for Bilingual Education, 2002). While **English second language (ESL)** students are diverse members of our population, they are not necessarily at risk. However, too many teachers have not been prepared to understand the ESL student, so this section presents several issues that may have an impact on their performance in schools. First we introduce some important terms that are used to describe ESL situations. People for whom English is a second language are sometimes designated as *nonnative speakers of English* or by the abbreviation *L2* for second-language speakers (Leki, 1992). They are sometimes called *ESL (English second language)* students. Families from other countries come to the United States for various reasons. Students who left their home countries with families who chose to move, seeking a different way of life, are **immigrants.** Other families fled their home countries because of unstable and dangerous conditions in their homeland; they might not have wanted to move but left because they were no longer safe in their own countries. They are **refugees.** In either case, students might be confused and intimidated by their new surroundings, but refugees may have more challenges to overcome.

How well ESL students settle into their new environment depends on several conditions. First, students should be encouraged to feel proud of and retain their cultural heritage; when they maintain their first language and culture and integrate as necessary, they are **acculturating** to English and the new country. If they feel forced to give up or deny their traditions, they may **assimilate** (become like others in this country)

What is the difference between an immigrant and a refugee? How might this difference influence learning?

What is the difference between acculturation and assimilation? How might this difference influence learning?

but lose an important part of themselves. In the case of assimilation, students may begin to resent the forced choice and develop low self-esteem. Schumann (1978) identifies conditions for successful acculturation and language acquisition in his now classic model. The best learning environment would include social variables such as an even balance between the target and native culture, so that the learner does not rely more heavily on the native culture; an expectation that the two cultures will intermingle; a balance of the two cultures so that one does not dominate; an expectation that acculturation will occur; and positive attitudes toward both cultures.

Monitor Model and five hypotheses

In his Monitor Model, Krashen (1982, 1989) argues for a balance between determinism and environmental factors as contributors to second language acquisition. His model comprises five hypotheses:

1. Any language is acquired unconsciously more than through direct learning. The power of acquisition ought to be used more effectively in teaching ESL. For instance, less reliance on organized learning through workbooks and more reliance on learner environment are necessary components of effective ESL instruction.

2. Learners monitor their learning, but they need sufficient time to focus on form and specific knowledge of when to apply rules. Because these conditions are difficult to meet during most communication—which demands quick responses—explicit rule teaching and error correction will slow down or impede progress.

3. The natural order hypothesis suggests that language learners acquire language rules in a natural, predictable sequence rather than by direct instruction. Grammatical features will evolve in spite of a prescribed sequence. Studies of English orthographic development (Bear & Templeton, 1996) seem to support this hypothesis.

4. As a logical extension, natural communication seems to provide a relaxed setting for language learning. Learners do best when language input is comprehensible and just beyond their current level of knowledge. Krashen calls this comprehensible input "*i* + 1," whereby *i* is input and 1 is the challenge level.

5. Socioemotional factors strongly influence language learning and may well account for older learners who master a second language in spite of the critical age factor. Krashen calls this the **affective filter hypothesis;** he writes that it is the single most important variable in language learning. When the filter is high, it represents a tense, highly anxious socioemotional climate. Learning is greatly impeded.

BICS and CALP

Cummins (1979, 1994) argues that a distinction must be made between conversational language proficiency, which he calls **Basic Interpersonal Communication Skills (BICS),** and **Cognitive Academic Language Proficiency (CALP),** which is more formal academic instruction. Stoller (1999) calls this **English for Academic Purposes (EAP)** and notes its importance in a school content-based curriculum. Learning English for conversational and functional purposes is less cognitively stressful and more immediately practical than is learning English for academic purposes.

This notion supports Krashen's fourth hypothesis, that natural communication in a relaxed setting is the best vehicle for learning English.

Several second-language experts discuss the variable of time in language acquisition. Cummins (1994) suggests that achieving conversational proficiency might take approximately two years, whereas achieving academic proficiency might take as much as five to seven years. Leki (1992) writes that time is the single most important factor in learning ESL, as do Peregoy and Boyle (1997). A study by Lee and Schallert (1997) suggests that solid second-language proficiency is a better facilitator of literacy acquisition in a second language than is literacy proficiency in the first language. This second-language proficiency takes time, as Snow, Burns, and Griffin (1998) indicate when they recommend that ESL children develop oral proficiency before beginning reading instruction; they indicate that oral proficiency may take as much as a year. The process of helping students make the transition from a first to a second language involves special attention to "linguistic bridges" that show the learner how the languages are similar and different (Gibbons, 2003).

Learning a new language takes time.

ENGLISH LANGUAGE LEARNERS

Public Law 93-380 (enacted in 1974) requires provisions for bilingual education in virtually every aspect of the educational process. This law recognizes that students with limited English proficiency have special educational needs and that teachers must take into account the cultural heritage into which the student was born (Harris & Smith, 1986). With demographers continuing to predict increasing numbers of immigrant and refugee students from Central and South America, eastern Europe, and Asia, teachers must consider how instruction can be modified to meet the special needs of those with limited English proficiency.

Cultural discontinuity is how Reyhner and Garcia (1989) describe the serious internal conflict brought about by a disparity between the language and culture of the home and the language and culture of the school. Both immigrants and refugees may experience a home language and cultural environment that differs significantly from the school environment. Pronounced differences may cause conflict for some students. A student may have to choose between the school and the home language and culture. According to Reyhner and Garcia (1989), such a choice is counterproductive to educational development. Rejecting the home background may damage self-esteem, while rejecting the language and culture of the school may result in lost educational opportunities. This dilemma is called **culture shock.** When learners are refugees, the rejection is compounded by feelings of loss and guilt about fleeing, often called **survivor guilt.**

Culture shock and survivor guilt defined

Teachers should learn about the different cultures represented in their classrooms and provide instruction that encourages acceptance of native languages and cultures while facilitating the learning of English (Au, 2001; Mohr, 2004). Equally important is enlisting support from the home. When the entire family is involved, cultural discontinuity will be less severe. Shanahan, Mulhern, and Rodriguez-Brown (1995) describe project FLAME, which helps Latino parents support their children's school learning.

In fact, if a student must struggle with functioning in two disparate cultures, the child's literacy learning may actually be impeded (Schmidt, 1995). Differences among cultures with respect to social style and attitudes also have implications for instruction. A number of studies (Downing, 1973; Downing, Ollila, & Oliver, 1975; Heath, 1986; Schieffelin & Cochran-Smith, 1984) confirm that students from non-school-oriented cultures do not have the same literacy skills as students from school-oriented cultures. The value and utility of literacy in the culture, and particularly in the home environment, influence the development of literacy skills. A study by Lee, Stigler, and Stevenson (1986) found that the superior reading performance of Chinese students in Taiwan, compared to their American counterparts, was related to social and cultural variables such as time spent in class, amount of homework, and parental attitudes. This study suggests that the Chinese students were better readers because they worked harder and were encouraged and supervised more frequently by parents and teachers. High motivation is the most powerful factor in successful learning of a second language (Leki, 1992).

School Programs for English Language Learners

When ESL students arrive at school with some proficiency, but not fluency, in English, they are often labeled as *Limited English Proficient (LEP)* or as *Students with Limited English Proficiency (SLEP)*. However, a more recent and less deficient-sounding term is **English Language Learner (ELL).** Some designate these ESL students as *speakers of other languages.*

The most representative term is ELL.

Two types of programs prevail in American schools for ELL pupils: an ESL–TESOL approach or a bilingual approach. These programs are usually conducted by a specialist in teaching English as a second language. When students receive language instruction in special programs, content teachers should be aware of what the specialist is doing and monitor student progress to ensure that students receive adequate classroom opportunities to develop English, reading, and writing skills (Mason & Au, 1990; Mohr, 2004).

The first type of program—ESL (English second language) or **TESOL (Teaching English to Speakers of Other Languages)**—emphasizes learning English exclusively. Instruction in English progresses from oral skills (listening and speaking) to written skills (reading and writing). The methodology emphasizes English language skills and learner-centered activities that stress meaningful communication. ESL/TESOL is somewhat similar to programs that teach English-speaking students a second language. The latter usually focuses more on cognitive academic language proficiency (CALP), whereas the former focuses on basic communication. The main goal of ESL/TESOL is to help students attain the language skills needed for success in school as quickly as possible. Most ESL/TESOL programs now include not only oral but also reading and writing skills. Chamot and O'Malley (1994) describe the **cognitive academic language-learning approach (CALLA)** as a "method of reading instruction for second language learners which provides students with authentic texts that include both content area material and literature to integrate oral and written language skills so that students can develop all aspects of academic language and develop strategic reading and writing through explicit instruction in learning strategies" (p. 94). The goal of ESL/TESOL classes is to move students to the regular classroom as soon as possible. Many ESL/TESOL classrooms have learners from 10 or more different countries, and the only common language is English.

The second type of program is **bilingual education,** which provides instruction in both English and the native language in the same classroom. Separate instructional periods are provided, one in English and one in the students' native language. In a variation of this approach—transitional bilingual education—bilingual teachers begin instruction in the students' native language and gradually introduce English. A review of the history of bilingual education indicates that this approach can be very effective (Rothstein, 1998). Of course, it works only where all learners speak a common language and need to learn English as their second language.

Instructional programs for ELL students may emphasize English, may emphasize the students' first language, or may give equal attention to both languages. Mason and Au (1990) caution that teachers should realize that bilingual education is a controversial topic. Teachers must be aware of the view of the community and school system concerning bilingual education. In some communities, parents may feel strongly that their children's education should emphasize bilingual competence; in other communities, parents want their children to speak and read only in English.

Instructional Guidelines for Working with ELL Students

Russell (1995) describes a program called **sheltered content instruction,** which focuses on "teaching subject matter through the principles of second language acquisition" (p. 30). First the teacher activates students' prior knowledge and introduces new experiences. Next, new concepts and ideas are added; students are then encouraged to apply the new knowledge. This method is similar to the PAR system. Russell explains that sheltered language instruction calls for a balance of top-down (emphasis on prior knowledge, context, and cognition) and bottom-up (emphasis on text and language features) because the needs of the ESL learner differ from those of a proficient user of English. But the focus is on subject matter. Sheltered language instruction might best occur in an ESL classroom rather than in a regular content classroom, but knowing about it may help regular classroom teachers accommodate ESL learners. Immersion in English without any sheltered instruction becomes most effective only by the third generation of English second language speakers (Rothstein, 1998).

When ELL students are included in regular classrooms, teachers of content subjects will be their instructors too. These students certainly can learn the same curriculum in language arts, science, and math as native English speakers (Minicucci et al., 1995). By studying eight schools with exemplary programs for ELL students, Minicucci and her colleagues identified several characteristics of successful instruction:

1. Innovative approaches encouraging students to become independent learners

2. Use of cooperative learning

3. Making parents feel comfortable at the school

4. Communication between teachers, parents, and community

5. "Families" within the school to create strong attachments

6. Innovative use of time, particularly so students have more learning time

7. Concentrated focus on the goal of learning English

Teachers should not underestimate ELL competencies. Verplaeste (1998) found that teachers issued more directives and asked fewer and lower-level cognitive questions of ESL students in their content classes. Teachers were protective but also impatient about waiting for ESL students' responses. To avoid such instructional traps when working with ELL students, teachers should keep the following guidelines in mind:

1. ESL students should be assessed and placed in appropriate programs. Specialists should be available in school districts to perform this kind of assessment. Content teachers should communicate with these specialists. Further, teachers should make sure they consistently evaluate student work and maximize ELL learning opportunities (Mohr, 2004).

2. Teachers need to learn as much as possible about students' language and culture. Ample evidence indicates that background knowledge is a significant factor in reading comprehension (see Chapters 5 and 6). Field and Aebersold (1990) suggest that the teacher answer the following questions: Is students' native culture literate? What is the common method of instruction in their native culture? Are the relatives living in the present home literate in English? Is English spoken in the home? Is reading (in any language) a part of their home activities? It is relatively easy for a teacher to find these answers by interviewing the student, parents, relatives, or other members of the culture. Using local reference sources such as community groups, libraries, and knowledgeable professionals can also provide insights about other cultures. *Culturegrams* (brief descriptions of a culture) can be obtained by writing embassies or searching on the Internet.

3. Model how oral language ability precedes reading. Students can read what they can say and understand. Accordingly, students should begin reading instruction in their native language, or they should receive instruction that focuses on language development before formal reading instruction. Snow, Burns, and Griffin (1998) recommend that "an adequate level of proficiency in spoken English" (p. 10) is necessary before reading instruction begins.

4. Whenever possible, use reading materials for instruction that reflect the background and the culture of the students. Teachers can supplement the existing reading materials with literature from the native cultures represented in the classroom. Daily teacher read-aloud sessions can use trade books that feature minority cultures. Students can be encouraged to contribute proverbs, recipes, and stories from parents and grandparents as the basis for experience stories (Reyhner & Garcia, 1989).

5. Create learning situations in which students can develop a sense of security and acceptance. Language proficiency is developed through oral and written activities that direct the students' attention to significant features of English.

Students can gain fluency in English through working with proficient English-speaking peers, learning key phrases for school tasks, and reading predictable texts. For instance, threaded discussion boards can facilitate practice in meaningful use of English in the content context (Bikowski & Kessler, 2002).

6. Employ thematic units (Chapter 5) and literature so ELLs can explore their own identities as they learn about your content (Vyas, 2004; Vann & Fairbairn, 2003).

7. Be conscious of the issues related to working successfully with students from other cultures, without feeling restricted by them. Teachers are in a unique position to positively affect the attitudes of children from differing cultures by adopting methods, materials, and ideas that are linguistically and culturally sympathetic to the students' backgrounds (Cooter, 1990). Field and Aebersold (1990) suggest, "What is most important is that we remain aware of how culture functions as a cognitive filter for all of us, shaping our values and assumptions, the ways we think about reading, and the ways we teach reading" (p. 410).

8. Practice patience. Time is the single greatest factor influencing success for ESL learners (Leki, 1992; Peregoy & Boyle, 1997); they need time to acculturate, to learn language, and to apply that learning to the act of reading. Teachers need to be willing to provide L2 students enough time, get to know them, consult with them often, and adapt their curriculum.

Techniques That Work Well with ELL Students

The majority of techniques and approaches ESL experts propose are centered around language arts, of course. These approaches use some of the strategies that we stress in this text, such as cooperative learning, response journals, higher-level thinking skills, use of visuals to teach vocabulary and concepts, directed readings, and use of predictions in reading. Ashworth (1992) concisely presents how listening and speaking, reading, and writing activities can be tailored to the needs of ESL students. Writing, discussed further in Chapter 10, is an excellent tool for content teachers. Purohit (1998), a teacher of Chinese immigrants, described how her students used science to learn English. They wrote letters expressing their knowledge, used the classroom as a community in which to learn, and started always from their own experiences.

Cook and Gonzales (1995) suggest that ESL students be encouraged to visualize and manipulate literature they read because "second language learners need a social context for both understanding and producing English." Although such activities are not new—visualization through drawing is much like postgraphic organizers—they encourage students to use what they already know in making connections to a new language and culture. ESL learners who regard text as "only a tool to learn that language" (p. 639), rather than as a way to learn about a new culture, do not learn as effectively and efficiently (Chi, 1995).

The **group frame** from the Guided Language Experience model is recommended for reading and writing and is directly applicable to content area material (Brechtel, 1992). Using this strategy, the teacher takes dictation (pertaining to the content area) from the class and records the information on a chart. This information is used to model revising and editing for the group. The revised dictation is reproduced and used for the reading lesson. Activity 2.1 shows a group frame from an elementary mathematics lesson on flowcharts and algorithms. In this example, the teacher can begin with the child's native language (in this case Spanish) or start with English and dictate later in the second language.

A modified anticipation guide (introduced in Chapter 6) can net very positive results. A group of 10 adult ESL students, 7 men and 3 women from Vietnam, Egypt, Bangladesh, China, El Salvador, Colombia, and Hong Kong, reacted to the statements shown in Activity 2.2. First the teacher wrote the statements on the chalkboard to encourage reading in English. Class discussion about the students' opinions, based on their experiences in the United States, was conducted. After discussion, a passage about an American family was read. The students were eager to volunteer information and were interested in finding out about family life in one another's cultures as well as in the United States. The teacher noted that she had fewer requests during the reading time for explanation of vocabulary, and she speculated that coming to the passage with a good idea of the concepts helped the students use context clues to make sense of unfamiliar vocabulary. This activity engaged ESL students in listening, speaking, and reading in English, and it respected their various cultures.

Another effective activity has ELLs work in pairs to write sentences about new words. The teacher selects words from the text and defines each one. She also uses the word in a sentence. Then students work in pairs to practice the word in context and write sentences with the word. Then they read the sentences in text using the word. This activity, Capsule Vocabulary, is also presented in Chapter 9, with an ESL example.

ACTIVITY *2.1* GROUP FRAME: ELEMENTARY MATHEMATICS

Dictation from Students	**Dictation from Students**
We use a series of steps to solve a problem.	Usamos una serie de pasos para resolver un problema.
We can make a chart showing how we solved the problem.	Podemos hacer un esquema que nos muestra cómo resoldimos el problema.
The answer to the problem should be at the end of the chart.	La solución del problema debería estar al final del esquema.
Revised Dictation	**Revised Dictation**
A series of steps to solve a problem is called an *algorithm*.	Una serie de pasos para resolver un problema se llama un "algorithm."
The picture of this is called a *flowchart*.	El diagrama se llama un "flowchart."
Shapes of things in the flowchart tell you something.	Las formas de los pasos en el esquema te indican algo.

_____ **Most marriages last a long time.**

Most students felt that marriages in the United States do not last a long time. Discussion turned to the question "What is a long time?" The students decided it meant a lifetime. We talked about divorce in the United States and how divorce is viewed in other cultures.

_____ **Television is bad for children.**

Although the class generally disagreed with the statement, several students commented that television can be both good and bad for children. We talked about the need for parents to be selective and to monitor programs. Watching TV is one way to learn English.

_____ **Women in America are equal to men in the United States.**

Most students agreed that women in the United States are equal to men. After much laughter, the Vietnamese men commented that American women seem to be superior to American men because they always get to go first!

_____ **Working mothers neglect their children.**

This statement generated the most controversy and debate among the students. The student from Egypt felt that mothers needed to be with children for long times; other students brought up the idea of quality time.

Developed by Karen Curling.

Multitext activities are especially important for ESL learners. When books at many levels and on many topics are provided, ESL learners have opportunities to select, read, reread, and practice (Gee, 1999; Koskinen et al., 1999). Hadaway and Mundy (1999) share how they used picture books about science topics to create compare/contrast maps, poetry, semantic maps, and jot charts with secondary ESL students. Watching videos and movies and then discussing the content and American culture depicted in them is a good way to combine oral and written media (Pally, 1998). Sadly, books representing children from other countries are not as available as teachers and students would prefer. Barry's (1998) review indicates that Hispanic representation in literature is sparse.

SPECIAL-EDUCATION STUDENTS[*]

Special education is defined as schooling for students "very different in one or more ways in intellectual, physical, social, or emotional development from the usual student" (Harris & Hodges, 1995, p. 238). Special-education students are diverse learn-

[*]Special thanks to Dr. Joseph Boyle, Special Education professor at Virginia Commonwealth University, for reviewing this section.

ers, and their differences may place them at risk unless they receive appropriate accommodations. If their differences are severe, students are usually placed in special classrooms for all or part of their accommodations. The current educational preference, however, is **collaboration**—called **mainstreaming** in the 1990s and **inclusion** in the early 2000s—designed to include students in regular classrooms as often as possible. The terms **collaboration** or **inclusion** are often used interchangeably today.

Laws govern special education, as well as ELL instruction.

PL (Public Law) 94-142, Education of All Handicapped Children, was renamed the **Individuals with Disabilities Education Act (IDEA)** in 1990. This law states that all children with disabilities will receive a free and appropriate education in the least restrictive environment. In 1997 the act was amended to become IDEA 97. The most significant change for regular education teachers was the expansion of the term *Other health impaired* to include specific language for students with ADD or ADHD. Final regulations for IDEA 97, released in March 1999, ensure that all children with disabilities will receive a free, appropriate public education, with special education emphases and services that meet the children's needs. The effectiveness of educational efforts must be assessed.

In 1999–2000, 6.1 million children (ages 3–21) were eligible for special-education services; this is an increase of 65 percent from 3.7 million in 1976–1977 (Horn & Tynan, 2001). Those diagnosed with learning disabilities more than doubled in this same period (Kidder-Ashley, Deni, & Anderton, 2000). When students are included in regular classrooms, content teachers must understand what special-education needs their students possess and how to accommodate them. In this section we introduce some terms that may be helpful, issues that content teachers should be aware of, and suggestions and strategies for content teachers.

Groups of Disability

Some students possess significant developmental disabilities. These are usually children born with birth defects, serious sensory or physical disabilities, or cognitive delays. They are often diagnosed early in life and begin receiving intervention before kindergarten. While PL 94-142 was originally passed for this group, it constitutes only 10 percent of children now included in special education (Horn & Tynan, 2001). Accommodations made for them include interpreters, Braille resources, curb cuts for wheelchairs, and enough space to use appropriate learning equipment.

A second group of special-education students comprises those with emotional or behavioral problems. These students might be labeled as having "oppositional defiant disorder" or "conduct disorder." They are often enrolled in special programs to help them become accountable for their behavior and develop coping strategies for social problems.

The largest group of students with special-education needs includes those with processing problems—learning disabilities (often labeled as **SLD** for **specific learning disorder**) in seven areas: listening, speaking, basic reading of words, reading comprehension, written expression, mathematics problem solving, and mathematics calculations. The number of students classified as SLD has increased dramatically over the past 20 years (Swanson, 2000). Also included are students with mild forms of neurological dysfunction or mild mental retardation, such as educable mentally retarded (EMR) students and those with attention deficit disorder (ADD). These students are often included in the regular classroom and must receive some appropriate accommodation.

While not usually thought of as having a disability or as special-education students, gifted students with learning disabilities also require accommodation in their learning to challenge them beyond the regular curriculum. These students are a challenge because teachers must ensure that they will become autonomous learners who have appropriate skills and attitudes. Gifted students need a differentiated curriculum so that they can learn at their own pace within the classroom (Betts, 2004).

Gifted children present special challenges also.

Issues in Special Education

Whereas procedures for diagnosing a developmental disability or a behavior disorder seem to have recognized criteria, there is no validated diagnostic criterion to determine SLD (Horn & Tynan, 2001). IDEA has guidelines for identifying SLD, but procedures may vary from state to state. This poses a considerable problem because often students are misdiagnosed and receive either no services or services inappropriate for their needs. For instance, Gunderson and Siegel (2001) caution that the use of intelligence testing to classify ESL students as learning disabled is risky because such tests rely on proficient use of the English language.

Minority children are overrepresented in special education (Agbenyega & Jiggetts, 1999; Cox, Matthews, & Associates, 2001). According to Agbenyega and Jiggetts, some students are "railroaded" into special-education programs so their test scores will not be included in a school profile. These authors also write that 38 percent of minority students are classified as special-education students, including 1.3 percent Native American, 1.5 percent Asian, 10 percent Hispanic, and 25.1 percent African-American students. African-American students are three times more likely to be classified as mentally retarded than are Caucasian students (Cox, Matthews, & Associates, 2001). Some minority students may be at risk due to low socioeconomic profiles, low self-esteem, limited English proficiency, or low literacy contact in home environments, but these factors do not make them special-education students. A related issue concerns the type of instruction received in some special-education classrooms. Cox, Matthews, and Associates, after reviewing 14 studies, warn that some students are "subject to less demanding work, more restrictive classrooms, and isolation" (p. 22). However, Gallagher (1998) points out that gifted students do not receive the challenge they need; their test scores often inflate a school's test performance, but they themselves do not benefit from the curriculum they should have. Gifted students who are also learning disabled present a special challenge. They do best when identified early, especially when their specific gifts are recognized. They require a supportive environment that stresses resilience (Dole, 2000).

Technology is an excellent resource to tap the creativity of gifted children (DelSiegle, 2004).

Retention and transfer of knowledge learned in school is a critical problem for special-education students (Gersten & Baker, 1998). Mastropieri, Scruggs, and Butcher (1997) found that 35 percent of students with learning disabilities could not transfer a general rule of physical science when 95 percent of average-ability students could do so. "Nearly every student with whom we worked used an approach to solving word problems that was mechanical and procedural, rather than based on an attempt to understand the problem. . . . Students consistently attempted to use the irrelevant information in every problem we gave them. They demonstrated poor comprehension of the problems they were being asked to solve" (Goldman et al., 1996, p. 201).

Some special-education students show poor postschool outcomes (Cimera, 2000). In 1984, Will proposed a bridge model for transition and adjustment for special-education students after the completion of high school studies. But his model has not been actualized as yet. Cimera writes that the goal "should be to give students the skills they will need to accomplish whatever they wish to achieve" (p. 124), but many are not able to make life decisions for themselves or become self-sufficient.

Teaching Special-Education Students in the Content Classroom

Teachers of content subjects will teach special-education students. Instruction must be in the best interest of the special-education student, while also serving all other students in the classroom. Here are some suggestions from experts in special education:

Universal design, a feature of special education, should be a feature of all education.

- **Universal design** should guide all instruction. Instruction that takes into account the needs of special education will be good for all students in the classroom.
- Borden and Lytle (2000) provide a checklist and scoring procedure to make us aware of special-education students' instructional needs. The instructional setting should include social support, such as parent support groups, resources, and classroom volunteers. The instructional setting should encompass a team approach that includes parents, teachers, students, and administrators; steady positive comments to parents and students via telephone, notes, or e-mail; and a consistent emphasis on strengths rather than weaknesses.
- Gersten and Baker (1998) recommend that teachers know and practice a variety of strategies and effective adaptations. For example, *situated cognition*—placing or situating activities into the context and concepts being studied—makes sense. Situated cognition anchors learning and application in real-world problems.
- Gallagher (1998) proposes *differentiated education*—allowing different opportunities for students to learn the content beyond the regular curriculum. One way to provide differentiation is to encourage learners to pursue inquiry into areas of personal interest related to subject matter.
- Lankutis (2001) encourages teachers to provide instruction in more than one mode. Brain research tells us that when learners receive information in more than one way, they process it more effectively. Using technology can be an aid to multimode presentation (see Chapter 4). For instance, Co-Writer 4000, a software program (Don Johnston, Inc.), helps a student who has difficulty moving ideas from thought to print. The program "guesses" what word the student might mean to write from clues given so the student can make good

writing choices: "I want to r____" might be translated as "I want to read." L & H Kurweil 3000 is a program that scans and reads text to students. It also has study skills features.

- Maroney (1990) tells teachers that to make it easier for students to do what is expected, teachers should *tell* students exactly what is expected; *teach* by modeling; *watch* students in action to see if they understand; *coach* students who seem unsure; *remind* students frequently; and *practice, practice, practice* to make perfect!

READING INSTRUCTION FOR STRUGGLING STUDENTS

Proficiency in reading stands at the center of academic learning. The student who is struggling in reading avoids reading at all costs. Such students read when instructed to do so but only to "get through" the assignment. Their view of themselves as helpless and unable to overcome failure results in lack of participation and passive reading at best. In short, these students do not learn how to read to learn. Those who struggle with reading from elementary school onward are more likely to become violent and to engage in delinquency and substance abuse (Fleming et al., 2004). Bad behavior and poor reading habits are difficult to break. However, through modeling and guided practice in using techniques such as those listed for good readers in Table 2.1, even the poorest students can change their reading patterns. A dramatic improvement for poor readers results when they are taught to apply intervention strategies to content text.

We know that virtually all students can learn to read. We also know a great deal about how to succeed with students who are at risk of reading failure. Success with these students is not always easy; in some cases, it is extremely difficult. The routes to success, however, are not mysterious (Au, 1992; Gambrell, 1990). The work of Allington (1991) and Pallas, Natriello, and McDill (1989) suggests that improvement in the teaching and learning of struggling students does not lie in special remedial programs. Rather, we need to change the approaches we use with these students in the regular classroom (Au, 1992). Ivey and Broaddus (2000), for instance, encourage teachers to "tailor the fit" of their instruction by being responsive to the needs and interests of their students.

> Struggling readers often manifest other problems in a classroom.

Factors to Consider

Vacca and Padak (1990) identify four factors associated with the learned helplessness that typifies many struggling students:

1. Struggling students may lack knowledge of the reading process and, as a result, may have trouble identifying appropriate purposes for reading and resolving comprehension failure. Struggling readers must become aware of the demands of the reading task and learn how to handle these demands. This awareness is important for readers to choose the strategies needed either to meet their purposes or to resolve their comprehension difficulties.

TABLE 2.1	Contrasting Good and Poor Readers

Good Readers	Poor Readers
Before Reading	
Build up their background knowledge on the subject. Know their purpose for reading. Focus their complete attention on reading.	Start reading without thinking about the subject. Do not know why they are reading.
During Reading	
Give their complete attention to the reading task. Keep a constant check on their own understanding. Monitor their reading comprehension and do it so often that it becomes automatic. Stop only to use a fix-up strategy when they do not understand.	Do not know whether they understand or do not understand. Do not monitor their own comprehension. Seldom use any of the fix-up strategies.
After Reading	
Decide if they have achieved their goal for reading. Evaluate comprehension of what was read. Summarize the major ideas in a graphic organizer. Seek additional information from outside sources.	Do not know what they have read. Do not follow reading with comprehension self-check.

A dramatic improvement for poor readers results when they are taught to apply intervention strategies to content text.

From Orange County Public Schools (1986). *Contrasting Good and Poor Readers, in Middle School Curriculum Planning Guide for Reading.* Orlando, Florida. Used with permission.

2. Struggling readers typically view themselves as poor, ineffective readers rather than competent, proficient readers. This self-view may make them avoid reading. These students don't read because they don't believe they will be successful.

3. When students fail to value reading as a source of information and enjoyment, they are at risk of reading failure. As explained in Chapter 12, motivation is a central component of the reading comprehension process (Gambrell, 1996; Guthrie, 2000; Mathewson, 1976). When students are motivated, they will want to pick up books. Encouraging students to choose reading as an activity should be a primary goal of reading instruction. The teacher plays a critical role in motivating students to read. One key factor is a teacher who values reading and is enthusiastic about sharing a love of reading with the students. If a teacher enjoys reading, students will be more likely to become voluntary lifelong readers (Wilson & Gambrell, 1988).

4. Struggling readers may lack the ability to monitor their own comprehension. Because they lack experience in constructing meaning, they read words passively instead of actively questioning their understanding (Walker, 1990).

Comprehension monitoring is the conscious control of one's own level of reading comprehension (Brown, 1980). Comprehension monitoring occurs when readers begin to scrutinize their comprehension processes and actively evaluate and regulate them. In short, comprehension monitoring occurs when readers think about their own comprehension. This awareness of processing allows the reader to take remedial action to rectify comprehension failure. Before readers can independently employ specific strategies to enhance comprehension, they must be aware that their comprehension is less than adequate.

Forgan and Mangrum (1997) discuss many possible causes of reading failure. They use the acronym **PLEASE** to remind content teachers what to consider:

Use PLEASE to help guide understanding of struggling readers.

1. **P**hysical factors may have caused difficulties, such as poor vision, hearing, or health at an early age.

2. **L**anguage problems or delays may cause a child to lag in development.

3. **E**nvironment: the home or the community may not stress literacy or may distract from learning.

4. **A**ptitude may be over- or underestimated, causing lower or higher expectations than are fair.

5. **S**ocioeconomic status may influence the will to learn; interests and attitudes may conflict with learning.

6. **E**ducational factors may play a role—for example, poor educational facilities, teachers without the proper background, or lack of materials.

Steps for Content Teachers

Refer to the reading specialist for help with content instruction that incorporates reading.

In order to help struggling readers, the first step is for content teachers to rely on the reading specialist in their school. Yes, every school should have a reading specialist on board! According to Tatum (2004), the reading specialist should be ready to assess students who are struggling and share assessment results, along with suggestions that incorporate appropriate strategies within content classrooms. Also, this specialist should select and demonstrate curriculum materials and resources to aid content teachers. Dole (2004) suggests that reading teachers should become coaches to show teachers how to teach reading within their subject areas.

Second, content teachers need to understand how their students view literacy in the first place. The story of Jacques (Knobel, 2001) provides a sobering illustration. Jacques declared that he was "not a pencil man" (p. 407). He used many avoidance strategies, such as fooling around to distract attention from the reading task assigned; remarking on "how boring" the assignment was; and not listening or pretending not to listen. When teachers realize what these avoidance behaviors might be, they can counter them with relevant use of text and activities that pull those "nonpencil" students into literacy.

Third, content teachers need to ask hard questions and seek answers, rather than abdicating responsibility. Ganske, Monroe, and Strickland (2003) pose some of these hard questions and provide brief responses. One such question is, "Why don't students come to each grade level more prepared?" (p. 126). The answer is not easy, but the authors point out that early literacy experiences, background knowledge, choice of materials used in classrooms, and test difficulty all contribute. This text presents information about each of these issues. The next section provides concrete suggestions.

Strategy Repertoire

Striving readers often do not realize that reading calls on them to know what to do at a given point with the text they are reading (Gee, 1996). Even if they know they should take action, their repertoire of strategies to comprehend material is limited (Olshavsky, 1975; Paris, 1986). Proficient readers use such strategies deliberately and flexibly, adapting them to fit a variety of reading situations (Duffy & Roehler, 1987). When used for resolving comprehension difficulties, these are often referred to as **fix-up strategies.** Struggling readers who encounter difficulty with text may "shut down," stop, or give up because the text is too difficult. The proficient reader, in contrast, has specific strategies—such as visual imagery, self-questioning, and rereading—that can fix up or resolve the comprehension difficulty (see Activity 2.3).

Research suggests that proficient readers spontaneously use fix-up strategies, whereas struggling readers do not—even though they can and do use fix-up strategies under teacher direction (Gambrell & Bales, 1986). Kletzein (1991) investigated students' self-reports of strategies when reading different kinds of materials. He found little difference in the strategies used by good and poor readers, but he found that good readers were more flexible and persistent. Poor readers did not seem to know when to use appropriate strategies. In fact, the most important goal of reading instruction for the struggling reader may be to develop the ability to use strategies to enhance comprehension (Winograd & Paris, 1988). Embedding strategy instruction within content is an efficient way to help struggling readers in content classrooms (Hinchman et al., 2004). To do so, teachers must have a repertoire from which to draw. The following activities are especially effective with struggling readers, and numerous other effective activities are described in each chapter of this text.

RECIPROCAL TEACHING

Palincsar and Brown (1986) describe a strategy to promote independent learning from a text. In this strategy, called **reciprocal teaching,** students and teachers establish a dialogue and work together in comprehending text. At the heart of reciprocal teaching are four shared goals: prediction, summarization, questioning, and clarification. First the teacher assigns a paragraph. Next the teacher summarizes the paragraph and asks students several questions about it. The teacher then clarifies any misconceptions or difficult concepts. Finally, the students predict in writing what will be discussed in the next paragraph or segment. When the next cycle begins, roles are reversed and students become the modelers.

We recommend this strategy because reciprocal teaching uses small segments of reading; thus the struggling reader is not overwhelmed by too much reading. It is a highly structured method that incorporates all the language arts—listening, writing,

Visualization

Visualize a tree house that you and your friends would like to build in your backyard or in nearby woods.

How would you measure it? In yards? In feet? In inches?

Visualize how big it would be and your measuring of it.

Visualize some objects that are one inch long.

Visualize some objects that are one foot long.

Visualize some objects that are one yard long.

Visualize something that is one mile long.

Self-Questioning

What are the standard units of length?

Why do I need to know them?

Why do we measure in fractions?

What if we couldn't measure in fractions?

---

reading, and speaking. According to Palincsar and Brown (1986), this technique succeeds with small and large groups, in peer tutoring, in science instruction, and in teaching listening comprehension.

REQUEST

Manzo (1969) describes a questioning strategy called **ReQuest** that encourages students to ask informed questions. This procedure seems to work especially well in a remedial situation or with poor readers. The key to this technique is that it requires students to "open up" their thinking, to question and think critically. Also, a short selection is involved, usually a paragraph, which doesn't overwhelm the slow reader.

With this technique, the teacher and students first read silently a selected portion of the text (usually one or two paragraphs). The students then ask the teacher questions about what they read. The teacher must keep the book closed during this phase. When the students exhaust their questions, the teacher begins asking questions. During this phase, the students must also keep their books closed. The activity can be repeated with other paragraphs, as time allows. The teacher then sets purposes for reading the remainder of the lesson, referring to the questions asked and information received during the ReQuest. Because Manzo had remedial readers and small groups in mind when designing ReQuest, some modifications for the content class are in order. The teacher probably should select a small but representative portion of text and limit the questioning time. It is likely that students' questions will be mainly literal; the teacher can then concentrate on inferences and applications. If ReQuest is used often, students will readily adapt to asking more sophisticated questions. After focusing on listening, speaking, and reading in this activity, teachers can follow the same steps using written rather than oral questions. Written questions tend to be

ReQuest was used to introduce the chapter on integers. Students read the first two pages of the chapter, then asked the teacher questions directly pertaining to those pages. The students referred to their pages, but the teacher could not. After two minutes, the teacher had students close their books and she asked questions. The teacher, Beverly Marshall, comments:

> This activity was enjoyed by all—teacher and students. I noticed that even students who don't participate orally did so with "stump the teacher." Students were better able to answer the questions I asked them because they had already listened to the answers I had given to their questions. Overall, comprehension was greatly increased over past reading.

Students' Sample Questions

What was the coldest temperature recorded in the United States? (80 below)

What was the name of the weather station? (Prospect Creek Camp)

In what state was the weather station located? (Alaska)

How do you write a negative integer? (-4)

Teacher's Sample Questions

What are some examples other than those on these pages where integers are used? (profit/loss; elevation . . .)

Which number is larger, 0 or -5? (0—it is farther to the right on the number line.)

Describe the location of 2 and -2 on the number line. (Positive 2 is two units to the right of 0, and negative 2 is two units to the left of 0.)

Developed by Beverly Marshall.

more intricate than oral questions and will thus enhance students' levels of sophistication with writing as well. A sixth grade mathematics teacher using ReQuest obtained the results reported in Activity 2.4.

Ciardiello (1998) added a training model to ReQuest that encourages formal questioning. In stage one, divergent questions are identified; in stage two, divergent questions are classified; in stage three, divergent questions are generated. The model enhances ReQuest by enabling struggling readers to comprehend at higher levels.

MYSTERY CLUE GAME

The mystery clue game, described in Chapter 7, is useful for helping students understand the sequential listing organizational pattern. The example provided in Activity 2.5 is adapted for first graders in an inner-city school. The teacher used this activity to help students recognize the sequence of steps in a science experiment about fire and air. The question they were to answer was "Can fire burn without air?" The teacher wrote each step on a different card. When she presented the cards to the students, she said that she had "dropped them and needed to get the cards back in order." She had "found" the first card and placed it at the top of the pile. Their job was to put the rest of the cards in order. She read each card aloud, pointing to the picture and

CAN A FIRE BURN WITHOUT AIR?

First — Use a knife to cut off the top of the pumpkin.

Fifth — Put the top back on the pumpkin.

Third — Put a candle inside the pumpkin.

Then

Relight the candle.

Second — Clean the inside of the pumpkin with a spoon.

Next

Cut eyes, nose, and a mouth in the pumpkin.

Fourth — Light the candle.

Last

Put the lid back on.

Developed by Megan K. Houston.

word clues. After the students sequenced the cards, they completed the experiment. For follow-up, students received an ordered copy of the clues, which they cut apart and then pasted in correct sequence again. The teacher found that her students, often distracted, paid attention and participated enthusiastically. She thought that their understanding was greatly enhanced.

ANALOGIES

Analogies (see Chapter 6) are especially helpful to struggling readers, who often require relational (concrete, gestalt, example-oriented, relevant) rather than analytical (abstract, detail- and lecture-oriented, definitional) learning experiences (Anderson & Adams, 1992). At-risk readers might be better equipped to understand what they read after hearing analogies such as these:

> When I begin a new year of teaching mathematics, I always draw a little house on the board, starting with a foundation of bricks, and I explain that the foundation in math is being able to do the four basic operations—first with whole numbers, then with decimals, then with fractions. As we get into time, measurement, money, percents, and geometry, having a good foundation is absolutely necessary in order to do the work. So I tell my students that we cannot have any "loose bricks," or else doing multistep problems, story problems, solving for one or more unknowns, and graphing will be impossible. Students seem to appreciate the foundation analogy and can accept that doing calculations well is as important as grasping the new concept. The teaching of the new concepts must be "laid down" on a solid understanding of old concepts and the ability to apply them.
> —Kerry Blum, middle school mathematics teacher

> When a student does not understand new words or does not have any prior knowledge to link with new content, the student is likely to reject the new information. For example, deoxyribonucleic acid is a complex molecule made up of different nucleotides linked together and is difficult to understand. However, Watson and Crick's double helix model of DNA can be taught easily by comparing it to something the students already know. By drawing a picture in students' minds of a circular staircase, and by describing the links of nucleotides as building blocks that can match up only in specific pairs (cytosine to guanine and adenine to thymine), the mystery of the DNA molecule dissolves.
> —Diana Freeman, high school biology teacher

Additional Strategies for Struggling Readers and Nonreaders

What can the content area teacher do with the student who can barely read or who is a nonreader? The teacher can (1) pretend such a student is really not that bad a reader and do nothing, (2) get help from a reading specialist, or (3) assign extra work to help a student in this situation. Ideally, content area teachers do both (2) and (3). The reading specialist can help with basic skills while aiding the content teacher in adapting assignments for this type of student. Most of the techniques that we describe in this book will help the very poor reader or nonreader. Here we present some techniques that are especially important for the success of such students.

LANGUAGE EXPERIENCE APPROACH

The **Language Experience Approach (LEA)** has been used by reading specialists for a long time (Ashton-Warner, 1959). Fisher and Frey (2003) suggest its use once again, as part of what they term a "gradual release model." In this model teachers move from teacher control to student-directed writing. Students dictate to a teacher or another individual their thoughts about a topic; then they copy to their own notebooks the words they have said and now see. The words become the topic of discussion that can generate new words, phrases, and sentences. Next students are encouraged to try to write just a few more sentences. In the Fisher–Frey model, students go on to interactive writing, relying on models of good writing to expand their own writing, and generating sentences. Eventually students are able to expand their writing and move beyond the teacher's help with dictation. The model can also apply to reading. In the same way, by having struggling readers dictate their impressions about a subject, then using that dictation to talk about the subject and add to it, a beginning reader—even in a content classroom—will have some text material to read and use for study.

AUDITORY AND VISUAL DISCRIMINATION GUIDES

Auditory discrimination can be defined as a student's ability to differentiate between sounds, including differences in rhythm, volume, and tone. **Visual discrimination** is a student's ability to perceive similarities and differences in forms, letters, and words. As children mature and develop, they usually acquire basic auditory and visual discrimination abilities. However, auditory and visual discrimination problems may continue for many children into middle school and even high school. Weaknesses in these two important areas may mean that students will be severely hindered in learning to read. We suggest that content area teachers ask reading specialists to evaluate nonreaders on these two important factors. Nonreaders weak in these areas can be helped through auditory and visual discrimination games and activities. For instance, the teacher or another student can call out to the nonreader words similar or alike in beginning, middle, and ending sounds to selected words in the unit. This activity can be done in this manner: Are the beginning (middle, ending) sounds of these two words alike or different?

zygoma [*word in unit*], xylophone

CONCEPT-FORMATION STUDY GUIDES

The ability to create superordinate generalizations is a skill often completely lacking in reluctant readers and at-risk learners. **Concept-formation study guides** (Thompson & Morgan, 1976) are excellent motivational tools for such readers. Such guides use a fundamental learning operation: the categorization of facts (subordinate concepts) under more inclusive, superordinate concepts. Thompson and Morgan note that "once a key concept has been acquired, we use it at different levels of abstraction, complexity, and generality, depending upon our stage of motivation" (p. 132). The function of this type of study guide is to teach the key concepts of a passage and to provide practice in applying those concepts to more complex and more general situations.

Activities 2.6 and 2.7 present two examples of concept-formation study guides. The first is for elementary students, the second for high school social studies.

EMBEDDED QUESTIONS

Weir (1998) encourages the use of questions embedded in reading material to engage struggling readers. When they are confronted with questions during reading, they will more likely practice metacognitive strategies. She actually cut up reading material and inserted questions and response slots to keep students' attention while reading. Students began to make more and more elaborate responses as they answered embedded questions. Their test scores reflected increased comprehension.

Embedded questions must be carefully considered to maintain balance and variety. Selections can be physically cut up and pasted back together with questions and response slots, or a teacher can use a computer and a word processing program to create the activity. This fix-up activity is best reserved for struggling readers, but the investment of time does help students become active, more proficient readers.

BEGINNER-ORIENTED TEXTS

The texts used in content classes are too difficult for many struggling readers. Texts that contain fewer words per sentence and page, simpler words, less metaphoric language, fewer complex sentences, and illustrations that provide context will be more successful (Cole, 1998). Media specialists can help content teachers locate such texts. High-interest/low-readability, content-oriented books are also available from a few publishers. They are a good choice because they enable practice with material at the readers' instructional level (Ivey, 1999). Activity 2.8 lists some of these books and

---

ACTIVITY 2.6 CONCEPT-FORMATION STUDY GUIDE FOR ELEMENTARY STUDENTS

I. Read the story. Put an X before each statement you think is true.

———— 1. A person should find out how the neighborhood feels about pets.

———— 2. Some small pets grow into large pets.

———— 3. Someone must care for your pet if you are sick.

———— 4. A kangaroo will not make a good pet.

———— 5. Do not read about a pet before you buy it.

———— 6. It is hard to keep a pet in a small apartment in the city.

II. Put true statements from Part I where they fit below.

Choosing a pet depends on

Size   Care   Space

III. When you are finished, get together with a classmate and discuss your answers.

THE MOVE TO WINTER GRASSLANDS

Key Concept: Social transience

Main Idea: Interaction between people and the physical and social environment that surrounds them influences how the basic needs of life are met.

PART I

Directions: Think of a family you know who recently moved. What reasons did this family have for moving? In the chart below, complete a listing of reasons American families and Al'Azab families have for moving from one place to another.

Reasons for Moving

American Families	Bedouin Al'Azab Clan
1. Dad's new job	1. Good grasslands
2.	2.
3.	3.
4.	4.
5.	5.
6.	6.
7.	7.
8.	8.
9.	9.
10.	10.

PART II

From your list in Part I, answer the following questions:

1. Select those items under the "American" list that are related to making a living. Do the same thing for the Al'Azabs. How are the reasons different? Alike?

2. Based on the information you have organized above, make a list of the Al'Azab basic needs of life. Are they different from the American family's basic needs?

3. Based on the information you have organized above, define in your own words what you think *social transience* is.

From The Globe Readers' Collection (Globe Fearon, 4350 Equity Drive, Columbus, OH 43216):

Myths and Stories from the Americas
Stories of Adventure and Survival
Eight Plays of U.S. History

From The Reading Success Series (Curriculum Associates, Inc., P.O. Box 2001, North Billerica, MA 01862):

The Inside Story
Sneakers
Burgers
Jeans

Bikes
Skateboards

From Dominie Press, Inc. (1949 Kellogg Avenue, Carlsbad, CA 92008):

Global Views
American Voices
Knowing About Places

The Horn Book Guide, an interactive database, reviews more than 29,000 books, searchable by level and topic (Heinemann, 88 Post Road West, P.O. Box 5007, Westport, CT 06881).

---

publishers. An alternative to beginner-oriented text is rewriting (see Chapter 6). This requires an investment of time by the teacher, but it tailors the text to the specific content to be taught.

TEACHING DIVERSE LEARNERS IN THE CONTENT CLASSROOM

Horn and Tynan (2001) state that the most effective educational strategies for special-education students are the same ones that help most students in regular education. Likewise, the strategies we present here work for all students and especially for all diverse learners. This list of suggestions should remind the content teacher that PAR works for all content students:

- Gee (1999) encourages teachers to remember that reading is the best way to become a good reader. Good readers read. Practice makes perfect, and those who are at risk and struggling need to read also. Direct instruction in reading skills is important, but written language is too complex to master without extended practice in the actual process of reading. We feature this suggestion throughout the textbook.

- Technology can help the diverse learner put reading into practice in different and challenging ways. Use of discussion forums, e-mail, Internet treasure hunts and web quests, videotapes, and audiotapes will provide variety and use several

Plugger home entertainment system.

modes to stimulate learning (Dahlman & Rilling, 2001; Lankutis, 2001). We feature this suggestion in Chapter 4.

- Writing helps diverse learners reflect on their behavior and build literacy skills, and it increases willingness to learn (Haley & Watson, 2000). We feature this suggestion in Chapter 10.

- **Collaborative Strategic Reading (CSR)** promotes reading comprehension and content learning with support from other learners (Klinger & Vaughn, 1999). Students with different reading skill levels assist one another in small groups as they apply previewing, comprehension monitoring, retelling, and summarizing. Using such strategies—featured throughout this text, especially in Chapters 5 through 7—while instructing and relying on other learners is a good use of co-operative learning (discussed in Chapter 11). CSR goes beyond cooperative grouping because the learners in the group collaborate, making their own decisions and going beyond what the teacher has designated should occur in a co-operative group. Thus in successful group work there are no longer master and apprentice but "equally competent learners in a learning community" (Leki, 2001, p. 60).

ONE-MINUTE SUMMARY

This chapter has considered several groups of diverse learners: students at risk, students from low socioeconomic environments, students with low self-esteem, students with limited English proficiency, special-education students, and struggling readers. We suggested that at-risk learners can become successful, as studies of resilient students indicate. The types of intervention suggested for all diverse learners include cooperative grouping, teacher interaction, and high expectations; boosting students' confidence and encouraging an internal locus of control; and interesting, systematic, and strategy-based learning. Most of the techniques presented in this textbook are appropriate with some modifications. Some additional strategies were also suggested.

There is an old saying in education that teachers must work with the haves, the "halves," and the have-nots. You probably agree that one does not have to be a great teacher to teach the haves—students with the motivation to learn and the skills to do work above their grade level. The true art of teaching is in relating to the halves and the have-nots. The halves have marginal skills to learn a subject but are not motivated to do so. The have-nots usually are not motivated to learn and do not have the necessary thinking, reading, and study skills to be successful. This chapter presented unique strategies for unique individuals—diverse learners who need teacher assistance and empathy to help them become productive citizens in a technological society. The challenge that such students pose for teachers is great, and the rewards may be few. But these diverse students can and must be reached if our society is to prosper.

PAR Online

 Post a threaded discussion to share your ideas for high-needs activities. High-needs activities are targeted for diverse learners who may be hard to teach or have greater needs than many others.

Locate a website that provides information about one kind of diverse learner discussed in this chapter. Describe to others in your class how this website can be useful in content instruction.

Go to the website for IDEA 97 to learn more about the disabilities included in this legislation: http://www.ed.gov/offices/OSERS/Policy/IDEA/the_law.html

END-OF-CHAPTER ACTIVITIES

Assisting Comprehension

In a *jigsaw,* named for the jigsaw puzzle, cooperative reading and study occur as students read, share, and teach one another. Students in a base group (numbers 1–4) are given unique information about a topic. After reading the material, students meet in "expert" groups (all As together, all Bs together, and so forth) with their counterparts from other groups to discuss and master the information. Students share their "expert" knowledge in their base group, each taking a turn. In this way, the puzzle is completed. The following diagram illustrates the structure of this activity.

For this jigsaw, Group A is to read and teach the information on diverse learners: at-risk, low-socioeconomic, and low-self-esteem students. Group B is to read and teach the information about ESL and ELL students. Group C is to read and teach the information on special-education students. Group D is to read and teach the information about struggling readers and the chapter summary.

Base group 1

A	B
C	D

Base group 2

A	B
C	D

Base group 3

A	B
C	D

Base group 4

A	B
C	D

Reflecting on Your Reading

1. Read *Among Schoolchildren* by Tracy Kidder (1989), particularly the chapter entitled "The Science Fair," in which Chris, the teacher, confronts Robert about his failed science project. *Supporting Struggling Readers* by Barbara Walker (1992) gives many practical instructional suggestions. Also, Mary Ashworth's (1992) *First Step on the Longer Path: Becoming an ESL Teacher* will help you understand the ESL learner.

2. The International Reading Association (2003) has developed a set of standards that identify the performance criteria relevant to classroom teachers. Standard 1.3 indicates that teachers

Demonstrate knowledge of language development and reading acquisition and the variations related to cultural and linguistic diversity. They can de-scribe when students are meeting developmental benchmarks; they know when to consult other professionals for guidance.

Standard 2.2 indicates that teachers

Use a wide range of instructional practices, approaches, and methods, including technology-based practices, for learners at differing stages of development and from differing cultural and linguistic backgrounds.

Standard 2.3 indicates that teachers

Use a wide range of curriculum materials in effective reading instruction for learners at different stages of reading and writing development and from different cultural and linguistic backgrounds.

Standard 4.1 indicates that teachers

Use students' interests, reading abilities, and backgrounds as foundations for the reading and writing program.

Standard 4.2 indicates that teachers

Use a large supply of books, technology-based information, and nonprint materials representing multiple levels, broad interests, and cultural and linguistic backgrounds.

How were these elements addressed in this chapter? How does being informed about these elements aid in content instruction?

CHAPTER 3

A Guide to Evaluation and Assessment for Content Teachers

Often, teachers are required to operate under government mandates without government support. It is the "impossible" that leads to resourcefulness. You do not teach for your government; you teach for your students . . . and for yourself.

MEDITATIONS FOR TEACHERS BY GREG HENRY QUINN, APRIL 15 ENTRY

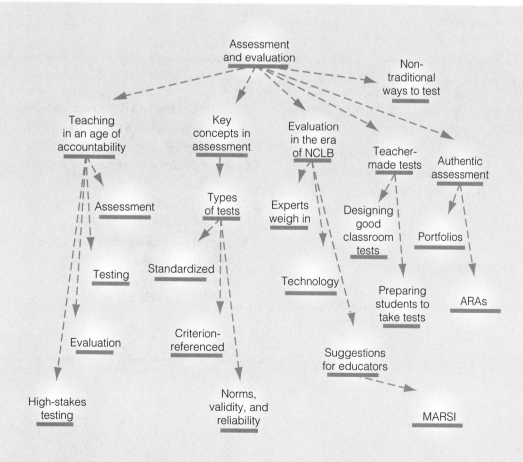

PREPARING TO READ

1. Before reading this chapter, read the International Reading Association (2003) Standard 3 and the four elements that the IRA expects classroom teachers to be able to perform. How do you rate your knowledge at this point? Could you do these tasks? Standard 3 is presented in the end-of-chapter activities.

2. Following is a list of terms used in this chapter. Some may be familiar to you in a general context, but in this chapter they may be used in unfamiliar ways. Rate your knowledge by placing a plus sign (+) in front of those you are certain you know, a check mark (✓) in front of those you have some knowledge about, and a zero (0) in front of those you don't know. Be ready to locate them in the chapter, and pay special attention to their meanings.

_____ assessment
_____ testing
_____ evaluation
_____ high-stakes testing
_____ informal assessment
_____ standardized test
_____ norm-referenced test
_____ validity
_____ reliability
_____ criterion-referenced test
_____ NCLB
_____ MARSI
_____ nontraditional test
_____ SCORER
_____ test-wise
_____ authentic assessment
_____ portfolio
_____ ARA

OBJECTIVES

As you read this chapter, focus your attention on the following purposes. You will

1. define the term *high-stakes testing* and describe its influence on assessment.

2. understand why the content teacher must take a large role in assessment, testing, and evaluation in today's classroom.

3. describe traditional tests, including standardized, criterion-referenced, and teacher-made tests.

4. understand the problems of traditional tests and learn some suggestions for improving them.

5. understand how to design a test whereby students complete a self-rating of their performance.

6. understand the importance of nontraditional testing.

7. understand how being test-wise affects student performance on tests.

8. learn about practical forms of authentic assessment for the content classroom.

9. learn about the value of portfolios and how to use them for effective assessment.

TEACHING IN AN AGE OF ACCOUNTABILITY

 We are living in an age of accountability (Johnson & Johnson, 2002; Stewart, 2004), high-stakes testing (Afflerbach, 2002; Worthy & Hoffman, 2000), and standards for learning (Valencia & Wixson, 1999). These expectations for accountability, testing, and standards cut across school divisions, states, and nations. It is no longer enough to focus on one's own content in one's own classroom. Educators recognize that all teachers must be accountable to a set of standards that permeate every classroom. For instance, the International Reading Association has prepared a set of standards about assessment, diagnosis, and evaluation specifically targeted to classroom teachers. (In the beginning of this chapter, you were asked to review the standard and its elements.) Knowing more about accountability issues is clearly becoming part of the content teacher's responsibility. Such knowledge helps teachers to discuss standards for learning, evaluation, assessment, and high-stakes testing in a manner that helps all learners receive the best education and all educators to provide it. In this chapter we present information about assessment, testing, and evaluation as it pertains to the content teacher. Both formal and informal means of assessment are discussed, and suggestions are provided.

"**Assessment** is the gathering of information about students from multiple measures or sources at multiple points in time" (Gottleib, 2003, p. 2). The purpose of assessment is to make educational decisions by collecting data (Salvia & Ysseldyke, 1998). Assessment is an ongoing process; it can include such data as formal test scores, but often does not. Each time a teacher begins a new unit of instruction, assessment should occur. We call this process "determining background," which we describe in Chapter 6, along with several assessment procedures. **Testing** is a part of assessment; it is one event, or data source, from one instrument given at one point in time. Tests are a "proxy for accomplishment" (Afflerbach, 2002, p. 9) because they provide a look—not an entire profile—at how a general population is doing on the factors being tested. Theodore Sizer (in Oppenheimer, 2003) has commented, "Tests tend to test how one individual performs on that kind of test. It's like taking a temperature in a hospital. It's one important index, but it's only one. We're judging kids on the basis of their temperatures" (Oppenheimer, 2003, p. 282). Tests are useful in providing a point of comparison and one measure of evaluation. **Evaluation** is a term usually reserved for making judgments about educational performance based on the assessment data collected. A test is one piece of data for an evaluation. When teachers give tests in their content areas, they are using the results to evaluate student knowledge. However, teachers often use many more sources of data than one test score in evaluating student learning. When *one* instrument is used to make an educational decision, that process is often labeled **high-stakes testing.** According to the International Reading Association, "*high-stakes testing* means that one test is used to make important decisions about students, teachers, and schools" (1999, p. 1). That one test is given specifically to determine how well students know content information.

Teachers are constantly assessing because they collect information about their students' performance regularly. In the past, such **informal assessment** was used to evaluate students and assign grades that should reflect student learning and success.

However, today such informal assessment is not considered adequate to demonstrate student progress. Uniform assessment procedures at the state level are now required to provide evaluation of educational progress. A formal measure, usually a designated test, is selected as the way to determine if students have learned what they "should know." Because of this trend toward consistent, uniform testing with one test as the single measure of success, all teachers must be aware of information provided in this chapter; becoming informed is the first step toward selecting appropriate assessment. Teachers must understand how to balance informal and formal means of assessment.

KEY CONCEPTS IN ASSESSMENT AND EVALUATION

Testing involves quantitative assessment; that is, its purpose is to quantify or ascribe numerical results to performance. Several types of tests are available to assess students. *Aptitude tests* predict potential for learning. *Diagnostic tests* designate areas of strength and needs. Suppose a student was not achieving and the teacher suspected that the student could do much better. An aptitude test might verify this observation and lead to an effective educational plan for that student, such as a program that challenges gifted students. Suppose a student was below level in reading performance but specific ways to help were not apparent. Then a diagnostic test could help pinpoint the areas of need. In these examples, the tests assess and the findings help activate an instructional plan. Usually, guidance personnel or specialists would administer such forms of assessment, which can be informal or formal measures. The initial observations that the teacher made, often including informal assessment of student class performance, started the testing process.

Achievement tests are intended to show what students have achieved or learned about a specific area. Teachers give achievement tests all the time, but in informal ways. Most schools have participated in annual evaluations of student achievement for decades. Such evaluations have focused on creating a picture that informs us about student progress, especially in math and reading skills. One national example, cited throughout this textbook, is the National Assessment of Educational Progress (NAEP), which publishes results of nationwide testing. School systems have systematically administered tests to determine how their schools are doing, but the tests they have used—and thus the information they have gathered—have differed from state to state and even district to district. Decisions about individual students' progress, or a school's standing, were seldom made from the results of such tests. Teachers of content subjects may have helped administer such tests in their classrooms, but they were not held accountable for the results of the testing. In today's content classrooms, however, teachers are being held accountable for testing results.

What are the three types of tests discussed here?

Standardized, Norm-Referenced Tests

Tests can be standardized and norm-referenced, or criterion-based and/or norm-referenced. A **standardized test** measures ability or achievement against an expectation (norm or standard). The major purpose of standardized, norm-referenced tests is to evaluate what students know about a subject. Examples you may know are *The Scholastic Aptitude Test (SAT)* and the *Graduate Record Examination (GRE)*, developed and published by Educational Testing Service (ETS), or *The Stanford Nine* (ninth edition of the *Stanford Achievement Test*). Such tests usually consist of multiple-choice or closure questions, which are readily and quickly scored by scan sheets or sometimes by hand. One correct answer is expected per item. Many classroom teachers follow the formats used on standardized tests as they construct classroom tests.

Standardized tests are used to compare the performance of groups, such as the results from one school compared to those of a school system, or a system to the state, or the state to the nation. The tests are designed with care by a group of experts and are pilot-tested on a representative sample of students. The results are studied, the test is modified, and a set of norms is developed. The norms become the basis for comparing results; hence the term **norm-referenced test** is often used to describe standardized tests. Scores on a standardized test are given in percentiles, stanines, standard-score equivalents, grade equivalents, or normal-curve equivalents.

Not all standardized tests are equally satisfactory to all users. Perhaps the norming groups are not representative of the particular population to be tested. Perhaps the items on the test do not reflect the content taught to the students tested. Perhaps the test purports to test content that, in fact, it does not really test. Standardized tests, however, are subject to a system of checks that help users make appropriate selections. These measurement concepts include validity and reliability. **Validity** is the "truthfulness" of the test—a check of whether the standardized test actually measures what it claims to measure. **Reliability** is the "consistency" of the test—whether it will produce roughly the same results if administered more than once to the same group in the same time period. Reliability is a check of how dependable the test is. Both validity and reliability contribute to confidence in a quantitative measure. The higher the validity and reliability, the better a test is reported to be.

A school system should select the standardized test best suited to its system by asking these questions:

1. Does this test measure what has been taught?

2. Can we depend on it to give about the same results if we administer it today and tomorrow?

3. Is the norming group similar to our group of students?

Criterion-Referenced Tests

Criterion-referenced tests are less formal than standardized tests, although their format is much like that of standardized tests—usually multiple-choice or closure questions. Criterion-referenced tests can be standardized, but their major purpose is not comparison, so they often are not normed. Because they are less formal, they may include short-answer, true/false, and other objective items. The purpose of criterion-referenced tests is to measure whether a student can perform a specific task or knows a specific body of knowledge. Thus their purpose resembles that of classroom tests.

The *criterion* is the level of performance necessary to indicate that a student "knows" the task. The clients decide this criterion. Thus two schools could use the same test but set different criteria. One school might set 85 percent as a passing score, and the other might set 90 percent as passing. The level of performance on the task is the score: a score of 85 percent means that the student responded correctly to 85 percent of the items. No grade-equivalents, stanines, or other scores are provided.

Because criterion-referenced tests indicate mastery of a task, they should be based on specific objectives. For example, this objective might be stated: "The student will demonstrate mastery by correctly identifying 48 of 50 states and their capitals." A student who has been taught 50 states and capitals and can identify 48 on the test has demonstrated mastery of the criterion. A school system that elects to use a criterion-referenced test developed by an outside source can select an appropriate test by asking these questions:

1. Do the objectives and criteria match our objectives in this content?

2. Are there enough items included to give us a good indication that our students have met the criteria?

3. Do the test items reflect the way in which we taught the information?

Criterion-referenced tests are not new, but their evolution into more uniform, formalized tests is. In fact, the concept of criterion mastery is what individual teachers rely on as they design classroom tests that are criterion-referenced but are for individual classroom use.

EVALUATION IN THE ERA OF NO CHILD LEFT BEHIND

A perception exists that public education in the United States is not adequate. Information cited in Chapter 1 demonstrates why this perception has formed: Over the past 35 years, national results (National Center for Educational Statistics, 2003) for fourth and eighth graders have shown a decline (although it is slight from 2002 to 2003); only 31 percent of fourth graders and only 32 percent of eighth graders attained a "proficient" level—a standard that test officials say all students should reach. Thirty-seven percent of fourth graders and 26 percent of eighth graders did not achieve a basic level of reading proficiency as of the NAEP 2003 report. Many have written that our schools are in crisis and standards must be established as a benchmark for all students. Such authors as Bloom (1987) and Hirsch (1987) led the "charge" several years ago. The charge today is being led in part by politicians. Legislation at the federal and state government levels has raised awareness of assessment and evaluation in schools. Although many experts contest the perception that public education is failing (Berliner, 2001; Bracey, 1997; McQuillan, 1998; Whittington, 1991), the voices of concern have led to new federal intervention such as the No Child Left Behind Act **(NCLB)** of 2001. As President George W. Bush stated when signing this act,

Our schools will have higher expectations—we believe every child can learn. From this day forward, all students will have a better chance to learn, to excel, and to live out their dreams. (Committee on Education and the Workforce, 2002)

NCLB was incorporated into the reauthorization for the Elementary and Secondary Education Act (ESEA), which indicates in part that stronger accountability is expected, as well as use of "teaching methods that have been proven to work" (www.ed.gov/programs/readingfirst/legislation.html). President Bush intends to expand the No Child Left Behind law by requiring two more years of testing in reading and math in high school, which would mean annual state testing in grades 3 to 11. Also, a requirement that national reading and math tests be given to representative samples of 12th graders in every state every two years may be added to this act. The National Assessment of Educational Progress is already required in grades 4 and 8 in every state. (For a direct link to the site, click on the web links option of Chapter 3 resources on our companion website.)

With this legislation, huge amounts of federal funds have been provided to states to ensure strong education for all students, and for teachers as well. A major goal of this act is to promote a strong emphasis on reading instruction, especially for children in the first few grades. Some professionals argue that this emphasis takes away support needed for older students who need reading instruction, and also for those who have special needs, as described in Chapter 2 (Paul, 2004; Conley & Hinchman, 2004). This funding comes with a condition: schools must demonstrate that the education resulting from funding has been effective. The way this demonstration takes place is through the results of mandated testing in grades 3 through 8. NCLB states that, if the test results show that adequate yearly progress is not being made, parents may move their children to other schools and federal dollars may be taken away from low-performing schools. Adequate yearly progress must be based on scientific and research-grounded instruction and evaluation.

Many states have decided, in the wake of NCLB, that they should require all schools to use a designated test that will better determine mastery of content deemed important in their states. They have created—or commissioned creation of—criterion-referenced tests that match their state standards for education, or they have chosen a nationally recognized standardized test they believe will demonstrate such competency. This has created a situation new to many content teachers: high-stakes tests are now a greater part of their instructional considerations.

Experts Weigh In

Many experts in education are quite concerned about the emphasis NCLB seems to place on the use of high-stakes tests, as this article title reflects: "The train has left: the No Child Left Behind Act leaves black and Latino literacy learners waiting at the station" (Paul, 2004). Calkins, Montgomery, and Santman (1998) explain that tests are not necessarily the "enemy," but they warn that teachers must learn how to understand what they reveal and cannot reveal about individual performance. Some professional organizations have developed position statements that raise cautions about

Did you realize that the NCLB Act repeated the words *scientific* or *scientifically* 115 times and the word *research* 245 times? (See pages 240 and 436 of Oppenheimer's *The Flickering Mind*.)

How has NCLB affected evaluation procedures?

What makes one test so important?

Does your professional organization have a position statement about high-stakes tests?

high-stakes testing (American Psychological Association, 2001; International Reading Association, 1999; National Council of Teachers of Mathematics, 2000).

Standardized and criterion-referenced tests have an important place in the evaluation process. They also create some concerns. One concern is the *washback* effect of tests (Bardovi-Harlig and Dornyei, 1998): through constant exposure, students and teachers become very familiar with the language of tests, and this familiarity itself can influence test results. Because the adoption of state and national standards may create too much emphasis on testing and not enough on learning content (Berube, 2004), students may end up learning more about how to take tests than what they should be learning. A major concern is that *one size truly does not fit all*. Often questions about what test to choose—such as those we have suggested be asked—do not yield satisfactory answers for a school system; nevertheless, school systems use the tests as a measure of performance. They do so because comparisons can be made across schools, divisions, states, and nations—and because demand for national testing, using the same test throughout every state, is increasing. This concern leads to the *high-stakes issue*. More educators and politicians are questioning why students should achieve a passing grade in a content class when they perform poorly on a designated test. They want the test to be the common denominator and the grade to be consistent with the test score.

But are high-stakes tests appropriate measures of academic success? They now seem to be "major influences on curriculum and instruction, on teachers and their professional development, on community–school relationships and on levels of school funding" (Afflerbach, 2002, p. 1). Gross (2003) points out that sometimes panic sets in when a statistic seems troubling—such as a ranking that places the United States lower in education than other countries—and the wrong choices are made, causing "American Education Flu." Should one test be used to make decisions about performance when other indicators, or a combination of other indicators, might better reflect progress? Will test results be used to take money from students such as those discussed in Chapter 2? Can a test really capture the learning that "involves complex, recursive processes of interpretation and meaning construction" (Afflerbach, 2002, p. 12)? Can tests really replicate the day-to-day tasks that students will be expected to perform after they graduate from high school?

On the positive side, NCLB brings to the surface an increasing awareness that many diverse students need more instructional attention. This can mean that subgroups such as ELLs or learning-disabled, at-risk, and poverty-stricken children (see Chapter 2) will receive much more attention and that teachers instructing them will be highly qualified to do so. Another benefit is that uniform testing will permit consistent comparison of learners and groups of learners on the same measure. And, most important for content teachers, it means that *all* teachers must become involved!

How Are High-Stakes Tests Constructed and Used?

The essential content information that students "should know" is determined by a group of experts that may include content teachers, administrators, state department personnel, and citizens. The "essential content knowledge" is usually written in the form of standards and competencies that all students are expected to meet. Once the

In Virginia, these are called "Standards of Learning" (see Chapter 1 for examples of these standards within the PAR discussion). For a look at California's Standards for Reading Assessment, go to www.cde.ca.gov/re/pn/fd/documents/lang-arts.pdf.

Oppenheimer provides an example of one comprehensive computerized assessment program, STAR, in his book *The Flickering Mind* (p. 284).

standards are developed and accepted by a state, they are used to formulate a test that students must take to demonstrate mastery of content. To meet the requirements of NCLB, such tests would be given in grades 3 through 8, but many states also test mastery at the end of content courses to make sure students know specific content before graduating from high school.

If students do not demonstrate mastery of the test material, they and their teachers are held accountable. The consequences of poor scores on this one test are often disturbing. Funding for the school may be withheld by the district, state, or nation; students may not be able to pass a grade or graduate until they pass the test, even if their grades in the content courses are passing; teachers may be asked to explain why their students have "gained so little" in their classrooms. Students who do not "pass" the mandated test are usually required to repeat the test until they do pass. Schools—and teachers—whose students consistently do not pass the test are being asked to explain why not and to provide remediation for their students. Many schools have come under fire for low test scores. Because it appears that only one measure of knowledge, the designated test, is being used to judge a student's, school's, district's, or state's performance, the stakes are indeed high.

What Role Can Technology Play in Assessment, Testing, and Evaluation?

Assessment, testing, and evaluation are not necessarily helped by technology. Because technology is one tool that can help with instruction, and must be considered only a means to the end of excellent content instruction, any electronic aids for assessment, testing, and evaluation must be selected using the same criteria presented in this chapter. Elaborate programs that include assessment procedures, placement into computer learning environments, and evaluation after learner interaction with the program are certainly available, but few of these computer programs measure up right now. This is probably because such programs must rely on mostly quantitative means of assessment and evaluation and are subject to the same pitfalls as the use of isolated tests rather than several sources of assessment. An appealing quality of computer-based assessment is that, once the software or online registration is purchased, individual learners can participate and their results can be computed, saved, and reported quickly without much time invested by the teacher or school. One drawback is the great cost of the more sophisticated programs. Another is that results are subject to the same issues of norming, validity, and reliability as any paper testing programs.

WHAT EDUCATORS CAN DO IN THE AGE OF ACCOUNTABILITY

Formal testing provides valuable information; it is a part of good assessment and evaluation of instructional success. What can content teachers do in this age of accountability? Professional organizations provide sound advice for teachers within their position statements (American Psychological Association, 2001; International Reading Association, 1999; National Council of Teachers of Mathematics, 2000).

- Teachers should explain the appropriate use of tests whenever they can, and they can point out the importance of using multiple measures.

- Teachers can "construct rigorous classroom assessments to help outside observers gain confidence in teacher techniques" (IRA, p. 1). Such action might demonstrate to outsiders that because instructional quality is high, pushing for extreme measures of accountability (that do not really account for progress) is not necessary.

- Teachers need to explain to parents and policymakers that classroom assessment is important and reflects students' achievement. Teachers need to teach students about tests, but not teach to a test. Informal and authentic assessment should be incorporated into instruction, as will be presented in the following sections of this chapter. One school recently took a stand that it will not teach to the test (Fisher, 2004). The principal explained that teachers had been spending too much time preparing students to take a test rather than on deepening student learning and integrating art and music into the classroom. The diversity of the students in this school (77 percent English language learners) meant that more creativity rather than less was necessary. The school expects to do well on the high-stakes test, but will no longer gear all of its instruction toward this one measure. Richardson (2000) found that high school students who had experienced a humanities curriculum (focusing on the impact of history on literature, philosophy, and art), with little emphasis on a high-stakes test, did as well as or better than students who had experienced in-depth test preparation.

- Teachers should understand the purpose of a test—or any other means of evaluation—well enough to describe it to parents, students, and other stakeholders. By assembling an "assessment team" (Murray, 2002) consisting of students, parents, teachers, and administrators, everyone can share this job, and all can be ready to help describe the how and why.

- Teachers need to practice accountability by choosing authentic, representative formats for assessment and evaluation that match the content being learned; this includes technological formats.

- Informed teachers might argue that some of the conflicts raised by high-stakes tests result from trying to equate different sources of data meant to demonstrate different aspects of education. By consistently raising questions and balancing test results with other measures, teachers can keep the role of standardized tests in perspective.

The most effective solution should be excellent instruction and multiple means of assessment that lead to solid evaluation.

A Standardized Test That Can Inform Instruction

Mokhtari and Reichard (2002) present the way in which they designed and developed their standardized test, the **Metacognitive Awareness of Reading Strategies Inventory (MARSI).** Their article can help classroom teachers understand how a test is built and how authors of the test can adhere to the requisite standards of norming, validity, and reliability. The intent of the MARSI is to help content teachers know what reading strategies their students use. The MARSI uses a self-report instrument that relies on students' metacognitive awareness and perceived use of reading to help them learn material. It is a good example of how a test is developed and of how teachers can add to their informal assessment of students' learning strategies with a test that provides more quantitative data. Activity 3.1 shows what questions students are asked, along with the Lickert scale used.

Teacher-Made Tests

Teacher-made tests are one way of being accountable. Teachers should test to determine what their students have learned and still need to learn. Their tests should reflect high academic standards but also should be based on what was taught. Tests are the culmination of periods of study about a content topic. Tests come in many forms, from informal observations of student learning to formal final examinations. Students' ages and the topics covered influence the type of evaluation to be made. Teachers do need to test in some way; that is part of their instruction.

Tests should match the learning, not vice versa. Beyer (1984) writes, "Much so-called teaching of thinking skills consists largely of giving students practice in answering old test questions, a procedure that probably focuses students' attention more on question-answering techniques than on the specific cognitive skills that are the intended outcomes of such activities" (p. 486). Rather than giving practice with stale questions, teachers will want to discover ways to improve their tests, thereby eliciting the cognitive skills that are the ultimate goal of instruction. A teacher's main purpose for giving a test is to evaluate whether students learned. Traditionally, teachers ask questions about what they have taught, and students answer them. Teachers then evaluate the answers to gauge how well students have learned the material. A secondary purpose is to provide test grades as one sign of progress in a report to students, parents, and administrators.

In addition, students' performance on a test should tell teachers how well the teachers presented content material. Overlooked in the past, this purpose for testing has the greatest potential for creating an optimal learning environment in classrooms. If students can produce fine responses to questions, teachers may conclude not only that students are confident with the topic but also that they as teachers are presenting the content in ways that assist comprehension effectively. If students cannot produce satisfactory answers, the material may need to be retaught with different instructional strategies. Teachers who consider tests as a way to evaluate their own instruction, as well as to evaluate students' knowledge and to assign grades, often alter

All items are graded on a 1 to 5 Lickert Scale:

  1 I never or almost never do this.

  2 I do this only occasionally.

  3 I sometimes do this (about 50 percent of the time).

  4 I usually do this.

  5 I always or almost always do this.

1. I have a purpose in mind when I read.
2. I take notes while reading to help me understand what I read.
3. I think about what I know to help me understand what I read.
4. I preview the text to see what it is about before I read it.
5. When text becomes difficult, I read aloud to help me understand what I read.
6. I summarize what I read to help me reflect on important information in text.
7. I think about whether the content of the text fits my reading purpose.
8. I read slowly but carefully to make sure I understand what I am reading.
9. I discuss what I read with others to check my understanding.
10. I skim the text first by noting characteristics like length and organization.
11. I try to get back on track when I lose concentration.
12. I underline or circle information in the text to help me remember it.
13. I adjust my reading speed according to what I am reading.

their instruction and revise their tests. The result is that both teachers and students begin to improve at their respective jobs.

The Role of Pop Quizzes

Pop quizzes have often been popular with teachers. Teachers may think that pop quizzes provide a means of control over "making" students learn. They may think that such quizzes demonstrate their instructional rigor. The usual scenario for pop quizzes is to find out whether students have read an assignment. But suppose students attempted to read the assignment and experienced difficulty? A pop quiz may penalize students for not understanding rather than for not reading the material. Students may require assistance before they will be able to demonstrate learning.

Nessel (1987) comments that question-and-answer sessions that do not develop understanding "amount to a thinly disguised test, not a true exchange of ideas" (p. 443). When question-and-answer sessions become drills, teachers will not be able to determine whether a question has been misunderstood or poorly phrased or whether the

14. I decide what to read closely and what to ignore.

15. I use reference materials such as dictionaries to help me understand what I read.

16. When text becomes difficult, I pay closer attention to what I am reading.

17. I use tables, figures, and pictures in the text to increase my understanding.

18. I stop from time to time and think about what I am reading.

19. I use context clues to help me better understand what I am reading.

20. I paraphrase (restate ideas in my own words) to better understand what I read.

21. I try to picture or visualize information to help remember what I read.

22. I use typographical aids like boldface and italics to identify new information.

23. I critically analyze and evaluate the information presented in the text.

24. I go back and forth in the text to find relationships among ideas in it.

25. I check my understanding when I come across conflicting information.

26. I try to guess what material is about when I read.

27. When the text becomes difficult, I reread to increase my understanding.

28. I ask myself questions I like to have answered in the text.

29. I check to see if my guesses about the text are right or wrong.

30. I try to guess the meaning of unknown words or phrases.

Developed by Kouider Mokhtari and Carla Reichard.

---

student has difficulty constructing a response. Unless teachers use pop quizzes for instruction rather than for grading, they will defeat their own purposes and send an incorrect message to students: It's not important to understand the material, just to recount it!

Instead, pop quizzes should be used to evaluate what teachers can be reasonably sure has been achieved. For instance, rather than "popping" questions for a grade, a teacher could check to see whether students followed instructions for reading an assignment. A teacher could also use a writing activity (such as those described in Chapter 10) to make certain that homework was attempted. If understanding the homework was the problem, the students' written comments will show the teacher that the attempt was made. If students do this, they demonstrate that they tried to read for the assigned purpose. This demonstration will accomplish the same purpose as a pop quiz.

One middle school mathematics teacher, Mary Broussard, allows students to accumulate points toward their final grade by doing homework. The students are also tested, and the homework points do not outweigh the test grade. This teacher encourages

On this paper (front and back) I want you to answer the following questions as completely as you can.

1. How did you study pages 192–194 in Social Studies?
2. What did you learn from these pages?
3. Do you see any similarities between your life and the life of the people mentioned?
4. Were there any passages, terms, or concepts you found difficult to understand?
5. What part of this reading did you find most interesting?
6. How do you feel you answered these questions?
7. Why do you feel the way you do?

Developed by Charles Carroll.

students to try, knowing that they can get some credit for doing so, and she uses the class review to clear up confusion. Activity 3.2 shows a homework comprehension sheet designed by a middle school social studies teacher to indicate whether students attempted their homework and also to help the teacher focus the lesson. Before assigning the reading as homework, the teacher asked the students to survey the reading and write three questions that they expected to answer from it. When they arrived in class the next day, the teacher distributed this exercise. The teacher could rapidly review the responses to the homework comprehension sheet to find out who had completed the assignment. Areas of student confusion as well as student interests could be ascertained. This activity serves as a check on homework and also as a way to determine student background for the rest of the lesson.

We encourage teachers to think carefully about why they plan to administer a pop quiz, then design the quiz to achieve their objectives. If the objective is to promote student independence and responsibility, then the social studies teacher's solution works well. If it is to "catch" students, we ask teachers to please think again about assisting versus evaluating comprehension.

Traditional Teacher Evaluation

Traditional test items include objective questions, essay questions, or a combination. Objective tests include multiple-choice, true/false, matching, and completion questions. Teachers find such items easy to grade but difficult to phrase. Students sometimes label objective items as "tricky," "confusing," or even "too easy." Essay tests require students to write about a given topic. Students sometimes label essay questions as "confusing," "too hard," or "not fair." Essay formats are also labeled "subjective" because teachers must spend time considering responses carefully when grading. However, essay questions are not subjective or difficult to grade when questions are written clearly and carefully. Furthermore, essay questions offer a viable way to evaluate critical thinking and the applied level of comprehension.

CREATING EFFECTIVE TEACHER-MADE TESTS

The single greatest problem with traditional tests is that the grades students receive are often disappointing to teachers. We think the best solution to this problem is for teachers to stop giving tests before students experience the preparation and assistance phases of the PAR Lesson Framework. Yet, even allowing for this solution, many other problems with traditional tests have been identified.

Captrends ("Window on the Classroom," 1984) reports a study of 342 teacher-made tests in a Cleveland, Ohio, school district. Administrators, supervisors, and teachers representing all subject areas reviewed tests from all grade levels. The format that these reviewers found throughout the tests was similar to the format that we described: objective, short-answer questions. Only 2 percent of all items in the 342 tests were of the essay type. The researchers found many problems with the presentation of the test items. Directions were often unclear, sometimes nonexistent. Poor legibility, incorrect grammar, and weak writing skills made some items difficult to read. Point values for test items and sections were noticeably absent. Ambiguity in questions led to the possibility of more than one correct response or student confusion about choices to make in responding to items. In addition, the types of questions asked were predominantly literal. Almost 80 percent of all the items concentrated on knowledge of facts, terms, and rules. The middle school tests used literal questions even more than the elementary or high school tests did. Questions at the application level of comprehension accounted for only 3 percent of all the questions asked. Hathaway (1983) provides a more complete description of this project.

One eighth grade English teacher took a "hard look" at her test and found that

> the primary comprehension focus was a mixture of all three levels, but more literal and inferential than application. . . . Comprehension was dependent on recall more than real learning. . . . The test was too long and looked hard. . . . I neglected to give point values or the weight of the test in the final grade. (Baxter, 1985)

This teacher revised her test and summarized her satisfaction with the new version:

> All in all, I feel that the best feature of my redesigned test is that it captures many concepts and is a more appealing form. In relation to the original test, I feel this test allows the student to demonstrate more of his/her knowledge of the material covered in the unit by giving specific responses, especially in the discussion section. I feel this test will net better student response because it appears shorter, looks more appealing, and is different from usual tests I would have given in similar teaching situations before. (Baxter, 1985)

We see five problems as characteristic of teacher-designed classroom tests:

1. Textbooks tend to bombard the learner with an abundance of facts without incorporating enough in-depth explanation.

2. Teachers seem to rely on the objective format, and factual questions dominate their tests. We infer that teachers find such items relatively easy to construct.

Perhaps they think knowledge of facts is especially important to test. Students won't learn how to think critically if we don't require that they demonstrate such thinking on tests. Note how Activity 3.3 provides a check on whether students understand a third grade mathematics lesson by asking students to demonstrate learning through interpretation and application.

3. Teachers seem to have difficulty expressing themselves clearly when they write questions and construct tests. The problem may be that teachers need practice in constructing good questions.

4. Students may not be ready for a test because they have not developed enough understanding of a topic. This problem might occur because teachers need to provide more assistance or because students have not assumed enough responsibility for their own learning.

5. Students must be responsible for demonstrating their learning. They need to take an active role in designing assessments that help them demonstrate what they know in relation to real-life situations. If teachers always design tests, then students have a very limited role—regurgitating information for the teacher. This is why so many students tend to quit rather than study; they don't see any point to a test that doesn't seem "real" to them.

HOW TO IMPROVE THE DESIGN OF TESTS

Many teachers like to use traditional tests. There is great value in what is known and experienced. By reviewing the flaws discovered in many tests, teachers can improve traditional tests immensely. Coombe and Hubley (2004) offer several suggestions for constructing classroom tests. Among them are that teachers need to test to course outcomes, to how and what has been taught; prepare unambiguous items; write clear directions; and take the test themselves! We offer these general guidelines:

1. Questions on a test should reflect a balance among the three basic comprehension levels.

2. The difficulty of questions should be related to the task required. Recall is harder than recognition; production is harder than recall. Questions with several parts are more difficult than questions with one part. Selecting is easier than generating. Teachers should try to vary their use of difficult and easy questions within a test.

3. Sometimes the answer that a student gives is unanticipated but better than the expected response. Teachers will want to write questions carefully to avoid ambiguity but still encourage spontaneous critical thinking.

4. The best-worded test items do not provide secondary clues to the correct answer. Carter (1986) found that teachers often give inadvertent clues to students, who are facile at discerning this giveaway. For instance, students learn that correct answers on a multiple-choice test are often keyed to choice *c* and that the longest choice is most likely to be the correct answer. Also, the stem often signals one obvious match among the multiple choices. Students realize that for

SUMMING UP YOUR MEASUREMENTS

These activities are designed to determine how well you have understood the chapter on measurements. You will demonstrate your knowledge and understanding by performing the following activities.

The first activity will be done with your assigned group. The next three will be performed on your own. Be careful and have fun!

1. Read the recipe first. Make the individual assignments. With your group, make a vanilla pudding.
    - Who will read the recipe?
    - Who will assemble the cooking utensils and cups?
    - Who will mix the ingredients?
    - Who will pour the hot mixture into the cups? (Use pot holders!)
    - Who will place the cups in the pan and take them to the refrigerator?

2. Read the outdoor thermometer at three different periods of the day (morning, midday, afternoon). Record the temperature at each period.

3. Use the scales to weigh your empty lunch box, your mathematics book, and your wallet/purse. Record each weight.

4. Measure the perimeter of your desktop, your closet cubbyholes, and any other item on the classroom floor. Record each.

Developed by Bessie Haskins.

both multiple-choice and true/false items, positive statements are more likely than negative statements to be correct choices. Teachers sometimes give answers away with grammatical clues. With Carter's study in mind, teachers will want to express themselves carefully!

5. When wording test items, teachers need to consider their students' language proficiency. A well-worded test that does not match the students' knowledge of language will result in poor comprehension even though the students' learning may be excellent. Drum, Calfee, and Cook (1981, pp. 488–489) caution that the abilities needed for successful performance on a comprehension test include the following:

Accurate and fluent word recognition

Knowledge of specific word meanings

Knowledge of syntactic/semantic clause and sentence relationships

Recognition of the superordinate/subordinate idea structure of passages

Identification of the specific information requested in questions

Evaluation of the alternative choices in order to select the correct "fit"

PREPARING AND ASSISTING STUDENTS TO TAKE TESTS

By using the PAR Lesson Framework, teachers can fulfill much of their instructional role in readying students to take tests. We find that some other techniques also prepare and assist students in test performance.

Chapter 4 describes uses of technology as a learning tool, such as creating an online or disk database that students can access on their own. The use of study questions can be facilitated by such an electronic database.

Using Study Questions   Teachers who encourage students to use study questions find this technique helpful. Study questions can be used in a variety of ways. The teacher can prepare a list of questions to be included on the test and distribute the list at the beginning of a unit so students can refer to it throughout the unit. Or the teacher can suggest possible test questions as instruction proceeds and then review all of the questions after completing the unit. This list can become the pool for essay test items. The teacher might tell students that the test will include only questions from this list. Such a technique has merit for two reasons: A test bank is acquired as the unit progresses, thus eliminating last-minute test construction; and students have a study guide that is familiar, thorough, and not intimidating. If the teacher creates questions that follow the question construction guidelines and covers representative content with these questions, the technique works well.

Some teachers tell students before testing what the specific test questions will be. This technique works better with essay questions than with objective questions. Although many teachers are hesitant about providing questions in advance, fearing that students will not study everything, this can be a wise way to prepare and assist students. The fact is that students cannot study everything anyhow, and they certainly cannot remember everything for a long time. If the essential information is covered in the proposed questions, then a question list can be effective. The pool of essay questions from which the specific question for a particular test is drawn can also be provided in an electronic environment.

A threaded discussion at a teacher's website can enable students to share their possible test questions with one another. Other students can respond, and the teacher can interject as well.

Having students themselves create the questions for a test is sometimes a good technique. This option requires that students understand the content thoroughly and also understand how to write good questions. An alternative for younger students and those not proficient at question construction is to have students use brainstorming to predict possible test topics and then informally generate questions. A first grader could speculate, "I think you might ask me to explain how fish breathe." Students can construct possible items for an objective as well as an essay test, or they can review items from sample tests that the teacher provides. Teachers who encourage students to create possible test questions should be sure to include some version of the students' questions on the actual test.

Any variation on student construction of the test questions will provide students with practice in questioning and answering, provoke critical thinking, and promote the students' responsibility for their own learning. Another bonus is that students who are familiar with the teacher's way of designing a test will be less anxious about being tested. Test anxiety accounts for much poor test response.

Using Open Books or Notes   Teachers find that allowing students to use open books or open notes—or both—enables students to concentrate on producing the best response on a test and assists them in the actual test-taking process. This tech-

If students
take their tests
in an elec-
tronic environ-
ment and they
cannot use
notes, be sure
the computer
is "clean" of
any aids and
the medium
for saving the
test (keydrive,
disk, or the
like) is also
"clean."

nique encourages good note-taking strategies and clear organization of information by promoting recognition and production rather than recall.

Nontraditional Ways to Assess

Everyone appreciates variety. Teachers may be pleasantly surprised to find that students increase productivity when an evaluation device looks more like the strategies that have been used to instruct than the same old test format. "Conventional policy-based testing . . . is the wrong kind of tool for thoughtfulness. It makes people accountable only for the development of very low levels of knowledge and skill" (Brown, 1987, p. 5). Although Brown's comments refer specifically to standardized tests, we think they apply to teacher-made, nontraditional tests as well. We encourage teachers to use new strategies for assessment, testing, and evaluation; we argue that even when poorly made objective tests are redesigned, they do not correlate with the type of achievement required in a world where concepts are more important than facts. We must alter our testing procedures if we want to produce critical, thoughtful readers. Creative thinkers often perform much better on tests that are nontraditional and reflect nontraditional instructional activities.

By employing some of the strategies we present in this book, teachers can construct tests that contain few traditional items. The most **nontraditional test** would eliminate questioning altogether. Although teachers may not wish to design an entire test with no questions, some nontraditional items might spark interest. Primary teachers are especially attracted by nontraditional tests, and intermediate and secondary teachers may prefer adding some nontraditional items to a more traditional test. The possibilities are as numerous as the types of activities presented in this text.

The following activities can be used as nontraditional test items. Teachers who have designed tests using such items report that they elicit more critical thinking from their students. We are sure that teachers will see the possibilities for designing many activities as nontraditional test items.

GRAPHIC ORGANIZERS

Graphic or-
ganizers are
used to begin
the chapters
of this text-
book. Their
construction is
explained in
Chapter 6.

Student- or teacher-produced visual representations of learned concepts and relationships are called *graphic organizers*. Research (Katayama & Robinson, 2000; Robinson & Schraw, 1994) has shown that notes and partial notes recorded as graphic organizers help students comprehend better than fully formed outlines. We feel so strongly about the worth of graphic organizers that chapters in this book begin with them. Similarly, a teacher can instruct by using a graphic organizer, map, structured overview, chart, or any such visual aid and then present the organizer with blanks on a test, where it becomes a nontraditional test item for eliciting responses that demonstrate knowledge of facts. Such is the case with the example in Activity 3.4, designed by an eleventh grade teacher. If the teacher provides a list of terms that could complete the organizer, then recognition of facts is tested. Such is the case in the example in Activity 3.5, designed for an elementary social studies class.

If the teacher asks students to explain why they positioned words at certain points on the organizer, then the interpretive level of comprehension is being tested. If the

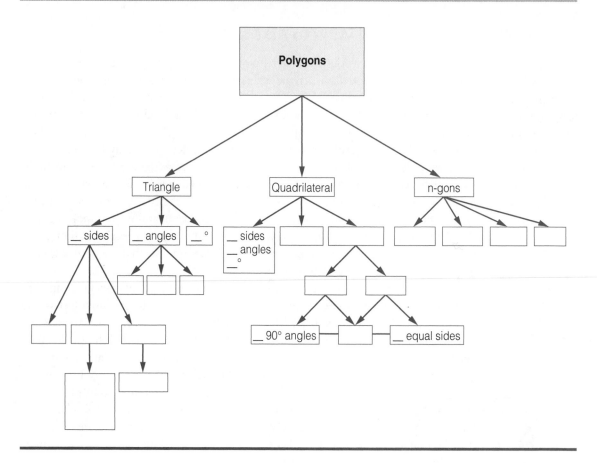

teacher asks students to create an organizer using terms they learned during the lesson, the applied level of comprehension is demonstrated. No traditional questions are asked, yet comprehension can be evaluated and graded. The test item might read as follows:

> Study the organizer I have drawn for you. It is like the one we studied in class, but in this one there are several blank spaces. Using the list of terms attached, fill in the term that fits best in each space (1 point each). Then write one sentence beside each term listed; this sentence should explain why you think the term belongs where you put it in the organizer (2 points each). Next, write an essay that includes the information in this organizer. Your first paragraph should provide four (4) details. Your last paragraph should summarize by telling what new information you have learned by reading this chapter (25 points).

Note that the directions are specific and that point values are given for each procedure. Factual knowledge is tested, but some interpretation and application are also required. Writing an essay is also part of this question. Because the components of the

Activity 3.4 *(continued)*

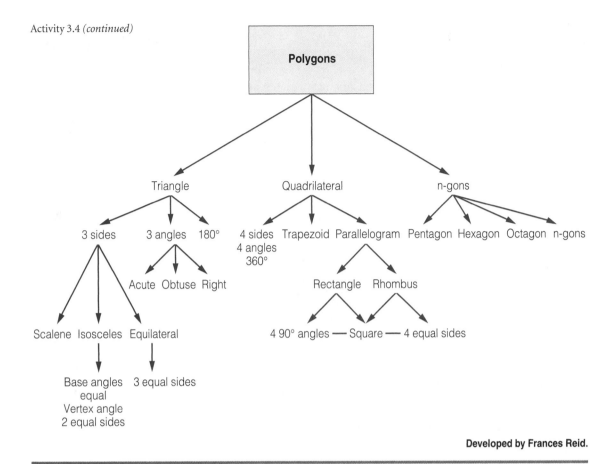

Developed by Frances Reid.

essay are defined, grading it should be simple. It is also possible to prepare a rubric for this essay:

> An A essay will contain three or four paragraphs that explain fully all the information on the organizer. Students not only will demonstrate factual knowledge but also will show inferences and applications. The entire list of terms will be appropriately placed and thoroughly defined. The essay will have a clear beginning and end.
>
> A B essay will contain two or three paragraphs that explain the information on the organizer. Students will demonstrate factual and interpretive knowledge. The entire list of terms will be appropriately placed and adequately explained. The essay will have a clear beginning and end.

FACTSTORMING

Factstorming is explained in Chapter 5 as a good preparation activity because students identify familiar terms in a topic before they study further. Students can add to the list produced by factstorming after their studying is completed; the additions become an evaluation of new learning. If students are asked to explain each addition,

Description of Activity: The students fill in a graphic organizer to determine comprehension. The overview was previously introduced on an overhead projector to help build background of key concepts in the unit. The students received a copy of the organizer to take home and study.

The graphic organizer is presented to the students as a test at the conclusion of the unit. Because students may have a difficult time remembering the concept names, an answer key has to be included with the organizer.

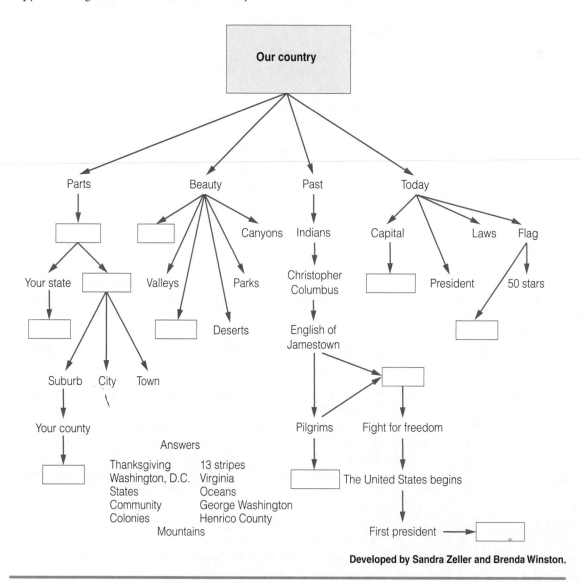

Developed by Sandra Zeller and Brenda Winston.

they are demonstrating interpretation of information. If students categorize the already known and new information and then write an essay about this categorization, they demonstrate application. The use of factstorming as a test item is similar to the last step in either a KWL or a What-I-Know Activity (WIKA), but it is graded (see the example in Chapter 1 and description in Chapter 5).

Other strategies discussed in this text can be used as tests. A number of strategies for writing that are explained in Chapter 10 can be used as effective tests. Some of these are cubing, quick-writes and free-writes, and student-generated questions.

Designing a Test with a Self-Rating

Teachers can design tests with a self-rating included on the test. Hoffman (1983) originated this rating technique to be used in journal entries, and Richardson (1992b) created a version for tests. The first questions on a test might be, How did you study for this test? How much did you study? How well do you think you will do? The answers show how the students prepared. Before the test is returned, a second set of questions should be asked: Now that you have taken the test, and before it is returned, was this test what you expected and prepared for? What grade do you think you will receive? These questions can help the student take responsibility for studying and producing a good test response. The third set of questions promotes reflection. It is answered after the teacher returns and reviews the test with the students: Now that you have gone over your test, would you say that you studied adequately? Was your grade representative of your learning? Why or why not? What have you learned about taking tests?

Such a three-step process built into the testing procedure will send the message that the student is ultimately responsible for demonstrating learning. If teachers use the procedure often on tests, the student should begin to take a more active role. Teachers will also be enlightened by students' views of studying and taking tests and can apply this information in their instruction and when constructing tests.

One requirement for designing good tests is to use previous tests as the basis for constructing new ones. Students learn how to take an individual teacher's tests by learning that teacher's style. Teachers should learn how to design tests based on students' styles of learning as well. Did students need clearer directions? Did they use appropriate study procedures? Do they need reminders about certain test procedures?

Helping Students Become Test-Wise

The acronym **SCORER** (Carmen & Adams, 1972; Lee & Allen, 1981) refers to a test-taking strategy. High SCORERs **s**chedule their time; identify **c**lue words to help answer the questions (the directions should contain them); **o**mit the hardest items, at least at first; **r**ead carefully to be sure they understand and fully answer the question; **e**stimate what to include in the response, perhaps by jotting down some notes or an outline; and **r**eview their responses before turning in the test. Teachers might teach SCORER to students and then insert the acronym into test directions or include it as a reminder on tests. Students even could be asked to account for how they used

SCORER while completing the test. This strategy places responsibility on students to take a test wisely, in an organized and comprehensive manner. SCORER can be used as part of any test design.

There are other ways to make certain students become **test-wise**—that is, able to use a plan of attack regardless of the specific test content. Students become used to taking tests. They gain confidence because they understand how tests are designed and can capitalize on that knowledge to demonstrate their learning. Being test-wise means knowing the program, to use Hart's (1983a) terminology—or, in other words, the system. When students know how to take a test, they can concentrate their energy on answering the items. Being test-wise helps alleviate test anxiety. Panic—the "blank mind" syndrome—can be avoided. The older mammalian brain can send encouraging messages to the newer mammalian brain, and the student can then apply thinking skills to show knowledge.

Carter's (1986) study, cited earlier, indicated that students discern the inadvertent clues teachers give in test items; this is a test-wise ability. Many teachers provide a bit of information in one question that can help students answer another question. Students who watch for these clues are SCORERs. Studies (Ritter & Idol-Mastas, 1986; Scruggs, White, & Bennion, 1986) indicate that instruction in test-wise skills can help students perform better on tests. An instructional session that reviews a list of test-taking tips is helpful, particularly with older students, in improving results on standardized tests. When a teacher wants students to improve performance on classroom tests, such test-wise instruction is best done in the content teacher's classrooms with application to a particular test. The following list of test-taking tips indicates the kinds of suggestions that teachers can give to help students become proficient test takers:

1. Be calm.

2. Read through the entire test before answering any items. Look for questions that might provide clues to other answers.

3. Plan your time. If one question is worth several points and others are worth much less, spend the majority of the time on the question or questions where the greatest number of points can be made.

4. Answer first the questions for which you are most confident about your answers.

5. On objective tests, remember to be logical and reasonable. Consider your possible answers carefully. Look for "giveaway" words that indicate extremes: *all, none, never, always.* They probably should be avoided when you select the correct answer. On multiple-choice items, think what the answer should be; then look at the choices. Also, eliminate implausible responses by thinking carefully about each choice.

6. For essays, jot down an outline of what you intend to write before you start writing. Be sure you understand the teacher's terms: *list* means to state a series, but *describe* means to explain the items. *Compare* means to show similarities; *contrast* means to show differences. Make sure you answer all the parts of a question.

Take a minute to consider when and how you became test-wise.

A Checklist for Designing a Test

The following questions constitute a checklist for test construction. The checklist is useful for teachers who want to review previously designed tests that have produced unsatisfactory results.

1. How did you prepare the class to study for this test? If you suggested certain study strategies, are you asking questions that will capitalize on these strategies? For instance, if you suggested that students study causes and effects by using a pattern guide, are you designing test items that will call for a demonstration of causes and effects?

2. Are you including SCORER, a self-evaluation of test preparedness, or some other way of reminding students about their responsibilities as test takers?

3. Do the items on your test reflect your goals and objectives in teaching the content? Test items should test what was taught. If a major objective is that students be able to name states and their capitals, how can this test measure that objective?

4. What is your main comprehension focus? Why? If you think that factual knowledge is more important on this test than interpretation or application, can you justify this emphasis? Remember that many tests rely too much on factual questions at the expense of other levels of comprehension. Be sure that the factual level is the most important for this test.

5. Do you require comprehension at each of the three levels? What proportion of your questions addresses each level? What is your reasoning for this division? Remember that tests imply the kind of thinking that teachers expect of their students. Have you asked your students to think broadly and deeply?

6. What types of responses are you asking of students? Will they need to recognize, recall, or produce information? A good balance of responses is usually preferable to only recognition, recall, or production. Production requires more thinking from students.

7. Did you phrase your test items so that comprehension depends on the learned material rather than on experience or verbatim recall? Remember that although the preparation stage often calls for students to identify what they already know before a topic is taught, your test should find out what they have learned since then.

8. Is the weight of the test in the final grade clear to students? Is the weight of each item on the test clear? Are the weights of parts of an item clear within the item?

9. Did you consider alternatives to traditional test items, such as statements (instead of questions) or graphic organizers? Is writing an important part of your test? Why or why not?

10. For objective tests, what format (multiple-choice, true/false, incomplete sentences, short answers) have you selected and why? How many of each type did you include? Why?

11. For essay tests, have you carefully asked for all the aspects of the answer that you are looking for? Are descriptive words (such as *describe* or *compare*) clear?

12. Is the wording on this test clear? Is the test uncluttered, with items well spaced? Does the test look appealing?

13. Have you considered the needs of diverse students in your test design?

AUTHENTIC ASSESSMENT

Many authorities (Herman, Aschbacher, & Winters, 1992; Wiggins, 1989) in education have pointed to "alternative assessment" as the solution to the dilemma of traditional testing. This movement is motivated by the feeling that alternative assessment methods facilitate good teaching, enhance learning, and result in higher student achievement (Linn, Baker, & Dunbar, 1991). Wood (1996) has noted that traditional multiple-choice tests may not suffice in today's educational climate of learning outcomes, higher-order thinking skills, and integrated learning. We prefer the term **authentic assessment** to describe a viable solution. This term often refers to assessment that takes place in naturalistic situations that resemble the settings where a skill or knowledge is actually used or applied. Teachers actively observe learner activities that demonstrate what the learners can do. While the term *assessment* implies finding out what students already know, authentic assessment is broader in application, including informal evaluation procedures as well as determination of prior knowledge. In this section we describe ways to use authentic assessment as a means of evaluating what students have learned.

When teachers employ some nontraditional test items, they are moving toward authentic assessment, which is alternative, performance based, and process oriented. Traditional tests are specific measures given at specified times. Authentic assessment measures or samples student performance over time to see how student learning develops, matures, and ultimately reflects knowledge of the concepts learned in a real context. Brady (1993) suggests that authentic assessment builds relationships among the physical environment, the people who live in that environment, the reasons for or beliefs about completing activities in that environment, and the manifestation of these beliefs in human behavior. In short, authentic assessment shows students why they are learning, as well as showing educators what students have learned.

Authentic assessment emphasizes realistic, challenging material used over time (Biggs, 1992) as evaluation and can link previously taught material and current instruction. As Hager and Gable (1993) indicate, the increased use of observational and performance-based measures and process instruments, as well as content- or course-specific instruction, is essential to authentic assessment. Students can help decide what should be assessed, thus gaining an important role in demonstrating their own learning. Students enjoy creating authentic projects. In 1995 a group of middle school students wrote a script for and produced a video about the hazards of drugs. As they graduated from high school in 1999, these students were still talking about the fun they had making the video. They would probably not have remembered the information learned about drug hazards so well if a test or paper assignment had been the measure of evaluation.

The contexts for authentic assessment might include observing a performance or simulation, or completing a task in a real-world situation. Students will want to do well because the real-world consequences are clear. For instance, actually driving a car yields a more authentic assessment than taking a paper test in a driver education course. Or encouraging the student to show what steps were followed to complete a math problem is a way of demonstrating the logical processing of information. Completing the task reveals as much—or more—about the student's learning as the test grade.

Lund (1997) has written about the importance of using authentic assessment in every classroom. She describes the following characteristics of authentic assessment:

1. Worthwhile tasks that have meaning for the student are designed to broadly represent a field of study.

2. There is an emphasis on higher-level thinking and more complex types of learning.

3. Criteria should always be given in advance so students know how they will be graded.

4. Assessments are deeply embedded in the everyday workings of the curriculum so that it is hard to distinguish between assessment and instruction.

5. The role of the teacher changes from dispenser of knowledge (or even antagonist) to facilitator, modeler, and ally in learning.

6. Students know they will publicly present their work.

7. Students know that there will be an examination of both the processes they used in learning and the products that were produced as a result of the learning.

Developing Authentic Assessments

Tierney (1998) writes about the reform in assessment practices. He points out that developing better evaluation means more than just creating a new test. He argues that, if the point of literacy is to become immersed in text rather than to "be subjugated by it" (p. 375), then we must think about how we incorporate authentic assessment into our evaluation procedures. Because learning is a complicated process, evaluation must consider many complex ways to represent itself. Should observation be an assessment component? How? For how long? Under what conditions? Should learners select for themselves what will illustrate their learning? Worthen (1993) suggests that activities based on learning logs, double-entry journals (both explained in Chapter 10), and observation notes can reveal much about student performance over time. In Chapter 10 we describe an activity called C3B4Me that clearly shows how students improve their writing over time. We know teachers who keep gummed labels on a clipboard; as they walk around the classroom, they make notes on these labels, which they later stick into a student's folder. These notes often reveal important learning patterns. Such notes can be kept in any content classroom; they could be particularly useful during science labs, reading or writing workshops, cooperative group work, or library work. Performance measures might include oral debates, postgraphic organizers, or even presentations developed using the computer program PowerPoint (see Chapter 4). Wiggins (1990) suggests that a hands-on science test may be more logical than a paper-and-pencil test.

Rhodes and Shanklin (1991) suggest three ways to increase the authenticity of assessment in the classroom from the very start:

1. Provide students with opportunities to use language in natural social contexts.

2. Give students choices in materials and activities to ensure they will discover genuine purposes for reading and writing.

3. Follow students' natural leads to focus on communication through interaction with others.

Portfolios as a Means of Authentic Assessment

Research (Green & Smyser, 1996) has found that the use of portfolios helps students take a much more active role in their own learning. A **portfolio** is a representative sampling of artifacts that demonstrate a feature or specialty about a person. It is not simply a collection but a showcase. A student might collect many samples of work, but only one artifact might be selected for inclusion in the portfolio because it demonstrates best what the student is showing about herself or himself. Unlike traditional tests, many portfolios demonstrate growth over time.

Portfolios can be used at any grade level. Wagner, Brock, and Agnew (1994) advocate the use of portfolios in teacher education courses, to help students develop a greater understanding of themselves as readers and language users. Young and associates (1997) explain how portfolios can engage secondary students more effectively in their academic work.

Portfolios work well with both elementary and secondary students (Abruscato, 1993; Cleland, 1999). Activity 3.6 is an artifact selected by a third grader to show the many facts he learned over 12 weeks while he studied animals. Activity 3.7 is a list of history trade books that a fourth grader included in his portfolio to show how much he had read in four weeks.

When students are involved in an authentic assessment plan from the start of the grading period, they become more active participants in the learning process. Wilcox (1997) notes that an active portfolio—one in which the student, teacher, and even possibly the parents actively engage in the selection and presentation process—is a "working portfolio that changes and grows with new input as it creates and generates new input" (p. 96). Students should be encouraged to develop goals for their progress during the period and indicate possible ways in which they can demonstrate their growth at the end of the period. Teachers can guide students toward realistic and reasonable goals; students then collect their own evidence of their learning from the very beginning of a grading period. Teachers should give each student a folder, and teacher and students decide together what types of work will be kept in it. At the end of a

My
Fantastic
Animals

Did you know that
snakes eat bats?

Did you know that the Indian
Python is one of the largest snakes
in the world?

The smallest snakes can fit in
your hand.

Hummingbirds can fly backward
and hover motionless.

This is my mini-page about animals. I wanted to include this page in my portfolio to show what I
learned about animals.

This page was created with *The Writing Center,* from The Learning Company, 6943 Kaiser Drive, Fremont, CA 94555.

specified period, students designate which pieces of work in the folder show progress or demonstrate a particular accomplishment. It is a good idea to keep the portfolio folders in the classroom in a storage file. This ensures that papers will not be lost and provides easy access for students wishing to peruse or upgrade their portfolios. Products they select may reflect their learning much more fully over a long time than a traditional test—which captures only one moment in time—could do.

What types of samples should be collected during weeks one, two, three, and so on? What types of samples should be collected to demonstrate the achievement of course goals? Some measures of prior knowledge of the topic, such as anticipation guides, would provide a baseline measure (see Chapter 6). For instance, pre- and post-unit attitude surveys might be the first and last pieces collected. Work samples, such as jot charts (explained in Chapter 7), two-column notes (explained in Chapter 8), and graphic organizers, might be included. Quizzes, tests, and corrections could be saved. At grading time, the most representative piece and a "best" piece could be selected. Both process activities and products can be collected.

Abruscato (1993) describes Vermont's adoption of writing and math portfolios as a major means of statewide assessment. The assessment includes evidence of problem-solving and communication skills. Samples included in the writing portfolio are a

Books I read in History:

Meet Martin Luther King, Jr.

Meet Maya Angelou

The Story of Harriet Tubman, Conductor of the Underground Railroad

The Story of George Washington Carver

If You Traveled on the Underground Railroad

I chose this list of books I read to put in my portfolio because I never liked to read before. I did not know very much about history, but now I have practiced reading and learned a lot too! I like to read about real people and find out about real things.

---

table of contents, a "best piece," a letter, creative writing, a personal response, a prose piece from a content area, and an on-the-spot writing sample. Samples included in the math portfolio are five to seven "best pieces," such as puzzles, a letter to the evaluator, and a collection of math work. Results so far indicate that the students who score highest on their writing read at least once a week for pleasure. The greatest problem discovered by studying the math portfolios is that students have trouble presenting their results clearly and lack variety in their approaches to solving problems. Such findings will help educators build a more effective curriculum and enhance learning.

Here are some general guidelines for assembling a portfolio:

1. Organize with a table of contents and section divisions. Select categories to best represent your progress, such as "favorite activities," "activities I did not like," and "what I am most proud of."

2. Include representative samples of your work over time. Be sure to date the samples and make clear why you included them.

3. Annotate each sample to explain why it is included. The focus here is on individual samples, not the total progression.

4. Conclude with a reflective but brief summary that explains your progress in relation to the portfolio contents: What were your goals? What was learned? How, *overall*, do these artifacts demonstrate this?

5. Make sure that the number of samples is reasonable and representative of the depth and breadth of your learning (at least one sample per week during a 10- or 12-week grading period).

Teachers need to establish what they expect their students to demonstrate in the portfolios. Will specific knowledge be expected? Will some example of weekly progress be necessary? How will the portfolios be graded, if at all? Will they constitute the total grade or a portion of the grade? Who will read the portfolios—just the teacher and student, the parent, the principal, other students? After making the expectations clear to students, teachers need to encourage students to take ownership and make their own choices within the established parameters. It is a good idea to hold at least a midpoint conference so that students can practice articulating their choices and the teacher can guide the process. Activity 3.8 is an example of a portfolio guideline for high school English students.

Getting Started with Authentic Assessment

In the classroom, content area teachers can begin focusing on authentic assessment by keeping a checklist of essential developments that they want students to demonstrate. The checklist presented in Activity 3.9 can be modified as new criteria are added and then removed as students' developmental needs are met. Such a checklist can help teachers record subtle developments in the students' reading, writing, and thinking abilities.

Managing and analyzing authentic assessment results are facilitated by use of an electronic database and templates so each student record can be quickly updated.

A small start such as using a checklist is the easiest way to begin authentic assessment. At this level the students' development—trial and error, dialogue, self-criticism—can be assessed most readily. Samples can be taken over time, and students can be involved in designing the assessment and collecting the samples. Also, the teacher can make certain that both process and product are measured and that audiences—such as the students, their parents, and administrators—will be able to understand the samples and how they demonstrate progress in learning. Authentic assessment is the ultimate nontraditional evaluation. It is a challenge that can bring new enthusiasm to learning in every content area.

Once a teacher tries a few of these ideas for nontraditional testing and authentic assessment, the next step might be combining the data collected with the test data required by NCLB and/or state evaluations. Boyd-Batstone (2004) suggests that teachers can fill in gaps left by questions arising from what a test score means for instruction,

---

ACTIVITY 3.8 PORTFOLIO REQUIREMENTS FOR ENGLISH 11/FIRST GRADING PERIOD

This portfolio will count as 25 percent of your grade. Include pieces that YOU think best represent your learning about Early American History and Literature.

You should have at least eight pieces, one per week. Each should be annotated to explain why it represents your learning for this marking period. You may include more than one piece of the same type (two–three maps), but there should be some variety also.

You should write a summary of no more than two pages that explains how you met the objectives for this unit.

Suggestions for Selections:

Completed jot chart of Early American authors: their work, language style, and representative vocabulary

Quizzes taken

Essays written—this can include any drafts that you think show your progress in writing and thinking about the topic

Three-level guides completed and annotated

Notes from any day's discussions

Postgraphic organizer of *The Crucible*

Favorite quotes from *The Crucible*

Maps of *The Crucible*: acts, characters

★ Excellent   √ Good   ✕ Average   ◆ Lacking—needs to improve

Name	Student Self-Evaluation	Decision Making	Questioning	Problem Solving	Attitude and Motivation	Inferential Thinking	Clarity of Writing
Bobby	√	★	★	√	★	√	✕
Felicia	✕	√	✕	◆	√	✕	✕
Beverly	★	√	★	★	√	√	★
Joan	◆	◆	✕	◆	√	√	✕
Juan	✕	√	✕	✕	√	√	◆

and also attend to immediate classroom needs by collecting informal observations and data and matching the collections to state and national standards (as might be on state and national test assessments). This might be described as standards-based teaching, where both the standard, the test of the standard, and the classroom performance can be integrated. He calls his method **ARA (anecdotal records assessment).** Teachers can organize this electronically by creating templates with a standard listed and several notes collected over time for each student that describe how the student is meeting the standard. In this way, what the learner knows and can do are featured, but the learning is also matched to the standard and should substantiate any testing done. As Boyd-Batstone writes, "A quality assessment is like a well-woven fabric" (p. 236).

ONE-MINUTE SUMMARY

Assessment and evaluation are crucial components of ensuring good instruction. In an age of accountability in the United States, content teachers must play a larger role in assessment than ever before. Federal legislation and state standards have prominently influenced classroom instruction. In this chapter we presented key concepts about testing. We discussed the design of successful tests and the role of tests in the larger picture of assessment and evaluation. We presented viewpoints from several experts about the impact of NCLB on the state of assessment in this era. We described teacher-made tests and authentic assessment as ways to measure whether desired learning outcomes are taking place. We explained ways to evaluate both traditionally and in a more authentic manner, especially by introducing portfolios into classroom instruction, and incorporating anecdotal records with standards-based instruction.

PAR ONLINE

Post a threaded discussion to share your ideas about high-stakes testing and the role of authentic assessment.

Look at a website that provides information about some aspect of assessment that attracted you. Describe to others in your class how this website can be useful in your content instruction:

- American Psychological Association (2001). Appropriate use of high-stakes testing in our nation's schools. *APA Online:* http://www.apa.org/pubinfo/testing.html

- Assessment in math: nces.ed.gov/nceskids

For direct links to sites for topics in this chapter, including works by S. J. Gross, J. Murray, the International Reading Association, the National Council of Teachers of Mathematics, as well as a site for alternative assessment of ESL students, clink on the web links option of the Chapter 3 resources on our companion website.

END-OF-CHAPTER ACTIVITIES

Assisting Comprehension

1. Adopt one way to introduce authentic assessment into your content classroom. Relate this assessment to a standard about which you need to instruct. How can using and recording student performance on this authentic assessment technique demonstrate student progress in achieving the standard?

2. Read about the following:
   - NCLB: (www.ed.gov/programs/readingfirst/legislation.html)
   - Your professional organization's standards for teaching important content (search online for the name of your organization)
   - A history of testing starting with Binet (Oppenhimer, 2003, p. 276)

Reflecting on the Reading

The International Reading Association (2003) has developed a set of standards that identify the performance criteria relevant to classroom teachers.

Standard Three delineates four elements of assessment, diagnosis, and evaluation that a classroom teacher should possess. The teacher should

- 3.1: *Select and administer appropriate formal and informal assessments including technology-based assessments . . . understand the requirements for technical accuracy of assessments and . . . select technically adequate assessment tools . . . interpret the results of these tests and assessments.*

- 3.2: *Compare, contrast, and analyze information and assessment results to place students along a developmental continuum . . . recognize the variability in reading levels across different subject areas . . . identify students' proficiencies and difficulties . . . recognize the need to make referrals for appropriate services.*

- 3.3: *Analyze, compare, contrast, and use assessment results to plan, evaluate, and revise effective instruction for all students within an assessment/evaluation instruction cycle.*

- 3.4: *Interpret a student's reading profile from assessments and communicate the results to the students, parents, caregivers, colleagues, and administration.*

How were these four elements addressed in this chapter? How does being informed about these elements aid in content instruction?

The best education is to be found in gaining the utmost information from the simplest apparatus.

ALFRED NORTH
WHITEHEAD (1929)

Technology in Today's Content Classrooms

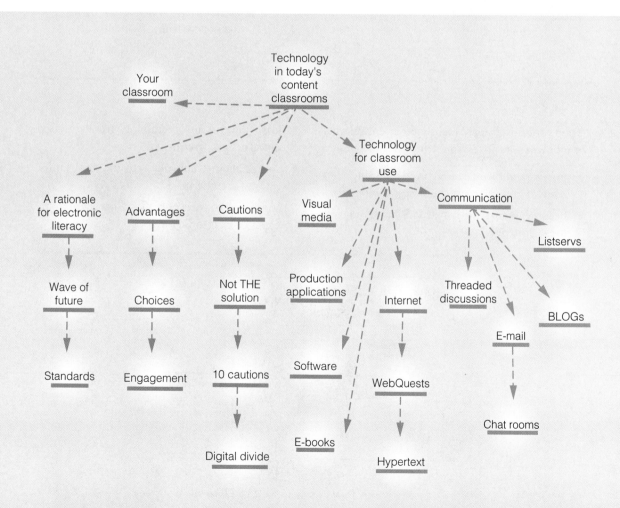

PREPARING TO READ

Following is a list of terms used in this chapter. Some may be familiar to you in a general context, but in this chapter they may be used in unfamiliar ways. Rate your knowledge by placing a plus sign (+) in front of those you are sure that you know, a check mark (✓) in front of those you have some knowledge about, and a zero (0) in front of those you don't know. Be ready to locate them in the chapter, and pay special attention to their meanings.

_____ technological literacy
_____ electronic literacy
_____ information literate
_____ electronic text
_____ digital divide

_____ database
_____ electronic book, e-book
_____ e-classroom
_____ WebQuest
_____ hypertext
_____ synchronous
_____ electronic mail, e-mail
_____ instant messages
_____ chat rooms
_____ discussion group
_____ threaded discussions
_____ asynchronous
_____ BLOG
_____ listserv
_____ distance learning

OBJECTIVES

As you read this chapter, focus your attention on the following purposes. You will

1. understand the need for complementing content area instruction with technology.

2. become familiar with instructional standards for technology.

3. learn about several technology resources used in today's classrooms.

4. appreciate the value of electronic communication for students.

5. compare two ways of reading this chapter: in paper or electronic form.

© Columbus Dispatch/Dist. by Newspaper Enterprise Association, Inc. Reprinted with permission.

IT'S A NEW WORLD

The word *technology* is derived from the Greek word *techne*, which refers to the "clever manipulation of natural artifacts to reach a desired goal" (Dwight, 2001, p. 22). **Technological literacy** is "the ability to use computers and other technology to improve learning, productivity, and performance" (U.S. Department of Education, 1997). Oppenheimer (2003) notes that Arthur Luehrmann coined the term *computer literacy* in 1971. In 1981 Don Rawitsch of the Minnesota Educational Computing Consortium (MECC) commented, "We've got to get computers away from the image of being separate from everything else" (Mace, 1981).

To indicate how pervasive technology has become in our culture, consider this study in which Yahoo! (a search engine) participated. Researchers wanted to find out how people would respond to having no access to the Internet for two weeks. The researchers, recounts Barnako (2004), had a hard time even finding people who would agree to participate because they were not willing to give up their Internet access. Of those who did participate, across all age, income, and ethnic groups, the participants recounted feelings of withdrawal, loss, frustration, and discontent. We have, indeed, become globalized (Bean & Readance, 2002; Schaeffer, 2003).

Turbill (2002) calls our new century "the age of multiliteracies" (p. 2003), when one reads text plus "color, sound, movement, and visual representations" (p. 2003). Education today must respond to a widely networked society (Davis, 2000). Cornu (2001) notes, "Society is changing, schools are changing, and students are changing." Many educators now recognize that technology must play an important role in classrooms (Anderson & Speck, 2001; Atkinson & Hansen, 1996). Grabe and Grabe (1998) and Anderson and Speck (2001) cite the great need for practical information about integrating technology in K–12 instruction. In this chapter we discuss **electronic literacy,** which refers specifically to a means of reading in the technologically literate environment. Although the authors cannot provide an in-depth study of instructional technology, as a book devoted to just that topic can do, we present a brief rationale for technology, some advantages and disadvantages, forms of technology that contribute to electronic literacy skills, and applications for the content classroom.

A Brief Rationale for Electronic Literacy

Two great waves of change influenced human history up to the twentieth century, according to Nettle and Romaine (2000): the development of agriculture and the industrial revolution. A third wave, which Rifkin (2002) calls the "hydrogen economy" (to account for a new source of fuel that will change the way we live), is the wave of the twenty-first century. Each new wave has influenced cultures and literacy, changing how we view the importance of literacy and how we use it. Expectations for readers in this new wave include learners who are **"information literate"** (Henderson & Scheffler, 2004)—that is, able to find and use information in any form, whether paper or electronic. Teachers cannot afford to maintain the "industrial age mindset" (Frand, 2000) of one who seldom knows much about or uses technology. Instead, teachers need "the information age mindset" of one who does know and regularly use technology. Unfortunately, many teachers may possess limited technology skills, as Newman's (2000) study indicates. Of 30 teachers surveyed, "only a handful had experience with more than e-mail and a word processing program" (p. 777). To avoid a clash of cultures and miscommunication between teachers and students, teachers must begin to change and implement technology in their instruction. Paper text is not enough any more; **electronic text** is the wave of the future.

Visit http://www.iste.org to view the NETS

Standards for instructional technology have become a national reality. The National Educational Technology Standards (NETS), developed by the International Society for Technology in Education (ISTE), outline core technological competencies that teachers, as well as students and administrators, should meet. In fact, at least 31 states have now adopted, or rely on, the NETS in developing state technology plans (Loshert, 2003). The use of technology in schools has increased exponentially, as a visit to the site of the National Center of Educational Statistics shows: http://nces.ed.gov/pubs2002/internet/Tables.asp. Note, for instance, that the percentage of schools with Internet access has increased from 35 percent in 1994 to 99 percent in 2001.

See # 8 at http://www.ncte.org/standards/standards.shtml

The International Reading Association and National Council of Teachers of English set the following standard for students, thus assuming that teachers can instruct accordingly: "Students use a variety of technological and information resources (e.g., libraries, databases, computer networks, video) to gather and synthesize information and to create and communicate knowledge." However, while the information age is marching on—as demonstrated by the standards just cited—too many schools of education lack a systematic means of instructing teachers about ways to use technology in their teaching (Willis and Raines, 2001). A report from the President's Information Technology Advisory Committee (2002) indicates that while the teacher's role is changing, current teacher education and training in methods of using technology in the classroom are insufficient.

Visit: http://www.itrd.gov/pitac/

Technology is here to stay, and we need to use it effectively in content classrooms. The challenge for us as textbook authors is to show how seamlessly technology can be used, along with literacy, to create academically engaging content lessons.

Visit http://www.pen.k12.va.us/VDOE/Compliance/TeacherED/tech.html to view the Technology Standards for Instructional Personnel in Virginia.

Comments from Teachers and Students

Teachers realize that they need to become electronically literate, and they recognize how difficult this can be. In a recent study (Watts-Taffe, Gwinn, Johnson, & Horn, 2003), three beginning teachers were followed for a year as they strove to incorporate technology in their classrooms. They found themselves using software for multiple purposes, such as creating graphic organizers and using encyclopedias on CD-ROM to gather information. They could integrate technology more easily as they practiced and gained confidence with it. Their students became more motivated and engaged in learning as they incorporated technology. By the end of their first year, they had lots of ideas for what to do with technology in their next year of teaching.

A student in one of the authors' classrooms noted that visual learners find technology very helpful. "This correlation of visual stimulus and learning is obvious. Our generation is a visually stimulated generation. The children of our generation are visually stimulated, and the generations from here on out will be visually stimulated. I feel that it cannot be avoided" (Evans 2004). Students generally know more than their teachers about technology and its uses. Indeed, in the area of technology, many teachers must become learners themselves, and thus a reciprocal learning environment can be created that facilitates true shared learning.

Advantages of Electronic Literacy

Technology presents choices in instruction that educators have never had before. Teachers and students can communicate from great physical distances with a rapidity not dreamed of in earlier ages. Learners can locate information without traveling to a physical library; instead they can visit virtual libraries by accessing the Internet and searching for the information by typing in a query on a search engine. People can hold conversations in real or virtual time, over any distance. Records can be kept within a small memory drive and transported on a key chain. Learners can "be there" without leaving their homes.

Maurer and Davidson (1999) encourage teachers to use technology "to help children become brilliant" (p. 458). They suggest that with technology learning is streamlined and less boring—it is like speed learning. They say that use of technology "shifts power into the hearts of children" (p. 460). Ruddell (2000) says about a commercial in which children are promoting a website, "We need classrooms that crackle with the kind of energy I saw in the dot.com commercial" (p. 2). She encourages teachers to embrace the possibilities of technology to promote "fully engaged learners who are excited, exhilarated, and passionately involved in school" (p. 2).

Reinking (1997) comments that, although technology itself is neutral, the way we use it to learn enables learners to be more creative and engaged. If technological instruction focuses on meaning, stresses comprehension, and allows students to become actively involved with whole texts, then the technology is an advantage to advancing literacy. Electronic text, as opposed to paper text, is beneficial because it is easy to modify with the "delete" or "cut" key. It can be adapted to the reader; it can be programmed to accept reader responses. Moving from place to place is easy in electronic text.

Cautions about Electronic Literacy

A series of panels about April, a teenager in the comic strip *For Better or for Worse*, was written by Lynn Johnston in early December 2004. April has finished her homework, which was to write an essay. Her mother discovers that she "wrote" it by visiting the Internet and copying and pasting from some sources there. Her mother makes her sit down with text material, including an encyclopedia, and read these materials in paper format, then write her own original essay. April mutters, "I was just told to do an essay. I wasn't told to LEARN anything." This comic strip points out the difficulties caused by easy access to multiple sources, most of which can be readily copied and pasted right into a student's paper without attribution or rephrasing. Although

Read Ruddell's online article about project-based learning in an electronic environment at http://www.readingonline.org/articles/ruddell/index.html.

Anderson-Inman (1998) provides a list of several repositories of electronic text, one of which is "The Online Books Page" found at http://digital.library.upenn.edu/books. This site is a directory of full-text books available for reading on the Internet.

plagiarism has always been a problem, the Internet makes it easier and more tempting. Some solutions might be for more Internet posters to provide their documents in pdf (portable document format) form, which is harder to copy, and for teachers to find activities for their students that require them to manipulate the information they find online and rewrite that manipulated material into innovative papers and projects. We will provide some ideas for this as we discuss different forms of Internet communication.

Technology and computers cannot teach: they can only facilitate. "It may be unreasonable to think that any innovation—technological or otherwise—would bring radical change to an institution as old, large, and as established as education (Oppenheimer, 2003, pp. 23–24). When technology helps educators do their job better, this is a great bonus. But technology is no more the final solution to educational challenges than were movies or television. As Steve Jobs commented to Wolf (1996) in an interview for *Wired*, "You're not going to solve the problems just by putting all knowledge onto CD-ROMs. We can put a website in every school—none of this is bad. It's bad only if it lulls us into thinking we're doing something to solve the problem with education" (p. 102). For instance, Wepner (2004) identifies 10 "techno-blunders" that can occur if educators assume that technology is a panacea. Her cautions are these:

- Always have a backup plan (of course, this should be true for any taught lesson).
- Make sure that a technological tool is really easier and more effective than another way.
- Do not assume that students can use the technology.
- Understand that using technology takes time—it is not a quick fix.
- Use technology in creative ways—why replicate what can be done as effectively or better with paper?
- Select a website if it fits the learners' skills, not because it is there.
- Beware of publisher claims (of course this should be true for paper materials too).
- Make sure there is a support system for the technology you plan to use.
- Make sure assistance is available.
- Make sure the technology works before starting the lesson.

The globalization of communication that technology has provided has also created a **digital divide** between those who have the resources to access and use electronic literacy and those who do not. In affluent communities, schools, and homes, students and teachers may either own or have access to computers at almost any time. However, not all communities, schools, and homes are so fortunate. Teachers and students in poorer communities may find that trying to access electronic literacy creates a chasm between their educational progress and that of the technologically advanced. Oppenheimer (2003) describes the digital divide as "the shortage of technological gear that has supposedly cheated the poor out of social and economic opportunities, but which is actually a very different problem" (p. xviii).

Wepner, Seminoff, and Blanchard (1995) caution that teachers who understand the goals and are involved in planning for technological innovation will be more successful than those who do not understand what the cautions are. They encourage teachers making curricular decisions to ask the following questions:

Where are we?

Where do we want to be?

How do we get there?

How do we know we are there?

In the rest of this chapter we describe several varieties of technological resources. This information may help teachers answer questions and make wise decisions about integrating technology into their classroom instruction. Because this field is changing so rapidly, we invite the reader to use the CD that accompanies this textbook for access to current information.

> This chapter will be available in a hypertext format so that readers can read and also follow any links that the electronic text provides.

TECHNOLOGY FOR CLASSROOM USE

TV, Video, and Movies

> When films first became popular, Wise (1939) cautioned that films have benefit depending on the circumstances such as teacher, students, environment, and objectives. He noted that film is not a panacea.
>
> The Gersten/Tlusty project could be replicated via CD or an interactive distance learning session.

The use of TV, video, and movies as an educational resource is well established. Students today thrive on these forms of technology. Videotape has pretty much replaced the film projector and film strips, which have become brittle with age. DVDs are about to replace videos. Digital musical devices are beginning to replace DVDs. These visual and auditory electronic devices can bring students closer to a topic, making it real. For instance, Gersten and Tlusty (1998) describe a video exchange between Czech and American students. Each group created a video that represented their lives and exchanged these videos. Content came alive through the careful planning, production, and viewing of different cultures through the medium of video.

Many studies report that children today watch a great deal more TV than children watched several years ago. Many organizations, including the International Reading Association, sponsor "no TV" days or weeks to highlight the importance of an environment where children can discover resources other than TV. Yet Neuman (1991) comments that just turning off the TV does not lead to more reading. When watching TV is simply a way to pass time, it probably is not stimulating much learning. As Elley (1992) reports in an international literacy study, those who watch TV a lot tend to score at lower levels of literacy than those who watch less TV. However, in some countries with high literacy scores, the average number of hours watched is three or four. In these countries, many foreign films with subtitles and informational films are shown on TV. Unfortunately, the United States fell in the category with high hours of TV watching and low literacy scores.

After reviewing 30 years of research, Reinking and Wu (1990) state that the evidence does not clearly show TV as a detriment to literacy. Channel 1, controversial as its use is, provides instant information to schools for a fairly low cost (Celano & Neuman, 1995; Johnston, 1995). It is reasonable to conclude that TV—documentaries, drama, and news shows, for example—can be a vehicle for powerful learning opportunities (Reinking & Pardon, 1995). The United States may need to create opportunities for using TV, video, and movies to better advantage.

What makes these media so popular? They appeal to many of the senses, fostering visual literacy and more. We see, hear, and are entertained by them. Our eyes move from place to place rather than remaining focused on a page. When programs are taped—or recorded on CD or DVD—the video can be used on many different occasions as a learning resource.

Students often prefer to see a videotape and compare it to the text. For instance, a video can animate a topic that otherwise might be covered in only two or three pages in a textbook chapter. The movie *Pocahontas* was quite disappointing to many teachers because history seemed to suffer for the sake of plot. Yet teachers found that they could start with the movie, guide children to read several resources such as biographies or historical accounts, and then compare the information.

The movie *Clueless* barely credited the novel *Emma* by Jane Austen, yet it became a starting point for discussing Austen's novel. *Clueless* can guide students to the movie titled *Emma* and on to the novel itself. However, caution is urged in moving from movies to literature (Baines, 1996). Films often use less sophisticated vocabulary and language and "reduce the complexity of dialogue, plot, characters, and theme" (p. 616). But video does lure students and can be the springboard to many projects linking movies and literature.

A great new use of video and television is their combination into video conferences. People at geographically distant sites can connect via video and talk to each other in real time. Guest speakers need not travel away from home; field trips are not always necessary. This is distance learning at its best (see the "Technology in Your Classroom" section of this chapter).

Word Processing and Other Production Applications

Maurer and Davidson (1999) tell the story of a first grader who seemed to be "giving up on school." When he realized that he could write on the computer, his whole attitude changed. He had power to accomplish a literacy task in a way that enticed him. Children's own work can become a learning resource for others. Term papers and reports submitted for only the teacher's eyes can be banished in favor of presentations for all learners to enjoy.

Many teachers know that writing is an effective means of learning. Learning logs and journals are two means of enabling students to express what they are learning and clarify difficult concepts. In Chapter 10 we explore more fully the benefits of writing in the content areas. In this chapter we wish to point out that writing can take place both on paper and on a computer. In fact, to write this edition of our textbook, we used word processing software, whereas our first edition was much more a pencil-and-paper product. Furthermore, we used many aids such as comments embedded in electronic text, highlighting, and change tracking to communicate with each other over geographic distance. We sent each other our chapter drafts via e-mail attachments.

Many word processing programs are available. They range from simple ones such as the Student Writing Center to sophisticated applications such as Microsoft Word. Some software applications, such as PowerPoint—a part of the Microsoft Office Suite—let the user create slide shows with text. Audio and animation can be included if the user has reached that level of sophistication. Word processing programs enable users to create and edit text, insert pictures and graphics, and make appealing book-like products. Software tools such as Inspiration allow teachers to create maps, graphic organizers, Venn diagrams, outlines, and writing opportunities for—and with—students. Such software is not content specific but provides numerous opportunities for content teachers to produce specific instructional materials.

Applications such as FrontPage and Dreamweaver enable users to create presentations that can be published on the World Wide Web. Iannone (1998) shows possibilities for using traditional and electronic text in writing instruction. His article shows how teachers can incorporate online student resources in the writing-centered activities; he provides several websites. Alvarez (1998) suggests that students will think differently about their writing and be more enthusiastic as well as careful when they realize that anyone on the web might access their work. Creating resources that others will read is a great incentive for learners: literacy becomes very personal and applies the technological features that today's children find so compelling.

We know instructors who have published their textbooks on the World Wide Web with production applications. Their students can read electronic text, see the same illustrations included in the textbook, and also *hear* the instructor explain points about a graph or lead them through a complicated set of directions. At given points, students can click and soar to other locations (using the hypertext feature), escaping the linear nature of a textbook for a nonlinear world. Teachers can create such presentations or search the World Wide Web for such programs. Although studies have yet to be conducted that prove that more learning occurs with such resources, the informal evidence is all around us. Children are intrigued by the multisensual nature of production applications and seem to spend more time on learning when such resources are available. The addition of graphics to a report enhances student interest and understanding. Using scanners or digital cameras, learners can place graphics in text to create lively visual displays of their learning. Free sources of clip art, and clip art within such programs as Inspiration and Word, can be found. Regular photographs can be transferred to computer via a scanner. Digital cameras feed pictures directly to the computer or printer. Sound can be introduced to a presentation using applications such as SoundEdit, SoundForge, or VisiCam, which enable audio of a fair quality but inexpensive form. Imagine how enticing it could be to show what a project looks like to viewers across the country or around the world.

Databases are increasingly popular, efficient means of storing information. In fact, some form of database is used to check on the supply of items in many stores. When a shopper goes to the Internet to make a purchase, a database is used to see whether that item is in stock. Teachers often use a database "to enter, store, update, access, and manipulate information" (Merkley, Schmidt, & Allen, 2001). For instance, a teacher might store activity ideas in a database such as Access (from Microsoft Office for Windows) or File Maker Pro. Or students could enter, store, and retrieve data on facts about planets.

Electronic Text Modification

With the use of devices that can read aloud electronic text, learners can hear as well as see the text. Talking word processors, such as WRITE: OUTLOUD and Kurzweil 3000 Instructional Technology, are especially valuable for ELL (English language learners), special-needs students, and struggling readers. Word prediction software, such as CO:WRITER, helps students build and write complete and correct sentences by predicting what might "fit" the text being typed in.

Instructional Software

Software is delivered on disk, CD-ROM, DVD, or via an Internet download, and it usually comes with a manual and supporting materials. Interactive computer books are available for students to read and respond to on screen (Chu, 1995). Programs like Oregon Trail and Amazon Trail have been around for some time and have undergone some improvements. Leonardo the Inventor takes learners to the Renaissance, where they experience da Vinci's ideas and inventions. Such programs simulate a situation and ask readers to make choices based on information. Careful thinking and interaction and literacy skills are required. Some software features a familiar text but provides multimedia such as read-alongs and question/answer interaction. Students are expected to respond; their responses are often tracked to provide a "score" for the learner and instructor. This can be a helpful monitoring device for teachers who want to record which types of resources a student used to learn about a topic and how effective that resource seemed to be.

Instructional software programs can be wonderful learning resources. Software can track what users are doing and keep records for students and teachers. As with textbooks, some programs are better than others. Willis, Stephens, and Matthew (1996) encourage teachers to look for attention to the subject matter, efficiency, approach to instruction, appeal, ease of use, and adaptability when they select software. Carter (1996) reviewed Accelerated Reader (AR), a software management program to record student reading of selected books, and found that 89 percent of AR books had never been reviewed by a reputable publication.

Quirk and Schwanenflugel review DISTAR, PHAST, Early Steps, Reading Recovery, and Reading Apprentice software programs.

Software should always be instructionally relevant as well as student and teacher friendly (Fox, 2003). When Quirk and Schwanenflugel (2004) analyzed the motivational appeal of five popular software programs for struggling readers, they found that each was somewhat stimulating, but all could have been much more motivating. Software is not good simply because it is there; it must conform to educational standards and facilitate achieving the instructional goals intended.

How the software is used makes a difference. Greenlee-Moore and Smith (1996) investigated the effects on reading comprehension when fourth grade students read either short and easy or difficult texts using either interactive software or printed text. When reading longer and more difficult narratives, the software group had higher scores. The authors speculate that students paid more attention to the computer text than to the text in the book.

Go to http://
www.soe.vcu.
edu/GCU/
and read Mod-
ules 6 (about
using the In-
ternet) and 7
(about using
software to as-
sist learners).
In either the
elementary or
secondary
modules,
Karchmer
(2003) pre-
sents lessons
on how to use
software and
the Internet.

Instructional software should teach about content as well as stimulate critical thinking rather than skill-and-drill or rote learning of isolated facts. One major advantage of software over Internet resources is that teachers can preview the software and be sure that the content is suitable for the age group. Another advantage is that the teacher does not depend on an Internet connection, which might be expensive, unreliable, or sometimes inaccessible. Teachers need to locate software that works for their content classrooms and embed it into lessons that help learners understand the content.

Electronic Books

An **electronic book**—or **e-book**—is a book presented on a computer; it is electronic text. The user's main focus is still on reading text, but the text can be augmented with pictures and hypertext links to create a nonlinear environment. *A Survey of Western Art* enables learners to view and read about art that they otherwise might never see. "Navigating learning" with electronic encyclopedias is an interesting and efficient new way to support textbooks with literature (Wepner, Seminoff, & Blanchard, 1995). *Compton's Interactive Encyclopedia* and *Grolier Multimedia Encyclopedia* are offered on CD-ROM. They rival print versions for number of articles. Ease of navigation from one article to another is good, and readability is fairly simple. Sound clips as well as pictures and animation are combined in these electronic books. But be careful! The package is modern, but these are still encyclopedias—which are secondary sources. Consider them as only one condensed source, not an inclusive treatment of any topic.

The Internet

The Internet makes electronic text easily accessible and has become "the medium of the future" (Anderson-Inman, 1998). The Internet is a collection of many resource networks—an electronic library of information. The most commonly used part of the Internet is the part that supports multimedia, the World Wide Web. Every minute something new is posted for viewers to find. A web search engine enables a learner to type in a topic—"key words"—and come up with many possible resources. Some are trash; many can enhance learning in content areas. Just as a reader would note the copyright date of a textbook, an Internet user should note when a website was posted and whether it has been revised (Rekrut, 1999). And just as a reader would want to know a text author's credentials, Internet users should be cautious about the source of the information they discover on the Internet; the learner must judge the quality and reliability of the information. Content teachers can help by checking possible sites in advance.

The Internet is changing what it means to be literate (Leu, 1997). First, Internet literacy requires new and sophisticated navigational skills. Getting around in the mass of information is a challenge. Second, learning is endless; just as one masters a new literacy skill on the net, a new challenge arises. Third, the Internet requires new ways of reasoning and thinking critically. Fourth, content on the net can be presented with

To find out more about important holidays for people of different lands and cultures, visit http://www.holidays.net.

multiple meanings and combinations. These literacy challenges are part of what makes the Internet appealing to students, but the challenge for teachers is to provide guidance so the Internet is used as a tool for effective learning. Teachers often find that the Internet can provide a means of extending literacy practice and proficiency (Karchmer, 2003). Students find the Internet an appealing source of information (Leu et al., 2004). They have opportunities such as responding to literature, viewing websites of authors, and learning about diversity.

A high school math teacher located a site that enlivens the study of the Pythagorean theorem. He found a high school posting about the short story "The Battle of Pythagorus." Here was a wonderful lesson about the theorem using the short story. Leu, Karchmer, and Leu (1999) provide numerous lessons in content areas that engage learners on the Internet. For example, they help learners find out about Japan by visiting "Kid's Web Japan" at http://web-jpn.org/kidsweb/index.html. This site provides steps by which students can learn about Japan's climate, culture, and art.

The Internet can make it easy to consult an expert. Rather than traveling to the expert, which can be expensive and limit the audience, we can visit the expert online. We might even see him or her talking to us, listening, and responding. Van Horn (1999) discusses the merits of such a conference, provides tips on setting up a live conference, and explains what equipment works best in various circumstances. He calls the setting for such conferences the **e-classroom.**

The Internet also provides access to many libraries. Electronic journals enable readers to locate resources for immediate consideration. Professional development occurs online (Anderson-Inman, 1998) when current and back issues of journals are available for easy retrieval. The "card catalog," where one used to look for reference material using an index card system in file cabinets, has been revised to the online catalog. One can visit the library from one's home via the Internet.

WebQuests are a means of using the Internet to send students on a problem-solving journey to several preselected websites. The teacher poses a question and provides clues that are found within the websites. WebQuests provide students with authentic problem-solving tasks. They guide purposeful reading and also can be used by cooperative groups of students. Teachers must carefully check each possible website to be used in a WebQuest, making sure the content is correct and suitable for the learners, and that the site does not link to any other "questionable" sites for their learners. Clues must be thoughtfully prepared. Creating a well-constructed WebQuest activity is time-consuming but effective as a learning tool. Activity 11.3 depicts a WebQuest designed by a teacher.

Visit http://webquest.sdsu.edu/ to learn more about WebQuests.

Treasure hunts are somewhat similar to WebQuests, although they are usually briefer and focus more on a fact-finding mission. Students have a question to answer by visiting teacher-selected sites. For both WebQuests and treasure hunts, the Internet offers numerous sites where teachers can follow directions to create and post their activities, at no cost.

A Hypertext Environment

Hypertext supports the use of a wide variety of resources in content classrooms. On the web, a student can start at one location and click on a hyperlink (an icon or underlined text) to immediately be linked to another site where more information is located. Reinking (1997) demonstrated how hypertext works in an online and print-format article as he discussed the possibilities of technology and literacy. The learner can go backward, forward, and sideways in many hierarchies. Instead of reading each line in order on each web page, the learner branches from here to there in a nonlinear fashion. The student can click to view a footnote, then click back to the main article. Readers can check a reference without turning a page. This environment is similar to that of a learner who leaps from one idea to another, who has piles of information on a desk and goes from one pile to the other as needed to take care of several tasks. In short, web hypertext and hyperlinks create a typical learning environment.

Read Reinking's article at http://readingonline.org.

E-Literacy Communication

The traditional view of communication and collaboration assumes face-to-face-same-time-same-place (**synchronous**) encounters. Online communication, however, is gaining in popularity. Learners are beginning to seek learning environments where they can work collaboratively over time and space in a variety of settings. Tse (1999) noted that participants who tend to be more passive in face-to-face interactions often take a more active role in electronic discussions. **Electronic mail** is sent over the Internet; unlike letters, **e-mail** can be received almost instantaneously. Sending letters by electronic mail enables learners to contact favorite authors or content experts who have made their e-mail addresses available. Many legislators provide their e-mail addresses for constituents, allowing students to write and receive immediate responses as they study political issues. Several studies have been conducted to determine the effect of e-mail correspondence on literacy skills and learning. Rekrut (1999) believes that e-mail is the best place to introduce the Internet to new users because it is so simple to learn.

Students today use e-mail and instant messaging to carry on conversations at least as often as they use cell phones! They are "tech-savvy" (Chandler-Olcott & Mahar, 2003). Such informal writing is prevalent and can be used to increase more formal writing and communication skills. **Instant messages** are sent as short notes from one writer to another over the Internet almost as quickly as a telephone conversation can be conducted; such messages can be sent between multiple users. However, having more than two to six users can mix up the communication because messages come so quickly and participants tend to get "lost" among the many message writers. Instant messages simplify the spelling and grammar of formal language. This is a mirror of what happens to language when many more users adopt it, and complexities are lost (Nettle & Romaine, 2000). Instant messages also contain references that are well known to the communicators but not to other speakers. Some might even call instant messaging a type of *pidgin* (an abbreviated form of communication adopted to allow speakers of two different languages to use one very simple language, such as a language of trade).

The possibilities for e-mail within content instruction are intriguing. The most obvious is that it provides a means for teachers, parents, and students to communicate outside the classroom hours. E Pals allow students from different schools—or even countries—to talk to each other about content topics. Two students can partner to instant message about a content topic and then "translate" it into more formal report language.

Chat rooms (Morgan & Beaumont, 2003) are found online at various locations, usually through a host Internet service provider. Here users talk to each other about a topic of common interest. Teachers can create their own chat rooms on a school server where their students can chat about a content topic. In chat rooms several people can talk, and the conversation can be instantaneous or at a convenient time for the user to submit a thought. Chat rooms are more effective for multiple speakers than is instant messaging.

Discussion groups allow many people to discuss a topic either in real time or over a period of time on a website. (Regular e-mail does not allow real-time communication.) A respondent can receive replies from several different people, all of whom can then read one another's responses. This **threaded discussion** offers opportunities for reflection over time and allows numerous visits to consider and reconsider other points of view. Knowlton and Knowlton (2001) define threaded discussions as " the **asynchronous** (not face-to-face-same-time-same-place but in-own-time-own-place) exchange of messages using a bulletin board or e-mail software" (p. 39). Discussion groups are an excellent vehicle for students to learn from one another, to "talk" about a forthcoming test or a point they do not understand. They provide a kind of online tutorial and can be an excellent resource for content instruction. Discussion groups are somewhat like chat rooms in that people "talk" to each other about a set topic. But discussion groups usually are more formal, and they follow a specific thread, or thought, for a while. Chat rooms tend to be more spontaneous forms of conversation and are often very informal. Figure 4.1 shows a threaded discussion board where topics to be discussed are posted. Figure 4.2 shows the "threaded" details for one of the threads in Figure 4.1.

Another form of communication with electronic text is a **BLOG,** which is a web log. It is a journal in which a person usually writes personal reflections and then shares them by posting them to a website. It is informal and written in one's natural voice. Once a BLOG is posted, others can visit it and add comments, although BLOG responses are not generally long or intense. The cyberjournal (Stefl-Mabry, 1998) is a type of BLOG. Dieu (2004) notes that BLOGs work best for content teachers as long-term assignments that can help students improve their writing and language fluency and competency. They can be excellent tools for English language learners, but they are also useful in content subjects when students are encouraged to write thoughts about their daily learning. Or teachers and students can BLOG.

Participation in **listservs** is by subscription. People who are interested in the same topic subscribe to an information source—a listserv—much like subscribing to a magazine. When someone writes a message, it is sent to everyone on the listserv by

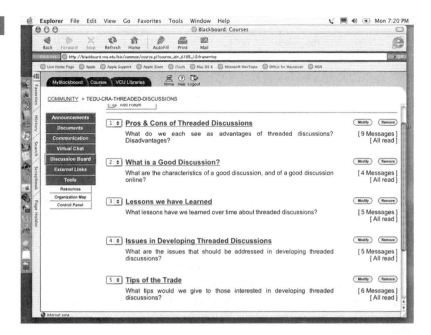

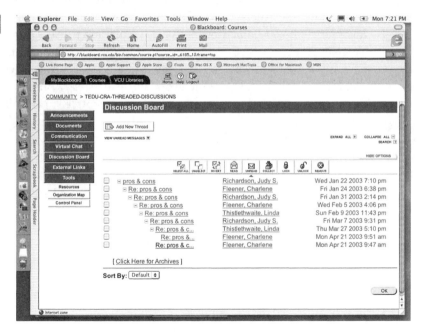

e-mail. All the members on the list can read other members' comments. Listservs are a good means of disseminating information quickly to many people who have a common interest. Teachers might subscribe to a listserv where the common topic is lesson plans on teaching grammar. When one subscriber posts his or her plan, all the other members of the listserv receive it. A teacher who is intrigued but does not yet have classroom access to the Internet and the forms of communication described in this section can use floppy disks to create a discussion community (Cole et al., 1998). One student writes a journal entry on disk and then passes the disk to another student, who reacts and passes the disk to another student. The teacher can read the final product.

These resources for electronic literacy create a community of learners. Students who might not speak out in class feel freer to communicate via e-mail, discussion groups, and listservs. Thus many diverse perspectives become available in the learning environment (Morrison, 1999).

Technology in Your Classroom

Free website construction for teachers is available at sites such as yahoo-geocities (http://geocities.com). Many school systems have purchased versions of BlackBoard and WebCT for teacher use in distance communication.

What will technology resources look like in future classrooms? They will surely take advantage of **distance learning** opportunities such as videoconferencing. Two-way communication is improving, whereby students in one classroom can connect via Telnets with other classrooms in geographically distant locations for real-time, or synchronous, discussion. Or individuals can go online for learning opportunities, choosing a convenient time to participate in a threaded discussion or locate Internet resources. Although many learners might access the same site, they may be there at different times, thus participating in an asynchronous manner.

Teachers will develop more websites, where they will post homework assignments, independent lessons, clarifications, notes to students and parents, streamed videos for computer home viewing about a topic, and treasure hunts and WebQuests that guide students to appropriate sites to find content information. Websites will be showcases for student work, so that others in schools far away—even relatives—can see. Students will send their homework and papers electronically, ask questions of teachers via e-mail, and share notes with other students, all in an online environment. Some of these innovations take place regularly in classrooms today—students are now taking courses online. More electronic devices will be brought to classrooms and used along with or instead of books. Some of these will be Personal Digital Assistants (PDAs), handheld computers, laptop computers, and cell phones.

All these possibilities can enhance content instruction and open new resources far beyond what a static, concise textbook can provide. Why should we consider technology as a resource for learning? "This is a nonquestion," according to Bruce (1998). Technology engages learners by providing motivation, a reason to learn, and a need to know within a new environment. Technology engages learners by developing their contextual knowledge—showing the world in new ways. For instance, writing to pen pals via e-mail creates a new and vital use for reading in a social environment (Baker, 2001) because learners can compose questions to experts in distant locations and read replies to those self-generated questions. Technology can make personal inquiry and purposeful reading and writing powerful tools.

Technology engages learners because learners want to know effective strategies they can use to find discussion groups and listservs to read what others said about a topic, to locate websites, and to access databases. Technology can engage learners because it provides the means to a social process—from remote locations we can learn together.

Throughout this textbook, the authors provide technological applications and notes that will help readers make electronic literacy connections. Each chapter ends with PAR Online, where a threaded discussion topic may be suggested and several websites are provided. The authors recognize that the field of electronic literacy is far outpacing paper literacy—information in this chapter will be out of date very soon, if it is not already as you read these words! That is why we offer some technological alternatives along with this textbook.

ONE-MINUTE SUMMARY

Faced with an ever-expanding amount of content to be digested and learned in every content area subject, teachers increasingly realize that no single textbook can deliver all the concepts in, and differing viewpoints on, any unit of study. Thus many content area teachers are turning to electronic resources that complement textbooks. This chapter has presented information about technological literacy that demonstrates what it means to be information literate and how such knowledge can facilitate instruction. A rationale for electronic literacy was provided, featuring changes in culture and history that have led to electronic literacy and standards for instructional technology. Some advantages of electronic literacy were presented, such as communication over great distances, more fully engaged learners, organization and management of instructional needs, and hypertext features. Several cautions about electronic literacy were also addressed: possibilities for plagiarism, techno-blunders that can occur, the digital divide, and the need to combine technology with other resources.

Ideas were presented for the seamless incorporation of technology with literacy to create academically engaging content lessons. We discussed technology for classroom use, including visual media, production applications, software, e-books, the possibilities of the Internet in instruction, and e-literacy/communication. Many locations for further reference to technology mentioned were provided in margin notes. Production applications teachers use daily, such as word processing, presentation, and database programs were discussed as a way to incorporate technology easily into classrooms. The possibilities of good instructional software were considered. We wrote about wise uses of the Internet in instruction. Because students today use the Internet for communication, special emphasis was given to how instant messaging, chat rooms, threaded discussions, and listservs can be used in content assignments. Descriptions of each medium and some suggestions for its use in content classrooms were provided. We ended with a brief look at the future, which—for some—is already happening.

PAR ONLINE

Participate in a threaded discussion about the digital divide in electronic literacy today. What are your experiences and thoughts about this issue?

Here are several web links that provide important information to complement this chapter:

- To learn more about the third wave: http://www.foet.org/JeremyRifkin.htm
- To read the story "Life without the net is unbearable": http://cbs.marketwatch. com/news/archivedStory.asp?archive=true&dist=ArchiveSplash&siteid= mktw&guid=%7BB0361CD7%2D6B85%2D4808%2D860B%2D9EE55739 D9BE%7D&returnURL=%2Fnews%2Fstory%2Easp%3Fguid%3D%7BB0361 CD7%2D6B85%2D4808%2D860B%2D9EE55739D9BE%7D%26siteid%3 Dmktw%26dist%3Dnbc%26archive%3Dtrue%26param%3Darchive%26 garden%3D%26minisite%3D
- To view the NETS standards for instructional technology: http://www.iste.org

Using WebQuests in your classroom:

- WebQuest
  http://btsdmail.brick.k12.nj.us/lrms/Webquestmain.html
- Web Quest Academy
  http://warrensburg.k12.mo.us/webquest/class/
- What is a WebQuest?
  http://rcs.rcps.k12.va.us/creativeways/webquest.html
- Another WebQuest template: http://edweb.sdsu.edu/webquest/templates/ lesson-template1.htm

END-OF-CHAPTER ACTIVITIES

Assisting Comprehension

1. Read this entire chapter online to experience a hyperlinked, electronic text environment.
2. Here is a list of the applications and instructional software mentioned in this chapter:
   - Microsoft Word (www.microsoft.com)
   - The Learning Company's Student Writing Center (www.sonicfoundry.com)
   - Microsoft PowerPoint (www.microsoft. com)
   - Microsoft FrontPage (www.microsoft.com)
   - Macromedia Dreamweaver (www. dreamweaver.com)
   - Macromedia SoundEdit (www. macromedia.com)
   - Sonic Foundry's SoundForge (www. sonicfoundry.com)

- *Oregon Trail,* Broderbund (www. broderbund.com)
- *Amazon Trail,* Broderbund
- *Leonardo the Inventor,* Softkey, One Athenaeum Street, Cambridge, MA 02142
- *A Survey of Western Art,* Ebook, Inc., 32970 Alvarado-Niles, Suite 704, Union City, CA 94587
- *Compton's Interactive Encyclopedia,* Compton's New Media (www. comptons.com)
- *Grolier Multimedia Encyclopedia,* Grolier Publications (www.grolier.com)
- Inspiration Inc.'s Inspiration software (www.inspiration.com)
- *Write:Outloud* from Don Johnston, Inc., at http://www.donjohnston.com

- *CO:WRITER* from Don Johnston, Inc., at http://www.donjohnston.com
- *Kurzweil* at http://www.kurzweiledu.com/

Reflecting on the Reading

The International Reading Association (2003) has developed a set of standards that identify the performance criteria relevant to classroom teachers. Standard Four delineates two elements for creating a literate environment that a classroom teacher should possess. The classroom teacher should be able to

4.1 Use technology to gather and to use this information in instructional planning. They can articulate the research base that grounds their practice.

4.2 Select books, technology-based information, and nonprint materials representing multiple levels, broad interests, and cultural and linguistic backgrounds. They can articulate the research that grounds their practice.

How were these two elements addressed in this chapter? How does being informed about these elements aid in content instruction?

CHAPTER 5

*Through literature I become
a thousand people and yet
remain myself.*

C. S. LEWIS

Moving Beyond the Traditional Textbook

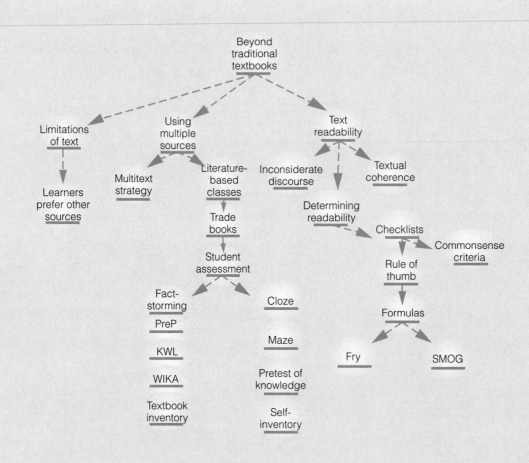

PREPARING TO READ

1. Did you ever serve on a textbook adoption committee or select material for classroom use? As you read this chapter, think of how you can use the information in it when selecting textbooks and other content material.

2. Following is a list of terms used in this chapter. Some may be familiar to you in a general context, but in this chapter they may be used in unfamiliar ways. Rate your knowledge by placing a plus sign (+) in front of those you are sure that you know, a check mark (✔) in front of those you have some knowledge about, and a zero (0) in front of those you don't know. Be ready to locate them in the chapter and pay special attention to their meanings.

_____ multitext
_____ literacy context
_____ read-alongs
_____ read-alouds
_____ trade books
_____ reading–writing connection
_____ literature-rich environment
_____ readability
_____ inconsiderate discourse
_____ textual coherence
_____ dumbed-down text
_____ rule of thumb
_____ readability formulas
_____ independent-level reading
_____ refutational texts
_____ cloze
_____ maze

OBJECTIVES

As you read this chapter, focus your attention on the following purposes. You will

1. learn why no textbook can stand alone as the only text reading in a content classroom.

2. understand the importance of using multiple resources in the classroom.

3. understand how to determine the match between a reader and the material to be read.

4. be able to define the term *readability*.

5. learn to judge the readability of textbook material.

6. become acquainted with situations that may cause a textbook to be less readable.

7. become acquainted with several activities that can help shape the match between a reader and the material to be read.

8. improve your own ability to select textbooks.

9. understand the roles of author, teacher, and student in improving textbook selection.

*A*s was discussed in the previous chapter, literacy is being redefined to take into consideration the growing number of resources such as CD-ROM encyclopedias, interactive videos, and websites (Leu, 2000; Richardson, 2004). Leu and colleagues (2004) recommend combining children's literature activities with the Internet to expand the response to reading in new and more powerful ways. Coiro (2003) maintains that such a combination prepares students for the new forms of literacy that will increasingly define their future. Because understanding these new text formats requires cognitive processing that is similar to reading traditional texts, researchers (Tyner, 1998) postulate that it is more important than ever to learn how meaning is created in both traditional textbooks and the new technologies. To this end, Thoman (1999) recently identified a number of critical questions teachers need to consider when evaluating alternative texts:

1. Who created the message?
2. Why did they create it?
3. What points of view are represented?
4. What techniques are used to attract reader attention?
5. How might the message be interpreted by different readers?
6. What is missing from the message?

These questions are equally relevant for both alternative and more traditional texts.

More teachers are digressing from the old norm and choosing books and text readings to add to the designated or assigned textbook. They do so because research (Guthrie, 2004) shows that students are more motivated when texts and readings are interesting. This chapter has two purposes: to validate the use of books and texts with traditional textbooks and to explain ways to determine how suitable any chosen text is for students who will read it. This chapter content represents the teacher's first step in PAR: preparing learners. Without planning for appropriate resources to teach the content, teachers and students will not be prepared. We are not advocating abandonment of the traditional textbook, but teachers need to explore other options for reading. Dove (1998) suggests that "it is no longer unrealistic to consider the textbook as only one of several resources that teachers can use to plan instruction. . . . Given the diversity of students in today's schools, the one-textbook approach is no longer viable" (p. 29).

WHY TEXTBOOKS CANNOT STAND ALONE

The Limitations of the Traditional Textbook

Learning today is often "disjointed and piecemeal" (Jetton & Alexander, 2000). Total reliance on textbooks as the single resource for learners contributes to this disjointed approach. The traditional notion of using one textbook for all classroom assignments limits success. Textbooks present condensed information about topics and thus are somewhat like encyclopedias. They offer an overview of a topic; they do not offer in-depth reporting. They are often secondary sources that are, of necessity, brief and condensed. In secondary reports much of the story behind a topic is omitted, and the original flavor of the authors' enthusiasm and style may be lost. Generally, when teachers assign homework to guide students to find out more about a topic, they want students to research multiple resources. However, teachers are often frustrated when students submit reports for which the only source was obviously an encyclopedia. Teachers prefer that students read widely on a topic and choose primary sources (those written by the authors who originally considered or researched the topic) rather than secondary sources (materials written as brief summaries). However, by using textbooks as single classroom resources, teachers model a single-resource approach, and learners imitate this style.

Using a solitary website for information is much like using only the dictionary.

Because textbooks condense information, their treatment of subject matter can be dry and boring. Hiebert (1999) makes the analogy between a variety of reading resources and a balanced diet. Someone using only one type of reading material may not receive all the nutrients needed to nourish the reading experience—or, we add, balanced knowledge about a content area. Guillaume (1998) proposes complementing textbooks with multiple resources, including trade books, fiction with content information, magazines, newspapers, and computer software.

Textbooks have been criticized for their conceptual density (Hurd, 1970) and for their doggedly factual presentation of material (Calfee, 1987). They also have been characterized as difficult for students to read and comprehend because the presentation lacks coherence (Armbruster & Anderson, 1984). Too many textbooks are bland collections of facts with not enough emphasis on showing students the relationships between facts or concepts. Textbook writing is often uneven, resulting in some sections that are much harder to read than others. Furthermore, the expository writing found in textbooks is often more difficult—and usually less interesting—for readers than a narrative or journalistic style. At times teachers use textbooks that are old and outdated and contain numerous errors in light of factual and conceptual changes within a field of study. The textbook used in a class may not be the one the teacher wants or needs for that particular class but one chosen by a textbook adoption committee or by the teacher who formerly taught the class.

Learners Prefer Other Resources

The modern world provides many resources as learning tools. Technological advances have created choices such as television, video, computer-based instruction, Internet access, and conversations with experts (much of this was explored in the previous chapter). It is small wonder that students sometimes view a textbook with boredom, skepticism, or distaste. Textbooks as a stand-alone resource simply do not fit today's learner.

Don't forget about electronic resources!

To illustrate this point, Thomas Bean (1999) conducted an informal study using his two adolescent daughters as subjects. He asked them to chart their functional uses of literacy for two weeks. Included as literacy tasks were text reading, novel reading, magazine reading, computer use, telephone use, and viewing TV, movies, and videocassettes. The TV/video category accounted for the greatest usage; the telephone was second, the computer third.

Why do we teach our students to use a textbook as the main instructional aid in classrooms? It is the rare classroom—even at the primary level—that does not issue textbooks to students. Only a rare curriculum guide does not list specific chapters as the way to teach topics in content subjects. But our students know better. They often express an aversion to learning when they think they will need to read a textbook. Bintz (1993) suggested that students "do not lose interest in reading per se" (p. 613) but lose interest in the textbooks as the reading resource.

The Strength of Using Multiple Resources

See Chapter 2 for more discussion of diverse learners.

The American student population is growing ever more diverse. It is not unusual for a classroom to include a half-dozen nationalities and cultures or for students to speak several languages. There is growing concern that teachers in all content subjects must become adept at offering reading choices that reflect students' interests, cultures, and customs. A **multitext** approach is necessary. What resources are the best for reading to learn? Literature is valuable. In the following sections we discuss the benefits of using literature as a learning resource.

The most comprehensive motivator to reading and writing is the development of a **literacy context** (Turner & Paris, 1995). The tasks that teachers assign send messages to students about what is important. Conceptions about what literacy is and involves influence students' feelings about reading and writing, the roles of literacy, and how much students integrate such roles in their own lives. In their study, Turner and Paris found that "the most reliable indicator of motivation was the actual daily tasks that teachers provided students in their classrooms" (p. 664). Specifically, they advise teachers to

- provide authentic choices and purposes for literacy.
- allow students to modify tasks so the difficulty and interest levels are challenging.
- show students how they can control their learning.
- encourage collaboration.
- emphasize strategies and metacognition for constructing meaning.
- use the consequences of tasks to build responsibility, ownership, and self-regulation.

USING MULTIPLE RESOURCES IN ADDITION TO TEXTBOOK INSTRUCTION

How can the resources that we have discussed be used to support, augment, and move beyond the textbook? Excerpts of literature, such as read-alouds and read-alongs, thematic units, and personal inquiries, are three good ways to start. All three can capitalize on literature and technology.

Read-Alongs and Read-Alouds

Literature and technology can be easily incorporated into existing instruction with no major restructuring of lessons. The teacher can collect and use excerpts of literature as adjuncts to the content being taught. Two plans of action are read-alongs and read-alouds. Using **read-alongs,** the teacher shares an excerpt with students, who read the piece individually, in small groups, or with the teacher. Using **read-alouds,** the teacher generally reads the excerpt to the entire class.

Teachers need to look for passages of literature that illustrate concepts in their field of study. Over time, teachers can compile a collection of examples. Activity 5.1 provides a map of possible resources for art, English, foreign language, mathematics, music, science, and social studies classes. It was generated by a group of teachers who all contributed at least one piece of literature that they found useful for instruction in a content area. For each content area, a resource is listed. For foreign language, the novel *After Long Silence* by Sheri Tepper describes how settlers on a planet learn to communicate with native crystalline structures by unlocking the secret of their language. A bibliography accompanies the map.

This map was prepared with *Inspiration* software.

Content teachers might start a personal database of literature selections to augment a content topic. As they come across an appropriate excerpt, they can enter it into the database along with suggestions for its use. Read-alouds sometimes work more effectively than read-alongs, at least initially, because the teacher can stimulate interest and regulate how much attention is given to the excerpt. Read-alouds have been shown effective in engaging students in learning (Erickson, 1996; Richardson, 1995b, 2000). However, teachers seem to abandon this practice by the time students start middle school, even though students of all ages enjoy and learn from it (Fisher, Flood, Lapp, & Frey, 2004; Richardson, 1994).

A social studies teacher tried read-alouds as an assisting activity to help her students understand myths, legends, and fairy tales of different cultures. After listening to read-alouds, students were expected to read stories from Eastern and Western cultures, then write their own myths. These students were ninth grade honors level, resistant to "baby" activities. Every day during the first unit on India, and every other day during the second and third units on China and Japan, the teacher read a myth, a legend, or a fairy tale during the last 5 to 10 minutes of class. The class then discussed the characteristics of these stories, as well as their historical merit. Next came the study of ancient Greece, after which students wrote their own myths, legends, or fairy tales based on one of the civilizations studied. Students were given two weeks to complete this writing assignment, which was worth a test grade; students also could present their stories orally for a quiz grade. The products generated were of high quality. Although good work is expected from honors students, the enthusiasm with which these students participated was greater than usual for this unit. They began to remind the teacher when to start the daily read-aloud time. When the teacher asked her students to evaluate the read-alouds, 63 percent responded that they would like them to continue for other units, and this percentage probably understated their enthusiasm. The teacher recalled, "I really believe more students enjoyed this than even said

Art
Mordecai Gerstein. (1984). *The Room.* New York: HarperCollins.
Andre Kertesz. (1971). *On Reading.* New York: Grossman.

English
F. Scott Fitzgerald. (1925). *The Great Gatsby.* New York: Scribner.

Richard Lederer. (1987). *Anguished English.* New York: Dell.
Lois Lowry. (1979). *Anastasia Krupnik.* Boston: Houghton Mifflin.

Foreign Language
Bruce Chatwin. (1987). *Songlines.* New York: Viking Penguin.
Sheri Tepper. (1987). *After Long Silence.* New York: Bantam Books.

Activity 5.1 *(continued)*

Mathematics

Pat Hutchins. (1986). *The Doorbell Rang.* New York: Morrow.

Catherine Neville. (1988). *The Eight.* New York: Ballantine Books.

Mark Twain. (1917). "On Cutoffs and Stephen" from *Life on the Mississippi.* New York: HarperCollins.

Music

Cynthia Voight. (1983). *A Solitary Blue.* New York: Fawcett Juniper/Ballantine.

Science

Vera and Bill Cleaver. (1970). *Where the Lilies Bloom.* Philadelphia: Lippincott.

Michael Crichton. (1990). *Jurassic Park.* New York: Knopf.

Annie Dillard. (1990). *Pilgrim at Tinker Creek.* New York: HarperCollins.

Social Studies

Sook Nyul Choi. (1991). *The Year of Impossible Goodbyes.* Boston: Houghton Mifflin.

Clyde Edgerton. (1985). *Raney.* Chapel Hill, NC: Algonquin.

Cynthia Voight. (1981). *Homecoming.* New York: Atheneum.

---

they did, because they kept looking at each other's papers. I had several students talk with me about the survey after we completed it. The comments orally were much more positive."

In science, one teacher found an Internet site that described the very expensive error in calculations made when the Mars Climate Orbiter was sent into space. It never reached its target because one set of scientists calculated using kilometers, while the other used miles. This site provided the perfect read-along "hook" to entice his students into real-world reasons to study metric measurement systems. Another science excerpt can be drawn from Robert C. O'Brien's novel *Mrs. Frisby and the Rats of NIMH* (1971), in which a science experiment works better than expected. The scientists divide rats and mice into three groups—control, experimental A, and experimental B—and then inject serums and conduct experiments. The serum works so well for group A that those rats and mice escape and set up their own society. Because this excerpt is several pages long—a whole chapter—it might best be shared with students reading silently and then discussing what constitutes experimental design.

Go to the book companion website to locate links that support these examples.

Teachers can find several literature excerpts and many instructional uses for read-alouds in the column "Read It Aloud," which appeared in the *Journal of Adolescent and Adult Literacy* four times a year (Richardson, 1994–1997), or in the monograph *Read It Aloud! Using Literature in the Secondary Content Classroom* (Richardson, 2000).

Issues Related to Using Multiple Resources in the Classroom

The physical environment of the classroom can facilitate the use of literature and technology to support the textbook because the way a classroom is arranged affects the climate for learning and teaching (Kowalski, 1995). According to Gambrell (1995), the availability of books, opportunities not only to read but also to choose what to read, and curiosity appear to motivate both good and poor readers. A classroom arranged to entice readers meets these criteria. When teachers provide bookshelves with literature, folders with newspaper clippings, magazines on racks, and baskets of books on topics being studied, students will be as enticed as anyone who browses in bookstores or libraries and feels the itch to pick up a book! A designated quiet reading spot is a friendly, encouraging touch. If possible, at least five or six computers should be available in the classroom so that students have easy access when they need to practice, write, enter data, send or receive e-mail, or find information on the Internet.

Locating and obtaining these resources may be less difficult than it first seems. In this textbook we mention several resources located by other teachers. Many parent organizations raise money for purchases. Libraries—either public or school—often lend books for extended classroom use. Students may donate books. Sometimes teachers receive "bonus" books from book club orders. If a school cannot afford several computers for each classroom, perhaps it can establish a "rolling" computer lab or a stationary lab.

As teachers integrate more literature into their content teaching, they should include multicultural literature. Bieger (1995) describes a four-level hierarchical framework for teaching multicultural literature: (1) looking at the contributions of people from other cultures; (2) adding information about other cultures to the curriculum; (3) changing the curriculum to help students see different cultures from new perspectives; and (4) identifying as well as proposing solutions to social problems that occur in multicultural environments.

Supporting the textbook with literature and technology enhances the teacher's ability to distinguish between the relevant information that textbooks offer and any incorrect, outdated, or abbreviated information they may present. Exemplary programs do this all the time. For instance, Lafayette Township School in New Jersey was granted the International Reading Association Exemplary Reading Program award (Mahler, 1995). The school integrated instruction in numerous ways—for example, by organizing a Renaissance fair where middle school students read about the Renaissance era, wrote stories, built inventions inspired by Leonardo da Vinci, staged a play, and coordinated activities for students in the lower grades to learn more about the Middle Ages. Mahler points out that this school developed a literature-based program for grades 2 through 8. Alvarez and Rodriguez (1995) describe how high school students in an exploratory project called "Explorers of the Universe" learned not only subject matter but also how to think and ask questions as a result of searching in teams for information beyond the classroom textbooks. One group of students began to correspond with two astronomers via telecommunication.

See the book companion website for a link to this site.

Teachers need to know how to encourage students to respond to supplemental literature through writing, discussion in response groups, and even art and drama renderings. In later chapters we describe cooperative learning response groups (Chapter 11), writing activities and learning logs (Chapter 10), postgraphic organizers and other visuals (Chapters 8 and 10), and cooperative drama (Chapter 11), as well as ways to guide students to respond through directed reading.

Using Literature in the Content Classroom

Over the past several years, the use of trade books has increased dramatically, especially in elementary and middle schools. **Trade books** are books that are considered to be in general use, such as books borrowed from a library or bought at the local bookstore, rather than textbooks bought and studied as a major course resource. Most trade books are written in either a journalistic or a narrative style; they are interesting resources but are not specifically intended as instructional tools. Trade books are often literature but can also be informational books. Sloan (1984) summarized the importance of the literature component of a classroom:

> The literate person . . . is not one who knows how to read, but one who reads: fluently, responsively, critically, and because he wants to. . . . Children will become readers only if their emotions have been engaged, their imaginations stirred and stretched by what they find on printed pages. One way—a sure way—to make this happen is through literature.

Because of the numerous limitations inherent in using a single textbook, researchers are calling for the use of "real" literature in all content area subjects (Wilson, 1988; Allen et al., 1995). Reading literature that augments textbook topics also provides necessary practice with enjoyable materials. All readers need practice, but for the struggling learner, practice is crucial. In interviews with 12 successful people labeled as dyslexic, Fink (1996) found that they enjoyed reading challenging books of personal interest, books that took them beyond textbook information.

Calfee (1987) noted that trade books offer causal relationships between concepts and provide a better framework for students to answer their own questions about the reading. Although trade books may have uneven readability, they possess several advantages over textbooks. Guzzetti, Kowalinski, and McGowan (1992) confirmed that using trade books improves the affective domain of learning for students; the researchers were impressed "with students' enthusiasm for self-selection of 'real books'" (p. 115). Haussamen (1995) stresses the value of reading literature for pleasure and interest versus reading to extract information. Because textbooks lend themselves to efferent or extraction-type reading, the aesthetic is often lost, and thus any act of reading is devalued. Allowing for personal responses to literature can encourage students to value reading (Villaune & Hopkins, 1995). Textbooks can be supplemented by fiction—novels and short stories—and nonfiction trade books in psychology, philosophy, religion, technology, history, biography, and autobiography. Also useful in a broad-based literature approach are reference books, magazines, and teacher-created materials from outside sources such as newspapers. Richardson (2000) shows teachers how to present lessons that integrate literature with content topics.

More and more teachers are showing interest in using literature in their curriculum (Allen et al., 1995). There are several reasons for such interest. One compelling reason is that when teachers bring complementary reading selections to their students, they can help revitalize instruction by opening new avenues for student and teacher alike. A number of recent research reports call for the use of Asian-American literature (Pang et al., 1992; Au, 2001), literature that focuses on minority groups (Bealor, 1992), literature in content areas such as social studies (Guzzetti, Kowalinski, & McGowan, 1992), and literature for special populations such as deaf teenagers (Hartman & Kretschner, 1992). We know of a vocational education teacher in a shipbuilding class who regularly reads to his students from books about ships, such as "Getting It Right at Swan Hunter" from *The Naval Architect,* and books about the sea, such as *World Beneath the Sea* from the National Geographic Society. He also provides reading lists to supplement each unit of study about shipbuilding. Such a class is intellectually stimulating, and the teacher is constantly modeling his positive feelings for reading with his use of literature.

Characteristics of Effective Literature-Based Classrooms

When content area teachers wish to supplement textbooks with literature-based materials and trade books, the teachers, the classroom curriculum, and the school as a whole should have certain characteristics.

1. Teachers themselves must be readers.   Only by reading will teachers model the importance of many resources from which to learn. They cannot model what they do not know and practice. Morrison, Jacobs, and Swinyard (1999) found that teachers who choose reading as a leisure activity report using more literacy practices in their classrooms than do teachers who do not read often. Because familiarity with a book influences whether a teacher will use it in the classroom, teachers need to familiarize themselves with a wide variety of literature that reflects the diverse population they serve.

2. Teachers must be flexible in their work habits.   To incorporate literature from outside sources in the classroom, teachers must be willing to rearrange topics in the curriculum to take advantage of current articles or stories about a particular topic. Teachers also must be prepared to abandon lesson plans on occasion to follow a gripping news or personal interest story. The entertainment value of these stories is fleeting and usually cannot last until some other unit is finished. In other words, teachers must be able to adapt the curriculum to fit the materials available, not vice versa. In addition, teachers need to become adept at saving interesting articles. Students—the teacher's greatest resource—can help as researchers in finding new material. Students need to be challenged from the beginning of the school year to bring in items of interest or items related to what they are studying. These can be shared with other classes in an effort to convince others that they too should bring in new materials.

3. Books and resource materials must be everywhere throughout the school. It is essential that students have access to many books in the classroom, in the school library or media center, and in a nearby public library. In the international study *How in the World Do Students Read?* (1992), Elley reports that the countries with the highest literacy scores also had large school and classroom libraries, regular book borrowing, frequent silent reading in class, frequent story reading aloud by teachers, and more hours scheduled for language activities. Teachers and librarians/media center specialists need to work together to find informational books at a wide range of read-

Teachers can post suggested book and resource material at the school or class website.

ability levels and interest levels related to content area units in both academic and vocational subjects. Teachers in all disciplines within the school need to make up reading lists of acceptable literature and other supplemental books. Reading specialists and librarians/media center specialists can help compile as many books as possible or borrow from nearby public libraries books not easily located.

4. Teachers must plan how to use literature.   Teachers need to develop the philosophy that literature is an integral part of any content area curriculum and is an important resource for studying any discipline. In literature-based classrooms, teachers actively plan to use literature and make it as important as the textbook in their teaching. Teachers should plan their instruction to get children interested in these books and in researching the topics in small groups. Teachers also should provide time for students, after they become accustomed to a literature-based environment, to brainstorm and explore their own ideas about topics and how they would like to research them. All this does not just happen; careful planning by teachers is needed to make such exploratory classes work.

5. Students should be given numerous ways to respond to literature.   Students become personally involved in reacting cognitively and affectively to literature. There is additional emphasis on the reflection step of the PAR Lesson Framework to allow students, both orally and in writing, individually and in groups, to respond to the meaning they derive from the reading. Guzzetti (1990) reports on the importance of students responding visually through cognitive maps, charts of character traits (visual illustrations), and written paradigms (creation of a new product based on the author's ideas and students' experiences) to historical fiction and novels. According to Guzzetti, such visual responses help students clarify their thinking and help motivate them through creative activity related to the interpretation of meaning from text.

Visual responses are conducive to technological display.

6. The reading–writing connection must be emphasized in each content area classroom.   Students learn to write to get ready to read, to read, and then to write about the meaning they derived from reading. This is the **reading–writing connection,** and in this atmosphere writing ability improves dramatically as students read and respond to varied literature. Students become used to combining reading and writing in this manner; it happens naturally in the literature-based classroom.

7. The media center should be a hub of learning for the school.   Literature-based programs rely on close cooperation among administrators, teachers, and reading and media specialists to make books a central focus for the school. One vocational education school that we know about utilizes a research-based curriculum in which the media specialist plays a central role in helping students do research. Teachers in the school stress the use of directed reading–thinking activities in each vocational and academic class. When students have unanswered questions remaining on their What-I-Know activity sheets, teachers create a committee and give students on the research committee a number of days to find the answers. The teacher and students sign a special form and deliver it to the media specialist. The media specialist, in turn, signs the form to acknowledge the research question and helps the student committee find reference and other material sufficient to answer the students' questions. In this manner the media specialist, teacher, and students team up to answer research questions emanating from student inquiry in reading.

8. Reading should be perceived as important.　A recent study by Duke (2000) found that fewer than four minutes a day were spent teaching literacy through nonfiction texts in first grade classrooms. In another study, Moss and Hendershot (2002) found the situation is not much better in middle schools, where students do not find nonfiction in classroom libraries. In such cases reading might not be perceived as important. In addition, in many schools reading is offered as a carrot to those students who finish their regular classroom assignments. This practice lowers the value of reading. Consider the lament of a content area teacher who said, "You would ask me to have students read in class? My students don't read in class. They go home and read!" When reading is done only as homework, students assign it a lesser value and often do not even bother to do the homework assignment because it has such little interest to them. For some learners, reading at home is often impossible due to the environment (see Chapter 2). When teachers read in the classroom, they demonstrate how important reading is. Rose (1999) implores teachers to keep reading in the classroom, especially aloud, because reading increases understanding and enjoyment, as well as providing context for learning. In a **literature-rich environment,** the teacher reads to students daily, students are allowed to read silently on a subject or story of interest, and they read and do research in groups on topics assigned by the teacher or self-selected by the group. Students also keep records and daily logs of reading and writing abilities so that a portfolio is built of their successes in the class.

9. Teachers should model an effective reading process.　Teachers in literature-based classrooms read aloud to students to motivate them to read further on a topic or to complete a story. Teachers also direct students to maturity in reading by modeling correct reading process, using many of the techniques mentioned in this text, such as directed reading–thinking activities and the question–answer relationship (QAR). When students are reading silently, the teacher also reads silently, to model good reading behavior and show interest in the lesson. Teachers also share what they are reading and writing with the students and generally provide an intellectually stimulating environment.

10. Teachers should stress the affective domain in reading.　Through reading aloud and encouraging the sharing and discussion of books, teachers emphasize the affective domain of reading—how students feel about what they are doing. In our study skills chapter (Chapter 8) we present a study log for students to keep so they can self-evaluate how they are doing in the classroom. Through such a device, teachers can allow students to become more internally motivated and to move toward an internal locus of control (discussed in Chapter 12). If students enjoy what they are doing, they tend to feel more "in control" of what is happening in the class. This emphasis on the affective domain is especially evident in the reflection phase of the PAR Lesson Framework. If students are given real opportunities, in an unhurried environment, to think critically and share their thoughts on reading material, their attitude toward class will improve. Allowing more time for sharing and reflection can be done in any grade and in any subject, from kindergarten to the most abstract and difficult twelfth grade subject.

11. Intellectual curiosity should be encouraged.   In literature-based classrooms, teachers always encourage questions from students about topics related to the subject being studied. Teachers point students in directions to find their own answers rather than simply telling students what they need to know. Teachers also try to get parents involved in stimulating their children's intellectual curiosity. Teachers can send letters to parents asking them to read to their children, and include a book list, in an attempt to stimulate reading. The book list may include a brief description of each book, its level of difficulty, topics covered, and whether it is fiction or nonfiction. This is an excellent way to encourage parents to stimulate the natural curiosity of their children.

ASSESSING THE READABILITY
OF TEXTBOOKS AND RESOURCES

This chapter so far has stressed the importance of using multiple resources instead of relying entirely on a textbook to convey content information. Unfortunately, some studies indicate that as much as 95 percent of classroom instruction and 90 percent of homework assignments for elementary students are based on textbook materials (Sosniak & Perlman, 1990). From our personal experience the situation seems to be similar at the secondary level. Too often, teachers organize their instruction around the textbook rather than around the topic. Apple (1988) writes, "Whether we like it or not, the curriculum in most American schools is not defined by courses of study or suggested programs, but by one particular artifact, the grade-level-specific text" (p. 85). It makes sense that any textbook or resource material being considered by the teacher needs to undergo thorough examination. Wilson (2004) has recently called for classroom assessment to be the cornerstone of accountability for teachers. We feel that an important aspect of classroom assessment that often goes lacking is assessment of the textbook and/or ancillary resource materials. In short, teachers need to determine what the textbook (or other supplementary content material) has to offer. Careful consideration of readability can ensure the selection of material not only is content-rich but also facilitates reading to learn. The first step is to assess the match between the reader and the material. If the match is poor, then the teacher must find better materials for the readers' background and level of expertise. To do otherwise handicaps the readers.

What is this notion of readability, and how does the teacher determine the readability match? Dreyer (1984) has written that "the goal of readability research is to match reader and text" (p. 334). Simply stated, **readability** is that match. Readability suggests that content is clear, well expressed, and suited to the reader.

Readability is not a formula. It is an exploration of what characteristics within the reader and within the text will create a successful marriage. By examining readability, teachers can prepare readers appropriately to learn. Professional judgment is essential in determining readability; no score or formula can do more than help teachers understand the problems that may arise with reading material. Too many factors are involved for teachers to settle for simple solutions. For instance, careful consideration of grammar and its complexity is necessary when evaluating why students find written material more difficult than oral discussion of a topic. Unsworth (1999) discusses how English writing "packs" many content words into expository text, many more than in the spoken form. One can determine the lexical or grammatical density of a piece of writing by using Halladay's (1994) formula, which divides the number of lexical items by the number of clauses. Unsworth notes that this technique requires a functional grammatical perspective on English.

> Readability is a great deal more than a formula.

Inconsiderate Discourse

"Your ring adjusters will shape to fit you right by following these simple steps." Wait a minute! Are the "ring adjusters" going to follow some simple steps? As this is written, the subject, *ring adjusters,* is going to follow simple steps. Doesn't the author mean the reader is supposed to follow simple steps? And will the ring adjusters change shape to fit the reader, or fit the ring, or help the ring fit the reader? The author has written an ungrammatical sentence in which the relationships between subject, verb, and direct object are confused.

Readers need to work extra hard to understand the meaning of such text passages. When confronted with careless text, the reader must make a decision. Too often students decide that the text is simply not worth the energy. How many readers abandon or postpone the mastery of a new software program because its documentation is poorly written or presented? How many parents become exasperated with the poorly written instructions for assembling a toy? Similarly, some content material, particularly that found in textbooks, may be poorly written and therefore place unnecessary stress on a reader. If so, teachers must identify the difficulties in the material to help their students expend the least energy for the greatest gain.

Poorly written material is recognizable because of its loose organization, its lack of a discernible style, its incorrect syntax, and/or its incoherent passages. Armbruster and Anderson (1981) call such material **inconsiderate discourse.** When Olson and Gee (1991) surveyed 47 primary grade classroom teachers about their impressions of expository text for their students, 23 percent of them identified text characteristics such as "sentence length, page format, inadequate arrangement and unfamiliar presentation of topics, and lack of aids on how to read expository text" as the greatest problems, and 69 percent cited unfamiliar words. College students indicated in a survey (Smith, 1992) that textbooks are generally boring because passages are too long, the writing style is hard to follow, graphics don't seem to relate to text, and information is either too detailed or repetitive. High school students who were asked to rate their textbooks and indicate how often they read and studied them said that they used mathematics texts most often, followed by social studies, science, and English texts. However, they reported the text they liked *least* was the mathematics text because it was "hard to understand, boring, not specific enough, and poorly arranged" (Lester, 1998).

Fortunately, textbooks are changing for the better. Walpole (1999) found that newer science texts are more enticing to readers. She compared science textbooks for third graders written in 1992 and 1995 and found significant improvements in format, organization, text coherence, and illustrations. These factors all enter the mix that makes text considerate or inconsiderate, coherent or incoherent.

Textual Coherence

For a text to be readable, it must exhibit textual coherence (Beck & McKeown, 1988). **Textual coherence**—the clear presentation of material to facilitate comprehension—can be divided into two categories: global coherence and local coherence.

Global coherence refers to the big picture. Major ideas should span the entire text so that readers are made aware of the global nature of the material and can follow the ideas without becoming confused. The way a text is structured can ensure global coherence. For example, the organization of ideas according to logical patterns, such as clear sequences of cause and effect, aids global comprehension. The style of text is also significant. A narrative style is usually easiest for readers, followed by a more journalistic style. Hardest to read is exposition. It is confusing when a writer mixes expository and narrative styles but doesn't cue the reader. "This is a story about" or "The following description explains" provides clear cues about the style of text to follow. The frequent use of one style also helps the reader recognize and understand the structure of the text. Of course, the content of the material and how well the author matches it to the structure are also important for global coherence.

Local coherence involves the many kinds of aids that connect ideas at the more immediate, or local, level. These aids include cues within sentences—phrases or clauses, for example—between sentences or within paragraphs. When an author clearly identifies the subject and then uses a pronoun to refer to that subject, coherence is much greater than when the pronoun referent is vague and the reader is forced to guess about to whom or what the author may be referring. Consider these passages, which Lederer (1987) quotes as an example of text ambiguity:

> Guilt, vengeance, and bitterness can be emotionally destructive to you and your children. You must get rid of them.

> After Governor Baldwin watched the lion perform, he was taken to Main Street and fed 25 pounds of raw meat in front of the Cross Keys Theater. (p. 156)

Another type of poorly written text is that in which the author oversimplifies the context. Former Secretary of Education Terrell Bell (Toch, 1984) expressed concern over such textbooks, calling them "dumbed down." In **dumbed-down text,** global coherence may be so simplified that the author can't do justice to the content, and local coherence may be absent because there isn't enough complexity to the text. When important points and intricacies are missing, the reader loses both content and cues. To determine whether textual coherence is a problem, students are really the best resource. Britton and colleagues (1991) found that college students were able to select with 95 percent accuracy which of two texts on the same topic was easier to learn.

What is the difference between global and local coherence?

How to Determine Readability of Textbooks and Resources

 ## Checklists

One way to determine the readability of text material is to use a checklist to aid in judging the overall strengths and weaknesses of the text. Creating an evaluative checklist, which the teacher can then use as a guide, ensures both "readability and relevance" (Danielson, 1987, p. 185). One fairly extensive checklist to help teachers consider readability carefully and efficiently is Bader's (1987) textbook analysis chart (see Figure 5.1 on pages 140 and 141). The chart identifies several areas of concern and lists specific items for teacher evaluation. The user is encouraged to summarize the textbook's strengths and weaknesses after completing the checklist and then to decide the implications of the summary for teaching the material evaluated.

The Bader analysis encourages teachers to consider several factors that contribute to readability. The "linguistic factors" category, for example, describes word difficulty in six ways, whereas a readability formula considers only the length of a word. The "writing style" category considers four measures of style, whereas a readability formula considers only sentence length. The four other categories are not considered at all in a formula. "Conceptual factors" and "organizational factors" include criteria that many teachers identify as having a crucial effect on text difficulty. In addition, the teacher is asked to think about "learning aids" because such aids can make otherwise difficult material easier for students to handle. The "learning aids" category also gives teachers direction in how to guide the reading of otherwise difficult material. For instance, visual aids often make difficult material readable. Because features such as typography, format, illustrations, and book appearance can enhance meaning in a text, Bader includes these items in her last category.

We must issue several cautions when promoting the use of checklists. First, no one checklist can cover all factors of teaching. In addition, checklists must be general, and they rarely cover instructional content. But armed with tools such as those presented in this chapter and with some knowledge of why determining the difficulty of reading material is important, teachers can proceed wisely.

The Rule of Thumb

A quick and reader-centered way to determine readability is to teach students to use the **rule of thumb** (Veatch, 1968). Younger students are told to select a book they want to read and open it to a middle page. If they spot an unknown word while reading that page, they press a thumb on the table. For each hard word, they press down another finger. If they press down five or more fingers by the time they finish the page, the book may be too hard. Three or fewer fingers indicate a more reasonable challenge. No fingers means the book might be very easy. Older students can determine readability by using two hands and closing their fingers into fists. One closed fist indicates that the book is just right, two closed fists may indicate difficulty, and only one or two closed fingers may indicate easy material.

Of course, students should read the chosen book even if it looks too easy or too hard, if that is their wish. The rule of thumb is not scientific and is intended only to help readers make decisions. It is not intended to discourage a reader from trying any book. Its value is that it encourages the reader to be responsible for determining difficulty. This involvement of the reader promotes independence.

Readability Formulas

Readability formulas are a major resource for determining the difficulty of material. Fry, a noted expert on readability formulas, quotes Farr as estimating that "over 40 percent of the state and local school districts in the United States use readability formulas as one criterion in textbook selection" (Fry, 1987, p. 339). Readability formulas are fairly reliable measures—if not always the most effective ones—for making instructional decisions about texts.

Readability formulas are a narrow measure of readability.

A quick first look at material to spot potential problems with difficulty can be accomplished by using a readability formula. Because formulas identify a certain grade level of difficulty, they are used most often to report information about textbook difficulty in terms of reading-level scores. A formula can be helpful when a prediction of difficulty is necessary, such as when a textbook adoption committee considers several texts but cannot try out the books on real students. Similarly, a formula may be useful and efficient when a teacher wants to assess the difficulty of several materials that students are to read on their own in the library. A readability formula offers a quick measure and can be used independently of student interaction. However, the teacher must not rely on the grade level obtained as an exact measure; it is only a predictor.

HOW READABILITY FORMULAS WORK

Over the years, reading researchers have developed and statistically validated many readability formulas. Some are cumbersome in that they necessitate checking long lists of words. Both the Dale and Chall (1948) and the Spache (1953) measure "word familiarity"—that is, whether students should be expected to know a word within a given passage—by relying on lengthy word lists. The Lexile Framework developed in the mid-1980s is based on the words found in textbooks. Mosenthal and Kirsch (1998) developed a comprehensive measure that focuses on the structure and density that create complexity. Their measure demonstrates that difficulty in reading a document may be due more to the document's complexity than to the reader's abilities.

Essentially, two measurements are used for almost all of these formulas: sentence difficulty and word difficulty. The underlying assumption is that the longer sentences and words are, the harder the material will be. Usually, this assumption holds true; sometimes, however, it is questionable. For instance, in William Faulkner's novel *The Sound and the Fury,* several sentences are as much as one and one-half pages long, and most readers would agree that the length of Faulkner's sentences makes for challenging reading. But could one say that because Ernest Hemingway's sentences are shorter, his

FIGURE 5.1 Bader's Textbook Analysis Chart

+	✓	−
Excellent/ Evident Throughout	Average/ Somewhat Evident	Poor/ Not Evident

Book Title _____

Publisher _____

Grade Level _____

Content Area _____

Linguistic Factors   *Comments*

_____ _____ _____ This book is generally appropriate
to intended grade level(s)
according to _____ formula.   _____

_____ _____ _____ Linguistic patterns are suitable to most
populations and fit intended level(s).   _____

_____ _____ _____ Vocabulary choice and control are suitable.   _____

_____ _____ _____ New vocabulary is highlighted, italicized,
in boldface type, or underlined.   _____

_____ _____ _____ New vocabulary is defined in context.   _____

_____ _____ _____ New vocabulary is defined in margin
guides, glossary, or beginning or end
of chapter.

Conceptual Factors

_____ _____ _____ The conceptual level is generally
appropriate to intended grade level(s).   _____

_____ _____ _____ Concepts are presented deductively.   _____

_____ _____ _____ Concepts are presented inductively.   _____

_____ _____ _____ Major ideas are highlighted, italicized,
in boldface type, or underlined.   _____

_____ _____ _____ Appropriate assumptions are made
regarding prior level of concepts.   _____

_____ _____ _____ New concepts are sufficiently developed
through examples, illustrations, or
redundancy.   _____

_____ _____ _____ Sexual, racial, economic, cultural, and
political bias are absent.   _____

Organizational Factors

_____ _____ _____ Units, chapters, table of contents, and
index present clear, logical
development of subject.   _____

_____ _____ _____ Chapters of instructional segments
contain headings and subheadings
that aid comprehension of subject.   _____

_____ _____ _____ Introductory, definitional, illustrative,
and summary paragraphs/sections
are used as necessary.   _____

_____ _____ _____ Topic sentences of paragraphs are clearly
identifiable or easily inferred.   _____

_____ _____ _____ Each chapter/section/unit contains a
well-written summary or overview.

+ Excellent/ Evident Throughout	✓ Average/ Somewhat Evident	− Poor/ Not Evident		

Writing Style   *Comments*

_____ _____ _____   Ideas are expressed clearly and directly.   _____

_____ _____ _____   Word choice is appropriate.   _____

_____ _____ _____   Tone and manner of expression are appealing to intended readers.   _____

_____ _____ _____   Mechanics are correct.   _____

Learning Aids

_____ _____ _____   Questions/tasks are appropriate to conceptual development of intended age/grade level(s).   _____

_____ _____ _____   Questions/tasks span levels of reasoning: literal, interpretive, critical, values clarification, and problem-solving.   _____

_____ _____ _____   Questions/tasks can be used as reading guides.   _____

_____ _____ _____   Suitable supplementary readings are suggested.   _____

_____ _____ _____   The book is clear and convenient to use.   _____

_____ _____ _____   Helpful ideas are presented for conceptual development.   _____

_____ _____ _____   Alternative instructional suggestions are given for poor readers, slow-learning students, and advanced students.   _____

_____ _____ _____   The book contains objectives, management plans, evaluation guidelines, and tests of satisfactory quality.   _____

_____ _____ _____   Supplementary aids are available.   _____

Binding / Printing / Format / Illustrations

_____ _____ _____   Book size is appropriate.   _____

_____ _____ _____   Cover, binding, and paper are appropriate.   _____

_____ _____ _____   Typeface is appropriate.   _____

_____ _____ _____   Format is appropriate.   _____

_____ _____ _____   Pictures, charts, and graphs are appealing.   _____

_____ _____ _____   Illustrations aid comprehension of text.   _____

_____ _____ _____   Illustrations are free of sexual, social, or cultural bias.   _____

Summary

_____ _____ _____   Totals   _____

The strengths are:

The weaknesses are:

As a teacher, I will need to:

Original text analysis chart by Dr. Lois Bader, Michigan State University. Used with permission of Lois Bader.

material is easy to read? In these cases, one reads to understand style and theme, and sentence length is of little importance. These two sentences better illustrate the point:

The children played on the playground with the elephant.

We reneged on all prior briefs.

A readability formula would score the first sentence as more difficult, but would it be more difficult for children to comprehend?

The syntactical structure of sentences probably deserves more attention than it receives in readability formulas (Richardson, 1975; Singh, 1995). For example, sentences in the active voice may be easier to understand than those in the passive voice. Readability formulas do not measure with such sensitivity. Also, word length may be a fairly accurate indicator of difficulty. Just as short sentences seem easier to read, short words generally are also easier on a reader. First graders recognize a lot of one-syllable words. But *elephant* might be an easier word for young readers than *the*. *Elephant* may be longer, but it's a lot easier to picture an *elephant* than to picture *the*! Because seeing words in the mind's eye facilitates comprehension, the longer word is easier in this case. Few readers wish to encounter a lot of long words all at once, but they will be bored by too many short ones. Given these qualifiers, the way most readability formulas measure reading material is common, if not commonsense. A few formulas remain popular because they are easy to apply and seem reliable. We describe the Fry readability formula here and the SMOG formula in Appendix B.

The Fry Readability Graph

The Fry readability graph (see Figure 5.2) was developed by Edward Fry in the 1960s for African teachers who taught English as a second language. In 1977 Fry revised the graph to include explanations, directions, and an extension to the 17th grade level. The Fry graph offers a quantifiable, efficient way to measure text difficulty.

To use this graph, teachers select at least three 100-word passages from different parts of the material. For each 100-word passage, two counts are made: the number of syllables and the number of sentences. The three counts of syllables are added, then averaged; the three counts of sentences are added, then averaged. The teacher locates the average for the number of syllables across the top of the graph and the average for the number of sentences along the side of the graph. The point at which these two averages intersect is the readability score. The point will fall within a fanlike, numbered segment on the graph; this number corresponds to the grade-level score. Fry says to count all words, including proper nouns, initials, and numerals, and he defines *word* as well as *syllable*. If a point falls in a gray area, the score is unreliable and should be recalculated by using additional 100-word passages.

EXPANDED DIRECTIONS FOR WORKING THE FRY READABILITY GRAPH

1. Randomly select three (3) sample passages and count out exactly 100 words each, beginning with the beginning of a sentence. Do count proper nouns, initializations, and numerals.

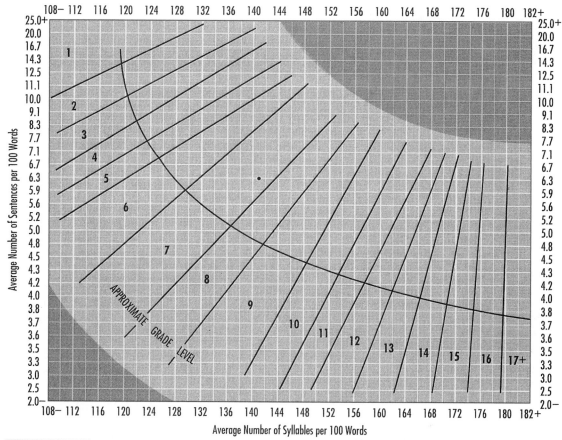

FIGURE 5.2 The Fry Readability Graph. From *Journal of Reading, 21,* 242–52.

2. Count the number of sentences in the 100 words, estimating the length of the fraction of the last sentence to the nearest one-tenth.

3. Count the total number of syllables in the 100-word passage. If you don't have a hand counter available, an easy way is to simply put a mark above every syllable over 1 in each word; then when you get to the end of the passage, count the number of marks and add 100. Small calculators can also be used as counters by pushing the numeral 1, then pushing the + sign for each word or syllable when counting.

4. Enter the graph with the *average* sentence length and the *average* number of syllables; plot the dot where the two lines intersect. The area where this dot is plotted will give you the approximate grade level.

5. If a great deal of variability is found in syllable count or sentence count, putting more samples into the average is desirable.

6. A word is defined as a group of symbols with a space on either side; thus *Joe, IRA, 1945,* and & are each one word.

7. A syllable is defined as a phonetic syllable. Generally, there are as many syllables as vowel sounds. For example, *stopped* is one syllable and *wanted* is two syllables. When counting syllables for numerals and initializations, count one syllable for each symbol. For example, *1945* is four syllables, *IRA* is three syllables, and & is one syllable.

The Fry formula is more usable for upper elementary and higher-level materials than for lower-level material because at least 100 words are needed for computation. Forgan and Mangrum (1985) developed a way to adapt the Fry for shorter materials, and their procedure is described and illustrated in Appendix B.

For **independent-level reading**—materials that students will read on their own with 90 percent or more comprehension—the SMOG formula of McLaughlin (1969) may be used. Directions for using it are presented in Appendix B. In choosing between Fry and SMOG, remember that these two formulas are used for different purposes and that their readability scores are read differently. The Fry formula measures the readability of material used in an instructional setting. Because the teacher explains difficult words and sentences, the Fry score is based on students' understanding 65 to 75 percent of the material at a given grade level. The SMOG formula is intended to measure the readability of material that a teacher will *not* be teaching, such as material that the teacher has suggested a student use independently. Because the teacher will *not* be explaining the difficult words and sentences, the SMOG score is based on students' understanding 90 to 100 percent of the material. If a Fry and a SMOG were calculated on the same material, the Fry score probably would be lower.

What is the difference between the Fry and the SMOG?

Readability Statistics from Your Word Processor

Word processing programs such as WordPerfect and Microsoft Word provide readability statistics for any document being processed. In WordPerfect they can be found under "Grammatik" on the toolbar. In Microsoft Word they can be found by clicking on "Tools" and then clicking on "Spelling and Grammar," "Options," and "Show readability statistics."

Both provide the Flesch-Kincaid grade level, which measures readability based on the average number of syllables per word and the average number of words per sentence. The score is reported as a grade level similar to the Fry grade-level score. Some programs provide various measures with which to compare the Flesch-Kincaid grade-level scores. Simply by typing a few passages into the computer and using the readability measures the program provides, you can get a feel for the readability of text without counting words and syllables.

Technology tip

Cautions about Readability Formulas

In recent literature, professionals warn teachers to be aware of the limitations of readability formulas. They are not precise determiners of the difficulty of material; they only predict how difficult the material might be for readers.

1. A readability formula gives a grade-level score, which is not a specific measure of difficulty because grade level can be so ambiguous. Cadenhead (1987) describes this ambiguity as the "metaphor of reading level" and claims that it is a major problem of readability formulas. What does 17th grade level mean when applied to a topic such as "electrical attraction of dielectric insulation" without consideration of the reader's interests, background, and knowledge? A grade-level readability score gives teachers a start in their considerations of text difficulty, not a complete picture.

2. The lengths of sentences and words are convenient and credible indicators of readability and fit neatly into a formula, but they are not comprehensive measures. The various factors that make a text coherent are difficult to quantify. Remember that readability formulas cannot get at the depth of the ideas inherent in a text. One cannot "compute" such factors in a simple mathematical formula.

3. Measures of word and sentence length are sometimes not the most accurate indicators of difficulty. In one study (Carson et al., 1992), college students read texts measured by a formula as being at their level; however, the texts were not equally readable because of the conceptual difficulty of the material. To further illustrate this point, we refer readers to noted author E. B. White's (1951) essay "Calculating Machine," which recounts White's reaction when he received a "reading-ease calculator" developed by General Motors and based on the Flesch Reading Ease Formula. "Communication by the written word," writes White, "is a subtler (and more beautiful) thing than Dr. Flesch and General Motors imagine" (p. 166). His point—that it is dangerous to reduce language to such simplistic evaluation—is well taken. (For further information about the Flesch formula, see the references.)

4. The fewer sections of material measured, the less consistent and reliable the resulting score is likely to be. Even three sections may be too few. If three or fewer sections are measured, the teacher should be cautious about accepting the results. We include the Fry Short Formula in Appendix B, but we ask the reader to realize that it is already a shortcut: the Fry Short Formula should be used only when the material contains fewer than 100 words, such as in textbooks for young readers. However, almost always in such a case, the teacher can assess readability efficiently by relying on checklists and professional judgment.

There is more to readability than formulas. Much research has been conducted about texts and text-related matters since readability formulas were developed in the 1920s (Davison, 1984). We know enough to move beyond rigid adherence to mathematical formulas. Although formulas can tell us some things—they yield levels based on the percentage of readers who have performed well at those levels—they tell us a lot less than we want to know. Fry (1989) argues that some reading professionals may not like formulas because they are "so objective." When others argue that readability formulas are not comprehensive enough, his response is, "Readability formulas do not deny all this, they simply state that in general, on the average, the two inputs of sentence length and word difficulty accurately predict how easily a given passage will be understood by the average reader" (p. 295).

A report by Guzzetti and colleagues (1995) recommends that students themselves give considerable input about the readability of texts. The researchers found that a broad sample of students in science classes preferred **refutational texts,** in which both sides of an argument are presented and debated. Also, they found that students prefer expository texts over narrative ones. The students gave researchers specific ideas about how the sample text material they were reading could be improved. The researchers recommend that teachers send students' critiques and suggestions to publishers to make textbooks more interesting and comprehensible.

The concept of readability and the efficacy of readability formulas stir much controversy. We maintain that formulas provide only one measure and should be used with checklists and commonsense criteria to judge the readability of a text for a group of students.

ASSESSING STUDENTS' ABILITY TO USE BOOKS

 Several activities can help teachers assess students' comprehension of text and general background knowledge. The cloze procedure, the maze, pretests, and self-inventories are usually constructed by the teacher. As students understand their own role in the process, they will discover that they can play an important part in their own learning, such as practicing factstorming and completing WIKA sheets (both described later in this chapter).

Cloze Procedure

The cloze procedure offers an interactive way to assess the match between the reader and the text. The term **cloze,** first used by Wilson Taylor in 1953, reflects the gestalt principle of closure, or "the tendency to perceive things as wholes, even if parts are missing" (Harris & Hodges, 1995, p. 33). In the cloze procedure, a passage is cut up so that students can fill it in. The premise is that readers rely on prior knowledge and use of context as they close, or complete, the cut-up passage. Ebbinghaus (1908), in the late 1800s, used a modified form of closure when he conducted his verbal learning and retention studies (described in Chapter 8).

Cloze is from the German word meaning "to cut up."

When Taylor designed the cloze procedure, as we now use it, his purpose was to determine the readability of material for different readers. In the strict format that Taylor designed, a passage of 250 words or more is chosen and words are deleted at regular intervals—every fifth, tenth, or nth (any predetermined number) word. The beginning and ending sentences remain intact. Blanks replace the deleted words, and no clues other than the context of the material are provided to the reader, who must fill in those blanks. In a review of the research, Jongsma (1980) found that the cloze procedure is useful at any grade level if the pattern of deletions is sensitive to the students' familiarity with language. We recommend that, generally, every tenth word be deleted for primary students, because young students need more clues than older, more proficient readers with greater reading experience. Every fifth word should be deleted for older students (fourth grade and above) because they have had more experience with reading and using context.

USING CLOZE TO DETERMINE BACKGROUND KNOWLEDGE

By using a cloze test, a teacher can find out whether students have prior knowledge about upcoming material and are able to adapt to the author's style. The readers can demonstrate their prior knowledge because they have to apply it when choosing the best words to insert in a cut-up passage. Their background knowledge helps them fill in gaps; their prior knowledge of language also helps them make good choices. If students complete the cloze with ease, they achieve an *independent-level score,* indicating that they can read the material on their own. If they can adapt when the teacher provides instruction about the material, they achieve an *instructional-level score.* A *frustration-level score* indicates that the material is difficult for readers to understand even with instruction.

The *use* of the cloze activity determines the scoring procedure.

Because the purpose of the cloze procedure is to help a teacher quickly see whether students have adequate background knowledge and understand the language clues used in the material in question, scoring should be rapid and efficient. When cloze is used to determine prior knowledge, students are not expected to see the cloze exercise again, and the teacher should not use it as a teaching tool. When cloze is used in this way, exact word replacement is the most efficient scoring procedure. In Taylor's presentation of cloze, only the exact word that was deleted is counted as a correct answer, and research (Bormouth, 1969) indicates that the exact word score is the most valid. When synonyms are accepted, the scoring criteria must be raised and the cloze must be modified. Although scoring seems stringent, the criteria for achieving an instructional level of readability are quite relaxed to compensate for inadequate prior knowledge and the synonym factor. A score of 40 to 60 percent correct is acceptable.

Here are directions for constructing a cloze test to ascertain a reader's comprehension in kindergarten through third grade:

1. Select a passage of about 125 words.

2. Leave the first sentence intact.

3. Delete consistently every tenth word thereafter until a total of 10 deletions occurs. Make all blanks uniform in length.

4. Leave the last sentence intact, or include the remainder of the paragraph to give the passage continuity.

5. Make a key of the exact words that have been deleted.

6. Write directions for your students that stress the purpose of the activity—to determine prior knowledge, not to test them. Explain that they are to fill each blank with the word they think the author might have used. Make certain you familiarize your students with the topic by brainstorming about the topic to be covered on the cloze. Remember it is your job to get real scores from the students, not inflated or deflated ones. Therefore it is important to "warm them" to the task to get the most accurate picture you can of their reading abilities.

7. For each student, count the number of correct responses and multiply by 10 (if 10 blanks were used) to express a percentage.

8. Use these scores to determine whether students will (a) be independent in reading the passage, (b) simply be able to understand the passage, or (c) be frustrated in their reading. A score of 60 percent or higher indicates the independent level; a score between 40 and 60 percent indicates the instructional level. The material is suitable for teaching students with those scores. A score of less than 40 percent indicates the frustration level; the material may be too hard for students achieving such a low score. It may help to list your students under each of these three levels, as follows:

Independent	Instructional	Frustration
(Scores above 60%)	(Scores 40% to 60%)	(Scores below 40%)
Material is easy	Material is suitable	Material is too difficult
(List students)	(List students)	(List students)

Here are directions for constructing a cloze test for use with students in the fourth through twelfth grades:

1. Select a passage of 250 to 300 words.

2. Leave the first sentence intact.

3. Delete consistently every fifth word thereafter until a total of 50 deletions occurs. Make all blanks uniform in length.

4. Leave the last sentence intact, or include the remainder of the paragraph to give the passage continuity.

5. Make a key of the exact words that have been deleted.

6. Write directions for your students. As in number 6 for the younger students, go over the directions and discuss the topic with your students before they do the cloze.

7. For each student, count the number of correct responses and multiply by 2 (if 50 blanks were used) to express a percentage.

8. Use these scores to determine whether students will (a) be independent in reading the passage, (b) simply be able to understand the passage, or (c) be frustrated in their reading. A score of 60 percent or higher indicates the independent level; a score between 40 and 60 percent indicates the instructional level. The material is suitable for teaching students with those scores. A score of less than 40 percent indicates the frustration level; the material may be too hard for students achieving such a low score. It may help to list your students under each of these three levels, as follows:

Independent	Instructional	Frustration
(Scores above 60%)	(Scores 40% to 60%)	(Scores below 40%)
Material is easy	Material is suitable	Material is too difficult
(List students)	(List students)	(List students)

EXAMPLES OF CLOZE TO DETERMINE BACKGROUND KNOWLEDGE

An English teacher facing a new textbook and eleventh graders in a school new to her wondered how the students might perform with the textbook and what accommodations she might need to make. These students had been labeled "high ability," but she knew that labels often do not indicate true performance. So she developed a cloze on a 300-word passage from the introduction to the textbook. The passage compared the origins of early American literature to men landing on the moon: both were adventures and initial explorations of a new era. Would her students have sufficient background to understand this analogy? Would they have enough language skill to read this and ensuing passages with facility?

She administered the cloze during the first week of school, before issuing textbooks, so that she could anticipate difficulties before starting the year. Students were instructed to do their best to fill in the words they thought would fit, as a way to help the teacher get to know them better; the teacher assured them that they would not be graded. She never returned the cloze to the students; the exercise was for diagnosis, not instruction. She scored it using the exact-word criterion. In this way she was able to develop a quick profile for 55 students in two sections. One student scored at the independent level; two scored at the frustration level. She decided that with proper guidance the majority of students would bring adequate knowledge to the textbook. She made a note to watch the two students who scored poorly, as well as the high scorer.

As the first weeks passed, she learned that one of the low-scoring students came from an abusive home and could not concentrate on academics even though he was capable. The other low scorer was unhappy to have been placed in a high-ability class because all she wanted to do was play in the band and coast through school. The teacher was able to find appropriate help for each of them. The high scorer continued to perform almost flawlessly on the assignments during the beginning weeks of school. The teacher discovered that this student was new to the school but had been in advanced classes in her previous school. Within the first three weeks, the teacher was able to recommend that the student be placed in an advanced class; the cloze results provided supporting documentation. The teacher might have missed an opportunity to help these three students had she not administered the cloze. Helpful diagnostic information was learned from an activity that took little time; it was administered to 55 students in one 15-minute period.

Activity 5.2 is a cloze for an elementary grade social studies chapter about St. Petersburg, Russia. Activity 5.3 is an example of a cloze for a high school reading from a technology textbook on the construction of the small gasoline engine.

Caution: A cloze procedure can reveal what students already know about a subject and can indicate whether the material is appropriate. The better students do, the more they probably know about the topic. If most students fall in the frustration level, the material is inappropriate because they may not bring enough background to it. Ashby-Davis (1985) cautions, however, that the cloze procedure is not like the usual reading that students do. Reading speed, eye movements, and use of context are likely

A VISIT TO ST. PETERSBURG, RUSSIA

St. Petersburg was first called Lovingood. It is on the delta of the Neva River. __1__ is at the eastern end of the Gulf of __2__. The city is built on both bodies of the __3__ and on islands in the river. It is the __4__ largest city in Russia. The city is a major __5__. St. Petersburg is famous for its elaborate palaces and __6__. One of the city's most visited attractions is the __7__ Palace. It was the winter home of the Czars __8__ the 1917 Russian Revolution. The Hermitage is a museum. __9__ has a great art collection. Visitors to St. Petersburg __10__ its beauty and history. It is a majestic city.

ANSWER KEY:

1. it
2. Finland
3. Neva
4. second
5. seaport
6. churches
7. Winter
8. before
9. It
10. love

to be different when reading a cloze. Therefore, although a cloze may help indicate a student's background in a particular topic, it should not be relied on to tell a teacher about a student's specific reading skills.

USING CLOZE TO BUILD ON BACKGROUND KNOWLEDGE

When a cloze is used for instructional purposes instead of assessment, the range of possible cloze constructions increases. Instead of exact replacement of vocabulary, synonyms can be considered. In constructing an instructional cloze, the teacher leaves beginning and ending sentences intact, but the deletions can serve different instructional purposes. For example, the teacher may delete all the verbs and then ask students to predict what part of speech the words to replace deleted words must be. Such a cloze activity builds awareness of verbs and helps students become proficient readers of their grammar books. An instructional cloze can also include clues. For example, in Activity 5.4 the teacher deleted important terms about the structure of a cell and provided a diagram of an animal cell. Clues from the reading give a student the answers. At the same time the student sees visual clues on the drawing to help in decision making.

Whatever the design, the instructional cloze can be used to help teachers learn what their students already know and, along with discussion of the choices made, build their knowledge of the material. Discussion also should whet readers' appetites for the reading material that follows, thus giving students a purpose for reading and assisting their comprehension of the material. Because discussing the students' choices is an obvious part of the activity when it is used for instruction, cloze also fosters listening and speaking opportunities. Although word choice is limited to single-word entries, some writing is occurring as well. Some teachers find cloze useful as a

Student Directions: Below is a passage taken from your technology textbook. Some of the words the author wrote have been deleted. Your job is to write in the blank the word that you *think* the author might have used in the same space. Your choices will help me get to know you as readers of this textbook. Good luck and do your best!

CONSTRUCTION OF THE SMALL GASOLINE ENGINE

The internal combustion engine is classified as a *heat* engine; its power is produced by burning a fuel. The energy stored in __1__ fuel is released when __2__ is burned. *Internal combustion* __3__ that the fuel is __4__ inside the engine itself. __5__ most common fuel is __6__. If gasoline is to __7__ inside the engine, there __8__ be oxygen present to __9__ the combustion. Therefore, the __10__ needs to be a __11__ of gasoline and air. __12__ ignited, a fuel mixture __13__ gasoline and air burns __14__; it almost explodes. The __15__ is designed to harness __16__ energy.

The engine contains __17__ cylindrical area commonly called __18__ *cylinder* that is open __19__ both ends. The top __20__ the cylinder is covered __21__ a tightly bolted-down plate __22__ the *cylinder head*. The __23__ contains a *piston*, which __24__ a cylindrical part that __25__ the cylinder with little __26__. The piston is free __27__ slide up and down __28__ the cylinder. The air/fuel __29__ is brought into the __30__, then the piston moves __31__ and compresses it into __32__ small space called the __33__ chamber. The *combustion chamber* is __34__ area where the fuel __35__ burned; it usually consists __36__ a cavity in the __37__ head and perhaps the __38__ part of the cylinder. __39__ the fuel is ignited __40__ burns, tremendous pressure builds __41__. This pressure forces the __42__ back down the cylinder; __43__ the untamed energy of __44__ is harnessed to become __45__ mechanical energy. The basic __46__ within the engine is __47__ of the piston sliding __48__ and down the cylinder, __49__ *reciprocating* motion.

There are __50__ many problems, however. How can the up-and-down motion of the piston be converted into useful rotary motion? How can exhaust gases be removed? How can new fuel mixture be brought into the combustion chamber? Studying the engine's basic parts can help answer these questions.

Answers:

1. the	10. fuel	19. at	27. to	35. is	43. thus
2. it	11. mixture	20. of	28. within	36. of	44. combustion
3. means	12. When	21. with	29. mixture	37. cylinder	45. useful
4. burned	13. of	22. called	30. cylinder	38. uppermost	46. motion
5. The	14. rapidly	23. cylinder	31. up	39. When	47. that
6. gasoline	15. engine	24. is	32. a	40. and	48. up
7. burn	16. this	25. fits	33. combustion	41. up	49. a
8. must	17. a	26. clearance	34. the	42. piston	50. still
9. support	18. the				

From George E. Stephenson (1996). *Power Technology* (4th ed.). Albany, NY: Delmar Publishers, Inc. Reprinted with permission of Thomson Learning.

CLOZE ACTIVITY ON IDENTITY

Cells are made of smaller parts that do certain jobs. Look at the diagram of an animal cell below. This drawing is about 1,600 times larger than the actual size of the cell. Notice the cell has a large (1) _____ floating in cytoplasm.

The cell has an outer covering called the (2) _____ _____. The cell membrane lets nutrients, water, and other materials in and out of the cell. The inside of the cell is filled with cytoplasm—a clear, jellylike material. Cytoplasm is mostly water, but it also contains dissolved nutrients and cell parts called (3) _____.

The organelles in the cytoplasm have different jobs. Some organelles help make proteins in the cell. Others release energy from nutrients.

The saclike organelles in the picture—called (4) _____ —store nutrients, water, and wastes.

Find the nucleus in the cell. The nucleus is a large organelle. It has a membrane that surrounds a mesh of structures called chromosomes. The chromosomes are made of (5) _____ —deoxyribonucleic acid. The chromosomes contain instructions that control all the cell's activities. For example, chromosomes control how fast the cell grows and when the cell reproduces.

Different kinds of organisms have different numbers of chromosomes in their cells. Most of your cells have 46 chromosomes. A crayfish has 200 chromosomes in most of its cells, while a sunflower has 17 chromosomes in most of its cells.

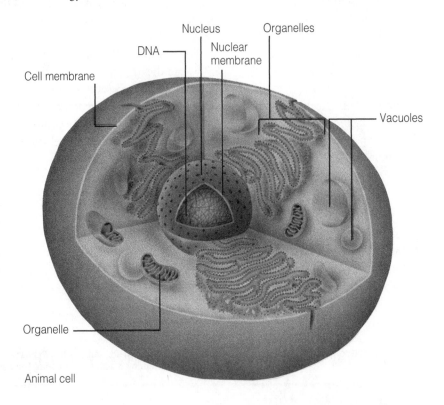

Animal cell

From *Scott Foresman Discover Science, Grade 6,* by Michael R. Cohen et al. Copyright © 1989 Scott Foresman and Company. Reprinted by permission of Pearson Education, Inc.

technique for reflection. Such an activity, the interactive cloze procedure, is explained in Chapter 9 for vocabulary skills.

The Maze

A strategy similar to cloze but easier for students to respond to is a **maze** (Guthrie et al., 1974), which is especially useful for ascertaining students' prior knowledge and understanding of a subject. The teacher selects a passage of 100 to 120 words from a representative part of the textbook and deletes every fifth or tenth word. The students are then given three choices: (1) the correct word, (2) a grammatically similar but incorrect word, and (3) a distracter, which is a grammatically different and incorrect word. Because a maze is easier for students to complete than a cloze, the scoring criteria are more stringent. A maze is a bit harder to construct than a cloze because the teacher must provide three choices for each deleted word; nevertheless, many teachers prefer it. Activity 5.5 shows a maze for primary science material.

Like cloze, a maze builds background as it reveals it. Because choices are given, students who lack prior knowledge have some material to react to. This interaction promotes the use of partial associations. Many teachers prefer maze to cloze for building background because it is less threatening to students and promotes discussion successfully. From the maze, students can move right into reading the whole material, practicing the use of context clues.

What is the difference between cloze and maze?

Pretests of Knowledge

Pretests of knowledge are quick, sensible ways to discover students' background knowledge. Students' self-perceptions on such tests are important factors in how likely students are to achieve. Teachers construct the tests for students to take before they begin reading. The tests are not graded; the teacher and students use them to see what students already know and what they should learn. Pretests can be developed in various ways.

RECOGNITION PRETESTS

Recognition pretests provide a good way to find out what students know about the content to be taught. Holmes and Roser (1987) recommend the recognition technique as an informal pretest. Teachers can use the subheadings in a chapter as stems for a multiple-choice format; alternatives are derived from chapter content. Sometimes a teacher designs a pretest from the important points to be learned in a text. One high school drama teacher wrote questions about 10 major ideas in a chapter on the origins of the theater (see Activity 5.6). Student answers helped him see what points needed the most emphasis in the lesson.

SELF-INVENTORIES

A discriminative self-inventory (Dale, O'Rourke, & Bamman, 1971) helps the teacher identify which words in the text the students know. The teacher chooses the important words and presents them along with a symbol system, such as check marks for

WHAT CAN MAKE THINGS MOVE?

Air can make things move. It can make a toy frog jump. Squeezing pushes $\begin{cases} \text{art} \\ \text{are} \\ \text{air} \end{cases}$ through a tube.

Air fills the legs under the $\begin{cases} \text{frog.} \\ \text{fig.} \\ \text{from.} \end{cases}$ The legs push the frog to make it jump. $\begin{cases} \text{And} \\ \text{Air} \\ \text{At} \end{cases}$ can make a horn blow.

Squeezing pushes air through $\begin{cases} \text{the} \\ \text{them} \\ \text{tug} \end{cases}$ horn. Then the horn makes a sound.

Moving air $\begin{cases} \text{also} \\ \text{as} \\ \text{ago} \end{cases}$ makes this party blower work. Moving air is a $\begin{cases} \text{poor.} \\ \text{push.} \\ \text{pin.} \end{cases}$

Wind is moving air. Wind can fill the sails $\begin{cases} \text{of} \\ \text{on} \\ \text{or} \end{cases}$ a boat and push it across the water.

Wind $\begin{cases} \text{cane} \\ \text{coat} \\ \text{can} \end{cases}$ push a pinwheel and turn a windmill. Water can $\begin{cases} \text{made} \\ \text{make} \\ \text{mask} \end{cases}$ things move, too.

Water can make a water wheel $\begin{cases} \text{turn.} \\ \text{torn.} \\ \text{told.} \end{cases}$ It can also push people and things.

Developed by Marvette Darby.

older students or faces for younger students. Students then react to each word. The self-inventory in Activity 5.7 was developed by a teacher to determine background for reading an eighth grade mathematics text. After students judge for themselves whether they know the words and rate each word, both teacher and students will be ready to focus attention when they meet those words in the material to be read. Such inventories also help the teacher discover who is having problems with certain words and concepts. Research indicates that students who need help the most are least likely to seek it from the teacher or from peers (Karabenick, 1998). This activity can help students gain self-confidence in analyzing words and seeking to learn on their own. Self-inventories are also discussed (word inventories) in Chapter 9.

WHAT I KNOW ABOUT THE ORIGINS OF THEATRE; OR, IT'S ALL GREEK TO ME!

Directions: Circle the answers you think are correct.

1. The Great Dionysia was
   a. a famous Las Vegas magician.
   b. Celine Dion's first stage name.
   c. a Greek celebration with play competitions.

2. "Komos" is
   a. Kramer's last name on *Seinfeld*.
   b. a Japanese robe.
   c. the root of the word "comedy."

3. The "skene" was used for
   a. making skinny Greek actors look good on stage.
   b. Greek acne medication.
   c. scene-building.

4. Thespis was
   a. the first Greek scholar to write a thesis.
   b. Memphis's original name before Elvis.
   c. the first actor.

5. The "chorus" was
   a. that awful group of singers before the Show Choir.
   b. a virus during Greek times.
   c. an important element in Aeschylus' plays.

6. The "deus ex machina" was used to lift a
   a. rude and self-centered actor off the stage.
   b. rude and self-centered director off the stage.
   c. "god" from backstage and plop him in the middle of the action.

7. Greek audiences loved to
   a. pay attention and absorb the whole theatrical experience.
   b. go to Augustus Starbucks after the play.
   c. applaud, hiss, cheer, and even get into fights over the action on stage.

8. True or false:
   Women sat alone and in the back of Greek audiences.

9. True or false:
   The altar was always in the center of the stage.

10. Euripides' play *Medea* was
    a. about the media.
    b. about medical miracles of the time.
    c. the Greek equivalent of *The Young and the Restless*.

Developed by Stephen D. Rudlin.

FACTSTORMING

Factstorming is another form of pretest that teachers can conduct easily. Factstorming is useful for assessing reader background. A whole class can participate at once, informally, with no paperwork. The activity proceeds from a single generative question. Factstorming is similar to brainstorming but focuses on facts and associations pertinent to the topic, whereas brainstorming focuses on problem solving. The teacher asks students to tell anything they can think of about the topic to be read—for instance, "Tell anything you know about the internal combustion engine." Responses are written on the chalkboard or on a transparency and discussed as they are entered.

Below is a list of terms and symbols that we will use while working in Chapter 14. This exercise will not be graded; it will help you and me to know what you already know.

Place a + beside the ones you know; place a ✓ beside the ones you know something about; place a 0 beside the ones you don't know.

_____ range   _____ median

_____ mode   _____ mean

_____ outcomes   _____ favorable outcomes

_____ probability   _____ sample space

_____ compound probability

_____ ∩   _____ ∪

_____ ⊂   _____ ⊃

Developed by Sherry Gott.

PREP STRATEGY

A sophisticated version of factstorming is PreP, a prereading plan (Langer, 1981). PreP has three phases: (1) initial associations with the concept, as in factstorming; (2) reflections on the initial concept, when students are asked to explain why they thought of a particular response, thus building an awareness of their prior knowledge and associations; and (3) reformulation of knowledge, when new ideas learned during the first two phases are articulated. PreP helps ascertain prior knowledge and also builds background. The steps encourage the reader to use whatever prior knowledge is available by listening carefully to the opinions of others. Misperceptions can be corrected in a nonthreatening way, with whole-group discussion as a supportive environment for expression. Listening, speaking, and reading all take place in a PreP activity. In Activity 5.8 students categorize the words they have generated during the PreP into three general categories: characteristics, habitat/environment, and associations. Students then use the categories to guide their reading.

KWL ACTIVITY

Another activity designed to find out what students already know about the content to be studied is KWL (Carr & Ogle, 1987, 1992; Heller, 1986; Ogle, 1986). The *K* stands for what students know before they begin to read. The teacher asks students to state facts they know in the first of three columns. The *W* stands for what students want to know. When students tell the teacher this information, the teacher can determine what they think is important about the material. These responses are recorded in the middle column. The *L* stands for what was learned. After reading, the students consider the third column and match what they knew in advance and what they wanted to learn with what

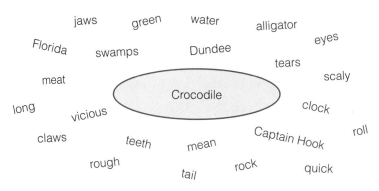

Categories:

Characteristics   *Habitat/environment*   *Associations*

---

they did learn. This activity not only helps the teacher and students determine prior knowledge; it also models an appropriate reflection strategy after reading has occurred.

WHAT-I-KNOW ACTIVITY

The What-I-Know Activity is a variation on KWL.

An alternative to KWL is the What-I-Know Activity (WIKA). The steps that students employ better reflect the terminology and steps of the PAR Lesson Framework. To use this activity (see Activity 5.9), students, before reading, discuss what they already know about the topic in the first column. In the second column they formulate questions about what they would like to learn from the reading. During and after the reading they record, in the third column, the answers to the questions. If they can't find an answer to a question, the question gets shifted to the fourth column, "What I'd Still Like to Know." When students fill in the column labeled "What I Already Know," they give the teacher information about their prior knowledge. If students are encouraged to add to their own lists after listening to and learning from class discussion, they build background by using other students' knowledge. This information can be placed in the "What I'd Like to Know" column. Another way to complete this column is to make questions of the subheadings in the material. "What I Know Now" is the column in which students record information learned from the text. Completing the "What I'd Still Like to Know" column encourages development of comprehension and reflective thinking. The class discussion and recording of associations integrate the communicative arts.

Activity 5.9 represents the results of a What-I-Know Activity produced by a reader of a chapter about the basic telephone system. The reader already knows some information, and she uses her knowledge to create questions based on the subheadings to complete the second column. In the third column, she answers the questions posed in column two. In the fourth column, she indicates the gaps in her knowledge.

Before Reading	During Reading		After Reading	
What I Already Know	**What I'd Like to Know**	**Interesting or Important Concepts from My Reading**	**What I Know Now**	**What I'd Still Like to Know**
The telephone works by electricity.	How does electricity make the phone work?	Electrical circuits.	A circuit is completed.	I need a simpler book about this topic!
You shouldn't use the phone in a lightning storm.	Why shouldn't you use the phone in a storm?	Electricity travels and current jumps.	The current might jump—electricity might be conducted beyond the normal current by lightning.	A clearer explanation about telephones and lightning.
I can hear another voice and speak in return.	What is the role of vibration in carrying sound from one place to another?	There is a diaphragm in my telephone!	Sound vibrates and causes changes in air pressure. When air pressure hits the diaphragm, it vibrates again, reconstructing the original sound.	I need to be able to explain about the diaphragm.

Textbook Inventories

At the beginning of a school year, content teachers might use a textbook inventory as a class activity to help them learn about their students' proficiency in using textbooks. This activity assesses students' knowledge of the parts of a book and can be effective at any K–12 grade level. Activity 5.10 is based on the "Textbook Treasure Hunt" (Bryant, 1984) and could be used with the textbook you are reading now. Activity 5.11 is a parts-of-the-book search developed to help students in a computer class become familiar with a word processing manual.

BEING THOROUGH WITH TEXTBOOK SELECTION

Textbook authors, teachers, and students share responsibility for improving the quality of textbooks. Some authors are inconsiderate of their readers. Authors need to keep their readers in mind as they write. If a passage includes many concepts, its organization should be made clear. Such clarity lets teachers develop instructional activities that can help students learn the important concepts. Authors should include important terms in the material, but if an author suspects these terms will be new to

TEXTBOOK TREASURE HUNT

There are many hidden treasures in your textbook. After you have completed the path below, you will have discovered some interesting facts! Write your answers and the page number(s) on which you found the information on a clean sheet of notebook paper.

1. Locate the example of a Textbook Treasure Hunt in your text. What kind of book was used in this hunt?

2. The PAR Framework in Chapter 1 is a framework for _____ instruction.

3. How many chapters are in your text?

4. In the Elementary Reading Attitude Survey, feelings are noted by the expressions of _____.

5. Give the names of the authors. Where do they teach?

6. How many appendixes does this book contain? Name the topics of each.

7. DRTA stands for _____.

8. Each chapter ends with a One-Minute Summary and _____.

9. The six sides of a cube in a cubing exercise are:

10. Activity 5.4 is a _____ procedure about _____.

11. Name and describe at least one reading procedure developed by A.V. Manzo.

12. How many lines are in a cinquain?

13. What does a Bader Textbook Analysis Chart help you do?

14. Find the PAR Cross-Reference Guide to classroom activities at the back of your textbook. What activities would be suitable for a middle school math class?

BECOMING FAMILIAR AND COMFORTABLE WITH THE MANUAL

1. What are the titles of the three people named in the acknowledgments section of the book?

   a. _____

   b. _____

   c. _____

2. On what page do you find the explanation of the special symbols used in the table of contents? How many special symbols are used in the manual?

   Page _____

   Number of special symbols _____

3. How many appendixes does the manual contain? _____ Which appendix explains the features bars? _____

4. On what page does the manual begin talking about using columns, and how many different types of column does WordPerfect allow you to choose from?

   Page _____ Types of column _____

5. What two things do you find at the end of each section?

   a. _____

   b. _____

6. What are the two types of "objectives" found in the manual? Explain the difference.

   a. _____

   b. _____

7. On what page will you find an explanation of the icons for drawing tools used in WP Draw? Page _____

8. On what page will you find an explanation of how to insert columns or rows into a table? Page _____

9. Where did you look to find the page number to answer the previous question—the table of contents or the index? _____ Would either one work?

   Yes _____   No _____

10. On what page would you find a table listing the different custom box types? Page _____ How many types are available to you?

    _____

11. Name the three major topics covered in the manual.

    a. _____

    b. _____

    c. _____

12. Where do you find an explanation of the keyboard shortcuts?

    _____

Developed by Mary L. Seward.

the reader, then meaning and pronunciation keys should be provided. In his foreword to Allan Bloom's *The Closing of the American Mind,* Saul Bellow (1987), a noted novelist, admits that "it is never easy to take the mental measure of your readers." Although textbook writers can know neither the individual literacy levels of prospective readers nor their interests and attitudes, they can be sensitive to the general needs of a group of readers. Authors should take into account what readers should be expected to know and what the authors, themselves, can help the reader learn. In this way, authors can become more considerate of their readers.

Teachers must make accommodations that help students read effectively.

Certainly teachers play an important role in identifying text-based problems and finding solutions. Shanker (1984) discussed the importance of evaluating textbooks and laid the responsibility for doing so on the teacher. He called for training in education courses to enable teachers to evaluate textbooks. Teachers must understand that text coherence comprises many factors, and that a readability formula does not provide enough information on which to judge a text. Teachers can determine a great deal about readability, but they also need help from other educational personnel. For example, Speigel and Wright (1983), reporting on a study of biology teachers' impressions of the readability of the text materials they used, comment that teachers were aware of many readability factors. Teachers, they write, should be encouraged to apply this intuitive understanding in their selection of text materials. Such encouragement must come from administrators and textbook selection committees.

The ultimate consumer of the content material is the student. Students need to move toward independence in assessing their own background for reading as soon as possible in their school careers. They must begin to ask questions about their reading material by applying the factors discussed in this chapter: Is this material too difficult for me? Is it poorly written? What do I already know about this topic? What aids in this textbook will make my reading easier? Questions such as these will not occur to many students until teachers model their importance by helping students understand why they should be asked. Even first graders are capable of discovering the difficulty of a book by using the rule of thumb. A fifth grader can ask, "What do I already know about fractions?" A tenth grader can assess whether poetry causes her difficulty. Ultimately, the buck stops with the students. But too great a burden is placed on students if authors and teachers offer them little help in assuming responsibility in reading.

Wray (1994) describes the roles of text author, student, and teacher as interactive. He encourages students to consider the author's role in clarifying meaning through text. This can be done only when teachers support students in becoming critics rather than remaining passive recipients. When asked to provide an example of dumbed-down text, one graduate student stated that he could not think of an example because he wouldn't read a book like that. We wish that all students were so empowered.

One-Minute Summary

This chapter addressed the importance for the teacher of going beyond the traditional textbook when searching for reading materials for the content classroom. We explained why textbooks can no longer stand alone in our new century and why multiple resources are sometimes necessary and even favorable in aiding learning. We showed how to supplement the traditional textbook with multiple resources and discussed some issues in using multiple resources. We also showed why it is important to bring literature into the content classroom and described ways for doing so.

We explained how teachers have at their disposal certain strategies to help them assess how readable a text or literature assignment is. We described many of these strategies in this chapter: readability formulas, checklists, cloze procedures, maze techniques, pretests of knowledge, and teacher-constructed textbook inventories. In addition, we provided strategies for improving the selection of textbooks for teachers. Finally, we emphasized that textbooks can be improved when authors, teachers, and students are aware of readability issues and assume responsibility for improving the reading material.

PAR Online

Web links that provide important information about lesson plans and rubrics for grading to complement this chapter can be found at the web links option of the Chapter 5 resources on our book companion website.

END-OF-CHAPTER ACTIVITIES

Assisting Comprehension

1. Think about why it is important to use both a Fry readability formula on the text and a cloze procedure with your students to accurately measure how readable any text is for your students. Why do the two go together? Which do you feel better about—readability formulas or cloze—and why?

2. Read *Anguished English* by Richard Lederer (1987). Besides laughing a lot, you will enjoy learning about textual coherence from his many examples.

Reflecting on Your Reading

Standard 2.3 of the International Reading Association (2003) for reading specialists and classroom teachers states that teachers should plan for the use of a wide range of curriculum materials in the classroom. Furthermore, according to the IRA guidelines, the curriculum materials should be chosen to accommodate the developmental, cultural, and linguistic differences of students.

Think back over this chapter and reflect on how the chapter helped you to think about using multiple resources to aid in curriculum development. Ask yourself two central questions. Did the chapter aid you in planning to use a range of curriculum materials? Also, did the chapter help you in selecting resources that accommodate developmental, cultural, and linguistic differences in students?

CHAPTER 6

*Oz never gave nothing
to the Tin Man that he
didn't already have.*

AMERICA (ROCK BAND),
"TIN MAN"

Preparing Learners

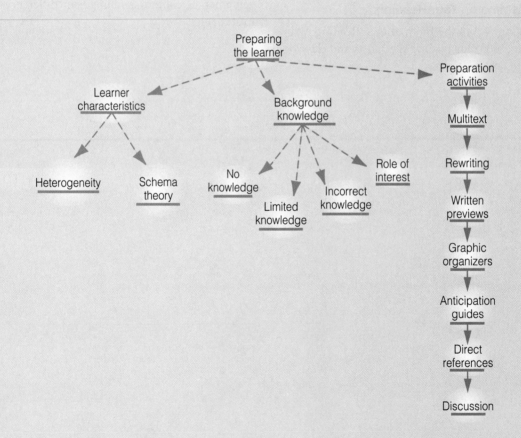

PREPARING TO READ

1. Study carefully the following statement: *what the learner already knows is the most important factor in future learning.* What do you think about this idea?

2. Following is a list of terms used in this chapter. Some may be familiar to you in a general context, but in this chapter they may be used in unfamiliar ways. Rate your knowledge by placing a plus sign (+) in front of those you are sure that you know, a check mark (✓) in front of those you have some knowledge about, and a zero (0) in front of those you don't know. Be ready to locate them in the chapter, and pay special attention to their meanings.

_____ heterogeneity

_____ schema, schemata

_____ cognitive dissonance

_____ multitext strategy

_____ graphic organizer

_____ anticipation guides

_____ reaction guides

_____ analogies

_____ direct references

OBJECTIVES

As you read this chapter, focus your attention on the following purposes. You will

1. understand the importance of building students' background knowledge.

2. learn why it is sometimes difficult to build the background knowledge of students.

3. identify pertinent research that supports the concepts of schema theory and prior knowledge.

4. learn how to adapt text for the needs of your students.

5. become acquainted with several activities that help build the match between the reader and the material being read.

6. understand the decisions that teachers must make in building background knowledge while using text materials to guide readers appropriately.

Growing research evidence shows that students do not like to read textbooks. (Maria & Junge, 1993; McKeown, Bede, & Worthy, 1992). Moreover, recent research suggests that many students who can read often choose not to do so (Purcell-Gates et al., 2002). We believe that both of these are true because many students lack background knowledge in the subjects they are studying. What students learn is greatly determined by their background knowledge (Byrnes, 1995; McDonald & Stevenson, 1998). In this chapter we discuss the importance of background knowledge in preparing the learner to read. We also detail how teachers can build on limited stores of student knowledge to allow students to learn and retain more information while reading.

THE IMPORTANCE OF DETERMINING BACKGROUND KNOWLEDGE

Many studies have shown the importance of background knowledge in reading (Hmelo, Nagarajan, & Day, 2000; Muller-Kalthoff & Moller, 2003). Within this context, researchers (Reynolds, Sinatra, & Jetton, 1996) have placed a strong emphasis on the social construction of knowledge and the idea that students have to pull from shared knowledge to complete a task. In problem solving, students with considerable subject background knowledge use strategies more effectively than those with little background knowledge (Alexander & Judy, 1988). More specifically, learners with high background knowledge can focus on what is important in the learning task, whereas those with inadequate background knowledge often search frantically because they cannot distinguish relevant material.

Research (McDonald & Stevenson, 1998) indicates that background knowledge plays an important role in how well students find and understand material on the computer and perform computer research. Hogan, Natasi, and Presseley (2000) studied the processes involved with eighth grade students in the construction of shared understanding. They determined background knowledge of groups of students on a science topic and then examined which groups improved significantly in knowledge and why. Background knowledge was very important in how well a group finally understood the topic; further, the most successful groups agreed with, confirmed, and accepted others' ideas.

Students with low background knowledge of a topic are also unable to formulate goals adequately (Last, O'Donnell, & Kelly, 1998) and often have trouble asking questions concerning the material (Miyake & Norman, 1979). For these reasons, teachers must be able to determine the background knowledge of their students on any topic to be studied. However, in doing so, they encounter an almost overwhelming problem caused by the differences in background knowledge from student to student.

Student Heterogeneity and Background Knowledge

Most of us prefer to feel comfortable with the material we read. Good readers usually browse before they start to read because they want to see how comfortable they will be with the material. They note how much they already know about the topic, how interested they are in the topic, and what strategies they might employ to read the material. They size up the material by asking, Is it easy to follow? Is the content clear? Do I have a purpose in mind for reading this? Good readers also assess the relative difficulty of the text. They ask questions such as these: Is it easy to read, like a story (narrative style)? Is it somewhat more difficult, like a newspaper article (journalistic style)? Or is it challenging to read, like many textbooks (expository style with many new facts and concepts)? After determining the difficulty and amount of challenge, they next ask, At

Think about your teaching. Do you treat all students exactly alike?

what speed should I read this text? Should I take notes as I read? A reader who knows what lies ahead and can chart a course feels more confident than a reader who opens the book and plunges into the text.

Mature, proficient readers may make this assessment almost automatically and unconsciously. Most students, however, need a teacher's guidance before reading material. Teachers need to carefully prepare the readers beforehand through discussion of the text. Teachers and readers who ignore this step neglect a crucial part of the preparation for reading. Reading comprehension, as well as time spent on instruction, will be lost.

Achieving a good match between reader and text makes sense. Suppose you are assigned to read the following passage on the pathology of viral hepatitis. Unless you are already highly interested in and knowledgeable about the topic, you may feel a little apprehensive. Read the passage now, not to learn the material but to grade it according to the criteria listed after the passage.

> The physical signs and symptoms that the person with hepatitis experiences are reflections of cellular damage in the liver. The hepatocyte has alterations in function resulting from damage caused by the virus and the resultant inflammatory response. The endoplasmic reticulum is the first organelle to undergo change. Since this organelle is responsible for protein and steroid synthesis, glucuronide conjugation, and detoxification, functions that depend on these processes will be altered. The degree of impairment depends on the amount of hepatocellular damage. The mitochondria sustain damage later than the endoplasmic reticulum. The Kupffer cells increase in size and number. The vascular and ductile tissues experience inflammatory changes. In most cases of uncomplicated hepatitis the reticulum framework is not in danger, and excellent healing of the hepatocytes occurs in three to four months.
> —From Chapter 68, "Disorders of the Liver," in *Medical Surgical Nursing: A Psychological Approach,* by J. Luckmann and K. Sorensen. Philadelphia: W. B. Saunders Company, 1980.

Rate this reading material on each of the following criteria by circling a grade from A to F:

The language and vocabulary are clear to me.

    A   B   C   D   F

The concepts are well developed.

    A   B   C   D   F

The paragraph is organized.

    A   B   C   D   F

The paragraph is well written.

    A   B   C   D   F

The paragraph is interesting to me.

    A   B   C   D   F

Now compare your impressions with those of 41 teachers, whose ratings were distributed as follows:

The language and vocabulary are clear to me.

A	B	C	D	F
2	0	7	16	16

The concepts are well developed.

A	B	C	D	F
2	3	19	8	9

The paragraph is organized.

A	B	C	D	F
6	12	14	3	6

The paragraph is well written.

A	B	C	D	F
2	9	14	12	4

The paragraph is interesting to me.

A	B	C	D	F
1	1	3	10	26

By considering the ratings—yours and those of 41 others—of that passage, you might gain insight into the problems inherent in reading textbook material. The 41 teachers constitute a fairly homogeneous group: they have a common profession and a recognized level of competence. Thus we might expect their reactions to the passage to be fairly similar. Yet they rated the paragraph differently. Although all 41 of them read the same material, the experiences and interests that each brought to the material, the interaction of each with the material, and the skill of each reader greatly influenced their reactions.

Note that the first and last ratings of the passage relate to prior knowledge and interest, both of which are inherent in the reader. The 41 teachers generally were neither confident about the language and the vocabulary of the material nor particularly interested in it. Teachers with background and interest in this field of study probably would give higher ratings. The middle three ratings relate to the text itself—concept development, organization, and style. These ratings involve characteristics of the text, not the reader. Note that the 41 teachers rated text characteristics higher. We can conclude that although they did not bring the requisite vocabulary, knowledge, or interest to this material, they recognized that the text was well structured. Reading the complete chapter would be challenging for them because they would be constantly trying to fit new information into a limited background of knowledge, but the text would help them because the writer presents the information well.

The challenge in the classroom is greater because the experiences, personal interactions, and reading skills of students are likely to be extremely diverse. This difference is called the **heterogeneity** of background knowledge of students, and it presents quite a problem for the teacher.

SCHEMA THEORY AND CONTENT READING

A number of researchers (Nuthall, 1999) believe that some students learn more than others because they are able to create a mental representation or an image of the new learning that is linked to knowledge structures already in their memory. Psychologists stress that learning new information depends on relating the new to something already known. That is, learning is better organized for good learners in a meaningful pattern of the mind.

Many psychologists maintain that learning takes place when what they call the "perceptual field" is organized in such a meaningful pattern. They define the *perceptual field* as a fluid organization of meanings existing for an individual at any instant. It is the basis for a person's reactions to any new event. To make sense of the world, the learner attempts to relate new information to already known information by drawing a **schema** (plural, **schemata**), or mental blueprint, of the way in which reality is constructed.

Schema theory offers a way of explaining how prior knowledge is stored in memory. The information a learner acquires about a topic is organized cognitively into a framework, or schema. The framework grows to include other topics, thus creating larger and larger schemata, arranged in a hierarchy. Learners retrieve information by understanding how newly encountered material links to what they already have organized cognitively. Interrelationships among schemata aid understanding. Rumelhart (1980) stresses that schemata, which may be likened to diagrams or drawings stored in the brain, are fundamental to all processing of information. Often the diagrams are incomplete, but they create a fuller picture as more information is found to complete them.

Learning occurs by a process of planning and building information in the brain. Frank Smith (1994) explains the process this way: Just seeing words (page-to-eye) or even saying words (page-to-eye-to-mouth) is fairly superficial. Connecting the intent of the words to what is already stored in one's schemata (eye-to-brain) is real reading. Thus what learners already know helps them read more effectively. Smith concludes that the eye-to-brain connection is far more complex than the mere intake of information.

Gestalt psychologists probably introduced the term *schema* in the 1930s (Anderson & Pearson, 1984). Bartlett (1932) used the term to explain how information that has been learned is stored in the brain and, with repeated use, becomes part of a system of integrated knowledge. Piaget (1952) used the term extensively, believing that children form a mental image of previous experiences, which in turn facilitates learning from new experiences. In this manner, learners chunk knowledge in an organized fashion by connecting a new segment to what they already know. Only by so doing can a learner move the new chunk of information from short-term memory to

There are excellent sections on how the brain chunks information in Chapter 8 on study skills and in Chapter 12 on the affective domain of learning.

WHAT'S IN A SHAPE? THE PROPERTIES OF QUADRILATERALS

The procedures were as follows:

1. Introduce students to a new chapter by having them read only one page of that chapter.

2. Ask students to point out examples of the different types of quadrilaterals using pictures on pages in the chapter—squares, rectangles, parallelograms, trapezoids, rhombuses.

3. Have students put their desks together with a partner; then give each pair a compass, protractor, ruler, and worksheet.

4. Read the worksheet directions aloud: "Find as many true properties about quadrilaterals as possible. Draw lines, measure with a ruler and a protractor, and use a compass to assist in making conjectures. List at least four conjectures for each type of quadrilateral."

5. After group work, discuss the conjectures. Create a master list and have the class agree or disagree with each conjecture.

6. State that conjectures will be verified by information in the chapter.

Developed by Jeannette Rosenberg.

---

long-term memory. Hirsch (1987) writes that schemata are essential to literacy in two major ways: information is stored so it can be retrieved, and it is organized so it can be used quickly and efficiently by the reader.

Content teachers will find schema theory useful as they prepare their students to read an assignment. One middle school mathematics teacher created a "discovery activity" designed to build her students' background by helping them see relationships between what they already knew and what they were about to learn. She was preparing them for a unit on the properties of quadrilaterals, showing them how to use what they already knew about parallel lines, perpendicular lines, and angles. This activity (see Activity 6.1) exemplifies the concept of building background by connecting the known to the new while making the content interesting.

B.C. Reprinted with permission of Johnny Hart and Creators Syndicate, Inc.

The Role Background Knowledge Plays
in Heightening and Lessening Interest

 The protagonist in the cartoon reads the first direction for making an angel food cake. She expects the verb *separate* to mean "set or keep apart." In her schema, the verb *separate* does not include a picture for "detach," so she puts each egg in a different location rather than detaching the egg whites from the yolks. Fortunately, she seems intent and interested in what she is doing. If she were in a home economics class, the teacher would need to help her build a more sophisticated schema.

Drum (1985) found that fourth grade science and social studies texts that were equal in vocabulary frequency, syntactic complexity, and overall structure were not equally easy for fourth graders to read. Prior knowledge seemed to play a significant part in making the social studies texts easy for these students. In other words, no matter how well written material is, if students do not possess background knowledge or interest in reading the material, they will find it hard to read.

If learners cannot find relevance in a selection, they are likely to ignore it. Thus teachers must become aware of their students' knowledge of and experiences in a particular topic and build on that knowledge. Discovering whether students have developed any schemata can help the teacher generate content reading lessons that are directed, meaningful, and highly personal. Teachers need to help students build programs for learning. For example, going from an easy text to a more difficult one can build and strengthen schemata. Gallagher (1995) had much success pairing adolescent literature with adult literature by "bridging" (Brown & Stephens, 1995). Studying the theme of the power of love in Harper Lee's novel *To Kill a Mockingbird* made it easier for students to grasp that same theme in Nathaniel Hawthorne's *The House of the Seven Gables*.

> Think about how teaching background knowledge can be a problem for you as well as the student.

Background knowledge and interest are problems both for the student and for the teacher. As we saw in the teachers' ratings of the hepatitis passage earlier in this chapter, the text is only one part of the necessary interaction. Even though readers thought that text was well written, they did not rate it highly in the categories relating to themselves as readers. In the same way, we cannot hold the author of the angel food cake recipe at fault because the cartoon protagonist does not know the meaning of the verb *separate*. The responsibility falls on the teacher and the learner.

Limited Background Knowledge

Readers usually have some background for a topic they are to study. It is likely they have some related experience, limited information, or even incorrect information. Even if they know little about the specific content, they may understand a related concept. For instance, fifth graders may not know much about the Pilgrims, but they may know what it's like to be uprooted and have to relocate to a strange place. These students, then, would have some background that the teacher could use in introducing the reading. The following dialogue illustrates how difficult it is to understand material when one has limited prior background:

"Do I deserve a mulligan?" asked Bob.

"No, but don't take a drop," said Al. "Use a hand-mashie, then fly the bogey high to the carpet and maybe you'll get a gimme within the leather."

"You're right," said Bob. "I'll cover the flag for a birdie and at least get a ginsberg if I'm not stymied." (Morgan et al., 1986, pp. 2–3)

Unless you are a golfer, reading this dialogue might be more an exercise in pronouncing the words than in understanding the text. Try to answer the following questions about the passage:

1. Does Bob deserve a mulligan?
   a. Yes
   b. No
   c. Maybe

2. What does Al think Bob should do?
   a. Catch a gimme
   b. Take a drop
   c. Use a hand-mashie
   d. Fly a kite

3. What does Bob decide to do?
   a. Cover the flag
   b. Take a drop
   c. Birdie-up

4. How can Bob get a birdie?
   a. By getting stymied
   b. By getting a ginsberg
   c. By covering the flag

5. If Bob is not stymied, what will he get?
   a. A hickie
   b. A birdie
   c. A mulligan
   d. A ginsberg

The answers are b, c, a, c, and d. The test was factual in nature. You probably scored 100 percent because you were able to look back at the passage and find the facts. But do you know what this passage is about? To comprehend it fully, you need broad prior knowledge about golf.

What is a mulligan? What is a birdie? Readers who don't know golf may try to create meaning for these words by calling on their store of information. Likewise, many students are able to answer rote questions after a reading without really understanding the passage. The following translation shows how paraphrasing by using more familiar language—more likely to be present in one's background—makes the passage meaningful:

"Do I deserve a mulligan?" asked Bob.

Bob asks if he deserves a second shot without a penalty.

"No, but don't take a drop," said Al. "Use a hand-mashie, then fly the bogey high to the carpet and maybe you'll get a gimme within the leather."

Al says no but warns Bob not to take the option of moving his ball from a difficult location and dropping it at a better spot, which may cost him a penalty stroke. Another (illegal) move is to kick the ball out of trouble with his foot (a "foot-mashie" or "hand-mashie"). He then can hit the ball with a high trajectory to the green, or "carpet" (where the hole is). If Bob gets the ball within 18 inches of the hole, or cup ("leather"), he can pick up his ball and give himself one stroke (a "gimme") rather than having to actually putt the ball.

Can you think of some other topic that someone has discussed or you have read about where you had limited knowledge, as in the golfer passage here?

"You're right," said Bob. "I'll cover the flag for a birdie and at least get a ginsberg if I'm not stymied."

Bob will attempt to hit the ball close to the hole so that he has a chance for a "birdie" (one stroke under par). If he gets on the green, he can lay up his putt to the hole ("get a ginsberg"). In earlier days, golfers did not mark their balls, so they could get stymied by another ball—that is, have to shoot around the ball of another player. Bob is being facetious here. In modern golf a player cannot get stymied by another player's ball on the green.

Incorrect Prior Knowledge

Sometimes readers have incorrect knowledge about material to be studied. Grace Hamlin, a teacher, wrote this "telegram" to illustrate how incorrect knowledge can influence one's reading:

won trip for two st. matthew's island pack small bag meet at airport 9 am tomorrow.

Readers who "know" that islands are tropical, have a warm climate, and are surrounded by beaches for swimming and sunbathing will pack a suitcase with sunglasses, shorts, bathing suits, and suntan lotion. St. Matthew's Island, however, is off the coast of Alaska, where the average temperature is 37 degrees. Incorrect knowledge in this case will impede comprehension. Similarly, readers who "know" that the dinosaurs were destroyed by other animals will have difficulty reading and understanding a theory proposing that dinosaurs were destroyed by the consequences of a giant meteor.

Maria and MacGinitie (1987) discuss the difference between having correct, though insufficient, prior knowledge and having incorrect prior knowledge. They conclude that students are less likely to overcome a problem of incorrect knowledge because the new information conflicts with their supposed knowledge. In this situation, building students' knowledge is essential because material will be most "unreadable" to the students who try to refute the material as they read.

Heightening Interest

Even the most proficient reader experiences difficulty in understanding and thinking about a subject that he or she is not interested in. Remember that a majority (26) of the 41 teachers who graded the paragraph in this chapter gave it an F for interest! Yet they were good readers. We might speculate that their lack of interest in viral hepatitis negatively influenced their match with this material. Several studies indicate that interest in a topic plays a very important role in students' comprehension (Lin, Zabrucky, & Moore, 1997; Schumm et al., 1992; Wade & Adams, 1990). When asked to address textbook issues, 41 percent of teenage respondents commented that they would "include topics in their textbooks that would interest them" (Lester & Cheek, 1998).

Put another way, cognitive dissonance brings about muddied, unclear, and disorganized thinking on the part of learners.

If teachers recognize that their students bring little interest or negative attitudes to the content material, they can use many activities to stimulate interest and, hopefully, some appreciation for the subject. A teacher who simply assumes that students are interested in the subject is likely to be disappointed in the students' reaction to it. This situation can be seen as a form of **cognitive dissonance,** defined in *A Dictionary of Reading* (Harris & Hodges, 1995) as "a motivational state of tension resulting from an inconsistency in one's attitudes, beliefs, perceived behaviors, etc." (p. 34). In short, students' reading proficiency may conflict with their lack of interest to impede learning.

We are reminded of an old story, told by one of our reading professors, about a little girl who goes to the library and asks for a book about penguins. Excited that this small child is requesting information, the librarian selects a large volume on penguins and offers it to her. The child takes the book, almost staggering under its weight, and trudges home. The next day she returns it. "How did you like that book about penguins?" the librarian eagerly asks. "To tell you the truth," the girl replies, "this book tells more about penguins than I care to know." A similar situation occurs when teachers misinterpret a little interest as a lot and thus do not match the reader with a suitable text. In Chapter 12 we cover this situation in depth and offer several means to determine students' interests and attitudes, as well as activities to stimulate positive feelings. The activities we offer in this chapter can also help determine interests and attitudes if teachers are sensitive to students' responses.

PREPARING THE LEARNER BY BUILDING BACKGROUND KNOWLEDGE

 The major factor in building background knowledge in students and in improving the quality of interaction with text is preparation. Many activities can help the teacher and students prepare for a text. In the rest of this chapter we describe tried-and-true activities that prepare readers by building their backgrounds. The activities represent possibilities but are not an exhaustive list. By considering why an activity could help build background, teachers will build their own backgrounds for creating other activities.

Using a Variety of Texts

By enlisting the help of a media specialist or reading specialist, the teacher may discover several trade books that treat the topic to be studied. The teacher should study those books to ascertain whether they match the reading levels and backgrounds of students. The teacher may use checklists and readability formulas (see Chapter 5). The newly selected trade books can be assigned as preparation for the regularly assigned textbooks. Students can read books matched to their own levels and thus build background about a topic before reading textbook material.

The **multitext strategy**—using a variety of texts—offers versatility. Different reading levels within a classroom can be accommodated when many books are used. The lists of books can be expanded over the years with the help of professional journals. However, teachers must thoroughly know the content of the required material and then familiarize themselves with each new book that might be included on the multiple-text list. In addition, most teachers will want to consider a readability test for each book to ensure a good reading match. This activity requires extra planning time.

We like multitext strategies at the preparation stage because we want our students to experience not only the required text but also varied resources that build background. At times, however, the teacher will decide to substitute multiple texts for the original textbook. In that case, the strategy can be classified as one to assist comprehension.

Another popular way to use multiple texts is in a reflection activity, when the teacher gives students a list of books from which to do independent reading. The teacher can assemble books that seem suitable as background material, make them available, but leave the responsibility of selection to the readers. Ammons (1987) demonstrates such a procedure with a class of fifth graders preparing to learn about dinosaurs. First the students pose questions they want to answer. Next Ammons introduces several trade books that might give them answers. Then the students select their own books and read to find the answers. They can use the rule of thumb to help them in their selections. In this way students build their background knowledge by using a multitext strategy.

Rewriting as an Adaptation Strategy

One form of adaptation involves rewriting the material. Rewriting can be used to prepare students before introducing them to the original material. By using rewritten material as an introduction to the original text, teachers can simplify writing styles and clarify concepts that students may have difficulty understanding. However, in returning to the original text, teachers will still be using required materials, and students will receive the message that the text material is important.

Siedow and Hasselbring (1984) found that when eighth grade social studies material was rewritten to a lower readability level, the comprehension of poor readers improved. Currie (1990) rewrote text by shortening sentences, replacing unfamiliar words, changing metaphors to more literal phrases, and clarifying. Teachers using these materials reported that students, whether high or low achievers, significantly improved their grades. Beck and associates (1991) revised a fifth grade social studies text to create a more casual and explanatory style, then compared students who read the original version with those who read the revised version. Students who read the revised version recalled and explained the events better and answered more questions correctly.

The assignment to revise Virginia Woolf's essay "Professions for Women" (1966) illustrates rewriting (see Activity 6.2). Rewriting this essay was a desperate move. The teacher had assigned the essay to stimulate the writing of a freshman college English class. The students interpreted Woolf's metaphoric angel literally and thought that Woolf had a ghost looking over her shoulder. They also could not understand why Woolf mentioned buying an expensive cat. Woolf's writing was not at fault; the readers did not possess the appropriate background for the essay. Their backgrounds apparently did not include the metaphors or experiences that Woolf had selected, and they did not know how to relate to the allusions in her essay. Rewriting was chosen because the essay was required reading for the course: No other could be substituted for it even though it was clearly difficult for the readers.

Students read the rewrite first, as an introduction; then they read the original essay and compared the two versions. The results were satisfactory: students understood clearly the concepts that Woolf was conveying, and, as an unexpected bonus, they realized how much better written Woolf's essay was than the rewrite. As a preparation strategy, rewriting in this case proved successful.

Rewriting can bring down the readability level, as measured by a readability formula, sometimes to a significant degree. In the case of Woolf's essay, the original was found to be at ninth grade level and the rewrite at seventh grade level (according to the Fry graph). Sometimes a revision does not lower the readability level but does clarify difficult material. The goal should be to present necessary material in an understandable form, as a prelude to reading the original, not to show a change in a readability formula.

Like so many other activities, rewriting can be used at every step of the PAR Lesson Framework. If a rewrite is used in place of the original material, then it is no longer being used to prepare the reader; in this case, rewriting assists comprehension. One teacher once rewrote portions of the Georgia Juvenile Court Code because the code was too hard for tenth graders to understand in its legal form (measured at the fourteenth grade level). The rewrite, to seventh grade level, enabled students to read with attention to the main points. Rewriting also can be used as a reflective reading technique. A teacher might ask students to think about the material and try to rewrite it for younger students. In this way, students gain writing practice and demonstrate their learning, and an integration of the communicative arts takes place. Rewriting also can be a useful tool for the at-risk reader who needs to learn the same content as classmates but has difficulty reading at their level.

I was asked to speak to you about women as professionals and tell you about what has happened to me. This is difficult because my experiences in my job as a writer may not be that outstanding. There have been many famous women writers before me who have learned and shown me the best way to succeed at writing. Because of their reputations, families today accept women who become writers. They know that they won't have to pay a lot of money for writing equipment or courses!

My story is this. I wrote regularly every day, then submitted an article to a newspaper. The article was accepted, I got paid; I became a journalist. However, I did not act like a struggling writer who spends her hard-earned money on household needs; I bought a Persian cat.

My article was a book review. I had trouble writing it and other reviews because something nagged at me. I felt that because I am a woman, I should be "feminine": have sympathy, be charming, unselfish, keep the family peaceful, sacrifice, and be very pure. When I began to write, this is what women were supposed to be like, and every family taught its girls to be this way. So when I started to write criticisms of a famous man's

novel, all of the things I had learned about being a woman got in the way of my writing critically instead of writing just nice things. This problem was like a ghost whispering in my ear. I called this problem ghost "The Angel in the House" because it was always there, in my "house," telling me to be nice rather than truthful.

I got rid of this problem. I realized that being nice is not always the most important thing. Also, I had inherited some money, so I felt I didn't have to do what others expected of me in order to earn a living! I had to get rid of this obsession with being feminine rather than being truthful in order to write clearly. I killed my problem ghost before it could kill my true thoughts and reactions. This is really hard to do because "feminine" ideas creep up on you before you realize that what you're writing is not a true criticism but something you were raised to believe. It took a long time to realize what was my idea and what was society's idea about what I should write.

Readability as measured by the Fry formula:
Original passage = 9th grade
Rewritten passage = 7th grade

The biggest drawback to rewriting is the time that it takes. On one rewrite of a 15-page social studies selection, one teacher spent four hours. The Woolf rewrite consumed two hours. Because a teacher's time is precious, teachers will want to weigh their options carefully in attempting to overcome text-based problems. If rewriting is the best choice, we suggest these six steps:

1. Read and restate the ideas in your own words.

2. Identify the concepts that are especially important for students to know.

3. Keep rewrites short and to the point.

4. Explain difficult concepts in the rewrite. Exchange particularly difficult words for words you think students already know.

5. Make sentences short, and use the active voice whenever possible.

6. Underline specialized vocabulary to make it easier to note difficult words.

Written Previews

Graves, Prenn, and Cooke (1985) suggest that teachers write brief previews of the material to be read by students. These previews—especially valuable for difficult material—provide a reference point and offer students a way to organize new information. The written preview should be fairly short and usually is read aloud to the class before silent reading of the original material is done. Teachers can use the information gained from their own reading of the material to write the preview. In writing previews, a teacher can follow these steps:

1. Select a situation familiar to the students and relevant to the topic. Describe the situation and pose questions that will enhance interest in the topic.
2. If the material demands background knowledge that students do not have, include a brief section providing the necessary information.
3. Provide a synopsis of the material.
4. Provide directions for reading the material to facilitate comprehension.

Written previews and rewrites take time to prepare. However, they are worth the effort in heightening student achievement and interest.

After a teacher reads the first few sentences of the preview, time should be allotted to discuss the questions posed therein. And immediately after the teacher reads the remainder of the preview, the students should begin reading the text material. Activity 6.3 is a preview of "Two Kinds" by Amy Tan (1993), written for ninth grade English students.

Written previews are less time-consuming than rewrites, and they accomplish similar purposes. They build the reader's background and help the reader organize the forthcoming text material. If a teacher writes previews carefully, the structure of the text will be more apparent to its readers.

ACTIVITY 6.3 A WRITTEN PREVIEW OF "TWO KINDS" BY AMY TAN

Have you ever had a conflict with your parents or guardian about their expectations of you? How about when you were moving to a new school or area? For example, I remember when my family and I moved into our new house. Everybody in the neighborhood knew one another and thus expected us to join this community family too. But my mother made it known to all the neighbors that we were different. We couldn't play with the other children in the neighborhood. As far as she was concerned, her daughters were not going to join the other teen mothers. She had high expectations of her children. Sometimes I thought she was totally ridiculous. She was suspicious of every male. As a result, we sometimes got into arguments.

How did you handle your conflicts with your parents, such as what they expected from you? How did you react when you were not in agreement with them? How did you resolve the conflict?

Activity by Etta Malcolm.

Augmenting Text with Graphic Organizers

Like written previews, **graphic organizers** help prepare readers by presenting a pictorial road map of the text. A graphic organizer is a visual overview that demonstrates how the important concepts, as represented by the vocabulary in a reading selection, fit together. Promoting *visual literacy* (the ability to interpret visual and hierarchical information), a graphic organizer is effective because readers are asked to interpret a concise, comprehensive, and compact visual aid. At the beginning of each chapter in this book we present a graphic organizer to help readers see the relationships among the concepts and the key terms in the chapter through a visual representation of its content.

A structured overview (Earle & Barron, 1973) is one type of graphic organizer that is normally used in the preparation phase before reading. This type of visual aid is in the form of a hierarchical diagram of words, sometimes described as a *tree diagram*. Structured overviews are constructed by teachers, whereas other types of graphic organizers may be constructed by students (or by teachers and students together) in the reflection phase of the lesson. Activity 6.4 represents a structured overview of a first grade lesson on maps and continents.

A number of studies (Lambiotte & Dansereau, 1992; Rakes, Rakes, & Smith, 1995) support the notion that graphic overviews and displays help organize students' thoughts. When readers understand the relationships among concepts in a selection, they can begin to connect the new relationships to their previous knowledge. Robinson's (1998) review of 16 studies on graphic organizers indicates that they facilitate memory for text. This outcome is most likely because they connect schemata and help students see links between the new and the known.

This overview was created with *Inspiration.*

ACTIVITY 6.4 GRAPHIC ORGANIZER FOR FIRST GRADE

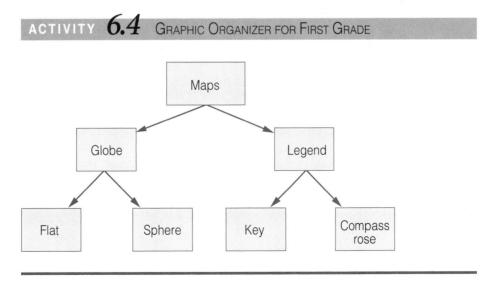

Teachers usually find graphic organizers challenging to prepare but very much worth the effort. To construct one, follow these steps:

1. Identify the superordinate, or major, concept; then identify all supporting concepts in the material.

2. List all key terms from the material that reflect the identified concepts.

3. Connect the terms to show the relationships among concepts.

4. To show relationships between new concepts and already-learned ones, add any terms that are from the previous lesson or that you feel are part of students' background knowledge.

5. Construct a diagram based on these connections, and use it to introduce the reading material.

When developing a graphic organizer, you don't need to use every word that might be new to readers; some new words may not contribute to the diagram. Including words already known to the students is useful when these words represent key concepts, because familiarity will aid understanding. Teachers should explain to students why they prepared the graphic organizer as they did, noting the relationships. This presentation should include a discussion to which students can contribute what they know about the terms as well as what they predict they will be learning, based on the chart. Students should keep the organizer available for reference while they are reading, so they can occasionally check back to see the relationships as they encounter the terms.

After reading, students can use the graphic organizer as an aid for refocusing and reflecting on the learning. It can even be used to check comprehension. Thus the graphic organizer can be useful at each of the PAR steps and promote integration of the communicative arts. Activity 6.5 provides an example of a graphic organizer prepared by a teacher for middle school science. It uses students' prior knowledge about animal kingdoms and begins to link that knowledge to new information.

Anticipation Guides

Anticipation guides, sometimes called **reaction guides** or prediction guides, prepare readers by asking them to react to a series of statements that are related to the content of the material. In reacting to these statements, students anticipate, or predict, what the content will be. Once students have committed to the statements, a purpose for reading has been created. Students' curiosity about their predictions can help maintain a purpose for thoughtful reading. In this way, the guide provides assistance for the learner while reading. In the reflection phase of the lesson, student group and teacher-led discussions attempt to come to final consensus on the answers to the guide. Remember that if some statements are intentionally vague to arouse curiosity and discussion, consensus might not be reached in all cases. We use an anticipation guide at the beginning of this chapter (see item 1 in "Preparing to Read"): we ask our readers whether they agree with a statement and why. Erickson and associates (1987) cite three reasons why anticipation guides are valuable:

Creating a template in a word processing program for an anticipation guide can save teacher time.

Directions: Chapters 10–14 in our textbook are about animals. Using these chapters, you will fill in the chart below. This chart will then be kept in your notebook.

Draw or name two examples.

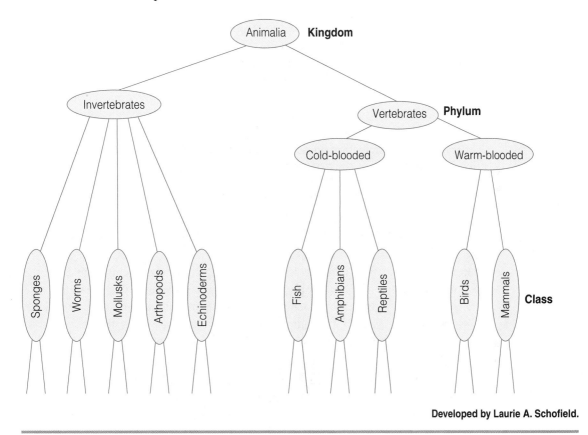

Developed by Laurie A. Schofield.

1. Students need to (a) connect what they already know with new information and (b) realize that they do already know something that will help them comprehend.

2. Students exposed to anticipation guides tend to become interested and participate in lively discussion, which motivates reading.

3. Reading and writing instruction are easily integrated when anticipation guides are used.

Suppose a high school health teacher has introduced the term *integumentary system* to a less than enthusiastic class. In fact, no one in the class ventures an idea of what the term means. When the teacher starts to discuss the skin, it becomes apparent that the students don't understand that the skin is a vital organ of the body, just like the heart. They do not know that the skin is so waterproof that it prevents the escape of fluids that bathe body tissues. In short, they have no schema of the importance of the skin for our existence. To overcome such misconceptions about skin, the teacher prepares the anticipation guide in Activity 6.6. As groups of students discuss the guide, they verbalize their prior knowledge and begin to reformulate their knowledge concerning this vital organ.

Anticipation guides involve students in discussion and reading and also can include writing if students are asked to respond in writing to the statements. Many teachers have students refer to the guide as they read, which enhances comprehension. If students return to the guide after reading to clarify or rethink previous positions, every phase of PAR is applied throughout the administration of the guide. Conley (1985) argues that such guides are excellent tools for developing critical thinking and promoting cross-cultural understanding. Truly eclectic, anticipation guides are well received by both teachers and students.

Making an anticipation guide takes some thought but becomes easier with practice. The basic steps for constructing an anticipation guide are as follows:

1. Read the content passage, and identify the major concepts to be learned in the lesson.

2. Decide which concepts are most important to stimulate student background and beliefs.

3. Write three to six statements about the concepts. The statements should reflect the students' background and be thought-provoking. Choose statements that might make students disagree with one another and provide valid evidence for a side of an argument. General statements, rather than statements that are too specific, work best. Well-known quotations and idioms are successful.

4. Use some statements that are intuitively appealing to students but that will prove incorrect on reading the text. Keep the exercise from turning into rote "decoding" by writing statements that require students to interpret large segments of text.

5. Display the guide on the chalkboard, with an overhead projector, or on worksheets. Give clear directions. (These will vary depending on the age group and variations in the guide.) Leave space for original student responses.

6. Conduct class discussion based on your concept statements. Students must support their responses; "yes" and "no" are not acceptable answers. Students should be told by the teacher to argue based on their experiences and always explain any decision they make.

7. After reading with the assistance of the guide, have students form small groups and attempt to come to consensus on the answers to the guide. Bring the class back together to discuss group answers; attempt to bring closure to the lesson. Students discuss what they have learned, and the teacher clarifies any concepts that are still foggy.

NAME _____ DATE _____

Before reading the selection: In the space to the left of each statement, place a check mark (✔) if you agree or think the statement is true.

During or after reading: Add new check marks or cross through those about which you have changed your mind. Keep in mind that this is not like a traditional "worksheet." You may have to put on your thinking caps and "read between the lines." Use the space under each statement to note the page(s) and paragraph(s) where you are finding information to support your thinking.

_____ 1. A person's skin might weigh about five pounds, be about 10 to 11 square feet in area, and have an outermost layer that is composed of overlapping scale-like cells almost like a fish.

_____ 2. Of the principal functions of skin, one of them is clearly more important than the other three.

_____ 3. The evidence of the problem with overweight people is to be found in their skin, and one successful way to lose weight is to remove one layer of the skin.

_____ 4. Human skin protects people from solar radiation.

_____ 5. Skin is made of the same substance as bone tissue, and it can be broken like a bone.

_____ 6. Keratin is found in all layers of the skin.

_____ 7. You can tell how healthy a person is by looking at that person's fingernails.

_____ 8. The skin is almost totally waterproof.

8. Take advantage of the opportunity to review and reinforce the use of the skill of predicting. Point out to students that they can use the skill in any reading in any subject area to engage themselves and to make the reading more interesting by setting a purpose for reading and by keeping that purpose in mind during the reading.

Activities 6.7, 6.8, and 6.9 are anticipation guides constructed by teachers of primary science, high school art, and vocational education welding classes, respectively. There is no "right" way to create a guide. Anticipation guides that reflect sound instructional principles and research are developed every day by enterprising teachers. Note that in Activity 6.8 some statements are quite creative; students might be quick to agree with them if they do not think carefully. Such statements are designed to make students think more critically about reading material.

Analogies

Analogies compare known and unknown concepts. Analogies are like previews in that both begin with a connection point to the reader's background. However, analogies carry out a comparison, whereas previews focus more directly on the material to be read.

Directions: Read these statements to yourself as I read them aloud. If you agree with a statement, be ready to explain why. We will check all statements we agree with in the prereading column. Then we will read to see if we should change our minds.

PREDICTION GUIDE FOR MAMMALS

Before   After

_____   are mammals.   _____

_____   are mammals.   _____

_____   All mammals have four .   _____

_____   are mammals.   _____

_____   Some mammals can .   _____

Analogies are excellent tools for content reading teachers because they are simple to create and highly relevant for students. They can be presented in oral or written form as an informal introduction to content material. They also promote listening and speaking, and if students are encouraged to write their own analogies after reading certain material, then analogies become useful reflection and writing activities as well. The example in Activity 6.10 on page 187 was developed by a third grade teacher.

We can liken practicing for a basketball game to preparation for reading by relating a familiar concept to a less familiar one. Playing the game actually takes up the smallest amount of time; the greatest amount of time is spent in workouts, strategy sessions, viewing game films, and concentrated practice—all intended to ensure success in the game itself. After the game, more time is spent analyzing what occurred on the court, and then preparation for the next game begins. The question is asked, "Why did we do well in this game," or "Why didn't we do well?" So it is with reading. A

NAME _____ DATE _____

Before reading: In the space to the left of each statement, place a check mark (✓) if you agree or think the statement is true.

During or after reading: Add new check marks or cross through those about which you have changed your mind. Keep in mind that this is not like a traditional "worksheet." You may have to put on your thinking caps and "read between the lines." Use the space under each statement to note the page(s), column(s), and paragraph(s) where you are finding information to support your thinking.

_____ 1. Reading a painting is like reading a book.

_____ 2. You might look at a painting the same way that you look at a beautiful sunset.

_____ 3. Painting is a more effective way to communicate than writing or speaking.

_____ 4. Artists use styles of painting in the same way that authors use grammar and vocabulary.

_____ 5. Careers related to painting are limited to the fine arts.

_____ 6. All paints are composed of three types of ingredients.

_____ 7. Art, from prehistory to the present, has reflected what was most important to the culture that created the art.

_____ 8. Art styles have stayed pretty much realistic over time.

_____ 9. There is more than one philosophy about how paintings should be made and used.

_____ 10. The greatest advances in art came after World War II.

proficient reader spends time getting ready to read by determining and building background. Instead of plunging into the reading, the reader must prepare. Good comprehension is a natural result, just as playing a game successfully is the natural result of hard work in practice. Teachers who are aware of this phenomenon and aid students in the preparation stage of reading are like good coaches. The coach is there at every step to help and encourage the students as they take responsibility and work through the lesson. Students who realize that preparation for reading is like court practice will reap benefits in higher achievement and better grades.

When a high school junior resisted reading a history chapter that explained the circumstances leading to the American Revolution, his parent (a reading specialist, of course!) tried this preparation strategy:

"Suppose," the parent suggested, "that your parents decided to go to Europe for six months, leaving you on your own at home. You would have the car and access to money; you would be able to make all your own decisions. What would your reaction be?" As you might imagine, the high school junior thought this would be an excellent arrangement. "However," the parent continued, "we would arrive home again and take charge once

Directions: Carefully read each statement below. Check either *agree* or *disagree* to show what you think. Do this both before and after reading. You should be able to defend your answers.

Prereading		Statements	Postreading	
Agree	Disagree		Agree	Disagree
_____	_____	1. Skill in performing welding operations requires practice.	_____	_____
_____	_____	2. The first basic operation is learning to strike an arc and run a curved bead.	_____	_____
_____	_____	3. The current used in a welding operation depends only on the size and type of electrode used.	_____	_____
_____	_____	4. A proper arc length between the electrode and the work is required to generate the heat needed for welding.	_____	_____
_____	_____	5. Using the correct electrode angle will ensure proper penetration and bead formation.	_____	_____
_____	_____	6. It is safe to touch the welding bench with an uninsulated holder.	_____	_____
_____	_____	7. It is important to have correct welding heat to make a sound weld.	_____	_____

more. We would want our car back, and you would have to ask for permission to do the things you'd been doing freely. Now how would you feel?" The junior did not like the turn of events. "Would you still love us?" the parent inquired, assuming, of course, that teenagers do love their parents even though they have funny ways of showing it!

"Well, yes," the junior reluctantly agreed. "But I'd be insulted, and family life wouldn't be the same."

"Exactly," agreed the parent. "That's the way it was with the British and their American colonies. The British had to attend to problems in Europe and in their own government. They let the American colonists have free rein for a while. Then they turned their attention back to the Americans. But the Americans didn't appreciate the intervention after this period of time. Many of them still 'loved' the British, but they deeply resented the renewed control. While you're reading this chapter, you might want to keep in mind your own reactions to this hypothetical situation and compare those feelings to the reactions of the colonists."

Much later in the month, this junior grudgingly reported to his parent that the chapter had turned out to be "pretty easy to read" because he understood the circumstances better than for most of the other chapters in the book.

This on-the-spot analogy was simple enough to construct. The teacher/parent understood several characteristics of 16-year-olds and applied them to building an analogy that would hook the reader to the content material. The informal analogy was a

Goal: To enable students to connect new knowledge with existing knowledge.

Directions: Read the following paragraphs as a primer for small-group discussion comparing cars with bodies.

Materials: Paper
Pencils

"Your body is very similar to a car in the way that it acts. You may have been told to 'rev up your engine' one time. When a car revs up, it begins to go.

"A car needs many different substances to keep it running well. It might need oil for the parts and air for the filters, as you would need oil for your joints or air for your lungs.

"Actually, there are many other things that a car and your body have in common. A car needs gasoline to make it go. What do you need?" (food)

Now divide the students into small groups and let them list on paper the ways that cars and bodies are similar. Some suggestions that you will be looking for are:

Fats/oil
Protein/gasoline
Carbohydrates/spark plugs
Vitamins/fuel additives, super grade gasoline
Minerals/paint, rustproofers
Air/air conditioning
Muscles/wheels
Heart/engine

Return to the class in 15 or 20 minutes and share the group information. Write the analogies on the board. Ask for comments or changes.

Developed by Kathy Feltus.

---

simple preparation strategy. It worked because the reading took on new meaning for the student. His comprehension was enhanced, enough so that he admitted it to a parent!

Direct References and Simple Discussion

Sometimes teachers find that students have incorrect knowledge. What is the best way to build on background knowledge for readers with misconceptions? When Dole and associates (1991) compared the use of interactive and teacher-directed strategies, they found that teacher direction increased students' comprehension of a passage. In this regard, **direct references** and discussion can be effective.

Maria and MacGinitie (1987) conducted a study in which they asked students in the fifth and sixth grades to read two types of materials. The first referred specifically to the misconceptions that the researchers had identified during a pretest and contrasted those misconceptions with correct information. The second was written with the correct information but no direct refutation of predetermined misconceptions. The researchers found that student recall was significantly better on the text that confronted the misconceptions.

Guzzetti, Snyder, and Glass (1992) conducted a meta-analysis of studies about children's misconceptions. They found that some type of intervention was enough to establish for students a degree of discomfort with their prior beliefs (p. 648). Three strategies were effective:

- Using refutational text—providing a passage directly refuting the misconception.
- Using activities to initiate discussion and then to supplement the material generated with the correct information, similar to what might occur with fact-storming and PreP or anticipation guides.
- Using a discussion web (Alvermann, 1991) to make students articulate and defend their positions by referring to text and discussing results with peers.

Regardless of which specific activity is used, dissatisfaction with incorrect prior knowledge must be created before the misconception will be altered.

As a final point, the authors would like to remind our readers that determining and building background knowledge in students is important, but the process is never an exact science. This is so precisely because students are so special and unique, enigmatic, and often refreshingly unscripted in their thoughts and habits. One of the authors was visiting a first grade class recently where the teacher was getting students to ask questions about the lesson. The author posed a question to the class: Who made the first American flag? None of the 14 students seemed to know, and no student ventured a guess. Fully 10 minutes after the question was asked and seemingly forgotten by all, the visiting author told the class goodbye and started to leave. While the visitor smiled, waved, and walked toward the door, a small, red-faced, smiling boy, seated in the front, ran up and tugged on the pants of the visitor and whispered in an almost inaudible voice, "Betsy Ross."

ONE-MINUTE SUMMARY

This chapter has noted the importance of students' background knowledge in reading and the necessity of building on students' background knowledge throughout the reading lesson. Careful preparation by the teacher may help overcome both the students' limited or incorrect prior knowledge about a topic and their lack of interest in the topic. We described the difficulty teachers have with determining and building background knowledge of students because of heterogeneous student backgrounds.

We included many activities—some developed by classroom teachers—for building background knowledge throughout the reading lesson. Although textbook material sometimes needs adaptation, it should not be eliminated from the curriculum. Preparation activities can promote reading, writing, speaking, and listening and can incorporate all the steps of PAR. We emphasized that the way a teacher uses an activity is more important than rigorous adherence to prescribed steps, and we included variations of activities that demonstrate the creativity of the teachers who constructed them. In this chapter we described strategies to prepare the learner such as multitext strategies, rewriting, written previews, graphic organizers, anticipation guides, analogies, direct references, and simple discussion.

PAR ONLINE

Go to *Reading Online* and locate the article by Thomas Bean about social constructivism. Read it and share your comments with classmates. (The URL is located in the references section where Bean is cited.)

Create a template for one of the activities presented in this chapter, such as the anticipation guide or the structured overview.

Visit one of the websites where teachers post their activities (provided on the book companion website). Select an activity that you think features good preparation, and be able to explain why.

END-OF-CHAPTER ACTIVITIES

Assisting Comprehension

Select a chapter from a content area textbook. Using the following questions as a guide, reflect on what your text offers to help you as a teacher build your students' background knowledge for reading the text:

1. What aids are provided in the text chapter to help you build on students' prior knowledge?

2. Is there a chapter preview or summary that could be used to build on it?

3. Are there any statements, such as those identifying objectives, that could be used in an anticipation guide?

4. Is there a graphic organizer?

5. Are these aids suitable for your students?

6. Are these aids sufficient for your students?

7. As a teacher, should you construct some aids to help yourself build on student prior knowledge? If so, what will you construct?

Reflecting on Your Reading

1. Refer to the statement in item 1 of the "Preparing to Read" section of this chapter. Would you answer any differently after having read this chapter? Has this chapter changed your thinking in any way? If so, how?

2. The International Reading Association (2003) Standard 1.4 asks classroom teachers to recognize the major components of reading. One important element they list in this standard is building the background knowledge of students. They maintain that the classroom teacher should know and be able to articulate the research that supports the importance of background knowledge and prior knowledge in reading. To help you in your deliberations on this, think about the research we cited on all of these topics:

   a. Student heterogeneity in learning
   b. Schema theory in reading
   c. Limited background knowledge
   d. Incorrect background knowledge
   e. Lack of background knowledge
   f. Heightening interest
   g. Cognitive dissonance

   From the study of these topics, try to come to a coherent vision and purpose statement as to why building background knowledge is the most important aspect of preparing the learner. We hope it will be a vision and purpose statement you can articulate to others in the profession.

CHAPTER 7

Assisting Comprehension and Reflecting on Learning

If everyone is thinking alike then somebody isn't thinking.

GEORGE S. PATTON

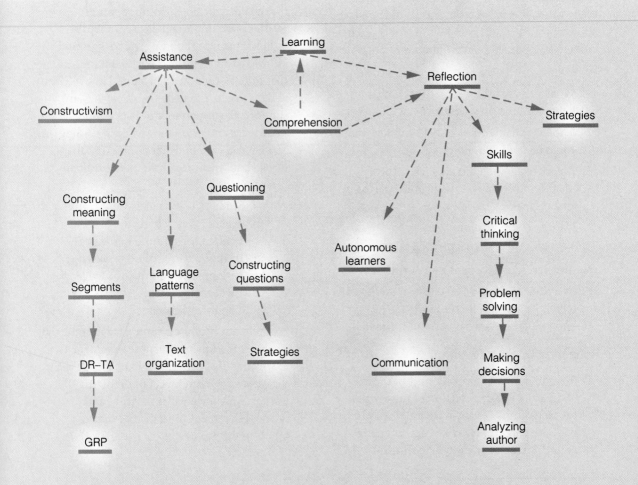

PREPARING TO READ

1. What does it mean to assist students as they read? Before beginning to read this chapter, can you name any ways you can help students comprehend as they read?

2. Why is it important to reflect about learning after we finish reading?

3. Following is a list of terms used in this chapter. Some may be familiar to you in a general context, but in this chapter they may be used in unfamiliar ways. Rate your knowledge by placing a plus sign (+) in front of those you are sure that you know, a check mark (✓) in front of those you have some knowledge about, and a zero (0) in front of those you don't know. Be ready to locate them in the chapter, and pay special attention to their meanings.

   _____ adjunct strategies
   _____ constructivism
   _____ superordinate
   _____ subordinate
   _____ directed reading–thinking activity (DR–TA)
   _____ guided reading procedure (GRP)
   _____ patterns of organization
   _____ discourse analysis
   _____ collaborative reasoning
   _____ jot charts
   _____ metacognition
   _____ question–answer relationship (QAR)
   _____ comprehension monitoring
   _____ free rides
   _____ propaganda
   _____ brainstorming
   _____ literary gift exchange
   _____ text lookbacks

OBJECTIVES

As you read this chapter, focus your attention on the following purposes. You will

1. be able to define *reading comprehension,* using a historical perspective when forming your definition.

2. understand constructivism, constructivist learning, and the theory underlying the construct.

3. be able to help students construct meaning while reading.

4. learn strategies for teaching short segments of text.

5. learn the importance of how writing is organized and patterned.

6. learn a number of activities that assist and guide students to better understand text.

7. be able to use questioning strategies to teach comprehension.

8. understand the importance of the reflection phase to reading and learning.

9. learn specific skills that are important in reflection.

10. understand a number of strategies that help foster reflective thinking.

ASSISTING WITH COMPREHENSION

As we have discussed, it is well established that a reader's background knowledge strongly affects text comprehension (Moravcsik & Kintsch, 1993). According to Dole and associates (1991), both novice and expert readers use existing knowledge to construct meaning from text. This is why in previous chapters we described ways teachers can both determine the background knowledge of their students and use effective strategies to build background knowledge of students in the preparation phase of reading. Two very important steps in the PAR Lesson Framework are the assistance and reflection phases, where students develop and deepen their understanding of any learning activity.

If we are to assist with comprehension, we must first understand the nature of the construct. William S. Gray (1941/1984) wrote that comprehension "assumes that the reader not only apprehends the author's meaning but also reflects on the significance of the ideas presented, evaluates them critically, and makes application of them in the solutions of problems" (p. 18). Sixty years later reading is often described by researchers as analytic, interactive, constructive, and strategic (Guthrie et al., 2000; Lederer, 2000). These recent definitions imply that apprehension and reflection are requisites of comprehension. A reader must grab hold of—apprehend—and ponder the significance of the content. This analysis must be active (Principle 2 in Chapter 1), generating strategies that aid the reader now and in future reading.

Comprehension strategy instruction by teachers is widely used throughout the country. Recent national surveys reported that 98 percent of teachers in grades 3–5 provide strategy instruction (Baumann et al., 1998). That instruction may include summarizing, self-questioning, and self-monitoring in using text. Unfortunately, this instruction is often hit-or-miss rather than systematic (Garner, 1985). Pressley and colleagues (1998) have stated that, despite 20 years of attention to research in the area, comprehension instruction in our classrooms remains inadequate. It is the teacher's role, then, to teach students about comprehension strategies as well as text information (Fielding & Pearson, 1994). Teachers can do this best by using **adjunct strategies** to reinforce learning during reading rather than before or after the reading is completed. Teachers use adjunct strategies more often than pre- or postreading strategies (Rakes & Chance, 1990). Of the students polled by Rakes and Chance, 78 percent (of

182) at the secondary level and 59 percent (of 156) in the elementary grades said that teachers had taught them strategies to use as they read. Reviews of research show that, with careful and directed instruction, students can acquire effective strategies for reading comprehension (Fielding & Pearson, 1994). How the teacher presents the content material, complemented by adjunct strategies, will make a difference in how well students learn the material. In this chapter we focus on ways to assist students to comprehend as they read content material.

Constructivist Learning

In constructivist learning theory the student makes his or her own meaning with the teacher acting as facilitator or helper.

Although historically the study of reading comprehension has reflected different schools of thought at different times, the changes in definition over time exhibit more continuity than contrast. Huey (1908/1968) and then Thorndike (1917) defined *reading* as a thinking process, implying that comprehension is not only recognizing letters and words but also thinking about what those symbols mean. Sixty years later, Hillerich (1979) drew the same conclusion when he identified reading comprehension as "nothing more than thinking as applied to reading" (p. 3). A little earlier, Frank Smith (1971), drawing from his study of communication systems, argued for a definition of *comprehension* as "the reduction of uncertainty" (p. 17). Smith explained that as readers gain information by reading, they rely on what they know to "reduce the number of alternative possibilities" (p. 17). Pearson and Johnson (1978) picture reading comprehension as the building of bridges between the new and the known. The continuity among these definitions, which span 70 years, is apparent.

The definition of *comprehension* has not changed substantially, but the way we study comprehension has changed. New interest in how to teach reading comprehension has been generated by the recognition that comprehension is not a passive, receptive process but an active, constructive, reader-based process. While reading is occurring, the reader is seeking assistance in understanding the material. The reader wants to sort facts from implications, identify the organization of the material, and use picture clues and text aids to help with this understanding. **Constructivism** is a term used by psychologists and reading experts of this era to explain what happens as a reader processes text (Pearson & Stephens, 1994). Applefield and associates (2000) have stated,

> The field of education has undergone a significant shift in thinking about the nature of human learning and the conditions that best promote the varied dimensions of human learning. As in psychology, there has been a paradigm shift in designed instruction: from behaviorism to cognitivism and now to constructivism. (p. 36)

Researchers call constructivism one of the most influential views of learning during the last two decades. Dalgarno (2001) has noted that constructivism is emerging as a significant learning theory that emphasizes a student-centered approach to learning. In a constructivist model, teachers are not transmitting knowledge to passive learners; instead, learners are building information from the assistance that teachers provide (Weaver, 1994). The reader must actively construct meaning by relating new material to the known, using reasoning and developing concepts. The process is not only individual but also social, because "by articulating ideas and experience through writing, speaking, and/or visually representing, students deepen their thinking and construct and organize their understanding of new material" (Gill & Dupree, 1998, p. 95).

In addition, some recent research suggests that constructivist learning is useful for improving interactivity in online learning (Rudestam & Schoenholtz-Read, 2002). By discovering what readers do as they read, and how they constantly strive to construct meaning while reading, we can design strategies for assistance that enhance their learning. This can be illustrated by an encounter one of the authors had in helping a young boy read a passage on log cabins. The boy could not say the two words "oil lamp" as he read the passage orally. Throughout the reading he was not given the pronunciation of these two words. After the reading the boy was asked several questions to help him recall the story, including one concerning what kind of lighting was used in the log cabin. The child quickly answered, "Oh, they had an oil lamp." This child was thinking as he read, trying to put together the clues. He was processing what he knew was "unknown data." When he reached the stage of retelling the story, he realized that he did know; he had put the clues together. If the teacher had interpreted as a final product his failure to pronounce the words while he was reading, he would have thought the boy did not know the words. In fact, all along the boy was constructing meaning. Ultimately, his processing led to a correct understanding. As this experience illustrates, we must give our students every chance to process information, thus discovering meaning as they read, before we measure their understanding.

Helping Students Construct Meaning

Comprehension is influenced by how much teachers help students to understand the way texts are organized and presented. Students need to first understand that a text is organized through the presentation of **superordinate** information: information spread over whole chapters and sections of chapters. Put another way, superordinate concepts are the overall concepts the author wishes to impart to readers. **Subordinate** information consists of smaller ideas that are specific to the major concepts. Readers need to keep in mind the major thrust of the material to understand the relationship between superordinate ideas and subordinate information. For instance, in this textbook, the major—superordinate—theme is the PAR Lesson Framework. Each chapter explains aspects of the framework—subordinate information.

Look at the templates and examples in the *Inspiration* software to see many ways that mapping can be useful.

Mapping is one adjunct strategy whose use has been effective in organizing information into major and subordinate ideas (Ruiz-Primo & Shavelson, 1996; Zelik et al., 1997). This activity, sometimes called *concept mapping,* provides a way for both the teacher and student to remember and organize key elements of knowledge (Romance & Vitale, 1997). Furthermore, the activity can assist readers in understanding concept relationships and thereby avoid fragmented or simple rote learning outcomes (Romance & Vitale, 1999). Mapping has in fact become a popular activity for helping readers develop comprehension. Just as travelers use a map to help them find their way, readers can use a diagram that shows the route to understanding a passage, and they themselves can make maps to show their understanding.

The primary purpose of mapping is to portray the relationship of major and supporting ideas visually. Because maps encourage students to refer to the reading material and engage in interactive learning, reading educators recognize their value in assisting comprehension. Mapping can teach vocabulary and introduce outlining and note taking, and can be a study aid (see our vocabulary and study skills chapters). Mapping can introduce a topic before any reading takes place. In this case, the teacher probably has already made the map or is relying on students' prior knowledge to construct the map; thus the strategy is to use prior knowledge to prepare the reader. Mapping also can aid reading reflection, because after the map is made it becomes a study aid. The following are suggestions for developing a map (based on Santeusanio, 1983):

1. Identify the main idea of the content passage. (Sometimes just the topic or a question may stimulate map generation.) Write the main idea anywhere on the page, leaving room for other information to be written around it.

2. Circle the main idea.

3. Identify secondary categories, which may be chapter subheadings.

4. Connect the secondary categories to the main idea.

5. Find supporting details.

6. Connect supporting details to the idea or category that they support.

7. Connect all notes to other notes in a way that makes sense.

Although mapping a whole chapter may be time-consuming, we recommend it for portions of a chapter that a teacher identifies as very important, to help readers understand the superordinate/subordinate relationships.

Maps engage readers as they read, reread, and study, and they demonstrate the hierarchical nature of exposition. Muth (1987) reports that mapping, because it is a hierarchical strategy, has been found highly successful in helping students to understand expository text. Once teachers have mapped several times with students, students will become proficient at making their own maps. Because a map is a diagram of information, it is a visual learning aid. Often, especially for younger readers, drawings added to the map will stimulate learning. Such visual reinforcement capitalizes on visual literacy and right-brain functions. Activity 7.1 shows how a technology teacher used mapping to show the parts of a computer.

Integration of all the communicative arts occurs when mapping is used. Class discussion must take place for the map to be developed. This requires students to listen to one another and talk about the topic. Reading is the source of the information mapped, and writing can be incorporated if the teacher asks students to use the map as a frame of reference for writing about the reading topic. For instance, students could be assigned to write a six-paragraph essay about the parts of the computer, as generated from the map. A science teacher who wants students to write reports about

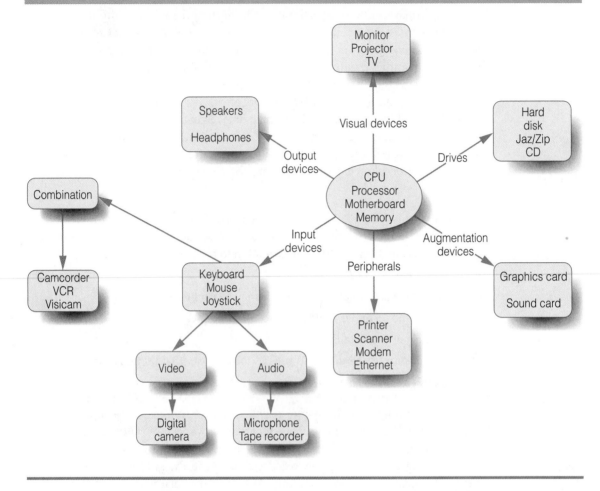

planets could have students map the information on a planet provided in an encyclopedia. Then students might refer to primary sources to find out more about each portion of the map. The map in Activity 7.2 was constructed by fifth graders as they read about and discussed the five kingdoms of living things. Students were able to refer to the text material and worked in groups.

Gaining Meaning by Emphasizing Segments of Text

Authors usually organize text by dividing it into meaningful sections or segments. These are usually signified by subheadings. Readers must pay attention to these segments of text to gain information and focus on important information. Teachers can use strategies that provide directed readings over small segments of text. Two important strategies for doing this are explained next: the directed reading–thinking activity and the guided reading procedure.

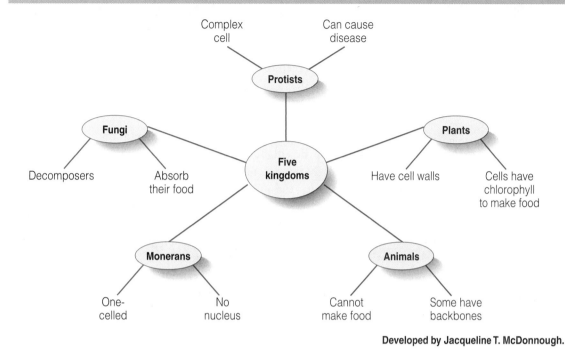

Developed by Jacqueline T. McDonnough.

DIRECTED READING–THINKING ACTIVITY

The **directed reading–thinking activity (DR–TA)** helps students understand that each segment of text can help them figure out the next segment. As advocated by Stauffer (1969a), the DR–TA has three basic steps: predicting, reading, and proving. Predicting involves asking readers to use not only what they already know but also whatever they can learn from a quick preview of the material to predict what the material is going to be about. Predicting prepares the reader for comprehension. It is an extremely important DR–TA step, but it cannot stand alone. Because students can be encouraged to predict aloud and to justify their predictions, the DR–TA offers a lively listening and speaking opportunity within a social context. Although an overall prediction may be made, teachers encourage readers to make predictions about specific portions of text and then to read the appropriate portion to confirm or alter the predictions. Students reflect aloud on those predictions before going on to read another segment. If teachers are worried that students will be reticent to make predictions, they can use a simple prediction guide, shown as Activity 7.3. Students predict in the left column and write what actually happened in the right column. This also can provide a check for the teacher of whether the student is actively predicting and taking part in the process. The teacher guides the DR–TA process, making sure that each student is actively involved in understanding each segment before continuing to the next. WIKA and KWL activities, discussed in Chapter 5, are similar to the DR–TA

The DR–TA is important because it teaches the correct reading process— predicting, reading, and proving the reading has occurred. Also, the DR–TA uses all three phases of the PAR Lesson Framework.

in promoting the strategy of involving the reader before, during, and after reading. With the DR–TA, learners also apply the strategies of prediction and segmenting text.

Figures 7.1 and 7.2 outline the DR–TA steps to apply to fiction and nonfiction material, respectively. Note that step 2 in the fiction DR–TA requests that readers read to find out whether the predictions they made were accurate. Step 4 in the nonfiction DR–TA requests that readers read to find the answers to questions they have generated, and step 5 calls on students to think critically by defending responses. These steps focus on purposeful reading; they are the foundation for a successful DR–TA. A teacher must decide in advance how to segment the material for a DR–TA. The organization of the material is the key factor affecting this segmentation.

The predicting steps of the DR–TA build purpose for reading. When readers are asked what they think might happen next and then read to verify their predictions, they are being encouraged to read purposefully. Readers become excited about this predictive involvement in their own reading. Often they share their predictions orally before the individual reading occurs. This activity incorporates listening and speaking. If students are asked to write down on the prediction guide what they predict during various portions of the reading and then review those written predictions at the end of the DR–TA, writing is used as a way to determine purpose within the DR–TA.

Our experience with the DR–TA shows that students are quite imaginative when formulating predictions about fiction but can be dreadfully boring when trying to do

ACTIVITY **7.3** DR–TA PREDICTION GUIDE

My Prediction	What Really Happened

FIGURE 7.1

DR–TA for
Fiction

1. Previewing
   Preread: Title
               Pictures
               Subtitles
               Introduction (if story is long enough)
   Close book and make hypotheses: What do you think will happen?
               Why do you think that? (What gives you the clue?)

2. Verifying
   Read: To find whether predictions were right

3. Reflecting on reading
   Developing comprehension by
               Checking on individual and group hypotheses
               Staying with or redefining hypotheses

FIGURE 7.2

DR–TA for
Nonfiction

1. Previewing
   Study: Title
               Introduction
               Subtitles
               Pictures
               Charts
               Maps
               Graphs
               Summary or conclusion
               End-of-chapter questions

2. Decision making
   What is known after previewing?
   What do we need to learn?

3. Writing
   Writing specific questions students need to learn

4. Reading
   Finding the answers to students' written questions

5. Reflecting on the reading by
   Determining answers to students' questions
   Having students defend their inferences by referring to text
   Finding out what we still need to know

the same for nonfiction. The reason for the difference may lie in the fact that they are not predicting the nonfiction outcome in the same sense as they do for fiction. The procedure for nonfiction DR–TA's is to survey, question, and then read for answers. The result, without proper preparation, can be similar to just "doing the questions at the end of the chapter." This defeats the purpose of the DR–TA, which is to allow students to create their own purpose in reading. One way we have found to help students write higher-level questions is through use of the "Higher-Level Questioning Bookmark" shown as Activity 7.4. Adapted from one developed by the Maryland State Department of Education, students are given the bookmark to keep and use with each nonfiction reading to think of more creative and interesting prediction questions for the reading. Roughly analogous to Bloom's (1956) taxonomy of cognitive objectives—knowledge, comprehension, application, analysis, synthesis, and evaluation—the bookmark can teach students the importance of asking probing questions that tap higher levels of thought.

The dialogue in Activity 7.5 gives teacher and student responses in a fiction DR–TA read for the story "The Wildest Ride in the World" by Paul Gallico. Another dialogue in Activity 7.6, transcribed from a fourth grade social studies teacher's DR–TA lesson on Virginia's Piedmont Region, shows how well PAR is incorporated in a nonfiction DR–TA.

ACTIVITY 7.4 HIGHER-LEVEL QUESTIONING BOOKMARK

QUESTION MARK: QUESTIONING FOR QUALITY THINKING

Knowledge: Identification and recall of information
Who, what, when, where, how _____?
Describe _____.

Comprehension: Organization and selection of facts and ideas
Retell _____ in your own words. What is the main idea of _____?

Application: Use of facts, rules, principles
How is _____ an example of _____?
How is _____ related to _____?
Why is _____ significant?

Analysis: Separation of a whole into component parts
What are the parts or features of _____?
Classify _____ according to _____.
Outline/diagram/web _____.
How does _____ compare/contrast with _____?

What evidence can you list for _____?

Synthesis: Combination of ideas to form a new whole
What would you predict/infer from _____?
What ideas can you add to _____?
How would you create/design a new _____?
What might happen if you combined _____ with _____?
What solutions would you suggest for _____?

Evaluation: Development of opinions, judgments, or decisions
Do you agree _____?
What do you think about _____?
What is the most important _____?
Prioritize _____.
How would you decide about _____?
What criteria would you use to assess _____?

Maryland State Department of Education; adapted by Mark Forget.

Teacher: What would you guess the "wildest ride" in the world is?

Students: A roller coaster ride.

> A bucking bronco.
>
> I think it is a roller coaster too.
>
> An Indy 500 type race at 200 miles an hour.
>
> I think it is being in a little boat in the middle of the ocean in a hurricane.

Teacher: OK, let's read the first page to see if anyone is correct in their prediction. Don't read past the first page, now. Close your books when you get to that point. . . . Was anyone right in their prediction?

Students: No.

Teacher: Then read the part that shows what the wildest ride really is. (One student reads out loud about what the Cresta Run is and that a 59-year-old is going to try to race a steel skeleton down the run.) What is unusual about the man?

Student: He is old!

Teacher: Yes, 59, which may be old to you but is not extremely old. Anyway, what do you think might happen to him in this race?

Student: He is going to win.

Teacher: Why do you think that?

Student: Because it says he is "qualified." He just didn't decide to do it at the last minute. He has had practice.

Teacher: Good thinking! Now what else could happen to him?

Student: I think he will make it down and be proud because he is writing about it and wants to brag a little.

Student: I think he will win also.

Teacher: Why do you think that?

Student: Because I just think so. I don't have a reason.

Student: I think he will have an accident.

Teacher: Why do you think that?

Student: Because he is too old to do this.

Student: I think that is true and I think he will have a minor accident too. Maybe just some bumps and bruises.

Teacher: Good predictions! Now let's read to see if anyone is correct in their prediction. Read the next two pages of the story down to the word "saying" on page 134.

Note: After reading, the teacher asks if anyone is correct, and the students who said that he was going to "just make it down" say they are correct. The teacher asks them to read orally the part that shows they are correct. After this they predict a third, and last time, about the author's second run down Cresta. The author does have an accident, and several students predicted the accident. These students seem to take delight in orally reading to the group the part that describes the accident. They are happy that they made the correct prediction.

Next the teacher asks the students whether they liked the story. All said they did like it. The teacher asks each student to read a part of the story either where the main character did something they particularly liked or where there was a good descriptive paragraph or paragraphs that they liked.

One thing to note in Activity 7.5 is that the teacher did not ask traditional after-the-reading comprehension questions. When strictly adhering to the DR–TA process, the predictions themselves act as a barometer of whether the students are comprehending the story. The postreading reflection phase enables the teacher to have students do higher-level thinking in evaluating whether they liked the story. Such

VIRGINIA'S PIEDMONT REGION

Objective: Students will describe the characteristics of the Piedmont Region in Virginia.

Building Background

Teacher: Who remembers studying the coastal plain last week?

Students: We do! (many raised hands)

Teacher: What types of things did we talk about when we discussed the Coastal Plain?

Students: Rivers—pony roundups on Chincoteague—Hampton Roads Harbor.

Teacher: How did we organize the information?

Students: A graphic organizer.

Previewing and Decision Making

Teacher: Good. Today we are going to begin our study of the Piedmont Region. Take a look at the first page of this chapter and tell me if you see some of the same things we had on the graphic organizer last week.

Student: There is a map with rivers and cities.

Student: It talks about the Fall Line.

Student: It shows some places to live.

Teacher: OK. Let's write down some of the things from your background knowledge and what you see here. Write down some things you think you know about the Piedmont Region of Virginia. Make certain you bring in what you have already learned about the Coastal Plain Region. (Students write what they know after the preview and share

first in groups and then with the teacher.) Now let's write out some questions we would like to know about the new region we are about to study, the Piedmont Region. (Students write questions.) Let's share some of our questions on the board.

Student: What is a Fall Line?

Student: Does the Fall Line have mountains?

Teacher: Good questions. Any more questions?

Student: What kind of cities are at the Fall Line?

Student: What are the rivers?

Student: What happens at the state capital? At Richmond.

Student: Why does the president have to live in Richmond?

Teacher: Good questions. Are there any more questions?

Student: What is a plateau?

Student: What are some other towns and cities besides Richmond?

Student: What are some places of interest in the Piedmont Region?

Teacher: Do you think we have some good questions now? Good. I have written them on the board now, and let's read silently and try to find the answer to just these nine questions. If you have other questions, save them for now and we will come back to them later. Again, just read to find the answers to the nine questions we have shared and written up here on the board.

---

evaluation and concomitant critical thinking are needed for students to truly understand and appreciate a story.

DR–TA lessons help teachers to model the reading process at its best. They are also compatible with constructivist theory, discussed earlier in this chapter. What good readers do as they read is predict and speculate; read to confirm; and stop reading and carry on a mental discussion of what they understand. Students are very active during reading. Through the prediction process, the material is divided into manageable units. DR–TAs provide a vehicle for figuring out content as the reading occurs; they emphasize reading as a constructive process rather than a measurement

Activity 7.6 (continued)

Reflection on the Reading

Teacher: Let's see what we learned. Take our first question: What is a Fall Line?

Student: It is a small line of waterfalls and rapids.

Teacher: What is a rapid?

Student: Places in a river that go quickly and roughly.

Teacher: Do you think boats could move well in a river with rapids?

Students: No!

Teacher: OK. What else did you learn besides the definition of a rapid?

Student: People traveled by boat to the Fall Line on their way to the western part of the state. People had to go around the rapids and waterfalls.

Teacher: Now we know why we had to learn about the Fall Line. It slowed down travel, didn't it? What did they do with their boat if they had to go around the Fall Line?

Student: They left it sometimes. Sometimes they got help to carry it with them.

Teacher: So what did people also do some of the time?

Student: They stayed there. They didn't continue the journey. They would live there.

Teacher: What do we call a place where people live?

Student: A city.

Teacher: Do you think that maybe that is how Richmond and other cities got started?

Students: Yes!

Teacher: Was there anything in the chapter about mountains?

Student: Yes. "Piedmont" means "foot of the mountains."

Teacher: Does that mean the Fall Line has mountains?

Student: No, it is at the foot of the mountains. Not in the mountains.

Teacher: Good. Did we answer any of our other questions?

Student: Yes. Where are the cities on the Fall Line? Petersburg, Richmond, Fredericksburg, and Alexandria are some cities on the Fall Line.

Student: And the question about the president living in Richmond. The governor lives there, not the president.

Teacher: Class, you have done a great job. I think we will answer the rest of these questions—let's see, we have five more left to answer—by reading more of the chapter. So save these questions and we will try to answer them as we read more of the chapter tomorrow. Now, for homework, I want you to reread the first part of the chapter that we read today and try to answer the questions you came up with on your own. Not the nine here on the board but the ones you wrote. When you come back to school tomorrow we will go over your questions and answers and turn them in for homework. Then we will read further into the chapter. Good work, boys and girls!

Developed by Sandra Harlan with her fourth grade class.

of comprehension. DR–TAs also build the self-concept of readers. When readers know that predictions help them understand better, and that everyone's speculations are important whether or not they prove to be what the author concluded, they feel more confident about their reading. At the elementary level, teachers can encourage readers to become "reading detectives." Playing a game of detection motivates students to read and to take charge of their own reading. We cannot stress enough the pervasive benefits of using DR–TAs in teaching both fiction and nonfiction.

One final note: the DR–TA makes use of all phases of the PAR Lesson Framework. The teacher does not have to worry whether she is preparing and assisting students, as

When you teach the DR–TA and ask students to predict, you are teaching *convergent inference.* When you ask them to tell you why they liked or disliked the story, or ask them to do some creative follow-up activity, you are teaching *divergent inference.*

this is an integral part of the strategy. Also, there are plenty of opportunities to reflect over the reading and learning in the DR–TA.

GUIDED READING PROCEDURE

The **guided reading procedure (GRP)** (Manzo, 1975) offers an excellent way to teach students to gather and organize information around main ideas. GRP uses brainstorming to collect information as accurately as possible and then rereading to correct misinformation and fill in conceptual gaps. The second reading is very important because it brings heightened motivation—students read to prove their statements are correct or disprove fellow students' statements. In conducting the GRP, we have noted students' intensity of purpose and focus during this second reading segment. According to Colwell and associates (1986), GRP is a very effective teacher-directed technique. It can be used to aid students in becoming more independent in their thinking and studying. Here are the steps teachers use to apply the guided reading procedure:

1. Prepare the students for the lesson by clarifying key concepts about the reading; assess students' background knowledge. The teacher may ask students to clarify vocabulary terms or make predictions concerning concepts inherent to the reading.

2. Assign a selection of appropriate length, and ask students to remember all they can about the reading. Manzo (1975) gives these general guidelines for passage length: primary students—90 words, 3 minutes; elementary students—500 words, 5 minutes; junior high school students—900 words, 7 minutes; high school students—2,000 words, 10 minutes.

3. After the students have completed the assignment, have them close the book and relate everything they know about the material they just read. Then list statements on the board without editing, whenever possible assigning two students to act as class recorders. Using student recorders makes it easier for the teacher to monitor and guide the class discussion. Of course, for early elementary classes the teacher will have to do all the recording.

4. Direct students to look for inconsistencies and misinformation, first through discussion and then through reading the material.

5. Add new information. If reading a narrative, help students organize and categorize concepts into a loose outline. For nonfiction, students can put information into two, three, or four categories and title each category.

6. Have students reread the selection to determine whether the information they listed is accurate.

7. To strengthen short-term recall, test students on the reading.

Part I of Activity 7.7 lists the statements that students made in the first phase of a GRP. Listed in Part II of the activity are the categories in which students chose to group the facts they listed. Students placed the facts in Part I under one of the three categories listed. In this manner students created their own "categories of learning" as an aid to comprehension.

Part I

Statements from ninth grade earth science
students after the first reading:

1. The word *planet* comes from the Greek word
   for wanderer.

2. 11 kilometers per second is escape velocity.

3. Newton's third law of motion is that every
   action has an equal and opposite reaction.

4. Inertia is a little thing that doesn't let a planet
   travel in a straight line in space travel.

5. Newton has a theory of universal gravitation.

6. A reflecting telescope uses mirrors instead of a
   lens.

7. Heliocentric is a model of the solar system.

8. Astronomers used to think the sun and other
   planets revolved around the earth.

9. The earth's inertia combines with the sun's
   gravity to make us orbit around the sun.

10. Inertia is an object that keeps moving in one
    direction.

11. Refracting telescopes are tubes with lenses
    that bend the light from the stars.

12. Reflecting and refracting telescopes can only
    be used at night, so you have to use radio-
    telescopes during the day.

13. A satellite is an object in orbit around another
    large body.

14. Probes travel out to the other parts of the
    solar system.

15. In 1610, an Italian nobleman named Galileo
    was the first to use a telescope.

16. Isaac Newton was from England.

17. Sputnik was the first orbiter in 1957.

18. Nine planets orbit around the sun.

19. Reflecting telescopes use two or more mirrors
    to reflect stars' light.

Part II

CATEGORIES:

Celestial Bodies
Celestial Mechanics
Measuring Instruments

Recorded and developed by Brian Alexander.

The Importance of the Organization of Language

As many as 17 **patterns of organization**—ways in which segments of language can be
ordered—have been identified in good writing. A few of them predominate in textbooks. When readers learn to recognize organizational patterns and the relationship
between superordinate ideas and subordinate information, they take a giant step toward
independence in reading. We have combined research identifying several basic patterns
(Kolozow & Lehmann, 1982) to target seven that often are recognizable in content textbooks: simple listing, sequential listing, analysis, cause and effect, comparison and contrast, definition, and analogy/example. We describe and illustrate each one in turn.

SIMPLE LISTING

A simple listing is an enumeration of facts or events in no special order. The superordinate information is the topic or event; the facts or traits that follow are the subordinate

or supporting information. Some words that may signal this pattern are *also, another,* and *several.*

Example: "We presented several principles in Chapter 1. For the most part, each can be considered independently of the others. One stresses the relationship of the communicative arts to content reading instruction. Another states that reading should be a pleasurable experience."

SEQUENTIAL LISTING

In a sequential listing, chronological or some other logical order of presentation is important. The superordinate information is the topic or event; the facts or traits then presented in appropriate order are the subordinate information. Henk and Helfeldt (1987) explain that even capable readers need assistance in applying the sequence patterns used in directions. Some words that signal this pattern are *first, second, next, before, during, then,* and *finally.*

Example: "Gray's may be the simplest and friendliest of the taxonomies. Gray said that one must first read the lines and then read between the lines; then one can read beyond the lines."

ANALYSIS

Analysis takes an important idea (superordinate information) and investigates the relationships of the parts of that idea (subordinate information) to the whole. Some words and phrases that signal this pattern are *consider, analyze, investigate, the first part suggests,* and *this element means.*

Example: "Consider how the child concluded that the word he had been unable to pronounce was *oxygen.* The first portion of his behavior, when he skipped the word, indicated that he did not know the word at all. Yet he was able to recognize it when he had a context for it during the recall stage. This means that he was processing information all along."

CAUSE AND EFFECT

The pattern of cause and effect takes an event or effect (the superordinate information) and presents discourse in terms of the causes (subordinate information) of that event. The effect is thus shown to be a result of the causes. Some words and phrases that signal this pattern are *because, hence, therefore, as a result,* and *this led to.*

Example: "When teachers prepare students to read content material, they help students understand better. As a result of such preparation, teachers will see that students are more interested, pay more attention, and comprehend better."

COMPARISON AND CONTRAST

Sometimes a writer seeks to highlight similarities and differences between facts, events, or authors. The basic comparison or contrast is the superordinate information, and the specific similarities and differences are the subordinate information.

Some words and phrases that signal this pattern are *in contrast, in the same way, on the one hand, on the other hand, either . . . or,* and *similarly.*

Example: "On the one hand, a checklist offers less mathematical precision; on the other hand, it provides more qualitative information."

DEFINITION

A definition provides an explanation of a concept or topic (superordinate information) by using synonyms to describe it (subordinate information). Some words and phrases that signal this pattern are *described as, synonymous with, is,* and *equals.*

Example: "Reading can be described as analytic, interactive, constructive, and strategic. The active, integrated thinking that leads to a conclusion as a result of reading is comprehension."

ANALOGY/EXAMPLE

Analogies were introduced in Chapter 6 as a way to prepare readers. Sometimes a writer uses an example—a specific instance or a similar situation (subordinate information)—to explain a topic or concept (superordinate information). Analogies are a type of example. Some words and phrases that signal this pattern are *for example, for instance, likened to, analogous to,* and *is like.*

Example: "Reading is like a game of basketball. To play one's best game, lots of preparation and practice are necessary. In reading, this is analogous to preparing by determining and building background for the material to be read."

> One way to help students see a pattern is to ask them to underline or highlight the signal words. If the text material can be posted electronically, students can use the highlighting feature of a word processing program to experiment with locating signal words.

Often more than one pattern is apparent in a single section of text. A writer may analyze by means of comparison and contrast. Definition is often accompanied by example. Some patterns appear frequently in particular content subjects. Table 7.1 suggests some possible patterns of organization and how they are used in content textbooks, but it is only a guide. Also, teachers need to consider the grade level they teach and the specific materials they use, because different patterns may dominate at different grade levels and in different subjects.

The study and identification of patterns of organization in written material as well as student and teacher verbal interaction and reaction to text structure is called **discourse analysis.** Gee (1996) has noted that students use discourses such as networking, talking, and interacting to learn about the world. Chinn (Chinn et al., 2001)

TABLE 7.1 Some Patterns of Organization Used Frequently in Content Textbooks

Science	Math	Social Studies	English	Health
Sequential listing	Sequential listing	Cause/effect	Cause/effect	Comparison/contrast
Cause/effect	Simple listing	Simple listing	Comparison/contrast	Simple listing
Definition	Analysis	Example	Example	Definition
	Definition	Analysis		

includes in discourse analysis such behaviors as teacher and student turn taking in discussions, teacher questions, taking authority in decision making, and control of the topic of discussion. Chinn recommends the use of a technique called **collaborative reasoning** (Waggoner et al., 1995), which was found to be better than recitations in improving student engagement and in teaching higher-level thinking. Collaborative reasoning is an approach to literature discussion intended to stimulate critical thinking. After reading a selection, the teacher poses a central question that is worded to force students to take a position for or against the question. Students discuss the question and must defend the position they take concerning the question. In this manner, students collaboratively construct arguments through a complex network of reasoning and shared evidence (Chinn & Anderson, 1998). After getting the discussion going with the central question, the teacher acts only as a moderator and mostly stays out of the discussion. Students are encouraged to weigh evidence offered and decide whether to maintain or change their original positions.

Strategic instruction shows readers how to identify patterns of organization. General comprehension of the material—understanding the text overall—is enhanced for the reader. One simple activity to raise awareness of organization is to have students peruse the table of contents of a textbook and ask, "How did the author organize this writing? What overall patterns of organization do you see in the table of contents?" Also, a teacher may simply ask students to identify the pattern of organization in a chapter, a subchapter, or even a paragraph. Teachers can devise activities to assist readers in identifying patterns, as we explain in the next section. When readers learn to recognize organizational patterns and the relationship between superordinate ideas and subordinate information, they move toward independence in reading.

Activities for Teaching Understanding of Text Organization

When the teacher uses activities to assist understanding of text organization, reading to learn is much easier. Activities assist students and create an interesting learning environment. Here we present some of our favorites.

MYSTERY CLUE GAME

The group mystery clue game is designed to help readers understand sequence. It works well when it is important for students to understand a sequence of events. The idea for this activity comes from *Turn-ons* (Smuin, 1978); we have adapted it to fit content materials.

1. To construct a mystery clue game, the teacher first studies the sequence of events in the material and writes clear, specific clue cards for each event. More than one card may be made for each clue.

2. The teacher divides the class into small groups and gives each group member at least one clue card. Each group can have one complete set of cards, but each group member is responsible for his or her own cards within that set.

3. No student may show a card to another in the group, but cards can be read aloud or paraphrased so that all group members know what is on each card. In this way, students who are poor readers will still be encouraged to try to read and to participate.

4. Each group of students must use the clues the teacher gives them to solve the mystery. For example, they must find the murderer, the weapon, the time and place of the murder, the motive, and the victim. Or they must find the equation that will solve a problem, or the formula that will make a chemical.

5. A time limit is usually given.

6. A group scribe reports the group's solution to the whole class.

7. Students are instructed to read the material to find out which group came closest to solving the mystery.

Visit www.soe. vcu.edu/GCU. Select Secondary Modules; select Module Four and then Video; watch Kenya Brown teach using a mystery clue game.

This cooperative activity promotes oral language as well as reading, and it works well in most content areas. For instance, science teachers can write clues to performing an experiment, mathematics teachers can write clues to deriving a formula, and social studies teachers can write clues to sequencing historical events. The goal of the activity is for students to approximate the sequence of events before reading and then read with the purpose of checking their predictions. It is not necessary for students to memorize specific details. As they read, they will think back to their clues and construct meaning.

Activity 7.8 is a mystery clue game for a French lesson to assist students in mastering the Paris Metro. Students in small groups have to read (translate) the 10 clue cards (without referring to their textbooks) and put the cards in the correct chronological order. In doing so, students learn the logical steps in taking the Paris Metro and grasp the relationship between the Metro, the grammar, and the vocabulary presented in the French textbook.

Pattern guides (Herber, 1978) are most useful in helping students recognize a predominant pattern such as cause and effect or comparison and contrast. To construct them, the teacher locates the pattern, decides on the major ideas to be stressed, and designs the pattern-oriented guide. Pattern guides can help students see causal relationships. Students need to learn to distinguish cause and effect when reading text materials, especially in social studies, science, and vocational education. Simply asking students to search for causes is often not successful; students tend to neglect—or worse, misunderstand and misuse—this pattern without the teacher's intervention, support, and patience. Moreover, finding causal relationships is difficult because the cause of an event or situation may not be known or traceable. Even so, students should endeavor to distinguish cause and effect for the practice in thinking that it affords. Activity 7.9 provides an example of a cause-and-effect guide at the middle school level. Teachers can also encourage students to make contrast–contrast maps such as the one reproduced here as Activity 7.10. These graphic organizers or concept maps stress similarities and differences, as in the case here of comparing brown widow spiders with black widow spiders. Teachers may help children by constructing some of the map to get them started. Or teachers can "talk" students through the map

Luc et Jérome veulent aller au Louvre pour apprendre quelque chose pour leur classe d'art.

A la bouche du métro ils regardent le plan et ils comprennent qu'il faut prendre une correspondance.

Ils prennent la direction Porte de Clignancourt et ils prennent une autre correspondance aux Halles.

Bon! Ils sont là!

Après le musée, ils font des achats.

Ils n'ont pas de voiture. C'est trop loin—ils ne peuvent pas aller à pied ou prendre leurs vélos. Le taxi est trop cher, ainsi ils veulent prendre le métro.

Ils vont au métro—c'est la station Maubert-Mutalité. Ils achètent deux billets de seconde.

D'abord, ils prennent la direction Boulogne–Point de St Cloud, et ils changent à Odéon.

Ils prennent la direction Pont de Neuilly. Ils descendent à Louvre.

Ils entrent dans le Louvre où ils voient la Joconde (Mona Lisa) et la Vénus de Milo.

ENGLISH TRANSLATION IN CHRONOLOGICAL ORDER

1. Luke and Jeremy want to go to the Louvre in order to learn something for their art class.
2. They don't have a car. It is too far—they can't walk or take their bikes. A taxi costs too much, so they want to take the Metro.
3. At the Metro entrance, they look at the map and they understand that they will have to transfer to another line on the Metro.
4. They go into the Metro station "Maubert-Mutalité." They buy two second-class tickets.
5. First, they take the "Boulogne–Point de Saint Cloud" direction, and they change at "Odéon."
6. They take the "Porte de Clignancourt" direction, and they make another change at "Les Halles."
7. They take the "Pont de Neuilly" direction. They get off at "Louvre."
8. Good! They are there.
9. They enter the Louvre, where they see the *Mona Lisa* and the *Venus de Milo*.
10. After the museum, they run errands.

Developed by Laura Clevinger.

and in this way build the map together with the students. Such maps provide excellent ways to teach patterns of organization inherent in print material.

ORGANIZATIONAL (JOT) CHARTS

Jot charts organize text information by showing comparisons and contrasts. Students complete a matrix as a way to see how ideas are alike and different. Jot charts are relatively simple to construct and can be used at any grade level and in any content area. The teacher usually sets up the matrix and encourages students to fill it in as they read. In this way, students understand the relationships and build meaning as they read. When completed, jot charts become a good study aid. If they are filled in by groups of students, the social aspects of learning are also included in the activity.

NAME _____

Based on information from the reading selection, match the effects listed in the second column to the causes listed in the first column. Be prepared to explain your choices.

CAUSES	EFFECTS
_____ **1.** Inland, away from the ocean, the influence of salt spray decreases.	**a.** Maritime forests and inland marshes are protected from the ocean.
_____ **2.** Grasses disappeared in the bay waters around 1980.	**b.** Water circulation was cut down, and the salinity (saltiness) of the water in the bay decreased.
_____ **3.** There was a great amount of dredging and development along the northern part of the bay.	**c.** Stormwater management regulations were made to control runoff from new development, and new development was limited upstream from Back Bay.
_____ **4.** Residential subdivisions, a golf course, and farms use chemicals to eliminate weeds and fertilize land.	**d.** Low shrubs and trees are able to grow, forming the maritime forest habitat.
_____ **5.** The Civilian Conservation Corps built dunes up along the seashore.	**e.** The bay water gets cloudy and blocks the sunlight needed to grow grasses.
_____ **6.** In the absence of grasses, algae feed on the nutrients.	**f.** Food depended on by the waterfowl disappeared, sediment at the bottom of the bay was free to erode, and fish lost their cover.
_____ **7.** Currituck Inlet closed naturally, and the Knotts Island Causeway was built in 1890.	**g.** 40% of the citation largemouth bass caught in Virginia came out of Back Bay by 1978.
_____ **8.** Eurasian milfoil grass was planted and spread to cover 88% of the bay floor.	**h.** Erosion is reduced, nutrients are recycled, and habitats for many species of fish and other wildlife are created.
_____ **9.** Marsh grass is abundant in the tidal flatlands.	**i.** Nitrogen and phosphorus levels in the bay water exceed state reference levels and pose a serious water quality problem.
_____**10.** City officials commissioned a study of Back Bay.	**j.** Sediment flooded into the bay from streams and tributaries, causing loss of sunlight reaching the grasses.

Developed by Mark Forget.

We present two examples of jot charts to demonstrate their diversity in activating comprehension. The chart in Activity 7.11 was developed for an elementary science unit. Activity 7.12 depicts a chart of mathematical formulas.

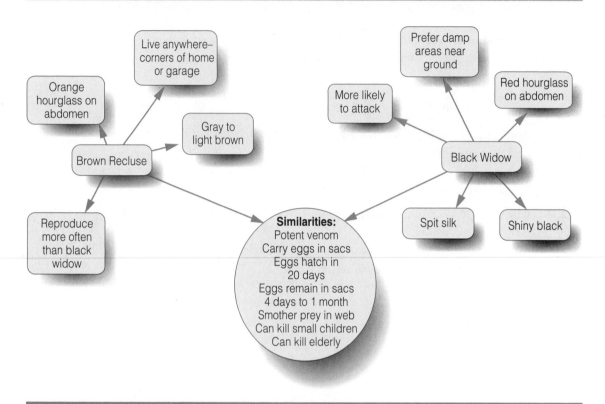

Nutrient	How This Nutrient Helps Your Body	Examples of Foods That Contain This Nutrient
Protein	Helps your body make new cells	Peanuts, eggs, beans, fish, almond butter
Carbohydrate	Gives you quick energy	Pineapples, bananas, rice, pasta, strawberries, green beans, corn, potatoes
Fats	Give your body energy to store	Bacon, peanuts, cheese, steak, butter, walnuts
Vitamins and minerals	Help your body use proteins, carbohydrates, and fats	Bananas, milk, orange juice, whole wheat bread, whole grain cereal
Water	Makes up half of your body weight	Almost all foods and liquids contain some water

Developed by Mendy Mathena.

	Shape	Picture	Perimeter/Surface area	Area/Volume
2-dimensional	Circle		$2\pi r$	πr^2
	Triangle		$a + b + c$	$\frac{1}{2} bh$
	Square		$4x$	x^2
	Rectangle		$2l + 2w$	lw

	Shape	Picture	Surface area	Volume
3-dimensional	Cone		$\pi rh + \pi r^2$	$\frac{1}{3}\pi r^2 h$
	Rectangular box		$2(lw) + 2(lh) + 2(hw) =$ surface area	lwh

Developed by Serena Marshall.

Assisting Comprehension and Reflecting on Learning ~ 213

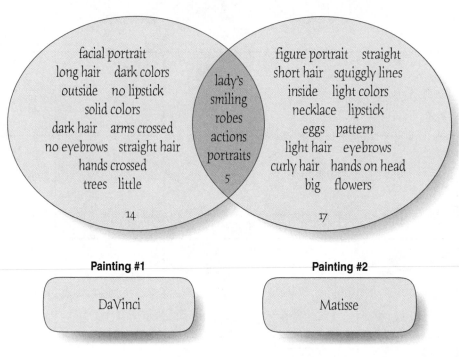

Painting #1

DaVinci

Painting #2

Matisse

Developed by Susan Protich and her students.

VENN DIAGRAMS

Venn diagrams provide another way to demonstrate similarities and differences. Facts or ideas about the topic from two different perspectives or eras are listed in two different columns. Then similarities are listed in a third, central column. The differences and similarities are enclosed in two circles that overlap, with the overlapping portion listing the similarities and the nonoverlapping portions listing the differences. This graphic depiction helps readers see, understand, and remember the patterns. Activity 7.13 is a Venn diagram for comparing and contrasting the paintings of DaVinci and Matisse in a third grade classroom.

USING QUESTIONING STRATEGIES TO IMPROVE COMPREHENSION

Many researchers feel that dialogue between teachers and students should be the most important medium for teaching and learning (Hillocks, 2002; Langer, 2001). The best dialogue may come in the form of teacher–student questions. Classroom questioning strategies and questioning instruction can help with memory for what was read, can improve information-finding abilities of students, and can lead to more in-depth processing of text (McKeown & Beck, 2003). When questioning works, it works well. Studies show that the most effective teachers encourage higher-level thinking through questioning techniques (Taylor et al., 2002). Questions can help teachers to know whether students understand text and can guide readers to consider many aspects of material. Question-generated discussions create meaning for readers (Alvermann, O'Brien, & Dillon, 1990; Barton, 1995). Questions are excellent probes. Robert Sternberg (1994) argues that the ability to ask good questions and to know how to answer them is the most essential part of intelligence. Well-considered questions are essential to guide students' thinking and reasoning abilities (Marashio, 1995). Often, however, questioning does not work well because teachers fall into some common traps.

A major reason why questioning is not successful is that teachers confuse the *product* of comprehension with the *process* of learning when they question. A teacher who requires students to close their books and recite information before they have a chance to assimilate that information is testing a product rather than assisting the process of constructing meaning. Furthermore, recitation relies on the literal level and does not encourage higher-level thinking.

A second trap is writing questions that focus on literal comprehension. Gusak (1967) reported that 78 percent of the questions asked in second grade were literal, 65 percent in fourth grade were literal, and 58 percent in sixth grade were literal. Observing at the upper elementary level, Durkin (1979) found that teachers asked mostly literal questions, expecting a specific response. Durkin (1981) then studied teachers' manuals for basal reading instruction and discovered that low-level literal questions with one correct response were the major instructional strategy provided for teachers. Newer research shows the emphasis has not changed. Armbruster and colleagues (1991) studied science and social studies lessons for fourth graders and found that 90 percent of the questions were teacher generated and explicit. In a study of two American history classes, Sturtevant (1992) found that teachers stressed textbook reading and factual information. Reutzel and Daines (1987) reached the same conclusion after a study of seven major basal readers. When Young and Daines (1992) looked at the types of questions that students and their teachers asked, they found that students were more likely to ask interpretive questions and teachers asked literal questions about the same material.

Getting little practice in answering higher-level questions, students are ill equipped to think critically. Elementary students are trapped into expecting only literal questions; secondary students will remain in the trap because the literal question has been their previous experience. Research shows, however, that when instructional strategies are altered so that the focus is on inferences and main ideas, students respond with improved recall and greater understanding (Hansen, 1981; Hansen & Pearson, 1983; Raphael, 1984). Cooter, Joseph, and Flynt (1986) were able to show that third and fourth graders who were asked no literal questions in a five-month period performed significantly better than a control group on inferential comprehension and just as well on literal comprehension. Menke and Pressley (1994) encourage teachers and their students to use *why* questions because their use greatly increases factual memory.

When students are encouraged to develop their own questions, they develop higher-level understanding. Ciardello (1998) argues that the process of asking questions helps students to focus on and learn content, as well as develop cognitive strategies that will help them understand new and challenging material. Ciardello describes a technique called *TeachQuest,* in which the teacher guides students through a series of steps to identify and classify divergent-thinking questions. The goal is for students to generate their own divergent-thinking questions. Crapse (1995) reports that "through the experience of honest questioning, I have observed students celebrating their own insights and solutions to problems posed" (p. 390). Remember that students can also develop their own questions using the "higher-level questioning bookmark" discussed earlier in this chapter and shown in Activity 7.4.

Another trap that teachers sometimes fall into is misjudging the difficulty of the questions they are asking or failing to match the questions to the students' ability. Generally, questions are simplest when students are to recognize and locate answers in the text rather than close their books and try to recall the same information. Easy questions also include those asked during reading or shortly after reading, questions that have only one or two parts, oral questions rather than written ones, and those that allow students to choose an answer from among several alternatives. We are not suggesting that all questions should be asked in the simplest manner; we are cautioning that many times teachers do not consider the difficulty of their questions and their students' ability to answer them.

A final trap that often snares teachers is focusing more on the questions asked and the responses expected than on the students' actual responses. Recall that Durkin's research cited earlier in this discussion found that teachers too often expect one response and do not consider an alternative. As Dillon (1983) remarks, we should "stress the nature of questions rather than their frequency and pace, and the type of student response rather than the type of teacher question" (p. 8). Students' answers can tell a lot about their understanding of the topic. We need to listen for answers that let us know how well we are assisting the development of comprehension.

How to Construct Good Questions

We have learned much about how to question from the extensive studies of reading comprehension conducted over the past few decades. Although much of this research has been conducted with elementary students, the implications are relevant for secondary instruction as well. Students who have not received a firm foundation in reading comprehension in elementary school will not be well equipped in secondary school. To help teachers construct good questions, we summarize here what we consider the most important research considerations:

1. Simplify your questions! Although teachers want to challenge their students, they should challenge within a range that allows students to succeed. Consider using these guidelines:

   a. Identify the purpose of the question. (Will it measure fact, implication, or applied levels of comprehension? Is there a particular organizational pattern? Is there a superordinate or subordinate idea?) Is this purpose justified? Does it contribute to a balance of comprehension levels within the lesson?

    b. Identify the type of response demanded by the question (recognition, recall, production, or generation of a new idea from the information). Is this expectation justified, given the age and ability of the group? Have you provided an example of what you want? If you wish students to produce a modern dialogue for a character in *Hamlet,* can you give them an example first?

    c. Might the question elicit more than one reasonable response? If this is a possibility, will you be able to accept different responses and use them to assist instruction?

    d. Does this question contain several parts? Will these parts be clear to the students, and can they remember all of the parts as they respond?

    e. Write the question clearly and concisely. Then decide whether to pose it orally or in writing.

2. Share with students the reasons for your questions. Let them know the process you use to develop questions and the process you would use to answer them. This knowledge helps them see what types of questions are important to you in this area (Pearson, 1985). It also helps them understand how they should be thinking when they respond and what you are thinking when you question. This process—thinking about thinking—is called **metacognition** (Babbs & Moe, 1983). It uses two very important operations in the learning process: self-appraisal and self-management (Jacobs & Paris, 1987). Recent research points to the value of teaching students metacognitive behaviors during and after reading (Mevarech, 1999). Helping students think about both their own reasoning and reading processes should produce large rewards in learning. This sharing is a form of think-aloud (Davey, 1983) and think-along (Ehlinger & Pritchard, 1994). Such metacognitive activities are discussed in Chapter 11.

3. Encourage students to ask questions about your questions and to ask their own questions. Goodlad (1984) suggests that students will thrive when they can participate in classroom questioning more directly than they do in the typical classroom. Beyer (1984) says that teacher-dominated questioning inhibits student independence and limits thinking. "Instruction that leads to systematic question-asking by students would be more appropriate, but such an approach is rare indeed" (p. 489).

4. Provide plenty of practice in answering questions at different levels of comprehension. Check yourself occasionally to make sure that you are not leaning on the literal level too heavily. Training and practice result in learning the material (Brown, Campione, & Day, 1981; Paris, Cross, & Lipson, 1984) and in learning how to understand material in sophisticated ways. Wassermann (1987) argues that students' depth and breadth of understanding improve when they are asked challenging questions. Also, students who learn to take another's perspective may become better readers as a result (Gardner & Smith, 1987). But students must have opportunities for practice to master this ability.

In Chapter 2 we discussed the ReQuest strategy, an excellent way for students to practice questioning techniques.

5. Allow discussions, which give students practice in asking and answering questions (Alvermann, 1987a; Alvermann et al., 1996; Perez & Strickland, 1987).

6. Ask students the types of questions you know they are able to answer. Try not to expect too much too soon, but do expect as much as students can give. For example, research indicates that students can identify main-idea statements earlier than they can make such statements (Afflerbach, 1987). If students seem consistently unable to answer a certain type of comprehension question even after you have followed these suggestions, we suggest that you review the most recent findings in the research literature for clues.

Several Excellent Questioning Strategies

THE QUESTION–ANSWER RELATIONSHIP

Raphael (1984, 1986) has studied and applied the **question–answer relationship (QAR).** QAR is a four-level taxonomy: (1) right there, (2) think and search, (3) the author and you, and (4) on your own. The best way to introduce QAR is with a visual aid showing the QAR relationship. Figure 7.3 shows one teacher's illustrated introduction to QAR. After introducing QAR, the teacher uses a short passage to demonstrate how QAR is applied. To model the use of QAR, the teacher provides, labels, and answers at least one question at each QAR level. The teacher then moves gradually to having students answer questions and identifying the QAR for themselves. At various times throughout the school year, the teacher should refer to QAR. Activity 7.14 lists QAR questions and a student's answers about the story *Clifford's First Halloween* in an early elementary class.

Because QAR is a straightforward procedure, easily implemented, quickly beneficial to students, and useful at any grade and in any content area, we encourage content teachers to use it in their instruction. QAR has been proved to increase students' comprehension more than several other questioning strategies (Jenkins & Lawler, 1990). Research (Ezell et al., 1996) shows that students who used QAR maintain good comprehension skills during their next school year. They show the most proficiency with text-explicit questions; they do not perform quite as well with implicit questioning. QAR fosters listening, speaking, and reading; and if students write their own questions, it also offers opportunities for writing.

GUIDE-O-RAMAS AND MARGINAL GLOSSES

A *guide-o-rama* (Cunningham & Shablak, 1975) alerts the reader to notice certain information in a reading passage. The teacher creates directions for these passages and encourages the students to use the directions as they read. For instance, if the teacher sees that the word *perverse* is used in an unusual way, he might write this: "On page 13, second paragraph, third line, the word *perverse* is used a little differently from what you'd expect. Pay attention to the meaning." When a teacher prepares several directions such as this and gives them to readers to refer to while reading, readers have a panoramic view of the reading—hence the name *guide-o-rama*.

Marginal glosses (Singer & Donlan, 1985) are often found in content textbooks. Glosses are comments that authors make to their readers as asides, sometimes in the margin of the page. Because the comments are intended to help the reader under-

FIGURE 7.3

Introduction
to QAR

Q A R

I. Where is the answer?

Right there!
_____

Words are right there
in the text.

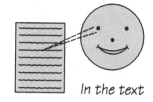

In the text

II. Where is the answer?

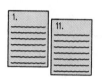

Think and search!
_____

Words are in the text but not
spelled out for you. Think about
what the author is saying.

Hmm! Gotta
think about this.

III. Where is the answer?

What I know

You and the author!
_____

Think about what you have learned
and what is in the text.

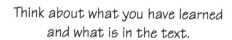

What the
author says

IV. Where is the answer?

On your own!
_____

Answer is in your head!

stand the passage, they assist the reader in developing comprehension. Teachers can write their own marginal glosses if texts do not include them or if additional ones are needed. Also, a guide-o-rama can be designed as a gloss.

Singer and Donlan (1985) suggest that teachers make marginal glosses as follows:

1. Fold a sheet of paper against the margin of a text.

2. Identify the book page at the top of the master, and line up numbers beside the teacher directives.

FROM *CLIFFORD'S FIRST HALLOWEEN*

Question 1: Right there!
What is the name of Emily Elizabeth's dog?   **Answer:** Clifford

Question 2: Think and search!
What did Clifford dress as for Halloween?   **Answer:** A clown

Question 3: You and the author!
Do you think Clifford had fun on Halloween?   **Answer:** Yes, but he was scared of the spider

Question 4: On your own!
If Clifford was your dog, what would you dress him as?   **Answer:** Woody or Buzz Lightyear

Developed by Jennifer Haczewski.

3. Write the marginal notes on the sheet of paper.

4. Duplicate and give students copies of these notes to match to text pages and lines as they read.

Marginal glosses and guide-o-ramas are like having the teacher go home with the students and look over their shoulders as they read, guiding their reading attention. These strategies can help students use features of text as well as help teachers facilitate comprehension by questioning. We suggest that the teacher select either very difficult portions of text to gloss or beginning portions, when the reading may be tougher. Making guide-o-ramas or glosses for use throughout a text would be very time-consuming. However, to provide assistance in developing comprehension of challenging reading, they are worth the time. Activity 7.15 is one for high school earth science.

THE REFLECTION PHASE OF LEARNING

A reporter once asked Coach John McKay, "What do you think about the execution of your team?" After little reflection, the coach replied, "I'm all for it." We are not certain that Coach McKay reflected sufficiently before answering, but we do know that reflective thinking is important in life. The third step in the PAR Lesson Framework is reflection, which takes place after reading has been completed. Many agree that postreading reflective strategies are crucial for extending comprehension beyond the literal level (Massey & Heafner, 2004).

Whereas the preparation phase of the lesson helps motivate students and the assistance phase helps build comprehension, the reflection phase helps clarify thinking and focus understanding. In this phase, students are aided in the retention of

How can I use this information?

1. Vocabulary word _____
   Definition in your own words:
   (Use the picture for help, if needed.)

2. What do you think *mass* is?

3. Why do you think ice floats in water?

4. Why do you think the average Earth density is greater than the average density of the Earth's crust?

5. Given a rock with a mass of 550g and a density of 2.75 g/cm³, calculate the volume of the rock.

6. BRING A ROCK TO CLASS TOMORROW—no larger than an egg!

7. What brand-name product has used density of the product in its advertising?

Place on top edge at p. ____ in binding.

Complete this side first.

Part I: What do I know?

Topic heading:

Vocabulary word:

Using words, give the density formula:

Recall: Volume = length × width × height

height
width
length

Average Earth density (include units):

Average density of Earth's crust (include units):

Recall from Chapter 1 two (2) materials found in the Earth's core:

1.

2.

Developed by Nancy S. Smith.

information. Full understanding cannot be achieved until reflection occurs. Although the teacher may guide students by providing instructional support, the student's role is crucial at this stage.

This third phase also has several important by-products. One is that it helps students think critically about what they have learned and have yet to learn about the lesson. Such critical thinking is necessary if students are going to become mature readers. A second by-product is that reflecting on the reading helps students retain understanding longer. The more we reflect on reading material or on the lesson at hand, the longer we will remember it and the more likely we will be to use the knowledge we retain. In this manner knowledge is related in a meaningful way to what is already known so that it will be retained and become the basis for further learning. A third by-product is that reflection provides a demonstration of one's learning through some system of evaluation. In this chapter we discuss all these aspects of reflection.

The Reflection Phase Builds Autonomous Learners

Remember that we said in Chapter 1 that a major goal of education is to create autonomous learners.

Erickson and Schultz (1992) note that little educational research has focused on the learner and the social, emotional, and cognitive interplay involved in learning. From the research on student learning, all indications are that readers must take charge of their own learning as soon as possible. The goal is to help students become *autonomous learners,* a term we defined in Chapter 1. Hawkes and Schell (1987) caution that teacher-set reasons to read may encourage dependence and a passive approach to reading. Student self-set reasons to read promote reading that is active and ultimately independent.

"By teaching us how to read, they had taught us how to get away," observe the rats in Robert O'Brien's *Mrs. Frisby and the Rats of NIMH* (1971). In this children's novel, scientists conduct experiments to teach rats to read. Because the rats are fed a superdrug to make them smart, the scientists anticipate that the rats will learn some letter–sound and word–picture relationships. They do not expect that the rats will actually ever understand and apply what they read. They underestimate what reading is all about. These rats want to escape from the lab, and their goal is vital: they are willing to work at reading so they can use this new skill to escape. The rats use all their communication skills. They study pictures presented to them, they listen to clues to the meaning of the pictures, and they consult with one another about what they are learning—the connections between letters and sounds, pictures and words. And then they read! Later, in their new home, they even begin to keep a written record of their progress.

The story of the rats of NIMH demonstrates how cooperative study and the communicative arts can produce reflective readers who think critically, enrich their environment, and use reading as a lifelong process. The key to the rats' success is that they became autonomous learners, and no test of their success could demonstrate their learning better than the self-supporting community the rats built. The rats had a great desire to escape NIMH and plenty of opportunities for practice as well as plenty of clues in their environment. The natural result was both comprehension and escape.

The scientists, to their misfortune, did not realize the important role of the learner in the success of their experiment.

Principle 10 in Chapter 1 states, "Content reading instruction enables students to become autonomous learners." Teachers help students achieve this independence by allowing students, as soon as possible, to take active, responsible roles. However, students may be left stranded unless teachers guide them toward independence by showing them how to use their own communication skills. Kletzein (1991) investigated adolescents' use of strategies for reading. She found that students used many strategies when they were reading independently, but students with poor comprehension were less flexible. Good readers are able to pause and demonstrate their comprehension by retelling and analyzing what they have read and by using certain strategies consistently. They are practicing **comprehension monitoring.** In contrast, poor readers seem to lose track of their reading and have no particular strategies for comprehending. In a recent study McInnes and colleagues (2003) found children 9 to 12 years of age with attention-deficit hyperactivity disorder (ADHD) were poorer at comprehending inferences and at comprehension monitoring of instructions than were normal groups of children.

In other words, poor readers do not function independently. Kletzein recommends that students be given more control over the strategies so that they can gain independence. Although teachers can point out what is important about content material, students must ultimately evaluate its worth for themselves (Cioffi, 1992). Thus, for example, Angeletti (1991) used question cards with her second graders to encourage them to express opinions about content they had read.

Bohan and Bass (1991) helped students in a fourth grade math class become independent by taking **free rides** in solving problems about fractions. "After the teacher covered multiplication of two fractions, the class was told the next type of problem, multiplying mixed numbers, was a free ride—a situation in which they were solving a seemingly new type of problem, but one that was not really new because they had previously acquired the knowledge needed to find the product" (p. 4). The next day, a student volunteered another case in which free rides could apply. This situation exemplifies the elements of reflection: the teacher provides a context and encourages students to manage their own learning at the application level. In this way students become self-managed and acquire skills to enhance their own attending, learning, and thinking. In the next section we examine some important skills necessary for reflective thinking on the part of students.

The Reflection Phase Teaches Communication Skills

The National Council of Teachers of English (1996) has called for the creation of classrooms where all children seek to become strategic, critical, independent, and lifelong readers and writers. Researchers (Duffy & Hoffman, 1999; Villaune, 2000) have asserted that the key to successful teaching of communicative arts is the training of independent, spirited teachers who understand that their job is to use methods and materials in ways to accommodate student needs. Such teachers need to teach through what Allen, Brown, and Yatvin (1986) call *informative communication*—describing the way children acquire knowledge through listening, speaking, reading, and writing and use that knowledge to make sense of their world. Such teachers also realize that just as students read to learn, they listen to learn, speak to learn, and write to learn.

Oppenheimer (2003) illustrates the importance of learning as communication by relating a story of a team of American researchers who journeyed to Japan in the late 1990s to attempt to ascertain why Japanese children rank near the top of all countries in standardized achievement tests. What they found surprised them. Instead of classes steeped in memorization and rote learning, the researchers found classes where students were engaged in "active exploration, argument, analysis, and reflection" (p. 360). Further, they found Japanese students didn't rush from topic to topic (as in the United States) but worked in depth on discrete problems, examining some questions for weeks at a time. Oppenheimer notes how much the classroom environment in Japan is at odds with America's notions of what happens in Japanese schools. And it appears that Japanese schools, with the highest-achieving students in the world, are conducting classes very compatible with the guidelines called for by the NCTE.

More than at any other stage, reflective learning depends on informative communication. A 15-year-old high school student recently said, "We need more class discussion. You can read stuff out of the book and answer questions, but you never really learn it unless you talk about it. We need more time to ask questions." Teachers have to let go, learn not to talk, and encourage students to ask their own questions and cooperate with one another in their learning (Barton, 1995).

Listening and speaking reflectively about reading reinforce learning in a social context. Such discussion reflects students' thinking. By listening to and considering the viewpoints of other participants, students may gain different and deeper insights about a topic. Other examples surface and new connections are made. Most important, students gain control of their own learning. Richardson (1999b) reports that students prefer discussion to lecture as a means of deep learning, although many students she interviewed reported that few discussions occurred in their classes. Students are aware of how discussions help them understand what they read. Alvermann and colleagues (1996) recommend that productive small group discussions be fostered by giving students frequent opportunities to discuss what they read; developing a sense of community in the classroom; attending to group dynamics; and building on students' keen sense of conditions that foster good discussion (p. 264). They further caution that teachers should take care to moderate rather than dominate a discussion and find topics that engage students.

The lecture method of instructing is not as popular with students as one might think. Students like discussion and questioning better.

Teachers must realize that the key element of the reflection phase of the PAR Lesson Framework is the type of communication just described. All of the communicative arts are present in some form in good communication. Next we describe what we feel are the most important skills students need to practice in the reflection phase of learning.

IMPORTANT SKILLS FOR REFLECTION

 ## Critical Thinking

Critical thinking is a "buzzword" in education today. Everyone seems to be talking about how to teach critical thinking. Some popular terms are bogus, but critical thinking is a real construct. Many of our students don't think critically as they read.

Oliver Wendell Holmes once said, "Every now and then a man's mind is stretched by a new idea and never shrinks back to its former dimensions." One of the most important ways to have students reflect on reading is to ask them to think critically about what they read. Yet Parker (1991), in a literature review on the pervasiveness of teaching critical thinking in social studies, found that the goal of teaching students critical thinking strategies was largely unrealized. Parker's findings mirror recent studies and national reports that indicate that critical thinking remains a neglected part of instruction. Kirsch and Jungeblut (1986) report that today's young adults are literate but have difficulty with the more complex and challenging reading that is required in their adult life. The study notes the inability of young people to analyze and understand complicated material. Sternberg (1994) laments the lack of correspondence between what is required for critical thinking in adulthood and what is being taught in schools today. Hynd (1999) encourages teachers to expose middle and high school students to historical documents and multiple texts. In this way, they will read different or even opposing views and begin to think like historians. As students experience the process that historians use in researching and writing about history, they may be able to apply the thinking process to other subjects as well. Thinking like a researcher enables students to think critically. By reinforcing the reading experience through critical thinking, teachers can challenge students to think about content material in new ways.

Too often, however, classroom teachers, especially at the elementary level, shy away from teaching critical thinking. One reason for this is that there is no clear definition of the construct. Another reason is that teachers mistakenly believe that *critical* means to find fault and emphasize the negative. Also, critical thinking is a difficult construct to measure through teacher-made tests, and critical thinking skills are not mandated for minimum competency in many subjects. Gronlund (1993) found that teachers are not well trained in the skill of test construction in general, much less in testing for critical thinking. In addition, some teachers have the notion that at-risk learners are not capable of critical thinking. Finally, teachers often say that they do not have adequate time to plan instruction in critical thinking and lack appropriate materials and books to teach it properly. Despite these perceived obstacles, the teaching of critical thinking should not be neglected at any K–12 grade level. This important ability leads to greater success in academic subjects and will be of use to students after graduation. In short, critical thinking is a skill that will aid students in all facets of life, during and beyond the school day.

Critical thinking as an important dimension of learning is emphasized in textbooks, in the research literature, and in published programs. Unks (1985) said that the ability to think critically is one of the most agreed-on educational objectives. But even though almost everyone agrees that some elements of critical thinking need to be taught across the curriculum, the concept remains so vague that educators are not certain about its meaning, about the best ways for classroom teachers to teach it, or even about whether it can be taught. After examining a textbook that contained practice examples in teaching critical thinking, a reviewer once remarked, "It was a good book, but it really didn't contain much critical thinking." This comment underscores the subjective nature of the concept.

The literature, in fact, supports two interpretations of critical thinking. One is a narrow definition of critical thinking as the mastery and use of certain skills necessary for the assessment of statements (Beyer, 1983). These skills take the same form as logic or deduction and may include judging the acceptability of authority statements, judging contradictory statements, and judging whether a conclusion follows necessarily from its premises. A more encompassing definition includes these skills as well as inductive types of skills, such as hypothesis testing, proposition generation, and creative argument (Facione, 1984; Sternberg & Baron, 1985). We agree with the latter definition and emphasize critical thinking in this broader sense throughout this text.

We can clarify our view of critical thinking by studying what happens when the skill is put to use. McPeck (1981, p. 13) identified 10 features of critical thinking:

The World Wide Web is full of conflicting and unsubstantiated information, as well as being a good source of excellent information. Think about developing a WebQuest (see Chapter 4) that helps students think critically and formulate new knowledge within your content area.

1. Critical thinking cannot be taught in the abstract, in isolation. It is not a distinct subject but is taught in content disciplines. It is critical thinking "about something."

2. Although the term may have one correct meaning, the criteria for its correct application vary from discipline to discipline.

3. Critical thinking does not necessarily mean disagreement with, or rejection of, accepted norms.

4. Critical thinking describes the student's skills to think in such a way as to suspend or temporarily reject evidence from a discipline when the student feels data are insufficient to establish the truth of some proposition.

5. Critical thinking includes the thought process involved in problem solving and active thinking.

6. Formal and informal logic are not sufficient for thinking critically.

7. Because critical thinking involves knowledge and skill, a critical thinker in one discipline may not be a critical thinker in another discipline.

8. Critical thinking has both a "task" and an "achievement" phase. It does not necessarily imply success.

9. Critical thinking may include the use of methods and strategies as exemplars.

10. Critical thinking does not have the same scope or boundaries as rationality, but it is a dimension of rational thought.

McPeck suggests that at the core of critical thinking is practicing the skill of reflective skepticism. In our complex and rapidly changing society, the ability to be reflective and skeptical when weighing evidence before making decisions is of great importance. More than 70 years ago John Dewey (1933) spoke of the importance of reflective thinking:

> When a situation arises containing a difficulty or perplexity, the person who finds himself in it may take one of a number of courses. He may dodge it, dropping the activity

that brought it about, turning to something else. He may indulge in a flight of fancy, imagining himself powerful or wealthy, or in some other way in possession of the means that would enable him to deal with the difficulty. Or, finally, he may face the situation. In this case, he begins to reflect (p. 102).

Students in kindergarten through twelfth grade are seldom taught to reflect, to solve problems by "facing the situation," except in published programs on thinking or in "critical thinking" sections of basal reading materials. The first of McPeck's features calls into question the effectiveness of any published program that teaches critical thinking as a skill, isolated from content. Reyes (1986), in a review of a social studies series, found that publishers did not deliver material that developed strong critical thinking, even though they promised it. In another study, researchers (Woodward, Elliott, & Nagel, 1986) found that the critical thinking skills emphasized in elementary basal materials were those that could be most readily tested, such as map and globe skills.

Evidence indicates that teachers do not need published "thinking" programs and that they cannot depend on basal reading materials to teach critical thinking skills. However, they do need to integrate their own critical thinking lessons with those of the textbook they are using. For example, to teach critical thinking, teachers might present study guides that emphasize critical thinking, then have small groups of students practice a problem-solving exercise. In this manner, students are taught critical thinking in a concrete context of carefully guided thinking. Studies indicate that, especially in early adolescence, formal reasoning and thinking can best be taught through the teacher's use of guided prompts such as graphic overviews and study guides, which enable students to structure their thinking more easily (Arlin, 1984; Strahan, 1983).

In addition to asking teachers to emphasize critical thinking, noted educator Art Costa has called for a school environment in which principals and other school leaders encourage teachers "to look carefully at the intelligent behavior of their own students" (Brandt, 1988, p. 13). Further, Costa calls for administrators to model intelligent behavior themselves by spending more time discussing thinking, encouraging teachers themselves to engage in critical thinking, and purchasing materials to support the teaching of critical thinking.

Problem Solving and Decision Making

Research (Montague & Applegate, 2000) attests to the importance of problem-solving skills in content area subjects. Critical thinking leads to problem solving, which in turn leads to effective decision making. Students who use critical thinking will be more effective thinkers; both their creative and contemplative abilities will improve (Parnes & Noller, 1973). We offer the following steps in problem solving:

1. *Gather ideas and information.* Students brainstorm to generate enough information to begin defining the problem. They can play a "reading detective" game or do research to gather information from all possible sources.

2. *Define the problem.* Students recognize the need to resolve a situation that has no apparent solution. They should be asked to clarify the nature of the task and completely describe the situation in writing.

3. *Form tentative conclusions.* This is a creative phase in which students suggest possible solutions from available data.

4. *Test conclusions.* Students discuss in groups which conclusions work best as solutions to the problem. Poor choices are eliminated until workable solutions remain. Students also may establish criteria for evaluating outcomes.

5. *Make a decision.* Students select one of the remaining solutions and give reasons for their choice.

Study guides, such as the one in Activity 7.16, can be constructed by teachers to provide cognitive activities to assist students in using these problem-solving steps. It is especially important to start these types of activities in early elementary classrooms because unsophisticated learners seldom let their minds journey across stories to think about possible similarities.

Group decision making can also be taught through the use of a group-and-label technique. The teacher begins by writing the topic on the board and telling students that they will be reviewing important terminology. Then students volunteer any terms they can think of that fall under the topic heading. The teacher may ask leading questions or even eliminate this step by preparing the list in advance on the board or on a worksheet. Students reorganize the list into smaller lists of items that have something in common. Each of these sublists is then given a label. Students may work individually or in small groups to reorganize and label the words. Activity 7.17 shows how grouping and labeling might work for a first grade social studies unit on communities.

ACTIVITY 7.16 CRITICAL THINKING GUIDE: PROBLEM SOLVING

- Problem arises.
- Why do we need to solve problem?

Ways to Solve Problem	Reasons for Choosing Method
Method 1	Positive outcomes Negative outcomes
Method 2	Positive outcomes Negative outcomes
Method 3	Positive outcomes Negative outcomes
Best way to solve problem	Reasons for choosing to solve problem in this manner

Adapted from a decision-making model by J. McTighe and F. T. Ryman, Jr. (1988), Cueing Thinking in the Classroom: The Promise of Theory-Embedded Tools, *Educational Leadership* 45(7), 18–24.

From a jumbled list of words, the students will be asked to divide the words into four groups, according to their similarities. The teacher will write these four groups of words on the chalkboard. The students will label these groups. These labels will be written by the teacher on the board as titles for the groups of words.

Getting to School

school bus   "The bus driver brings me to school."

walking   "I walk to school with my sister."

Mom's station wagon   "My mom drives me to school in her station wagon."

Daddy's pickup truck   "My daddy drives me to school in his pickup truck."

Bicycle   "I ride my bicycle to school."

Things Used at School

ruler

books   "I learn to read in first grade."

writing tablet   "I write in my tablet."

pencils   "My teacher sharpens my pencil every day."

crayons   "I like to color pictures with my crayons."

glue

scissors   "I cut the paper with my scissors."

Rooms at School

office   "I'm scared to go to the principal's office."

classroom

library   "I like to check out books at the library."

cafeteria   "We eat in the cafeteria."

nurse's clinic

auditorium

gymnasium   "I play in the gym."

People at School

teacher   "My teacher helps me to read."

coach   "The coach is my friend."

librarian   "The librarian always reads us a story."

principal

secretary

nurse   "The nurse is nice."

bus driver

cafeteria workers

janitors and cleaning workers

guidance counselor

Developed by Gail Perrer.

Analyzing Authors' Techniques

Rarely are students asked to examine an author's background to determine whether the author is noted for a particular bias. However, as students evaluate content information, they should note the source of that information. Most important, they should ask who the writer is and what his or her qualifications are. This analysis is especially important when reading from the World Wide Web. Anyone can post a website, but the discriminating reader must decide whether the author is really qualified to do so.

Baumann and Johnson (1984, p. 78) ask that students read with these questions in mind:

1. What is the source? Is anything known about the author's qualifications, the reputation of the publisher, and the date of publication?
2. What is the author's primary aim—information, instruction, or persuasion?
3. Are the statements primarily facts, inferences, or opinions?
4. Does the author rely heavily on connotative words that may indicate a bias?
5. Does the author use negative propaganda techniques?

Students can think about and discuss these questions in groups after they read a narrative or an expository selection. Also, students can be supplied with multiple-choice items, such as those in Activity 7.18, to help them learn to ascertain an author's qualifications for writing accurate and unbiased statements on a subject. Such an activity can be used to begin class discussion on a reading or to initiate debate after reading.

ACTIVITY 7.18   EVALUATING THE RELIABILITY OF SOURCES

Supply students with multiple-choice items like the following. The student checks the source that is the most reliable of the three suggested.

1. Japan has the highest per capita income of any country in the world.
   _____ a. Joan Armentrag, salesperson at Bloomingdale's
   _____ b. Bob Hoskins, star golfer
   _____ c. Dr. Alice MacKenzie, economic analyst, the Ford Foundation

2. Mathematics is of no use to anyone.
   _____ a. Bob Brotig, high school dropout
   _____ b. Bill Johnson, editor, *The Mathematics Teacher*
   _____ c. Susan Winnifred, personnel, the Rand Corporation

3. We have proved that honeybees communicate with each other.
   _____ a. John Bowyer, salesman, Sue Ann Honey Co.

   _____ b. Jane Maupin, high school biology teacher
   _____ c. Martha Daughtry, bank teller

4. Forty-six percent of all married women with children now work outside the home.
   _____ a. Sue Ann Begley, electrician
   _____ b. Carol Radziwell, professional pollster
   _____ c. Joe Blotnik, marriage counselor

5. We must stop polluting our bays and oceans.
   _____ a. Clinton Weststock, president, Save the Bay Foundation
   _____ b. Marjorie Seldon, engineer, Olin Oil Refinery, Gulfport, MI
   _____ c. Carl Kanipe, freelance writer of human interest stories

Separating Fact from Opinion

Separating fact from opinion is another higher-level thinking skill that can be taught to students starting in the early elementary years. To do so, teachers must train students to see relationships between facts, to distinguish fact from opinion, to grasp subtle implications, and to interpret the deeper meanings an author has in mind. Often the reader must bring to bear past experiences and background to derive accurate interpretations. With frequent practice, students can become adept at interpreting an author's point of view and detecting biases. Activity 7.19 presents a guide for fact and opinion to help students distinguish one from the other and to give students practice in writing facts and opinions.

Detecting Propaganda

Skilled readers know how to absorb important information and throw away what is of no use. They are especially adept at recognizing **propaganda**—persuasive, one-sided statements designed to change beliefs or sway opinion. Propaganda can be glaring or extremely subtle, and students need to be made aware, even in the elementary years, of the effects propaganda can have, particularly in the marketplace. The following are the most often used forms of propaganda:

1. Appeal to the bandwagon—aimed at the "masses"—to join a large group that is satisfied with an idea or product. Readers of this kind of propaganda are made to feel left out if they don't go along with the crowd.

2. Emotional language, which plays on the subtle connotations of words carefully chosen to evoke strong feelings.

3. Appeal to prestige—associating a person, product, or concept with something deemed to be important or prestigious by the reader or viewer.

4. Plain-folks appeal—the use of people in an advertisement who seem typical, average, or ordinary (sometimes even dull). The idea is to build trust by depicting people as "regular" folks.

5. Testimonial—the use of a famous person to give heightened credibility to a concept, idea, or product.

Propaganda is rampant on the World Wide Web. Locate a website about a topic in your content area and determine if it meets any of the tests listed here.

Teachers at all grade levels need to prepare students to recognize propaganda techniques. After the basic techniques have been explained, students can be asked to bring in examples of advertisements from newspapers and magazines. In literature classes, students can be asked to discover examples in plays, short stories, and novels. *A Tale of Two Cities,* for example, contains examples of each of these propaganda techniques. Master storytellers like Charles Dickens know how to use such techniques deftly to develop complicated plots.

When discussing environmental issues in a science class, would proponents of industry be likely to take a different position from Greenpeace? How might this difference be manifested in propaganda techniques? Activity 7.20 provides a sample

Directions: Place an *F* by the statements of facts and an *O* by the statements of opinions.

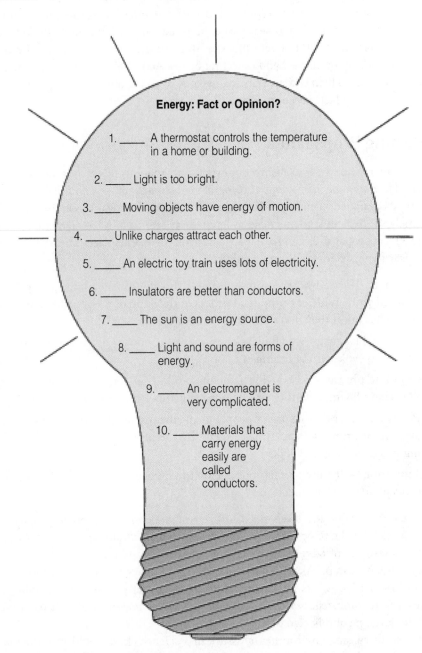

Energy: Fact or Opinion?

1. _____ A thermostat controls the temperature in a home or building.

2. _____ Light is too bright.

3. _____ Moving objects have energy of motion.

4. _____ Unlike charges attract each other.

5. _____ An electric toy train uses lots of electricity.

6. _____ Insulators are better than conductors.

7. _____ The sun is an energy source.

8. _____ Light and sound are forms of energy.

9. _____ An electromagnet is very complicated.

10. _____ Materials that carry energy easily are called conductors.

Developed by Laura Allin.

Match each statement with the propaganda technique used.

    a. Appeal to bandwagon
    b. Emotional language
    c. Appeal to prestige
    d. Plain-folks appeal
    e. Testimonial

_____ **1.** Come on down to Charlie Winkler's Auto before every one of these beauties is sold.

_____ **2.** Michael Jordan, former star basketball player, thinks Nike shoes are the best.

_____ **3.** You'll be glowing all over in your new Evening Time gown.

_____ **4.** Why, people in every walk of life buy our product.

_____ **5.** Join the American Dining Club today, a way of life for those who enjoy the good life.

_____ **6.** Already, over 85 percent of our workers have given to this worthy cause.

_____ **7.** I'll stack our doughnut makers up against any others as the best in the business!

_____ **8.** Even butcher Fred Jones likes our new frozen yogurt coolers.

_____ **9.** One must drink our wine to appreciate the truly fine things in life.

_____ **10.** Lift the weights that Arnold Schwarzenegger lifts—a sure way to a better body.

---

activity for teaching students to recognize propaganda. Students are asked to match each statement to the propaganda technique it employs.

STRATEGIES THAT PROMOTE REFLECTIVE THINKING

 BRAINSTORMING

Brainstorming—whole-class or group discussion of a topic in order to reach consensus or solve a problem—enhances reflective thinking and is appropriate to any grade level. Betts (1991) notes that brainstorming and similar types of student interactions are important for any constructivist classroom environment. Brainstorming is both reflective and creative in nature. Brainstorming sessions can last from 10 minutes to an hour and can be designed to teach any of the skills discussed in this chapter. An especially productive brainstorming session is one in which small groups of students list as many possible alternative solutions to a problem as they can. Group captains are chosen to report findings to the entire class. The teacher lists on the chalkboard alternatives that the students deem worthy. Discussion then centers on how to narrow the choices to one or two and why the final choices are the best ones. An important consideration is the size of the brainstorming group. Five-person groups seem to work best; however, three- and four-person groups are also suitable. The most vocal students tend to dominate groups of six students or more.

The "Ready Reading Reference Bookmark" (see Figure 7.4) developed by Kapinus (1986) can be used to get students ready to brainstorm after reading a passage. In the "After you read" section, students can use brainstorming to perform the five thinking operations called for: retelling, summarizing, asking, picturing, and deciding. Students also can brainstorm the "While you read" and "If you don't understand" operations at other points in the lesson—before reading, for example, or after reading specific sections.

TRIP CARDS

Another activity that uses cooperative groups and student discussion to build reflection skills is *TRIP (Think/Reflect in Pairs)*. For this activity, the teacher divides students into pairs. Students share information on TRIP cards, which list propaganda techniques or situational problems. Answers are printed on the back of the cards for

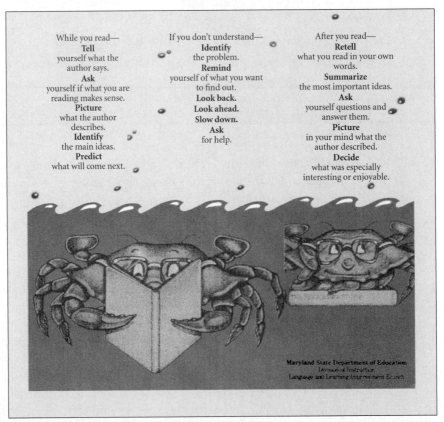

FIGURE 7.4

Ready Reading Reference Bookmark

While you read—
Tell
yourself what the author says.
Ask
yourself if what you are reading makes sense.
Picture
what the author describes.
Identify
the main ideas.
Predict
what will come next.

If you don't understand—
Identify
the problem.
Remind
yourself of what you want to find out.
Look back.
Look ahead.
Slow down.
Ask
for help.

After you read—
Retell
what you read in your own words.
Summarize
the most important ideas.
Ask
yourself questions and answer them.
Picture
in your mind what the author described.
Decide
what was especially interesting or enjoyable.

Maryland State Department of Education
Division of Instruction
Language and Learning Improvement Branch

immediate reinforcement. Points may be assigned for correct answers, with a designated number of points needed for a good grade in the class.

In a different TRIP activity, students are presented problems from a textbook. They first solve the problem in pairs, then write the problem on the front and the answer on the back of a card. In this manner, students create their own TRIP files for reinforcement or future use. Activity 7.21 shows eight TRIP cards made by an algebra class.

MULTITEXT ACTIVITIES

Many teachers' manuals suggest multitext activities as a way to encourage reflective thinking. Often teachers feel too rushed to cover curriculum and skip this enriching resource, although research supports the use of many reading materials to solidify learning about a topic. In Chapter 6 we described multitext activities in the preparation stage of PAR. A multitext approach also helps readers reflect by extending their knowledge of a topic after study.

LITERARY GIFT EXCHANGES

Schadt (1989) describes the **literary gift exchange** as a way to enrich readers. Each student brings to class an object reminiscent of a character or action from literature read in the content area and exchanges it with a designated partner. Students must be able to explain their gifts. Schadt noticed that students began to reread material after he initiated the exchange procedure.

POSTGRAPHIC ORGANIZERS

Designing postgraphic organizers is another reflection activity that students of all ages enjoy. We recommend the following steps to help students produce their own

---

ACTIVITY 7.21 TRIP CARDS FOR ALGEBRA I

FACTORING POLYNOMIALS

Front of Card	Back of Card	Front of Card	Back of Card
$(x + 2)(x + 9)$	$x^2 + 11x + 18$	$(5x + 2y)(x - 2y)$	$5x^2 - 8xy - 4y^2$
$(x + 1)(5x + 3)$	$5x^2 + 8x + 3$	Prime	$x^2 - 12x - 30$
$(2x + 5)(2x + 1)$	$4x^2 + 12x + 5$	$(x - 2)(x + 5)$	$x^2 + 3x - 10$
$(x + 7)(x - 7)$	$x^2 - 49$	$(x + 2)(x - 6)$	$x^2 - 4x - 12$

Developed by Ronda Clancy.

---

graphic organizers in order to create purpose for reading and to help one another construct meaning from the text after the reading:

1. Students preview the reading to determine the structure and main ideas.

2. Students work in small groups to hypothesize about what form the graphic organizer should take.

3. Students read the text silently, each student gathering information to be included in the group's graphic representation.

4. Groups meet to discuss the organization of the information each member has gathered. Each group makes a large model to be presented to the class.

5. Groups present their finished product to the class. A group of secondary advanced placement chemistry students created the postgraphic organizer shown in Activity 7.22. They titled the postgraphic organizer "Fluids in a Nutshell." Activity 7.23 is a graphic organizer for a first grade class.

TEXT LOOKBACKS

Many students feel it is wrong to reread a passage; we have to get students out of this mind-set.

Garner (1985) discusses the importance of reexamining text—backtracking, or **text lookback**—in overcoming memory difficulties. There is evidence that both children and adults fail to use this strategy (Garner, Macready, & Wagoner, 1985), even though research (Amlund, Kardash, & Kulhavy, 1986) shows that repeated readings and reinspection of text make a significant difference in recall.

Ruth Strang, the great reading educator, once remarked that she was disappointed when she entered a school library and found students reading for long periods without looking up to reflect on what they were reading and not glancing back over material during their study. We recommend that teachers ask students to use the lookback strategy after a reading by working in groups to clarify confusing points. For instance, students in a social studies class can be asked to reinspect a chapter on economic interdependence to find why credit and credit buying are so important to the American economy and to economic growth. Students can then be asked to write a group summary of what the text says about the important concept of credit.

For both summaries and text lookback, Garner (1985) stresses the following:

1. Some ideas are more important than others.

2. Some ideas can (and must) be ignored.

3. Students need to be taught how to use titles and topic sentences.

4. Students need to learn that ideas cross boundaries of sentences.

5. "Piecemeal" reading that focuses on comprehending one sentence at a time is not conducive to summarizing or gaining ideas from text.

6. Rules of summarization need to be learned and practiced.

7. Students must be taught how and when to apply both summarization and lookback strategies.

8. These strategies cannot be adequately accomplished in a hurried classroom atmosphere and environment.

FLUIDS IN A NUTSHELL

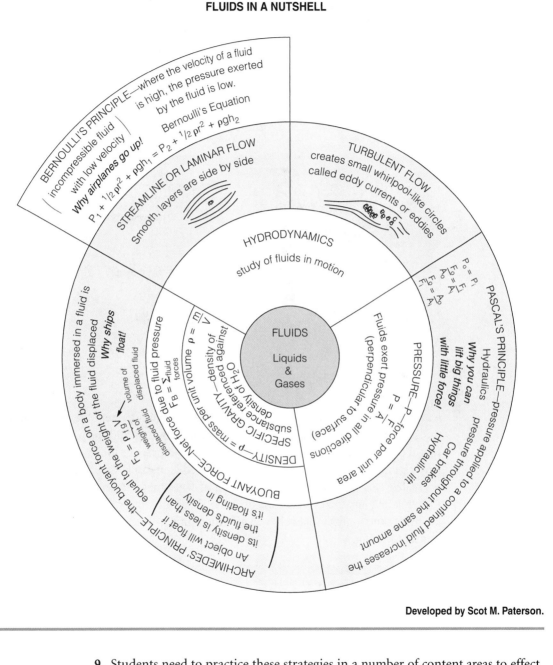

Developed by Scot M. Paterson.

9. Students need to practice these strategies in a number of content areas to effect transfer.

Garner and associates (Garner et al., 1984) also maintain that readers should be taught the following: why to use lookbacks (because readers can't remember everything);

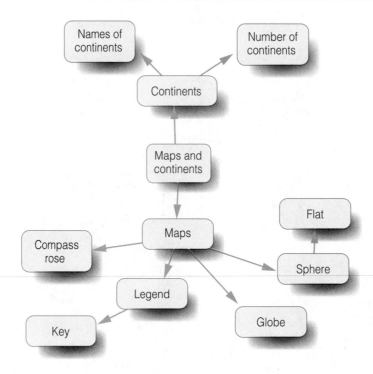

when to use them (when the question calls for information from the text); and where to use them (where skimming or scanning will help one find the portion of the text that should be read carefully). Next, readers should practice looking back for answers to questions asked after the reading is completed. Lookbacks are necessary when readers realize that they didn't understand all of what they read. Good readers evaluate their reading and make decisions on whether to look back. But poor readers rarely have this skill, so text lookbacks will give them much-needed practice in this aspect of critical thinking.

ONE-MINUTE SUMMARY

 This chapter described activities to be used in both the assistance and reflection phases of the PAR Lesson Framework for improving comprehension and retention of learning. We considered factors that facilitate comprehension: attention to constructivist principles of learning, using segments of text to facilitate "small chunks of learning," text features, and questioning strategies. Comprehension is enhanced when readers attend to all four of the factors mentioned. This chapter described activities such as the directed reading–thinking activity and guided reading procedure for teaching short segments of text. Also detailed were strategies for teaching text organization and for constructing and asking questions.

The importance of the reflection phase of learning in creating autonomous learners was explained. Also explained was how communication is the key element of the reflection phase of learning. These key skills of reflection were explained: critical thinking, problem solving, decision making, and analyzing authors' techniques of writing. Finally, strategies to teach reflection were described such as brainstorming, TRIP cards, multitext activities, literary gift exchanges, postgraphic organizers, and text lookbacks.

PAR Online

For a direct link to the resources below, click on the web links option of the Chapter 7 resources on the book companion website:

- Learn how to evaluate the web
- Visit Michael's Internet Finding Tips
- Thinking critically

END-OF-CHAPTER ACTIVITIES

Assisting Comprehension

1. Review some questions that you recently constructed for students to answer. Do they focus equally on each of the three levels of comprehension explained in this chapter? If they do not, what level of comprehension predominates?

2. Having read this chapter, what ideas for appropriate activities to assist your students' comprehension do you now have?

3. Why is it important to get students to reflect over the reading?

Reflecting on Your Reading

Standard 1.4 of the International Reading Association Standards for Teachers and Reading Professionals (2003) states that teachers need to demonstrate knowledge of teaching comprehension, a major component of reading. Take some time to reflect on how this chapter has helped your teaching concerning ways to (a) assist students to comprehend and (b) help students learn to reflect over reading and thereby build comprehension.

*All wish to know, but none
wish to pay the fee.*

JUVENAL

Study Skills

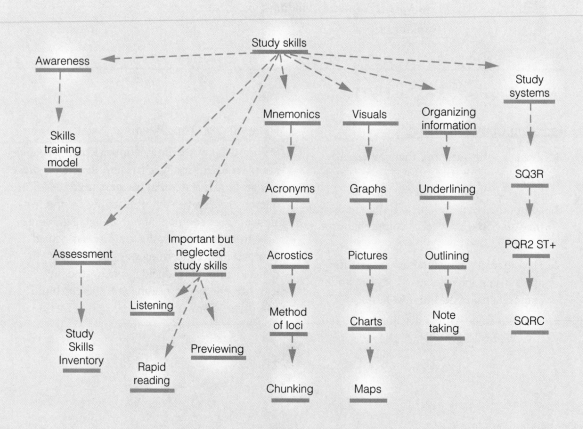

PREPARING TO READ

1. Do you teach study skills as you teach content? If so, list the study skills you teach. Now see how many are described in this chapter. Perhaps you can add to your repertoire of study skills training by reading and studying this chapter.

2. Following is a list of terms used in this chapter. Some may be familiar to you in a general context, but in this chapter they may be used in unfamiliar ways. Rate your knowledge by placing a plus sign (+) in front of those you are sure that you know, a check mark (✓) in front of those you have some knowledge about, and a zero (0) in front of those you don't know. Be ready to locate them in the chapter, and pay special attention to their meanings.

_____ skills training model
_____ previewing
_____ massed study
_____ mnemonics
_____ acronym
_____ acrostic
_____ saccadic eye movements
_____ skimming
_____ scanning
_____ mental push-ups
_____ rapid reading drills
_____ preview and rapid reading drill
_____ two-column note-taking system
_____ study system

OBJECTIVES

As you read this chapter, focus your attention on the following purposes. You will

1. understand the importance of developing students' ability to use study skills at all grade levels.

2. learn the importance of the skills training model.

3. be able to assess students at all grade levels in their use of study skills.

4. understand the importance of previewing and learn how to preview.

5. understand study strategies such as mnemonics and associational learning.

6. learn about teaching visual representations and other visual aids.

7. understand and be able to use rapid reading and previewing.

8. be able to show students how to organize materials through underlining, outlining, and note taking.

9. understand the systems of study described in this chapter and be able to use them in your own classroom.

*T*he opening quotation for this chapter is interesting because it definitely applies to study skills. Study is difficult and time consuming, and many students do not want to apply themselves sufficiently to become productive learners. Teachers can help students by providing opportunities whereby study leads to learning interesting information and where the payoff is worth the effort expended. Unfortunately, most teachers do not seem to know about or value study strategies and are unsure how to integrate study skills with content (Jackson & Cunningham, 1994). This is so despite research showing that students who use a range of study skills achieve greater success in school (Purdie & Hattie, 1999) and research suggesting that good study habits lead to academic success (Jones, Slate, & Marini, 1995). Indeed, a survey conducted by the American School Counselor Association (2000) had some alarming findings:

- Seventy percent of teachers say their students have poor study skills.
- Sixty percent of guidance counselors say students are not prepared adequately to do homework assignments.
- Around 50 percent of schools do not offer study skills courses.
- Of those that do, only 11 percent require students to take the course.
- Even though many counselors feel it is most effective for students to study in a group, 57 percent of students do their homework at home; only 9 percent study in a group.

Research suggests that study skill intervention programs do work (Hattie, Biggs, & Purdie, 1996). In this chapter we present many study skill strategies that have been shown to make a positive difference in learning and retention. We also explain the importance of study and discuss special study systems that enhance student learning. Strategies explained in this chapter represent a special emphasis on the reflection phase of the PAR Lesson Framework, which facilitates greater retention of the reading matter. The best place to teach students how to be reflective in studying is in the classroom. Because teachers have little control over study behaviors outside class, they must provide careful guidance and practice that will carry over to independent study.

THE IMPORTANCE OF STUDY SKILLS

In 1917 Thorndike described the process of reading a paragraph. Educators today can still profit from his remarkably clear interpretation of the reading process:

> Understanding a paragraph is like solving a problem in mathematics. It consists in selecting the right elements of the situation and putting them together in the right relations, and also with the right amount of weight or influence or force for each. The mind is assailed as it were by every word in the paragraph. It must select, repress, soften, emphasize, correlate, and organize, all under the influence of the right mental set or purpose or demand. (p. 329)

As Thorndike suggests, reading can be seen as a problem-solving task. This task can be difficult because it requires readers to have a positive attitude toward the purpose for reading, the demands of the text, and their own background experience. Most important, the reader must be in a good frame of mind—have a good mental set—and must have clarity of thought before beginning to read. Reading for study cannot occur unless these conditions are met. In short, the combination of reading and study is a disciplined inquiry that demands training over many years of schooling.

The definition Harris and Hodges (1995) provide in the Literacy Dictionary states,

> *Study skills* is a general term for those techniques and strategies that help a person read or listen for specific purposes with the intent to remember; commonly, following directions, locating, selecting, organizing, and retaining information, interpreting typographic and graphic aids, and reading flexibly.

As you read this chapter, notice how many study skills we discuss can be taught in the early elementary grades—some as early as first grade!

Thus study skills are now viewed as a major component of reading processing skills, the problem-solving aspect of Thorndike's definition.

Although children are taught to read at an early age, often there is no concomitant emphasis on study or study skills (Durkin, 1979; Schallert & Kleiman, 1979). In middle school—or even high school—a teacher may announce that for a period of time students will be trained in how to study and better retain the information they read. We find two problems with this approach: (1) It is isolated from the reading process and transmits the message that study isn't really connected to reading. (2) This focus on study skills in middle school or high school transmits the message that study skills are pertinent and applicable only late in one's education.

There is growing evidence (Borkowski, Weyhing, & Carr, 1988; Salembier, 1999; Schunk & Rice, 1992) that convincing students of the value of study strategies will both promote student achievement and ensure that students will keep using strategies. Basic study skills should be introduced to children as early as first grade (Strauss, 2003). Making information relevant to students at all grade levels increases their motivation to study (Frymier & Schulman, 1995). When teaching study skills, teachers should remember that what is needed is a student-centered approach, based on constructivist theory (discussed in Chapter 7). Kauchak and Eggen (1998) list four key components to learning that we believe teachers should keep in mind when teaching study skills:

1. Learners construct knowledge for themselves rather than waiting for the teacher to give them knowledge piecemeal.
2. New learning builds on prior knowledge.
3. Learning is enhanced by social interaction.
4. Authentic learning promotes meaningful learning.

One last note about the importance of study skills needs to be made. We will discuss the affective domain of learning and one's will to learn in Chapter 12. We maintain that one's will to learn is very important in creating a successful learning atmosphere. Corno and colleagues (1982) discuss the idea that teaching study skills gives students the means to learn, and doing so might also give them the will to learn. We cannot agree more. Teaching study skills is important not only in imparting the skill itself, but also in building in students the confidence to master any task.

MAKING STUDENTS AWARE OF STUDY SKILLS

The most important first step in teaching students study skills is to make them aware that they are learning a new study skill. To make students aware of the learning strategies they are employing, teachers should use a **skills training model:**

1. *Explain the skill being taught.* Explain to your students that they will be asked to think in a certain way, to make judgments, and to practice effective thinking.

2. *Introduce the lesson.* When introducing the content lesson, make certain that new information is related to the students' prior knowledge.

3. *Develop structured practice using the skill.* Explain how to use the skill appropriately. Have students practice using the skill for 20 to 30 minutes.

4. *Summarize how the skill was used in the content lesson.* Explain again why the skill is important for the students to master and how it helped them understand the lesson better.

5. *Continue practice with the skill.* Repeat these steps in at least five additional lessons. For elementary and middle school students, this practice should be with different content lessons, to ensure transfer of the skill to other disciplines.

Notice how the skills training model is compatible with the PAR Lesson Framework.

At any of the five steps listed here, the teacher can reference the skill that is being learned in the lesson. For instance, an anticipation guide (explained in Chapter 6) or previewing will teach the skill of predicting outcomes from printed material. When teachers use this paradigm they provide guided practice and direct teaching to help students acquire skills, internalize skills by repeated practice, and transfer skills to other learning contexts. When students know the plan of the lesson and the skill being taught, teachers can facilitate improvement in students' thinking ability. This type of teacher intervention is a necessary step in improving cognitive ability. Pearson and Tierney (1983), however, assessed the instructional paradigm most used by teachers— which features the use of many practice materials, little explanation of cognitive tasks, little interaction with students about the nature of specific tasks, and strong emphasis on one correct answer—to determine the extent to which teachers supply answers if there is any confusion over a task. Not surprisingly, Pearson and Tierney concluded that such a paradigm is ineffective. The skills training model creates an opportunity for students to assess, regulate, and evaluate their own comprehension, a crucial component of the complex process of reading (Meeks, 1991). Every study skill that we describe in this chapter can be introduced to students through the skills training model.

ASSESSING STUDY SKILLS

Most standardized achievement tests include subtests of study skills. However, these subtests are usually limited in scope, measuring the students' knowledge of "standard" items such as reference skills, alphabetization, and the ability to read maps, charts, and graphs. Often neglected are important skills such as following directions, presenting a report, test taking, note taking, and memory training. To address the need for a broader assessment of study skills, Richardson, Rhodes, and Robnolt (2004) used Harris and Hodges's definition of study skills (1995) to create seven categories of study skills. To clarify what each of these categories might mean and include, they referred to Rogers's list of study skills (1984). The study skills checklist they developed (see Activity 8.1) asks students to think about whether they use the skill with electronic and paper materials. Content area teachers could design tests for each of the areas on this checklist or have a reading specialist help question children, individually or in small groups, on how often and how comfortably they use the skills listed. A brief survey will most likely provide enough information for teachers to realize what study skills their students really know and use.

A particular area of concern in assessing study skills should be assessing homework study habits. Schneider and Stephenson (1999) call students today directionless, noting that they spend as much as 20 percent of time alone and that 60 percent of mothers work outside the home. The researchers postulate that students today are particularly disadvantaged when it comes to homework. Besides not having strong parental guidance, students also encounter homework that is too difficult or boring and not of any inherent interest to them. Teachers can help students learn how to better handle homework. One way is to challenge students to study homework in their usual way for a block of time (dependent on the age of the students) and then in the teacher's way for the same amount of time. While studying, students note how much they accomplish. Usually they discover by experimenting that at least some of the teacher's tips about a study environment really do help them study.

For many students, changing the study environment at home might be difficult. We work with children in inner cities who have witnessed murders, dodged bullets, and gone to bed hungry on numerous occasions. Experimenting with study environments at home will not work under such conditions, but arranging for the school or community to provide a study environment in another location may help (for example, in the school after hours or in a local community center or church).

Studies show that the amount of time spent doing homework has a positive correlation with achievement (Keith et al., 1986). Because of homework's importance, and because much study is done independently in the home, teachers also may want to assess how parents help students study and how students evaluate their own study habits. Activity 8.2 on page 248 provides examples of these kinds of assessment for kindergartners and first graders. The survey can be adapted for any grade level. Teachers who have compared parents' to students' responses have discovered a difference in perception of the two groups. For instance, parents indicate that students do have a special place to study (see "Survey of Parents," item 1), but students indicate

When teachers can post a website where homework is placed, the contents can be printed out or placed on disk so study environment supervisors in other locations can help students do the assignments.

Please complete the following checklist. Answer the questions in both columns.

Study Skills for Reading	How often do you use this skill when reading text from the computer screen? Circle one. A = always F = frequently S = sometimes N = never	How often do you use this skill when reading a paper text? Circle one. A = always F = frequently S = sometimes N = never
Following directions	A F S N	A F S N
I read to understand important information.	A F S N	A F S N
I read to understand important relationships.	A F S N	A F S N
I read to understand important details.	A F S N	A F S N
Locating information		
I can use an online library catalog.	A F S N	A F S N
I can find reference materials.	A F S N	A F S N
I can use a card catalog.	Not applicable	A F S N
I can use a search engine to find information.	A F S N	Not applicable
I can find information in a dictionary.	A F S N	A F S N
I can use guide words or letters to find a word.	A F S N	A F S N
I can find word origins.	A F S N	A F S N
I can find information in a preface.	A F S N	A F S N
I can find information in a table of contents.	A F S N	A F S N
I can find information in a book chapter.	A F S N	A F S N
I can find information in headings.	A F S N	A F S N
I can find information in footnotes.	A F S N	A F S N
I can find information in a glossary.	A F S N	A F S N
I can find information in an index.	A F S N	A F S N
I can find information in an appendix.	A F S N	A F S N
I can find information in an encyclopedia.	A F S N	A F S N
I can find a phone number.	A F S N	A F S N
I can find a map and driving directions.	A F S N	A F S N
I can find specific information in a newspaper.	A F S N	A F S N
I can find information using book parts such as title, author's name, edition, and publisher.	A F S N	A F S N
I can find information about the copyright of a text.	A F S N	A F S N

Activity 8.1 *(continued)*

Study Skills for Reading	A = always F = frequently S = sometimes N = never				A = always F = frequently S = sometimes N = never			
When I want to show that something is important, I highlight the text so it will pop out at me.	A	F	S	N	A	F	S	N
When I want to show that something is important, I underline the text so it will pop out at me.	A	F	S	N	A	F	S	N
When I want to show that something is important, I mark the text in another way that will pop out at me (bold, text changes, etc.).	A	F	S	N	A	F	S	N
Selecting information								
I can use subheadings in text to find what I need to know.	A	F	S	N	A	F	S	N
I ask myself questions while I am reading and studying so I can remember better.	A	F	S	N	A	F	S	N
Organizing information								
I can create a way to remember information, such as mnemonic aids (like 3Rs = read, review, reflect).	A	F	S	N	A	F	S	N
I study in a way that follows a system: such as Survey, Question, Read, Recite, Review= SQ3R).	A	F	S	N	A	F	S	N
Retaining information								
I remember what I read by repeating the information.	A	F	S	N	A	F	S	N
I remember what I read by taking notes.	A	F	S	N	A	F	S	N
I remember what I read by drawing a picture or creating a graphic.	A	F	S	N	A	F	S	N
I remember what I read by writing a summary.	A	F	S	N	A	F	S	N
I remember what I read by making an outline.	A	F	S	N	A	F	S	N
I use text editing to make notes on electronic text.	A	F	S	N	Not applicable			
Interpreting typographic and graphic aids								
I can usually look at a picture, chart, comic, or graph and understand it.	A	F	S	N	A	F	S	N
Reading flexibly								
I use search and find to locate information.	A	F	S	N	Not applicable			
I can change how fast I read when I want to find only one piece of information.	A	F	S	N	A	F	S	N
I can change how fast I read when I need to think and remember important information.	A	F	S	N	A	F	S	N
I know how to preview—read over the text quickly to get the general idea.	A	F	S	N	A	F	S	N
Demonstrating good study habits								
I know how to select a good environment for study: Few distractions; equipment at hand; plan time to study effectively; use time to study effectively	A	F	S	N	A	F	S	N

Developed by J. S. Richardson, J. Rhodes, and V. Robnolt (2004). Used with permission.

Survey of Parents

Please circle YES or NO in front of each statement.

YES   NO   **1.** My child has a special place to study. Where?
    _____

YES   NO   **2.** My child has an independent reading time each night.
    When? _____

YES   NO   **3.** My child watches television while completing homework.

YES   NO   **4.** I always supervise my child's homework period.

YES   NO   **5.** I sometimes help my child with homework.

YES   NO   **6.** I listen to my child read.

YES   NO   **7.** My child has a set bedtime. When? _____

YES   NO   **8.** I check over my child's homework.

YES   NO   **9.** My child has a place to put materials that must be returned
    to school.

YES   NO   **10.** My child eats breakfast daily.

YES   NO   **11.** I discuss with my child how he or she does in school
    each day.

YES   NO   **12.** I read to my child often.

Survey of Students

Circle the true sentences as you read them.

1. I bring my books to school each day.
2. I listen in class.
3. I read the directions when I begin my work.
4. I ask questions when I don't know what to do.
5. I do my homework every night.
6. I have a special place to do my homework.
7. No one helps me with my homework.
8. I watch TV when I do my homework.
9. I bring my homework to school.
10. I am a good student.

These two surveys were adapted with permission from surveys done by Cornelia Hill.

that they do not ("Survey of Students," item 6). Discussing such findings early in the school year, perhaps at a back-to-school meeting, can help establish positive study environments from the beginning of the school year.

The surveys in Activity 8.2 also provide several indicators about environments conducive to studying. Without a good study environment, study strategies will not be very effective. The only environment over which the teacher has control is his or her classroom. Modeling in the classroom the study skills presented in the next part of this chapter will benefit students as they learn new study strategies.

THE NEGLECTED STUDY SKILL OF LISTENING

Listening is the foundation for all other study skills, and it can enhance learning in any classroom. Listening is a prerequisite for taking good notes from an oral presentation. Listening in conjunction with teaching keywords and previewing has been found to increase oral reading proficiency among low-achieving students (O'Donnell, Weber, & McLaughlin, 2003; Skinner, Cooper, & Cole, 1997). Gold (1981) describes the directed listening technique as a strategy for motivating and guiding students to improve listening. Teachers motivate students before the lesson by asking them to listen for certain information in the lecture or in the oral reading. In this prelecture discussion phase, students brainstorm areas of interest and questions to be answered. Teachers then deliver a lecture or read to the students portions of a chapter from a textbook. In this way, students are trained to know what they must listen for and what they are expected to learn from listening.

Such an activity provides a means of study in a social context, which learners often find productive.

As a variation, listening guides, similar to the extended anticipation guides explained in Chapter 11, can be constructed to point to parts of the lecture or oral reading that need to be emphasized. In this manner students are taught to listen more carefully for details and key points. Through such an active listening strategy, even primary students can be trained to be better listeners. Activity 8.3 presents such a listening guide for a high school class on the topic of genetics.

Alvermann (1987a) developed a strategy called *listen-read-discuss (LRD)*. With this technique, the teacher first lectures on a selected portion of material. Students then read that portion with the purpose of comparing lecture and written content. Afterward, students and teacher discuss the lecture and reading. LRD works best to promote discussion if the material is well organized.

ACTIVITY 8.3 LISTENING ACTIVITY: GENETICS

Listening purpose: Listen for the three aspects of genetics.
Directions: As you listen to the lecture, circle all of the topics you hear discussed. Feel free to make notes on the subjects as you hear about them in the lecture.

Heredity	**DNA**	**Mutation**
Traits	Replication	Inbreeding
Genes	Proteins	Hybridization
Dominant	Chromosomes	Producing insulin
Recessive		Cloning
Genotype		
Homozygous		
Heterozygous		
Phenotype		

Note: After listening to the lecture, get together with several of your classmates and see if they circled the same words you did. Discuss the meanings of the words.

The *student listening activity (SLA)* (Choate & Rakes, 1987) is another technique for improving listening skills. In this strategy the teacher first discusses concepts in the material and sets a clear purpose for listening, then reads aloud, interspersing several prediction cues with the reading. Finally, the teacher questions students about what they heard, using three levels of questions: factual, inferential, and applied.

Another technique developed by the authors is *First Step to Note Taking,* which promotes listening and purpose setting and offers practice in group note-taking strategies. Thus First Step to Note Taking is a listening activity, a note-taking activity, and a cooperative grouping activity. The activity can be modified for teacher-based instruction or for an independent student learning experience, depending on the ages of students. The activity consists of five steps:

1. Either the teacher or a student defines a listening purpose. If, for instance, the student is completing the activity for independent practice, perhaps he or she will listen to the evening news to identify the major stories and two significant details of each story.

2. Listening with a purpose commences. Students might listen to the teacher read, listen to the news on television, or listen to a tape recording, for example. No writing is allowed during the listening.

3. The students react by listing what they heard in relationship to the stated purpose. Responses are now recorded, but no modifications are made.

4. Students listen to the material again, with the list in sight. No writing is allowed during the listening. (If students listened to the evening news, then either a recording of that news broadcast or a late-evening news show would provide an appropriate second listening.)

5. Individually or in small groups, students edit the list—adding, deleting, or modifying information—and organize it into a logical pattern. They have now generated notes for study.

> Students can organize the listening and note taking in two-column format, as shown in a later example in this chapter when we discuss two-column note taking.

PREVIEWING: THE MOST IMPORTANT STUDY SKILL

Chapter 7 describes the directed reading–thinking activity (DR–TA: Stauffer, 1969a), which is a technique that teachers can use to model correct reading process. Fundamental to the DR–TA is **previewing,** a process that is important for clarifying thinking before students read textbook material. Previewing has been found to help improve comprehension and achievement in students, especially low-achieving students (O'Donnell et al., 2003; Skinner et al., 1997).

In the previewing stage, students select strategies appropriate to the depth and duration of study needed. To select proper strategies—whether note taking, underlining, or rapid reading—students must spend time clarifying their thinking about the topic. Then they need to ask themselves questions such as the following:

How interested am I in this selection?

How deeply do I need to think and concentrate to learn this material?

How fast can I read this material?

What do I still need to learn about this topic?

Teachers might take students step-by-step through the previewing phase, then ask them to write down how they will study the material.

Just as one might size up a piece of clothing and decide whether it is too big and needs altering, a reader can size up a reading selection and realize that "mental alterations" are needed. Such assessment is the purpose of previewing. Sometimes the preview yields all the information the reader needs, so the material need not be read. In many instances, however, the preview builds anticipation for material that is not familiar to the reader.

The Preview Process

Previewing to clarify thinking reduces uncertainty about the reading assignment, allowing students to gain confidence, read in a more relaxed manner, gain interest, and improve their attitude toward the material. In addition, previewing strategies enable students to decide how much of the material is in their own background of experience. As a result of the previewing strategy, learners are clearer about what they know and what they need to know. In effect, they set a purpose for reading before they begin.

When previewing a technical chapter or a report, students should examine and think about the following:

1. *Title and subtitle*—We need to discover the overall topic of the chapter or article. This part of the chapter is often skipped entirely by students. This is where the student should ask herself what she knows about the chapter as a whole and what this chapter has to do with the chapter that went before it. What will this chapter be about?

2. *Author's name*—We might ask whether the author is a recognized authority. What is the author's point of view?

3. *Copyright*—This is examined to see whether the material is current.

4. *Introduction*—Here we find out what the author intends to talk about. The main points that will be covered usually are discussed here, and sometimes objectives and goals are stated in the body of the paragraph(s) or highlighted in marginal notes.

5. *Headings and subheadings*—Identification of the topics of the sections that follow (forming these headings into questions gives purpose to the reading).

6. *Graphs, charts, maps, tables, pictures*—These are an aid in understanding specific aspects of the chapter. Important information might be gleaned here that is nowhere else in the reading.

7. *Summary*—Here we get an overview of what has been discussed in the reading. This is important to study in the preview to get a sense of where the entire reading is going.

8. *Questions*—These are examined to review important topics covered in the chapter.

Students enjoy previewing, and their interest in the reading material is greatly heightened by using the strategy.

In practicing with a group or a class, the teacher assists students in deciding what they already know about the material and what they need to learn. The reader turns those things that are not known into questions, which provide a purpose for reading. Students reading fiction need to preview the title, illustrations, and introduction in order to make hypotheses about the outcome of the story. This preview heightens suspense and aids in maintaining interest. Most important, predicting story structure gives the reader a purpose for reading—namely, to find out whether the predictions are correct.

Whether students are reading fiction or expository or informational material, previewing forces them to do the sophisticated kind of thinking required for drawing inferences and developing interpretations. Thus students think critically about the chapter or story before the reading, operating at times at higher levels of cognition.

We find that students at any level generally will not preview material on their own unless teachers model and provide practice in this important skill. First, teachers should make students aware that they are teaching both content and the strategy of previewing. Students can be made aware by following the skills training model described earlier in this chapter. Second, teachers need to review with students the table of contents of a textbook to help them discover the theme or structure of the course material. In this way, students will get the gist or overall idea of what the author is attempting to teach in the textbook. The teacher might ask, for example, why the author chose to organize the table of contents in a particular manner.

Students can learn to preview through using a preview guide that is easy to construct. Students fill in the guide as they preview the chapter, or part of a chapter, under the guidance of the teacher. Activity 8.4 is an example of such a guide.

For each new reading or unit of instruction, the teacher can ask students to return to the table of contents to see how this particular segment of learning fits into the overall textbook scheme or pattern. Teachers with a class of poor readers can model the previewing strategy by using preview questions they have constructed and annotated. Previewing can be done for any type of reading material, including a website. Some of the eight steps in previewing may not apply to a particular website, but most will. Activity 8.5 on page 255 shows how to preview a web page to get the most out of research and study.

VISUAL LEARNING AS A STUDY SKILL

 Visual representations are visual aids and graphic clues designed to help readers comprehend a content textbook. Yet one of the most common responses of students when questioned about such aids is that they "skip over them" (Gillespie, 1993). It is very important for teachers to teach visual representations and never skip them. So often, readers incorrectly assume that such visuals represent a "free page"! Richardson and Forget (1995) illustrate the calculations that Mark Twain used in "proving" that the

1. Title of chapter _____   From page _____ to page _____
    Subtitle of chapter_____

2. Name of author(s) _____   Is author an authority?
    _____   Proof: _____

3. Copyright _____   Is material current? _____
                                          _____

4. Introduction _____   Tell what you know after reading this
    _____   introduction: _____
    _____   _____
    _____   _____

5. Headings and subheadings _____   Subheading: _____
    _____   _____

                                          Page: _____

                                          Subheading: _____
                                          _____

                                          Page: _____

                                          Subheading: _____
                                          _____

                                          Page: _____

                                          Subheading: _____
                                          _____

                                          Page: _____

                                          Subheading: _____
                                          _____

                                          Page: _____

                                          Subheading: _____
                                          _____

                                          Page: _____

6. Graphs, charts, maps, and pictures   Page: _____
    _____   Description: _____

                                          Page: _____
                                          Description: _____

                                          Page: _____
                                          Description: _____

(continued) ➤

7. Summary _____   Write about the summary in your
    _____   own words: _____
    Where summary section is found: _____   _____
    _____   _____
    _____   _____
                                          _____
                                          _____

8. Vocabulary terms   Word: _____
                                          Page found: _____
                                          Meaning: _____
                                          _____

                                          Word: _____
                                          Page found: _____
                                          Meaning: _____
                                          _____

                                          Word: _____
                                          Page found: _____
                                          Meaning: _____
                                          _____

                                          Word: _____
                                          Page found: _____
                                          Meaning: _____
                                          _____

Mississippi River would be shortened to a length of a mile and three-quarters 742 years from the time he wrote *Life on the Mississippi.* By reading a graph that applies the formula for slope, readers can see how slope always reflects the relationship of one variable to another. Both Twain's humorous essay and the formula for slope are more interesting and clear when the graphic information is available.

Many standardized state tests of learning consist of, in large measure, graph, chart, and map reading. When teachers attend to the detail of reading visuals, they are directly helping students prepare for standardized achievement tests.

Reading Visuals on the Internet

If students are having particular difficulty reading visual information, teachers can use a modified textbook treasure hunt (see Chapter 5) to teach the skill. Activity 8.6 shows how this procedure can be used to help upper elementary and middle school students read about manatees while searching Internet sites on the subject.

Eastern Virginia Medical School
Community Based • Nationally Recognized

Search   Home / Site Map / About EVMS / Patient Services
          Education / Research / Departments / Library

I need to research medical schools. This looks like a good place to start.

Department Information

Francis J. Counselman, M.D. Chairman

Here is the chairman.

Emergency Medicine Department

Residency Program
Clinical Faculty
Core Faculty CVs
Awards
Publications
Tidewater Emergency Medical Services

Here are the faculty.

What are CVs? Maybe by clicking here I will find out.

The Department of Emergency Medicine at the Eastern Virginia Medical School is a fully accredited PGY-I through PGY-III program, approved by the Emergency Medicine Residency Review Committee. There are eight resident positions in each class. The program has maintained Continued Full Accreditation status since its inception in 1981. We received independent academic departmental status in 1992; we were only the twenty-sixth such academic department in the United States at that time.

Read the introductory paragraph.

All of the faculty of the Department of Emergency Medicine are board-certified or board-prepared in Emergency Medicine. A number of our faculty are double-boarded. In addition, all are members of our private practice group, Emergency Physicians of Tidewater, one of the country's oldest private practice Emergency Medicine groups. The faculty provide clinical supervision at all of our training sites, providing a uniformity of supervision and the guidance of academic practitioners as well as Emergency Medicine physicians in private practice. This provides a unique opportunity to experience first hand the different career paths available in Emergency Medicine.

◀

Home / Site Map / Search / About EVMS / Patient Services
Education / Research / Departments / Library

Feedback | Revised: November 29, 2001 | Copyright © 1999-2000 Academic Computer Center

What kind of library do they have?

I will click here to learn about the different departments.

Reading Pictures and Maps

Pictures make a textbook interesting and vital. Teachers should frequently ask students to "read" the pictures in an effort to clarify thinking about concepts in the chapter. Cartoons are specialized pictures that carry significant messages or propaganda. What meaning does the cartoon on page 258 convey to you? Does it convey irony?

Introduction

Surf's up! Grab your brain and head for the further reaches of cyberspace. There is a lot to learn in this information age. Using the web allows you to discover tons more than you may have ever known possible. Below is a list of questions about manatees. Surf the Internet links provided by your teacher to find answers to the questions. Don't forget to go after the monster learning wave, the Big Question. Have fun and avoid any watery danger.

Questions

1. Give a detailed description of a manatee (color, size, weight, and so on).

2. Is the manatee population increasing or decreasing? Why?

3. Where does the West Indian manatee live? Does it migrate?

4. Do manatees have teeth?

5. Are manatees omnivores, carnivores, or herbivores? Give an example of their diet.

Internet Resources

Your teacher will show you how to do an Internet search on manatees and provide you with some web links.

The Big Question

How can we protect this endangered species?

Good luck and go find out about those manatees!

Developed by Jody Irvin.

Pessimism? Is it a satire about the world of education? Activity 8.7 demonstrates how teachers can teach students to label maps. Labeling may be done either after students memorize a map or as they consult maps in their textbook. We recommend map labeling as the primary way to get students to learn to use maps and to better remember certain important locations on a map.

STUDYING THROUGH THE USE OF MNEMONICS

Students need to know that learning is difficult but always rewarding. Sternberg (1991) noted that learning and retention are enhanced when students study in fairly equal distributions over time rather than in what he calls **massed study**—last-minute cramming before a test or exam. Many students cram because it is human nature to put off study to the last minute. Also, students form this habit because teachers do not explain to them how distributed study enhances retention. The famous Ebbinghaus (1908) findings almost 100 years ago described the difficulty of learning. Ebbinghaus postulated that tremendous amounts of information are forgotten in a short period

Complete this map. Use the map of the Colonial Southeast on page 210 to help you complete this activity.

1. Color the water area BLUE.

2. Color the area covered by the 11 states of the Southeast LIGHT YELLOW.

3. Print the names of the states in the proper places on the map.

4. Print these names in the proper places:
   Mountains: Appalachians, Blue Ridge
   Plains: Atlantic Coastal, Gulf Coastal
   Rivers: Potomac, James, Savannah, Mississippi, St. Johns

   Bays: Chesapeake, Delaware

5. Print these names of early settlements in the proper places on the map:
   Jamestown   St. Mary's
   Charleston   Williamsburg
   Savannah

6. With a BLUE crayon trace over each of the rivers listed above.

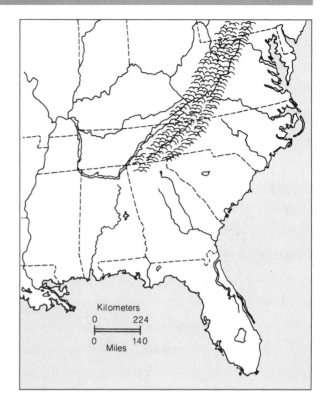

With Mac computers, "sticky notes" can be programmed to pop up on the screen to remind students to study at a certain time. Microsoft Word has a feature that reminds a reader to review a certain document at a prescribed time.

of time—up to 60 or 70 percent in only a few days. He also made these important discoveries, which still seem to hold true:

1. Fatigue affects one's ability to remember.

2. Earlier study and learning tend to get buried by later learning.

3. Learned images may decay over time and end up changed in meaning from what was originally perceived.

4. Memories erode, and most information (an estimated 90 percent) is forgotten over prolonged periods.

In short, forgetting is natural and remembering is difficult.

Fortunately, the use of **mnemonics**—devices and techniques to improve memory—can help students in what Ebbinghaus describes as the difficult task of learning. Peters and Levin (1986) found that mnemonics benefited both above- and below-average readers when they read short fictional passages as well as longer content passages. Students instructed in mnemonic strategies remembered significantly more information on names and accomplishments than did those in the control group.

Reprinted by permission of H. L. Schwadron.

Similarly, Levin, Morrison, and McGivern (1986) found that students instructed in mnemonic techniques scored significantly higher on tests of immediate recall and on recall tests administered three days later than did either a group taught to memorize material or group members who were given motivational talks and then used their usual methods of study. Mnemonics instruction also has been found effective for learning new words in foreign language classes (Cohen, 1987) and as an aid in learning Chinese and Japanese characters (Lu et al., 1999). Studies (Levin et al., 1992; Scruggs et al., 1992) have found that key-word mnemonics significantly affect retention of text material, attesting to the benefits of mnemonic techniques.

Mnemonics seem to work by taking the load off working memory, or short-term memory, by retrieving learning directly from long-term memory. This is completed through a single association with an existing memory code (Levin, 1993; Wang & Thomas, 1995). Not all research on the efficacy of using mnemonics has been positive, however. Hwang and Levin (2002) found that students have trouble applying complex mnemonic strategies independently. They state that the teacher in the learning situation must provide much auxiliary support for the mnemonic strategy to be effective. It is not altogether certain that children can discover effective learning strategies—such as mnemonics—on their own or apply them in the learning environment (Pressley & Schneider, 1997).

Despite mostly favorable studies, teachers do little memory training with their students, even though it takes only a small effort to get students to try mnemonics. For example, a teacher can give vocabulary or chapter terms that need to be memorized and ask students to form groups in which they create their own mnemonics and share them with the class. The teacher can give rewards for the ones judged to be the best. Through such practice, students form the habit of creating mnemonics for themselves.

In the remainder of this section we describe acronyms, acrostics, the method of loci, and other mnemonic learning techniques. These can be welcome learning aids, especially for poor readers who find that they forget material too quickly (remember Ebbinghaus's studies showing that forgetting is natural). If we could help students to remember from 10 to 30 items with ease, think how their self-concepts and self-images might be improved. With practice, there seems to be almost no limit to improvement in long-term memory skill. We recommend familiarizing children in primary grades with these memory-enhancing techniques. Then they will possess a skill useful throughout the rest of their education.

Remember that mnemonics have been used successfully for centuries!

Acronyms

The most time-honored of mnemonics, an **acronym,** is a word or phrase composed entirely of letters that are cues to the words we want to remember. PAR is an acronym for the instructional framework that we explain in this book. For another example, suppose that you are reviewing musculoskeletal systems for a test, and among the things you want to remember are the six boundaries of the axilla: apex, base, anterior wall, posterior wall, medial wall, and lateral wall. The initial letters are A, B, A, P, M, and L. You could rearrange these letters to form the acronym A.B. PALM. Or consider the following list of the six branches of the axillary artery: supreme thoraces, thoracromial, lateral thoracic, anterior humeral circumflex, posterior humeral circumflex, and subscapular. You could use the initial letters S, T, L, A, P, and S to form the name of a fictitious patron saint of arteries: ST. LAPS. Here are a few examples of commonly used acronyms:

HOMES: the Great Lakes—Huron, Ontario, Michigan, Erie, Superior

ROY G BIV: the colors of the spectrum—red, orange, yellow, green, blue, indigo, violet

FACE: the notes represented by the spaces of the treble clef

Acrostics

An **acrostic** is a phrase or sentence in which the first letter of each word is a cue. For example, another way of remembering the boundaries of the axilla—initial letters A, B, A, P, M, and L—would be to create a phrase such as "**a**bove, **b**elow, **a**nd **p**retty **m**uch **l**ost." To remember the names of the planets—**M**ercury, **V**enus, **E**arth, **M**ars, **J**upiter, **S**aturn, **U**ranus, **N**eptune, **P**luto—you might use the following acrostic: **m**y **v**ery **e**legant **m**other **j**ust **s**at **u**pon **n**ine **p**orcupines.

Acrostics can be made for any area. To improve reading study skills, ask students to **relax** by doing the following:

Rest plenty.

Exude enthusiasm.

Laugh often.

Anticipate what's coming.

Xcite yourself about the reading.

Suppose you had to remember these nautical terms: **b**ow, **s**tern, **c**abin, **t**raveler. You could use this acrostic: **b**ig **s**torms **c**ause **t**rouble.

Associations

Students can be taught to memorize words by associating the words to be learned with outrageous images. For instance, to memorize the words in the left column, students can imagine the images in the right column:

WORD	IMAGE
sweater	sweater
horse	a gigantic horse wearing a gigantic sweater
surf	a huge horse surfing
iron gate	a surfer on a high surfboard flying over an iron gate
typewriter	tiny iron gates spewing out of a typewriter

In this manner, one word leads to the next to make a long list of associations.

Another means of associational learning is a *peg-word system,* which associates a target word with a numbered peg word. Listed below are 10 peg words that name familiar places found at many schools:

1. Computer center
2. Guidance office
3. Cafeteria
4. Auditorium
5. Library
6. Classroom
7. Hallway
8. Principal's office
9. Nurse's clinic
10. Gymnasium

The words to be memorized—*plot, setting,* and *character*—are linked to the peg words through outrageous images. You can remember the words *plot, setting,* and *character* by associating each with one of the numbered peg words:

5. A criminal with a *plot* to blow up the *library*

3. Someone *setting* a tray down in the *cafeteria*

6. A drunken *character* sitting in the back of a *classroom* filled with disbelieving students

The peg words do not have to name places. They can be words that sound similar to or rhyme with the words to be learned. An example would be the peg word *commotion* for *commodities* in an economics class or *this criminal* for *discrimination*.

Method of Loci

The method of loci (Latin for "places") improves students' ability to remember lists of unrelated objects. It also can be a sequencing task, enabling a student to remember items in a definite order. In this ancient method, used by Roman orators, a person mentally walks through a house that has familiar surroundings. Cicero and other classical orators constructed "memory places" and linked sections of their speeches to architectural features. Then, as they spoke, they imagined the place where they had established the link. This process enabled them to remember huge amounts of information.

An electronic drawing of loci adds interest and permanence.

By choosing from 15 to 20 distinct loci—for example, the stove, the closet, the desk, the kitchen sink—students can mentally place objects to be learned in strategic spots throughout the house. In a variation, students memorize words by placing them in strategic places in each of the six or seven rooms where they have classes each day or in various places around the school.

Chunking

The chunking of large amounts of information into categories can help students remember information more readily and retrieve it faster. Suppose you have to learn these 15 items in a language arts unit on puppetry:

director	equipment	props	create	purchase
lights	story development	size of puppets	analysis	microphone
copyright	budget	sound	stories	spotlight

Chunking information into categories makes learning the 15 items much easier:

SCRIPTS	TECHNICAL
director	lights
copyright	equipment
story development	props
budget	size of puppets
create	sound
analysis	microphone
stories	spotlight
purchase	

Chunking information through categorization exercises (which can be used to review for tests) is an excellent way to help poor readers understand text material. Chunking capitalizes on connecting prior knowledge to new knowledge, thus enhancing learning. Once students become more practiced at chunking, they can construct hierarchies of mnemonics to learn 15 to 50 items. Activity 8.8 provides an example from a "Teen Living" class in home economics, where the total number of items to be learned is 17.

Remember that complicated hierarchies of mnemonics are best constructed by middle school and high school students who have considerable experience with using simple acronyms and acrostics. This level of chunking is the most difficult mnemonic to construct, but it allows students considerable leeway in memorizing prodigious amounts of information.

Go MAD

Children have a better chance to successfully use mnemonics if they make their own mnemonics to help them learn certain concepts. One way to familiarize primary and upper elementary children with mnemonics is to go MAD—use the Mnemonic-A-Day technique. Have students work in groups to make a mnemonic a day for 10 days; each new mnemonic has to be in a different content area than the one created the day

---

ACTIVITY 8.8   CHUNKING THROUGH CATEGORIZATION

BEING A SUCCESSFUL BABYSITTER

Acronym = JOG

(J)ob acceptance	(O)n the job	(G)etting started
P — Parents' permission		
A — Address of family	N — No TV	
D — Day and time	A — Attend to task	P — Prompt for arrival
	M — Make file of family after job	A — Address where couple will be
M — Meet children	E — Exploring in house is out	R — Reaching doctors, firefighters, etc.
O — Offer fee	S — Stay awake	
M — Meet family		

---

before. Children keep MAD logs and periodically refer to the logs to make certain they remember all the accumulated mnemonics. By making a game of it, teachers can reward individuals or groups who can create a MAD example for the most days consecutively. This can be an enjoyable yet purposeful activity.

RAPID READING

 One of Edmund Burke Huey's tenets in *The Psychology and Pedagogy of Reading* (1908/1968) was that children should be taught, from the first reading instruction, to read as fast as the nature of the reading materials and their purpose will allow. Huey recommended speed drills to help students get information efficiently and effectively. After Huey, William S. Gray, in a 1925 review of the literature on speed of reading, endorsed rapid reading by concluding that such training could result in increased speed without a concurrent drop in comprehension. Unfortunately, many professionals have forgotten Huey's and Gray's work, and rapid reading has fallen into disfavor as a bona fide reading skill that students should be acquiring. More than 90 years after Huey's pronouncement, probably no area of reading is as controversial as speed-reading (Carver, 1992). The very mention of speed-reading carries with it a negative connotation for many teachers at all levels of education. In studies of adult readers, Carver (1985, 1992) concluded that the speed-readers he tested comprehended less than 75 percent of eighth grade material when reading faster than 600 words per minute. He also found that much of what passes as speed-reading is really skimming—glossing material at between 600 and 1,000 words per minute at fairly low comprehension levels. Other studies question the quality of speed-reading research (Collins, 1979; Fleisher, Jenkins, & Pany, 1979), the limited utility of eye movement training (McConkie & Rayner, 1976; Rayner, 1978), and the limits to speed in the act of reading (Carver, 1985; Spache, 1976). Yet much more research on speed-reading is needed, as evidenced in a study by Just, Carpenter, and Masson (1982), which found fairly positive results for speed-readers when they answered higher-level comprehension questions.

Perhaps one problem with speed-reading is the misconception that one can read faster just by accelerating a physical activity. Simply stated, the physical process of reading requires the eyes to move in a jerky pattern over the page, stopping to let the brain take in information, then moving again. These **saccadic eye movements,** or eye fixations, constitute the physical process of reading. A reader could get quite a headache by trying to accelerate this physical process too much. What is important is how readers manipulate the information taken in with a fixation or, as Frank Smith (1988) puts it, what goes on "between the eye and the brain" rather than from the page to the eye. This mental process requires the chunking of information into the largest meaningful units that one can assimilate and relating those chunks to an existing schema. We described this type of brain activity in the preceding section on mnemonic associations.

We do not recommend speed-reading per se, but we do advocate rapid reading or speeding up one's reading along with an emphasis on previewing the material. Previewing (explained earlier in the chapter) brings purpose to the reading by letting the reader decide what he or she needs and wants to know. We maintain that students can find answers to their questions quickly by reading more rapidly after the previewing stage. We also suggest that it is better to read a chapter several times rapidly than it is to read the chapter one time at a laboriously slow rate. Providing verification for several rapid readings, Samuels (1979) found that repeated reading enhanced reader fluency and comprehension. We are not advocating reading 1,000 words or more a minute, but we do believe that some study reading should be done at rates well above 300 words per minute.

Timed readings can be created within some software programs.

Skimming and Scanning

Skimming is rapid glancing through text to find out generally what the reading is about (Jacobson, 1998). **Scanning** is rapid reading for some specific purpose—for instance, to find out where, when, or how something happened. When scanning, a person may read an introduction or opening paragraph, a summary, and the first and last sentences of each paragraph; note material in bold print; and glance at visual aids. Unlike skimming, in which the reader glances at the whole text to get a general sense of the piece, scanning is searching for specific information, such as a word or detail. Researchers have reported on the importance of skimming content materials for organizing details and making inferences (Sherer, 1975). Carver, as noted earlier, mentions the importance of scanning to find particular target words.

Skills in skimming and scanning allow students to preview information. Students need to be reminded that previewing, as described earlier, helps to clarify thinking and set a purpose for reading and that they will learn further details in the full reading. Students need much practice (beginning at an early age) to acquire these skills. We recommend scanning drills, in which teachers ask students to scan rapidly, looking for answers to *who, what, when,* and *where* questions in the chapter. Students need to be reminded to skim one or two sentences in each paragraph in addition to the title, author, headings, and so on, as described earlier. Scanning can be practiced as students demonstrate how they confirmed predictions, or found a word's meaning, by returning to that place in the material.

Rapid Reading Exercises

Teachers can use four easy exercises to get students to practice in order to increase student reading speed. The first of these, **mental push-ups,** consists of rate and comprehension drills. At the beginning of class, the teacher asks students to use a 3-by-5-inch card to "mentally push" themselves down one page of a content chapter or story so quickly that they cannot absorb all the information on the page. (Older students who have had practice in the technique and who have better fine motor control can use a finger to pace themselves.) Then students close the book and write down what they learned. After the first reading, the amount retained is usually two or three words. The students repeat the procedure as many times as needed (usually two to four) until there is a "rush" of information—that is, until they comprehend and can write out or verbalize most of what is on the page. With extended practice, students will need fewer readings to comprehend the material. This technique can be used to clarify cognitive structure and increase student attention at the beginning of a class period. With practice, it will help make students more facile and mentally alert when reading short passages.

Another rapid reading activity is a variation on mental push-ups. Teachers can conduct three-minute **rapid reading drills** at the beginning of classes. In a straightforward rapid reading drill, students are asked to read as fast as possible. Again, young children can use a 3-by-5-inch card as a pacer; later they can use the finger-pacing technique. The teacher can conduct one or two three-minute drills without taking away too much time from the day's lesson. Students taking rapid reading drills are not asked to write out what they learned. As a variation, however, they could be asked to form groups in which each person discusses what she or he remembers from the reading.

A third exercise, the **preview and rapid reading drill,** can be used when the teacher is directing the reading of a content chapter. The teacher monitors the previewing phase, culminating with students' writing specific questions that they wish to have answered in the reading. The previewing phase can be done by the whole class, in groups, or by individuals working on their own. The teacher asks the students to read more rapidly than usual to find the answers to their preview questions.

A fourth excellent activity to practice with students is using a finger-pacing technique. Teachers can show students how to use their index fingers lightly to pace themselves in their reading. The students glide their fingers lightly across the page and down the page at a swift pace to make their eyes go faster as they read the print. This technique will get students used to reading faster in their everyday reading. Teachers should start with simple, easy-to-read material to ensure students have initial success at the activity.

These four activities can be accomplished in any content area and can be started with better readers at the second grade level. Students generally express interest in such activities. They can see immediate results and appreciate being able to improve their own reading rate.

ORGANIZING INFORMATION

Teachers can help themselves and their students gather information by subscribing to online services for deciphering and organizing incoming information, such as the free service InfoBeat or a paid service such as Lexis-Nexis Universe. InfoBeat offers a way to keep abreast of news without spending money, but it can quickly overwhelm an e-mail account with the volumes of information that it will register.

Underlining is often cited in the literature as a way to help students organize their thinking enough to begin an outline. Underlining, then, can be a first step to outlining. McAndrew (1983), in a review of the literature on underlining, made several suggestions for teaching this skill if students own their textbooks. To begin, teachers should create "pre-underlining" reading assignments in handout materials that coincide with the textbook. Teachers need to show students how to underline relevant material. Students need to learn how to underline superordinate statements rather than subordinate details. When they learn this, students will underline relatively little, but what they underline will be important. McAndrew notes that teachers should remind students that with underlining, less is more, and that any time they save by underlining can be put to good use in further study of the material. Teachers also need to teach students when to use techniques other than underlining. Even when underlining in textbooks is not possible, pre-underlining is an important study strategy for students to learn.

Outlining

Outlining is the more traditional method by which students organize information. There is no agreement, however, on the best way to teach this skill. Outlining is an organizational tool that allows readers to create for themselves a condensed presentation of the chapter that they want to understand. Outlining is particularly useful because it actively involves the reader and because the notes are made on a separate sheet of paper, not in the textbook, which the student might not own. A well-made outline shows the relationship to the overall topic of main ideas, supporting details, definitions of terms, and other data. Mapping can be an early and unstructured form of outlining. Outlines are valuable because they help students understand difficult texts, take notes, write papers, and give oral presentations.

When students first begin to practice outlining, they should not concentrate on form (no need for a B for every A). Teachers can help students learn to outline by preparing outlines with key words missing. By replacing missing words or terms, even very young children can begin to learn outlining. Teachers can give students partially completed outlines to complete as they read a chapter. This example is from first grade:

MAPS
- I. Maps
  - A. Legend
    - 1. Key
    - 2. Compass rose
- II. Flat
- III. Sphere
  - 1. Globe

The following are some features of successful outlines:

1. The material itself determines the number of headings and subheadings.
2. Each heading expresses one main idea.
3. Ideas are parallel. All ideas recorded with roman numerals are equally important.
4. All subheadings relate to the major heading above them.
5. In a formal outline, each category has more than one heading.
6. Each new level of heading is indented under the heading above it.
7. The first letter of the first word in each heading and subheading is capitalized.

An outline enables students to organize material in a hierarchical fashion. This can be accomplished by using a graphic pattern as well as in traditional ways.

Note Taking

Note taking, an often-used study skill, produces good study results. Research focusing on the time students spent on constructing their own study notes showed that their notes were more effective than instructor-provided notes (Crooks & Katayama, 2002). McAndrew (1983) offers teachers these suggestions to help their students become effective note takers (p. 107):

1. Be certain students realize that the use of notes to store information is more important than the act of taking the notes.
2. Try to use a spaced lecture format.
3. Insert questions, verbal cues, and nonverbal cues into lectures to highlight structure.
4. Write material on the board to be sure students will record it.
5. When using transparencies or slides, compensate for possible overload of information.
6. Tell students what type of test to expect.
7. Use handouts, especially with poor note takers.
8. Give students handouts that provide space for student notes.

To the students who are taking notes, Morgan and associates (1986) offer some practical advice:

1. *Do not use a spiral notebook (contrary to what is often advocated).* A two- or three-ring notebook filled with loose-leaf paper enables students to rearrange their notes or any other material and permits the easy addition or subtraction of material.
2. *Write on every other line whenever possible or when it seems logical to separate topics.* By leaving a lot of white space, students give themselves room to correct errors or add points they missed. In addition, every-other-line note taking makes for easier reading when students review or study for an exam.
3. *Develop a shorthand system.* Students should reduce frequently used words to a symbol, such as "w" for *with*. Other commonly used words should be abbreviated. Morgan and colleagues (1986) offer examples of such abbreviations:

compare	comp	data bank	db		
important	imp	evaluation	eval		
advantage	advan	developed	dev		
introduction	intro	literature	lit		
continued	cont	definition	def		
organization	org	individual	ind		
information	info	psychology	psych	example	ex

Content words should be recorded in full and spellings checked with a dictionary or a textbook.

4. *Underline, star, or record the teacher's pet theories or concepts.* Listen for key statements such as "I particularly agree with this theory" or "You'll probably be seeing this information again." Statements like those might mean that the material will appear on an exam. If the teacher writes terminology or math examples on the board, always record them word for word (or figure by figure). If the teacher lists or numbers remarks, such as "three significant facts stand out," those should be numbered and indented in the notes.

5. *Do not try to outline notes according to a roman numeral system with main ideas and supporting details.* No one thinks in roman numerals. Important points may be missed if students worry too much about how they are taking the notes. Until notes are organized later, students should not worry about the numerals.

6. *Do not disregard related discussions.* Teachers frequently use questions as a teaching tool. Students should write down questions that are introduced for discussion purposes. Often such discussions stray from the subject, but the teacher always has a reason for asking the question.

7. *Ask questions when there is misunderstanding.* If one student is confused by a concept or misses a point in the lecture, usually other students have missed it too. Students should not be embarrassed to ask for clarification.

8. *Review often and with different purposes in mind.* When rereading textbook assignments, students should coordinate the chapter with their notes. Make certain main ideas from the chapter are included directly in the lecture notes. For some students, rewriting notes is a helpful memory device. Even though this process is time-consuming, it may be worth the effort if it helps students retain the material.

Remember that note taking is usually somewhat messy. The process the mind uses while thinking and taking notes may resemble a webbing or mapping approach.

Richardson (1996) offers a tip for teachers. When teachers allow students to use notes during a test, they will see a great improvement over time in students' use of note taking. Of course, students should not be able to find the answers to test questions directly in the notes, but should be required to use inference and application skills when forming their answers.

REST SYSTEM OF NOTE TAKING

The REST system (Morgan et al., 1986) has been proposed as a way to prepare for note taking before a lecture. This system emphasizes the importance of note taking to help integrate the lecture with the textbook. Using the REST system, students should follow these steps:

1. *Record:* Write down as much of what the teacher says as possible, excluding repetitions and digressions.

2. *Edit:* Condense notes, editing out irrelevant material.

3. *Synthesize:* Compare condensed notes with related material in the textbook, and jot down important points stressed in both the lecture and the textbook.

4. *Think:* Think and study to ensure retention.

To help students practice REST, teachers should distribute handouts for note taking that include space for writing notes on the lecture, for making notes to oneself, and for summarizing main ideas. An example of such a handout completed by a high school student in art history is shown in Activity 8.9.

TWO-COLUMN NOTE TAKING

The Cornell system (Pauk, 1997), a practical approach to taking notes, is an alternative to the REST system. Pauk's **two-column note-taking system,** or "5r's," has an advantage over REST in that it can be used with younger children. To use this system, students divide the page in the following way. The main heading, the notes students make for themselves, and key words all go in the narrow left column. The students also may use the left side as their side to record topics, questions, key phrases, definitions, comments, and summaries of information from the lecturer or textbook. The wider right column is for information from the lecturer or the textbook.

The key to two-column note taking is space. Just as adolescents and even younger students need physical space, they also need intellectual space—that is, space to think. The left column provides space for students to question themselves about the big picture of the lesson and the major concepts to be learned. The system is based on the

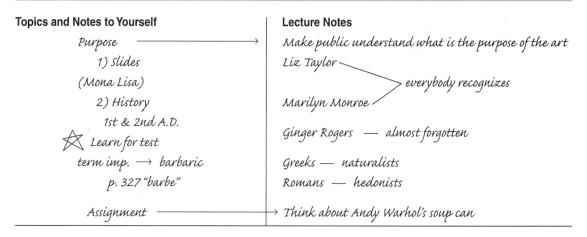

ACTIVITY 8.9 ART HISTORY NOTE-TAKING HANDOUT

Topics and Notes to Yourself

Purpose ⟶
　　1) Slides
　　(Mona Lisa)
　　2) History
　　1st & 2nd A.D.
　☆ Learn for test
　term imp. ⟶ barbaric
　　p. 327 "barbe"

Assignment ⟶

Lecture Notes

Make public understand what is the purpose of the art
Liz Taylor
　　　　　　⟶ everybody recognizes
Marilyn Monroe

Ginger Rogers — almost forgotten

Greeks — naturalists
Romans — hedonists

⟶ Think about Andy Warhol's soup can

Summarization and Main Ideas

Art is a reflection of history.
Need to study both the purpose
and the style.

sound theory of categorization, with subordinate concepts consolidated and organized under superordinate headings. Students practice these steps (the 5r's):

Step 1: They *record* the information as they hear it or read it.

Step 2: They *reduce* the information by putting their abbreviated notes about it in the narrow left column.

Step 3: They *recite* the information by using their reduction notes with the recorded notes in the wider right column.

Steps 4 and 5: They *reflect on* and *review* the notes over time.

Two-column notes are often referred to by other names, such as double-entry notes or split-column notes.

The two-column system allows great flexibility. Pairs of students can "call" the notes to each other, covering either column and asking each other what belongs in that column. Teachers can put students into groups at the beginning or end of class to brainstorm two or three recently covered major topics (to go in the left column). In this manner note taking is made an integral part of all the operations of the class. When this system is used effectively, students improve markedly. However, studies (Spor & Schneider, 1999) show that only 30 percent of teachers work with students on any outlining or note-taking procedure at all. Many simply tell students to "put a line down the page about one-third of the way across the page, creating two columns, and take notes like this from now on." Students do not continue (or even start) to use the method because they have no practice in using it.

Activity 8.10 is an example of a two-column note-taking handout from an early elementary classroom. The teacher is discussing a story and asks students to complete the notes. Teachers can prepare such handouts and give them to students before a lecture or before students read a chapter to provide practice with the two-column method. This handout employs a modified cloze procedure: students fill in gaps as they listen to the lecture or read the chapter. In subsequent lessons, more and more notes are omitted (more blanks are used) until eventually students complete all the note taking themselves.

Activity 8.11 is an example of a two-column note-taking handout from a high school health class on brain functioning through diet and eating habits.

SYSTEMS OF STUDY

 As soon as children in the first grade are ready, they should begin reading stories under the teacher's direction using the DR–TA technique (Stauffer, 1969b). If such guided practice continues, teachers gradually give more and more responsibility for learning to students, as illustrated in Pearson's (1985) model (see Figure 8.1 on page 273). If practice in using the DR–TA is schoolwide and responsibility is taught, students will receive a firm foundation in study reading. By the fourth or fifth grade, students can be taught a **study system**—a systematic set of steps for studying text. Study systems are a natural outgrowth of previewing, skimming, and teacher-modeled reading lessons such as the DR–TA. In this section we examine three study systems.

NAME _____ DATE _____

Directions: Listen very closely as I discuss *Franklin Fibs* by Paulette Bourgeois. Fill in the missing words to complete these notes.

Main characters   Franklin, Bear, _____, Beaver, Mom, and

                     _____.

Setting   Franklin's _____.

Beginning   Bear, Hawk, and _____ were _____ about things they could _____.

Middle   Franklin said he could eat _____ flies in the _____ of an eye.

End   Franklin did _____ seventy-six flies, but he ate them in a _____.

Problem   Franklin told a _____.

Solution   Franklin told the _____ and did something that he could brag about.

Developed by Stephanie Hunter.

The following systems of study are sometimes referred to as "the best systems of learning that no one ever uses"! Students do not use them because teachers do not model them. Such learning systems need to be modeled in the classroom as many as 10 times.

SQ3R

SQ3R (Robinson, 1961)—which stands for Survey, Question, Read, Recite, Review—is a study system that has been practiced for many years. Table 8.1 on page 274 summarizes the SQ3R steps. Lipson and Wixson (2003) call it the grandfather of study strategies. Spor and Schneider (1999) found in a survey of 435 teachers that 44 percent of teachers knew of the SQ3R study strategy and 31 percent said they would use it in their classrooms. Studies (Bhat, Rapport, & Griffin, 2000) generally speak to the benefits and positive results of using the approach. In a recent review of research concerning SQ3R, Huber (2004) found mixed results but overall asked for a renewed emphasis on researching the usefulness of the technique. An alternative to SQ3R is REAP, described in Chapter 10 as a writing-to-learn activity. REAP is also useful for improving study skills because when students annotate they pay attention and reinforce their reading by writing.

Study systems such as these have not really permeated schools across the country. Researchers Spor and Schneider (1999) found that even though 44 percent of teachers had heard about the SQ3R method, only 17 percent had used it with students. There are probably three reasons for this low percentage. First, teachers themselves did not learn through such a study system; thus they often give only lip service to the techniques described. Second, teachers may have been required to use a study system

Your brain	It is always _____.
	It is selective in the way it gets _____.
Two amino acids are important for brain function	Tyrosine is an amino acid that helps with _____ _____ , long term _____ , and feelings of being _____ .
	From tyrosine, the brain makes _____ and _____ .
	Tryptophan slows _____ time and makes you _____ .
	Scientists believe you can control the activity _____ of the mind with the foods you eat.
If you want to get tyrosine to the brain	eat _____.
If you want to get tryptophan to the brain	eat _____.
Protein lunches	enhance _____ performance.
Carbohydrates	can _____ thought processes of the brain.
	are good for helping you _____.
	can _____ people with seasonal affective disorder (SAD).
Fats	are important for thinking.
	Brain _____ are made largely of fat.
	Take _____ hours for fats to reach the brain and affect thinking.
	Saturated fats _____ ability to think.
	Polyunsaturated fats _____ ability to think.

imposed by their own teachers, but they did not understand the underlying reasons for the system. Teachers themselves need to practice previewing and study systems before they can believe in and teach such systems to others. Third, study strategies are not systematically introduced throughout educational systems from the early elementary years.

PQR2 ST+

The PQR2 ST+ study system developed by Morgan, Forget, and Antinarella (1996) is a complete study system. It includes the following steps:

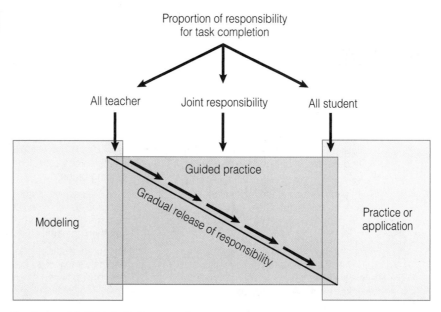

Proportion of responsibility
for task completion

All teacher Joint responsibility All student

Guided practice

Gradual release of responsibility

Modeling

Practice or
application

PQR2 ST+ is a variation on the SQ3R study system. We feel that this approach adds touches that improve the SQ3R system.

Preview: This is a very important step that good readers always perform. Students quickly skim the material before they start reading. Here is what to look for in the preview:
- Title
- Introduction
- Subtitles
- Pictures
- Charts, maps, graphs
- Bold print and italicized words
- Summary
- Review questions

Question: In the left column of a page formatted for two-column notes, students write the question or objective to be achieved. A good way to do this is to turn the heading that introduces a passage into a question.

Read: Students read the subsection silently, thinking about how to express the information in personal terms.

Remember: In the right column of the notes, with the book closed, students write down the details of what they read. These notes must be in the student's own words! The students recall as much as possible but do not worry about missing some details.

Scan: Students rapidly scan the same subsection of the text to see whether they missed any details that were important or got anything wrong in their notes.

Touch Up: Students add any important details to their notes.

TABLE 8.1 SQ3R

Technique	Procedure	Values
Survey	Read questions and summary at end of the chapter. Skim-read divisions of material, which usually are in boldface type. Read captions under pictures and graphs.	Highlights major ideas and emphases of chapter; helps organize ideas for better understanding later.
Question	Turn each heading into a question. (Practice will make this skill automatic.) Write questions in outline form.	Arouses curiosity; increases comprehension; recalls information known; highlights major points; forces conscious effort in applying the reading process.
Read	Read each section of the material to answer questions from headings.	Promotes active search for answers to specific questions; forces concentration for better comprehension; improves memory; aids in lengthening attention span.
Recite	After reading entire section, close book and write the answer to your question plus any significant cues; use your own words; write key examples; make notes brief.	Encourages students to use their own words and not simply copy from book; improves memory and ensures greater understanding.
Review	Study the topical outline and notes; try to see relationships; check memory by trying to recall main points; cover subpoints and try to recall them from seeing main points.	Clarifies relationships; checks short-term recall; prepares students for class.

+ **(Plus):** The last step should be done within 24 hours of the reading. Students return to study from the notes by folding the page so that only the question shows. Students see whether they can remember the details noted on the right side. Because of the way the notes are taken, students can usually recall important details. Students go over the notes one more time before the test.

SQRC

Sakta (1999) proposed another study system similar to SQ3R. The SQRC procedure, which works best with expository readings, has four steps: State, Question, Read, and Conclude. It is carried out in three phases of the reading process: before, during, and after reading. First, students are given a general statement that they must support or refute based on what they find in the reading. Here are the phases of the strategy:

Phase 1—Before reading: The teacher introduces the topic and activates prior knowledge. Students then get a guide sheet (an example of such a guide sheet is shown as Activity 8.12), on which they write whether they are for or against the position statement given by the teacher, and why. Next students rewrite their position statement in question form.

Phase 2—During reading: Students read the text to find information that supports their position. They also are instructed to take notes of salient points while reading. Immediately after reading, students review their notes and write a brief conclusion.

NAME _____ CLASS _____

TITLE OF READING ASSIGNMENT: _____

Directions: Before reading the assignment, state your belief or position about the topic by selecting one of the two statements supplied by the teacher, or write your own position statement. Restate your position in the form of a question and write it in the space labeled "Question."

As you read, use this question to guide your reading and thinking about the topic. Take notes on (1) facts that support your position and (2) facts that refute, or do not support, your position. When you are finished reading, review your notes and write your conclusion. The conclusion may or may not support your original position statement.

Statement: _____

_____

_____

_____

Question: _____

_____

_____

Facts that support my position statement:

_____

_____

_____

_____

_____

Facts that refute my position statement:

_____

_____

_____

_____

Conclusion:

_____

_____

_____

_____

_____

From Sakta, C. G. (Dec. 98/Jan. 99). SQRC: A strategy for guiding reading and higher level thinking. *Journal of Adolescent and Adult Literacy 42*(4), 265–269. Reprinted with permission of Cathy G. Sakta and the International Reading Association. All rights reserved.

Phase 3—After reading: The class is divided into two groups, each group representing a position. With several students from each side acting as judges, students representing each position present arguments. The teacher serves as a consultant but does not offer opinions. After debate, the judges render a decision as to which side presented the stronger case.

Sakta (1999) presents results of a study she conducted that points to the effectiveness of the SQRC strategy for systematic study. The strategy is beneficial because, like

SQ3R and PQR2 ST+, it combines key elements of cognitive learning theory and constructivist approaches.

ONE-MINUTE SUMMARY

Study skills need to be taught systematically and emphasized in early elementary grades through high school. As students mature and progress through school, the skills that are taught may include locating information, previewing materials, organizing material for study, and using study systems. This chapter described an assessment technique designed to find out whether students use adequate study skills. The teaching of study skills cannot be left to chance. Students at all levels need to be made aware of good study practices through the use of a skills training model.

Students must be convinced that study practices really will help more than hinder and that the hard work involved will pay off. Teachers' modeling and involving students in practicing good study skills are the most effective way to impart this message. Table 8.2 summarizes the strategies discussed in this chapter and indicates where each can be introduced in the school continuum.

TABLE 8.2 Introducing and Teaching Reading–Study Skills: A Kindergarten through Grade 12 Timetable

	K	1	2	3	4	5	6	7	8	9	10	11	12
Skills training model		■	■	■	■	■	■	■	■	■	■	■	■
Locating information				■	■	■	■	■	■	■	■	■	■
Interpreting charts and graphs			■	■	■	■	■	■	■	■	■	■	■
Analyzing pictures	■	■	■	■	■	■	■	■	■	■	■	■	■
Reading maps			■	■	■	■	■	■	■	■	■	■	■
Mnemonics			■	■	■	■	■	■	■	■	■	■	■
Previewing		■	■	■	■	■	■	■	■	■	■	■	■
Rapid reading					■	■	■	■	■	■	■	■	■
Outlining				■	■	■	■	■	■	■	■	■	■
Note taking				■	■	■	■	■	■	■	■	■	■
Text lookbacks					■	■	■	■	■	■	■	■	■
SQ3R				■	■	■	■	■	■	■	■	■	■
PQR2 ST+				■	■	■	■	■	■	■	■	■	■
SQRC				■	■	■	■	■	■	■	■	■	■

PAR ONLINE

Find further information on, and activities dealing with, study skills and cooperative learning. Go to the web links option of the Chapter 8 resources on the book companion website.

END-OF-CHAPTER ACTIVITIES

Assisting Comprehension

Either use the two-column note taking system to take notes in a class that you are presently attending, or practice the REST system or PQR2 ST+. If you feel the system is a good aid to learning, use it with your students in a forthcoming lesson. Ask students whether they enjoyed the activity.

Reflecting on Your Reading

Standard 4.3 of the International Reading Association's Standards for Reading Professionals and Classroom Teachers (2003) states that teachers should model reading and writing strategies "enthusiastically" in the classroom:

> "Model and share the use of reading and writing for real purposes in daily life. They use think-alouds to demonstrate good reading and writing strategies. They can articulate the research that supports modeling think-alouds and read-alouds to students."

Think about the study skills that were described in this chapter. Can you model them in your classroom? Think and reflect on ways you can model these strategies in your classes.

CHAPTER 9

A word is not a crystal, transparent and unchanged; it is the skin of a living thought and may vary greatly in color and content according to the circumstances and time in which it is used.

OLIVER WENDELL HOLMES

Teaching Vocabulary

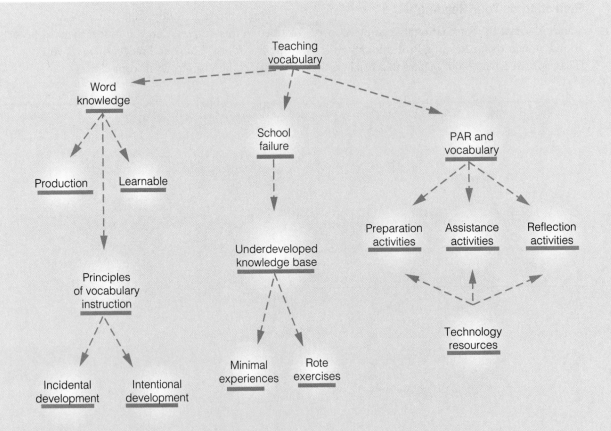

PREPARING TO READ

1. What personal connections and associations come to mind when you think of vocabulary development? What do you remember about the ways in which you were taught vocabulary? Are your memories and associations pleasant or painful? Before beginning this chapter, list some ways in which you think content area teachers can generate enthusiasm for word study. How can we get students more interested in finding out the meanings of unfamiliar words? As you read the chapter, consider how your ideas can be added to or blended with those presented in the chapter to make vocabulary study appealing as a lifelong habit for your students.

2. Following is a list of terms used in this chapter. Some may be familiar to you in a general context, but in this chapter they may be used in unfamiliar ways. Rate your knowledge by placing a plus sign (+) in front of those you are sure you know, a check mark

(✓) in front of those you have some knowledge about, and a zero (0) in front of those you don't know. Be ready to locate them in the chapter, and pay special attention to their meanings.

_____ production knowledge
_____ learnable knowledge
_____ contextual knowledge
_____ incidental vocabulary development
_____ intentional vocabulary development
_____ conceptual base of understanding
_____ free morphemes
_____ bound morphemes
_____ categorization
_____ closed word sort
_____ open word sort
_____ TOAST
_____ key-word strategy
_____ magic squares
_____ vocabulary illustrations

OBJECTIVES

As you read this chapter, focus your attention on the following purposes. You will

1. understand the importance of vocabulary in reading comprehension.

2. know and understand the underlying theory and research for vocabulary development in content areas.

3. understand the four necessary mental operations for mastering new vocabulary.

4. realize that a student's lack of understanding of concepts and vocabulary can contribute significantly to failure in school.

5. be able to use teaching strategies to increase a student's conceptual understanding of words.

6. identify research-based practices to include strategies and activities for teaching vocabulary before, during, and after reading.

7. learn a wide range of vocabulary enrichment activities that consider student developmental, cultural, and linguistic differences.

8. understand the role of oral language in vocabulary development.

9. identify technology tools and applications for vocabulary development and enrichment.

*I*n 1839 Edward George Earle Bulwer-Lytton first declared in writing that "Beneath the rule of men entirely great, the pen is mightier than the sword." The words of language convey the essence of our thoughts, ideas, musings, and emotions. Having a command of our language, and more specifically the vocabulary within that language, puts power in our hands. A strong vocabulary equips us to actively participate in society as educated citizens and consumers.

Vocabulary plays a critical role in reading through the facilitation of comprehension (Blachowitz & Fisher, 2000; Pressley, 2002; Snow, Burns, & Griffin, 1998). The National Reading Panel (NRP, 2000), upon examining numerous studies in the field, identified vocabulary instruction as one of the five key emphasis areas necessary for successful reading among children. Booth and Hall (1994) found that older students (16 years) used many more sophisticated words than younger students (13 years), probably because of greater exposure to text reading. Booth and Hall speculate that skilled reading comprehension depends on sophisticated word knowledge. Nagy and Scott (2000) explain that word usage within language indicates degrees of metalinguistic awareness that ultimately affect academic achievement. In the next section we take a closer look at what is meant by *word knowledge* and ways in which it is both developed and encouraged.

A CLOSER LOOK AT WORD KNOWLEDGE

Over a half-century ago, Davis (1944) and Thurstone (1946) wrote that knowledge of word meanings is one of the most important factors in reading comprehension. More recent studies (Anderson & Nagy, 1991; Baker, Simmons, & Kame'enui, 1998; Blachowitz & Fisher, 2000; Cunningham & Stanovich, 1998; Pressley, 2002; Snow, Burns, & Griffin, 1998), as well as the National Reading Panel's review of research in reading instruction (2000), have revealed a strong link between vocabulary and reading comprehension. Simply stated, if readers do not know the meanings of most of the words in a passage, they will be unable to understand the passage. Research attests to the correlation between vocabulary knowledge and unit test scores, oral reading rates, and teacher judgment (Lovitt, Horton, & Bergerud, 1987) as well as comprehension (Medo & Ryder, 1993). What constitutes vocabulary knowledge?

It is generally agreed that even if readers "know" a word, each person may relate it to a different experience. The sentence "John took a plane," for example, could be interpreted in different ways. A young child reading it might imagine playing with a toy; a high school student would imagine a scene in an airport; and an adult who is a carpenter might imagine a carpenter's tool. Simpson (1987) notes that "word knowledge is not a static product but a fluid quality that takes on additional characteristics and attributes as the learner experiences more" (p. 21). Knowing a word involves more than identification and pronunciation. Word knowledge has been described in various ways as being on a continuum (Dale, 1965; Stahl, 1999). We may think of word knowledge as being similar to coming to know a person. Initially a word is a stranger, one we have not seen or heard before. Then that word becomes an acquaintance; we have seen or heard it and know a little about it. As our depth of understanding grows and we become confident using the word in a variety of contexts, it takes on the status of friend.

Kibby (1995) proposes a continuum of word knowledge progressing from **production knowledge** to potentially **learnable knowledge.** Production knowledge is evident when a student knows a word so well that she or he can use it with facility in speech and writing. A student does not have learnable knowledge until background knowledge and pertinent information are provided concerning a concept about which students are unclear. Figure 9.1 shows this model.

When an association or a concept is known only vaguely or not at all, teachers need either to provide learning opportunities or to postpone instruction until students learn prerequisite knowledge. Teachers need ways to determine when to spend time on vocabulary. If they find that students already know a concept and words associated with it, time spent on vocabulary will be wasted. If they assume that students know something that they do not know, not spending time on vocabulary will cripple the lesson. Biemiller (2001) and Stahl and Schiel (1999) argue that direct instruction of reading vocabulary is needed and appropriate for most students. However, the typical prereading vocabulary instruction provided is one Nagy (1988) calls the "definition only" method, in which students are asked to find definitions of 10 to 20 words in a dictionary and copy down the meanings before reading. This prescriptive approach has been described by researchers (Irvin, 1990; Ryder & Graves, 1994) as minimally effective, resulting in temporary retention of material, student disengagement, and little student understanding of text. Jitendra, Edwards, Sacks, and Jacobson (2004) attest to the effectiveness of intervention and direct instruction that go beyond definitional learning for vocabulary growth among students with learning disabilities. Nagy and Scott (2003) describe true word knowledge as being applied knowledge or "being able to do things with it: to recognize it in connected speech or in print, to access its meaning, to pronounce it—and to be able to do these things within a fraction of a second" (p. 273).

Unlike the "definition only" method of learning vocabulary, if concepts and words are to be learned it is best for the teacher to start with concrete experiences. Consider this story:

> A nine-year-old was visiting a theme park with his parents. They walked past a ride named "Ribbault's Adventure." Although the father pronounced the ride's name, the boy kept asking when they would get a chance to ride "Rabbit's Adventure." In exasperation, the father turned to the mother and asked, "Why can't he remember the name of the ride?"
>
> The mother pointed out that the boy had read *Alice in Wonderland* and *Peter Rabbit* and had picked a name that was close in looks and sounds to "Ribbault's Adventure." "Perhaps," she suggested, "when he gets on the ride, he will call it what it is."
>
> Sure enough, the guide on Ribbault's Adventure explained who Ribbault was. And when the boy exited the ride, he remarked, "That was fun. I'd like to ride Ribbault's Adventure again before we go home."

A Model of the
Relation of
Things and
Words in
an Individual's
Lexicon.
Note: A "thing"
is any real or
imaginable
object, feeling,
action, or idea.

**Potentially
learnable knowledge**
Thing not known and cannot be
learned with current prior knowledge;
additional learning is required before
thing may be learned: e.g., *kurtosis*

**Immediately
learnable knowledge**
Thing not known, but have sufficient
prior knowledge to conceptualize
thing with verbal or graphic descriptions or
definitions: e.g., *pentimento*

**Unorganized
knowledge (trivia)**
Fragmented knowledge of thing
that cannot be recalled without external
prompt, but is capable of incorporation into
schema: e.g., *cadenza*

**Organized
prior knowledge**
Thing known and organized
in schema, but not activated by
oral/written word and may be communicated
only by description: e.g., *philtrum*

**Recognition
knowledge**
Word and thing are
comprehended in listening
and reading but are not used in
speaking and writing: e.g., *shrift*
(as in "short *shrift*")

**Production
knowledge**
Word and thing
are used in speech
or writing: e.g., *toe*

From M. W. Kibby, November 1995, The organization and teaching of things and the words that signify them. *Journal of Adolescent & Adult Literacy, 39*(3), 208–223. Reprinted by permission of the International Reading Association and Michael W. Kibby.

This child was probably at what Kibby calls the stage of "immediately learnable knowledge." He did not know about Ribbault's adventure but had enough prior knowledge about adventures to "get it" once he received more information and an experience to link with the words.

Full-concept learning of vocabulary, according to Simpson (1987), requires four mental operations:

1. Recognizing and generating critical attributes—both examples and non-examples—of a concept

2. Seeing relationships between the concept to be learned and what is already known

3. Applying the concept to a variety of contexts

4. Generating new contexts for the learned concept

The first of the four operations can be developed by asking students to exclude a concept from a list of concepts to which it does not belong. Note the following:

·   muezzin   mosque   minaret   *mangrove*

Also, students can brainstorm attributes and nonattributes of a given concept, as shown in Activity 9.1.

Students can better understand relationships (operation 2) by brainstorming about targeted vocabulary concepts, then writing possible definitions. For mental operation 3, students can apply what they know about a vocabulary concept by being exposed to the word in different contexts. Stahl (1983) calls this teaching comprehension through developing **contextual knowledge.** Students can learn how to generate new contexts for a learned vocabulary term (operation 4) by creating new sentences using previously learned concepts. To encourage frequent practice at this task, Simpson (1987) recommends a technique called *paired-word sentence generation:* two words are given, and students are asked to write a sentence demonstrating the relationships between them. Possible examples are *method–analysis, genes–environment, graph–plot,* and *juvenile delinquency–recession.* A sentence for *juvenile delinquency–recession* might be, "Incidents of juvenile delinquency occur more frequently during a recession."

Word knowledge results from both incidental and intentional learning experiences. Considerable word knowledge is developed naturally through exposure and daily living through incidental experiences. There is neither time nor is it necessary to teach every word that becomes a part of an individual's store of knowledge (Beck, McKeown, & Kucan, 2002; Biemiller, 2001; Brabham & Villaume, 2002). Purposely setting up an environment for encouraging language play, inquiry, and discovery in addition to planning explicit instruction provides a means for positively influencing vocabulary acquisition to include both intentional and incidental learning pathways.

ACTIVITY 9.1   CONCEPT LEARNING: WORLD HISTORY

Use the textbook to brainstorm attributes and nonattributes of *nationalism.*

ATTRIBUTES		NONATTRIBUTES
honor	imperialism	maturity
pride	prestige	democracy
superiority	force	cooperation
wealth	fascism	isolationism
power		equality

Blachowicz and Fisher (2000, p. 504), in their review of the research on vocabulary instruction, found and identified four guiding principles. Students should

1. be immersed in words (incidental).

2. personalize word learning (intentional and incidental).

3. continue to add to their word knowledge through varied and repeated exposures (intentional).

4. be actively engaged in their own vocabulary development both to come to an understanding of words and to choose and apply strategies for independent word learning (intentional).

Incidental Vocabulary Development

Word knowledge is developed incidentally through conversation, word play (such as puns, rhymes, and jingles), exposure to spoken words from a variety of sources (such as friends, television, radio, and video), and wide reading. Our earliest experiences with language are exposures to spoken words as parents and caregivers respond to our needs. Language development begins as a spontaneous and natural process that occurs as we listen, experiment, approximate, and put our understanding into practice (Johnson, 2001). Through incidental experiences words are initially categorized and filed away in the mind based on personal connections and conceptions. Naive understandings may occur until explicit and intentional instruction is provided to clarify and realign faulty reasoning. For example, young children believe that the sun actually "comes up" before learning the full meaning of planetary movements and distinctions between revolving and rotating.

As children are read stories and literature steeped in rich vocabulary, the initial and repeated exposures to language beyond daily conversation add to personal vocabulary growth. Cunningham and Stanovich (1998) found, in their study examining vocabulary used in sources of spoken and written language, that rare or "rich" words are more frequently found in children's literature than in adult conversation, except for that which may occur in courtroom testimony. As children begin reading on their own, wide and extended independent reading experiences further contribute to vocabulary growth (National Reading Panel, 2000).

Though language begins with listening and speaking experiences and moves and develops into reading and writing, all four channels contribute to our continued growth as literate individuals. In their review of the literature on oral language development, Pinnell and Jaggar (1991) found evidence that students need time and opportunities to participate in various types of classroom talk including discussion, project work, role playing, storytelling, and drama. Activities that encourage classroom talk are important for continued vocabulary development and are not reserved exclusively for young children.

Francis and Simpson (2003) found that one way of improving secondary and college students' vocabulary knowledge is through actively involving them in oral expression activities. Effective practices identified in their study included teachers making concerted efforts to apply and use new vocabulary in their daily classroom conversations. Students in such settings are given opportunities to try out and understand appropriate use and application of the terms they are learning. This level of vocabulary implementation takes learning beyond memorization for a test.

For an interesting view, read about Pulido's (2004) study of the role of culture in incidental vocabulary development in *The Reading Matrix* 4:2. For a direct link, click on the web links option of the Chapter 9 resources on the book companion website.

Intentional Vocabulary Development

Making time to develop full word knowledge through intentional instruction for depth and breadth of concept understanding has proved beneficial (Francis and Simpson 2003; Nagy and Scott, 2000). Research supports practices that help students connect new vocabulary to known vocabulary and concepts. Francis and Simpson found that when teachers engaged students in explicit discussions identifying synonyms, antonyms, connotations, and nuances of language, students were helped to clarify misunderstandings and were redirected to improve their reading comprehension.

Through direct instruction teachers may think aloud, model, and provide opportunities for practice and clarification to scaffold strategies and techniques for independent word learning. Interactive strategies, in which students work together focusing on semantic connections using semantic maps, semantic feature analysis, and word sorts, have been identified in research as effective means for vocabulary development (Blachowitz & Fisher, 2000). The personal components of vocabulary learning that research supports include involving students in selecting words for study as well as choosing the strategies that work best for independent reading. Finally, instruction should go beyond introducing words prior to reading, the most common practice found in classrooms (Scott, Jamieson-Noel, and Asselin, 2003). Vocabulary instruction, just like comprehension and skills instruction, needs to be addressed before, during, and following the reading of text, providing repeated and reflective experiences with the words targeted for study.

VOCABULARY AND SCHOOL FAILURE

Often a mismatch occurs between school expectations and students' achievement, especially in the case of struggling readers (discussed more fully in Chapter 2). This is true despite a plethora of compensatory educational programs designed to reduce the conceptual and language deficits of culturally disadvantaged and minority children (Bryant, Goodwin, Bryant, & Higgins, 2003; Jitendra, Edwards, Sacks, & Jacobson, 2004; Moats, 2001). These children are often taught vocabulary through rote exercises that require dictionary definitions for extensive numbers of technical and specialized terms (Konopak & Williams, 1994). In a typical exercise, the teacher informs students that before reading a chapter they must look up in the dictionary and define 30 words found in the chapter. It's no wonder reading is often thought of as dull by students who have to perform such rote tasks! This method of teaching vocabulary and concepts is product oriented: the rote production of the written word is the product.

Rather than in-depth or thoughtful word exploration, what occurs is "considerable mentioning and assigning and little actual teaching" (Scott, Jamieson-Noel, & Asselin, 2003, p. 14). Such vocabulary exercises are used despite the fact that most disadvantaged students, at-risk populations, and poor readers use action words in much of their communication ("he gone," for example); they use process to facilitate information rather than memorization of an extensive written vocabulary. Because rote vocabulary exercises present words and terms in the abstract, these students seem unable to grasp either their surface or their underlying meaning.

You can read online about a vocabulary intervention developed specifically for struggling adolescent readers. An article by Curtis and Longa can be accessed through a direct link in the Chapter 9 resources on the book companion website.

To help these students—and all students learning words for which they seem to have no prior experiences or concepts—teachers need to present concepts in a concrete manner, through direct and purposeful experiences followed by varied and repeated exposures (Bryant, Goodwin, Bryant, & Higgins, 2003; Jitendra, Edwards, Sacks, & Jacobson, 2004; Moats, 2001; Piaget & Inhelder, 1969). Bryant and colleagues (2003) found, in their review of the research on vocabulary instruction for students with learning disabilities, a clear need for explicit, systematic instruction that includes opportunities for word manipulation, planned intervention, and personal connections and associations. It is especially important for instruction to include word examination that provides a means for deeper processing and retention at the word meaning level. Mnemonic devices and the key-word strategy were some techniques found to be effective for retention of content area vocabulary.

When teaching students with learning disabilities, teachers should limit the number of words for study to those most needed; and multiple, varied exposures are critical. Snow (2002) has suggested that productive approaches that make the most of word learning may accelerate the process and provide help for future learning. This may be done by creating semantic maps or by examining and manipulating word parts such as prefixes, suffixes, and roots. When hands-on experiences are not possible, students need activities of observation, such as field trips, demonstrations, graphics, and visuals, to build a knowledge base for learning. Attention should be given to building and enriching oral language and basic concepts of study in an environment that encourages focused classroom talk and word play. "Just as a house needs a strong foundation, so reading comprehension depends on a strong base of oral language and concept development" (Blachowitz & Fisher, 2004, p. 67).

Remember that a reader's background knowledge is very important in determining how much vocabulary she or he will understand and absorb. Students with broad background and understanding of the world will have an easier time learning vocabulary because of their wider experience. This view has been substantiated in research literature for decades (Blachowicz & Fisher, 2004; Ausubel, 1968; Carr & Wixson, 1986; Drevno et al., 1994; Graves, 1985; Henry, 1974). For instance, students who have toured historic Philadelphia can relate to a passage about the influence of the Constitution more easily than can those lacking such firsthand experience. Teachers who follow this view emphasize building on background knowledge in all phases of the

PAR Lesson Framework. For example, a teacher might ask students what they know about small loan agencies in a business mathematics lesson on small loans. She might carefully present new vocabulary such as *collateral, passbook savings, debt,* and *consolidation loans.* At each phase of the lesson, she would try to identify how much students already know about the topic. In this manner, the teacher is helping build students' general background knowledge.

Effective readers consider their own background of understanding when trying to solve for unknown words encountered in a text. A former student told the story of her 6-year-old son trying to figure out the word *Kentucky* in a book he was reading. He asked for her help but explained that he knew the word had something to do with chicken. He apparently was drawing from his own experience with takeout food.

Much of the discussion in this chapter so far has addressed ways to help students establish a **conceptual base of understanding**—an underlying knowledge of the subject matter—with which to grow in knowledge of vocabulary. We feel that vocabulary instruction can be beneficial in increasing the base of knowledge at any phase of a lesson. Teachers need to make their own vocabulary lessons that will aid students before, during, and after reading. They cannot always rely on basal reading series or textbook manuals' vocabulary exercises, because these mostly stress teaching vocabulary before reading in the "definition only" method mentioned earlier. Teachers' manuals may target words already known to your students or select words not particularly useful beyond the text selection. Letting students read freely in class or at home is important to vocabulary development but not sufficient for large vocabulary growth (Carver, 1994; Cunningham & Stanovich, 1998; Nagy, Herman, & Anderson, 1985). Students struggling with reading simply either cannot or do not independently read the volume of material necessary to make a significant difference in vocabulary growth (Baker, Simmons, & Kame'enui, 1998).

Students need preparation in vocabulary before reading a chapter or a lesson (the preparation phase of the PAR Lesson Framework), but it should not stop there. Often students need assistance with vocabulary during or immediately after the reading (the assistance phase of PAR). For in-depth word learning, students need longer periods of reflection to study vocabulary and attempt to understand how the terms convey meaning and relationships (the reflection phase of PAR). Research by Memory (1990) suggests that vocabulary development can be effective when taught at any of these stages—before, during, or after the reading assignment.

This three-step approach supports the specialized type of language development needed for students to reach full understanding of the academic and content-specific vocabulary necessary for study and life application. Content area learning involves gaining a clear understanding of sets of terms that are critical to new concept development. This adds to the load because not only are the terms unfamiliar, the concepts are new. The type of vocabulary associated with content area learning requires instruction that provides in-depth treatment going beyond superficial introduction. Because concepts often build on one another, gaining a clear understanding of terms basic to a concept is important for later learning and the complexity of advanced study. For example, students need to understand, remember, and use the terms learned in basic mathematics as they move into algebra and geometry.

In the remainder of this chapter we describe several research-based practices and strategies for developing vocabulary. They can be used before, during, or shortly after reading. They also can be used as follow-up activities (usually the next day) to reading. We describe how teachers can use these strategies to teach vocabulary through understandable activities that are meaningful to students.

Teaching Vocabulary in Preparation for Reading

Research by Carney and associates (1984) shows that vocabulary instruction before reading improves student comprehension regardless of a student's reading ability. Teaching vocabulary before reading involves not so much the teacher "teaching" the terms as the students exploring and attempting to make sense of them before beginning the reading. As strategic learners, students need to recognize whether a link exists between words in the content material and their own knowledge. Douglas Barnes (1976) speaks to the matter in this way:

> Children are not "little vessels . . . ready to have imperial gallons of facts poured into them until they were full to the brim," as Dickens put it. They have a personal history outside the school and its curriculum. In order to arrive at school they have mastered many complex systems of knowledge; otherwise they could not cope with everyday life. School for every child is a confrontation between what he "knows" already and what the school offers; this is true both of social learning and of the kinds of learning which constitute the manifest curriculum. Whenever school learning has gone beyond meaningless rote, we can take it that a child has made some kind of relationship between what he knows already and what the school has presented. (p. 22)

Several activities—word inventories, graphic organizers, mapping, modified cloze, possible sentences, vocabulary connections, and capsule vocabulary—can be used before reading to strengthen the relationship between what the student already knows and what is provided in the text.

Word Inventories

Included in this book as self-inventories, word inventories are used consistently at the start of each chapter. This activity encourages readers to assess their own prior knowledge and rate themselves. Although teachers can use such ratings to instruct, readers are in charge of their own assessment of conceptual knowledge. Activity 9.2 is an example of a word inventory developed for elementary school students.

Graphic Organizers

Reviews of graphic organizer research (Armbruster, 1992; Dunston, 1992; Egan, 1999; Rice, 1992; Swafford & Alvermann, 1989) conclude that graphic organizers significantly aid students in remembering text. Graphic organizers can be an effective strategy for getting students on the same wavelength as the teacher in understanding the

Directions: Use the happy faces to tell how well you know these words. This isn't a test and you won't be graded. Remember: You aren't supposed to know all the words.

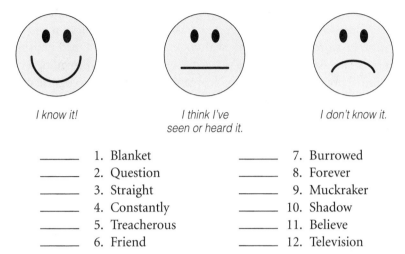

I know it!   I think I've seen or heard it.   I don't know it.

_____	1. Blanket	_____	7. Burrowed
_____	2. Question	_____	8. Forever
_____	3. Straight	_____	9. Muckraker
_____	4. Constantly	_____	10. Shadow
_____	5. Treacherous	_____	11. Believe
_____	6. Friend	_____	12. Television

Developed by Terry Bryce.

direction a lesson is taking. The teacher interacts with students by displaying the diagram and discussing why it is arranged in a particular way.

You can visit the CAST website sponsored by the National Center on Assessing the General Curriculum for more information on a variety of graphic organizers and the research base that supports their use. This site illustrates several types of graphic organizers and suggests ideas for use. Clink on the web links option of the Chapter 9 resources on the book companion website.

A semantic map (Johnson & Pearson, 1984) is one of the most popular types of graphic organizers because it is excellent at depicting the interrelationships and hierarchies of concepts in a lesson. Research (Bos & Anders, 1990) demonstrates the effectiveness of semantic mapping for increasing reading comprehension and vocabulary learning. Mapping was introduced in Chapter 7 as a way to develop comprehension. A semantic map can be used as a prereading or postreading exercise. To use semantic mapping before reading, follow these steps:

1. Select an important word from the reading assignment.

2. Ask students to think of as many related words and key concepts as possible that will help in understanding the key word.

3. List these words on the board as they are identified.

4. As an extension of this activity, have students rank the words or categorize them as "most important" and "least important." This activity may help

students begin to see that all words in the lesson are not equally important and that information needs to be categorized.

5. Organize the words into a diagram similar to the one in Activity 9.3 (for elementary language arts).

Software like Inspiration and Kidspiration may fit seamlessly into a lesson using features like Rapid Fire to create graphic organizers with visual elements and vocabulary connections. The teacher may select a target word from the lesson and have students contribute words they associate with it. As the words are typed in using Rapid Fire, they are immediately added to a web with connecting lines, providing a visual for all to see. Initial organizers can then be reorganized as students recognize groupings, headings, and subheadings. From the Chapter 9 resources on the book companion website, you can visit Inspiration online to find and experience an interactive presentation/

ACTIVITY 9.3 SEMANTIC MAP IN ELEMENTARY LANGUAGE ARTS

ROTTWEILERS

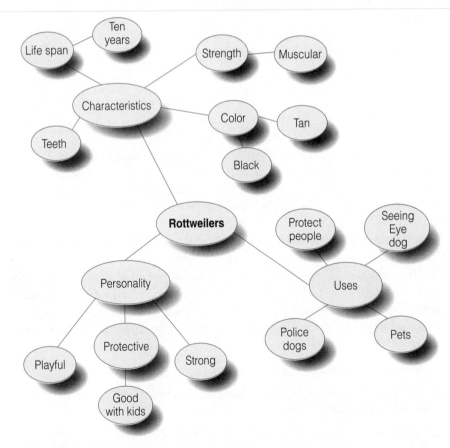

CHILI PEPPERS

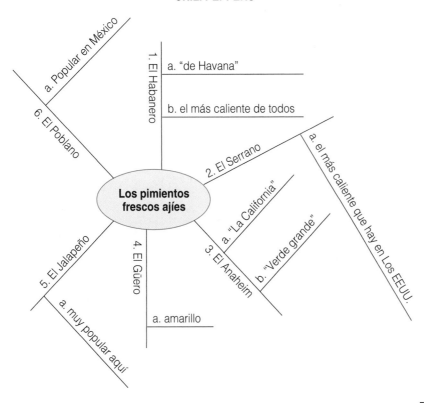

Developed by Brian Littman.

demonstration using graphic organizers and to discover further information about this product's utility. Activity 9.4 shows a variation of a semantic map in which a Spanish teacher helped students learn about types of chili peppers.

Using the semantic map as their base, Schwartz and Raphael (1985) designed a word map. Directly under the key word, which is circled or boxed, examples that remind students of that word are placed. To the right of the key word, properties are written. The teacher might ask, "What is it like?" Directly above the key word, the concept of the word is represented as a definition or description. In this way students are led in their understanding from concrete examples to abstract definitions and concepts. Activity 9.5 is a word map for the key word *metaphor*. Activity 9.6 presents a type of word map sometimes called a *spider map* because the graphic organizer resembles a spider's web. This activity is from an early elementary lesson on the benefits of music. Both semantic maps and word maps provide excellent ways of getting students to clarify their thinking before reading an assignment.

WORD MAP SIMILE
<KEY>

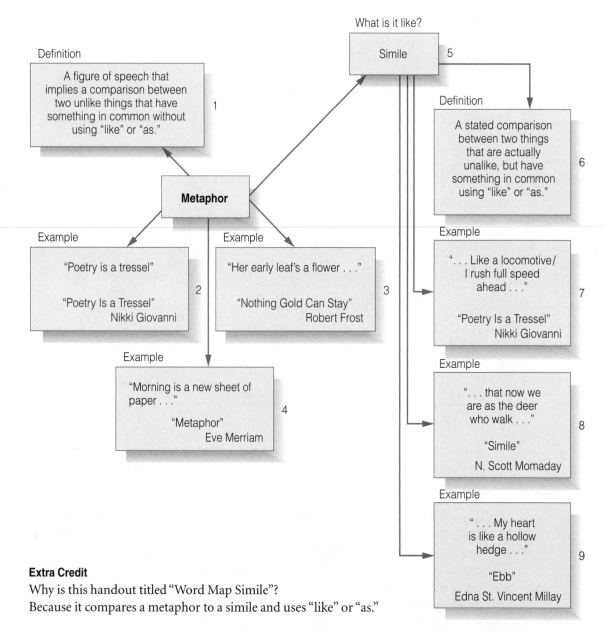

What is it like?

Simile 5

Definition

A figure of speech that implies a comparison between two unlike things that have something in common without using "like" or "as."   1

Metaphor

Definition

A stated comparison between two things that are actually unalike, but have something in common using "like" or "as."   6

Example

"Poetry is a tressel"

"Poetry Is a Tressel"
Nikki Giovanni   2

Example

"Her early leaf's a flower . . ."

"Nothing Gold Can Stay"
Robert Frost   3

Example

". . . Like a locomotive/
I rush full speed
ahead . . ."

"Poetry Is a Tressel"
Nikki Giovanni   7

Example

"Morning is a new sheet of paper . . ."

"Metaphor"
Eve Merriam   4

Example

". . . that now we
are as the deer
who walk . . ."

"Simile"
N. Scott Momaday   8

Example

" . . . My heart
is like a hollow
hedge . . ."

"Ebb"
Edna St. Vincent Millay   9

Extra Credit

Why is this handout titled "Word Map Simile"?

Because it compares a metaphor to a simile and uses "like" or "as."

Developed by Tara Furges.

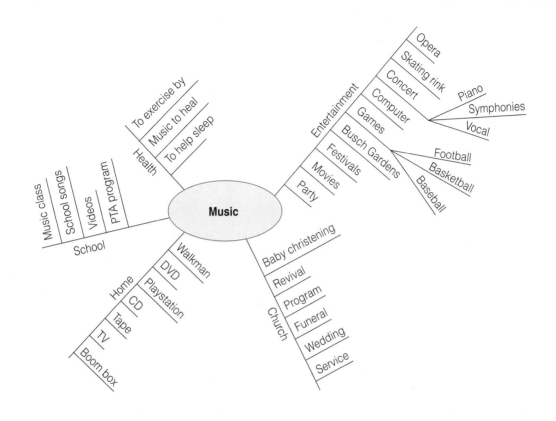

Developed by Audra Jones and her students.

Modified Cloze Procedures

Chapter 5 introduced cloze as a means of determining reader background. Cloze passages can also be constructed to teach technical or general vocabulary. Passages used in this manner are modified for instructional purposes. Instead of deleting words at predetermined intervals, as when measuring readability and checking students' reading ability, teachers select an important passage from the text and delete key words. Teachers may also create their own cloze passages of 50 to 100 words to assess students' knowledge of vocabulary and concepts on a certain topic. Activity 9.7 presents a passage of more than 100 words constructed by a teacher to assess students' knowledge of the first settlers in North America. Students can fill in the blanks individually, then discuss their answers in small groups. The best, or most unusual, answers can eventually be shared with the entire class.

The United States of America is a young country. It is only about _____ years old. North America had been explored for more than _____ years before any settlers came to live here. After the first settlement at _____ in 1607, many more European settlers came to North America. Some wanted to find _____ freedom. Others came for the chance to own _____. Still others came to teach _____ to American Indians. At first, it was _____ for the colonists. Many did not know how to _____ the land and were not used to wild _____. As a result, many colonists _____.

Possible Sentences

Possible sentences (Moore & Arthur, 1981) is an activity that combines vocabulary and prediction. It is designed to acquaint students with new vocabulary that they will encounter in their reading and guide them as they attempt to verify the accuracy of the statements they generate. Additionally, it arouses curiosity concerning the passage to be read. This activity is best used when unfamiliar vocabulary is mixed with familiar terminology. When using this technique, the teacher might give students a worksheet such as the one shown in Activity 9.8. Teachers pick between five and eight vocabulary terms, such as those from elementary science in Activity 9.8. For each term, students write a possible sentence on the left side of the worksheet. Then, during reading, they look for the real meaning of the term and write this meaning in a sentence. In doing so, students create a mnemonic, with the possible sentence cueing them to the real meaning of the word. This is a simple but powerful strategy for learning words. Research attests to the advantage of using such mnemonic devices to learn vocabulary (Levin et al., 1992; Moore & Surber, 1992; Scruggs et al., 1992). Mnemonic devices are discussed later in this chapter and in detail in Chapter 8.

Vocabulary Connections

Iwicki (1992) describes a strategy whereby students use a term from a previous book in shared literature study to describe a situation in a book currently being studied. In this way, connections are made between old vocabulary and the new book. For example, the word *pandemonium,* found in *Welcome Home, Jelly Bean* (Shyer, 1988), can be related to events in *The Black Stallion* (Farley, 1941). In other content areas, words from a previous chapter can be used to see relationships in a new one. In occupational mathematics, for example, the term *conversion* may be used with *product volumes* in one chapter and again in a chapter on the use of mathematics in leisure activities (converting international track-and-field times from English measurements to metrics). Iwicki reports that vocabulary connections retain their appeal to students throughout schooling. They provide an excellent way for students to use higher-level thinking in comparing vocabulary from one content area subject to another.

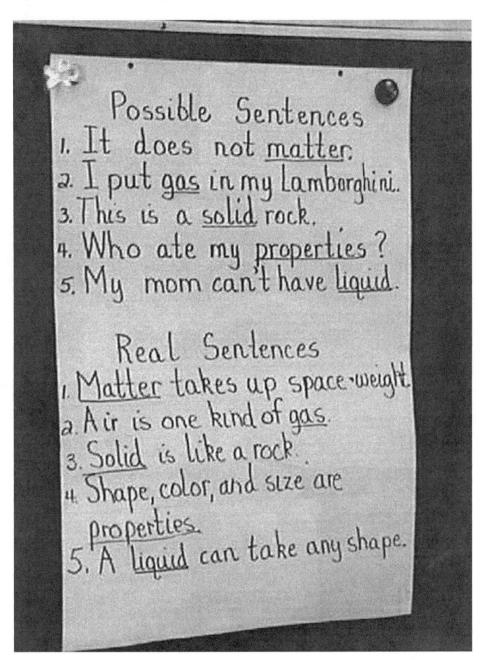

Possible Sentences
1. It does not <u>matter</u>.
2. I put <u>gas</u> in my Lamborghini.
3. This is a <u>solid</u> rock.
4. Who ate my <u>properties</u>?
5. My mom can't have <u>liquid</u>.

Real Sentences
1. <u>Matter</u> takes up space·weight.
2. Air is one kind of <u>gas</u>.
3. <u>Solid</u> is like a rock.
4. Shape, color, and size are <u>properties</u>.
5. A <u>liquid</u> can take any shape.

Developed by Suzanne McDaniel.

Capsule Vocabulary

Capsule vocabulary (Crist, 1975) is an activity that helps readers explore meaning relationships among words and helps students connect those relationships to what they already know. The teacher selects a list or capsule of several words either found in the text or useful for understanding the text material. After the teacher briefly defines each word and uses it in a sentence, students work in pairs to use the terms in sentences. Next students write sentences or a summary using the words. Then they check their sentences against the text material.

Here is an example of the use of capsule vocabulary in an English as a second language class. Students worked in pairs to write sentences about new words they had encountered. Eighteen students from Cambodia, Vietnam, Korea, and Russia with widely different levels of English proficiency participated. Some had been in the United States for three years, some for less than two weeks. The teacher, Barbara Ingber, prepared a list of numbered words pertaining to shopping in a supermarket: *supermarket, cashier, coupons, groceries, food, detergent, diapers, bag, shopping cart, money,* and *change.* She dictated these words, and students wrote them in their notebooks using temporary spellings. Then the teacher asked for students to call the words back to her as she wrote each one on the chalkboard using the correct spelling. Students tried to define words as they were written on the board. For those they could not define, the teacher provided a definition with a sentence or an action (she pretended to push a shopping cart). Next the students worked in pairs, orally making sentences for each word. She was careful to pair students from different countries so that each had to communicate in English, the common language. Students then wrote their sentences on the board. The group studied each sentence and made corrections for standard English, with the teacher's help. Students then copied the corrected sentences and read them aloud to their partners. This activity utilized paired learning as well as listening, speaking, reading, and writing.

> *Note Ingber's use of listening, temporary (inventive) spelling, and oral interaction, as well as modeling and demonstration to prepare students for using vocabulary in writing and reading.*

TEACHING VOCABULARY TO ASSIST STUDENTS IN THEIR READING

Mealey and Konopak (1990), in an excellent review of the research on preteaching content area vocabulary, questioned the value of solely preteaching content terms. Like these researchers, we maintain that students need to be assisted in all content areas and at every grade level in interpreting unfamiliar words. Teachers cannot "protect" students from words by teaching before reading every difficult term that they will encounter. McMurray, Laffey, and Morgan (1979) found that students skipped over unfamiliar words when they had no strategy for learning vocabulary. Hynd and associates (1995) report that students tend to skip over text that does not confirm their prior knowledge, unless their attention is directed specifically to it. Teachers need to assist students in understanding words that clarify text for the reader. Encouraging students to develop word consciousness (Graves, 2000) may help them become aware of unfamiliar words that interfere with their understanding of the text. Using sticky notes, highlighting tape, or flags to mark difficult or interesting words in the text engages the reader in actively attending to and identifying words for further consideration. Five excellent techniques for assisting readers are context clue discovery, structural analysis, DISSECT, word attack paradigms, and vocabulary lists. Activities already introduced in this text, such as organizational (jot) charts, can also be adapted to assist readers.

Context Clue Discovery

To begin to understand the importance of "concepts in context," think of any word in isolation; then try to define it. Take, for example, the word *run*. It is not difficult to give a synonym for the word, but it does not have a clear meaning until it is placed in a context. You may have thought immediately of the most common definition, "to move with haste," but "to be or campaign as a candidate for election," "to publish, print, or make copies," or even "to cause the stitches in a garment to unravel" would have been equally accurate. A precise meaning cannot be determined until *run* is seen in context. One way to help students recognize the importance of context to meaning is to do a brief word association activity (see Activity 9.9) with them. Have them number a sheet of paper from 1 to 10 and write a one- or two-word definition/association that comes to mind as you call the words out orally. Select words that clearly have multiple meanings and words for which the students probably know two or three of the meanings.

ACTIVITY 9.9   WORD ASSOCIATION ACTIVITY

Word	Possible Definition	Possible Definition
1. Record	Musical disk	Data/information
2. Tie	Clothing for neck	Interlocking
3. Mouse	Furry animal	Computer device
4. Bad	Not good	Good
5. Story	A tale	Building level
6. Column	Newspaper story	Stone pillar
7. Break	Tear up	Brief relaxing period
8. Cell	Jail	Body part
9. Bank	Building for money	Land next to river
10. Bill	Bird part	Money owed

Students often use context clues to help determine the meaning of a word (Konopak, 1988). Sometimes, however, students fail at using context clues because they lack a systematic strategy for figuring out unknown words (Hafner, 1967). To help students develop the ability to use context to discover the meaning of unfamiliar words, teachers can discuss specific clues that they should look for in the text.

DEFINITIONS

Authors often define a word in the sentence in which it first appears. This technique is used frequently in textbooks when an author introduces terminology. Note the following examples:

> The *marginal revenue product* of the input is the change in total revenue associated with using one more unit of the variable input.

> The *peltier effect* is the production of heat at the junction of two metals on the passage of a current.

SIGNAL WORDS

Certain words or phrases may be used to signal the reader that a word or a term is about to be explained or that an example will be presented. Some of the most frequently used signal words are listed here, followed by two sentences using signal words:

for example	these (synonym)	in (the way) that
this way	especially	such
such as	like	

> Martin Luther King was more than just a leader in America, *in that* he was recognized worldwide.

> The man lost the sympathy of the judge, *especially* when he was found in a drunken stupor shortly after being let out of jail.

DIRECT EXPLANATIONS

Often authors provide an explanation for an unfamiliar term that is being introduced. This technique is used frequently in complex writing.

> Joe was a *social being,* whose thoughts and behaviors were strongly influenced by the people and things around him and whose thoughts and behaviors strongly influenced the people he was around.

> Mead emphasized that the mind is a social product; indeed, one of the most important achievements of socialization is the development of *cognitive abilities*—intellectual capacities such as perceiving, remembering, reasoning, calculating, and believing.

SYNONYMS

A challenging term may be followed by a simpler, more commonly understood word, even though the words may not be perfect synonyms. Again, the author is attempting to provide the reader with an explanation or definition—in this instance, by using a comparison. In the first example here, *obscure* is explained by comparison to the word *unintelligible.* In the second sentence, *attacks* helps explain *audacious comments.*

> The lecture was so *obscure* that the students labeled it *unintelligible.*

> There were *audacious comments* and *attacks* on prominent leaders of the opposition.

ANTONYMS

An author may define or explain a term by contrasting it with words of opposite meaning:

> The young swimmer did not have the *perseverance* of her older teammates and *quit* at the halfway point in the race.

> All this is rather *optimistic,* though it is better to err on the side of hope than in favor of *despair.*

INFERENCES

Students can often infer the meaning of an unfamiliar word from the mood and tone of the selection. In this case, meaning must be deduced through a combination of the author's use of mood, tone, and imagery and the reader's background knowledge and experience. The author thus paints a picture of meaning rather than concretely defining or explaining the word within the text. In the passage that follows, the meaning of *opaque* is not made clear. The reader must infer the meaning from the mood and tone of the paragraph and from personal experience with a substance such as black asphalt.

> This is it, this is it, right now, the present, this empty gas station, here, this western wind, this tang of coffee on the tongue, and I am patting the puppy, I am watching the mountain. And the second I verbalize this awareness in my brain, I cease to see the mountain or feel the puppy. I am *opaque,* so much black asphalt. But at the same second, the second I know I've lost it, I also realize that the puppy is still squirming on his back under my hand. Nothing has changed for him. He draws his legs down to stretch the skin out so he feels every fingertip's stroke along his furred and arching side, his flank, his flung-back throat. (From *Pilgrim at Tinker Creek* by Annie Dillard. New York: Harper's Magazine Press, 1975)

Research suggests that students can use context clue strategies to unlock the meaning of unfamiliar terms (Stahl, 1986). Therefore, it is a good idea to have these six clues (with explanations and sample sentences) posted at points around the classroom or on handouts to be kept in students' work folders.

CONTEXT CLUE TYPES AND EXAMPLES

1. **Definitions:** An *extemporaneous* speech is one that is given on the spot without prior preparation.
2. **Signal words:** There are several forms of *precipitation* like rain, sleet, snow, and hail.
3. **Direct explanations:** Carl was *despondent,* feeling so downhearted that he didn't want to participate in anything.

4. **Synonyms:** When we looked into the jar we saw the *larva* stage, or worm, of the beetle we were studying.

5. **Antonyms:** Tamara was quite *gregarious* while her sister, Mary, was instead very shy.

6. **Inferences:** It was a good thing the locksmith charged only a *nominal* fee to unlock John's car because John had only a few dollars in his pockets.

Structural Analysis

Even if students practice and remember the strategy, context clues sometimes are not of much help in decoding unfamiliar words (Blachowicz and Fisher, 2000; Nagy & Stahl, 2000; Schatz, 1984). For example, readers probably would have trouble guessing the meaning of the following italicized terms from clues in the context:

Nations impose burdens that violate the laws of *equity*.

A very important finding about the effects of mass media relates to *latency*.

They put a *lien* on our house.

Using context clues alone in these sentences would probably give readers a vague idea of the meaning or no idea at all. In these cases, it may be more helpful to use structural analysis along with contextual analysis to derive the meaning. Structural analysis provides a way to examine words looking for roots or affixes as keys to unlocking word meanings. Roots, prefixes, and suffixes are all morphemes. Morphemes are the smallest meaning-bearing units that make up words. In the word *unlock* there are two morphemes, *un* and *lock*. A **morpheme** can be **free** to stand alone like *lock,* or **bound** like *un,* which must be joined to another morpheme. Research by Biemiller (2001) and Baumann, Edwards, Boland, Olejnik, and Kame'enui (2003) provides evidence to support the use of morphemic analysis along with contextual analysis for inferring the meanings of unknown words.

Consider the following passage concerning sexual dimorphism:

An interesting relationship between sexual dimorphism and domestic duties exists among some species. Consider an example from birds. The sexes of song sparrows look very much alike. The males have no conspicuous qualities which immediately serve to release reproductive behavior in females. Thus courtship in this species may be a rather extended process as pair-bonding (mating) is established. Once a pair has formed, both sexes enter into the nest building, feeding, and defense of the young. The male may only mate once in a season, but he helps to maximize the number of young which reach adulthood carrying his genes. He is rather inconspicuous, so whereas he doesn't turn on females very easily, he also doesn't attract predators to the nest.

The peacock, on the other hand, is raucous and garish. When he displays to a drab peahen, he must present a veritable barrage of releasers to her reproductive IRMs. In any case, he displays madly and frequently and is successful indeed. Once having seduced an awed peahen, he doesn't stay to help with the mundane chores of child rearing, but instead disappears into the sunset looking for new conquests. (From R. A. Wallace, *Biology: The World of Life.* Copyright 1975 by Goodyear Publishing Co., Santa Monica, California)

After reading this passage we know the following:

A relationship exists between sexual dimorphism and some species.

Sparrows share domestic duties.

Peafowl do not share domestic duties.

Mating and pair-bonding are different for sparrows and peafowl.

Take a look at some of the online sources of common prefixes, roots, and suffixes. Click on the web links option of the Chapter 9 resources on the book companion website.

What is the cause of the difference? Your response should be "sexual dimorphism." If you know that *di* means "two" and *morph* means "form or shape," then you can figure out the term *sexual dimorphism*. (The CD contains a list of prefixes, suffixes, and roots of words, with their meanings and examples.)

Semantic maps make good vehicles for illustrating morphological relationships. Kidspiration and Inspiration, the software tools for creating semantic maps noted previously in this chapter, provide a way to include picture examples along with words and word parts being studied. Open and closed word sorts (explained later in this chapter) also work well for assisting students as they develop their understanding of words that share common morphemes. In working with young students, an activity called Affix Animals offers a playful way to experiment with prefixes and suffixes. Students are given a list of numbers and characteristic affixes that they may consider in order to draw, create, and appropriately name an imaginary animal (see Figure 9.2).

FIGURE 9.2

Biheaded, Trilegged Hydrosaur

DISSECT

This mnemonic, created by Deshler and Schumacher (1988), provides a ready reminder of several factors that may help when determining a word's meaning. When modeled and practiced it may be a helpful tool for independent reading:

Discover the word's context.

Isolate the prefix.

Separate the suffix.

Say the stem or root word.

Examine the stem or root word.

Check with someone.

Try the dictionary.

Several free online dictionary sources are available. For a direct link, click on the web links option of the Chapter 9 resources on the book companion website.

Word Attack Paradigms

Aguiar and Brady (1991) suggest that vocabulary deficits of less skilled readers stem from difficulty in establishing accurate phonological representations for new words. Their research points to the importance of structural analysis and the following strategy, called a *word attack paradigm,* to help students recognize words. In this activity, students are given a card with a series of steps to help them decipher new words when they encounter them in reading. Such a paradigm might look like this:

1. Figure out the word from the meaning of the sentence. The word must make sense in the sentence.
2. Take off the ending of the word. Certain endings, such as *s, d, r, es, ed, er, est, al,* or *ing,* may be enough to make the word look "new."
3. Break the word into syllables. Don't be afraid to try two or three ways to break the word. Look for prefixes, suffixes, and root words that are familiar.
4. Sound the word out. Try to break the word into syllables several times, sounding it out each time. Do you know a word that begins with the same letters? Do you know a word that ends the same? Put them together.
5. Look in the glossary if there is one in the back of the book.
6. Ask a friend in class or the teacher. No one should be ashamed of asking someone for help in figuring out a word.
7. Finally, as a last option, find the definition of the word in the dictionary.

Dictionaries should be the last source one uses in figuring out the meaning of a word, after all other sources are exhausted. Unfortunately, teachers often tell students to use the dictionary as a first option in discovering the meaning of words. Earlier in this chapter we discussed Kibby's (1995) continuum of word knowledge (see Figure 9.1). His model makes clear that background knowledge must be built before learnable knowledge can be effectively addressed. Thus by encouraging students to consider what is known those first levels of knowledge are activated. If students understand how context, affixes, roots, and syllables may be used to help unlock the meaning of words, they are provided techniques that may quickly aid them as independent learners. Dictionaries as a first choice may often serve to confuse by using vague terminology or derivatives of the word under examination to define that word. In essence, a word attack paradigm as we have described gives students a way to attempt newfound words without opening a dictionary. Students should keep the paradigm in their folders, or a large one should be posted on the wall by the teacher.

Vocabulary Lists

Students can be encouraged to make vocabulary lists of new terms they have mastered, whether by context clue discovery, structural analysis, or word attack paradigm. Students may keep such lists in notebooks or on file cards. If they use cards, first they can write the word and its dictionary pronunciation on the front side. Then on the back they can write the sentence in which the word was found and the dictionary definition or paraphrased definition in their own words. Dictionary use is more appropriate at this point because students have mastered the words and are finalizing and demonstrating understanding of various aspects of each term. Periodically, students can exchange their notebooks or file cards and call out vocabulary terms to one another, as they often do when spelling words: one student calls out the term, and another gives the definition and uses the word in a sentence. In this manner, students can make a habit of working daily and weekly with words to expand their content vocabulary. Activity 9.10 is an example of a vocabulary list with several words recorded.

Organizational (Jot) Charts

Students can compare and contrast words using organizational (jot) charts, as described in Chapter 7. For instance, a Spanish teacher had third-year students chart command words so they could see at a glance on one simple chart the relationship of

---

ACTIVITY 9.10 BEGINNING VOCABULARY LIST

Word	Page	Possible Definition	Verified Definition
Dwelling	132	Living area	A place where people live
Fossil	133	To harden or make like stone	The remains, trace, or impression of an animal or plant that lived long ago

Key	Tú		Ud.		Uds.	
afirmativo hablar comer escribir	**-ar** **-er, ir**	habla- come escribe	**-ar** **-er, ir**	hable coma escriba	**-ar** **-er, ir**	hablen coman escriban
irregulares	decir-di hacer-haz ir-ve poner-pon	salir-sal ser-se´ tener-ten venir-ven	dar-de´ estar-este´ ir-vaya saber-sepa	ser-sea	dar-den estar-este´n ir-vayan saber-sepan	ser-sean
escribir **negativo** hablar comer	**-ar** **-er, ir**	no hables no comas no escribas	**-ar** **-er, ir**	no hable no coma no escriba	**-ar** **-er, ir**	no hablen no coman no escriban
irregulares	**dar-** **ir-** **estar-** **ser-**	no des no vayas no este´s no seas	dar- estar- ir- saber- ser-	no de´ no este´ no vaya no sepa no sea	dar- estar- ir- saber- ser-	no den no este´n no vayan no sepan no sean

Developed by Heather Hemstreet.

the three types of commands in negative and affirmative statements. Activity 9.11 shows the chart. The table creation tool in any word processing program provides an interesting and useful computer technique for this strategy.

TEACHING VOCABULARY AS A REFLECTION ACTIVITY

Even though considerable research shows the benefits of teaching vocabulary before reading (Carney et al., 1984; Medo & Ryder, 1993), an intriguing finding consistently emerging from reading research is that it can be as beneficial—or more so—to teach vocabulary after reading as before the reading (Mealey & Konopak, 1990; Memory, 1990). For years the conventional wisdom has been that vocabulary is best taught before reading. In fact, however, the more students are asked to discuss, brainstorm, and think about what they have learned, the more they comprehend and retain the material. Thus the reflection phase of vocabulary development holds much promise in helping students thoroughly grasp the meaning of difficult terms in their reading. In this section we offer a number of strategies for reflection. We feel that these are best carried out by students working in small groups.

Interactive Cloze Procedure

Meeks and Morgan (1978) describe a strategy called the *interactive cloze procedure*, which was designed to encourage students to pay close attention to words in print and to actively seek the meaning of passages by studying vocabulary terms. They offer the following paradigm for using the interactive cloze:

1. Select a passage of 100 to 150 words from a textbook. It should be a passage that students have had difficulty comprehending or one that the instructor feels is important for them to comprehend fully.

2. Make appropriate deletions of nouns, verbs, adjectives, or adverbs. The teacher can vary the form and number of deletions depending on the purpose of the exercise.

3. Have students complete the cloze passage individually, filling in as many blanks as possible. Set a time limit based on the difficulty of the passage.

4. Divide students into small groups of three or four. Instruct them to compare answers and come to a joint decision about the best response for each blank.

5. Reassemble the class as a whole. Read the selection intact from the text. Give students opportunities to express opinions on the suitability of the author's choice of terms compared to their choices.

6. Strengthen short-term recall by testing using the cloze passage.

Use the web links option of the Chapter 9 resources on the book companion website to locate and visit a page from a reading WebQuest that spotlights semantic feature analysis.

Meeks and Morgan describe using the technique to teach imagery by omitting words that produce vivid images. Activity 9.12 is such a cloze, based on a passage from H. G. Wells's *The Red Room* (1896).

Semantic Feature Analysis

Semantic feature analysis (Pittleman et al., 1991) is a technique for helping students understand deeper meanings and nuances of language. To accomplish the analysis, first the teacher lists terms vertically on the chalkboard and asks students to help choose the features that will be written across the top of the chalkboard. (Teachers can also

---

ACTIVITY 9.12 INTERACTIVE CLOZE: H. G. WELLS

I saw the candle in the right sconce of one of the mirrors _____ and go right out, and almost immediately its companion followed it. There was no mistake about it. The flame vanished, as if the wicks had been suddenly _____ between a _____ and a thumb, leaving the wick neither _____ nor smoking, but _____. While I stood _____, the candle at the _____ of the bed went out, and the _____ seemed to take another step towards me.

Vocabulary words:
finger
gaping
wink
black
shadows
foot
glowing
nipped

---

choose the features beforehand.) Students then complete the matrix by marking a plus sign (+) for features that apply to each word. In certain situations, students can be asked to make finer discriminations: whether a vocabulary term always (A), sometimes (S), or never (N) happens with a feature. We recommend students do this analysis after reading the lesson, having used a technique such as the guided reading procedure or the directed reading–thinking activity (see Chapter 7). Activity 9.13 shows a semantic feature analysis used in a science class on energy.

ACTIVITY 9.13 GRID FOR SEMANTIC FEATURE ANALYSIS

Topic: ___Energy___ (Chapter 11)

Directions: Mark those features that apply to each vocabulary term.

A = the vocabulary term always applies to the feature
S = the vocabulary term sometimes applies to the feature
N = the vocabulary term never applies to the feature

Features

Vocabulary Terms	Renewable resource	Nonrenewable resource	Fossil fuels—direct use	Nuclear material	Naturally occurs	Manmade materials	Conservable	Pro-environment	Pollutant
Uranium^{235}									
Hydrogen									
Biomass									
Geothermal energy									
Hydroelectricity									
Wind energy									
Passive solar heating									
Active solar heating									
Deuterium + Tritium									
Oil									
Coal									
Natural gas									

Developed by Wendy Barcroft.

We feel the semantic feature analysis is an excellent activity for teaching vocabulary—perhaps the best activity there is. It is powerful because students make fine gradations of meaning concerning vocabulary terms, stating whether a term is affiliated always, sometimes, or never with a given concept or feature. With some low achievers teachers will need to fill out both the vocabulary terms and features beforehand. We recommend that after considerable practice in doing the technique this way, students be allowed in groups to (1) brainstorm words in the reading that they find difficult and (2) find the major concepts that they are learning in the chapter—that is, the features. Eventually, then, students can both determine and fill out the matrix themselves. One caution is in order, however. This technique was originally suggested as both a prereading activity and a postreading activity, but in our informal research we have found students do better with semantic features after they have completed the reading and have established a conceptual base of knowledge about the passage.

Word Puzzles

The Discover School's Puzzlemaker website provides numerous vocabulary activities and puzzlemaking options.

Almost all students enjoy word puzzles, and computer programs now make them easier to construct. The teacher enters the vocabulary terms and definitions, and the computer program constructs the puzzle. If a computer is unavailable, teachers can construct their own puzzles by graphically displaying the terms across and down and drawing boxes around the words. The boxes are numbered both across and down, and definitions are placed beside the grid. Activity 9.14 is a word puzzle in geography made for second grade.

Postgraphic Organizers

Earlier in this chapter, we discussed how students could help construct their own graphic organizers before reading to learn new vocabulary terms and to attempt to construct a hierarchical pattern of organization. To enhance concept development, students can return to the organizers after reading. Chapter 7 described postgraphic organizers for use in the reflection phase of learning. Here we present a variation specifically for vocabulary. Students can construct a postgraphic organizer directly after the reading. Activity 9.15 shows a postgraphic organizer completed by several college students on the subject of how best to construct graphic representations.

Numerous websites provide examples of graphic organizers and suggestions for their use. For some direct links, click on the web links option of the Chapter 9 resources on the book companion website.

ACTIVITY 9.14 Geographic Terms Word Puzzle

NAME ____

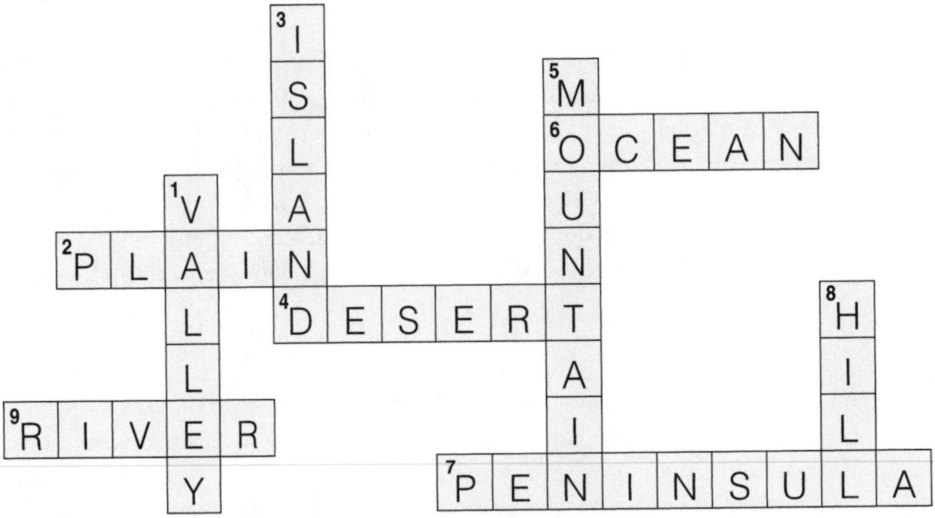
1 VALLEY
2 PLAIN
3 ISLAND
4 DESERT
5 MOUNTAIN
6 OCEAN
7 PENINSULA
8 HILL
9 RIVER

DOWN

1. Low land between hills or mountains.
3. Land that has water all around it.
5. The highest kind of land.
8. Land that rises above the land around it.

ACROSS

2. Flat land.
4. A dry place with little rain.
6. A very large body of salt water.
7. Land that has water on three sides.
9. A long body of water that flows across the land.

Developed by Laurie Smith.

Categorization

One of the best ways for students to learn relationships of concepts after a reading is through a categorization activity. **Categorization** is the act of assigning something to a class, a group, or a division. Categorization can be accomplished through a word relationship activity that begins with the teacher suggesting a topic and asking students to supply words that describe the topic. The teacher may supplement the words given by the students or skim the text to find more words. If students' abilities or backgrounds are limited, the teacher can provide the list. Activity 9.16 is a list of body systems, developed by a science teacher.

Students organize the list of words into smaller lists of items that have something in common, as shown in Activity 9.16. It is best during this phase for students to work in small groups to categorize and label the words. The groups explain their categories

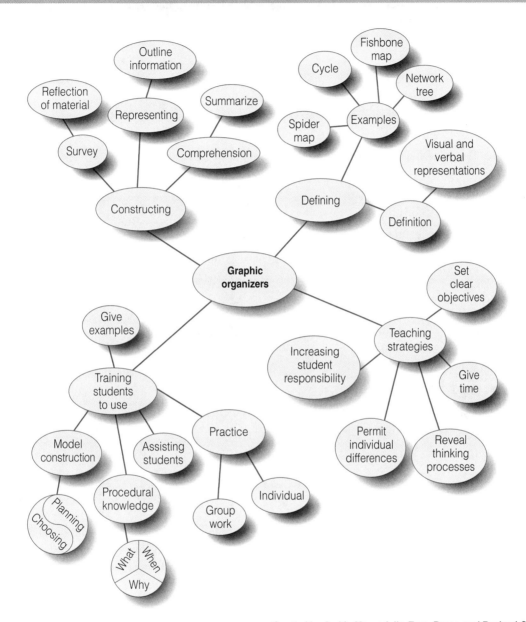

Created by Jackie Meccariello, Terry Bryce, and Racheal Curry.

Below are three categories that describe functioning systems in the human body—the digestive, respiratory, and circulatory systems.

DIGESTIVE	RESPIRATORY	CIRCULATORY

Place each of the following vocabulary terms in the correct category:

aorta	gastric juice	trachea
esophagus	diaphragm	flatus
ulcer	lung	artery
atrium	salivary gland	asthma
pneumonia	angina pectoris	hypertension
bronchi	ventricle	peristaltic waves

Answers:

DIGESTIVE	RESPIRATORY	CIRCULATORY
ulcer	asthma	aorta
gastric juice	pneumonia	atrium
salivary glands	bronchi	angina pectoris
flatus	diaphragm	ventricle
peristaltic waves	lung	artery
esophagus	trachea	hypertension

Developed by Kim Blowe.

and labels to the entire class; then the whole class tries to reach a consensus on what the correct labels are and where the particular words belong. During this final phase, the teacher needs to act as a guide to make certain that discussion and labeling are being channeled in the proper direction. It is also essential that students be allowed to provide a rationale for their decisions.

The focus on explanation and discussion in this activity makes it an excellent strategy for teaching difficult vocabulary, concept development, and critical thinking, especially because much learning depends on students' ability to create meaningful categories of information. Practiced in a relaxed and purposeful atmosphere, this activity can be an excellent tool for helping students develop concepts, improve comprehension, and retain information. Gillett and Temple (1983) call this type of categorization activity a *word sort*. In a **closed word sort,** students are given the categories in advance. This teaches classification and deductive reasoning. In an **open word sort,** students have to group words as concepts and title the relationship. This teaches inference, or reading between the lines, as discussed in Chapter 7.

Maggie's Teachers' Lounge online provides suggestions for word sorts focusing on science topics. These sorts are based on phonetic elements and principles. For a direct link, click on the web links option of the Chapter 9 resources on the book companion website.

DR–TA Vocabulary Search

When doing a directed reading–thinking activity in a content area classroom, the teacher can ask students to jot down difficult vocabulary terms. The student lists are given to the teacher without student names, and these terms become the words to be studied after the DR–TA or at the beginning of the next class period.

The teacher first teaches word recognition by using a "word families" phonics approach to sound out the word. If the word is *expressive,* for example, the teacher asks for other words in the same word family:

express

expression

press

pressure

Students work through the word family to sound out the word, thereby achieving word recognition.

Next comes a skimming and scanning exercise. The teacher begins by asking, "Who can find *expressive* first in the story? Give me the page, column, and paragraph number, and then read the paragraph the word is in." After the word search, the paragraph is read, and with the help of the teacher students try to figure out the meaning of the word in the context of the story or chapter. Here the teacher can ask students to use the context clue discovery strategy explained earlier in this chapter. This word search approach teaches word recognition, speed reading, and comprehension through the use of context clues. Keep in mind that the words to be studied are the ones with which students are actually having difficulty, not the ones a manual says are going to give them difficulty.

A Vocabulary Study System

Dana and Rodriguez (1992) proposed a vocabulary study system using the acronym **TOAST.** They found this system more effective for learning vocabulary than other selected study methods. The steps in this vocabulary study technique are as follows:

Test: Students self-test to determine which vocabulary terms they cannot spell, define, or use in sentences.

Organize: Students organize these words into semantically related groups; arrange words into categories by structure or function, such as words that sound alike or are the same part of speech; and categorize words as somewhat familiar or completely unfamiliar.

Anchor: Students "anchor" the words in memory by using a key-word method (assigning a picture and a caption to a vocabulary term), tape-recording definitions, creating a mnemonic device, or mixing the words on cards and ordering them from difficult to easy.

Say: Students review the words by calling the spellings, definitions, and uses in sentences to another student. The first review session begins 5 to 10 minutes after initial study and is followed at intervals by several more.

Test: Immediately after each review, students self-administer a posttest in which they spell, define, and use in context all the vocabulary terms with which they originally had difficulty. The response mode may be oral, written, or silent thought.

We recommend this vocabulary study system from early elementary grades through high school as a good method for getting students actively involved in the study of words. Keep in mind that TOAST encompasses all aspects of PAR.

The Webster site for Building a Better Vocabulary offers tips, games, and clear explanations for building a strong vocabulary base. For a direct link, click on the web links option of the Chapter 9 resources on the book companion website.

Vocabulary Self-Collection Strategy

Another effective strategy for use after reading is the vocabulary self-collection strategy, or VSS (Haggard, 1986). VSS is a cooperative vocabulary activity that allows both teachers and students to share words that they wish to learn and remember. The strategy begins after students read an assignment. Each member of the class, including the teacher, is asked to bring a word that is perceived as important for the class to learn. Words usually come from the content area textbook but also may come from what students have heard within or outside the classroom. Students share their words in class, defining and elaborating on the presented words as the teacher writes them on the chalkboard. Then as a whole class, students decide which words are most important and should be learned by the class. The students then record the chosen words in vocabulary notebooks. Class discussions ensue in which students use the words in purposeful sentences.

VSS can also be used as a cooperative assignment for groups. Each group member is expected to bring a word, and the groups decide what the words mean and which words are important enough for the entire class to learn. After working at length with their words, groups present their chosen words to the class. Words can be used for review and later study. A nice feature of VSS is that the set of vocabulary terms generated by this activity (with the exception of the one or two words suggested by the teacher) emanate from the students and are words for which they have shown interest.

Chase and Dufflemeyer (1990) have designed an adaptation of the VSS for English classes that they call *vocab-lit strategy*. To begin this strategy, the teacher introduces a new vocabulary term and, in a journal, the students write the term, the sentence where it is found, and a note as to whether the student is acquainted with the word. Then students can work as a group to define the word and write sentences telling how the word is used in the story. As the story progresses and students get familiar with the technique, they can offer words and define and use them in this manner.

LANGUAGE ENRICHMENT THROUGH REFLECTION

Students find many of the activities described in this chapter so enjoyable that their interest in words is heightened. In this section, emphasizing word play, we offer additional techniques that will help students experience the pleasure of working with words. Specifically, we present eight techniques: imaging through key words, word analogies, magic squares, vocabulary illustrations, vocabulary bingo, word bubbles, odd word out, and word inquiry.

Use of Key Words and Imaging

Probably no type of mnemonic device has been researched more thoroughly than the **key-word strategy** as an aid in learning new vocabulary terms. Much research over the past 20 years has demonstrated the usefulness of this activity (Levin et al., 1992; McGivern & Levin, 1983; Zhang & Schumm, 2000). Atkinson (1975) describes the key-word method as a two-stage strategy. First the learner imagines a concrete and easily remembered word that sounds similar to the word to be learned. Next an image is remembered that cues the learner to the key word and then, of course, to the word to be learned. For an example, say one wanted to remember the term *tryptophan* in a class on nutrition. The key word would be *fan*. The image that would be conjured up would be of an attic. Someone trips over a *fan* and falls in the attic. He tripped the *fan* in the attic (hence *tryptophan*).

Although key words have been shown to be effective, they do not work for all students and may not work with certain words. Also, some studies have found key-word gains in vocabulary growth have been temporary: sometimes the learned words stayed with students as little as a week before fading. As with all mnemonic strategies, it is best to get the students to make their own images and not have any key-word images dictated by the teacher. We included this strategy here because it has been shown to be effective in teaching vocabulary terms. Mnemonics were discussed more thoroughly in Chapter 8.

Amanda's Mnemonics Page has a rich listing of devices for use among a variety of subjects and topics. For a direct link, click on the web links option of the Chapter 9 resources on the book companion website.

Word Analogies

Word analogies are excellent for teaching higher-level thinking. To do word analogies, students must be able to perceive relationships between what amounts to two sides of an equation. This may be critical thinking at its best, in that the student is often forced to attempt various combinations of possible answers in solving the problem. At first, students may have difficulty with this concept; therefore, the teacher should practice with students and explain the equation used in analogies:

_____ is to _____ as _____ is to

_____.

or

_____ : _____ :: _____ : _____ .

For elementary students, teachers first spell out "is to . . . as" rather than use symbols. In addition, students say that analogies are easiest when the blank is in the fourth position, as in items 1 and 2 in Activity 9.17, an early elementary activity in language arts. More difficult analogies can be constructed by varying the position of the blank, as in items 3 through 6. Analogies can also present a sophisticated challenge for older students, as illustrated in Activity 9.18, a high school Spanish I activity.

Magic Squares

Any vocabulary activity can come alive through the use of magic squares, a technique that can be used at all levels—elementary, junior high, and high school. **Magic squares** are special arrangements of numbers that when added across, down, or diagonally always equal the same sum. Teachers can construct these vocabulary exercises by having students match a lettered column of words to a numbered column of definitions. Letters on each square of the grid match the lettered words. Students try to find the magic number by matching the correct word and definition and entering the number in the appropriate square or grid. Activity 9.19 gives explicit instructions in how to

---

ACTIVITY *9.17* WORD ANALOGIES: LANGUAGE ARTS

1. Hot is to cold as day is to _____ .
   up   night   long

2. Dog is to cat as small is to _____ .
   little   big   short

3. Puppy is to _____ as young is to old.
   playful   dog   kitten

4. _____ is to white as on is to off.
   Red   Black   Door

5. Happy is to _____ as stop is to go.
   glad   sad   frown

6. Slow is to _____ as long is to short.
   silly   happy   fast

Developed by Colleen Kean.

Directions: Choose the answer that best completes the analogy.

Model: hot : cold :: up <u>down</u>

over   wet   down   under

1. él : ella :: ellos : _____

Juan   son   las   ellas

2. mira : televisión :: gana : _____

poco   dinero   mucho   ganar

3. viajar : nadar :: viajo : _____

viajan   nadan   nado   México

4. Juan : él :: Pablo y Sara : _____

ellos   los   ellas   las

5. mal : bien :: un poco : _____

ahora   mucho   dinero   siempre

6. invierno: _____ :: primavera : llueve

frío   viento   nieva   verano

7. toco : _____ :: escucho : discos

canto   ahora   tocar   guitarra

8. cantan : canto :: _____ : hablo

hablan   cantar   hablar   música

9. como : estás :: _____ : tardes

buenos   días   noches   buenas

10. _____ : Srta. :: señor : Sr.

señora   usted   hola   señorita

Developed by William Cathell.

construct magic squares. Activity 9.20 gives various magic square combinations, and Activity 9.21 is an example of a magic square in elementary mathematics. Activity 9.22 represents a magic square history lesson on Greece, Rome, and the ancient world taught in an early elementary classroom.

Vocabulary Illustrations

Joe Antinarella, an English teacher at Tidewater Community College in Chesapeake, Virginia, developed a creative way to enrich students' study of vocabulary that he calls **vocabulary illustrations.** He has students first define a word on a piece of drawing paper, then find a picture or make an original drawing that illustrates the concept. Below the picture, students use the term in a sentence that clarifies or goes along with what is happening in the picture or drawing. Activity 9.23 is a vocabulary illustration completed by a student in an elementary language arts classroom. Activity 9.24 shows an example created by a student in a seventh grade English class. Finally, Activity 9.25 shows a vocabulary illustration of a first grade student in a science lesson.

1. Start with a range of numbers, such as 1 to 9 or 4 to 12, to fill 9 squares in a 3 3 3 magic square.
2. Add the first and last numbers: 1 + 9 = 10; 4 + 12 = 16.
3. Determine the midpoint and put that number in the middle of the square: Between 1 and 9, put 5; between 4 and 12, put 8.
4. Add the first and last numbers: 1 + 5 + 9 = 15.
5. Make combinations that add up to this magic square number and fill in the square.

8	1	6
3	5	7
4	9	2

As a shortcut to step 5, take the first number in your sequence, such as number 1; counting from that number, follow the directions below. In the diagram below, 1 is used as the first number.

1. Put the first number in the center of the top row.
2. Put the second number diagonally to the right; then place it in the corresponding position in the magic square.
3. Put the third number diagonally to the right; then place it in the corresponding position. Because you can't put the fourth number on the diagonal, you drop it below the third number.
4. Place the fifth number and then the sixth number on the diagonal.
5. You can't put the seventh number on the diagonal, so drop the seventh number down below the sixth.
6. Put the eighth number diagonally to the right, and move to the corresponding position.
7. Put the ninth number diagonally to the right; then move it to the corresponding position below.

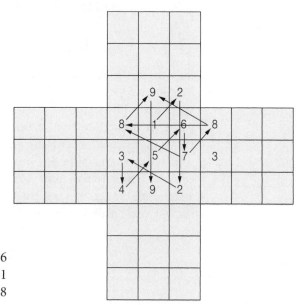

Variations on combinations:

672	294	438	618	492	834	276
159	753	951	753	357	159	951
834	618	276	294	816	672	438

9	2	7
4	6	8
5	10	3

18

16	2	3	13
5	11	10	8
9	7	6	12
4	14	15	1

34

19	2	15	23	6
25	8	16	4	12
1	14	22	10	18
7	20	3	11	24
13	21	9	17	5

65

ACTIVITY **9.21** MAGIC SQUARES: TWO-DIGIT SUBTRACTION

NAME _____ DATE _____

Directions: Put the number of the answer that best completes the statement listed in ABC order. Then place the number in the matching block. Check your answers to see if the sums of all rows, both across and down, add up to the magic number.

A. 56 minus 13 is
B. 72 minus 15 is
C. 40 subtract 10 is
D. 25
E. $68 - 24 =$
F. 75 apples less 45 apples is
G. 61
H. 80 apples less 22 apples is
I. $99 - 66 =$

1. 57
2. $78 - 17 =$
3. 30 apples
4. 33
5. 44
6. 43
7. $100 - 75 =$
8. 30
9. 58 apples
10. 32 apples

A. __6__	B. __1__	C. __8__	__15__
D. __7__	E. __5__	F. __3__	__15__
G. __2__	H. __9__	I. __4__	__15__
__15__	__15__	__15__	

The magic number is __15__ .

Developed by Laurie Smith.

NAME _____ DATE _____

Directions: Read each of the sentences below the magic square. Match the sentence to the correct word on the square. Put the number of the sentence in that box. If your answers are correct, the sum of the numbers when added across or down will be the same for each row.

Parthenon	Olympics	Slaves	
_____	_____	_____	_____
Athens	Columns	Arches	
_____	_____	_____	_____
Republic	Aqueduct	Rome	
_____	_____	_____	_____
_____	_____	_____	

1. The sporting event the Greeks invented to help train warriors.
2. This city ruled the largest empire in the world.
3. This city was the largest direct democracy in the world.
4. The type of government where citizens elect people to represent them.
5. The Greeks invented these to build temples and other important buildings.
6. These people could win their freedom by fighting in the Colosseum.
7. The Romans invented these to provide strong support for buildings.
8. The name of the temple built to honor the goddess Athena.
9. This carried water from the mountains to the city.

Developed by Ed Toscano.

Vocabulary Bingo

Bingo is one of the most popular of all games. Playing vocabulary bingo lets teachers work with words in a relaxed atmosphere. Steps in playing vocabulary bingo are as follows:

1. Students make a "bingo" card from a list of vocabulary items. (The game works best with at least 20 words.) Students should be encouraged to select words at random to fill each square.

Goalie
A goalkeeper

by Michael

If I played socer I would be a goalie.

Opulence

Definition - excessive wealth, grandeur

These four pictures are a good example of opulence because these things are things people with excessive wealth could afford to have.

The sun has light and is warm.

The sun has light and is warm.

Developed by Barbara Wood.

2. The teacher (or student reader) reads definitions of the words aloud, and the students cover the word that they believe matches the definition. (It's handy to have the definitions on 3-by-5-inch cards and to shuffle the cards between games.) The winner is the first person to cover a vertical, horizontal, or diagonal row.

3. Check the winner by rereading the definitions used. This step not only keeps everyone honest but serves as reinforcement and provides an opportunity for students to ask questions.

A sample bingo game in mathematics is shown in Activity 9.26.

Clues (also write on index cards):

Square—a shape with four equal sides and four right angles

Rectangle—a shape with four sides, two of them longer than the other two, and four right angles

Triangle—a shape with three sides

Circle—a round shape with no angles

Pentagon—a shape with five sides and five angles

Octagon—a shape with eight sides and eight angles

Trapezoid—a shape with four sides and four angles, which are not right angles

Cube—a solid with six equal square sides

Cylinder—a solid shaped like a can

Sphere—a solid shaped like a ball

Rectangular prism—a solid shaped like a box

Pyramid—a solid with sides shaped like triangles

Directions:

Each student should prepare a bingo card with 25 spaces. Write each term twice to fill up 24 boxes. The extra box can be a "free" box in the middle. The teacher shuffles the index cards and reads the *clues only.* The students decide which term matches the clue and cover one space with a chip. If all the clues are read without reaching a "Bingo," the cards can be reshuffled before continuing.

Square	Rectangle	Octagon	Trapezoid	Pentagon
Triangle	Circle	Cube	Cylinder	Sphere
Cylinder	Sphere	FREE	Rectangle	Rectangular Prism
Circle	Octagon	Square	Triangle	Trapezoid
Cube	Pentagon	Pyramid	Rectangular Prism	Pyramid

Developed by Mary Fagerland.

Bingo is an excellent game to play as a review. Most students enjoy the competition and participate enthusiastically. The constant repetition of the definitions can act as reinforcement for the aural learner. Bingo can be played in any content area. For instance, in chemistry students can make bingo cards with symbols of elements, and the names of the elements are called out. For a higher level of difficulty, the caller can use other characteristics of elements such as atomic number or a description—for example, "a silvery liquid at room temperature" or "used to fill balloons." As a variation on Activity 9.25 in mathematics, the bingo cards contain pictures of the shapes, and the caller names the shapes.

Word Bubbles

The word bubble game provides a good review of vocabulary. Students are given one clue to the word's meaning on a line below the bubble. Using this clue and the bank of words to be reviewed, they fill in the bubble and list other clues on the lines. Students are not limited to the word bank as they list new clues. Activity 9.27 is a sample word bubble for a third grade mathematics class.

Odd Word Out

Odd word out offers a way of considering similarities and differences among words and concepts as students try to determine which word does not belong and why. Students are given several groups of four words each. In each grouping one word must be selected as being different from the others. A rationale must be given for the word selected. Which word would you eliminate from each of these sets?

1. cottage, blue, American, cheddar
2. rectangle, triangle, quadrilateral, parallelogram
3. Lincoln, Ford, Johnson, Bush
4. condensation, evaporation, dehydration, precipitation

As you can see, there may be more than one right answer. In set 1 blue may be chosen as the only word that is a color, or American may be chosen as the only word that begins with a capital letter. You will probably think of other selections for that set with yet another justification. Students must carefully consider various aspects and attributes of each word to make their selections and state their rationale.

Another version of odd word out, created by Ur and Wright (1992), begins with six words all purposefully selected from a broad category.

committee   bills   congress   senator   vote   gavel

Students select one word that doesn't belong and state why. From the remaining words, students repeat the procedure until only two words are left. Students then decide on 10 ways in which the last two words are different.

MEASURE YOUR WORDS

Directions: Use the measurement word clue under each bubble to help you place the correct word from the word column in a bubble (in the example, "inch" is the word in the bubble). Then look at the word column again to add two more clue words on the blank lines extending below each bubble.

Words:

inch	pound
benchmark	temperature
foot	cup
yard	pint
mile	quart
perimeter	gallon
ounce	

Example:

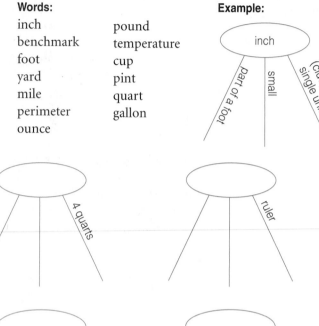

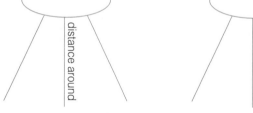

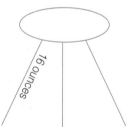

For extra credit, make your own word bubble game using words not found in this exercise.

Developed by Bessie Haskins.

Word Inquiry

Word inquiry uses the old "20 questions" format. Ten to 15 words are randomly placed on a page or transparency. Students work in groups of two (Partner A and Partner B). Each selects a word and writes it on a slip of paper so the partner will not see it. Partner A asks questions of Partner B that can be answered with "yes" or "no" to determine the secret word. As questions are asked, a tally is kept. The one who figures out the secret word using the fewest questions is the winner. The value in this activity is the close examination of the words as students consider what kinds of questions will narrow the field. Students can ask questions concerning prefixes, suffixes, word meanings, roots, compound words, parts of speech, and so on.

ONE-MINUTE SUMMARY

The main reason for vocabulary study is to develop concepts and help students see relationships inherent in reading. Having a good understanding of most of the words in a text is necessary for optimal comprehension and fluency to result as the text is read. Teachers need to take sufficient time to prepare for reading lessons by sometimes having students study difficult vocabulary terms before the reading. Preparation strategies help elevate word consciousness, provide personal connections, and build background to aid in understanding. Also, teachers need to assist students with long-term aids and strategies to help them grasp the meaning of unfamiliar words. These aids develop active reading habits as students negotiate meanings of unknown words encountered in the text. Often, however, it may be best to have students reflect on difficult vocabulary after the reading, when they have established a conceptual base of knowledge with which to learn. By reconsidering and reflecting on selected vocabulary, students get opportunities for in-depth vocabulary knowledge development for later reference as independent learners.

This chapter presented numerous vocabulary strategies that can be used in all phases of the PAR Framework. Students learn and grow intellectually when teachers spend more time teaching vocabulary and vocabulary strategies that students may use independently to enrich their own understanding. Research was cited throughout the chapter in support of the idea that increasing vocabulary knowledge is central to producing richer, deeper reading experiences for students.

PAR ONLINE

The Internet hosts numerous sites that students may reference for enriching and developing their vocabulary. However, as we all know, websites are moving targets, so frequent updating is necessary when suggesting or listing sites for use within the classroom. Look for a variety of currently available sites by clicking on the web links option of the Chapter 9 resources on the book companion website.

END-OF-CHAPTER ACTIVITIES

Assisting Comprehension

See how well you remember the following strategies by placing them in categories (preparation, assistance, reflection) on this organizational chart. Be ready to explain your choices to a peer.

Activity Name	Categories		
	Preparation	Assistance	Reflection
semantic map			
graphic organizers			
word bubbles			
odd word out			
structural analysis			
vocabulary self-collection			
key-word strategy			
context clue discovery			
word mapping			
modified cloze			
DISSECT			
word analogies			
word inquiry			
magic squares			
interactive cloze procedure			
semantic feature analysis			
word puzzles			
vocabulary connections			
vocabulary lists			
vocabulary illustrations			
capsule vocabulary			
postgraphic organizers			
word attack paradigms			
vocab-lit strategy			
word inventories			
possible sentences			

Activity Name	Categories		
	Preparation	Assistance	Reflection
TOAST			
categorization			
organizational (jot) charts			
DR–TA			
vocabulary search			
vocabulary bingo			
word sorts			
word inquiry			

Reflecting on Your Reading

The International Reading Association (2003) has developed a set of standards that identify the performance criteria relevant to classroom teachers. Standard 2 addresses three aspects of the use of instructional strategies and curriculum materials that a teacher should include. The teacher should

2.1 Match instructional grouping options to specific instructional purposes that take into account developmental, cultural, and linguistic differences among students. They model and scaffold procedures so that students learn to work effectively. They provide an evidence-based rationale for their selections.

2.2 Plan for the use of a wide range of instructional practices, approaches, and methods, including technology-based practices. Their selections are guided by an evidence-based rationale and accommodate the developmental, cultural, and linguistic differences of their students.

2.3 Plan for the use of a wide range of curriculum materials. Their selections are guided by an evidence-based rationale and accommodate the developmental, cultural, and linguistic differences of their students.

Considering the developmental, cultural, and linguistic differences of the students within your classroom, select a vocabulary strategy for each stage of PAR and explain how you plan to use each strategy to meet the needs of your students.

*How do I know what I think
until I see what I say?*

E. M. FORSTER

Writing to Learn in the Content Areas

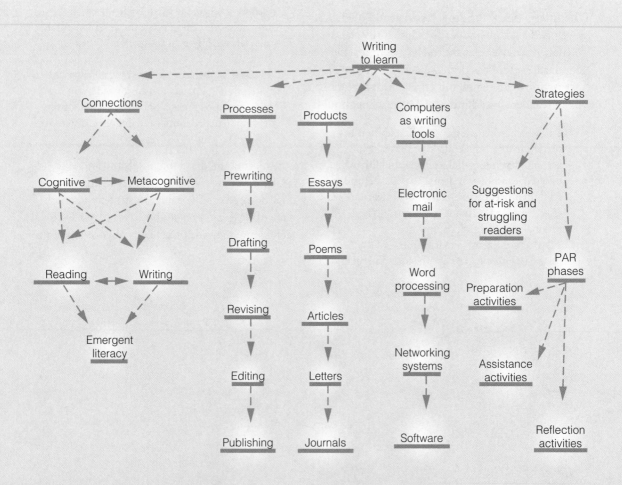

1. Anticipate what you will learn in this chapter by checking any of the following statements with which you agree. Be ready to explain your choices. After reading the chapter, return to decide whether you wish to reconsider any of your selections.

   Writing is the most complex of the communicative arts.

   Writing is often taught as a way of learning in the content areas.

   Writing should not be taught to young children in kindergarten.

   Elementary as well as college students may use metacognitive strategies to enhance their writing.

   All writing should lead to a formal product, or publication of the writing.

   Computers can provide an exciting way to help students improve their writing skills.

   Writers may make major changes in their material during what is called the drafting stage.

2. Following is a list of terms used in this chapter. Some may be familiar to you in a general context, but in this chapter they may be used in unfamiliar ways. Rate your knowledge by placing a plus sign (+) in front of those you are sure that you know, a check mark (✓) in front of those you have some knowledge about, and a zero (0) in front of those you don't know. Be ready to locate them in the chapter, and pay special attention to their meanings.

   _____ reading–writing connection
   _____ metacognitive
   _____ emergent literacy
   _____ process writing
   _____ cubing
   _____ brain writing
   _____ quick-write
   _____ free-write
   _____ student-generated questions
   _____ learning log
   _____ double-entry journal
   _____ annotating
   _____ REAP
   _____ biopoem
   _____ first-person summary
   _____ triangle truths
   _____ smart remarks
   _____ RAFT
   _____ guided-writing procedure
   _____ collaborative writing
   _____ C3B4Me
   _____ GIST
   _____ rubric

OBJECTIVES

As you read this chapter, focus your attention on the following purposes. You will

1. learn about the connection between reading to learn and writing to learn.

2. learn to distinguish between the process of writing and the products of writing.

3. see ways in which computers can aid students in learning to write.

4. identify the stages of writing, from prewriting through revision and publishing strategies.

5. learn strategies for preparing, assisting, and reflecting on writing.

6. see how writing can complement reading as a way to learn in the content areas.

7. learn ways to grade students' writing.

*W*riting may be the most complex communication process within the communicative arts. Writing challenges the learner to communicate, at the same time, with others and with herself or himself. It requires more than oral conversation in that organized thinking and planning must occur to ensure the message is clearly conveyed. The advantage afforded by vocal timbre, facial expression, and gestures must be accounted for in written communication through careful word choice and organization (Houston, 2004).

Writing is active involvement. Writing allows students to explore subject matter by progressing from a blank sheet to a page filled with statements about content learned, revelations about thoughts, and discoveries about self. Writing can challenge and enhance thinking skills more than any of the other communicative arts if it is viewed as a way of discovering, rather than solely as a means of testing knowledge. Writing requires abstract thinking, synthesis, and the ability and skill to apply several discrete skills as the writer describes or makes a case for his or her understanding of the content or topic. Brain research (Davis, 1997; Kotulak, 1996) as cited in Houston (2004) has provided evidence in the form of PET (positron emission tomography) scans that writing activates numerous areas of the brain with more intensity than other activities investigated.

Writing is the true complement to reading when it enables students to clarify and think critically about concepts that they encounter in reading. Reading and writing are often taught separately even though research has found that writing can be used in every content area as an effective means of learning (Bangert-Drowns, Hurley, & Wilkinson, 2004; Brown, Phillips, & Stephens, 1992; Durst and Newell, 1989). When reading and writing are taught as detached entities, students may adopt a superficial view of writing, seeing it as an essay exercise for the purpose of producing a particular form of writing without connection to learning or understanding information related to a subject or content. Vacca (2002) submitted that it is rare for students to assume or even consider writing a vehicle for exploring or interpreting concepts and ideas found in textbooks. Students have to be made aware through direct instruction, modeling, and practice that writing can be a tool for learning.

Unfortunately, writing is not used often enough as a way of learning in the content areas. Teachers may be reluctant to teach writing for some of the same reasons they often feel reluctant to teach mathematics and science concepts. They may lack confidence in their own abilities, which can contribute to frustration and uncertainty as they try to instruct their students. Graves (1994) has pointed out that not enough teachers receive in-service and preservice training in the effective teaching of writing. Although more needs to be done, writing programs and in-service training have increased with the emphasis and attention placed on writing scores and standardized testing in recent years. The National Center for Educational Statistics (2004) reported an improvement in writing performance for fourth and eighth graders between 1998 and 2002, while no significant change was found among twelfth graders.

Using writing as a means for learning as well as a tool to be learned and perfected provides a dual purpose contributing to achievement in writing as well as content. Content gives students something to write about. Bintz and Shelton (2004) explained that the power of a writing strategy and the potential of the curriculum for assisting students' learning are directly related to the teacher's adeptness for bringing the two harmoniously together.

The Importance of the Reading–Writing Connection

Students need to write about what they are going to read about, and after the reading use writing again as a culminating activity to clarify what was read. This write–read–write model is sometimes referred to as the **reading–writing connection.** As students embrace this model, they use writing as a tool for learning content. Content teachers, through direct instruction, can emphasize writing as a way to learn. In their meta-analysis on the effects of school-based writing on learning, Bangert-Drowns, Hurley, and Wilkinson (2004) explained, "Students are more effective learners when they possess a rich arsenal of learning strategies, awareness of their strategies, knowledge of the contexts in which the strategies will be effective, and a willingness to apply their strategies" (p. 32).

Both cognitive and **metacognitive** strategies may assist students in their learning as they engage in writing tasks. Weinstein and Mayer (1986) categorized cognitive strategies as rehearsal strategies, elaboration strategies, organization strategies, and comprehension-monitoring strategies. As students consider points read and discussed during the planning and drafting stages of writing, they repeat and rehearse. Organization and elaboration strategies come into play while students order, re-order, and describe points related to their own understanding and background. Self-monitoring and reflection, as well as peer review, offer opportunities for using comprehension-monitoring strategies. Finally, Bangert-Drowns et al. (2004) cite several studies supporting the power of metacognitive comprehension-monitoring strategies for improving learning among K–college populations. Metacognitive strategies give students a tool for determining their own use of strategies and for evaluating how well those strategies may work in each situation for future reference and use. It is like the old principle: Give the man a fish and he can eat for a day, but teach the man to fish and he can eat for a lifetime.

Besides implementation of metacognitive prompts, longer treatment length was found to positively impact academic achievement (Bangert-Drowns et al., 2004). Repetition may produce a cumulative effect over time so that students internalize the strategies and use them to learn content. But reduced effects in achievement were found when longer writing assignments were used. Longer assignments may present problems for several reasons. For students already struggling with writing, greater length requirements may be discouraging. Longer assignments may take away class time needed for other instruction and provide less time for content coverage. Reduced effects were also found when considering one population, students in grades 6–8. Researchers suggested that the low effects for this age group may be due in part to the typical shift in school organizational structure at this level, where subject matter is

Writing may improve academic achievement when meta-cognitive prompts are used and the length of the writing treatment is increased. Reduced effects may occur when longer writing assignments are given or writing-to-learn assignments are used among students in grades 6–8.

often distinctly differentiated. Developmental issues were also cited as a possible source of academic achievement difficulties. Studies of writing achievement among school populations must also recognize that students in control groups are capable of and participate in writing tasks about content being studied at least to some degree. This makes it particularly difficult to tease out and assess the power of writing to learn among populations.

We know now that writing can be taught to children at a younger age than was previously thought. Research on writing indicates that very young children can create forms of writing that they can explain to adults (Teale & Sulzby, 1986). Such writing includes pictures and scribbles, which Vygotsky (1978b) describes as gestures that represent the child's thought. Figure 10.1 shows two kindergartners' writings about and pictures of a bicycle and a bus.

Children in the early grades are capable of writing reports about content subjects (Calkins, 1986). Although these reports may contain inventive spelling and pictures that one might not expect to find in an older student's report, they reflect learning through language. Teachers are now encouraged to recognize this early reading and writing as a part of **emergent literacy** and to foster children's use of all of the communicative arts as early as possible in content subjects. Figure 10.2 contains two writing samples from a first grader. Both demonstrate learning about science through writing. The teacher made comments about the content of the writing, not about the inventive spellings.

WRITING AS A PRODUCT

Teachers often use the products of writing as a form of evaluation, such as evaluating a test essay or a research report. But teachers need to see products of writing not only as a versatile way of evaluating a student but also as a unique way to develop comprehension. For instance, many fiction writers confess that they did not know what a particular fictional character was going to do until they started writing. Their preparation gave them a direction but not exact knowledge of how the writing would turn out. Only by creating did they discover. The same held true for us as textbook writers. We learned more about our field of knowledge as we wrote this book. We discovered ways to express the information that we wanted to share with readers; before we drafted this text, we did not know all that we would write. In a similar way, readers learn as they read. Because both reading and writing can assist comprehension, it seems logical to use them in tandem when assisting readers. Unfortunately, writing is not used often as an activity to help students understand content material (Bader & Pearce, 1983; Pearce & Bader, 1984).

Teachers like Miss K in *Ralph S. Mouse* by Beverly Cleary (1982) would turn anything into a writing project. When Miss K and her class discover that Ralph the mouse came to school with Ryan, she inspires the students to write about mice and, later, to write rejoinders to a newspaper article that contained misinformation about their projects. Many teachers, in contrast, seem to use writing activities that are mainly

FIGURE 10.1
Writing to Learn
in Kindergarten

DaRius

Ride off To wfind
I can Not help
I see WhaTIlikeTow do
Isee a bicycle

I Like the buS   DeNNis

product oriented and graded. Products can take many forms, such as essays, poems, articles, journals, letters, and plays to name a few.

Research shows, however, that writing doesn't always need to have an end product to be successful—that is, writing can be a powerful tool to assist comprehension (Von Glaserfeld, 1996). Jacobs (1987) noted that writing can be compared to the ordering of thought. It is the formation of an idea, or a cluster of ideas, from the writer's experiences and imagination. It is a conscious shaping of the materials selected by the writer to be included in composition. In selecting what to put in and leave out, the child is using the elements of writing draftsmanship that he or she can manage.

A relationship exists between the process of writing and the products of writing. Much process-oriented writing results in a formal product. The best products are generated when students are given opportunities for prewriting, writing, and revising. Not all writing leads to a formal product, but all writing can be a means of learning.

Computers as Writing Tools

The personal computer (PC) provides an exciting venue for students to improve their writing skills. A growing body of research indicates that computer use has a positive effect on student learning in general and on student writing in particular (Russell & Abrams, 2004). A number of studies (Rekrut, 1999; Silva et al., 1996) recommend that students begin using the Internet by attempting electronic mail (e-mail) exchanges. Students can exchange e-mail with other students, sometimes called *key-pals,* and even with authors and experts. Silva and colleagues (1996) found that students using such telecommunications progressed more quickly than students who were asked to use the more traditional practice of grammar and textbook readings. Wagner (1995) describes how vocational students used Internet Relay Chat (IRC) to talk with other students and learn about other cultures and lifestyles.

You can visit Michelle Lemkuhl's article on The Electronic Classroom at the International Reading Association's readingonline website. For a direct link, click on the web links option of the Chapter 10 resources on the book companion website.

Word processing on computers allows students to improve their writing skills greatly. Students can write drafts quickly, revise, and save anything they have written. Word processing programs can help students check for errors before making final copies. Studies (Bangert-Drowns, 1993; Cochran-Smith, 1991; Goldberg, Russell, & Cook, 2003) have shown that when computers are used for developing writing skills, students make more revisions during writing and before the final draft than those using traditional paper tools. Students using computers for writing produced longer products and demonstrated a tendency to more often share their writing with one another during the process, thus involving the social aspects of learning. Overall, Goldberg, Russell, and Cook's (2003) meta-analysis of research on the effects of computers on student writing revealed significant positive results for both quantity and quality of student writing when computers were used as tools for developing writing skills.

Interestingly, despite positive effects found for using computers to develop writing skills among students, "across the nation, a higher percentage of teachers in urban

FIGURE 10.2

Writing to Learn
in First Grade

(*continued*) ➤

FIGURE 10.2

(continued)

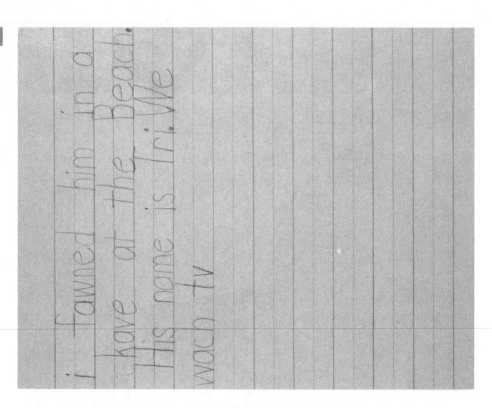

i Tawned him in a
kove at the Beach.
His name is Tri We
wach tv

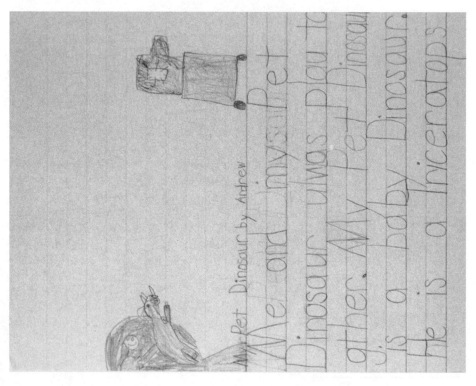

My Pet Dinosaur by Andrew

We and my Pet
Dinosaur Dinos Dau to
gther. My Pet Dinosaur
is a baby Dinosaur.
He is a Triceratops

locations and in lower-performing schools, as compared to suburban and high-performing schools, believe they have decreased instructional use of computers for writing because of the format of the state test" (Russell & Abrams, 2004, p. 1351).

Networking systems and databases available to students can assist and even motivate them to perform the research necessary for their writing. As Rekrut (1999) observed, "The depth and breadth of information available is virtually incomprehensible; the World Wide Web is indeed aptly named" (p. 546). When students assess information and write about their findings, they are using real-world practice that can only increase overall competence in writing. Teachers need to encourage students to use this tool both at home and at school when it is available. Many course-authoring programs enable teachers to produce websites where their students can participate in online threaded discussions. When students write about a topic to one another online, then read, consider, and reply within the threaded discussion, they improve their writing skills in an electronic format.

See Chapter 4 for more details and information on using technology for teaching reading and writing across the curriculum.

WRITING AS A PROCESS

Graves (1983) and Calkins (1994) have been influential in getting teachers to view writing as a process that has as its components the generation of ideas, drafting, conferencing, and revision. Writers must think about the topic in a prewriting phase and develop a first draft from their initial thoughts. In the drafting phase, students think, change direction, organize, and reorganize. During this phase, students do not focus on grammar, spelling, or any other aspects of mechanics.

Gone are the days when teachers maintained that one draft was all that students needed to produce. Students now are often asked to revise their initial work. Here, efforts can include major reorganization of the material, additions and deletions, and editorial changes. At this phase writers need to pay attention to their format. The emphasis becomes one of producing a product to be shared in the postwriting phase of the lesson.

The previous paragraphs describe **process writing,** whereby the student goes through many distinct phases in writing—from initial brainstorming of ideas to researching the topic and organizing information and ideas into a coherent piece of writing. The student working through this process may produce several drafts to clarify his or her message. An important part of the process is to have peers and others read drafts to help improve the writing. Activity 10.1 was developed by a primary science teacher to direct her students through the various phases of writing.

The prewriting phase just described matches what happens before reading, which corresponds to what we have called *preparation.* The drafting, revising, and editing phases match what happens during reading, or what has been called *assistance.* The act of producing a product can be likened to the *reflection* phase of learning that occurs after reading. Breaking down the writing process into several phases is advisable because this process is new to many students. The remainder of this chapter

I. Prewriting

The teacher will show the book *Desert Voices*, written by Byrd Baylor and Peter Parnall, to the class, and she will mention that these authors have worked together on three Caldecott Honor Books. (It may be necessary to refresh their minds about the annual Caldecott and Newbery Awards.)

"Byrd Baylor, who writes the words of the book, lives in the Southwest. I don't know which *particular* state in the southwestern portion of the United States. The title of this book has the word *desert* in it, and she has written another book called *The Desert Is Theirs*. If she lives in the Southwest and likes to write about deserts, could you guess a state where she *might* live?" (The students may remember that Arizona has desert land.)

"Peter Parnall illustrates the book. He lives on a farm in Maine with his wife and two children."

"If the title of the book is *Desert Voices*, who might be speaking? Who are the voices in the desert?" (Wait for responses.) "Byrd Baylor has written the words for 10 desert creatures as they tell us what it is like for the desert to be their home. I will read you what the jackrabbit and the rattlesnake have to say." (Teacher reads aloud.)

A. FACTSTORMING

The teacher will divide the class into small groups of four or five students. She lists on the chalkboard the names of the other creatures who "speak" in *Desert Voices:* pack rat, spadefoot toad, cactus wren, desert tortoise, buzzard, lizard, coyote. (The tenth voice is called "Desert Person.")

B. THE ASSIGNMENT

"Each group must select one of these creatures or any other desert animal or plant that has been mentioned in our unit. Each group member should jot down on a piece of paper any ideas he or she has about this creature's feelings relating to living in the desert. You may want to think about the appearance of this creature or thing. Does it have any body parts or habitat specifically suited to the desert's environment? After you jot down your ideas, place your paper in the center of the table and choose another member's paper. Add some of your ideas to his or her paper. After you have written something on every other group member's page, your group as a whole should compile the *best* list of ideas. Then we will begin to write our individual drafts."

II. Writing

III. Rewriting

Students may work in pairs to edit and proofread each other's work. The child's partner would be from another "creature's" group.

IV. Postwriting

Oral presentations

Room displays

Compilation of compositions dealing with the same "voice" into book form

Note: Naturally this project would continue for several days. Even the group factstorming might require more than one day, especially if some reference work were necessary.

Developed by Kathryn Davis.

discusses strategies for teaching writing during each of these distinct phases of the learning process.

THE PREPARATION PHASE OF WRITING

Pearce and Davison (1988) conducted a study to see how often junior high school mathematics teachers used writing activities with their students. They found that writing was seldom used to guide thinking and learning, especially in the preparation phase of learning. In a follow-up study, Davison and Pearce (1988b) looked at five mathematics textbook series to determine whether these texts included suggestions for writing activities. Not surprisingly, they found few suggestions, and almost none were suggestions for writing before reading. Writing prompts are found in subject area textbooks published in the late 1990s and in the 2000s but generally appear as follow-up or extension activities. Teachers in various content areas confirm that they find few suggestions in their textbooks for using writing as a preparation activity. Because teachers rely on textbooks and teachers' manuals for the majority of their instruction, they may be missing a rich source of preparation through writing activities.

Preparing to read through writing can be a powerful way for students to learn in the content areas. Davis and Winek (1989) noted that students who know little about a topic may have considerable difficulty even beginning to write. By providing their students with carefully directed lessons with plenty of opportunities to read, think, and write before reading, these authors found that their seventh grade social studies students produced some publishable articles.

In earlier chapters we presented a number of activities that pertain to writing in preparation for reading. Anticipation guides (Chapter 6), factstorming, PreP, and What-I-Know activities (Chapter 5) all use writing to prepare students to read. In this section we present additional writing activities to use before reading, to clarify students' thinking and spark interest in the material to be read.

A number web may be used as a prewriting strategy to help students recognize the role numbers play in their own lives. Students think of numbers that are important to them, such as phone numbers, home address, date of birth, number of brothers and sisters, number of pets, and so on. Students write each number on a sticky note and place the notes on a file folder in a web format. Under each sticky note students write the significance of each number. Students share number webs by asking a friend to guess the significance of each number. Answers are revealed and discussed. *The Math Curse* (Scieszka, 1995) complements this activity by providing numerous examples of the way math is used in daily activities.

Cubing

Cubing is an activity that can prepare students as both writers and readers by having them think on six levels of cognition. Cowan and Cowan (1980) originated cubing as a way to stimulate writing, especially when writers have a block and can't think of anything to write. The writer imagines a cube, puts one of the six tasks on each of the six sides, and considers each task for no more than five minutes. Because all six sides are considered, the writer has to look at a subject from a number of perspectives. When applied to reading (Vaughan & Estes, 1986), cubing can lead to purposeful reading and help to develop reading comprehension. Activity 10.2 shows the use of cubing in a mathematics class on linear equations.

The teacher may begin cubing by modeling the strategy on a simple construct such as a pencil. Then the teacher has students practice cubing on a concept that is in their sphere of prior knowledge. Finally, students practice cubing with difficult concepts to help clarify thinking.

When a teacher actually constructs a cube and uses it as a visual prop, students can gain a rapid understanding of the reading material. Making the cube is simple. Cover a square tissue box with construction paper, and label each side; or use the outline that we provide in Figure 10.3 to construct a cube from a strong material, such as cardboard. Most teachers, no matter what grade level they teach, find that the cube is an enticing prop for their students to manipulate. One teacher brought a cube to the classroom but did not have time to use it for several days. Left on her desk, the cube generated so much curiosity that the teacher was forced to use the activity!

A variation called *perspective cubing* (Whitehead, 1994) helps students consider concepts from perspectives other than their own. A number of teachers report excellent success with it. Students select a chart, map, graph, or picture in a textbook and then study and write about it from these six viewpoints:

Face One: Space   What would it look like up close? What would it look like from a distance?

Face Two: Time   What do we think about it today? What will people think about it in 100 years? What did people think about it 100 years ago?

Face Three: Location   What does it look like from above? What does it look like from the side? What does it look like from below?

Face Four: Culture   What would the indigenous people (first settlers of this land) think about it? What would visitors from another country think about it?

Face Five: Talk   If it could talk, what might it say?

Face Six: Size   If it changed size, how would that affect the way we might think about it?

Brain Writing

A variation of factstorming called **brain writing** (Brown, Phillips, & Stephens, 1992) can help students generate ideas. Small groups of students respond to a topic, write down their ideas, and then exchange and add to one another's lists. While working in the brain-writing groups, students could do any of the following:

1. Predict and write down the definition of a new word in the chapter.

2. Write what they think a visual aid is illustrating or could have to do with the topic.

3. Write how the new topic might fit with the previous topics studied.

Describe: It is the equation of a line, and it has two variables. It is written with the
y-variable all by itself on one side.

Compare: Compared to the standard form, $Ax + By = C$, it is easier to use to find
the line.

Associate: It makes me think of the coordinate plane with the *X* and *Y* axis.

Analyze: It is $y = mx + b$. The *y* is a variable, and so is the *x*. The *m* tells the slope
of the line (how steep it is). The slope, *m*, is the rise over run, the change in *y* over
the change in *x*. The *b* tells where the line crosses the *y*-axis. It is called the *y*-
intercept.

Apply: For the line written $y = mx + b$, which has a slope of *m* and a *y*-intercept at
b, there are an infinite number of solutions for *x* and *y*. For each *x*, there is a *y*, and
vice versa. An example is $y = 2x + 3$. The slope is 2, which means the rise in the *y*-
value is 2 for every increase in the run of the *x*-value. The line crosses the *y*-axis at 3.
So it looks like this:

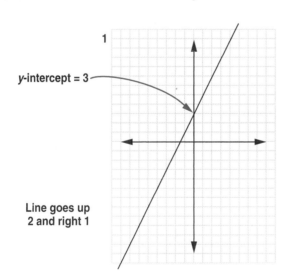

Argue: The slope-intercept form of writing linear equations is the easiest one
to be able to see the line quickly. It is better than the standard form because you
don't need to change the signs or anything to calculate the slope or intercept.
I can just look at the equation and picture the line in my head.

Developed by Mark Forget.

FIGURE 10.3

Cubing: Making
the Cube

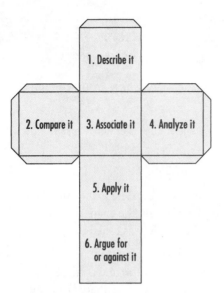

1. Describe it

2. Compare it   3. Associate it   4. Analyze it

5. Apply it

6. Argue for
or against it

Brown, Phillips, and Stephens, 1992

4. For mathematics, students could write out what they think a particular symbol might mean, what the possible steps for solving a problem could be, or why a particular unit of study is presented at a particular place in the text. For example, a fourth grade mathematics textbook starts the chapter on fractions with a picture of a sectioned pizza, but no explanation is given. Elementary students could be asked to write why they think this illustration has been selected.

5. For science, students could write what they anticipate to be the steps in an experiment, what a formula will produce, what the composition of a substance is, or why certain conditions facilitate certain results.

6. For social studies, students could write about problems people might face when they move from one place to another or after they have settled in a new place (Pearce, 1987).

7. For English, students could write why they think a particular punctuation rule might be necessary: What would happen if we didn't use commas in our writing?

Three Warm-Up Writing Activities

When students first enter the classroom, teachers can direct them to write as a warm-up to the intended instruction for the day. One activity is called a **quick-write** because teachers ask students to jot down ideas and write for one or two minutes on the topic to be studied. Also, the students can be asked to complete a **free-write,** writing that takes somewhat longer to complete, usually from three to five minutes. A free-write is an attempt to motivate students by getting them to write their perceptions of certain events or classroom operations. Students are encouraged to think and write without the encumbrance of worry over mechanics and correctness. The only rule is that once students put pencil to paper they cannot stop until they are completely out of ideas or until the teacher calls an end to the free-write. In this way, the student is guaranteed to exhibit a free association of ideas. If, however, students cannot sustain a free-write over five minutes, teachers can start with the easier quick-write for shorter practice and less frustration. Pope and Praeter (1990) found students preferred free-writing and brain writing over other writing to learn strategies in content areas.

A third writing activity to begin a class is **student-generated questions.** Students can be asked in small groups to write questions that they would like answered about the topic to be studied. As a variation, the questions can be about anything the students have studied about which they are unsure, so that concepts learned in the past few classes can be clarified. Activity 10.3 presents a quick-write from an English class. Activity 10.4 presents a free-write from a high school geography class. Activity 10.5 presents student-generated questions from an elementary science class.

THE ASSISTANCE PHASE OF WRITING

The drafting stage of writing is much like the assistance phase in reading. Process is emphasized, and writers begin to realize what they have to say and what they understand about a topic. The flow of thought is represented in the writer's draft as it is in the reader's discussion. According to Self (1987), using writing to assist in teaching content material fulfills the following purposes:

- Focusing students' attention
- Engaging students actively

ACTIVITY *10.3* QUICK-WRITE ON MARK TWAIN'S *HUCKLEBERRY FINN*

I believe Mark Twain is one of the better writers of American literature. I actually read this book for my 11th grade lt. English class (which is a surprise because I rarely read the books we're assigned in English). I can see how the book was so controversial, being that the best character (I think) is black. He is very real and down to earth. The book is very easy to read and hard to put down. My only problem with it is when the character of Tom Sawyer comes in. I'm not very fond of this character. In fact I hate him. He just makes the story drag on, making me think "UGH! When is this going to end?!" Although I realize that he is only trying to make things more adventurous but I still find it very stupid. I was very angry in the end when Tom explains that Jim had been set free by Miss Watson and the whole escape plan was unnecessary. So much time wasted! I could have gone out with my friends instead of reading that crap! Anyway, I think the book was done very well overall despite the Tom Sawyer character.

Dave N. Aznar

Students in a ninth grade geography class have been studying northern Eurasia (the former USSR). The teacher writes the following on the chalkboard

communism v. market economy
autocracy v. democracy

and asks students to discuss these terms in their own groups of three. After a few minutes of small-group discussion, the teacher informs students that they will perform a free-write as a prereading activity to prepare for the day's reading, the second chapter on northern Eurasia. The teacher reinforces the rules of free-write, stating to students that once they begin writing, they may not stop during the five minutes. Rather, they should rewrite the last phrase or sentence if they confront writer's block. The following are a few of the results. (They are reproduced with original student spelling and grammar.)

> Democracy is what we have in our country where the people have rights and freedoms. Autocracy is led by a couple of leaders and they own all the land. With a communist there is no freedom. The government does what it wants and there is no incentive to do well in life. The government gets the profits. Unlike with a democracy where the people keep the money that they make. So they want to do well in life and will work harder to make money and start new businesses. In communist countries the people must do what ever their government tells them to do and are not

have the freedoms of other countries such as speech and religion. Russia was once communist and after they were no longer comunist they became poor because they people weren't use to it and wanted a leader. They had the freedoms but didn't know what to do with it.

I know that capitalism is when you have ownership and it is not shared with the government. You are able to be richer or poorer than other people. Comunism is the complete opposite. Everything is owned and controlled by the government and you don't own anything you have. If you won a million dollars, you'd own 0% of it. Or if you've been working in a factory for 40 years you can never buy it. That's just the way it goes!!!!!!!!!!!!!!!!!!!!!!!

¡Yep!

Capitalism is a government that is more right wing and comunism is far left wing because of its government trying to take care of the people too much which causes no insentive for the people, but under capitalism people have different wages and therefore have an incentive to work hard.

Capitalism is when the businesses are owned by people. It is also called a market economy. Communist is when the government makes people work and get all the money. Democracy is when the people of a country get to select a leader. Autocracy is when a person is put into power without an election. In my view capitalism and democracy are the 2 top keys to true power of the people.

Developed by Mark Forget.

- Arousing students' curiosity
- Helping students discover disparate elements in the material
- Helping students make connections between the material and themselves
- Helping students "make their own meaning" from the material
- Helping students think out loud

- Helping students find what they do and do not know
- Helping teachers diagnose the students' successes and problems
- Preparing students to discuss material

Gebhard (1983) suggests four principles for developing writing activities that assist comprehension. First, students need an audience other than the teacher. Peers are a fine resource because they can provide supportive comments and suggestions. Often students become much more active and committed to writing when the audience is someone other than the teacher. The use of peers as an audience conveys the message that the process of writing is more important than the final product, which is the case when writing is an activity to assist comprehension. Writing for peers may eliminate the teacher's need to "grade" the writing at all. If the teacher does decide to grade, then the revision and the editing of the paper mean that the teacher will see a polished product. Correction will take second place to content.

A project at Tidewater Community College in Virginia Beach, Virginia, provided an interesting example of writing that is shared by peers. Students from nearby Salem High School shared their thoughts on poems and other readings with students in an English class at the college. Student at both schools used the correspondence to clarify ideas and concepts while simultaneously improving their writing skills. Activity 10.6 is a letter from a student at Salem High School to a college student on interpreting the poem "Poetry" by Nikki Giovanni.

Second, the writing task needs to be of some importance to the student. Simply knowing the teacher may grade a piece of writing does not motivate the student. Students need to be able to write about topics that interest them. The Foxfire books illustrate this principle of consequential writing very well. Eliot Wigginton (1986) inspired his English students in Rabun Gap, Georgia, to write about the crafts and habits of their own community. In this way he combined the subjects of English and social studies, using writing as the medium of instruction. This assignment itself was much more inspiring to students than receiving a grade. The audience consisted of their fellow students and their community. The work was collaborative, with many students planning and writing together. The collaboration assisted students in creating a cultural history of their community. The result of their writing is the Foxfire books, whose success has been phenomenal.

Third, writing assignments should be varied. No one wants to do the same old thing again and again. Copying definitions, answering questions at the end of the chapter, and writing summaries quickly get monotonous. Later in this section, we provide several teacher-tried ideas to vary writing assignments. Several publications also help content teachers find innovative and varied ways to introduce writing across the curriculum. Some are listed in the "Reflecting on Your Reading" section at the end of this chapter.

Fourth, writing activities should connect prior knowledge to new information, providing students with a creative challenge. As we have shown, cubing does this well. Another excellent activity to encourage this connection is the jot chart, introduced in Chapter 7 as a way to promote comprehension; obviously jot charts can have more than one purpose. Jot charts provide a matrix for learning by giving students an

Student-Generated Questions

1. What does the sun do for plants?
2. Do all plants have seeds, leaves, and flowers?
3. Can the sun harm some plants?
4. Which plants grow best in deserts?
5. What do you call plants that come back every year?
6. Which part of the plant makes the food?
7. Do all plants need the same things to grow?
8. What are the four things that all plants need?
9. Do people need the same four things?
10. Can we eat some plants?

Answers

1. The sun helps the plant make food.
2. Yes, all plants have seeds, leaves, and flowers.
3. Yes, some plants only like shade and filtered sun (filtered sun is sun that has something blocking some of its rays).
4. Cacti grow best in deserts. They need very little water.
5. Perennials are plants that come back every year.
6. The leaves make the food by taking in the oxygen and sun.
7. No, some plants need more sunlight than others. Some need a lot of shade.
8. All plants need air, water, sunlight, and soil.
9. No, people do not need soil because we move around freely.
10. Yes, we can eat a lot of vegetables such as beans, tomatoes, and corn.

Developed by Susan W. Hamlin.

organizational guide, a series of boxes in which they can enter their jottings about the content areas as they read and thereby see the connections between what they already knew, what they need to find out, and—when the chart is completed—what they have learned.

Four principles for developing writing activities that assist comprehension have been identified by Gebhard (1983):

1. Give students an audience for their writing beyond the teacher.
2. Give students opportunities to select and write about topics or aspects of topics that interest them.
3. Avoid monotony by varying writing assignments and activities.
4. Provide writing activities that assist students in connecting prior knowledge to new information.

Davison and Pearce (1988a, pp. 10–11), by modifying Applebee's (1981) classification system, divide writing activities into five types:

March 25, 1999

Dear Jason,

I, also must admit that I had to read "Poetry" by Nikki Giovanni, more than once to understand the poem secure enough to analyze it. Reading your letter and the verses in which you sighted, made me look at the poem in a different light. I didn't notice the "dark touch" it had.

My interpretation was much different. In lines 14-20 I understood it to say that poets, in general, are overwhelmed in their thoughts. They write what comes to mind, they understand it, but it really doesn't matter if we do. In lines 21-26 it sounds as if the writer is putting poets on a pedistool, that they are better than the average individual and their thoughts. The last three lines sum up the entire poem. I think the poem is not about poetry necessarily, but about the poets. There is a constant reinforcement of loniless, which you pointed out in your letter.

I enjoyed the poem and your letter. Please take in consideration my out look.

Sincerely,

---

1. Direct use of language—copying and transcribing information, such as copying from the board or the glossary
2. Linguistic translation—translating words or other symbols, such as writing the meaning of a formula
3. Summary/interpretation—paraphrasing or making notes about material, such as explaining in one's own words or keeping a journal
4. Applied use of language—presenting new ideas in written form, such as writing possible test questions
5. Creative use of language—using writing to explore and convey related information, such as writing a newspaper article, poem, or biographical sketch

In their study, Davison and Pearce found that copying tasks were predominantly used by junior high school mathematics teachers. Creative activities were seldom used, group writing opportunities were scarce, and the audience for the writing was usually the teacher. In practice, then, teachers do not seem to be following Gebhard's (1983) suggestions, probably because they do not realize how helpful writing activities can be in assisting students' comprehension. Yet the possibilities are great. Following are a number of ideas for content teachers, beginning with learning logs and annotations.

Learning Logs

Request that students write regularly in a journal called a **learning log,** under headings such as "Two new ideas I learned this week in science and how I can apply them to my life" or "How I felt about my progress in math class this week." These entries can be read by other students or by the teacher, but they should be valued for their introspective qualities and not graded. Richardson (1992a) found that such journal writing helps students work through problems they are having in learning material and verbalize concerns that the reader can respond to individually, also in written form. These types of activities tap the metacognitive aspects of learning to engage students in thinking about their own learning and the processes involved. Both a kindergarten study by Glaubman, Glaubman, and Ofir (1997) and a college student study by McCrindle and Christensen (1995) found evidence of positive academic achievement when writing activities involved metacognitive thinking.

Sheryl Lam, a vocational education teacher, discovered that journal writing enabled her to better monitor the progress of her cooperative education students as they worked in their placements: "Since I have 13 students in five different concentration areas, it is not always easy to deal with all of their problems at once. For me as the teacher, I can focus on each student's problems or successes one at a time; no one gets left out. For the student it's a catharsis."

Learning logs are a relatively simple yet effective way to get all students to write in content area classes. They stimulate thinking. Normally students write in their logs every day, either in class or out of class. Students can be asked to write entries that persuade, that describe personal experiences and responses to stimuli, that give information, or that are creative and spontaneous. Activity 10.7, a learning log from a high school science class, demonstrates how a log can be used to document students' problem-solving abilities.

Once students have practice in keeping a log, the teacher can ask them to respond in a more open-ended, less structured fashion. For instance, Page (1987) got the following response from a student, Carla, in exploring *Antigone* in a high school English class:

> I get Sophocles and Socrates mixed up. Socrates is a philosopher. Athena is talked about a great deal in mythology. Wow, they had dramatic competitions. I wonder if he had the record for the most wins at a competition. I bet if Polynices were alive, he would be very proud of his sister. I would! The chorus seems similar to today's narrator.

Page notes also that students are more motivated to learn when they keep a journal or log. She cites the positive comments of three students about such writing:

> I love the writing journals. Having to keep a writing journal is the extra push I need to expand my ideas, when otherwise I would not. My journal has brought to life many ideas that may have died if I had not been required to keep a journal. I am somewhat proud of it. —Carla

> Writing journals are my favorite. I like having a place to write down important events in my life, and literary ideas, poems, stories, etc. —Allison

The only preknowledge I brought to this activity was how to put batteries in a flashlight. Using that knowledge, I immediately put the two batteries together like this:

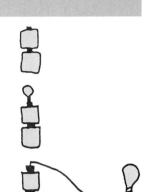

Then, I ignored the wires to see what would happen if I just placed the bulb on top of the battery, because that is how a flashlight seems to work. It didn't work.

One person in my group said, "Remember, it's a circuit." So I held the wires to either end of both batteries and twisted them together and touched the bottom of the bulb. That did not work either, so I untwisted the wire ends and touched the bottom of the bulb with them separate from each other, but simultaneously. However, the bulb would not light.

I had a lot of trouble holding everything together, so I reasoned that I probably only had to use one battery since a positive charge from one end and a negative charge at the other end was all that two (or more) batteries really amounted to. I thought that maybe the problem was that the circuit was broken because of all my fumbling around. I retried touching the ends of the wires to the bulb, but it still would not light.

Then I remembered when I installed a new phone last year, I had to wrap the end of a wire around something that looked like a screw. So I tried wrapping the wire ends around the bulb. The bulb still would not light.

I unwrapped one of the wires from around the bulb, intending to try twisting it again with the end of the other wire and then wrapping that whole thing around the neck of the bulb. However, before I did that, I accidentally touched the end of that wire on the bottom of the bulb and I saw a very quick flicker. For a moment, I wasn't sure what I had done to make it work. Then I deliberately touched the bottom of the bulb again and got the bulb to light.

Next, I wondered if I could reverse the wrapping wire and the bottom-touching wire to make the bulb light up. The bulb lit up this way as well.

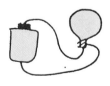

Next, I realized that my original "flashlight model" would work if I added a wire to complete the circuit, when working with my partner.

From Debby Deal (1998). "Portfolios, learning logs, and eulogies:
Using expressive writing in a science methods class." In Sturtevant, E. G., Dugan, J. A.,
Linder, P., and Linek, W. M. *Literacy and Community: The Twentieth Yearbook
of the College Reading Association.* Used with permission.

I feel that the writing journal by far is the most expressive and open writing that we have done in class. I always try to come up with original and creative entries. I feel that the journal has sparked some new creativity in me—and my essays (product paper) reflect it. They seem to be more imaginative than before. —Betsy

Another way of doing double-entry journals is using the left column for recording "what the author says" and the right column for "what you say."

Another journal activity, the **double-entry journal** (Vaughan, 1990), is a log in which students write on the left side of the page about their prior knowledge of a topic. After reading, they enter comments about what they learned on the right side of the page. These comments might include drawings or questions.

A class log, or class notebook (Richardson, 1992a), is a combined writing and note-taking activity that encourages students to take responsibility for writing about class content. Sometimes called *content journals,* they provide a way for students to review and interpret information to be discussed in class (Anderson, 1993). Students can write in the journals during class—for instance, during the reading of a passage or text. Students also can write in journals at home as a way to clarify their thinking.

Written Conversation

Part of the learning that occurs as students engage in writing tasks involves social aspects of learning theory (Vygotsky, 1978a). Written conversation uses to advantage a mechanism students typically like to use to communicate on the sly. The very nature of the task provides active engagement for all students. Students work in pairs or tri-ads to conduct a silent discussion. One sheet of paper and one pen or pencil are used to talk about a text, passage, or posed questions (Bintz & Shelton, 2004; Clyde, 1986). Written conversation can be structured in a variety of ways to encourage idea and viewpoint exchange before, during, or even after reading. Blintz and Shelton (2004) found in a study of written conversation among middle school students that the strategy encouraged students to really listen to one another, to take responsibility for their own participation and learning, and to take responsibility for supporting the learning of others. Different levels of participation and learning occurred based on partner satisfaction and compatibility. Data revealed several types of reading processes going on during written conversation: making a prediction, drawing an inference, making a personal connection, taking a position, asking a question, and detecting an anomaly. This writing strategy offers a means to engage students in active processing and critical thinking as they read and write to learn.

Annotations

Students need frequent chances to practice critical thinking in their reading and writing. One way of providing these opportunities for older students—middle and secondary level—is through a system of annotation. **Annotating,** making notes about a reading, will help students think about their understanding of the material and enable them to get their reflections down in writing. One such system is **REAP** (**r**ead, **e**ncode, **a**nnotate, **p**onder), developed by Eanet and Manzo (1976). This procedure is designed to improve comprehension skills by helping students summarize material in their own words and develop writing as well as reading ability. The four steps in REAP are as follows:

R—Reading to discover the author's ideas

E—Encoding into your own language

A—Annotating your interpretation of the author's ideas

P—Pondering whether the text information is significant

Creating annotations will help students increase their maturity and independence in reading. Although annotations may be submitted for grading—perhaps as homework or class grades—they are probably more valuable as written notes to facilitate understanding. Here we describe seven different annotation styles, which students can use singly or in combination.

1. *Heuristic* annotation is a statement, usually in the author's words, that has two purposes: to suggest the ideas of the reading selection and to provoke a response. To write the statement, the annotator needs to find the essence in a stimulating manner. The quotation selected must represent the theme or main idea of the selection.

2. *Summary* annotation condenses the selection into a concise form. It should be brief, clear, and to the point. It includes no more or less than is necessary to convey adequately the development and relationship of the author's main ideas. In the case of a story, summary annotation is a synopsis—the main events of the plot.

3. *Thesis* annotation is an incisive statement of the author's proposition. As the word *incisive* implies, it cuts directly to the heart of the matter. With fiction, it can substitute for a statement of theme. One approach is to ask, "What is the author saying? What one idea or point is being made?" Thesis annotation is best written in precise wording; unnecessary connectives are removed to produce a telegramlike but unambiguous statement.

4. *Question* annotation directs attention to the ideas the annotator considers most germane; the question may or may not be the same as the author's thesis. The annotator must first determine the most significant issue at hand and then express this notation in question form. This annotation answers the question, "What questions are the authors answering with the narrative?"

5. *Critical* annotation is the annotator's response to the author's thesis. In general, a reader may have one of three responses: agreement, disagreement, or a combination of the two. The first sentence in the annotation should state the author's thesis. The next sentence should state the position taken with respect to the thesis. The remaining sentences defend this position.

6. *Intention* annotation is a statement of the author's intention, plan, or purpose—as the reader perceives it—in writing the selection. This type of annotation is particularly useful with material of a persuasive, ironic, or satirical nature. Determining intention requires that the annotator bring to bear all available clues—both intrinsic, such as tone and use of language, and extrinsic, such as background knowledge about the author.

7. *Motivation* annotation attempts to speculate about the probable motive behind the author's writing. It is an attempt to find the source of the author's belief system and perceptions. Motivation annotation is a sophisticated form of criticism, often requiring penetrating psychological insight.

Poetry

Poetry, as a genre, may be used to introduce a concept, raise a question, provoke thought, or sum up an idea. Poetry, just like science, mathematics, social studies, and other content areas, involves reasoning, understanding, and making connections to the world. At the same time it provides a means for appreciating the power and subtleties found and expressed through words. Merging poetry with learning in content areas helps students develop basic understanding of principles and theories as well as experience ways such understanding can be described and enjoyed, engaging the senses, feelings, and beliefs (Howes, Hamilton, & Zaskoda, 2003). Dickson (2002) found that characteristics inherent in poetry, such as brevity, repetition, and rhythm, often help students see a concept or idea in a fresh new way. Several types of poetry and poetry adaptations are described in the paragraphs to follow.

Here is a brief sampling of poetry books with a science, social studies, or math connection:

Heller, R. (1983). *The reason for a flower.* Penguin Putnam Books.

Hopkins, L. B. (2001). *Marvelous math: A book of poems.* Aladdin Paperbacks.

Hopkins, L. B. (2002). *Spectacular science: A book of poems.* Aladdin Paperbacks.

Lewis, J. P. (2001). *A burst of firsts: Doers, shakers, and record breakers.* Dial Books.

Lewis, J. P. (2002). *A world of wonders: Geographic travels in verse and rhyme.* Dial Books.

Pollock, P. (2001). *When the moon is full: A lunar year.* Little, Brown.

Rice, D. L. (1997). *Lifetimes.* Dawn Publications.

Sceizska, J. (1995). *Math curse.* Viking Books.

Sceizska, J. (2004). *Science verse.* Penguin USA Viking Children's Books.

Shields, C. D. (2002). *American history fresh squeezed: 41 thirst for knowledge quenching poems.* Handprint Books.

Shields, C. D. (2003). *Brain juice: Science fresh squeezed!* Handprint Books.

Whitman, W. (2004). *When I heard the learn'd astronomer.* Simon and Schuster Children's Publishing.

BIOPOEMS

The **biopoem** is a poem in which the subject is the writer. Gere (1985, p. 222) provides the following pattern for writing biopoems:

Line 1: First name

Line 2: Four traits that describe the author

Line 3: Relative of ("brother," "sister," "daughter," and so on)

Line 4: Lover of (list three things or people)

Line 5: Who feels (three items)

Line 6: Who needs (three items)

Line 7: Who fears (three items)

Line 8: Who gives (three items)

Line 9: Who would like to see (three items)

Line 10: Resident of

Line 11: Last name

A biopoem can also be adapted to different subject matter, as illustrated in Activity 10.8. In this modified version, written by an elementary social studies teacher, the subject is the state of Virginia, and the poem is condensed to seven lines. An example of a biopoem written by an early elementary student is shown in Activity 10.9.

CINQUAINS

Another writing strategy similar to the biopoem is the cinquain. A *cinquain* (pronounced sin-kān) is a five-line poem with the following pattern: The first line is a noun or the subject of the poem; the second line consists of two words that describe the first line (adjectives); the third line has three action words (verbs); the fourth line contains four words that convey a feeling; and the fifth line is a single word that refers back to the first line. Students at all educational levels will be pleased to participate in this language enrichment activity. Cinquains require thought and concentration and can be tried in any content area. Activity 10.10 shows examples of cinquains written for middle and high school.

ACTIVITY 10.8 MODIFIED BIOPOEM

Virginia
Coastal, warm, fertile
Land, missionary, adventure
Planter, slave, farmer
First, tobacco, General Assembly
Smith, Rolfe, Pocahontas
Southern Colony

Written by M. J. Weatherford. Used with permission.

Note from the teacher: At the elementary grade levels I thought it was easier for the students to include what each line was trying to express. Upper elementary and above are capable of understanding the poem without the "clue words."

Andrea

who is blue-eyed, brown-haired, and nice
relative of Aunt Kathy
lover of Mom, Aunt Kathy, and Louie (my dog)
who feels good, happy, and tired
who needs more chapter books, friends, and long nails
who fears snakes, mom dying, mom's lupus
who gives clothes, toys, and money
who would like to see Spice Girls, 'N Sync, and Backstreet Boys
resident of Virginia Beach

Mathopoulos

Developed by Terry Bryce.

Junior high/middle school: After reading of the Boston Tea Party

Boston Tea Party
aggressive, risky
planning, breaking, entering
done for American independence
risk taking

High school business: After reading from *Introduction to Business*

Central Processing Unit
active, electronic
sorting, comparing, calculating
control center of computer
CPU

SEE WHAT I FOUND

This poetry pattern focuses on an object or concept critical to the area or topic being studied. Although the pattern is simple, it requires students to examine the object or idea critically "up close with new eyes." Here is the procedure:

1. Think of an object or item of significance that was part of the passage read.
2. Write the word/object you chose on the first line.
3. Tell something about it on the second line.
4. Tell where you might find it on the third line.
5. Tell what purpose(s) that object has on the fourth and fifth lines.
6. Say anything you would like about it on the sixth line.

Real objects may be used, as well as pictures of objects, to provide concrete examples and models. Activity 10.11 shows examples created for elementary science and math.

For more ideas, visit Denise Johnson's Poetry Workshop on the Electronic Classroom. For a direct link, click on the web links option of the Chapter 10 resources on the book companion website.

First-Person Summary

A **first-person summary** is an excellent writing activity in which students write about something in the first person, as if they were part of the enterprise or the action. Often students read an assignment or memorize information without a true understanding of the material. First-person summaries allow them to process information by writing in their own words about a topic. Using the first person encourages them to become personally involved in the material. Teachers may be able to recognize and correct any

---

ACTIVITY *10.11* SEE WHAT I FOUND

See What I Found

A wheel and axle
A type of simple machine
Right there on my bicycle
Makes my bicycle roll
Gets me from home to school
Awesome!

See What I Found

A STOP sign
A red octagon on the street
A signal meaning halt
Necessary for preventing crashes
A shape for saving lives

Another approach to first-person summary may take the form of an interview script. Students may take on the role of reporter and create a script to include relevant questions and responses.

deficiencies in students' understanding by reading their summaries. For instance, when studying photosynthesis in science, students might write a first-person essay in which they take the part of a water molecule. They must explain how they get into a plant, where they journey in the plant, what happens once they reach the chloroplast, and so on. In this way, students gain a deeper understanding of the photosynthesis process, and teachers can identify problems students are encountering. This type of assignment can work with a topic such as "A Day in the Life of a New Irish Immigrant in 1835" or "A Day in the Life of a Blood Cell," as demonstrated in Activity 10.12.

Triangle Truths and Smart Remarks

Two other activities described by Morgan, Forget, and Antinarella (1996) are triangle truths and smart remarks. **Triangle truths** can be described by students as they read or directly after they read a passage. In a log or a notebook, the student draws a triangle that contains four important pieces of information. One piece of information goes at each angle of the triangle (the clues), and one piece (the response that the reader must supply) goes in the center of the triangle. All the bits of information are connected to define, describe, or highlight a particular idea, person, or fact from the reading. The goal of the activity is to supply the correct response in the center of the triangle. A finished triangle could look like this:

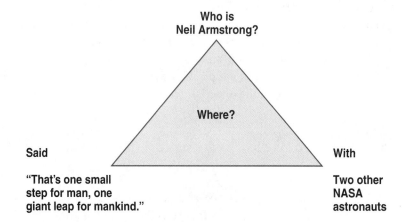

In the center of the triangle, one can use words to pose questions such as *who, what, where, when, how, why, tried, wanted, made,* and *found.*

Smart remarks are comments or questions that enable students to see in writing what they believe or need to know. The remarks are personal comments about what the reading says to the reader and how it makes the reader feel. The comments, when studied later by the students, show what was gained from the reading. After reading a passage in "Energy and Catalysts," a student might make the following remarks:

> What is a catalyst? Look up or ask. Adding salt to water should be a chemical change.
> Heat must be energy released. *Exothermic* and *endothermic*—these words remind me of a "thermos" bottle. Energy must *exit* in exothermic reactions. Remember the prefix "ex."
> How do rechargeable batteries fit into this? Ask! I'm not sure how you can *add* energy.

There I was, stuck on a boring day doing absolutely nothing. It was 1:32 in the afternoon. Agent 002 was in hot pursuit of the gangster known as Ned the Nucleus. Agent 0012 called me for backup because there was a shoot-out at the Cell Bank on 112 Membrane Street. I rode out there, but there was a backup in the bloodstream so I rode down the back way. Ned the Nucleus was threatening to blow the Cell Bank sky high. I snuck up and over the cell wall. I climbed up the Cell Bank with the help of Don the DNA. I went in and brought out Bob the Brain Cell. How could I be that stupid? Now Ned the Nucleus had a gun. He was shooting at the cops. What could we do?

I went back to the station and figured out a plan. I'd go in the bank disguised as a customer! He'd hold me hostage, then I'd hit him with my elbow and put him under arrest! I got into the building OK. Then I went up to the top floor. He had two other hostages. Their names were Rick the Red Blood Cell and Wally the White Blood Cell. He was arrested on the spot. I got promoted to Chief Lieutenant. Ned the Nucleus got 15–20 years and $500,000 cell bail. A very good lesson was learned today. Killing cells doesn't pay.

Headline!
Ned the Nucleus Breaks Out of Jail!
So now I had to get him back in jail. I went to headquarters so I could get all of the information. Then it hit me like a Mike Tyson jab. Where else would he be than Ned's Night Club in downtown Los Nucleus? So I took the bloodstream down there. He wasn't there, but I got some useful information. They told me he was at the dock. On San Fran Cellular's finest dock, Cells Wharf. I pulled up in the bad neighborhood. I wasn't alone, though. I had the help of Carl the Blood Clot and Priscilla the Spore. Ned the Nucleus was not alone; in fact, he had his whole gang there! I recognized some of their faces; they were Beau the Bruise, Cad the Cut, Rick the Red Blood Cell, and Wally the White Blood Cell, who had faked being a hostage at the bank. We called for backup and got out of there.

We missed the bullets shot at us and met the other cops at my house, where we had told them to go. We went back to the wharf with the SWAT team and the rest of the police squad. We had a stakeout. People shot at us from the water with their stun guns. Our snipers from the roof shot them. Then we had a shoot-out. But we had them surrounded, so they just gave up. I got a medal of honor and became head of the SWAT team and the police. But to me it was just another day in the life of a detective.

Written by Jon Morgan.

The goal of smart remarks is to write to clarify thinking as one reads and to think deeply about what has been read.

Other Assisting Activities

Many writing activities can be practiced with students at the assistance phase of learning. Students can write out the steps they would follow to solve a math problem or complete an experiment. The teacher can ask them to speculate on what would happen if they altered one step. Students also can practice writing about mathematics problems through writing questions about them: What is the sum of 15 and 30? The questions should reflect students' knowledge of the vocabulary and the correct operations.

In a history class students can rewrite a historic event by altering one cause or one effect. Then students can contrast the way the event really happened with their invented version. In the same way, students in an English class can choose a topic that they are studying and write about it from the perspective of the subject. For instance, one might become an author and, through the author's words, explain word choice or style or plot choices. In science, as was demonstrated previously in Activity 10.12, the student might take the role of a blood cell and describe a journey through the body.

THE REFLECTION PHASE OF WRITING

 A number of researchers (Atwell, 1987; Sanacore, 1998) maintain that the "publication" of writing is a natural way for motivation in writing to occur. Atwell believes that teachers should support student publication efforts because students write better when they know someone will read their writing.

When writing is to be published or finished as a product, writers should be concerned not only with content but also with form. This includes both revision and editing. Revision requires the writer to make decisions concerning content elaboration and organizational format to provide a clearly focused message. During revision, writers are still learning to express what they understand about the information, but they also are learning to consider their audience by putting the writing in a consistent, organized format. During editing, writers must attend to standard spelling, grammar, and mechanical issues to put the finishing touches on their work. After the writing has been revised and edited, an audience will read it and react in a formal way.

Teachers often confuse the evaluation stage with the drafting stage and expect students to produce writing that meets format considerations while they are writing to express content. This is a difficult chore even for the most experienced writers. Here is a rule of thumb to use when analyzing a student's piece of writing:

Fluency → Clarity → Correctness → Eloquence and style

Many students have poor handwriting, spelling, and grammar skills. In analyzing student writing, teachers first need to put much stock in the sincerity and fluency of the effort. Later they can ask for more clarity. Finally, the goal is to produce students who write correctly and with some style. Remember that, for the student, motivation to write may come from the teacher, who follows this progression in grading and analyzing student writing.

RAFT (Vanderventer, 1979) offers one way for writers and their teachers to keep the appropriate audience in focus. *R* stands for the *role* of the writer: What is the writer's role—reporter, observer, eyewitness? *A* stands for *audience:* Who will be reading this writing—the teacher, other students, a parent, people in the community, an editor? *F* stands for *format:* What is the best way to present this writing—in a letter, as an article, a report, a poem? *T* stands for the *topic:* What is the subject of this writing—a famous mathematician, prehistoric cave dwellers, a reaction to a specific event? When teachers are clear about the purpose of the writing and students keep RAFT in mind, the product will be clearer and more focused.

Whenever possible, as with RAFT, students should write for an audience, even if "publishing" means merely taking completed writing products home to their families. As students' writing skills develop, it becomes important to get students to write with attention to the finished product.

Activities for Reflective Writing

A number of activities are well suited to helping students write reflectively with a goal of building a product. Software like Inspiration and Kidspiration, which provides structure and tools for creating graphic organizers, is useful and motivational for students developing pre-, during, and postwriting webs, graphs, charts, and tables.

GUIDED-WRITING PROCEDURE

The **guided-writing procedure** (Smith & Bean, 1980) is a strategy that uses writing specifically to enhance comprehension. Because guided writing leads to a graded product, we classify it as a reflection activity; however, guided writing also involves the preparation and assistance steps. Smith and Bean give seven steps for its implementation, to be completed in two days. On the first day, the teacher (1) activates students' prior knowledge to facilitate prewriting, (2) has students factstorm and categorize their facts, (3) has students write two paragraphs using this organized list, and (4) has students read about the topic. On the second day, the teacher (5) has students check their drafts for functional writing concerns, (6) assigns rewriting based on functional needs and revision to incorporate the information from the reading, and (7) gives a quiz. Alternatives to giving a quiz include submitting the rewritten paragraphs, which we think is just as appropriate.

Activity 10.13 is an example of a modified guided-writing procedure used by a middle school English teacher to help her students write limericks.

BOOK DIARY

A book diary (Steen, 1991) is an exercise in which students respond in writing to the supplementary reading they have done. The teacher designs a form on which students write responses to specific questions about the material—for example, "This is what I already know about . . . ," "I liked this part of the book because . . . ," "The most important facts I learned were . . . ." Steen saw much progress in students' maturity as writers as a result of using book diaries. Teachers will be able to see immediately the learning that is taking place. Depending on how the teacher phrases the questions and designs the format, book diaries could be used equally well for younger students, as were Steen's, or for older students. At-risk learners may find them less threatening than assignments that start with a blank page.

CONTENT-FOCUSED DRAMA

Cooter and Chilcoat (1991) describe how high school students can cooperatively study and perform content-focused melodramas to stimulate connections between what they know and what historical texts describe. Students pick a topic of interest within a unit of study and, in groups of five or six, develop a melodrama by writing the plot, developing

Strategy: The purpose of this activity is to extend the students' abilities to compose a poem. They will achieve this purpose in a guided-writing exercise. I have students write poetry because they will understand poetry better after they have become poets. The exercise will begin with clustering, and from there the students will be guided through their first and final drafts. Because this is a guided exercise, I will first determine the students' background, build on that background, direct the study, and finally determine their comprehension. The final extension of this activity is publishing these poems.

First step: Prewriting (determining background) The teacher writes the word *limerick* on the board and then draws a circle around it. He/she then asks the students to think about the characteristics of that word. As they give answers, the teacher writes them on lines extended from the main word. Then the teacher directs them to look at some limericks in the text.

Second step: Prewriting (building background) The limericks are read and studied for rhyme scheme and rhythm. The characteristics are listed as further subtopics of the main topic, "limericks."

Third step: Guiding the first draft (developing comprehension)

1. Tell the students that instead of writing limericks, they will be writing pigericks.

2. Pigericks are like limericks, except they are always about pigs. They are short, have lines that rhyme, and contain a definite rhythm. Furthermore, they are humorous.

3. Pass out handouts on pigericks and show Arnold Lobel's book title *The Book of Pigericks*. Go over the poems, noticing the similarities between limericks and pigericks.

4. On the board or overhead, begin a line for a pigerick. Have the students continue brainstorming the remainder of the poem.

5. Assign the writing of a pigerick. Monitor.

Fourth step: Revising (reflection)

6. Have students exchange their poems and share suggestions.

7. Students then revise and rewrite onto large index cards. Next, they illustrate.

8. Post the finished products on the bulletin board.

---

characters, and making scenery. Students draft the writing in several stages: (1) the pre-writing stage, in which they research the topic, organize facts, and develop characters; (2) composing the initial draft of the script; and (3) conferencing with the teacher to revise, edit, and polish the final script. Cooter and Chilcoat advise that the teacher work with students on grasping the elements of melodrama: stereotyped characters, super-heroes, archvillains as ruffians and cads, romantic loves, excessive acting, overblown conflict, and plenty of action. The authors list a number of benefits of such drama: development of cultural literacy, student collaboration and responsibility training, teacher support, the teaching of creativity, and the teaching of reading–writing connections.

COLLABORATIVE WRITING

We mentioned **collaborative writing** in connection with the Foxfire books, cited earlier as an example of making writing relevant and relating it to students' backgrounds.

Activity 10.13 *(continued)*

Clustering

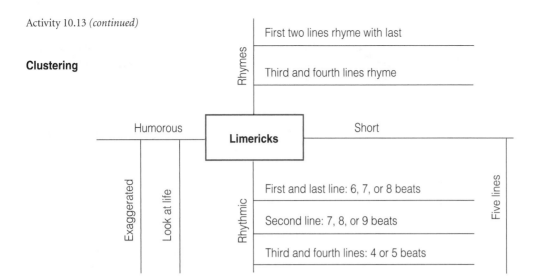

Students' Limericks:

There was a giant pig named Moe Cork
Who acted on a stage in New York
Said he, "Of we three
I am the greatest of thee
Because my head is made of more pork."

There once was a piggy named Lance,
Who wanted to do nothing but dance.
He danced every day,
In a very awkward way.
But that was okay for dancing Lance.

Developed by Frances Lively.

Collaborative writing is most effective in demonstrating to students the necessity of finished products that reflect consideration for the intended reader. When students work together, they are less intimidated by what they see as the immensity of the tasks involved in thinking, drafting, revising, and evaluating. Brunwin (1989) organized the students in an entire elementary school to produce a historical account of their neighborhood. They developed questions, targeted the best people to ask, conducted and transcribed interviews, organized their material, and wrote a book to report their findings.

Collaborative writing need not involve such large groups. One teacher divided her class into several groups. Each individual read an article and reacted to it independently. Then individuals brought their reactions to their assigned group. Within the group, a common draft was produced, using the individual reactions. Each group member then revised the draft and brought suggestions back to the group. Last, the group evaluated and rewrote the paper, which the teacher then graded. She discovered that students were able to demonstrate their knowledge of the content very well while practicing good writing skills—and, as a bonus, she received fewer papers to grade. Activity 10.14 presents a jot chart for peer editing of writing. While working collaboratively in teams, students can edit one another's papers using such a jot chart to help improve the final product of the writing.

C3B4ME

Yeager (1991) introduced **C3B4Me** (See Three Before Me) to remind students that writing that is to be turned in for a grade must be carefully reviewed and revised. Students should remember to see three other helpers before submitting the work to the teacher. First the writer should confer with himself or herself. Next the writer should confer with a peer, asking for specific advice about designated portions of the writing—not just "Do you like my work?" but "Do you think I have been clear enough in this section?" Last, the writer should be able to consult a "reading associate." Teachers can facilitate the revising/evaluating process by organizing the class into three types of associates. One type includes students who volunteer to be editors for other class members; they and the teacher agree that they have this skill. The second type comprises students who volunteer to illustrate others' written work. The third type helps writers find available editors and illustrators. In the C3B4Me process, students, or "associates," may find a jot chart (as in Activity 10.14) helpful during the peer review process.

GIST

Several strategies exist for teaching students to summarize text effectively. One, called **GIST** (Cunningham, 1982)—"**g**enerating **i**nteractions between **s**chemata and **t**ext"— has been found to effectively improve students' reading comprehension and summary writing (Bean & Steenwyk, 1984). With GIST, teachers must model and guide after the reading stage of a lesson. The reader is interrupted and directed to record a summary of the material just read. Cunningham recommends the following steps:

1. Select a short passage in a chapter that has an important main idea. A passage containing from three to five paragraphs works best. Type the paragraphs on an overhead transparency.

2. Place the transparency on the projector, but display only the first paragraph (cover the others). Put 20 blanks on the chalkboard. Have students read the paragraph, and instruct them to write a 20-word (or shorter) summary in their own words.

3. Have students generate a class summary on the board in 30 or fewer words. Their individual summaries will function as guides for this process.

4. Reveal the next paragraph of the text, and have students generate a summary of 30 or fewer words that encompasses both of the first two paragraphs.

5. Continue this procedure paragraph by paragraph until students have produced a GIST statement for the entire passage being taught. In time, they will be able to generate GIST statements for segments of text in a single step.

By restricting the length of students' GIST summaries, the teacher compels the students to use the three major strategies necessary for comprehension and retention of key ideas in any text. They must delete trivial information, select key ideas, and generalize in their own words (Kintch & Van Dijk, 1978). In this manner, GIST is beneficial for teaching reading and writing. Eventually GIST can be used after reading as an excellent reflective activity, although one should practice with the strategy at both

NAME _____ DATE _____

TOPIC _____

CONTROLLING IDEA _____

AUDIENCE _____

Major Points	Supporting Details	Transitions

A pumpkin is orange. It

is big and cold. You

can make a scary face

on it. It is funny.

Developed by Betty Henderson.

the assistance and the reflection phases of the lesson. Activity 10.15 presents a GIST done by a kindergarten student after reading about pumpkins.

SHORT STATEMENTS

Short pieces of writing can be quite motivational and provide a venue for exploring topics, synthesizing information, and expressing the most critical parts clearly and concisely. Yell (2002) describes the short statement strategy as a way for students to learn to express points and ideas precisely while using research techniques. Students explore a topic and write one, two, or even three "information-rich" paragraphs to describe their findings. The shorter task may appear less daunting to students, although it often requires as much reading, research, and thought as a longer assignment to accomplish writing an effective, concise product. Yell describes the steps for using this strategy to create a brief biography. First students are asked to explain the action, idea, or event for which the person is known. Next enough background information must be supplied to clarify the historical context. Writers must use action words, and finally, the information must be condensed into five or fewer sentences per paragraph (see Activity 10.16). This same strategy could be adapted to describe the procedure for solving a math problem.

Writing for At-Risk and Struggling Readers

Motivating poor readers and students at risk of failure requires techniques that engage them in both practical and creative writing. First, students need to be given adequate time to write. A homework assignment in writing is usually not successful with at-risk students. In the primary and intermediate grades, students will be motivated by pictures that the class can discuss and then use as a basis for a story. The class can discuss characters in a picture, and students can be asked what is happening in the picture, what may be about to happen, and what may have happened in the past. To accompany the picture, the teacher may construct partial sentences for the students to complete, such as these for a picture showing the signing of the Declaration of Independence:

1. The man in the picture is . . .
2. He is signing . . .
3. If I were at the signing, I would . . .
4. The men in the picture look . . .
5. There are no women in the picture because . . .
6. The men will soon be . . .

In addition to practicing with closure, students can be motivated to write by being given a beginning to a story, such as the following:

> The man knew it was not wise to refuse the mugger, who was young and strong and mean-looking. But he wanted to save his pocket watch. That watch was so special; it had a long history in his family. Should he refuse to give it to the thief?

By explaining why they would or would not surrender the pocket watch, students practice composing their own paragraphs.

Visit Wray and Lewis's article on using frames for writing factual texts. For a direct link, click on the web links option of the Chapter 10 resources on the book companion website.

The purpose of using writing as a means of learning is to help struggling students read and think better through awareness of their own ability to write. Research suggests that semiliterate students may have a writing vocabulary not exceeding 500 words

Christa McAuliffe was excited when she was chosen to be the first teacher to go up in space as an astronaut. She had been interested in space even as a youth when she saw some of the early rockets launched. It was a big honor to be chosen from among 11,000 applicants. McAuliffe took a year's leave of absence from her teaching position at Concord High School in New Hampshire to train and prepare for the mission. The Space Shuttle *Challenger* had flown nine successful missions.

McAuliffe knew there were risks involved. However, she could not have known that because of a faulty O-ring seal in the solid-fuel rocket, the unusually cold weather, and several questionable decisions, an explosion would occur. McAuliffe, along with six other crew members, was tragically killed on January 28, 1986. President Reagan recognized McAuliffe and the other crew members as true heroes. After much investigation and many modifications, space shuttle missions resumed on September 28, 1988, with the launch of the *Discovery*.

(Tonjes & Zintz, 1981). From an emphasis on paragraphs, teachers eventually can move to research and writing about larger amounts of information.

Perhaps the most important factor in motivating the writing of slow learners is making certain not to emphasize mechanics too soon. Many failing students have poor handwriting and often are weak in spelling and grammar. Such students get discouraged when teachers find fault and dwell on their inadequacies. Teachers should tell these students that they will be graded on the sincerity and fluency of their efforts. Later, teachers can ask for more clarity in student writing. Patience is the key when teaching students with these limitations.

At-risk students are generally characterized as passive learners who lack the ability to produce and monitor adequate reading behaviors (Harris & Graham, 1985; Torgensen & Licht, 1983). Yet, as Adler (1982) points out, "genuine learning is active, not passive. It involves the use of mind, not just the memory. It is a process of discovery, in which the student is the main agent, not the teacher" (p. 50). Writing that stresses discovery and active learning represents an excellent way for passive students to become active learners who are responsible for creating their own concepts as they write. Such techniques can aid even children with severely limited capacity to learn.

More than five decades ago, Strauss and Lehtinen (1947) successfully used writing to teach brain-injured children to read. They saw writing as valuable in developing the visual–motor perception and the kinesthetic abilities of these children. Researchers since that time, including Myklebust (1965), Chomsky (1971), Moffett (1979), and Graves (1983), have advocated that writing programs be adopted in the schools. Research also has documented the benefits of teaching the writing process to learning-disabled students and other students with special needs (Barenbaum, 1983; Douglass, 1984; Kerchner & Kistinger, 1984; Radencich, 1985; Roit & McKenzie, 1985). Zaragoza (1987) lists several fundamental elements of writing that, if followed, can help learning-disabled and at-risk children gain control and become more active and involved in their learning. She says that students need a 30-minute block of "time to write" each day—a period devoted expressly to writing so that they acquire the habit of writing. Zaragoza also calls for children to have considerable freedom in choosing the topic, to build self-confidence that what they say is important. The aim of process writing is to foster a feeling of control in the students so that they "learn that the influence of their choices extends beyond their work to the larger classroom environment" (p. 292). She also recommends that a revision be done after the first draft and that teachers edit this revised version. Later, children "publish" their work in the form of student-made books. According to Zaragoza, the critical element in the writing process is the teacher–student conference. These conferences, which can take place during any phase of the program, allow for one-on-one advising, editing, and sharing. The researcher believes that emphasizing the writing process can help develop in children traits that may keep them from being tagged with an unflattering educational label.

Research shows that poor readers have trouble identifying important ideas in a passage and have trouble using rules for summarizing (Winograd, 1984). Summary writing can help students by allowing them to reduce their thinking about the reading passage. The teacher can get these students to concentrate on the "big picture," or central theme, instead of getting caught up in minutiae. Zakaluk and Klassen (1992) report that Dan, a remedial ninth grader labeled as learning disabled, was taught to use check marks while reading so he could identify important points. He used the check marks to write headings for an outline. By going back to the text, he found supporting details. Then he was able to write summary paragraphs about what he had learned.

Another practical way to get students to concentrate on the gist of the reading is to start them with the ABOUT/POINT technique, discussed in Chapter 11: "This article on cumulus clouds is about, and the points are, and . . . ."

A number of reading professionals and researchers have formulated rules for condensing major ideas in a text (Brown, Campione, & Day, 1981; Kintch & Van Dijk, 1978). Here are six rules that students generally should follow:

1. *Delete unnecessary detail.* With practice, students will become adept at separating important text information from minor facts and trivial statements.

2. *Delete redundant information.* Students make lists and collapse information into broader categories of information as they notice redundancies.

3. *Use blanket terms.* Students should replace lists of smaller items of information with more encompassing terms.

4. *Select topic sentences; summarize paragraphs.* Often paragraphs have easily identifiable topic sentences. Sometimes there is no discernible topic sentence, however, and students have to create their own topic sentence for the summary. Doing this can be difficult for poor readers. Much practice is needed for these students to feel successful at this challenging step.

5. *Write a first draft of a summary.* Students need to integrate information by making more general certain topic sentences, key words, and phrases already compiled in steps 1 through 4. The first four steps prepare students to write the first draft of the summary.

6. *Revise the summary.* With the help of other students or the teacher, students re-work the summary to make it more readable. By doing so, students will get a clearer idea of the major points covered in the material.

Hare and Borchardt (1984) used similar rules in an experimental study with minority high school students. Compared to a control group, which made little progress, the experimental group improved in summary-writing ability as well as in the ability to use the rules to write summaries. It would appear from the results of this study and from our observation in the classroom that summary writing can be used to help all students.

Grading Reflective Writing

Teachers sometimes question whether they should accept writing from students when it contains grammatical errors, misspellings, and other errors. "Surely seventh graders can write better than this!" they admonish. However, teachers must allow students to start where they are and to focus on one stage of writing at a time.

Errors are a normal part of learning, and they will occur in student writing. The amount and types of writing practice that students have had will determine their level of sophistication. If the pressure to focus on errors is eliminated during the prewriting and drafting stages, when the focus should be on the content, then attention to errors can be greater during the revision and editing stages. If students have had prewriting and drafting opportunities, their revised writing will reflect both improved content and improved form.

Teachers can guide students in their writing activities by making clear their expectations for the final product. Students should understand exactly what will be evaluated. Of course, the content of the writing is most important. But "content" is a vague criterion. To clarify expectations and grading criteria for students, Pearce (1983) suggests that teachers use a checklist or a rubric. A **rubric** is an expectation guide that lists the qualities of a range of papers—from the strongest to the weakest (see Activity 10.17). A rubric helps students, who can refer to it as they revise, as well as the teacher, who can refer to it during grading. Similarly, checklists are useful because they list the features the teacher expects to find in the writing (see Activity 10.18). Teachers can use a checklist to quickly rate the features of a written assignment, and students can check their papers against this list during revision. Teachers might even provide their point scale for checklists or criteria for grading, as in Activity 10.19. Also, they can hand out the rubric or checklist when giving the assignment. In this way, students know in advance what factors will be considered in their grade, and they have a chance to organize their writing accordingly.

As with reflective reading, students should be involved at the evaluation and publishing stages of writing. Even if the teacher gives the final grade—as the teacher does if students take a test to demonstrate learning after reading—students should have every opportunity to evaluate their own writing before giving it to the teacher. Only when students know that their own analysis is a crucial part of the process will they take responsibility for it.

Paper topic: 1960s approaches to civil rights in the United States.

High-quality papers contain

An overview of civil rights or their lack during the 1960s, with three specific examples.

A statement defining civil disobedience, with three examples of how it was used and Martin Luther King's role.

At least one other approach to civil rights, with specific examples, and a comparison of this approach with King's civil disobedience that illustrates differences or similarities in at least two ways.

Good organization, well-developed arguments, few mechanical errors (sentence fragments, grammatical errors, spelling errors).

Medium-quality papers contain

An overview of civil rights during the 1960s, with two specific examples.

A statement defining civil disobedience, with two examples of its use and Martin Luther King's involvement.

One other approach to civil rights, with examples, and a comparison of it with King's civil disobedience by their differences.

Good organization, few mechanical errors, moderately developed arguments.

Lower-quality papers contain

A general statement defining civil disobedience with reference to Martin Luther King's involvement and at least one example.

One other approach to civil rights and how it differs from civil disobedience.

Fair organization, some mechanical errors.

Lowest-quality papers contain

A general statement on who Martin Luther King was or a general statement on civil disobedience.

A general statement that not all Blacks agreed with civil disobedience.

A list of points, poor organization, many mechanical errors.

Another way to facilitate such realization and responsibility is to allow preliminary review and revision opportunities. Teachers can give students the option of turning in drafts of assigned writing early for preliminary review at "no cost" to the grade. After receiving a graded writing assignment, students can be encouraged to rewrite the paper and receive an average of the first grade and a second grade. Using a computer and word processing program helps students become more receptive to polishing their writing (Bangert-Drowns, 1993; Brown, Phillips, & Stephens, 1992; Cochran-Smith, 1991; Goldberg, Russell, and Cook, 2003). Writing a draft and then returning to it with a critical eye is much easier when the major work does not have to be recopied. Cronin, Meadows, and Sinatra (1990) found that secondary students who used a computer for writing assignments across the curriculum improved their writing ability, attaining 100 percent success on a standard written essay test.

Content   **Weak**   **Average**   **Strong**

  1. Clear and interesting topic or main idea.

  2. Topic appropriate to the assignment.

  3. Ideas and details support and develop the topic.

  4. Ideas stated clearly and developed fully.

  5. Good use of language.

Form

  6. Introduction, body, and conclusion.

  7. Details arranged logically; appropriate to the topic.

  8. Coherent; paragraphs constructed well.

Mechanics

  9. Grammar and usage.

10. Spelling, capitalization, punctuation.

Comments:

Key:

Strong—10 points

Average/strong—7 points

Average—5 points

Weak—3 points

Developed by Dianne Duncan.

The Internet hosts numerous sites that suggest writing ideas for use by teachers as well as sites students may reference for enriching and developing their own writing skills and expertise. Visit Denise Johnson's article on Writing Resources in the Electronic Classroom. For a direct link, click on the web links option of the Chapter 10 resources on the book companion website.

ONE-MINUTE SUMMARY

This chapter has described how to teach, emphasize, and apply writing across the content areas and at different grade levels. Writing to learn in various curricular areas provides students opportunities to rehearse, elaborate, and organize their thinking about the content while monitoring their understanding. Concurrently, writing skills and techniques are practiced and reinforced. The connection between reading and

NAMES _____

_____

Used at least five facts	_____
Beginning	_____
Middle	_____
End	_____
Bat has a name	_____
Story has title	_____
Illustration(s)	_____

This is the evaluation form the teacher constructs for evaluating the students' performance. After the teacher completes this evaluation, it is kept and attached to the students' writing sample. These stories will be placed in a portfolio and made accessible to parents during visitation.

Developed by Polly Gilbert.

writing was discussed in this chapter, as well as the importance of teaching writing in the earliest elementary grades. We differentiated between processes and products of writing and described a number of phases of writing across the curriculum. We provided some computer writing applications, cited research, and gave examples of how writing quality and quantity can be improved through using computers. To demonstrate how easily writing to learn can be incorporated into content instruction, we explained activities to promote writing at each phase of PAR. Real classroom applications were included to show teachers how content writing works in action. Considerations and techniques for working with at-risk students were described. A section on grading students' reflective writing demonstrated how important it is to be concise in grading writing through the use of rubrics, checklists, and set criteria. Writing is a skill, an art, and a tool that can be effectively used in all curriculum areas for learning.

PAR ONLINE

For a sampling of currently available sites related to using writing in the classroom, click on the web links option of the Chapter 10 resources on the book companion website.

Threaded discussion suggestion: Given the challenges of limited numbers of computers within most classrooms, students not having computers in their homes, and the current mismatch between state writing assessments and the use of computers for writing, what actions would you suggest teachers take to resolve these issues while preparing students for writing and technology within the workplace?

END-OF-CHAPTER ACTIVITIES

Assisting Comprehension

1. Try keeping your own learning log to record your reactions as you use the writing strategies described in this chapter. Assess how each activity helps you teach the writing process. Learn to practice writing in your log every day. Share the writing in your log with your students.

2. Try cubing. Write a short paragraph about this chapter on each of the following six sides of the cube:

   How would you describe this chapter?

   To what would you compare this chapter?

   What does this chapter make you think of?

   How would you analyze this chapter?

   Apply this chapter to your own life.

   Do you agree with the tenets of this chapter? Argue for or against writing to learn in the content areas. Do you favor writing as a product or process writing?

Reflecting on Your Reading

1. The International Reading Association (2003) has developed a set of standards that identify the performance criteria relevant to classroom teachers. Standard Five describes four elements of literacy professional development necessary for a classroom teacher. The teacher should

5.1 Ensure that all individuals project ethical and caring attitudes in the classroom. They work with families, colleagues, and communities to support students' learning.

5.2 Identify specific questions related to knowledge, skills, and/or dispositions related to their teaching of reading and writing. They plan specific strategies for finding answers to those questions. They carry out those plans and articulate the answers derived. They indicate knowledge of and are members of some professional organizations related to reading and writing. They are informed about important professional issues and are effective advocates with administrators; school boards; and local, state, and federal policymaking bodies.

5.3 Actively engage in collaboration and dialogue with other teachers and reading specialists to obtain recommendations and advice on teaching practices and ideas. They can articulate the evidence related to these recommendations. They may conduct action research as a part of these collaborations.

5.4 Participate individually and with colleagues in professional development experiences.

a. Considering your own background of experience, training, and classroom practices, put into writing three to five questions you have concerning the role, skills, approaches, and your feelings about the teaching of writing within content areas.

b. Besides the material and suggestions in your text, what else will you do to find appropriate answers to your questions?

c. Now answer your questions, making use of the resources and plan you selected for locating answers.

2. The following textbooks provide excellent extension reading resources for finding out more about writing to learn in the content classrooms:

Atwell, N. (1989). *Coming to know: Writing to learn in the intermediate grades.* Portsmouth, NH: Heinemann.

Blasingame, J., & Bushman, J. H. (2005). *Teaching writing in middle and secondary schools.* Upper Saddle River, NJ: Pearson Education, Inc.

Bright, R. (1995). *Writing instruction in the intermediate grades: What is said, what is done, what is understood.* Newark, DE: International Reading Association.

Bromley, K. (1993). *Journaling: Engagements in reading, writing, and thinking.* New York: Scholastic.

Brown, J., Phillips, L., & Stephens, E. (1992). *Toward literacy: Theory and applications for teaching writing in the content areas.* Belmont, CA: Wadsworth.

Fulwiler, T. (1987). *Teaching with writing.* Portsmouth, NH: Boynton/Cook.

Gere, A. R. (Ed.). (1985). *Roots in the sawdust: Writing to learn across the curriculum.* Urbana, IL: National Council of Teachers of English.

Graves, D. (1994). *A fresh look at writing.* Portsmouth, NH: Heinemann.

Houston, G. (2004). *How writing works: Imposing organizational structure within the writing process.* Boston: Pearson Education, Inc.

Martin, N., D'Arcy, P., Newton, B., & Parker, R. (1976). *Writing and learning across the curriculum.* Montclair, NJ: Boynton/Cook.

Maxwell, R. (1996). *Writing across the curriculum in the middle and high schools.* Boston: Allyn and Bacon.

Murray, D. (1982). *Learning by teaching.* Montclair, NJ: Boynton/Cook.

Routeman, R. (2004). *Writing essentials: Raising expectations and results while simplifying teaching.* Portsmouth, NH: Heinemann.

Scarborough, H. A. (Ed.) (2001). *Writing across the curriculum in secondary classrooms: Teaching from a diverse perspective.* Upper Saddle River, NJ: Pearson Education, Inc.

Wolfe, D., & Reising, R. (1983). *Writing for learning in the content areas.* Portland, ME: J. Weston Walch.

Wollman-Bonilla, J. (1991). *Response journals.* New York: Scholastic.

CHAPTER 11

*We are each of us angels with
only one wing, and we can
only fly by embracing
one another.*

LUCIANO DE CRESCENZO

Cooperative Learning and Reading

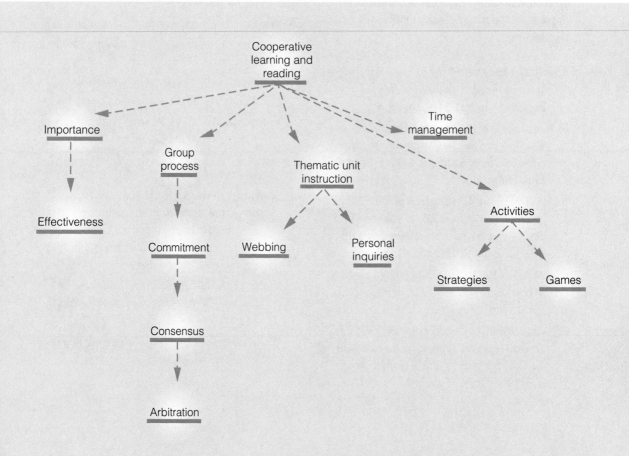

PREPARING TO READ

1. Assess your own study habits. Are you a "loner" or a "groupie"? If you like to study alone, list some of the benefits of individual study from your perspective. If you like to study in a group, list some benefits you derive from such study. Whatever your preference, as you read this chapter, keep an open mind concerning the flexibility of using both types of study behavior—quiet, individual study and group study.

2. Following is a list of terms used in this chapter. Some may be familiar to you in a general context, but in this chapter they may be used in unfamiliar ways. Rate your knowledge by placing a plus sign (+) in front of those you are sure that you know, a check mark (✓) in front of those you have some knowledge about, and a zero (0) in front of those you don't know. Be ready to locate these terms in the chapter, and pay special attention to their meanings.

_____ commitment
_____ consensus
_____ arbitration
_____ thematic unit instruction
_____ webbing approach
_____ personal inquiry
_____ time management
_____ extended anticipation guide
_____ ABOUT/POINT
_____ student-generated questions
_____ summarization
_____ jigsaw
_____ think-aloud
_____ interactive guide

OBJECTIVES

As you read this chapter, focus your attention on the following purposes. You will

1. understand the term *cooperative learning.*

2. learn why cooperative learning is effective.

3. learn about the group process and how grouping for instruction works.

4. learn how thematic unit instruction can foster cooperative learning.

5. learn how to utilize personal inquiries on the part of students.

6. understand the importance of time management.

7. be able to use some cooperative learning techniques to teach reading.

Shoe. Reprinted with permission of Tribune Media Services.

THE IMPORTANCE OF COOPERATIVE LEARNING

 Cooperative learning can be defined as students working in group and team situations on assigned tasks with an expectation that they will be rewarded for the success of the group. Cooperative learning has been found to be both an effective instructional method (Slavin, 1996) and a successful way to enhance social and academic development among children (Deen, Bailey, & Parker, 2001; Johnson & Johnson, 2003; Slavin, 2000). The end product of cooperative learning is collaboration and joint ownership. Studies show that cooperative learning benefits students by getting them more actively involved (Slavin, 1995). Also, researchers have found that students not only feel more engaged but also perceive that their learning task is more important when working in a small group than during large-group instruction (Peterson & Miller, 2004).

In contrast, some studies show that collaboration doesn't always happen in cooperative groups (Blumenfeld et al., 1997). Some students do not benefit from cooperative learning, especially those deemed by the group to be less competent. The success of the group depends, in large measure, on the cohesiveness of students in the group, individual students' willingness to complete the task, and whether the task is considered worthwhile (Leonard & McElroy, 2000).

Despite such negative findings, a growing body of research indicates that giving students opportunities to study cooperatively in the classroom can enhance learning (Abrami et al., 1992; Alexander & DeAlba, 1997; Hancock, 2004; Johnson & Johnson, 1987; Leinhardt, Stainton, & Bausmith, 1998; Rekrut, 1997). Research by Wiegel (1998) suggests that even kindergarten students can achieve more when they work for sustained periods in cooperative groups. A positive aspect of cooperative learning is that it may lessen stress reactions such as self-deprecation, lack of clear goals, disparagement, immature relationships with teachers, and pervasive depression (Gentile & McMillan, 1987). It especially enables low achievers to gain success without the feelings of failure and isolation that often accompany more traditional learning (Coleman, 1994; Kirkland, 1993). Most important, students learn the skill of working together as they discuss how material can best be learned. Students who work together also appear to have a higher regard for school and for the subjects they are studying and are more confident and self-assured. As a result, both motivation and achievement improve (Hancock, 2004).

One of the main goals in teaching is to help students become autonomous learners. Research has shown that students may not exhibit independent learning habits even when they know and use certain cognitive strategies (Borkowski et al., 1990; Paris & Winograd, 1990). Teachers need to help students become independent by encouraging group decision making and having students work in teams or small groups whenever possible. Learning is enhanced when such cooperative learning teams are emphasized in content teaching (Abrami et al., 1992; Johnson & Johnson, 1987; Meloth & Deering, 1992; Vermette et al., 2004). As evidence of this, Australian researchers Gillies and Ashman (1998) trained first and third grade students in formal and informal collaboration techniques during the teaching of 10 social studies units. They found these students learned more content while in cooperative teams and thereby improved decision making. The study pointed to the benefit of teaching young children to learn cooperatively and use decision-making techniques.

Slavin (1991) reviewed 60 studies that contrasted the achievement outcomes of cooperative learning and traditional methods in elementary and secondary schools. His conclusions were as follows:

1. Cooperative learning has positive effects on student achievement. The groups must have two important features: group goals and individual accountability.

2. When students of different racial or ethnic backgrounds work together toward a common goal, they gain liking and respect for one another. Cooperative learning improves social acceptance of mainstreamed students by their classmates and increases friendships among students in general.

3. Other outcomes include gains in self-esteem, time on task, attendance, and ability to work effectively with others.

Another reason for the use of cooperative learning is that it helps students set purposes for their reading and monitor whether those purposes are being met. Although at first teachers must help readers set purposes, readers need to begin setting their own purposes for reading as soon as possible. Hawkes and Schell (1987) caution that teacher-set reasons to read may encourage dependence and a passive approach to reading. Self-set reasons to read promote the development of readers who are active and ultimately independent. To wean readers from dependence, teachers can use many of the activities mentioned in this chapter until students are familiar with them and understand what purpose setting involves—that is, until students are able to perform alone what initially they could accomplish only with the aid of the teacher (Gavelek, 1986).

Researchers note that cooperative learning enables students to display more positive attitudes and helps them increase intrinsic motivation to learn (Wood, 1987). We tend to think of cooperative learning taking place mainly at the upper elementary and middle school levels. But cooperative learning can also take place at the kindergarten level (Vermette, 1994). When students work in small groups on an assigned task that has been clearly explained to them, they often prosper in their learning environment.

Cooperative learning and study are more than telling students to get together in groups and work. Rather, they form a structured experience in which students, preferably in groups of two, three, or four, practice learning content by using study skills emphasized by the teacher for a particular lesson. Glasser (1986) gives a number of reasons why cooperative study in what he calls "small learning teams" will motivate almost all students. Glasser says such group learning gives students a sense of belonging and motivates them to learn. Stronger students help weaker ones, and all students see that team effort brings rewards. In addition, the teams keep students interested, lessen dependence on the teacher, and improve communication skills through the continued and varied interaction within the team.

WHY COOPERATIVE LEARNING IS EFFECTIVE

Weinstein (1987) suggests that cooperative learning strategies are successful in aiding comprehension and retention because they fall into one or more of what she calls "categories of learning strategies"—processes and methods useful in acquiring and retrieving information. Weinstein proposes five categories of learning strategies:

1. *Rehearsal strategies,* such as cooperative reading activities and think-alouds
2. *Elaboration strategies,* such as jigsaw, paired reading, and student-generated questions
3. *Organizational strategies,* including techniques such as ABOUT/POINT and cooperative graphing
4. *Comprehension-monitoring strategies,* including extended anticipation guides and think-alouds
5. *Affective strategies,* such as paired reading and the positive rewards of learning in groups

In underscoring the importance of cooperative learning, we wish to reemphasize a point made frequently throughout this book: Learning is difficult in a hurried, pressured classroom environment. A first grader recently complained, "The teacher never lets me finish. I never have enough time to finish." This is a lament that holds true in all too many classrooms. Jeremy Rifkin, in his book *Time Wars* (1987), argues that we appear to be trapped in our own technology. Rifkin maintains that the constant pressure to become more efficient causes Americans to feel that they do not have enough time to get things done. This pressure, which permeates today's classroom, is detrimental because all types of classroom effort succeed best in a calm, unhurried atmosphere in which students are free to explore ideas, develop creativity, solve problems, and be thoughtful and reflective.

The Structure of Group Work

With group work, we recommend a stylized three-step process analogous to the steps in the PAR Lesson Framework described in Chapter 1. In the preparation phase, individual students should commit to something, usually written, to be shared later with the group. In this individual phase of the lesson, the teacher attempts to get a **commitment** from the student. This can be difficult because students today often do not wish to commit to anything; their cop-out is not to get involved in classroom activities. However, a sense of involvement is crucial to successful group interaction. Lack of commitment is the reason so much group work degenerates, with students getting away from the subject to be discussed or the problem to be solved. Rarely will commitment be generated by teacher assignment and the threat or reward of a grade. Students need to be invested in their learning, and this commitment phase will accomplish that (Leki, 2001).

The second phase involves the actual work to be done in groups. The key word here is **consensus.** In the group phase the students should share what they have done individually and arrive at a consensus, whenever possible, on the best possible answer. The teacher provides much assistance in this phase by moving from group to group to help students with areas of difficulty and to make sure groups are staying on topic.

In the third phase, involving reflection, the teacher may lead a discussion with the groups, an exercise in **arbitration.** The teacher acts as an arbiter or a mediator to resolve difficult points of the lesson on which students could not come to consensus. Also, in this phase groups may report to the whole class on their findings.

To recap, here are the three phases of good group process:

Phase I: individual phase; key concept = commitment

Phase II: group work; key concept = consensus

Phase III: teacher-led discussion; key concept = arbitration/mediation

> Try to practice the three steps for better grouping in your own classes in the near future. You will see that this approach works.

Teachers often express frustration with the results of group work. One solution is to have students role-play different scenarios in which certain group members might sabotage the group effort. When students consider for themselves possible obstacles to the success of their group work and possible solutions, they become more productive in groups. Swafford (1995) describes a technique she uses with college students. Groups are given one of three scenarios in which one person in a group is not participating at all, underparticipating, or overparticipating. By discussing these problems and acting out a solution for the rest of the class, everyone experiences the process of commitment, consensus, and arbitration in a friendly atmosphere.

The technique that Swafford (1995) used with her students can help students move toward successful cooperative group work. However, group work can cause significant problems in how students view themselves or are viewed by their peers (Alvermann, 1996). Some students feel left out; others feel unable to contribute. Alvermann cautions that just creating groups is not enough; the teacher must monitor progress and discuss with individual students their perceptions of group work. By considering the real problems that can occur and devising solutions themselves, students come to understand that they can succeed in cooperative groups. The goal is that the teacher gradually releases purpose-setting responsibility to the students, enabling them to become independent learners. This goal is especially difficult to meet with at-risk students, but it is equally as important.

McKeachie (2002) makes these four points concerning ways to improve what he calls "peer learning":

1. Have students take part in discussions of what makes a group effective and discuss why it is valuable to work together as a team.

2. Make sure students know exactly what the task is. To check on this, have students report on the nature of the task and what all the parameters are.

3. Move around the room a great deal to monitor the groups and make certain students are on the right course.

4. Help students develop skills necessary for effectively working together.

Cooperative Learning through Thematic Unit Instruction

Thematic unit instruction can be defined as effective teaching organized around a central topic or theme that uses related activities to initiate in-depth study (Gardner et al., 2003). To accomplish such in-depth instruction, teachers often move toward a saturated use of multiple resources and greater use of technology. Shanahan, Robinson, and Schneider (1995) explain that thematic teaching is popular because student knowledge, which tends to be superficial, is enriched when students develop fuller understanding by delving deeply during a thematic unit. Also, thematic units reflect the real world, because learners generally read broadly on a topic rather than confine themselves to one source. Thematic units help teachers become more time-efficient in presenting content. Students taught with multiple-resource units stressing a theme have shown higher achievement and better attitudes than those using only a content textbook (Jone, Coombs, & McKinney, 1994).

Shanahan, Robinson, and Schneider caution that thematic units should be developed around themes, not topics. A topical approach can lead to treatment similar to subject treatment, which can drag instruction right back to segmentation. A theme "states a point of view or perspective; it actually takes a position" (p. 718). Thus themes are dynamic and help students think deeply, pull together ideas, make connections among ideas, and blend subjects naturally.

We have seen many teachers construct thematic units with titles such as "The Vietnam Era," "Survival in the World in the New Millenium," and "Welcome to Planet Earth." Thematic units, however, can be on a smaller scale, such as the nine-step unit plan developed for a middle school English class around *The Call of the Wild,* shown in Activity 11.1. The theme for this activity might be stated as "*The Call of the Wild* is as modern as it is reflective of the past." Or thematic units can be encompassing; one teacher built a yearlong unit by adding poetry to other content lessons throughout the school year (Myers, 1998).

1. Read the novel during the Iditarod Sled Dog Races in Alaska. You will be able to find current pieces on climate, geography, living conditions, and the history of dog races. Use these to compare and contrast with the novel.

2. Read books or articles about gold mining. Help the students identify the physical hardships and dangers of this occupation.

3. Read poetry by Robert Service ("The Cremation of Sam McGee") about Alaska.

4. Read Jack London's short stories about Alaska. Identify and explain the similarities and differences.

5. Discuss types of conflict (human vs. human, human vs. nature, etc.). Read newspaper and magazine articles and ask students to identify the type of conflict; then ask them to do it for key scenes in the novel.

6. Study articles on modern sled dogs and their mushers. How are things different today?

7. Write to Alaska's tourist bureau (at least a month before you read the novel) and ask them to send all their brochures. You can also ask for information about a specific topic.

8. Compare the personalities of the main characters (including the dogs) to people prominent in the news. Students will have to read the newspaper and news magazines to make informed comparisons.

9. When bringing outside sources into the classroom, remember to bring ones that are topical and current. A book about a dog written 70 years ago suddenly becomes a modern adventure story if it is coupled with events taking place today. The students instantly see how the novel can relate to their lives. It ceases to be another old and boring book.

Developed by Beth Pallister, Bayside Middle School, Virginia Beach, Virginia.

Administrators should encourage teachers to meet in teams to plan activities across the curriculum for interdisciplinary units. Such a breaking down of the traditional disciplines into more favorable climates for interdisciplinary study is a trend that gained momentum in the 1980s and may become a notable aspect of all instruction in middle and secondary schools. Even at the elementary level, thematic units can become grade-level or school-level projects rather than just being taught within one self-contained classroom. We know of an elementary school where the administrators require grade-level planning by teachers around a theme. Teachers plan together during a Friday afternoon monthly; administrators teach the students while the teachers meet in the library.

If a thematic unit centered on *The Call of the Wild,* the English teacher could work with the social studies/geography teacher to develop collaborative activities such as tracing on a map of Alaska the route followed in the novel, identifying landmarks, and discussing Alaska's state history. Visiting a site about Alaska on the Internet would help students see what that environment is like and how a person could become isolated and unable to survive. The science teacher could explain Darwinism and account for Buck's regression, describe the stages of hypothermia, and discuss dogs' physical adaptation to the harsh Alaskan environment.

Even in situations where departmentalized classes undermine communication among teachers, coordination can take place if teachers can meet long enough to agree on some books and technological resources to use for a particular unit. For instance, high school history and language arts teachers could coordinate the study of the American Civil War by deciding to read and discuss books such as *Voices from the Civil War* (Metzger, 1989), *Civil War Trivia and Fact Book* (Garrison, 1992), *Touched by Fire: A Photographic Portrait of the Civil War* (W. C. Davis, 1985), *The Long Surrender* (B. Davis, 1985), *A Separate Battle: Women and the Civil War* (Chang, 1991), *Crowns of Thorns and Glory: Mary Todd Lincoln and Varina Howell Davis, the Two First Ladies of the Civil War* (Van der Heuvel, 1988), *Civil War: America Becomes One Nation* (Robertson, 1992), *Blood Brothers: A Short History of the Civil War* (Vandiver, 1992), *Forged in Battle: The Civil War Alliance of Black Soldiers and White Officers* (Glatthaar, 1990), and *Diary of a Confederate Soldier* (W. C. Davis, 1990). Then they could locate and suggest some sites that students might visit. Perhaps they also could use videos, such as the Ken Burns documentary *The Civil War,* as another resource.

> Thematic units can last as long as nine weeks or as little as a few days.

Activity 11.2 describes a cross-disciplinary thematic unit "A Journal of the Lewis and Clark Expedition," developed by a team of teachers working together in staff development sessions. This three-week unit was developed in Norfolk, Virginia, by Norview High School teachers of math, science, social studies, art, English, business, and vocational education working together over shared planning periods. Note

---

ACTIVITY 11.2 THEMATIC PLANNING ACROSS THE CURRICULUM:
A JOURNAL OF THE LEWIS AND CLARK EXPEDITION

THREE-WEEK THEMATIC UNIT

Goal: Students will write a 14-day journal describing the experiences of accompanying Lewis and Clark on their expedition.

Process objective: Students will integrate information and process skills across the curriculum to produce a mock journal of the expedition of Lewis and Clark.

Content areas:

MATH
Compass direction
Provisions and physical requirements
Calculating mileage
Computing time, distance, and mileage
Reading map scales
Averaging
Probability of completing the journey

EARTH SCIENCE
Latitude and longitude
Crude measurement
Weather
Map reading
Rocks and soil
Rivers
Altitudes and seasons
Physics of transportation
Identification of plants and animals
    along the route
Physical and survival needs
Food: identification of new food sources
Food preservation
Herbal medicines

HISTORY/GEOGRAPHY
Geography of the route
Cartography
Regions and climate

that many content areas are included in this unit. Planning such units can be time-consuming and difficult, but the benefits of adding new dimensions and vigor to the curricular offerings are certainly worth the effort. Such integrated instruction allows practice with skills and a focus on instructional unity (Shanahan, 1997).

When developing a unit plan, teachers may need to construct the unit in distinct phases. Moss (1990) lists four:

- Determining unit objectives and goals
- Determining the theme or focus of the unit
- Gathering resources to be used in the unit
- Deciding student activities for the unit and the sequence of the activities

In determining unit goals, be sure to examine both the curriculum to be taught and the students' backgrounds and abilities. If a unit is to be taught well into the school year, the teacher should know what the students can absorb emotionally and socially, as well as their abilities for reading supplemental literature and using technology. Templeton (1991) advises teachers to wait several weeks before starting a unit at the beginning of the school year, so that students can learn classroom procedures and the teacher can assess their abilities and characteristics.

Activity 11.2 *(continued)*

Landforms
Researching resources through the
    Internet/books/videostreams
Native American tribes and their customs and
    culture
Geological events of time
Dioramas
Purpose of journey

ART
Research pictures of the expedition on the
    Internet
Ansel Adams photographs
National Geographic
Student products: clay, sketching, beadwork,
    quilting
Native American arts and crafts
Native American traditions in art

ENGLISH
Journal writing and readings
Story of Sacagawea
Excerpts of Lewis and Clark diary
Other fiction about the time and areas involved

Poetry—write cinquain about journey
Other literature and authors of the time
Find newspapers of the time on the Internet

VOCATIONAL
Transportation used in the time
How cooking was achieved
Building tools for the trip
Survival guide/kit for journey
Make a plan for how to carry great loads of
    supplies
Surveying
Making clothes

BUSINESS
Cost of trip
Original budget given to explorers by President
    Jefferson
Your budget: comparing differences between
    today's budget and their budget
Obtaining financial backers
Marketing the expedition
Advertising campaign
Bartering

Look for webbing and other types of graphic organizers in other chapters of this text.

To begin determining the activities, teachers (either individually or with other teachers) can use the **webbing approach** to brainstorm ideas (Cullinan, Karrer, & Pillar, 1981; Huck, 1979; Huck, Hepler, & Hickman, 1987). The teacher first identifies large categories of information reflecting unit objectives and then narrows the focus to represent smaller concepts with numerous activities. The teacher does not have to use all the ideas that are generated, but the brainstorming session provides a springboard for determining how the final unit plan will appear. The teacher can choose themes and activities based on students' needs and interests, current events, and activities that were successful in other thematic units.

Concerning the collection of books, Lynch-Brown and Tomlinson (1993) advise that teachers should let the curriculum drive what resources are used, not vice versa. Teachers should avoid including books that are not really relevant, and they should not base the selection of a theme on one or two books that they have on hand. Teachers need to constantly watch for books and other materials that might be suitable for a particular unit of instruction. Also, whenever possible, they should ask students to help find books about subjects of interest to the class and of importance to class objectives. Students will be eager to help locate Internet resources and are likely to find more than the teacher has time or energy to locate. To find sources of interest, teachers can start with the databases, electronic library catalogs, and periodical indexes in the school library. If resources there are scanty, teachers should check the local public library for resources on a desired topic. The Internet is an amazing source of materials, but the teacher must make sure that the resources are factual and relevant.

In any search, the school media specialist and reading specialist (if available) should be called on for valuable assistance. The media specialist can show the teacher how to borrow materials from libraries elsewhere in the state and how to conduct electronic searches of libraries. When choosing literature, teachers may wish to use the SMOG readability formula (found in Appendix B) to obtain a quick estimate of how readable a book may be for students.

Today technology can be integrated into thematic unit instruction with some deliberate instructional planning. It must be stressed that any technological input into the lesson should be authentic, meaningful, and interactive (Gardner & Wissick, 2002). Such activities can promote general problem-solving skills or can teach specific skills (Robyler & Edwards, 2000).

A number of software programs on the market can provide students with scaffolding techniques to organize their writing. Draft Builder (Don Johnston, 2001) is an outlining program, and Inspiration 7 (Inspiration, 2002) allows students to create a web or map of any writing to be done. For younger students or students with disabilities, Kidspiration (Inspiration, 2000) provides webbing features and also includes text auditory feedback. In a review of how technology can aid thematic unit instruction, Gardner (Gardner et. al, 2003) describes how spreadsheets can help students with computational math, multimedia programs can support thematic unit activities, and Internet activities such as WebQuests can aid in the area of personal learning inquiries. Much of this has been explained in detail in Chapter 4 on the use of technology in the teaching of reading. A WebQuest developed by Christine Rauth, a teacher at Caroline High School in Virginia, for her tenth grade honors English class is reproduced here as Activity 11.3.

Personal Inquiries

A **personal inquiry** originates from questions that a student asks as a result of exposure to a topic about which she or he wishes to learn more. It is somewhat similar to the old-fashioned term paper traditionally required at the high school level, often in English class, when students may be given a choice of topics to research. But with personal inquiry, the students select their own topics and are encouraged to develop their own questions. Whereas thematic units are teacher generated, personal inquiries are student generated. Todd (1995) describes the pleasure of independent study that inquiry learning provides.

Emphasis on inquiry learning increased in the 1990s (Rasinski & Padak, 1993). Campbell (1995) declares that lifelong learning and inquiry are the best routes to learning. Examples have been available for many years, especially in literature. Omri, in *The Indian in the Cupboard* (Banks, 1990), finds himself so immersed in reading books about the Iroquois Indian who appears in his cupboard that he doesn't hear the school bell ring. Usually, Omri expresses great dislike for both school and reading. In *Canyons* by Gary Paulsen (1990), Mr. Homesley convinces Brennan to start collecting

---

ACTIVITY 11.3 A WEBQUEST PROJECT: CHEKHOV'S "THE BET"

Initially, the class will record answers to the KWL sheet that is provided regarding capital punishment and life imprisonment. After this brainstorming session, the class will form groups of four and work together at the computers on the following five subprojects:

1. Each group will have an assigned secretary to record all ideas discussed on the cause and effect handout and the character comparison chart that are both distributed to the groups.

2. For a direct link to sites for this activity, click on the web links option of the Chapter 11 resources on the book companion website. One student in each group will go to the website about lessons to print out the "pros" and "cons" worksheet contained at the site. The group will complete the pros and cons worksheet about the positive and negative sides of capital punishment.

3. One student will go to the same website and find information (in the section called INTO) on the life of Anton Chekhov. The student will share the information with the group. The student must find at least five facts about his life.

4. One student will go to the same website (in the section called BEYOND) and answer questions 1 through 3.

5. The remaining student will find the map on the website and color in the states that sanction capital punishment.

When all the data have been collected, students will rejoin their groups to complete the cause/effect guide and the character charts. The secretary will record all pertinent information.

Developed by Christine Rauth.

bugs; they learn about each one together. As a result, Brennan goes to Mr. Homesley when he needs help to find out about the skull he found in the canyon. When materials arrive from Mr. Homesley's friend, Brennan stays up all night reading to unravel his mystery.

Personal inquiry approximates how adults learn. We have a question, and we search for an answer. Our answers are often the result of using literature and the Internet to learn; most likely we do not use textbooks as our source material. Content teachers who encourage this lifelong learning technique may hook their students on learning just as Omri and Brennan were hooked. Perhaps the best way to begin supplementing content instruction with personal inquiry is to collect questions that students ask, encourage them to find answers, and promote sharing what is learned with all the students. Teachers who use authentic assessment in the form of portfolios can ask students to demonstrate within a portfolio the results of an inquiry.

To fully understand the value of personal inquiries, conduct some of your own. Questions can run the gamut. A teacher of drama and literature asked, "Can I make puppets that can be used effectively for telling stories, expressing different personalities in a variety of plots?" A geometry teacher asked, "What geometric properties are exhibited in soap bubbles?" A physics teacher asked, "What are the areas related to the topic of sound?" Davis (1998) tells how a beehive in a classroom generated questions that students set out to answer: Which one is the queen bee? Where is the queen? What does she look like? How is she different from other bees?

ENHANCING COOPERATIVE LEARNING THROUGH IMPROVED TIME MANAGEMENT

Time management has been defined by Francis-Smythe and Robertson (1999) as effectively using one's time through prioritizing, planning, and adhering to a schedule. Positive time management has been associated with higher achievement levels in students (Britton & Tesser, 1991) and with improved self-evaluations of academic performance (Macan et al., 1990). Incorporating time management into the content curriculum is an important way to teach students to work cooperatively. One of the most important factors in how well students do in cooperative study groups is how carefully they manage their time while studying with the group. Vaughan and Estes (1986) described two negative factors that affect many students: compulsiveness and distractibility. Students will attend to tasks better if they are taught to concentrate and think about what they are learning, to be responsible for their own learning, and to listen carefully to directions.

Responsibility can be fostered through daily work routines, especially in the early elementary grades. For example, after students complete assigned work, they can be offered a choice of activities. In elementary school, students whose names are written on a card in green can be allowed to choose a follow-up activity from four choices that the teacher has labeled on charts in the room. Students whose names are written in yellow can select from three choices. Figure 11.1 illustrates this method of allowing

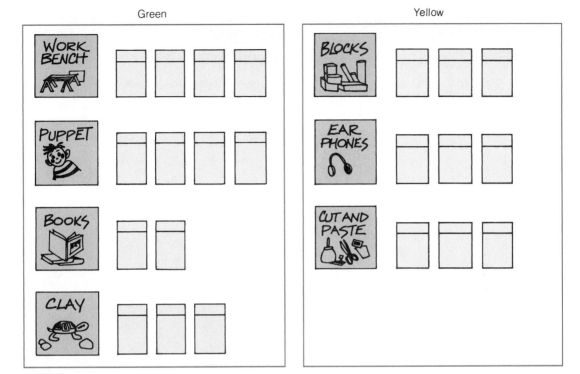

Green   Yellow

WORK BENCH   PUPPET   BOOKS   CLAY

BLOCKS   EAR PHONES   CUT AND PASTE

FIGURE 11.1   Room Chart for Student Activities

students to monitor their own learning and free time. Of course the activities would be numbered and explained on a sheet given to middle and high school students.

Another effective technique for teaching time management is to get students to monitor themselves on self-evaluation logs. Ross, Rolheiser, and Hoaboam-Grey (1998) found that self-evaluation training of fifth and sixth grade mathematics students helped greatly in clarifying students' understanding of curricular expectations. Activity 11.4 presents a student self-evaluation log for elementary grades. Activity 11.5 presents a student self-evaluation sheet for a middle or high school class.

By the time students enter the workforce or college, they often feel shortchanged in knowing how to manage their time (Britton & Tesser, 1991). An activity that can be modified for different grade levels is "How I Spend My Time." First students estimate how they think they spend their time. The teacher keeps these estimates. Next students record how they use their time for a given period. For first or second graders, one day is enough, from waking up until bedtime. Recording can be completed with teacher supervision during the school day. For upper elementary and middle school students, a week is an appropriate block of time. Students should keep records outside of school hours, but the teacher might provide some class time for "catching up." For high school and beyond, the block of time should be at least a week, with recording of all hours—even sleep—done outside class. Next students study their records and compare the activities on which they spent their time with their estimates of how they

LIFE IN THE OCEAN

Directions: At the end of each lesson, rate yourself using the number from the code below that best describes how you think you did on that lesson.

Date	Skill	Student Evaluation	Student Comment	Teacher Comment

#5
S.O.S.

#3
Storm
brewing

#2
Calm
seas

#1
Smooth
sailing

#4
Rough
seas

Day and Date	Activities Planned	Activities Completed	Self-Evaluation of Amount Learned	Self-Evaluation of Enjoyment of Activity	Teacher or Student Comments

Evaluation Scale:

Ugh! I learned little or nothing.		I learned some.		I learned a great deal.
1	2	3	4	5
I disliked doing this.		It was all right.		Wow! I liked it a lot.
1	2	3	4	5

thought they would spend it. Results are often revealing and help students see where they can make changes.

Eleventh graders who participated in such a time management study in their English class were asked to indicate

1. how much time they spent on study and recreation.
2. how much more study time was needed.
3. where time could be found in the schedule for more study.

The students wrote study goals such as "I will study 10 more minutes each evening for English class." They also wrote rewards that they might receive if they achieved the goal, such as "Because I studied wisely, I will probably get a better grade." A classmate had to sign the contract; a parent's signature was optional. Students were to consistently practice achieving their goals for a month. Below are some responses that they recorded in their journals:

1. What was your time management goal?
   - **K:** My time management goal was to spend more of my time studying— more quality time, that is—and thus achieve a better understanding of the material.
   - **J:** My time management goal was to increase preparation—for instance, for tests, quizzes, and essays.
   - **E:** My goal was to spend time studying and preparing for class.

2. Did you achieve this goal? Why or why not?
   - **K:** I achieved my goal because I studied the material more extensively instead of just reading over it.
   - **J:** I did not achieve my goal because of my lack of will and lack of time for preparation.
   - **E:** Sort of. I did spend some more time, but not enough.

3. What did you discover about managing your time for study in English?
   - **K:** I need to spend more time preparing for class instead of talking to friends on the phone. Also, I need to understand the material more fully.
   - **J:** I found out that I spend most of my time working. I spent at least 7 hours a day on school days and 16–19 hours on weekends working. The rest of my time went to being at school and some time—very little—sleeping.
   - **E:** I found that my priorities were not entirely in order. I previously would watch TV, eat dinner, and lie around before doing my homework. I now do my homework as soon as I get home, shower, and eat dinner, and then I take my leisure time. I sometimes study just before going to sleep as well.

4. Was this assignment helpful? Why or why not?
   - **K:** The assignment was helpful to me because the chart helped me to budget my time more wisely.

J: The assignment was helpful because it made me realize what I was doing and should be doing. I should spend more time on schoolwork, but at this time it is not possible.

E: This assignment was helpful because it allowed me to get somewhat of a schedule together in order to get things done. I seem to work much more efficiently now and my grades have improved.

The teacher observed progress in grades and attitudes. She attributed the success to students' involvement and control of their own progress. Students provided their own data about specific uses of time and then decided what they wanted to improve and how. The assignment did not take much class time, and responsibility improved.

ACTIVITIES FOR PROMOTING COOPERATIVE LEARNING

 In the remainder of the chapter we explain reading, writing, and listening activities that involve sharing, collaboration, and cooperative learning. They all work best in a relaxed classroom atmosphere where teachers can guide students in their efforts to work cooperatively.

Extended Anticipation Guides

A technique that can be adapted to cooperative learning is the **extended anticipation guide** (Duffelmeyer & Baum, 1992; Duffelmeyer, Baum, & Merkley, 1987). As noted in Chapter 6, anticipation guides can aid students in predicting outcomes. The extended guides can spark discussion, reinforce or verify information that students have learned, and enable them to modify predictions to take into account new insights and information. Activity 11.6 includes both an anticipation guide for high school students to complete individually before reading Upton Sinclair's muckraking novel *The Jungle* and an extended guide to be completed by students working in groups after reading *The Jungle.*

ABOUT/POINT

ABOUT/POINT is a versatile strategy for cooperative study (Morgan et al., 1986). In kindergarten and first grade, teachers can use it as a listening and speaking aid after reading a story aloud to students. An example of its use in first grade is shown as Activity 11.7. The student is identifying the sun as the source of light and heat. In upper elementary and junior high school, students can work in groups to recall information from content material. To use the ABOUT/POINT strategy, teachers ask students to reread a passage, then to decide in groups what the passage is "about" and what "points"—details—support their response. Teachers can provide study sheets such as the one in Activity 11.8 on high school consumer mathematics.

PART I: ANTICIPATION GUIDE

Instructions: Before you begin reading *The Jungle,* read the statements below. If you agree with a statement, check the Agree column. If you disagree with the statement, check the Disagree column. Be ready to explain or defend your choices in class discussion.

Agree	Disagree	Statement
		1. Anyone who works hard can get ahead.
		2. An employer has a responsibility for employees' safety and welfare.
		3. Companies that process packaged food should be responsible for policing themselves for health violations.
		4. Immigrants were readily accepted into the American system at the beginning of the twentieth century.
		5. Unions can remedy all labor grievances.

PART II: EXTENDED ANTICIPATION GUIDE

Instructions: Now that you have read *The Jungle* and information related to the statements in Part I, get into groups to complete this section. If you feel that what you read supports your choices in Part I, check the Support column below. If the information read does *not* support your choice in Part I, check the No Support column and write a reason why the statement cannot be supported in the third column. Keep your reasons brief and in your own words.

Support	No Support	Reason for No Support (in your own words)
1.		
2.		
3.		
4.		
5.		

Paired Reading

Another strategy that works with middle school and secondary students is paired reading, described by Larson and Dansereau (1986). Students begin by reading a short assignment and then divide into pairs. One partner is designated a "recaller" and the other a "listener." The recaller retells the passage from memory; the listener interrupts only to ask for clarification. Then the listener corrects ideas summarized incorrectly and adds important ideas from the text material that the recaller did not

NAME ____Porche v._____

Directions: Read the paragraph. Then ask yourself, "What was this selection about and the main idea?"

> The sun is a very big star. It heats the earth and moon. The sun lights the earth and moon, too. We play in the sunlight.

This paragraph is ABOUT ____Sun_____
and the main idea is ____Sun heats_____
____and lights the earth._____.

Developed by Dana S. Jubilee.

This reading is ABOUT:
   The high cost, including hidden costs, of automobile ownership.
And the POINTS are:
   Few people have cash enough to buy a car outright.
   Therefore, they borrow from banks, auto dealers, or small loan agencies.
   Costs are affected by the state and region in which the borrower lives.
   Few institutions will lend money unless the borrower purchases life insurance.

---

mention. During the time the listener is clarifying, the recaller also can add clarification. In this manner, the two students work together to reconstruct as much as possible of what they read. The pair can use drawings, pictures, and diagrams to facilitate understanding of the material. Students alternate the roles of recaller and listener after each reading segment, which may number four or five in one class period. Wood notes that paired reading succeeds because it is "based on recent research in metacognition, which suggests that without sufficient reinforcement and practice, some students have difficulty monitoring their own comprehension" (1987, p. 13). Paired reading is also based on elaboration strategy, which, according to Weinstein (1987), helps students learn new concepts by drawing on their prior experiences.

Self-Generated Questions

Recent studies center on **student-generated questions.** Davey and McBride (1986) found that children who were trained to develop probing questions after the reading, either individually or in small groups, scored better on a test of comprehension of the material. In a similar study MacDonald (1986) found that groups instructed in methods for asking questions had comprehension scores higher than the scores of groups without this training. Activity 11.9 presents questions generated by students in a fifth grade elementary social studies class upon getting ready to read about Native American tribes.

Group Summarization

A number of researchers address the importance of **summarization** for the study and retention of reading material (Garner, 1985; Scardamalia & Bereiter, 1984). Garner notes that summarization involves (1) judging ideas deemed important, (2) applying rules for condensing text, and (3) producing a shortened text in oral or written form. A study by Friend (2001) found that student summaries were improved when students looked for ideas in the text that were repeated a number of times, and when students tried to write summaries by generalizing—that is, keeping the gist of the passage uppermost in their mind. Studies consistently show that skilled readers have the ability to summarize, whereas unskilled readers almost always lack this ability (Brown & Smiley, 1977; Garner, 1985; Scardamalia & Bereiter, 1984). To learn to write effective summaries, students can be asked to work in groups and use the following six rules, suggested by Brown and Day (1983):

1. Delete all unnecessary material.
2. Delete redundancies.
3. Substitute a superordinate term for a list of items.
4. Use a superordinate term for a list of actions.
5. Select topic sentences from ones provided in the text.
6. Construct topic sentences when they are not provided explicitly in the text.

One way to have students summarize in groups is for group members to develop a concept map based on the ideas they believe to be important in a chapter or a portion of a chapter. Groups can share their mapping exercises on the board, and discus-

---

ACTIVITY *11.9* STUDENT-GENERATED QUESTIONS: NATIVE AMERICAN TRIBES

What was the environment of the Inuit tribe?
How did the Inuit obtain food and shelter?
How did the Pueblo obtain food and shelter?
Did the Sioux live on a reservation?
What is a shaman?
What is a longhouse?
Where did the Kwakiuti tribe live?
Were the Iroquois a peaceful or warlike tribe?
How did American Indian tribes act differently depending on where they lived?

sion can center on why groups chose to map different concepts. An example of a group-made concept map for vocational students is shown in Activity 11.10.

Mapping can be an excellent cooperatively generated activity for small-group interaction. Davidson (1982) suggests that such concept maps are "low-risk" activities for even the most limited students and can be an unobtrusive way for students to summarize what they learned in the reading. Finally, group summarizing can be accomplished through the use of the GIST (Cunningham, 1982) procedure described in Chapter 10 on writing. Students can work in small groups to make group GISTs and can share these with the entire class. The GIST procedure provides an excellent way to teach much-needed summarization skills.

Jigsaw

Aronson (1978) describes a cooperative learning strategy called **jigsaw,** named for the jigsaw puzzle. In this strategy, each student in a five- or six-member group is given unique information on a topic that the group is studying. After reading their material,

---

ACTIVITY *11.10* CONCEPT MAP: OFFICE TECHNOLOGY

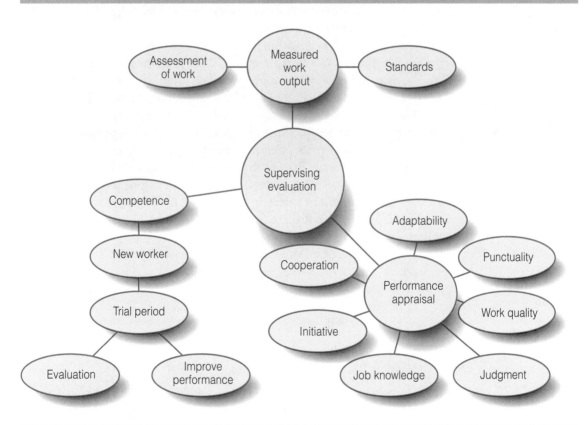

---

the students meet in "expert groups" with their counterparts from other groups to discuss and master the information. In a variation called jigsaw II (Slavin, 1980), all students are first given common information. Then student "experts" teach more specific topics to the group. Students take tests individually, and team scores are publicized in a class newsletter.

Jigsaw uses two distinct grouping patterns: heterogeneous study groups and homogeneous discussion groups. Study groups are arranged heterogeneously by ability or age level to learn about subtopics of the main topic. The purpose of the study group is to allow each member to become expert in a particular topic in common with other group members. Discussion groups are arranged homogeneously by ability or age level to discuss the different subtopics that members studied in their study groups. The purpose of the discussion group is to allow each member to share his or her expertise with others who share a common perspective.

The number of members in each discussion group must equal or exceed the number of study groups. This is to ensure that at least one discussion group member is in each study group. For example, a class of 22 students might be divided into three groups by reading ability—say, one group of seven grade-level readers, a group of six low-level readers, and a group of nine average-ability readers. These could be the homogeneous jigsaw discussion groups. Discussion groups would then count off by fours to establish the heterogeneous study groups, thus ensuring equal representation of the reading groups in each study group.

Suppose the topic under discussion is "The Life of the Native American," and the subtopics are "Traditional Myths and Legends," "Occupations and Products," "Lifestyles," and "Origin and History." Each study group is assigned a subtopic to research, dividing the available materials and informational resources among its members. After each member completes his or her assignment, the study group meets for a sharing session. Each member teaches the other members what he or she learned about the subtopic, so that all members become experts on the assigned subtopic. They bring the results of their study back to the discussion group to share with students who have become experts on other subtopics. In this way, all students have the opportunity to do a small amount of research, to present their findings about what they have learned, and to listen to and learn from other students.

Another technique similar to jigsaw is called *group investigation,* developed as a small-group activity for critical thinking (Sharan & Sharan, 1976). In this strategy, students work in small groups, but each group takes on a different task. Within groups, students decide what information to gather, how to organize it, and how to present what they have learned as a group project to classmates. In evaluation, higher-level thinking is emphasized.

Think-Aloud

Think-aloud, developed by Davey (1983), uses a modeling technique to help students improve their comprehension. Think-alouds are particularly effective as a diagnostic tool to assess students' ability to use inferences as they read (Laing & Kamhi, 2002).

Baumann, Seifert-Kessell, and Jones (1992) found that think-alouds were as effective as directed reading–thinking activities in teaching the skill of comprehension monitoring. In addition, students who performed the think-aloud strategy demonstrated more depth of comprehension-monitoring abilities. Finally, Anderson and Roit (1993) found that students who verbalize their thoughts while reading score significantly higher on comprehension tests. All of this research suggests that think-alouds are an important cooperative learning strategy for teaching reading.

To carry out a think-aloud, teachers verbalize their thoughts as they read aloud—modeling the kinds of strategies a skilled reader uses during reading and pointing out specifically how they are coping with a particular comprehension problem. The teacher models five reading comprehension techniques:

1. Forming hypotheses about a text's meaning before beginning to read
2. Producing mental images (spontaneously organizing information)
3. Linking prior knowledge with a new topic
4. Monitoring comprehension
5. Identifying active ways to "fix" comprehension problems

Using a difficult text, the teacher "talks" it through out loud while students follow the text silently. This training helps poor students realize that text should make sense and that readers use both information from the text and prior knowledge to construct meaning. To demonstrate the five techniques, teachers can make predictions and show how to develop a hypothesis, describe the visual images that come to mind, share analogies and otherwise link new knowledge to prior knowledge, verbalize a confusing point or problem, and demonstrate fix-up strategies such as rereading, reading ahead to clarify a confusing point, and figuring out word meanings from context.

After the teacher models think-aloud a few times, students can work with partners to practice the strategy, taking turns in reading orally and sharing thoughts. This strategy can become an excellent cooperative study technique. Teachers also can give student pairs a checklist to self-evaluate their progress, as shown in Activity 11.11.

ACTIVITY 11.11 THINK-ALOUD CHECKLIST

HOW AM I DOING ON THINK-ALOUDS?

	Not Often	Sometimes	Often	Always
Made predictions				
Formed mind pictures				
Used comparisons (*this* is like *that*)				
Found problems				
Used fix-ups				

Cooperative Reading Activity

Opitz (1992) describes a strategy for emphasizing cooperative study called *cooperative reading activity (CRA),* which he offers as an alternative to ability grouping. It entails locating a reading selection and breaking it into sections, having students individually read and identify important points of a particular section, and forming groups in which students who have read the same section come to an agreement on essential points. Each group, in turn, is expected to share its findings with the rest of the class. Opitz suggests the following steps for constructing a CRA:

1. Choose selections that are already divided by headings into sections roughly equal in length. A selection with an interesting introduction is helpful.
2. Count the sections of the selection and determine the number of students in each group. Generally, groups of four are ideal.
3. Prepare copies of the text you will use for the CRA. Prepare enough copies so that each group member will have a cut-and-paste version of the proper section and a card with the section heading, which will be used to assign students to groups.
4. Design a form that readers can use to record important information learned from the reading (see Activity 11.12 for an example from high school statistics).

To carry out a CRA, students should first read their sections and record important concepts. When students finish reading and completing their record sheets, they form groups, and each person reads the important points out loud from his or her

---

ACTIVITY 11.12 INDIVIDUAL RECORD SHEET FOR A COOPERATIVE READING ACTIVITY IN HIGH SCHOOL STATISTICS

NAME *Susan*

SECTION *Numerical measures of variability*

Important information:

> *The variability is the spread of the data set.*
> *Knowing variability can help us visualize the*
> *shape of a data set. Also we can know*
> *its extreme values.*
> *You need a measure of variability as well as a*
> *measure of central tendency to describe*
> *a data set.*

From M. F. Opitz. 1992, May. In the classroom: The cooperative reading activity: An alternative to ability grouping. *The Reading Teacher 45*(9), 736–738. Reprinted with permission of Michael F. Opitz and the International Reading Association. All rights reserved.

---

record sheet. After everyone has a turn, each group makes a list of important details, using a marker on a piece of chart paper. If details are similar, students still write them on the group list. Then other details that students feel are important are added. Students must come to an agreement before a detail goes on the list.

When the work is completed, each group in turn reads its list to the class. Students are held accountable for all the information presented. Lists are then posted for all to see. In this manner, the groups construct cooperatively the essential meanings of the textbook.

Cooperative Integrated Reading and Composition (CIRC)

Slavin (2001) describes a way of teaching reading and writing in upper elementary grades through stressing cooperative groups. In CIRC, teachers use basal reading texts and traditional reading groups but assign pairs of students from different reading groups to meet and work on specialized tasks. For instance, students in the pairs might read to each other, make predictions about the reading, summarize stories, write responses to stories, work together on getting the main idea of the story, and work on vocabulary skills. Writing is especially stressed in the groups, with the stated goal being to publish student writing. The teams have regular quizzes on their work, but one unique feature of this approach is that students do not take the quiz until teammates say they are ready. Slavin says research shows CIRC to be highly effective in teaching reading and writing to elementary children.

Interactive Guide

Wood offers the **interactive guide** as an effective solution for teachers who find that groups of students within a class need additional help with a difficult reading passage (Wood, 1992; Wood, Lapp, & Flood, 1992). The interactive reading guide allows for a combination of individual, paired, and small-group activity throughout a learning task. According to Wood, such a guide is based on two assumptions: (1) Students need differing amounts of time to complete a task. (2) Sometimes the best way for students to learn a subject is through interacting with other students.

After teachers "walk step by step" through the use of the guide, students are given group assignments and are asked to work portions of the guide individually, in pairs, in small groups, and with the class as a whole. The teacher may use the guide with the whole class or with a portion of the class that needs a slower pace on a particular phase of the lesson. Activity 11.13 provides an example of an interactive reading guide used in mathematics.

Cooperative Graphing

Another excellent activity for teaching cooperative study can be termed *cooperative graphing*. Students work in groups to rate the importance of concepts in a chapter; the ratings appear in the form of a graph. In the second part of the lesson, students work cooperatively to justify their ratings.

△ Work individually   ⊠ Work in groups

△△ Work in pairs   ☐ Work as a whole class

Factoring

☐ 1. Discuss instructions for each set of problems pp. 179–180.

☐ 2. Review important vocabulary; check for inclusion in notes.

△ 3. Work problems 9 & 10, p. 179.

△ 4. Work problems 21 & 22, p. 180.

⊠ 5. Complete problems 1–4. Discuss which factor is needed.

△△ 6. Complete problems 5–8. Compare with group and discuss results.

△△⊠ 7. Continue working problems 11–20. Check with other group members for accuracy.

⊠ 8. Work even problems 22–42. If disagreement occurs, first check g.c.f., then verify by distribution.

☐ 9. Question-and-answer time for general concerns. Time for extension problems.

Developed by Cheryl Keeton; adapted from Wood (1992).

Teachers can construct study guides for a cooperative graphing exercise such as the one shown in Activity 11.14. The activity can be modified for English classes or whenever story structure is being studied by changing the "most important–least important" continuum of the graph to "most liked–least liked" to enable students to rate how they empathized with characters in the story. This is an excellent activity for teaching both cooperative study and graphing.

COST FACTORS THAT INFLUENCE DECISIONS

Part I. Make a graph of how important the following concepts are, from most important to least important. An example is done for you.

		Income statement	Total costs	Unit cost	Variable costs	Sales	Cost of merchandise sold	Gross profit	Selling expenses	Administrative expenses	Net income
Most important	5										
	4										
Important	3										
	2										
Least important	1										

Part II. Work in small groups to justify your answers.

I gave _____ an importance of 5 (most important) because

_____ .

I gave _____ an importance of _____ because

_____ .

I gave _____ an importance of _____ because

_____ .

I gave _____ an importance of _____ because

_____ .

I gave _____ an importance of _____ because

_____ .

I gave _____ an importance of _____ because

_____ .

(*continued*) ➤

Activity 11.14 (*continued*)

I gave _____ an importance of _____ because
_____.

I gave _____ an importance of _____ because
_____.

I gave _____ an importance of _____ because
_____.

I gave _____ an importance of _____ because
_____.

Games Involving Cooperation in Learning

In Chapter 7 we introduced the activity TRIP (Think/Reflect in Pairs) as a way to help students think reflectively and review before a test. Activity 11.15 shows a TRIP card developed for the study of Shakespeare's *Othello;* students must work cooperatively in pairs to think reflectively, work together, practice writing, and hear each other's views about the play.

In Chapter 8 we described note-taking procedures. Cooperative group work is very helpful for teaching two-column note taking. After students record and reduce their notes, the teacher has students form pairs or small groups to compare their reductions. By discussing cooperatively what reduction terms each person in a group decided on, all group members learn from each other not only about the process of reducing notes but also about the material in the notes.

A physics teacher who wished to engage his students in discovery through group work devised an activity he calls "The Shover and the Shovee" (see Activity 11.16). The activity begins with students organizing themselves into groups of three; two people are "shovers" and one is the "shovee." One of the shovers gently pushes the shovee toward a wall. The students are then asked which way the shovee went, which is toward the wall. The vector (arrow) represents this motion as drawn on the chalkboard. The second shover now pushes the shovee toward a different wall. Again, direction is established and the vector drawn. Now both shovers gently push the shovee toward their respective walls, and this additional information is added to the chalkboard drawing. Students are asked what the effect of the shovers pushing with different relative velocities would be. Various combinations are illustrated. Finally, shovers experiment with the time it takes to go from a particular point to one wall while gently shoving the shovee at different speeds toward the second wall. They can see by doing that the time to go from the starting point to the wall will be the same in each case, thus illustrating the independence of perpendicular vectors. Activity 11.16 shows what would be drawn on the chalkboard.

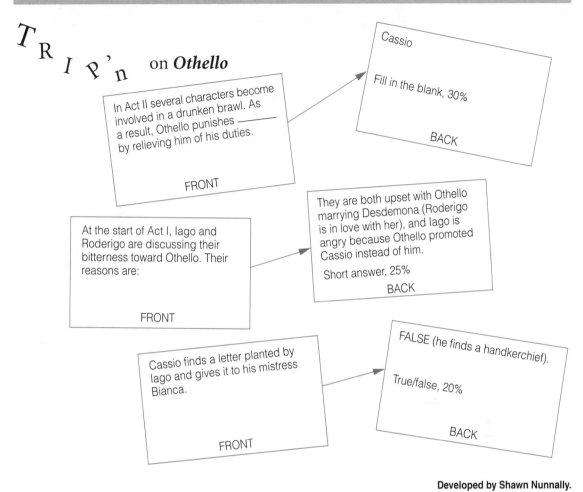

T R I P'n on **Othello**

In Act II several characters become involved in a drunken brawl. As a result, Othello punishes ———— by relieving him of his duties.

FRONT

Cassio

Fill in the blank, 30%

BACK

At the start of Act I, Iago and Roderigo are discussing their bitterness toward Othello. Their reasons are:

FRONT

They are both upset with Othello marrying Desdemona (Roderigo is in love with her), and Iago is angry because Othello promoted Cassio instead of him.

Short answer, 25%

BACK

Cassio finds a letter planted by Iago and gives it to his mistress Bianca.

FRONT

FALSE (he finds a handkerchief).

True/false, 20%

BACK

Developed by Shawn Nunnally.

ONE-MINUTE SUMMARY

This chapter has described cooperative learning strategies that help students to think and learn. By explaining and modeling strategies that foster cooperative learning, teachers can show students how to obtain the most from their learning experiences. Cooperative learning can enhance retention of content by providing an opportunity for students to practice, under a teacher's guidance, five important categories of learning: rehearsal, elaboration, organizational thinking, comprehension monitoring, and affective thinking. Cooperative learning requires an atmosphere of seriousness of purpose, confidence, assistance, and, above all, commitment to disciplined inquiry and study. In this chapter we presented a stylized three-step procedure for group

THE SHOVER AND THE SHOVEE

[Step 1]   Shover #1

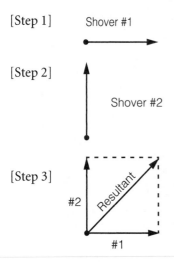

[Step 2]

Shover #2

[Step 3]

#2 Resultant

#1

[Step 4] Various combinations

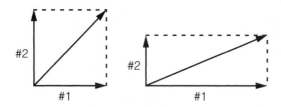

[Step 5] For constant #2, time to wall doesn't change, regardless of the magnitude of #1

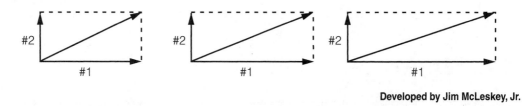

Developed by Jim McLeskey, Jr.

process to help cooperative groups to function better. We discussed the importance of thematic unit instruction, personal inquiries, and time management techniques. Finally, we described many actual reading and writing strategies that stress cooperative learning. Table 11.1 summarizes the specific techniques described in the chapter and indicates when each can be introduced to students in the content area classroom.

	K	1	2	3	4	5	6	7	8	9	10	11	12

TABLE 11.1 Introducing and Teaching Cooperative Study Skills: A Kindergarten through Grade 12 Timetable

	K	1	2	3	4	5	6	7	8	9	10	11	12
Grouping	▬	▬	▬	▬	▬	▬	▬	▬	▬	▬	▬	▬	▬
Extended anticipation guides				▬	▬	▬	▬	▬	▬	▬	▬	▬	▬
ABOUT/POINT						▬	▬	▬	▬	▬	▬	▬	▬
Paired readings					▬	▬	▬	▬	▬	▬	▬	▬	
Student-generated questions	▬	▬	▬	▬	▬	▬	▬	▬	▬	▬	▬	▬	▬
Summarizations			▬	▬	▬	▬	▬	▬	▬	▬	▬	▬	▬
Jigsaw						▬	▬	▬	▬	▬	▬	▬	
Think-aloud					▬	▬	▬	▬	▬	▬	▬	▬	▬
Cooperative reading activity					▬	▬	▬	▬	▬	▬	▬	▬	▬
Interactive guide				▬	▬	▬	▬	▬	▬	▬	▬	▬	
Cooperative graphing					▬	▬	▬	▬	▬	▬	▬	▬	▬

PAR ONLINE

Websites that provide information to complement this chapter can be found by clicking on the web links option of the Chapter 11 resources on the book companion website.

END-OF-CHAPTER ACTIVITIES

Assisting Comprehension

1. Think about and list ways in which you might change the daily operations of your class to incorporate some or all the techniques described in this chapter.

2. Try specific cooperative learning activities in your classes, and evaluate how well students receive them.

Reflecting on Your Reading

1. Ask students to take the "How I Spend My Time" test described in the section on time management. Have students reflect on whether their self-analysis shows that they spend study time wisely both in and out of school. (Try taking the test yourself.)

2. Standard 2.1 of the International Reading Association's Standards for Reading Professionals and Teachers (2003) states that teachers should use appropriate grouping options, such as individual, small group, whole class, and computer-based grouping plans. Classroom teachers are asked to model and use scaffolding procedures so that students learn to work effectively in groups. Strategies described in this chapter were mainly targeted for use in small-group instruction; all 14 strategies described can be used in cooperative learning classrooms. Decide if any of the strategies can be used for individual learning activities or for whole-class learning activities. Do you think any can be used for computer-based instruction?

*The greater thing in this
world is not so much where
we stand, as in what
direction we are going.*

OLIVER WENDELL HOLMES

Engaging Students through Teaching in the Affective Domain

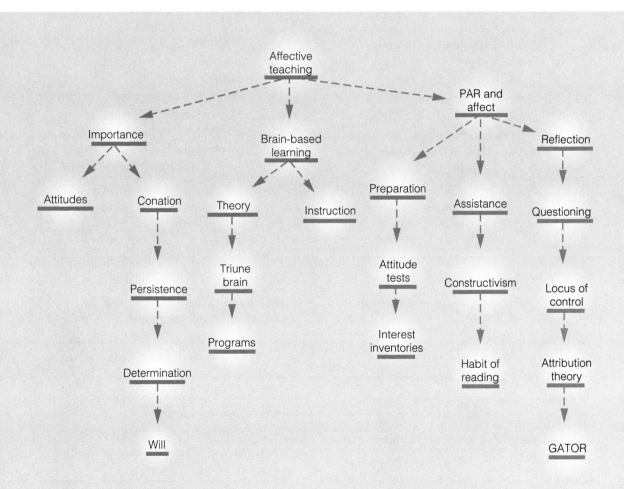

PREPARING TO READ

1. Before you read this chapter, try to answer the following questions to test your background knowledge concerning the affective domain of learning. Then read the chapter, expand your knowledge, and see how your answers change.

   a. Why is the affective domain of learning important?

   b. What are conative factors of learning?

   c. How can attitude affect learning?

   d. How can we use attitude tests and interest inventories to improve instruction?

   e. What is attribution theory?

   f. How can brain function influence students' actions?

   g. What is locus of control? Why is it an important construct for teaching?

   h. What is brain-based learning? Why is it important in teaching?

   i. What is constructivism?

2. Following is a list of terms used in this chapter. Some may be familiar to you in a general context, but in this chapter they may be used in unfamiliar ways. Rate your knowledge by placing a plus sign (+) in front of those you are sure that you know, a check mark (✔) in front of those you have some knowledge about, and a zero (0) in front of those you don't know. Be ready to locate them in the chapter, and pay special attention to their meanings.

   _____ affective domain

   _____ attitude

   _____ conation

   _____ brain-based learning

   _____ triune-brain theory

   _____ reptilian brain

   _____ old mammalian brain

   _____ new mammalian brain

   _____ downshifting

   _____ program

   _____ constructivism

   _____ internal locus of control

   _____ external locus of control

   _____ attribution theory

   _____ passive failure

   _____ learned helplessness

OBJECTIVES

As you read this chapter, focus your attention on the following purposes. You will

1. learn what is meant by *affective domain of teaching.*

2. understand why affect is important to reading.

3. learn the importance of attitudes in teaching.

4. learn the importance of conative factors in reading.

5. understand what constitutes a brain-based approach to learning.

6. understand the importance of attitude tests.

7. see three examples of attitude tests.

8. learn how to provide assistance in strengthening affective bonds.

9. better understand the construct of locus of control and its importance for content area instruction.

10. understand attribution theory and its importance for teachers.

11. be able to incorporate a number of affective strategies into the content area curriculum.

Why an Affective Teaching Chapter Is in This Textbook

What is the affective domain?

The quote from Oliver Wendell Holmes speaks to the importance of making meaning of one's life through self-directed learning. Such meaning can be gained not only through conscious thought, or cognition, but also through feelings, emotions, attitudes, and instincts that we display as we react to new learning. There are many kinds of emotional reactions that one exhibits in learning. Such evoked feelings and emotions are said to be part of the **affective domain** of learning. Affective constructs, such as feelings, emotions, attitudes, self-concepts, values, self-esteem, and locus of control, influence a student's ability to learn.

Students in kindergarten to twelfth grade dwell in the affective domain—that is, their lives are often ruled by strong feelings and emotions, and they often exhibit very positive or very negative attitudes about their school environment. However, teachers often dwell mainly in the cognitive domain, where student achievement is perceived as the single most important reason for schooling. Because of this perceptual mismatch, students and teachers often do not "meet" intellectually in the classroom. They are physically in the same classroom, but their needs are so different—teachers are driven to impart knowledge, students to discover the range of emotions inherent in living each new day—that real communication sometimes does not occur in classrooms where the focus of instruction is only on cognition. Throughout this book, we assert that it is the teacher's job to get students to think more often and more clearly. Sometimes students do not challenge themselves to think, and some students have not been trained to think. However, we also contend that teachers need to pay more attention to the affective domain, to make learning more interesting by making class more fun, functional, and rewarding. If teachers move toward the affective domain and students move toward the cognitive domain, discipline problems will be lessened, and students will learn more. We think that this is important enough to devote an entire chapter to engaging students through good affective teaching.

Cognitive plus affect = more effective learning!

For many decades, researchers (Adler, 1931; Bandura, 1986, 1997; Dechant, 1970; Glasser, 1986) have written about the importance of the social aspects of learning. As a consequence of late twentieth century publications concerning the "crisis in education" (see Chapter 1), research on such affective variables as attitude and self-concept has waned. Because initiatives and reform efforts have resulted in rigorous national standards, and specific performance measures have been mandated for students in many states, studies examining affective variables have been largely absent from funding proposals. This is so despite recent research showing that affective variables have an important connection to outcome performance measures such as memory and recall (Hager & Gable, 1993; Wolfe, 2001). However, times are changing: Glickman (2004) suggests that it is time to support students and teachers once more in their quest for the best instructional environment.

Glasser (1986) has noted the importance of the affective domain in his book *Control Theory in the Classroom*. He states that more than half of all students are making little or no effort to learn, mainly because they don't believe that school provides any satisfaction. In a spirited repudiation of stimulus–response theory, Glasser maintains that human behavior is generated by what goes on inside the person. In an interview (Gough, 1987) Glasser spoke of the importance of affect:

> Except for those who live in deepest poverty, the psychological needs—love, power, freedom, and fun—take precedence over the survival needs, which most of us are able to satisfy. All our lives, we search for ways to satisfy our needs for love, belonging, caring, sharing, and cooperation. If a student feels no sense of belonging in school, no sense of being involved in caring and concern, that child will pay little attention to academic subjects. (p. 657)

In this chapter we explain why we agree that the affective domain plays an important role in learning. We present both the theory and the application (strategies) to enhance the teaching of affect in content area classrooms.

IMPROVING STUDENT ATTITUDE

Attitude is the most outward manifestation of the affective domain.

The most outward manifestation of the affective domain is **attitude**—the mental disposition one exhibits toward others. For a long time educators have known that student attitude is a critical variable in reading achievement (Purves & Bech, 1972; Walberg & Tsai, 1985). Frank Smith (1988) noted that the emotional response to reading "is the primary reason most readers read, and probably the primary reason most nonreaders do not read" (p. 177). M. Cecil Smith (1990) found, in a longitudinal study, that reading attitudes tend to be stable over time from childhood through adulthood. It may be true that poor attitudes toward reading (or good attitudes) are inculcated early in schooling and tend to remain stable throughout one's life. Wolfe and Antinarella (1997) maintain that teachers are still able to win over and inspire students through developing in them attitudes and dispositions for learning that cause them to honor, respect, and value themselves and others. Currently, researchers such as Maurer and Davidson (1999) are calling for teachers not to ignore the affective domain, and what they call the "power of the heart," in using new technologies in the classroom for teaching the skills of reading and writing.

What teachers can do

Research by Heathington and Alexander (1984) indicates that although teachers see attitudes as important, they spend little time trying to change students' poor attitudes. To change student attitudes about reading, teachers first need to listen actively when students are commenting and discussing. Teachers need to concentrate on what students are saying and learn to reply to their comments, not formulate in advance a stock reply. Also, teachers need whenever possible to make reading fun and rewarding. They can do this by encouraging students to read on their own and making certain that reading assignments are not long and overwhelming. Teachers also can have students take part in frequent group sharing experiences. As another element of good teaching, the teacher should always speak well of reading and be a reader who shares the books she or he is reading. To promote affect, teachers should bring good literature into the classroom whenever possible, even in content area classrooms. Bottomley and colleagues (1999) found that a literature-based approach to reading and writing had a greater effect on intermediate-age children's affective orientations toward literacy than did whole-language or basal-reader literacy instruction.

Purkey and Novak (1984) suggest teachers can change student attitudes by making the classroom more affectively inviting. They outline four levels of invitation that have a direct impact on student learning. Figure 12.1 gives Purkey's four levels, from intentionally disinviting to intentionally inviting. Purkey stresses that at the highest level the teacher must make a conscious effort to help the students feel they are part of a learning community. The teacher must further be aware that students have a desire to learn and that each day teachers must nurture that innate thirst for knowledge.

If teachers follow Purkey's advice, a positive classroom environment will be maintained. Researchers (Fisher & Berliner, 1985; Palmer, 1998) have stressed the importance of creating a positive classroom climate. Teachers should provide a climate that says, "I am never going to give up on you; I believe in you." Many famous people did poorly in school—Albert Einstein, Woodrow Wilson, Thomas Edison, George Bernard Shaw, Pablo Picasso, William Butler Yeats, Henry Ford, and Benjamin Franklin. Paul Harvey, in *Destiny* (Aurandt, 1983), relates how Charles Schulz struggled with rejection in school for years. Schulz was a "loser" in school; no one had faith in him, yet he created *Peanuts,* one of today's most popular comic strips. If we emphasize the positive, each of us someday may play a central role in helping a future genius realize his or her potential. Most important of all, the teacher must truly value inquiry, problem solving, and reasoning. By keeping an open mind and letting students take part in open-ended discussions, the teacher makes a statement about the true art of teaching that even the most limited students cannot ignore or misinterpret.

FIGURE 12.1   Purkey's Four Levels of Invitation

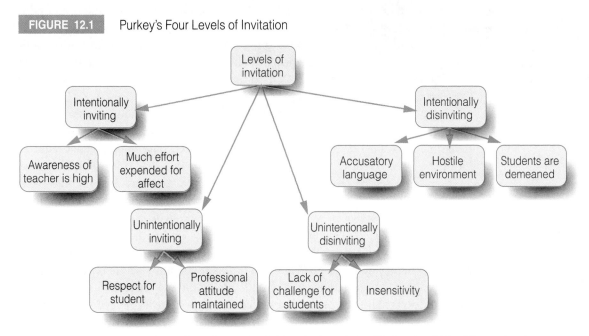

From W. W. Purkey and J. M. Novak, *Inviting School Success.* (1984). Adapted with permission of Wadsworth, a division of Thomson Learning.

"SOON AS YOU LEARN TO READ, JOEY, THE WHOLE WORLD'S AGAINST YOU."

Dennis the Menace © King Features Syndicate

THE ROLE OF CONATION IN TEACHING READING

What is the role of conation in the affective domain?

In *Hooked on Books,* Fader (1976) relates his encounter with remedial students in Los Angeles whom he "catches" reading an article in *Playboy.* They explain to him that it isn't that they can't read—they won't read. An aspect that teachers sometimes overlook is students' lack of determination, persistence, and will to gain information through reading. Energy, persistence, desire, determination, and will to learn define **conation** in learning (Cooter, 1994). Even though this term has been used for almost 200 years in psychological literature, it is fairly obscure.

Paris, Lipson, and Wixson (1983) were among the first modern researchers to affirm the importance of intrinsic motivation and determination in a student's ability to become an independent learner. They noted that becoming a good reader requires both the skills of reading and the will to learn in increasingly complex educational environments. Recent research (Wang and Guthrie, 2004) has corroborated what Paris, Lipson, and Wixson found on the importance of intrinsic motivation in reading comprehension.

Researchers such as Cooter (1994), Raven (1992), and Berlak (1992) have argued for the emergence and realization of the importance of conative components of learning. Researchers (Gholar et al., 1991; Snow, 1987)) see conative factors as separate from, but very close to, the affective domain of learning. All these researchers maintain that conative aspects of human behavior are necessary for a student to function cognitively.

Gholar and Riggs (2004) have written a powerful book called *Connecting with Students' Will to Succeed: The Power of Conation,* which may be the first text to deal entirely with conation. In it they offer a number of new conative strategies for engaging students in learning. They also offer (see Figure 12.2) a conative paradigm of learning. This paradigm progresses from what Gholar and Riggs call an "incongruent environment" to a "congruent environment." In an incongruent environment, much cognitive dissonance (see Chapter 6), apathy, and discord are evident because affective feelings and conation are not being nurtured. But in a congruent environment, students are empowered and actively engaged in learning. This is so, according to Gholar and Riggs, because teachers in this environment are supportive and nurturing. In such an environment, teachers stress intrinsic motivation through the use of positive conative experiences. According to the authors, conation can be stressed through (1) activities and strategies that give students choices in the learning experience, (2) pretend situations where students learn self-efficacy through being challenged to

FIGURE 12.2

A Conative Paradigm of Learning

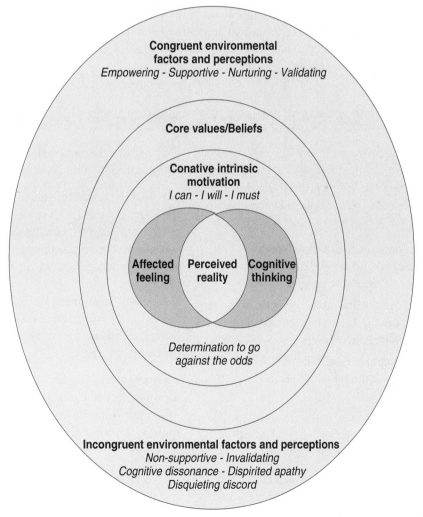

From *Connecting with Students' Will to Succeed,* by Cheryl R. Gholar and Ernestine G. Riggs. © 2004 by Pearson Professional Development. Reprinted by permission of LessonLab, a Pearson Education Company, www.lessonlab.com

succeed in difficult encounters, (3) use of activities that ask students to decide whether a real or imagined historical or fictional character exhibits good or bad intentions. WebQuests, discussed earlier in this text, can be set up for students to do all three of these activities. Activity 12.1 shows possible WebQuest questions for small groups of students to answer.

Fleener and associates (2000) propose that conation be treated as a viable component of the reading development of children. They suggest a model of literacy development that integrates conation, cognition, affect, and social environment as connecting domains that interact to enable successful teaching and learning. The researchers propose that literacy develops when teachers tend to affect and conation and demonstrate the value of inquiry, sharing, and curiosity about learning within a social context. The four key contexts in which these social attributes occur are child, teacher, text, and task. Table 12.1 lists the attributes of learning that these researchers feel are important for each of the four contexts.

In the next section of this chapter we will demonstrate the importance of conation by describing two students who find themselves in different classroom environments, and we will explain how classroom settings can motivate students in different ways.

ACTIVITY 12.1 SAMPLE WEBQUEST: TRAVELING TO RURAL AMERICA

The task: Four of you are to work as a group to travel America looking for historical links to our heritage through attending art festivals and historical festivals. Each of you will have a task to perform.

The accountant/treasurer will make spreadsheets and tables detailing trips and budgets for the entire group.

The reporter will compile the notes of all four investigators and lead the team to make a final report on the festival visits.

The photographer will take pictures of each visit and post them to the website created by the team.

The travel agent will make arrangements for all travel and budget all items. Data will be collected and shown for each trip.

The group should attempt to attend at least one festival in each of the following areas: the South, Northeast, Midwest, and West. A final report will be issued on what new insights were found about cultures through these cybervisits.

Tools for the task: Students in the group will use the Internet to find art festivals and other festivals of historical interest. Graphs will be drawn, and all "visitations" will occur through cyberspace adventures mapped out by the students themselves.

Informational sources: Websites will be posted for you, such as chamber of commerce sites and sites where the group can find festivals throughout the country.

Evaluation: The group will be evaluated on the thoroughness and accuracy of their final report. Also, the group will report to the class on their findings. The overall evaluation will show how well the group covered the topic in their final report. Each group member will document his or her own contribution to the final report, which will be verified by other group members and the teacher.

TABLE 12.1	Factors Contributing to Teaching and Learning Success

Child	Teacher	Text	Task
Quality of prior knowledge The learner's prior knowledge may be clear and factual, or unclear and represent false knowledge. **Task-intrinsic motivation** The child's readiness to perform an activity is a goal in itself. **Insight** Reflective awareness comes through cooperative interchange among students. **Perception of self as a reader** Children must see themselves as generators of information, not passive receptors of knowledge. **Will to succeed** Persistence and internal locus of control must be present.	**Quality of time on task** Teachers must develop caring relationships with children in completing the task. **Modeling the value of thought processes** Teachers must value thinking and discussion as tools to develop the thought processes of children. **Fostering curiosity** Teachers must believe that inquisitiveness and curiosity are most important in the learning process.	**Perception of difficulty** Students cannot perceive the book in a negative way, as being too difficult to comprehend. **Aesthetics** Texts must be appropriate for the audience, with pleasing formats. **Good writing** Subjects must come alive through the author's use of good writing.	**Interest** Tasks must be interesting to students. **Appropriateness** Tasks must be appropriate to the intellectual, psychological, social, and moral development of students. **Cohesive context** Students must perceive that the task assigned makes sense in relation to what is read. **Perception of difficulty** Students cannot perceive the task in a negative way, as being too difficult to perform. **Will to succeed** Internal locus of control and a desire to be competitive with others or oneself—that is, persistence must be operational.

From Fleener, C., Hager, J., Morgan, R. F., & Childress, M. (2000). The integration of conation, cognition, affect, and social environment in literacy development. In P. Linder, W. M. Linek, E. G. Sturtevant, & J. Dugan (Eds.), *Literacy at a New Horizon: 22nd Yearbook of the College Reading Association.* Used with permission of the College Reading Association.

HOW AFFECT IS DISPLAYED BY TWO STUDENTS

An example of the effects of conation on learning

Consider two students to see how persistence, determination, and will can be of paramount importance in a classroom environment. One student, Freddy, has had difficulty in school since the third grade. Now in middle school, he finds himself daily moving from classroom to classroom in which little or no talking is allowed among students except during the five minutes between classes. In his science class the typical lesson is going over the questions at the end of the chapter. He is supposed to, but doesn't, read the chapter for homework. The teacher gives a brief lecture about the reading material and addresses a stern lecture to the class about the value of homework and the apparent laziness shown by many students. This lecture is punctuated by the threat of a quiz at the end of the class and the warning that "all this will be on the test on Friday." Students are not allowed to talk to one another (although several

In Freddy's class, little discussion, reading, or writing has occurred. Although the personal notes students are writing might be sent via e-mail, it is likely that not even that use of technology is occurring!

write notes). The teacher spends a great deal of time and energy keeping the class "in order," preventing students from talking. Students spend the remainder of the period filling in words in spaces provided on textbook worksheets created by the publisher. To accomplish this task, Freddy does not have to read the text. He simply finds the answers by scanning for boldface words and other clues that show where he might find the answers that will fill the blanks. He seldom does well either on the end-of-class multiple-choice quizzes or on the tests, but he always acts as though he doesn't care. When the bell rings to change classes, Freddy feels as though he hasn't learned much. In fact, what he is concluding is that science is boring and that reading in science is pretty much about filling in spaces on worksheets to keep the teacher happy. In short, his will to be a good student is nonexistent and seems so suppressed that he has no extra energy to enjoy reading books on his own.

Becky is a ninth grade student who also has had some difficulty since third grade, but her day is different from Freddy's. She starts the day in a 100-minute interdisciplinary "earth class" in which the same teacher teaches both geography and earth science. The class begins with the teacher writing a single word on the chalkboard and then getting all the students involved by writing about what they think they will find out about the topic. The anticipation is obvious as the students busily make their predictions. The teacher asks each student to share aloud as she paraphrases each response on the chalkboard. Students at this point are simultaneously helping the teacher to find out about their prior knowledge and actively building on their own knowledge base through the sharing process. There is an air of importance to what each student has to offer, and the teacher frequently asks the students to explain why they gave certain responses. Both teacher and students respect the background knowledge each person brings to the pursuit of new understandings. The teacher then introduces a skill the students will use to make sense of the reading they are about to do. She points out what "good readers" always do when they read nonfiction text. Then she shows students how they can practice that skill in class that day.

In Becky's class, discussion, reading, and writing all occur in a content context. Students' predictions could be recorded in a word processing program and viewed by an LCD projector. The graphics could be created in a mapping program such as *Inspiration*. Thus information could be saved and edited.

She sets up a guided practice in which students are grouped in pairs to read silently and then reflect with each other on what they have read. Students spend 10 to 15 minutes actively reading a section of text and working with partners to practice recalling in their own words what they have learned. When each partnership has finished the reading, the partners collaborate to create a graphic representation of what they have learned. The teacher moves around the room to keep students on task, clarify important concepts, and answer any questions students might have. When students have finished the reading and shared their graphic representations with other groups in the classroom, the teacher puts six key terms on the chalkboard and asks each student to write a summary of what he or she learned today, using all the terms at least once in the summary. The teacher then collects the summaries for evaluation. Throughout the entire process, students in this class are active, engaged, and thoughtful. When Becky leaves her class, she knows she wrote a summary that will demonstrate her successful interpretation of the text. Becky never feels threatened in this class. She knows the teacher is interested not just in the teaching of geography and earth science but also in sharing important skills that Becky has found can help her in other subjects as well. Through the purposeful fun she is having in class, Becky is determined to be a better student and a better reader.

These two classroom descriptions illustrate the importance of student satisfaction in the learning process. Even if no more facts and concepts are learned in Becky's class than in Freddy's, Becky has more determination to learn than Freddy because she is learning how to learn in a nonthreatening, enjoyable atmosphere. Becky's teacher is employing strategies and paying attention to conative factors that are compatible with how students best learn new concepts. This technique, called *brain-based teaching,* deserves a close look.

Affect and Brain-Based Teaching

What is brain-based learning?

Modern discoveries about how the human brain functions are quite possibly among the most significant scientific discoveries in all of human history. Increasingly, educators are relying on **brain-based learning theory** to take advantage of a growing body of knowledge that neurologists are uncovering about how humans learn. The newest imaging technology has shown us how the brain is structured in an incredible network of approximately 100 billion neurons, each connected to thousands of other neurons to form more connections than there are atoms in the entire universe. Sylwester (1994) describes the brain as modular, with separate components learning over time to combine information to form complex cognitive environments. Sylwester maintains that the brain is powerfully shaped by genetics, development, and experiences. The brain works to shape the nature of our experiences and is active in formulating the very culture in which we live.

Caine and Caine (1994) stress the importance of brain-based learning for educators. They describe the brain as a parallel processor that performs many functions simultaneously, making all meaningful learning complex and nonlinear. Many researchers (Diamond & Hopson, 1998; Sylwester, 1995; Weiss, 2000) assert that the brain is constantly in a search for meaning. Green (1999) has asserted that "learning is enhanced by combining a rich environment with complex and meaningful challenges. Isolated pieces of information unrelated to what makes sense to a student [are] resisted by the brain" (p. 685).

Green and other researchers such as Healey (1990) and Jensen (1998), in discussing the roles and functions of the brain, stress the importance of the emotions of the learner. The brain uses emotions in learning to create patterns of learning that can be replicated at other occasions and in other environments. Emotion (certainly an integral part of the affective domain of learning) is needed, then, for learners to learn and make meaning out of their environment.

The role of affect, emotions, conation, and brain development just described should be of utmost importance to educators. To disregard what we are finding out about how the brain works in successful learning environments would be irresponsible. Yet most educators either are not aware of these findings or choose to ignore them. Schools continue to teach separate, often nonmeaningful, and segmented concepts to students who "chew" the bite-sized bits of uninteresting learning. Such an approach is inherently dull because it is not compatible with how the human brain works and has evolved. In addition, the primary means of controlling students who have difficulty learning in this stifling system is through the use of threats, either of failure or of disciplinary measures. Because the brain does not function at its best or at its highest level in a threatening environment, the use of threats can guarantee only failure in the learning process.

Researchers such as Restak (1982, 1984) have debunked the simplistic "left brain/right brain" literature to show that most learning tasks require both left-hemisphere and right-hemisphere processing. Cooperation rather than competition between the brain hemispheres is the prevailing mode in most learning. Moreover, Sinatra (1986) proposes the importance of the two subcortical brains in the emotional and motivational aspects of learning. He states,

> . . . since the neural pathways between the cortex and the reticular and limbic systems function all the time without our conscious awareness, educators must realize that curriculum content cannot be approached solely by intellectual reasoning. The systems regulating feeling, emotions, and attentiveness are tied to the very learning of information. (p. 143)

It can be further postulated that the teacher's attitude toward the reason for learning, and toward the learners themselves, may be a more important factor in how well something is learned than the specific content. In making learning interesting and challenging, teachers are, in reality, activating brain subsystems responsible for alertness and emotional tone. Sinatra criticizes dull worksheet drills as decoding exercises that negate students' eagerness to learn. Most brain researchers would agree that motivation, attention, and memory all operate in an interlocking fashion to enhance learning.

The triune brain theory has a significant impact on understanding student reactions to what they perceive as stressful learning situations.

Sinatra's work is compatible with the **triune-brain theory** described by MacLean (1978). This model clarifies how the brain works in general and precisely why affect is so important in reading. MacLean explains that the brain has evolved into three principal parts, each of which handles a different function. The most primitive is the brain stem, often referred to as the **reptilian brain** because reptiles as well as mammals possess this limited brain function. This lowest section of the brain deals with only the most basic needs, such as reaction to immediate threat. This part of the brain holds no memories, which is why, when the reptilian brain is in charge, we have no recollection of what occurred.

What is the reptilian brain?

The old mammalian brain is also called the *limbic system*.

The middle section of the brain—which MacLean calls the **old mammalian brain** because it is present in all mammals—is a larger and newer portion of the brain. It controls emotions and plays a great role in the learning process by determining whether the newest portion of the brain will be able to function fully. It is the seat of the *limbic system*, which secretes different chemicals when a mammal is confronted with stimuli. For instance, a negative event may stimulate chemicals that affect the reptilian brain, which may then produce an automatic response to danger, much like freezing or "shutting down." Hart (1983a) describes this process by which negative messages are sent from the old mammalian to the reptilian brain as **downshifting.**

What is downshifting?

The upper section of the brain—which MacLean calls the **new mammalian brain**—is the neocortex, the newest and largest portion of the brain. It is the source of abilities such as mathematical and verbal acuity and logical reasoning. This is the most complex part of the human brain and, as a result, the one that functions most slowly. The neurological makeup of the neocortex allows learning to take place through associations that can number in the high trillions. Medical researchers know that, through the release of limbic system neurotransmitters, cells of the neocortex are either helped or hindered in their functioning.

Possible applications of the triune-brain theory might include actions such as the following: for a student who perceives an academic climate as threatening, chemicals may be secreted to the reptilian brain, telling the brain to, in effect, revert to the instinct of freezing, thereby impeding learning and retention. The primary concern for educators ought to be that the neocortex function to its fullest potential through the elimination of the possibility of threats. Students such as Becky, who feel positive and happy about a learning experience, will be better able to process and retain information. Students such as Freddy, who are uncertain and unhappy in a learning situation, either at school or at home, will become emotionally unable to attend to a task for any length of time. Just as the reptilian brain takes over in situations of panic, the limbic system can take over from the highest levels of thinking possible in the neocortex if the emotional climate is threatening or stressful. Similarly, consider the teacher who is struggling to find a way to present content material but cannot seem to get it across to her students. She is using the chapter information, but it just isn't working. She becomes more frustrated and less effective. Again, a sort of downshifting may be occurring.

Research has shown that brain functioning increases significantly when novelty is present (Restak, 1979) and when subjects experience feelings of pleasure and joy (Sagan, 1977). Researchers have also found that removing touch and movement can result in increases in violent behavior (Penfield, 1975). All this gives credence to the importance of attitudes, feelings, emotions, motivation, and conative factors in thinking, reading, and learning. The neocortex, according to Hart (1983b), is what separates humans from most animals. It is the newest part of the brain, which enables us to make plans and carry them out. Hart suggests that pattern seeking—efforts to make sense out of complex and often chaotic realities—is the key to human intelligence. Such pattern seeking can be fostered by what Greenough, Withers, and Anderson (1992) call "enriched environments," where students encounter substantial and varied input, problem-solving efforts, and immediate feedback in the context of real-world problems.

The human brain did not develop because of evolutionary needs for rote memory, manipulation of symbols, or dealing with tight, sequential structures or work systems, which today constitute the main concerns of conventional schooling and much training. If a learner already knows at least something about a topic, then a logical, sequential, and fragmented presentation may serve well enough to transfer some new information about that topic to his or her neocortex. But if a learner is not already familiar with the topic, this kind of presentation produces consistently poor learning results.

Hart further suggests that we live by "programs" that we acquire and store for use in the brain. A **program** is a fixed sequence for accomplishing some goal. The goal may be learning a new way of approaching a math problem or something as simple as walking across a room. Human nature makes the working of a program a pleasurable experience; we can rely on its activation to help us achieve a goal. We can use only programs that are built on and stored through experience. Each individual develops his or her own unique programs. Efforts to impose a program on someone who has not developed it on his or her own are futile. Yet these brain programs are used to accomplish everything we do. In performing all tasks, we routinely use a three-step cycle: (1) evaluating the situation, (2) selecting the program that seems most appropriate from our store, and (3) implementing it. Fully acquired programs, though laboriously built, have an automatic quality that can easily lead one to forget that other individuals have not already acquired them. For instance, a good reader attempts to read difficult material by using a program developed over the years. Another person might implement a similar program but select a different way of previewing the material.

Inefficient readers have not yet developed an effective program for reading difficult material. They don't know what to do and try to keep implementing the program they "know" for reading easy material. Yet most teachers—as good readers—don't even realize that this is the problem; teachers are equipped with programs that have become automatic for them. Throughout this text we have advocated the PAR Lesson Framework as a program of learning that students can use to enhance their learning experience. Unfortunately, for many students today the programs acquired are negative. They often are programs of survival resulting from the lack of a brain-compatible environment. They may even be programs of failure and dropping out—a sense that school is "just not for me."

Focusing on what the latest brain research is telling us about how students learn (Diamond & Hopson, 1998; Jensen, 1998; Kotulak, 1996; Lowery, 1998; Wolfe & Brandt, 1998), we believe the following guidelines are important to teaching:

1. Students remember material best that is structured and meaningful.

2. Because the environment in which a brain operates determines to a large degree the functioning ability of that brain, the classroom should always be a rich environment in which students interact.

3. An enriched environment allows students to make sense of what they are learning.

4. Opportunities to talk and move about are important for heightening brain activity.

5. Threats and pressure need to be held to a minimum because they cause the neocortex (the newest and highest level of the brain) to function poorly.

6. Because the brain is essentially curious, learning must be a process of active construction by the learner, whereby students relate what they learn to what they already know.

7. Because learning is strongly influenced by emotion, when emotion is added to learner input, retention is enhanced.

8. Teachers should stress intuitive learning as much as step-by-step logic to allow creative thinking to emerge.

By taking advantage of what we now know about the way the human brain functions, we can create in our classrooms an environment in which all students can perform at their highest potential, developing patterns that will carry them through life as successful learners. In an affective environment that facilitates optimal use of the higher brain functions, students are empowered to become effective, self-motivated learners.

PREPARATION FOR AFFECTIVE TEACHING

 An important part of preparing to teach is to find out what attitudes students exhibit toward school in general and your course in particular. However, we suggest that before doing this, teachers conduct some self-assessment on whether they are exhibiting an enthusiastic and positive attitude about reading in their classroom. One factor found to be positively correlated with both teacher affectivity and attitudinal changes is teacher enthusiasm (Streeter, 1986). According to Collins (1977), teacher enthusiasm affects vocal delivery, eyes, gestures, body movements, facial expressions, word selection, acceptance of ideas and feelings, and overall energy. The teacher survey shown as Activity 12.2 helps teachers assess whether they are exhibiting an enthusiastic, positive attitude about reading in their classroom. Any K–12 teacher can use this survey for assessment.

Besides assessing their own enthusiasm for reading and proclivity to model affect, teachers also should assess students to determine positive and negative attitudes

| ACTIVITY *12.2* THE AFFECTIVE DOMAIN OF TEACHING |
| THE TEACHER'S VIEW OF READING—A SELF-ASSESSMENT |

Directions: Please read each of the following questions, and then circle *often, sometimes, seldom,* or *never* after each question.

1. Do you have patience with those who are having difficulty reading?
   Often   Sometimes   Seldom   Never

2. When you finish a guided reading lesson, do you ask your students whether they want to find out more about the topic?
   Often   Sometimes   Seldom   Never

3. Do your students ever get so interested in reading that they talk about the assignment after it is completed?
   Often   Sometimes   Seldom   Never

4. Do you ask thought-provoking, higher-order thinking questions about the reading assignments?
   Often   Sometimes   Seldom   Never

5. Do you check the prior knowledge of your students before assigning reading?
   Often   Sometimes   Seldom   Never

6. Do you ensure students are choosing reading material appropriate for their reading level?
   Often   Sometimes   Seldom   Never

(continued) ➤

7. Do you help students find resource books for assignments?

Often   Sometimes   Seldom   Never

8. Are you always careful to select reading material that is on the students' appropriate reading grade level?

Often   Sometimes   Seldom   Never

9. Do you explain or define new concepts and vocabulary in reading assignments?

Often   Sometimes   Seldom   Never

10. Do you praise students for good reading effort?

Often   Sometimes   Seldom   Never

11. Do you give reading assignments of appropriate length?

Often   Sometimes   Seldom   Never

12. Do you provide a quiet atmosphere for independent reading and study?

Often   Sometimes   Seldom   Never

13. Do you explain the importance of reading to your students?

Often   Sometimes   Seldom   Never

14. Do you modify the reading material to meet the needs of individual students, especially students with disabilities?

Often   Sometimes   Seldom   Never

15. Do you provide your students with extended literacy experiences?

Often   Sometimes   Seldom   Never

16. Do you know how interested your students are in reading?

Often   Sometimes   Seldom   Never

17. Are you interested in reading in your daily life?

Often   Sometimes   Seldom   Never

18. Do you read books for pleasure?

Often   Sometimes   Seldom   Never

19. Are you flexible in your reading—that is, do you read at different rates for different purposes?

Often   Sometimes   Seldom   Never

20. Do you find yourself exhibiting enthusiasm when discussing a favorite book?

Often   Sometimes   Seldom   Never

All 20 items should be answered *often* or *sometimes*.

Scoring key:

15–20 *often* or *sometimes* responses	Very effective
12–14 *often* or *sometimes* responses	Reasonably effective; fair in the affective areas
8–11 *often* or *sometimes* responses	OK; need some improvement
0–7 *often* or *sometimes* responses	Poor; do some rethinking!

Adapted from a questionnaire developed by James Laffey in *Successful Interactions in Reading and Language: A Practical Handbook for Subject Matter Teachers,* by J. Laffey and R. Morgan, 1983, Harrisonburg, VA: Feygan.

Before using any published inventories for other than classroom use, be sure to obtain permission from the authors!

toward reading. The *Mikulecky Behavioral Reading Attitude Measure* (Mikulecky, Shanklin, & Caverly, 1979) for older students (see Activity 12.3) and the *Elementary Reading Attitude Survey* (McKenna & Kear, 1990) for early elementary students (see Activity 12.4) were designed to cover a broad range of affective interest and developmental stages. Appendix A provides keys for interpreting these two surveys, along with technical information on their construction and validation. These tests can be given as pretests and again after several months as posttests to determine whether students' attitudes have improved significantly over the period.

Sometimes simply by finding out what students like to do in their spare time, but being aware of their goals and perceived needs, teachers can ensure a more positive

Following are 20 descriptions. You are to respond by indicating how much these descriptions are either unlike you or like you. For *very unlike* you, circle the number 1. For *very like* you, circle the number 5. If you fall somewhere between, circle the appropriate number.

Example:
You receive a book for a holiday present. You start the book, but decide to stop halfway through.

 Very Unlike Me 1 2 3 4 5 Very Like Me

1. You walk into the office of a doctor or dentist and notice that there are magazines set out.

 Very Unlike Me 1 2 3 4 5 Very Like Me

2. People have made jokes about your reading in unusual circumstances or situations.

 Very Unlike Me 1 2 3 4 5 Very Like Me

3. You are in a shopping center you've been to several times when someone asks where books and magazines are sold. You are able to tell the person.

 Very Unlike Me 1 2 3 4 5 Very Like Me

4. You feel very uncomfortable because emergencies have kept you away from reading for a couple of days.

 Very Unlike Me 1 2 3 4 5 Very Like Me

5. You are waiting for a friend in an airport or supermarket and find yourself leafing through the magazines and paperback books.

 Very Unlike Me 1 2 3 4 5 Very Like Me

6. If a group of acquaintances would laugh at you for always being buried in a book, you'd know it's true and wouldn't mind much at all.

 Very Unlike Me 1 2 3 4 5 Very Like Me

7. You are tired of waiting for the dentist, so you start to page through a magazine.

 Very Unlike Me 1 2 3 4 5 Very Like Me

8. People who are regular readers often ask your opinion about new books.

 Very Unlike Me 1 2 3 4 5 Very Like Me

9. One of your first impulses is to "look it up" whenever there is something you don't know or whenever you are going to start something new.

 Very Unlike Me 1 2 3 4 5 Very Like Me

10. Even though you are a very busy person, there is somehow always time for reading.

 Very Unlike Me 1 2 3 4 5 Very Like Me

(*continued*) ➤

11. You've finally got some time alone in your favorite chair on a Sunday afternoon. You see something to read and decide to spend a few minutes reading just because you feel like it.
    Very Unlike Me   1   2   3   4   5   Very Like Me

12. You tend to disbelieve and be a little disgusted by people who repeatedly say they don't have time to read.
    Very Unlike Me   1   2   3   4   5   Very Like Me

13. You find yourself giving special books to friends or relatives as gifts.
    Very Unlike Me   1   2   3   4   5   Very Like Me

14. At holiday time, you look in the display window of a bookstore and find yourself interested in some books and uninterested in others.
    Very Unlike Me   1   2   3   4   5   Very Like Me

15. Sometimes you find yourself so excited by a book you try to get friends to read it.
    Very Unlike Me   1   2   3   4   5   Very Like Me

16. You've just finished reading a story and settled back for a moment to sort of enjoy and remember what you've just read.
    Very Unlike Me   1   2   3   4   5   Very Like Me

17. You choose to read nonrequired books and articles fairly regularly (a few times a week).
    Very Unlike Me   1   2   3   4   5   Very Like Me

18. Your friends would not be at all surprised to see you buying or borrowing a book.
    Very Unlike Me   1   2   3   4   5   Very Like Me

19. You have just gotten comfortably settled in a new city. Among the things you plan to do are check out the library and bookstore.
    Very Unlike Me   1   2   3   4   5   Very Like Me

20. You've just heard about a good book but haven't been able to find it. Even though you've tried, you look for it in one more bookstore.
    Very Unlike Me   1   2   3   4   5   Very Like Me

Reprinted with permission of Dr. Larry Mikulecky, Professor of Education, Indiana University. Data regarding the construction, validation, and interpretation of this test are contained in Appendix A.

Example of how to use an interest inventory

atmosphere in the classroom. To this end, teachers can create general-interest inventories such as the one shown for middle school and high school in Activity 12.5, and the one for early elementary school in Activity 12.6. Through the use of an inventory a high school English teacher (Richardson, 1996) asked her eleventh graders to indicate what types of writing experiences they liked best. She discovered that they enjoyed writing letters but disliked writing essays. The curriculum expectation was that all students would learn and practice writing persuasive essays. While teaching "Sinners in the Hands of an Angry God" by Jonathan Edwards, the teacher talked about this sermon as an example of a persuasive essay. Then she asked the students to relate

SCHOOL _____ GRADE _____ NAME _____

1. How do you feel when you read a book on a rainy Saturday?

2. How do you feel when you read a book in school during free time?

3. How do you feel about reading for fun at home?

4. How do you feel about getting a book as a present?

5. How do you feel about spending free time reading?

6. How do you feel about starting a new book?

7. How do you feel about reading during summer vacation?

8. How do you feel about reading instead of playing?

9. How do you feel about going to a bookstore?

10. How do you feel about reading different kinds of books?

11. How do you feel when the teacher asks you questions about what you read?

12. How do you feel about doing reading workbook pages and worksheets?

13. How do you feel about reading in school?

14. How do you feel about reading your school books?

15. How do you feel about learning from a book?

16. How do you feel when it's time for reading class?

17. How do you feel about the stories you read in reading class?

18. How do you feel when you read out loud in class?

19. How do you feel about using a dictionary?

20. How do you feel about taking a reading test?

some of their own experiences in trying to convince someone of something important to them and to estimate how successful their efforts had been. After developing a list of successful persuasion strategies, she told the students to write a persuasive essay in the form of a letter to a real person, trying to persuade that person about an important issue. The assignment was a huge success.

Name _____

What do you prefer to be called? _____

Home address _____ Phone _____

Name of parent/guardian _____

Parent's place of employment _____

Parent's work phone _____

Your usual grade in Math _____, Social Studies _____, English _____, Science _____.

The grade you plan to earn this year in Math _____, Social Studies _____, English _____, Science _____.

What percentage of your grades should come from tests? _____.

In what other ways do you want to earn grades? _____

Complete the following:

My favorite subjects in school are _____.

My least favorite subjects are _____.

Circle all the words that describe you:

healthy	quiet	good sport	friendly
dependable	likable	hard worker	lazy
honest	nervous	cooperative	lonely
worthless	quick-tempered	shy	artistic
sense of humor	cheerful	easily upset	clean, neat appearance
forgetful	easygoing	good leader	easily discouraged

If I could change anything about myself, it would be _____ _____.

If I could change anything about school, it would be _____ _____.

My favorite hobby is _____.

My favorite sport is _____.

At home it is fun to _____.

I like to read about _____.

Ten years from now I would like to be _____.

Things I do well are _____.

What I dislike about classes are _____.

What I dislike about teachers are _____.

Sports I play at school are _____.

Clubs I belong to at school are _____.

My name is _____ .

I like myself because _____ .

My family likes that I am _____ .

I am good at _____ .

I think reading is _____ .

My favorite book is _____ .

My favorite thing to do is to _____ .

My hero is _____ because _____ .

My favorite time at school is _____ because _____ .

The assessment instruments described so far enable teachers to determine their own attitudes and interests as well as those of their students. This will allow teachers to design effective instruction that is sensitive to the students as individuals. When teachers show students that they are interested in them as people, significant changes can occur in student behavior. Affective assessments can be categorized anonymously and posted at a website (such as on WEB CT or BlackBoard course authoring tools). Responses can be entered into a database management system, such as File Maker Pro, so they can be searched and organized in different ways. In the next section we present ways to assist students and use the assessment results.

ASSISTANCE BY STRENGTHENING AFFECTIVE BONDS

Affective bonds can be strengthened for students when teachers assist students during the lesson by designing tasks that influence children's motivation. Turner and Paris (1995) explain how the context for literacy includes student choices, a challenge, personal control, collaboration, the construction of meaning, and specific consequences. Choice allows students to select from those areas in which they are most interested, thus ensuring greater attention during the task. Challenge keeps students from being bored, as long as the learning tasks are not at the frustration level. Students need to feel that a class is "their class" as much as the teacher's; students are more willing as learners when they feel that they control their own learning. Collaboration or social interaction motivates students to be more curious, confident about, and engaged in learning. In this way, the emotions come into play in learning. This is important, as we explained earlier in the section on brain-based learning.

When students can make sense of their learning, developing a knowledge base or constructing their own purposes for reading a selection and developing tasks on their own that demonstrate their learning, they are constructing meaning. That is, knowledge is not passively received but actively constructed by the learners on the basis of prior knowledge, attitudes, and values (Betts, 2001). This is called **constructivism,**

What is constructivism?

or the constructivist theory of learning. This theory emphasizes the important role of the learner in literacy tasks, allowing readers to feel comfortable with learning because they are so fully integrated in putting it all together. Concerning this theory, Sparks (1995) has said,

> Constructivists believe that learners build knowledge structures rather than merely receive them from teachers. In this view, knowledge is not simply transmitted from teacher to student, but is instead constructed in the mind of the learner. From a constructivist perspective, it is critical that teachers model appropriate behavior, guide student activities, and provide various forms of examples rather than use common instructional practices that emphasize telling and directing. (p. 5)

In a constructivist environment, students must be encouraged to use higher-order thinking skills to find meaning in classroom experiences. Teachers do not stress the "one correct answer" to every question, with that answer being the one supplied by the teacher. Student questioning must be encouraged, and a variety of possible interpretations will have to be accepted by the teacher in certain situations. Teachers who stress constructivism cannot simply rely on factual recall to questions and tests as the central proof that learning has taken place in their classroom. Betts (2001) has called for teachers in constructivist classrooms to reduce the amount of time spent in drill and practice exercises, increase open-ended questioning and discussions, and increase heuristic, trial-and-error type learning whereby teachers focus discussion on the reasoning that supports a variety of student-generated interpretations. Most of all, teachers should realize that we learn from our mistakes and that incorrect responses are not always bad but are a natural consequence of learning and of moving from inadequate knowledge to adequate knowledge about a given subject. In short, the teacher acts as a facilitator to help students discover from their own background knowledge any new learning that must take place.

An example of constructivist learning occurred when three professors separated geographically were implementing online instruction and shared insights over a threaded discussion (Richardson, Fleener, & Thistlethwaite, 2005). By "talking" with each other online, each built new understandings and applications of what a threaded discussion could add to their courses.

Providing Assistance in the Classroom Setting

Restructuring a classroom to assist in affective bonds

In a study of 11,794 school sophomores in 820 schools, achievement gains and engagement were significantly higher in restructured schools (Lee & Smith, 1994). Restructuring efforts included some of the following: school-within-a-school, keeping students in the same homeroom for the four years of high school, cooperative learning foci, teacher teams having common planning time, and flexible time for classes. Smaller schools enjoyed the most gains. Achievement, as tested in math, science, reading, and history, was consistently higher with restructuring. Students became more committed and involved in their learning. Thus both cognitive and affective areas showed improvement.

Individual teachers cannot restructure schools, but they can restructure their classrooms. Forget and Morgan (1995) found that when reading to learn was emphasized in a school-within-a-school setting in working with at-risk youngsters, attitudes and school attendance improved significantly. In addition, they found that students' ability to use and think critically about textbook material improved measurably. The way a classroom is arranged, or can be arranged readily, affects the learning and teaching climate. Students who always face forward to the teacher as the main focus in the classroom receive the message that learning takes place through lecture and teacher control. To engage all students in learning, redefinitions of the classroom climate must be made (Kowalski, 1995). A seminar approach, as is used in the Paideia schools (Strong, 1995), calls for long tables with all learners seated facing one another for intensive discussion. If such tables are not available, teachers and students might move several desks together to create the same effect. Group work calls for small clusters of chairs in several parts of a room.

Daily (1995) asks teachers to motivate students by modeling the classroom after the workplace. Students are "paid" as a reward for performing well in assignments and completing long-term projects. Activity 12.7 shows a teacher's adaptation of Daily's system. Teachers can also develop thematic units that cross content areas and that are developed around "themes of caring" (Nodding, 1995), such as "caring for strangers and global others by studying war, poverty, and tolerance" (p. 676). When teachers collaborate on such units, students see the value of collaboration more clearly.

Fostering the Habit of Reading

Students learn early that they can avoid reading. Bintz (1993) interviewed many students who were resistant to reading. He found that the majority avoided reading whenever possible, listening instead to the teacher for the basic information to be covered on tests. He concluded that by "resorting to shortcut and survival strategies, students were participating in their own deskilling" (p. 613).

Teachers must be careful to design instruction that includes reading as a crucial component and that ensures the consequences of reading are important as well as interesting. Richardson (1995a) shares a personal story of using three techniques to keep her middle school son reading: reading aloud from democratically chosen selections, reserving a period of time for sustained reading, and respecting her son's choices of reading material. Restrictions were not made, and the new climate of sharing, time, and choice fostered the reading habit. Teachers can implement all three of these techniques in some form in their classrooms. Enlisting parent support and being on the lookout for interesting newspaper articles in your content area are two ways to start.

Several websites provide recommended reading for children of all ages and reading levels. "Google" to find them!

Martin and Martin (2001) suggest a number of strategies for fostering reading habits in students who are having reading difficulty. First, they maintain that students should progress at a pace that is comfortable enough to bring success. Many poor readers are rushed to finish exercises, and this only brings more frustration. To help in monitoring pace, teachers can give students small, manageable portions of reading so students will find it easier to stay focused. Martin and Martin also recommend the idea of Paris and Oka (1989): acting as a coach to students to motivate them to acquire a habit of reading. Another important component is the motivational aspect of reading. Teachers

Materials

- Each student is issued a packet of five checks and one check register. (I go to the bank and beg for donations, but you could make your own for the students.)

Payments

- Each student is paid $50 per day based on a full day's attendance. Sickness and doctors' appointments are not excused. A student who is not there doesn't get paid even if the absence is not his or her fault.
- Paydays are the 15th and 30th of each month.

Deductions   (I don't distinguish between types of assignments.)

- Students lose $20 for each missed homework assignment in the first nine weeks, $25 in the second nine weeks, $30 in the third nine weeks, and $40 in the fourth nine weeks.
- Students lose $10 for a negative phone call home or a scheduled parent conference due to a student's not being responsible.
- Students lose $10 for being tardy.
- When a student is out of checks, he or she will be charged $25 for a new set.
- Students unable to make rent should be charged all that they have in their accounts and then docked a $20 late fee from the next paycheck in addition. (Consider taking away a privilege until enough money is earned to cover rent.)
- No checks or check registers are allowed to go home. Any student losing the checking materials is out of the game for the rest of the year.

Employees' Responsibilities

- Students must pay $600 in rent on the first of every month for the use of desks, books, cafeteria, playground equipment, computers, etc.
- September rent may be prorated at $15 per day because students won't have any money in their accounts. I actually charged my students rent for September at the end of September and then collected October's rent on the first of October. All other rent should be collected on the first (or the first available school day closest to the first) of each month.
- Students must endorse their checks when they are paid and then enter the amount correctly in their check registers. (Doing this as a class lesson with an overhead is very important for the first four or five payments until they get the hang of it.) You should have to write rent checks with them for only two months; they should be able to do it by themselves by November.
- Students write a check to you paying for items purchased in the auction (see below).

Auctions

- Auctions are held at the end of each nine-week period, for a total of four auctions. Good marketing in weekly newsletters to parents or sending home flyers can bring in donations to your auction that will save you time and money.
- Have as many parents volunteer for the auctions as you can. They can help move the merchandise to you as you auction it and help the students keep track of how much they are spending so no child spends more than allowed. Also, at the conclusion of the auction the students write you a check for the auction items they just purchased, and parents can help with this and help check the registers for accuracy.
- Allow time before the auction for students to browse and decide what they want to buy. Some will spend all their money on one large item; others will buy several small things.
- Allow time after the auction for students to admire their purchases and, in some instances, trade off with other students for something else.

- Students must always keep a balance in their accounts for emergencies (groceries, medical bills, etc.); thus they should not be allowed to go below $700 in their accounts. Most times, if rent has been paid, I let them go down to $150 but no lower. They write the amount of money they can spend on a piece of paper before the auction and deduct the amount every time they purchase something so they can keep a running total of what they have left to spend. At the end of the auction, they add up all that they spent and write a check to "Brain-Makers, Inc." for the correct amount, putting "auction" on the memo line of the check.

Hints

- Have students (or parent volunteers) cut out the checks, and always keep plenty on hand.
- Have a student fill in the date and the names on the checks so all the teacher has to do is write the amount owed.

- Sign the checks that the teacher uses to pay them before you photocopy them so you won't have to keep signing your signature.
- Consistently check the registers to help students who are having subtraction difficulties, aren't dating the transactions, or are placing their numbers in an incorrect area of the register. Ensuring that students keep accurate records all along is very important and will prevent them from not knowing their account balance because of errors in the register.
- No ink in the registers—pencils only.
- Get auction volunteers to help the students keep track of how much they are spending and to help at the end with check writing. You will be tired after talking the whole auction and trying to keep the students from playing with their new toys. Parents can help with classroom management.

BrainMakers, Inc.	
Pay to the Order of _____	$_____
_____	Dollars
Memo _____	
05100001: 9541 8741 0100	

Developed by Chris White, fourth grade teacher, Shady Grove Elementary, Henrico County, Virginia.
This activity was adapted from "A Glimpse of the Real World" by Garrison Daily.
Learning Magazine **(September 1995).**

should bring in the emotions of literature, making the reading more personal and relevant to the student. Finally, they recommend that student self-checks be employed often to give the students more responsibility and more of a stake in the activities.

No chapter on the importance of the affective domain in reading would be complete without a discussion of the particular problem we have in this country with boys and literacy. Researchers (Sommers, 2000) are documenting that by many measures boys are having far more problems with schooling than girls. Young and Brozo (2001) have gathered recent alarming statistics on literacy and learning for boys. According to some of the findings, boys are more violent than girls, get in trouble with the law with much greater frequency, have much more trouble with alcohol and drug abuse than girls, and are far more likely to commit suicide. As relates to schooling, the most outstanding statistic is that boys have far more reading problems than girls. Also, they are three to five times more likely to be diagnosed with attention deficit disorder and learning disabilities, as well as 50 percent more likely to be retained in school. Of course far more boys drop out of school than girls. These facts are so disconcerting that Brozo says boys "are fast becoming the culturally and academically dispossessed" (p. 318).

There is no easy answer for what can be done to help the plight (which Brozo says now amounts to a crisis in our nation) of boys in our schools. One thing for certain, though, is that ways must be found to foster the habit of reading in boys. Most boys still view reading as unmasculine. One of the authors still remembers playing at recess and in the school yard and how the subject of books simply never came up when boys got together. Sports heroes, television, movie stars, and events of the day were discussed. But no boy in the group ever said, "Let me tell you about a great book I am reading." Boys just did not make such statements, and maybe they still don't today. A way must be found to make reading a more acceptable pastime for boys. Certainly the first step is for the teacher to discuss with male students the books that interest them. Teachers, whenever possible, need to supply boys with readable books that have high interest for them.

STRATEGIES FOR AFFECTIVE REFLECTION

 Two strategies detailed in the next section will help students to become more reflective in their thinking and will aid them in being more responsible for their own learning.

Reinforcing Internally Controlled Behaviors

What is the difference between internal and external locus of control?

Magoon (1977) listed as one of the most important emphases of a constructivist classroom the fostering in students of an **internal locus of control.** People with an internal locus of control accept responsibility for the consequences of their own behavior. This is based on Rotter's (1966) social learning theory and suggests that individuals attribute their successes and failures to different sources. Those with an **external locus of control** blame fate, chance, other individuals, or task difficulty for their successes and failures. The concept of locus of control is a legitimate construct for affective teaching because it helps teachers understand certain behaviors in the classroom.

Studies have specifically tested locus of control and reading achievement (Culver & Morgan, 1977; Drummond, Smith, & Pinette, 1975). These studies support the notion that internally controlled students make greater gains in achievement in general, in reading achievement, and in classroom adjustment. More recent studies have found internally controlled individuals to be more cognitively active in the search and learning activities involved in reading (Creek, McDonald, & Ganley, 1991; Curry, 1990; DeSanti & Alexander, 1986). Recently Chan (1996) found that gifted students in Australia had greater motivation and confidence in their own ability to control successes or failures in school tasks than did a group of average-achieving peers.

Guidelines
help teachers
reinforce an
internal locus
of control.

Morgan and Culver (1978) have proposed certain guidelines to help teachers select activities that reinforce internally controlled behaviors. First, teachers need to minimize anxiety over possible failure by building patterns of success for each student in the class. They can accomplish this in several ways. To begin, teachers need to develop a realistic reward system of praise for work completed. The system of rewards can be kept simple if the teacher uses a contractual arrangement that specifies a sequence of graduated tasks, each of which is attainable. The teacher should stress the concept of mastery of the task in grading students, thereby eliminating arbitrary grading, which is a source of agitation to students who are external in their thinking. The teacher can deemphasize the concept of time and thus lessen compulsiveness by allowing students unlimited time to complete and master certain tasks. In addition, teachers should aid school guidance staff in counseling students toward realistic life goals, because externally controlled persons often have unrealistic aspirations or no aspirations at all.

Teachers also can adopt strategies that foster self-direction and internal motivation. For instance, they can let students make a set of rules of conduct for the class and start their own class or group traditions, to reinforce the importance of both the group and the individuals in the group. Such an activity, which relies on listening and speaking, can be implemented even in the early grades. Another excellent activity for older students is the "internal–external" journal. Students keep a record of recent events that have happened to them. In the journal they can explain whether the events were orchestrated and controlled by someone other than themselves and, if so, whether these externally controlled events frustrated them. As a variant on the journal idea, students can make a "blame list" to indicate whether positive and negative events that happen to them are their own fault or the fault of others. These activities rely on the use of writing, thus integrating another communicative art into affective education.

One of the most important classroom strategies for helping students develop an internal locus of control is to have them practice decision making whenever possible. Study guides and worksheets described in this text can be constructed in such a manner that individuals and groups are asked to reason and react to hypothetical situations in which decisions need to be made. Group consensus in decision making about a possible conclusion to a story can be a powerful way to teach self-awareness and self-worth and to teach about relationships with others. The directed reading–thinking activity (Stauffer, 1969b) is another excellent strategy for teaching group decision making through hypothesizing the outcome of a story. This activity, explained in Chapter 7, enables students to believe in themselves by feeling that what they have to say has dignity and worth.

How is attribu-
tion theory
similar to or
different from
locus of
control?

Locus of control is similar to **attribution theory** as proposed by a number of researchers in psychology (Butkowsky & Willow, 1980; Heider, 1958; Weiner, 1979). Attributions are assertions individuals make about the causality of and the responsibility for some observed behavior. This theory asserts that students often fail at tasks because they are influenced by their perceptions of the causes of past behavior. That is, students who see their performance in tasks as based mainly on chance factors, on luck, and on other factors they can't control get discouraged easily and give up when attempting to complete a difficult task.

What are passive failure and learned helplessness?

Unfortunately, teachers often reinforce negative attributions of students and contribute to what have been called **passive failure** and **learned helplessness** (Fenwick, 1995) by giving preferential treatment to high achievers. When teachers make it a point to never call on poor readers to answer questions or read a sentence out loud to prove a point of argument, they reinforce the students' negative feelings of failure and hopelessness.

The focal point for helping students who have fallen into the trap of learned helplessness is for the teacher to work diligently to get the student to accept responsibility for his or her own learning. Teachers need to interact with such students in a positive way and continually ask for their perceptions of how they are succeeding in the class. Teachers need to be very positive with all students and let everyone know they are cared for and appreciated. Teachers also should give self-evaluation checklists and learning logs, explained earlier in this text, to students so that they can monitor their own learning and set achievable goals for themselves in the class. Probably the most important commitment teachers can make for failing students is to use metacognitive strategies (metacognition was explained earlier in this text) to help students monitor their own comprehension and learning within any given lesson. Students who are asked to write down comments about whether they are succeeding and how they are succeeding, and are further asked to discuss these comments with the teacher, will begin to understand that they are responsible for their own learning and are actually putting in writing their own plans for success.

Questioning

Questions in the affective domain provide linkage among emotions, attitudes, and thoughts or knowledge (Jones, Morgan, & Tonelson, 1992). For example, when students examining the problems faced by Richard Nixon as president of the United States are asked to consider their feelings about these problems, they are connecting knowledge and feelings.

GATOR can help improve affective instruction.

The GATOR (Gaining Acceptance Toward Reading) system can improve instruction by allowing the teacher to ask more reflective questions. To help gain student acceptance of reading, the teacher announces that all questions asked about a lesson, by either the teacher or the students, must be based on "feeling," as must all responses. The entire lesson is taught with questions such as these:

How did that make you feel?

Why is this lesson important?

How did you feel about the main character? Why would you have done or not done what the main character did?

Why is this chapter important?

Tell us why you like what you just read.

GATOR also can be used when students are working in small groups. Students are asked to discuss only emotion-laden questions. As an example, consider these affective questions, which were generated by teachers and students during a brainstorming session after reading "Goodbye, Grandma" by Ray Bradbury (1983):

If you knew that a close relative of yours was about to die, would you treat him or her differently?

How do you think Grandma felt about the beginning and ending of her life?

What if you were given three years to live? How would you do things differently?

There is humor in this story. How do you feel about having humor in a story about death?

Do you feel Grandma is like anyone you know?

What lasting feeling were you left with at the end of the story?

During what parts of this story did you have a warm, happy feeling? Read these parts aloud to the class.

How do you think it will feel to be old?

Do we treat people differently when we know they are dying? Should we?

Using expository materials in a middle school lesson about seasons and climate from an earth science textbook, a teacher could ask the following affective questions:

How do you feel about today's weather?

Can weather affect your mood and how you feel? Give examples.

How do you feel about the seasons?

What if there were never any change of seasons? Describe what your feelings would be.

ONE-MINUTE SUMMARY

Students rarely achieve without having certain concomitant feelings, including a positive attitude and strong emotions of caring for other students, for the subject, and for the teacher. This chapter covered the affective domain—attitudes, emotions, interests, attributions, and conative factors that are important in content area teaching. The chapter began with a discussion of the importance of attitudes on learning. Strategies were discussed that help change student attitude toward the subject and the teacher. Next a section on conation and conative factors in learning was detailed. A brain-based approach to teaching and learning was explained. Brain-based learning strategies can heighten students' brain activity, thereby lessening threats and pressures.

Preparation, assistance, and reflection strategies aid teachers in emphasizing the affective domain. Teacher and student attitude tests were discussed, as well as general-interest inventories. Also, we presented ways to assist students in strengthening affective bonds and described two important reflection activities to help students achieve better in the classroom. Two important constructs—locus of control and attribution theory—were discussed, and strategies were discussed for stressing internal locus of control to improve learning and achievement.

Throughout the chapter we exhorted teachers to bring about lasting achievement by paying attention to not only cognition but also the affective domain of learning. Classroom teachers who stress affect in their teaching of cognitive skills and course content will be considerably more successful than those who omit such emphasis in their classrooms.

PAR ONLINE

Post in a threaded discussion an example of conation you have experienced or your response to the value of considering conation.

Create a model or diagram of the triune brain and downshifting, using a software program such as *Inspiration* or *KidPix*.

For direct links to topics such as Internet treasure hunts, creative writing, fun making postcards, online books, and poetry for children, click on the web links option of the Chapter 12 resources on the book companion website.

END-OF-CHAPTER ACTIVITIES

Assisting Comprehension

1. Why is it important for teachers to know about conation? What are some conative factors in teaching?

2. What is brain-based learning? What are some brain-based learning principles?

Reflecting on Your Reading

The International Reading Association's Standard 4.4 (2003) says that classroom teachers should display positive dispositions toward reading. In addition, Standard 5.1 says that teachers should motivate students to become lifelong readers. Both of these standards relate to ideas discussed in this chapter. Think of and then jot down ways this chapter has helped you to focus more positively on reading. Also, how have discussions in the chapter taught you to motivate students to read?

Assessing Attitudes toward Reading

Elementary Reading Attitude Survey

Directions for Use

The Elementary Reading Attitude Survey (ERAS) provides a quick indication of student attitudes toward reading. It consists of 20 items and can be administered to an entire classroom in about 10 minutes. Each item presents a brief, simply worded statement about reading, followed by four pictures of Garfield. Each pose is designed to depict a different emotional state, ranging from very positive to very negative.

ADMINISTRATION

Begin by telling students that you wish to find out how they feel about reading. Emphasize that this is *not* a test and that there are no "right" answers. Encourage sincerity.

Distribute the survey forms. If you wish to monitor the attitudes of specific students, ask all students to write their names in the space at the top. Hold up a copy of the survey so that the students can see the first page. Point to the picture of Garfield at the far left of the first item. Ask the students to look at this picture on their own survey form. Discuss with them the mood Garfield seems to be in (very happy). Then move to the next picture and again discuss Garfield's mood (this time, a *little* happy). In the same way, move to the third and fourth pictures and talk about Garfield's moods—a little upset and very upset. It is helpful to point out the position of Garfield's *mouth*, especially in the middle two figures.

Explain that together you will read some statements about reading and the students should think about how they feel about each statement. They should then circle the picture of Garfield that is closest to their own feelings. (Emphasize that the students should respond according to their own feelings, not as Garfield might respond!) Read each item aloud slowly and distinctly; then read it a second time while students are thinking. Be sure to read the item *number* and to remind students of page numbers when new pages are reached.

SCORING

To score the survey, count four points for each leftmost (happiest) Garfield circled, three for each slightly smiling Garfield, two for each mildly upset Garfield, and one point for each very upset (rightmost) Garfield. Three scores for each student can be obtained: the total for the first 10 items, the total for the second 10, and a composite total. The first half of the survey relates to attitude toward recreational reading; the second half relates to attitude toward academic aspects of reading.

INTERPRETATION

You can interpret scores in two ways. One is to note informally where the score falls in relation to the four nodes of the scale. A total score of 50, for example, would fall about midway on the scale, between the slightly happy and slightly upset figures, therefore indicating a relatively indifferent overall attitude toward reading. The other approach is more formal. It involves converting the raw scores into percentile ranks by means of Table A.1. Be sure to use the norms for the right grade level and to note the column headings (*Rec* = recreational reading; *Aca* = academic reading; *Tot* = total score). If you wish to determine the average percentile rank for your class, average the raw scores first; then use the table to locate the percentile rank corresponding to the raw score mean. Percentile ranks cannot be averaged directly.

Technical Aspects

THE NORMING PROJECT

To create norms for the interpretation of scores, a large-scale study was conducted in late January 1989, at which time the survey was administered to 18,138 students in grades 1 through 6. A number of steps were taken to achieve a sample that was sufficiently stratified (that is, reflective of the American population) to allow confident generalizations. Children were drawn from 95 school districts in 38 U.S. states. The number of girls exceeded by only 5 the number of boys. Ethnic distribution of the sample was also close to that of the U.S. population (*Statistical Abstract of the United States,* 1989). The proportion of blacks (9.5%) was within 3 percent of the national proportion, while the proportion of Hispanics (6.2%) was within 2 percent.

Percentile ranks at each grade for both subscales and the full scale are presented in Table A.1. These data can be used to compare individual students' scores with the national sample, and they can be interpreted like achievement test percentile ranks.

RELIABILITY

Cronbach's alpha, a statistic developed primarily to measure the internal consistency of attitude scales (Cronbach, 1957), was calculated at each grade level for both subscales and for the composite score. These coefficients ranged from .74 to .89 and are presented in Table A.2.

It is interesting that with only two exceptions, coefficients were .80 or higher. These were for the recreational subscale at grades 1 and 2. It is possible that the stability of young children's attitudes toward leisure reading grows with their decoding ability and familiarity with reading as a pastime.

Scoring Sheet

Student name _____

Teacher _____

Grade _____ Administration date _____

Scoring guide

4 points	Happiest Garfield
3 points	Slightly smiling Garfield
2 points	Mildly upset Garfield
1 point	Very upset Garfield

Recreational reading   Academic reading

1. _____   11. _____
2. _____   12. _____
3. _____   13. _____
4. _____   14. _____
5. _____   15. _____
6. _____   16. _____
7. _____   17. _____
8. _____   18. _____
9. _____   19. _____
10. _____   20. _____

Raw score: _____   Raw score: _____

Full scale raw score (recreational + academic): _____

Percentile ranks   Recreational   [ ]

Academic   [ ]

Full scale   [ ]

Raw Scr	Grade 1 Rec Aca Tot	Grade 2 Rec Aca Tot	Grade 3 Rec Aca Tot	Grade 4 Rec Aca Tot	Grade 5 Rec Aca Tot	Grade 6 Rec Aca Tot
80	99	99	99	99	99	99
79	95	96	98	99	99	99
78	93	95	97	98	99	99
77	92	94	97	98	99	99
76	90	93	96	97	98	99
75	88	92	95	96	98	99
74	86	90	94	95	97	99
73	84	88	92	94	97	98
72	82	86	91	93	96	98
71	80	84	89	91	95	97
70	78	82	86	89	94	96
69	75	79	84	88	92	95
68	72	77	81	86	91	93
67	69	74	79	83	89	92
66	66	71	76	80	87	90
65	62	69	73	78	84	88
64	59	66	70	75	82	86
63	55	63	67	72	79	84
62	52	60	64	69	76	82
61	49	57	61	66	73	79
60	46	54	58	62	70	76
59	43	51	55	59	67	73
58	40	47	51	56	64	69
57	37	45	48	53	61	66
56	34	41	44	48	57	62
55	31	38	41	45	53	58
54	28	35	38	41	50	55
53	25	32	34	38	46	52
52	22	29	31	35	42	48
51	20	26	28	32	39	44
50	18	23	25	28	36	40
49	15	20	23	26	33	37
48	13	18	20	23	29	33
47	12	15	17	20	26	30
46	10	13	15	18	23	27
45	8	11	13	16	20	25

Raw Scr	Grade 1 Rec	Aca	Tot	Grade 2 Rec	Aca	Tot	Grade 3 Rec	Aca	Tot	Grade 4 Rec	Aca	Tot	Grade 5 Rec	Aca	Tot	Grade 6 Rec	Aca	Tot
44			7			9			11			13			17			22
43			6			8			9			12			15			20
42			5			7			8			10			13			17
41			5			6			7			9			12			15
40	99	99	4	99	99	5	99	99	6	99	99	7	99	99	10	99	99	13
39	92	91	3	94	94	4	96	97	5	97	98	6	98	99	9	99	99	13
38	89	88	3	92	92	3	94	95	4	95	97	5	96	98	8	97	99	10
37	86	85	2	88	89	2	90	93	3	92	95	4	94	98	7	95	99	8
36	81	79	2	84	85	2	87	91	2	88	93	3	91	96	6	92	98	7
35	77	75	1	79	81	1	81	88	2	84	90	3	87	95	4	88	97	6
34	72	69	1	74	78	1	75	83	2	78	87	2	82	93	4	83	95	5
33	65	63	1	68	73	1	69	79	1	72	83	2	77	90	3	79	93	4
32	58	58	1	62	67	1	63	74	1	66	79	1	71	86	3	74	91	3
31	52	53	1	56	62	1	57	69	0	60	75	1	65	82	2	69	87	2
30	44	49	1	50	57	0	51	63	0	54	70	1	59	77	1	63	82	2
29	38	44	0	44	51	0	45	58	0	47	64	1	53	71	1	58	78	1
28	32	39	0	37	46	0	38	52	0	41	58	1	48	66	1	51	73	1
27	26	34	0	31	41	0	33	47	0	35	52	1	42	60	1	46	67	1
26	21	30	0	25	37	0	26	41	0	29	46	0	36	54	0	39	60	1
25	17	25	0	20	32	0	21	36	0	23	40	0	30	49	0	34	54	0
24	12	21	0	15	27	0	17	31	0	19	35	0	25	42	0	29	49	0
23	9	18	0	11	23	0	13	26	0	14	29	0	20	37	0	24	42	0
22	7	14	0	8	18	0	9	22	0	11	25	0	16	31	0	19	36	0
21	5	11	0	6	15	0	6	18	0	9	20	0	13	26	0	15	30	0
20	4	9	0	4	11	0	5	14	0	6	16	0	10	21	0	12	24	0
19		2	7		2	8		3	11		5	13		7	17		10	20
18		2	5		2	6		2	8		3	9		6	13		8	15
17		1	4		1	5		1	5		2	7		4	9		6	11
16		1	3		1	3		1	4		2	5		3	6		4	8
15		0	2		0	2		0	3		1	3		2	4		3	8
14		0	2		0	1		0	1		1	2		1	2		1	3
13		0	1		0	1		0	1		0	1		1	2		1	2
12		0	1		0	0		0	0		0	1		0	1		0	1
11		0	0		0	0		0	0		0	0		0	0		0	0
10		0	0		0	0		0	0		0	0		0	0		0	0

Grade	N	Recreational Subscale				Academic Subscale				Full Scale (Total)			
		M	SD	S_eM	Alpha[a]	M	SD	S_eM	Alpha	M	SD	S_eM	Alpha
1	2,518	31.0	5.7	2.9	.74	30.1	6.8	3.0	.81	61.0	11.4	4.1	.87
2	2,974	30.3	5.7	2.7	.78	28.8	6.7	2.9	.81	59.1	11.4	3.9	.88
3	3,151	30.0	5.6	2.5	.80	27.8	6.4	2.8	.81	57.8	10.9	3.8	.88
4	3,679	29.5	5.8	2.4	.83	26.9	6.3	2.6	.83	56.5	11.0	3.6	.89
5	3,374	28.5	6.1	2.3	.86	25.6	6.0	2.5	.82	54.1	10.8	3.6	.89
6	2,442	27.9	6.2	2.2	.87	24.7	5.8	2.5	.81	52.5	10.6	3.5	.89
All	18,138	29.5	5.9	2.5	.82	27.3	6.6	2.7	.83	56.8	11.3	3.7	.89

[a]Cronbach's alpha (Cronbach, 1951).

VALIDITY

Evidence of construct validity was gathered by several means. For the recreational subscale, students in the national norming group were asked (a) whether a public library was available to them and (b) whether they currently had a library card. Those to whom libraries were available were separated into two groups (those with and without cards), and their recreational scores were compared. Cardholders had significantly higher ($p < .001$) recreational scores ($M = 30.0$) than noncardholders ($M = 28.9$), evidence of the subscale's validity in that scores varied predictably with an outside criterion.

A second test compared students who presently had books checked out from their school library with students who did not. The comparison was limited to children whose teachers reported not requiring them to check out books. The means of the two groups varied significantly ($p < .001$), and children with books checked out scored higher ($M = 29.2$) than those who had no books checked out ($M = 27.3$).

A further test of the recreational subscale compared students who reported watching an average of less than one hour of television per night with students who reported watching more than two hours per night. The recreational mean for the low televiewing group (31.5) significantly exceeded ($p < .001$) the mean of the heavy televiewing group (28.6). Thus the amount of television watched varied inversely with children's attitudes toward recreational reading.

The validity of the academic subscale was tested by examining the relationship of scores to reading ability. Teachers categorized norm-group children as having low, average, or high overall reading ability. Mean subscale scores of the high-ability readers ($M = 27.7$) significantly exceeded the mean of low-ability readers ($M = 27.0$, $p < .001$), evidence that scores were reflective of how the students truly felt about reading for academic purposes.

The relationship between the subscales was also investigated. It was hypothesized that children's attitudes toward recreational and academic reading would be moderately but not highly correlated. Facility with reading is likely to affect these two areas similarly, resulting in similar attitude scores. Nevertheless, it is easy to imagine children inclined to read for pleasure but disenchanted with assigned reading and children academically engaged but without interest in reading outside school. The intersubscale correlation coefficient was .64, which meant that just 41 percent of the variance in one set of scores could be accounted for by the other. It is reasonable to suggest that the two subscales, while related, also reflect dissimilar factors—a desired outcome.

To tell more precisely whether the traits measured by the survey corresponded to the two subscales, factor analyses were conducted. Both used the unweighted least squares method of extraction and a varimax rotation. The first analysis permitted factors to be identified liberally (using a limit equal to the smallest eigenvalue greater than 1). Three factors were identified. Of the ten items composing the academic subscale, nine loaded predominantly on a single factor while the tenth (item 13) loaded nearly equally on all three factors. A second factor was dominated by seven items of the recreational subscale, while three of the recreational items (6, 9, and 10) loaded principally on a third factor. These items, however, did load more heavily on the second (recreational) factor than on the first (academic). A second analysis constrained the identification of factors to two. This time, with one exception, all items loaded cleanly on factors associated with the two subscales. The exception was item 13, which could have been interpreted as a recreational item and thus apparently involved a slight ambiguity. Taken together, the factor analyses produced evidence extremely supportive of the claim that the survey's two subscales reflect discrete aspects of reading attitude.

GARFIELD REVISITED: PERMISSION TO USE THE ERAS

Michael C. McKenna / Georgia Southern University
Dennis J. Kear / Wichita State University

Educators wishing to use the scale should copy and paste the legend on each page of the scale.

Since its appearance, the ERAS has grounded a number of research studies of reading attitudes, and each of these studies has contributed to an understanding of the instrument. The following sources may be useful to educators who have used the ERAS:

Allen, L., Cipielewski, J., & Stanovich, K. E. (1992). Multiple indicators of children's reading habits and attitudes: Construct validity and cognitive correlates. *Journal of Educational Psychology, 84,* 489–503.

Bromley, K., Winters, D., & Schlimmer, K. (1994). Book buddies: Creating enthusiasm for literacy learning. *The Reading Teacher, 47,* 392–399.

Grisham, D. L. (1993, December). *The integrated language arts: Curriculum enactments in whole language and traditional fourth grade classrooms.* Paper presented at the meeting of the National Reading Conference, Charleston, SC.

Kush, J. C., Watkins, M. W., McAleer, M. T., & Edwards, V. A. (1995). One-year stability of the elementary reading attitude survey. *Mid-Western Educational Researcher, 8,* 11–14.

McKenna, M. C., & Kear, D. J. (1990). Measuring attitude towards reading: A new tool for teachers. *The Reading Teacher, 43,* 626–639.

McKenna, M. C., Kear, D. J., & Ellsworth, R. A. (1995). Children's attitudes toward reading: A national survey. *Reading Research Quarterly, 30*:4, 934–956.

McKenna, M. C., Stratton, B. D., & Grindler, M. C. (1992, November). *Social desirability of children's responses to a reading attitude survey.* Paper presented at the meeting of the College Reading Association, St. Louis, MO.

McKenna, M. C., Stratton, B. D., Grindler, M. C., & Jenkins, S. (1995). Differential effects of whole language and traditional instruction on reading attitudes. *Journal of Reading Behavior, 27,* 19–44.

Payne, D. A. (1994, April). *Two-year evaluation of a continuous progress K–3 program.* Paper presented at the meeting of the American Educational Research Association, New Orleans.

Rasinski, T. V., & Linek, W. (1993, November). *Do students in whole language classrooms like reading more than students in traditional classrooms?* Paper presented at the meeting of the College Reading Association, Richmond, VA.

Reinking, D., & Watkins, J. H. (1996). *A formative experiment investigating the use of multimedia book reviews to increase elementary students' independent reading* (Technical Report). Athens, GA: National Reading Research Center.

Stanovich, K. E. (1993). Does reading make you smarter? Literacy and the development of verbal-intelligence. In H. Reese (Ed.), *Advances in child development and behavior* (Vol. 24, pp. 133–180). Gilsum, NH: Academic Press.

Whitney, P. (1994). *Influences on grade-five students' decisions to read: An exploratory study of leisure reading behavior.* Unpublished doctoral dissertation, University of British Columbia, Vancouver.

Mikulecky Behavioral Reading Attitude Measure

 Norming and Validation Information[*]

The *Mikulecky Behavioral Reading Attitude Measure* (MBRAM) was developed to be a sound reading-attitudes measure appropriate for use with mature readers. To establish the instrument on sound theoretical foundations, all items were written with direct

---

[*]Mikulecky, L. J. *The developing, field testing, and initial norming of a secondary/adult level reading attitude measure that is behaviorally oriented and based on Krathwohl's Taxonomy of the Affective Domain.* Unpublished doctoral dissertation, University of Wisconsin–Madison, 1976.

Mikulecky Behavioral Reading Attitude Measure

Name _____ Instructor's Name _____

Age _____ Sex _____ School _____

Example

You receive a book for a holiday present. You start the book, but decide to stop halfway through.

VERY UNLIKE ME   1   2   3   ④   5   VERY LIKE ME

1. You walk into the office of a doctor or dentist and notice that there are magazines set out.

   VERY UNLIKE ME   1   2   3   4   5   VERY LIKE ME

2. People have made jokes about your reading in unusual circumstances or situations.

   VERY UNLIKE ME   1   2   3   4   5   VERY LIKE ME

3. You are in a shopping center you've been to several times when someone asks where books and magazines are sold. You are able to tell the person.

   VERY UNLIKE ME   1   2   3   4   5   VERY LIKE ME

4. You feel very uncomfortable because emergencies have kept you away from reading for a couple of days.

   VERY UNLIKE ME   1   2   3   4   5   VERY LIKE ME

5. You are waiting for a friend in an airport or supermarket and find yourself leafing through the magazines and paperback books.

   VERY UNLIKE ME   1   2   3   4   5   VERY LIKE ME

6. If a group of acquaintances would laugh at you for always being buried in a book, you'd know it's true and wouldn't mind much at all.

   VERY UNLIKE ME   1   2   3   4   5   VERY LIKE ME

7. You are tired of waiting for the dentist, so you start to page through a magazine.

   VERY UNLIKE ME   1   2   3   4   5   VERY LIKE ME

8. People who are regular readers often ask your opinion about new books.

   VERY UNLIKE ME   1   2   3   4   5   VERY LIKE ME

9. One of your first impulses is to "look it up" whenever there is something you don't know or whenever you are going to start something new.

   VERY UNLIKE ME   1   2   3   4   5   VERY LIKE ME

10. Even though you are a very busy person, there is somehow always time for reading.

    VERY UNLIKE ME   1   2   3   4   5   VERY LIKE ME

11. You've finally got some time alone in your favorite chair on a Sunday afternoon. You see something to read and decide to spend a few minutes reading just because you feel like it.

    VERY UNLIKE ME   1   2   3   4   5   VERY LIKE ME

12. You tend to disbelieve and be a little disgusted by people who repeatedly say they don't have time to read.

    VERY UNLIKE ME   1   2   3   4   5   VERY LIKE ME

13. You find yourself giving special books to friends or relatives as gifts.

    VERY UNLIKE ME   1   2   3   4   5   VERY LIKE ME

14. At holiday time, you look in the display window of a bookstore and find yourself interested in some books and uninterested in others.

    VERY UNLIKE ME   1   2   3   4   5   VERY LIKE ME

(continued)

Mikulecky Behavioral Reading Attitude Measure (*concluded*)

15. Sometimes you find yourself so excited by a book you try to get friends to read it.

    VERY UNLIKE ME   1   2   3   4   5   VERY LIKE ME

16. You've just finished reading a story and settle back for a moment to enjoy and remember what you've just read.

    VERY UNLIKE ME   1   2   3   4   5   VERY LIKE ME

17. You *choose* to read nonrequired books and articles fairly regularly (a few times a week).

    VERY UNLIKE ME   1   2   3   4   5   VERY LIKE ME

18. Your friends would not be at all surprised to see you buying or borrowing a book.

    VERY UNLIKE ME   1   2   3   4   5   VERY LIKE ME

19. You have just gotten comfortably settled in a new city. Among the things you plan to do are check out the library and bookstores.

    VERY UNLIKE ME   1   2   3   4   5   VERY LIKE ME

20. You've just heard about a good book but haven't been able to find it. Even though you're tired, you look for it in one more book store.

    VERY UNLIKE ME   1   2   3   4   5   VERY LIKE ME

reference to the Hovland-Rosenberg tricomponent model of attitude and to the stages of Krathwohl's *Taxonomy of the Affective Domain*. A pool of 40 items, each of which was designed to reflect a specific Krathwohl substage, was reduced to 20 items after considering the evaluations of a panel of judges familiar with Krathwohl's taxonomy and after an item analysis that eliminated all items that correlated at $r = .600$ or less with the sum of items reflecting the Krathwohl stage appropriate to each item. The hierarchical framework hypothesized by Krathwohl was supported by an analysis of subjects' item responses using a method for Scaling a Simplex developed by Henry Kaiser (*Psychometrika*, 1962). The MBRAM hierarchy gave evidence of a .933 out of a possible 1.000 goodness-of-fit to an ideal hierarchy. This was interpreted as empirical support for the Krathwohl theoretical foundation of the MBRAM.

A graduate-level seminar on affective domain measurement helped survey and refine all items to reflect everyday reading-related behaviors, thereby establishing *face validity*. Correlations of *concurrent validity* ranging from .446 to .770 were established with such formal reading attitude measures as the Estes Scale, the Dulin-Chester Scale, and the Kennedy-Halinski Reading Attitude Measure. The MBRAM correlated more highly with the Estes Scale and the Dulin-Chester Scale than either of those measures did with the other.

To establish *construct validity,* five informal criteria for reading attitude (self-reported liking and amount of reading, teacher and classmate judgment of reading attitude, and number of books read in six months) were administered along with the MBRAM. All MBRAM correlations with these informal criteria were significant to the $p < .001$ level, and the majority of correlations ranged from .500 to .791. The MBRAM correlated significantly more highly with these informal measures than did the other, formal reading attitude measures used in the study. Analysis of variance statistically demonstrated the ability of the MBRAM to discriminate subjects of high, average, and low reading attitude as measured by the informal criteria.

The MBRAM demonstrated a test–retest reliability of .9116.

The MBRAM was administered to 1,750 subjects ranging from seventh grade through college–adult. 1,343 of the subjects were public school students selected from urban, suburban, and rural populations. These subjects were randomly sampled to create a composite, stratified Wisconsin Population Model. Norms for the MBRAM are reported for each grade level in terms of this model and also in terms of urban, suburban, and rural populations. For ease of interpretation of scores, attitude-level scoring bands are provided. No significant differences in scores of urban, suburban, or rural subjects were found from seventh to tenth grade, but rural subjects exhibited slightly higher MBRAM mean scores in the upper grades. Reading attitude scores decreased slightly in all locations with each year in school. (See Tables A.3 and A.4.)

Stages of Krathwohl's Taxonomy as Reflected by Mikulecky Behavioral Reading Attitude Measure Items

Stage 1 (attending) of Krathwohl's taxonomy is reflected by items 1, 3, 5, and 7 (see Table A.5). Each item provides from 1 to 5 points. A perfect score at this stage would be 4 items × 5 points, or 20 points. A student can be said to have attained a stage if he or she has 75 percent of the possible points at that stage. By interpreting items and stages, a deeper understanding of a student's reading attitude is possible.

TABLE A.3 Summary Statistics: Junior High School (Grades 7–9) and Senior High School (Grades 10–12); Urban, Suburban, and Rural Subjects, MBRAM Scores

	Urban				Suburban				Rural			
Level	N	Mean	Range	S.D.	N	Mean	Range	S.D.	N	Mean	Range	S.D.
Jr	127	55.93	27–90(63)	12.11	276	59.60	25–98(73)	14.33	182	60.81	22–92(70)	13.91
Sr	332	55.24	20–90(70)	12.51	144	58.29	24–95(71)	15.55	190	59.28	29–97(68)	15.17

Attitude Bands for Junior and Senior High School by Location

	Urban		Suburban		Rural	
Attitude Level	Jr. High	Sr. High	Jr. High	Sr. High	Jr. High	Sr. High
Above average	66–100	62–100	68–100	67–100	69–100	68–100
Average	53–65	49–61	52–67	59–66	54–68	52–67
Below average	20–52	20–48	20–51	20–49	20–53	20–51

TABLE A.4	Adult Norms: Results of Analyses of Variance and Post Hoc Scheffe Tests of Attitude toward Reading (MBRAM Score) by Each Demographic Variable				

All Cases	N	Mean	S.D.	F-Ratio	*Post Hoc* Test of Significance
Sex					
M	118	65.02	14.15	33.58	***
F	166	74.47	13.10		
Race					
W	262	70.78	14.36	.43	Not significant
B	20	67.90	14.22		
O	2	65.50	0		
Education					
Less than high school	40	66.87	12.13	2.48	*
High school	88	68.69	15.79		
Post high school	93	71.07	14.19		
College	42	73.71	13.34		
Graduate work	22	77.09	11.13		
Family Income					
Less than 3,000	13	69.38	12.72	2.79	*
3–5,000	17	70.12	13.37		
5–10,000	39	71.69	10.76		
10–20,000	112	69.26	15.23		
Greater than 20,000	86	73.85	12.89		
No response	17	60.94	19.46		
Employment					
Full time	141	68.38	15.75	3.008	**
Part time	20	75.45	11.80		
Housewife	49	74.96	11.45		
Unemployed	9	78.67	17.33		
Student	36	67.81	11.57		
Retired	29	71.10	12.26		

*$p<.05$
**$p<.01$
***$p<.001$
From Mikulecky, Shanklin, & Caverly (1979).

TABLE A.5   Measure Items

Krathwohl Stages	Items (1–5 Points Possible Each Item)	Criterion Score (75 Percent of Possible Points)
I. *Attending:* The individual is generally aware of reading and tolerant of it.	1, 3, 5, 7	15 pts.
II. *Responding:* The individual is willing to read under certain circumstances. He or she begins to choose and occasionally enjoy reading.	11, 14, 16	11 pts.
III. *Valuing:* The individual begins to accept the worth of reading as a value to be preferred and even to extend to others.	13, 15, 17 18, 19, 20	23 pts.
IV. *Organization:* For the individual, reading is part of an organized value system and is so habitual that it is almost "instinctive."	9, 10, 12	11 pts.
V. *Characterization:* For the individual, reading is so much a part of life that both the reader and others see reading as crucial to this person.	2, 4, 6, 8	15 pts.

Readability Information
Using the Fry Graph for Short Selections

The Procedure

The Fry graph can be used with selections of fewer than 100 words if some conversions are made (Forgan & Mangrum, 1985). This technique will be useful to teachers of primary grades, where material is partly visual and partly verbal, or for teachers using newspaper or magazine articles to supplement instruction. It also can help teachers measure the difficulty of word problems in math or of essay questions on tests. The material should contain fewer than 100 words; if the material contains at least 100 words, then the Fry graph can be applied. To use this short-selection version, a teacher should do the following:

1. Count the total number of words.

2. Round *down* to the nearest 10.

3. Refer to the conversion chart (Figure B.1), and identify the conversion number corresponding to the rounded number.

4. Count the number of syllables and sentences in the rounded-down number of words (see steps 1 and 2).

5. Multiply the number of syllables by the number on the conversion chart; multiply the number of sentences by the number on the conversion chart.

6. Plot the final numbers on the regular Fry graph.

FIGURE B.1	If the number of words in the selection is:	Multiply the number of syllables and sentences by:
Conversion Chart for Fry's Graph for Selections with Fewer Than 100 Words	30	3.3
	40	2.5
	50	2.0
	60	1.67
	70	1.43
	80	1.25
	90	1.1

From *Teaching Content Area Reading Skills*, 3rd ed., by Harry W. Forgan and Charles T. Mangrum II, copyright © 1985. Merrill Publishing Co., Columbus, OH. Used with permission.

An Example

The following two essay questions have been assessed using this procedure.

Syllables

1. To what extent do you believe it is possible for people of different races, religions, or political beliefs to live together in harmony? What suggestions can you make to help people become more tolerant?

17

21

16

6

2. It is often said that communism develops fastest in those countries where people do not have the basic necessities of life. Why do you think this might be possible?

16

16

6

60 words *Total*   98

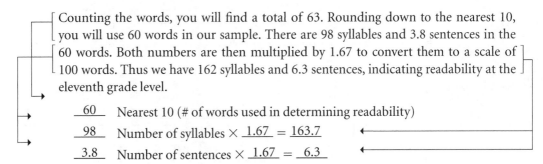

Counting the words, you will find a total of 63. Rounding down to the nearest 10, you will use 60 words in our sample. There are 98 syllables and 3.8 sentences in the 60 words. Both numbers are then multiplied by 1.67 to convert them to a scale of 100 words. Thus we have 162 syllables and 6.3 sentences, indicating readability at the eleventh grade level.

  __60__ Nearest 10 (# of words used in determining readability)

  __98__ Number of syllables × __1.67__ = __163.7__

  __3.8__ Number of sentences × __1.67__ = __6.3__

  __11th__ Estimate of readability

USING THE SMOG FORMULA

McLaughlin (1969) named his readability formula SMOG as a tribute to another formula—the FOG—and after his birthplace, London, where "smog first appeared" (p. 641). Some have said that SMOG stands for the Simple Measure of Gobbledygook! Although its name is very lighthearted, this formula is a serious solution to the problem of measuring the readability of material that students may have to read on their own.

The SMOG formula is very easy to compute. However, the teacher needs to use a calculator that computes square roots or have a table of square roots handy. To use the SMOG formula, follow these steps:

1. Count three sets of 10 sentences (a total of 30 sentences).
2. Count all words of three or more syllables.
3. Take this number, and determine the nearest perfect square root.
4. Add 3 to this square root.
5. The final number is the readability level.

Differences between the Fry Graph and the SMOG Formula

 The differences between the Fry graph and the SMOG formula are important to note. Each formula is based on a different premise, so the readability scores must be read differently. The Fry formula measures the readability of material used in an instructional setting. Because the teacher will explain the difficult words and sentences, the score is based on students' understanding 65 to 75 percent of the material at a given grade level. The SMOG formula is intended to measure the readability of material that a teacher will not be teaching. Perhaps it is material that the teacher has suggested a student use independently. Because the teacher will not be explaining the difficult words and sentences, the score is based on students' understanding 90 to 100 percent of the material. If a Fry and a SMOG were calculated on the same material, the Fry score would probably be lower. Table B.1 illustrates the basic differences between these two popular measures of readability.

TABLE B.1   A Comparison of the Fry Graph and the SMOG Readability Formula

Readability Measure	Provides Readability Score for	Teacher Will Be Assisting Instruction?	Student Is Expected to Comprehend	Readability Score May Be	Apply This Formula When
Fry	Instructional reading settings	Yes	65–75% of material	Lower*	Teacher will instruct the group using the material being measured
SMOG	Independent reading settings	No	90–100% of material	Higher*	Student will be reading the measured material on her or his own, as in report writing, homework, etc.

*As measured on the same passage.

References

Abrami, P. C., Chambers, B., d'Apollonia, S., Farrell M., & DeSimone, C. (1992). Group outcome: The relationship between group learning outcome, attributional style, academic achievement, and self-concept. *Contemporary Educational Psychology, 17*, 201–210.

Abruscato, J. (1993). Early results and tentative implications from the Vermont portfolio project. *Phi Delta Kappan, 74*, 474–477.

Adams, M. J. (1990). *Beginning to read: Thinking and learning about print.* Cambridge, MA: MIT Press.

Adler, A. (1931). *What life should mean to you.* New York: Capricorn.

Adler, M. J. (1982). *The Paideia proposal.* New York: Macmillan.

Adler, M. J. (1994). *Socrates: Art, the arts, and the great ideas.* New York: Simon and Schuster.

Afflerbach, P. (1987). How are main idea statements constructed? Watch the experts. *Journal of Reading, 30*, 512–518.

Afflerbach, P. (2002). The road to folly and redemption: Perspectives on the legitimacy of high-stakes testing. *Reading Research Quarterly, 37*(3), 348–360.

Agbenyega, S., & Jiggetts, J. (1999). Minority children and their overrepresentation in special education. *Education, 119*(4), 619–628.

Aguiar, L., & Brady, S. (1991). Vocabulary acquisition and reading ability. *Reading and Writing: An Interdisciplinary Journal, 3*(3), 413–425.

Albright, J. (2001). The logic of our failures in literacy practices and teaching. *Journal of Adolescent & Adult Literacy, 44*, 644–658.

Alexander, D. S., & DeAlba, L. M. (1997). Groups for proofs: Collaborative learning in a mathematics reasoning course. *Primus, 7*(3), 193–207.

Alexander, P. A., & Judy, J. E. (1998). The interaction of domain-specific and strategic knowledge in academic performance. *Review of Educational Research, 58*, 375–404.

Allen, R., Brown, K., & Yatvin, J. (1986). *Learning language through communication: A functional approach.* Belmont, CA: Wadsworth.

Allen, V. G., Freeman, E. B., Lehman, B. A., & Scharer, P. L. (1995). Amos and Boris: A window on teachers' thinking about the use of literature in their classrooms. *The Reading Teacher, 48*, 384–389.

Allington, R. L. (1991). How policy and regulation influence instruction for at-risk learners: Or why poor readers rarely comprehend well and probably never will. In L. Idol & B. F. Jones (Eds.), *Educational values and cognitive instruction: Implications for reform* (pp. 277–299). Hillsdale, NJ: Erlbaum.

Altea, R. (1995). *The eagle and the rose.* New York: Warner Books.

Alvarez, M. (1998). Developing critical and imaginative thinking within electronic literacy. *NASSP Bulletin, 82*, 41–47.

Alvarez, M. C., & Rodriguez, W. J. (1995). Explorers of the universe: A pilot case study. In *Generations of literacy, seventeenth yearbook of the college reading association* (pp. 221–236). Commerce, TX: East Texas State University.

Alvermann, D. (1987). Discussion strategies for content area reading. In D. Alvermann, D. R. Dillon, & D. G. O'Brien (Eds.), *Using discussion to promote reading comprehension* (pp. 34–42). Newark, DE: International Reading Association.

Alvermann, D. (1991). The discussion web: A graphic aid for learning across the curriculum. *The Reading Teacher, 44*, 92–98.

Alvermann, D. (1996). Peer-led discussions: Whose interests are served? *Journal of Adolescent & Adult Literacy, 39*, 282–289.

Alvermann, D. (1999). Modes of inquiry into studying engaged reading. In J. Guthrie & D. Alvermann (Eds.), *Engaged reading: Processes, practices, and policy implications* (pp. 134–149). New York: Teachers College Press.

Alvermann, D. E., O'Brien, D. G., & Dillon, D. R. (1990). What teachers do when they say they're having discussions of content reading assignments: A qualitative analysis. *Reading Research Quarterly, 25*, 296–321.

Alvermann, D. E., Young, J. P., Weaver, D., Hinchman, K., Moore, D., Phelps, S., Thrash, E. C., & Zalewski, P. (1996). Middle and high school students' perceptions of how they experience text-based discussions: A multicase study. *Reading Research Quarterly, 31*(3), 244–267.

American Psychological Association (2001). Appropriate use of high-stakes testing in our nation's schools. *APA Online.* Retrieved Sept. 7, 2004, from *http://www.apa. org/pubinfo/testing.html*

American School Counseling Association (2000) *Study skills survey.* Alexandria, VA: Author.

Amlund, J. T., Kardash, C. A. M., & Kulhavy, R. W. (1986). Repetitive reading and recall of expository text. *Reading Research Quarterly, 21*, 49–53.

Ammons, R. I. (1987). *Trade books in the content areas.* Tempe, AZ: Jan V.

Anderson, J. (1993). Journal writing: The promise and the reality. *Journal of Reading, 36*, 304–309.

Anderson, J., & Adams, M. (1992, Spring). Acknowledging the learning styles of diverse student populations: Implications for instructional design. In L. L. B. Border & N. Van Note Chism (Eds.), *Teaching for Diversity, 49*, 21–33.

Anderson, J. & Lee, A. (1995). Literacy teachers learning a new literacy: A study of the use of electronic mail in a reading education class. *Reading Research and Instruction, 34*, 222–238.

Anderson, R. C., & Nagy, W. E. (1991). Word meanings. In R. Barr, M. L. Kamil, P. B. Mosenthal, & P. D. Pearson (Eds.), *Handbook of reading research: Vol. II* (pp. 690–724). New York: Longman.

Anderson, R. C., & Pearson, P. D. (1984). A schema-theoretic view of basic processes in reading comprehension. In P. D. Pearson (Ed.), *Handbook of reading research* (pp. 255–291). New York: Longman.

Anderson, R. S., & Speck, B. W. (2001). *Using technology in K–8 literacy classrooms.* Upper Saddle River, NJ: Merrill Prentice Hall.

Anderson, V. A., & Roit, M. (1993). Planning and implementing collaborative strategy instruction for delayed readers in grades 6–10. *The Elementary School Journal, 94*, 121–137.

Anderson-Inman, L. (1998). Electronic journals in technology and literacy: Professional development online. *Journal of Adolescent & Adult Literacy, 41*(15), 400–405.

Anderson-Inman, L. (1998). Electronic text: Literacy medium of the future. *Journal of Adolescent & Adult Literacy, 41*(8), 678–682.

Anderson-Inman, L., & Zeitz, L. (1993). Computer-based concept mapping: Active studying for active learners. *The Computing Teacher, 21*(1), 6–10.

Angeletti, S. (1991). Encouraging students to think about what they read. *The Reading Teacher, 45*, 288–296.

Apple, M. (1998). *Teachers and texts: A political economy of class and gender relations in education.* New York: Routledge and Kegan.

Applebee, A. N. (1981). *Writing in the secondary school.* Urbana, IL: National Council of Teachers of English.

Applebee, A. N., Langer, J., & Mullis, I. (1987). *Learning to be literate in America: Reading, writing, and reasoning.* Princeton, NJ: Educational Testing Service.

Applefield, J. M., Huber, R. L., & Moallem, M. (2000). Constructivism in theory and practice: Toward a better understanding. *High School Journal, 84*(2), 35.

Arlin, P. K. (1984). *Arlin test of formal reasoning.* East Aurora, NY: Slosson Educational Publications.

Armbruster, B. (1992). Content reading in RT: The last two decades. *The Reading Teacher, 46*, 166–167.

Armbruster, B., & Anderson, T. (1984). *Producing "considerate" expository text: Or easy reading is damned hard writing* (Reading Education Report No. 36). Champaign: University of Illinois, Center for the Study of Reading.

Armbruster, B., Anderson, T., Armstrong, J., Wise, M., Janisch, C., & Meyer, L. (1991). Reading and questioning in content areas. *Journal of Reading Behavior, 23*, 35–59.

Armbruster, B. B., Anderson, T. H., & Meyer, J. L. (1991). Improving content area reading using instructional graphics. *Reading Research Quarterly, 26*(4), 393–416.

Armbruster, B. B., Anderson, T. H., & Meyer, J. L. (1992). Improving content area using instructional graphics: Erratum. *Reading Research Quarterly, 27*(3), 282.

Aronson, E. (1978). *The jigsaw classroom.* Beverly Hills, CA: Sage.

Ashby-Davis, C. (1985). Cloze and comprehension: A qualitative analysis of critique. *Journal of Reading, 28*, 585–593.

Ashton-Warner, S. (1959). *Spinster.* New York: Simon & Schuster.

Ashworth, M. (1992). *First step on the longer path: Becoming an ESL teacher.* Markham, Ontario: Pippin.

Atkinson, R. C. (1975). Mnemotechnics in second language learning. *American Psychologist, 30*, 821–828.

Atkinson, R. C., & Hansen, D. N. (1996). Computer assisted instruction in initial reading: The Stanford project. *Reading Research Quarterly, 21*, 5–25.

Atwell, N. (1987). *In the middle: Writing, reading, and learning with adolescents.* Portsmouth, NH: Heinemann.

Atwell, N. (1989). *Coming to know: Writing to learn in the intermediate grades.* Portsmouth, NH: Heinemann.

Au, K. H. (1992). *Literary instruction in multicultural settings.* Fort Worth, TX: Harcourt Brace Jovanovich.

Au, K. H. (2001). Culturally responsive instruction as a dimension of new literacies. *Reading Online, 5*(1). Retrieved Dec. 7, 2004, from *http://www.reading online.org/newliteracies/lit_index.asp?HREF=/ newliteracies/xu/index.html*

Aurandt, P. (1983). *Destiny.* New York: Bantam Books.

Ausubel, D. (1960). The use of advance organizers in learning and retention of meaningful verbal material. *Journal of Educational Psychology, 51,* 267–272.

Ausubel, D. (1963). *The psychology of meaningful verbal learning.* New York: Grune and Stratton.

Ausubel, D. (1968). *Educational psychology: A cognitive view.* New York: Holt, Rinehart and Winston.

Babbs, P., & Moe, A. (1983). Metacognition: A key for independent learning from text. *The Reading Teacher, 36,* 422–426.

Bader, L. (1987). *Textbook analysis chart: Reading, writing, speaking, listening, and critical thinking in content area subjects.* Unpublished manuscript, Michigan State University.

Bader, L., & Pearce, D. (1983). Writing across the curriculum, 7–12. *English Education, 15,* 97–106.

Baerwoald & Fraser (1992). *World geography.* New Jersey: Prentice-Hall.

Baines, L. (1996). From page to screen: When a novel is interpreted from film, what gets lost in the translation? *Journal of Adolescent & Adult Literacy, 39*(8), 612–622.

Baker, E. A. (2001). The nature of literacy in a technology-rich, fourth grade classroom. *Reading Research and Instruction, 40,* 159–184.

Baker, S. K., Simmons, D. C., & Kame'enui, E. J. (1998). Vocabulary acquisition: Research bases. In D. C. Simmons & E. J. Kame'enui (Eds.), *What reading research tells us about children with diverse learning needs* (pp. 183–218). Mahwah, NJ: Erlbaum.

Bandura, A. (1977). Self-efficacy: Toward a unifying theory of behavioral change. *Psychological Review, 84,* 191–215.

Bandura, A. (1986). *Social foundations of thought and action: A social-cognitive theory.* Upper Saddle River, NJ: Prentice-Hall.

Bandura, A. (Ed.). (1995). *Self-efficacy in changing societies.* New York: Cambridge University Press.

Bandura, A. (1997). *Self-efficacy: The exercise of control.* New York: W. H. Freeman.

Bangert-Drowns, R. L. (1993). The word processor as an instructional tool: A meta-analysis of word processing in writing instruction. *Review of Educational Research, 63*(1), 69–93.

Bangert-Drowns, R. L., Hurley, M. M., & Wilkinson, B. (2004). The effects of school-based writing-to-learn interventions on academic achievement: A meta-analysis. *Review of Educational Research, 74,* 29–58.

Banks, J. A. (1995). Multicultural education: Historical development, dimensions, and practice. In J. A. Banks & C. A. M. Banks (Eds.), *Handbook of research on multicultural education* (pp. 3–24). New York: Macmillan.

Banks, L. R. (1990). *The Indian in the cupboard.* Garden City, NY: Doubleday.

Bardovi-Harlig, K., & Dornyei, Z. (1998). Do language learners recognize pragmatic variations? *TESOL Quarterly, 32*(2), 233–259.

Barenbaum, E. (1983). Writing in the special class. *Topics in Learning and Learning Disabilities, 3,* 12–20.

Barnako, F. (2004). Life without the net is unbearable. Retrieved Sept. 23, 2004, from *http://cbs.marketwatch. com/news/archivedStory.asp?archive=true&dist= ArchiveSplash&siteid=mktw&guid=%7BB0361CD7% 2D6B85%2D4808%2D860B%2D9EE55739D9BE% 7D&returnURL=%2Fnews%2Fstory%2Easp%3Fguid %3D%7BB0361CD7%2D6B85%2D4808%2D860B %2D9EE55739D9BE%7D%26siteid%3Dmktw% 26dist%3Dnbc%26archive%3Dtrue%26param%3D archive%26garden%3D%26minisite%3D*

Barnes, D. (1976). *From communication to curriculum.* New York: Penguin Books.

Barry, A. L. (1998). Hispanic representation in literature for children and young adults. *Journal of Adolescent & Adult Literacy, 41*(8), 630–637.

Bartlett, F. C. (1932). *Remembering.* Cambridge: Cambridge University Press.

Barton, J. (1995). Conducting effective classroom discussions. *Journal of Reading, 38,* 346–350.

Baumann, J. F., Edwards, E. C., Boland, E. M., Olejnik, S., & Kame'enui, E. J. (2003). Vocabulary tricks: Effects of instruction in morphology and context on fifth-grade students' ability to derive and infer word meanings. *American Educational Research Journal, 40,* 447–494.

Baumann, J., Edwards, E., Font, G., Tereshinski, C., Kame'enui, E., & Olejnik, S. (2002). Teaching morphemic and contextual analysis to fifth-grade students. *Reading Research Quarterly, 37,* 150–176.

Baumann, J., Hoffman, J., Moon, J., & Duffy-Hexter, A. M. (1998). Where are teachers' voices in the phonics/whole language debate? Results from a survey of U. S. elementary teachers. *The Reading Teacher, 51*, 636–652.

Baumann, J. F., & Johnson, D. D. (1984). *Reading instruction and the beginning teacher: A practical guide.* Minneapolis: Burgess.

Baumann, J. F., Seifert-Kessell, N., & Jones, L. A. (1992). Effect of think-aloud instruction on elementary students' comprehension monitoring abilities. *Journal of Reading Behavior, 24,* 143–172.

Baxter, J. (1985). *Designing a test.* Unpublished paper, submitted in partial fulfillment of course requirements for Reading in the Content Areas. Virginia Commonwealth University, Richmond.

Bealor, S. (1992). Minority literature book groups for teachers. *Reading in Virginia, 17*(1), 17–22.

Bean, T. W. (1988). Organizing and retaining information by thinking like an author. In S. Glazer, L. Searfoss, & L. Gentile (Eds.), *Reexamining reading diagnosis* (pp. 103–127). Newark, DE: International Reading Association.

Bean, T. W. (2001). An update on reading in the content areas: Social constructivist dimensions. *Reading Online, 5*(5). Retrieved Dec. 7, 2004, from *http://www.readingonline.org/articles/art_index.asp?HREF=handbook/bean/index.html*

Bean, T. W., Bean, S. K., & Bean, K. F. (1999). Intergenerational conversations and two adolescents' multiple literacies: Implications for redefining content area literacy. *Journal of Adolescent & Adult Literacy, 42*(6), 438–448.

Bean, T. W., & Readance, J. E. (2002). Adolescent literacy: Charting a course for successful futures as lifelong learners. *Reading Research and Instruction, 41*(3), 203–210.

Bean, T. W., & Steenwyk, F. L. (1984). The effect of three forms of summarization instruction on sixth graders' summary writing and comprehension. *Journal of Reading Behavior, 16,* 297–306.

Beane, J. (1990). *A middle school curriculum: From rhetoric to reality.* Columbus, OH: National Middle School Association.

Bear, D. R., & Templeton, S. (1996). Explorations in developmental spelling: Foundations for learning and teaching phonics, spelling, and vocabulary. *The Reading Teacher, 52,* 222–242.

Beck, I., McKeown, M., & Kucan, L. (2002). *Bringing words to life: Robust vocabulary instruction.* New York: Guilford.

Beck, I. L., & McKeown, M. G. (1988, August–September). Toward meaningful accounts in history texts for young learners. *American Educational Research Journal,* 31–39.

Beck, I. L., McKeown, M. G., Sinatra, G. M., & Loxterman, J. A. (1991). Revising social studies text from a text-processing perspective: Evidence of improved comprehensibility. *Reading Research Quarterly, 26,* 251–276.

Bellow, S. (1987). Foreword. In Allan Bloom, *The closing of the American mind* (pp. 11–18). New York: Simon and Schuster.

Bergenske, M. D. (1987). The missing link in narrative story mapping. *The Reading Teacher, 41,* 333–335.

Berlak, H. (1992). The need for a new science of assessment. In H. Berlak et al. (Eds.), *Toward a new science of educational testing and assessment.* New York: State University of New York Press.

Berliner, D. C. (2001). Mythology and the American system of education. In K. Ryan & J. M. Cooper (Eds.), *Kaleidoscope: Readings in education* (pp. 106–115). Boston: Houghton Mifflin.

Berube, C. T. (2004). Are standards preventing good teaching? *The Clearing House, 77*(6), 264–267.

Betts, F. (1991). What's all the noise about? Constructivism in the classroom. In K. Ryan & J. M. Cooper (Eds.), *Kaleidoscope: Readings in education.* Boston: Houghton Mifflin.

Betts, G. (2004). Fostering autonomous learners through levels of differentiation. *Roeper Review, 26*(4), 190–192.

Beyer, B. K. (1983). Common sense about teaching thinking skills. *Educational Leadership, 41,* 44–49.

Beyer, B. K. (1984). Improving thinking skills: Defining the problem. *Phi Delta Kappan, 65,* 486–490.

Bhat, P., Rapport, M. J., & Griffin, C. C. (2000). A legal perspective on the use of specific learning methods for students with learning disabilities. *Learning Disabilities Quarterly, 23*(4), 283–297.

Bieger, E. M. (1995). Promoting multicultural education through a literature-based approach. *The Reading Teacher, 49,* 308–311.

Biemiller, A. (2001). Teaching vocabulary. *American Educator,* 143–148.

Biggs, S. A. (1992). Building on strengths: Closing the literacy gap for African-American students. *Journal of Reading, 35,* 624–628.

Bikowski, D., & Kessler, G. (2002). Making the most of discussion boards in the ESL classroom. *TESOL Journal, 11*(3), 27–30.

Bintz, W. P. (1993). Resistant readers in secondary education: Some insights and implications. *Journal of Reading, 36,* 604–615.

Bintz, W. P., & Shelton, K. S. (2004). Using written conversation in middle school: Lessons from a teacher researcher project. *Journal of Adolescent & Adult Literacy, 47,* 492–507.

Blachowicz, C. L. Z., & Fisher, P. (2000). Vocabulary instruction. In M. Kamil, P. Mosenthal, P. D. Pearson, & R. Barr (Eds.), *Handbook of reading research: Vol. III* (pp. 503–523). Mahwah, NJ: Erlbaum.

Blachowicz, C. L. Z., & Fisher, P. (2004). Vocabulary lessons. *Educational Leadership, 61*(6), 66–69.

Blasingame, J., & Bushman, J. H. (2005). *Teaching writing in middle and secondary schools.* Upper Saddle River, NJ: Pearson Education.

Bloom, A. (1987). *The closing of the American mind.* New York: Simon and Schuster.

Bloom, B. C. (1956). *Taxonomy of educational objectives: Cognitive domain.* New York: David McKay.

Blumenfeld, P. C., Marx, R., Soloway, E., & Krajcik, J. (1997). Learning with peers: From small group cooperation to collaborative communities. *Educational Researcher, 25,* 37–40.

Bohan, H., & Bass, J. (1991, Fall). Teaching thinking in elementary mathematics and science. *Educator's Forum, 1,* 4–5, 10.

Booth, J. R., & Hall, W. S. (1994). *Relationship of reading comprehension to the cognitive internal state lexicon.* (Reading Research Report No. 14). Athens: University of Georgia National Reading Research Center.

Borden, J., & Lytle, R. K. (2000). All together now . . . ? *The Exceptional Parent, 30*(9), 79–82.

Borkowski, J. G., Carr, M., Rellinger, E., & Pressley, M. (1990). Self-regulated cognition: Interdependence of metacognition, attributions, and self-esteem. In B. F. Jones & L. Idol (Eds.), *Dimensions of thinking and cognitive instruction* (pp. 53–92). Hillsdale, NJ: Erlbaum.

Borkowski, J. G., Weyhing, R. S., & Carr, M. (1988). Effects of attributional retraining on strategy-based reading comprehension in learning-disabled students. *Journal of Educational Psychology, 80,* 46–53.

Borman, G. D., & Overman, L. T. (2004). *The Elementary School Journal, 104*(3), 177–197.

Bormouth, J. R. (1969). *Development of a readability analysis.* (Final Report, Project No. 7–0052, Contract No. OEC-3-7-070052-0326). Washington, DC: USOE, Bureau of Research, U. S. Department of Health, Education, and Welfare.

Bormouth, J. R. (1975). Literacy in the classroom. In W. D. Page (Ed.), *Help for the reading teacher: New directions in research* (pp. 60–90). Urbana, IL: National Conference on Research in English and ERIC/RCS Clearinghouse.

Bos, C. S., & Anders, P. L. (1990). Effects of interactive vocabulary instruction on the vocabulary learning and reading comprehension of junior-high learning disabilities students. *Learning Disabilities Quarterly, 13*(1), 31–42.

Bosworth, K. (1996). Caring for others and being cared for: Students talk about caring in school. *Phi Delta Kappan, 76,* 686–693.

Bottomley, D. M., Truscott, D. M., Marimak, B. A., Henk, W. A., & Melnick, S. A. (1999). An affective comparison of whole language, literature-based, and basal reader literacy instruction. *Journal of Research and Instruction, 38*(2), 115–130.

Boyd, W. L. (2004, February). Relaunching the *American Journal of Education* in "interesting times." *The American Journal of Education, 110,* 105–107.

Boyd-Batstone, P. (2004). Focused anecdotal records assessment: A tool for standards-based, authentic assessment. *The Reading Teacher, 58*(3), 230–239.

Brabham, E. G., & Villaume, S. K. (2002). Vocabulary instruction: Concerns and visions. (Questions and answers). *The Reading Teacher, 56,* 264–269.

Bracey, G. (1992). The condition of public education. *Phi Delta Kappan, 74,* 104–117.

Bracey, G. (1997). *Setting the record straight: Responses to misconceptions about public education in the United States.* Alexandria, VA: Association for Supervision and Curriculum Development.

Bradbury, R. (1983, July). Goodbye grandma. *Reader's Digest, 23,* 139–142.

Brady, M. (1993). Critical issues that will determine the future of alternative assessment. *Phi Delta Kappan, 74,* 444–456.

Brandt, R. (1988). On teaching thinking: A conversation with Art Costa. *Educational Leadership, 45,* 10–13.

Brechtel, M. (1992). *Bringing the whole together: An integrated whole-language approach for the multilingual classroom.* San Diego: Dominie Press.

Brendtro, L. K., Brokenleg, M., & Bockern, S. V. (1990). *Reclaiming youth at risk: Our hope for the future.* Bloomington, IN: National Educational Service.

Bright, R. (1995). *Writing instruction in the intermediate grades: What is said, what is done, what is understood.* Newark, DE: International Reading Association.

Britton, B. K., & Tesser, A. (1991). Effects of time-management practices on college grades. *Journal of Educational Psychology, 83,* 405–410.

Britton, B. K., Van Dusen, L., Gulgog, S., Glynn, S. M., & Sharp, L. (1991). Accuracy of learnability judgments for instructional texts. *Journal of Educational Psychology, 83,* 43–47.

Bromley, K. (1993). *Journaling: Engagements in reading, writing, and thinking.* New York: Scholastic.

Brotherton, P. (2000). Diverse solutions. *Techniques, 75*(2), 18–21.

Brown, A. L. (1980). Metacognitive development and reading. In R. J. Spiro, B. Bruce, & W. F. Brewer (Eds.), *Theoretical issues in reading comprehension* (pp. 453–481). Hillsdale, NJ: Erlbaum.

Brown, A. L., Campione, J. C., & Day, J. D. (1981). Learning to learn: On training students to learn from texts. *Educational Researcher, 10,* 14–21.

Brown, A. L., & Day, J. D. (1983). Macrorules for summarizing texts: The development of expertise. *Child Development, 48* 1–8.

Brown, A. L., & Smiley, S. S. (1977). Rating the importance of structural units of prose passages: A problem of metacognitive development. *Child Development, 48,* 1–8.

Brown, J., Phillips, L., & Stephens, E. (1992). *Toward literacy: Theory and applications for teaching writing in the content areas.* Belmont, CA: Wadsworth.

Brown, J., & Stephens, E. (1995). *Teaching young adult literature.* Belmont, CA: Wadsworth.

Brown, R. (1987). Who is accountable for thoughtfulness? *Phi Delta Kappan, 69,* 49–52.

Bruce, B. (1998). Dewey and technology. *Journal of Adolescent & Adult Literacy, 42*(3), 222–226.

Brunwin, B. (Ed.). (1989). *The Bucktrout swamp.* Written by first- to sixth-grade students at Greenbriar Elementary School, Chesapeake, VA.

Bryant, D. P., Goodwin, M., Bryant, B. R., & Higgins, K. (2003). Vocabulary instruction for students with learning disabilities: A review of the research. *Learning Disability Quarterly, 26,* 117–128.

Bryant, J. A. R. (1984). Textbook treasure hunt. *Journal of Reading, 27,* 547–548.

Burns, M. (1975). *The I hate mathematics! book.* New York: Little Brown and Co.

Butkowsky, I., & Willow, D. (1980). Cognitive-motivational characteristics of children varying in reading ability: Evidence for learned helplessness in poor readers. *Journal of Educational Psychology, 72,* 408–422.

Byrnes, J. P. (1995). Domain specificity and the logic of using general ability as an independent variable or covariable. *Merrill-Palmer Quarterly, 41,* 1–24.

Cadenhead, K. (1987). Reading level: A metaphor that shapes practice. *Phi Delta Kappan, 68,* 436–441.

Caine, G., & Caine, R. (1994). *Mindshifts.* Tucson: Zephyr Press.

Caine, R. N., & Caine, G. (1991). *Teaching and the human brain.* Alexandria, VA: Association for Supervision and Curriculum Development.

Calfee, R. C. (1987). *The role of text structure in acquiring knowledge: Final report to the U. S. Department of Education* (Federal Program No. 122B). Palo Alto, CA: Stanford University, Text Analysis Project.

Calkins, L. (1986). *The art of teaching writing.* Portsmouth, NH: Heinemann.

Calkins, L., Montgomery, K., & Santman, D. (1998). *A teacher's guide to standardized reading tests.* Portsmouth, NH: Heinemann.

Calkins, L. M. (1994). *The art of teaching writing* (2nd ed.). Portsmouth, NH: Heinemann.

Campbell, D. (1995). The Socrates syndrome: Questions that should never be asked. *Phi Delta Kappan, 76,* 467–469.

Carmen, R., & Adams, W. (1972). *Study skills: A student's guide to survival.* New York: Wiley.

Carney, J. J., Anderson, D., Blackburn, C., & Blessing, D. (1984). Preteaching vocabulary and the comprehension of social studies materials by elementary school children. *Social Education, 48*(3), 195–196.

Carr, E., & Ogle, D. (1987). KWL plus: A strategy for comprehension and summarization. *Journal of Reading, 30,* 626–631.

Carr, E., & Wixson, K. K. (1986). Guidelines for evaluating vocabulary instruction. *Journal of Reading, 29,* 588–595.

Carson, J., Chase, N., Gibson, S., & Hargrove, M. (1992). Literacy demands of the undergraduate curriculum. *Reading Research and Instruction, 31,* 25–50.

Carter, B. (1996, Fall). Hold the applause! Do Accelerated Reader and Electronic Bookshelf send the right message? *School Library Journal,* 22–25.

Carter, K. (1986). Test-wiseness for teachers and students. *Educational Measurement: Issues and Practices, 5,* 20–23.

Carver, R. P. (1985). How good are some of the world's best readers? *Reading Research Quarterly, 20,* 389–419.

Carver, R. P. (1990). *Reading rate: A review of research and theory.* New York: Academic Press.

Carver, R. P. (1992). Reading rate: Theory, research, and practical applications. *Journal of Reading, 36*(2), 84–95.

Carver, R. P. (1994). Percentage of unknown vocabulary words in text as a function of the relative difficulty of the text: Implications for instruction. *Journal of Reading Behavior, 25*(4), 413–437.

Celano, D., & Neuman, S. (1995). Channel One: Time for a TV break. *Phi Delta Kappan, 76,* 444–446.

Chall, J. (1958). *Readability: An appraisal of research and application.* Columbus: Ohio State University, Bureau of Educational Research.

Chall, J. (1983). *Stages of reading development.* New York: McGraw-Hill.

Chamot, A. U., & O'Malley, J. M. (1989). The cognitive academic language learning approach. In P. Rigg

(Ed.), *When they don't all speak English: Integrating the ESL student into the regular classroom* (pp. 108–125). Urbana, IL: National Council of Teachers of English.

Chamot, A. U., & O'Malley, J. M. (1994). Instructional approaches and teaching procedures. In K. Spangenberg-Urbschat & R. Pritchard (Eds.), *Kids come in all languages: Reading instruction for ESL students* (pp. 82–107). Newark, DE: International Reading Association.

Chan, L. K. S. (1996). Motivational orientations and metacognitive abilities of intellectually gifted students. *Gifted Child Quarterly, 40*(4), 184–193.

Chandler-Olcott, K., & Mahar, D. (2003). "Tech-savviness" means multiliteracies: Exploring adolescent girls' technology mediated literacy practices. *Reading Research Quarterly, 38,*(3), 356–385.

Chang, I. (1991). *A separate battle: Women and the Civil War.* New York: Lodestar Books/Dutton.

Chase, A. C., & Dufflemeyer, F. A. (1990). VOCAB-LIT: Integrating vocabulary study and literature study. *Journal of Reading, 34*(3), 188–193.

Chi, F. (1995). EFL readers and a focus on intertextuality. *Journal of Reading, 38,* 638–644.

Chi, K. (2004, Spring). No Child Left Behind and emerging trends. *Spectrum.* Retrieved Nov. 26, 2004, from *http://www.csg.org*

Childress, H. (1998). Seventeen reasons why football is better than high school. Retrieved Nov. 26, 2004, from *http://www.pdkintl.org/kappan/kchi9804.htm*

Chinn, C. A., & Anderson, R. C. (1998). The structure of discussions that promote reasoning. *Teachers College Record, 100,* 315–368.

Chinn, C. A., Anderson, R. C., & Waggoner, M. A. (2001). Patterns of discourse in two kinds of literature discussion. *Reading Research Quarterly, 36*(4), 378–411.

Choate, J. S., & Rakes, T. A. (1987). The structured listening activity: A model for improving listening comprehension. *The Reading Teacher, 41,* 194–200.

Chomsky, C. (1971). Write first, read later. *Childhood Education, 47,* 296–299.

Chu, M. L. (1995). Reader response to interactive computer books: Examining literacy responses in a nontraditional reading setting. *Reading Research and Instruction, 43,* 352–366.

Ciardello, A. V. (1998). Did you ask a good question today? Alternative cognitive and metacognitive strategies. *Journal of Adolescent & Adult Literacy, 42*(3), 210–219.

Cimera, R. E. (2000). From bridges to beyond: A perspective of special education's future. *Journal of Disability Policy Studies, 11*(2), 124–125.

Cioffi, G. (1992). Perspective and experience: Developing critical reading abilities. *Journal of Reading, 36,* 48–52.

Cleary, B. (1982). *Ralph S. Mouse.* New York: William Morrow.

Cleland, J. V. (1999). We can charts: Building blocks for student-led conferences. *The Reading Teacher, 52*(6), 588–595.

Clyde, J. A. (1986). Talking on paper: Exploring the potential of a quality language experience. *Forum in Reading and Language Education, 2*(1), 1–10.

Cochran-Smith, M. (1991). Word processing and writing in elementary classrooms: A critical review of related literature. *Review of Educational Research, 61*(1), 107–155.

Cohen, A. D. (1987). The use of verbal and imagery mnemonics in second-language vocabulary learning. *Studies in Second Language Acquisition, 9,* 43–61.

Cohen, M. R., Cooney, T. M., Hawthorne, C., McCormack, A. J., Pasachoff, J. M., Pasachoff, N., Rhines, K. L., & Siesnick, I. L. (1991). *Discover science.* Glenview, IL: Scott, Foresman.

Coiro, J. (2003). Reading comprehension on the Internet: Expanding out understanding of comprehension to encompass new literacies. *The Reading Teacher, 56,* 458–464.

Cole, A. D. (1998). Beginner-oriented texts in literature-based classrooms: The segue for a few struggling readers. *The Reading Teacher, 51*(6), 488–501.

Cole, R., Raffier, L. M., Rogan, P., & Schleicher, L. (1998). Interactive group journals: Learning as a dialogue among learners. *TESOL Quarterly, 32*(3), 556–568.

Coleman, M. W. (1994). *Using a collaborative learning project to teach information literacy skills to twelfth grade regular English students.* M. S. Practicum, Nova Southeastern University, Ft. Lauderdale, FL (ERIC Document Reproductive Service No. ED 371 398).

College Board, Touchtone Applied Science Associates. (1986). *Degrees of reading power.* New York: College Board.

Collins, C. (1979). Speedway: The action way to speed read to increase reading rate for adults. *Reading Improvement, 16,* 225–229.

Collins, M. L. (1977). *The effects of training for enthusiasm on the enthusiasm displayed by pre-service elementary teachers.* Unpublished doctoral dissertation, Syracuse University, Syracuse, NY.

Colwell, C. G., Mangano, N. G., Childs, D., & Case, D. (1986). Cognitive, affective, and behavioral differences between students receiving instruction using alternative lesson formats. *Proceedings of the National Reading and Language Arts Conference.*

Committee on Education and the Workforce. (2002). *President Bush signs landmark reforms into law* [press release]. Washington, DC: White House Committee on Education and the Workforce.

Conley, M. (1985). Promoting cross-cultural understanding through content area reading strategies. *Journal of Reading, 28,* 600–605.

Conley, M. W., & Hinchman, K. A. (2004). No child left behind: What it means for U. S. adolescents and what we can do about it. *Journal of Adolescent & Adult Literacy, 48*(1), 42–48.

Connell, J. P., & Ryan, R. M. (1984). A developmental theory of motivation in the classroom. *Teacher Education Quarterly, 11,* 64–77.

Cook, L. & Gonzales, P. (1995). Zones of contact: Using literature with second language learners. *Reading Today, 12,* 27.

Coombe, C. A., & Hubley, N. J. (2004). *Fundamentals of language assessment.* Presentation and booklet, TESOL conference, Long Beach, CA.

Coopersmith, S. (1967). *The antecedents of self-esteem.* San Francisco: Freeman.

Cooter, R. B. (1990, October/November). Learners with special needs. *Reading Today,* 28.

Cooter, R. B., Jr. (1994). Assessing affective and conative factors in reading. *Reading Psychology, 15*(2), 77–90.

Cooter, R. B., & Chilcoat, G. W. (1991). Content-focused melodrama: Dramatic renderings of historical text. *Journal of Reading, 34,* 274–277.

Cooter, R. B., Joseph, D., & Flynt, E. (1986). Eliminating the literal pursuit in reading comprehension. *Journal of Clinical Reading, 2,* 9–11.

Corno, L., Collins, K. M., & Capper, J. (1982). *Where there's a way there's a will: Self-regulating the low achieving student.* ERIC Document Reproduction Service No. ED 222 499 (TM 820 465).

Cornu, B. (2001). *Winds of change in the teaching profession.* The report of the French National Commission for UNESCO. Paris: UNESCO.

Covey, S. (1990). *Seven habits of highly effective people.* New York: Simon and Schuster.

Cowan, G., & Cowan, E. (1980). *Writing.* New York: Wiley.

Cox, J., & Wiebe, J. (1984). Measuring reading vocabulary and concepts in mathematics in the primary grades. *Reading Teacher, 37,* 402–410.

Cox, Matthews, & Associates. (2001). Blacks are more likely to be placed in special education. *Black Issues in Higher Education, 18*(3), 22.

Crapse, L. (1995). Helping students construct meaning through their own questions. *Journal of Reading, 38*(5), 389–390.

Creek, R. J., McDonald, W. C., & Ganley, M. A. (1991). *Internality and achievement in the intermediate grades.* (ERIC Document No. ED 330 656).

Crist, J. (1975). One capsule a week—painless remedy for vocabulary ills. *Journal of Reading, 31,* 147–149.

Cronbach, L. J. (1951). Coefficient alpha and the internal structure of tests. *Psychometrika, 16,* 297–334.

Cronbach, L. J. (1957). *Psychological tests and personnel decisions.* Urbana: University of Illinois Press.

Cronin, H., Meadows, D., & Sinatra, R. (1990). Integrating computers, reading, and writing across the curriculum. *Educational Leadership, 48,* 57–62.

Crooks, S. M., & Katayama, A. D. (2002). Effects of on-line note-taking format on the comprehension of electronic text. *Research in the Schools, 9,* 22–23.

Cullinan, B. E., Karrer, M. K., & Pillar, A. M. (1981). *Literature and the child.* New York: Harcourt Brace and Jovanovich.

Culver, V. I., & Morgan, R. F. (1977). *The relationship of locus of control to reading achievement.* Unpublished manuscript, Old Dominion University, Norfolk, VA.

Cummins, J. (1979). Linguistic interdependence and the educational development of bilingual children. *Review of Educational Research, 49,* 222–251.

Cummins, J. (1994). The acquisition of English as a second language. In Spangenberg-Urbschadt and R. Pritchard (Eds.), *Kids come in all languages.* Newark, DE: International Reading Association.

Cunningham, A. E., & Stanovich, K. E. (1998). What reading does for the mind. *American Educator 22*(1, 2), 8–15.

Cunningham, J. W. (1982). Generating interactions between schemata and text. In J. A. Niles & L. A. Harris (Eds.), *New inquiries in reading research and instruction: Thirty-first yearbook of the national reading conference* (pp. 42–47). Rochester, NY: National Reading Conference.

Cunningham, P. (1995). *Phonics they use.* New York: Harper Collins.

Cunningham, R., & Shablak, S. (1975). Selective reading guide-o-rama: The content teacher's best friend. *Journal of Reading, 18,* 380–382.

Currie, H. (1990). Making texts more readable. *British Journal of Special Education, 17,* 137–139.

Curry, B. A. (1990). *The impact of the Nicholls State Youth Opportunities Unlimited Program as related to academic achievement, self-esteem, and locus of control.* Master's thesis, Nicholls State University, Thibodaux, LA.

Dahlman, A., & Rilling, S. (2001). Integrating technologies and tasks in an EFL distance learning course in Finland. *TESOL Journal, 10*(1), 4–8.

Daily, G. (1995, September). A glimpse of the real world. *Learning*, 62–63.

Dale, E. (1965). Vocabulary measurement: Techniques and major findings. *Elementary English, 42*, 395–401.

Dale, E., & Chall, J. (1948). A formula for predicting readability. *Educational Research Bulletin, 27*, 11–20, 37–54.

Dale, E., & O'Rourke, J. (1976). *The living word vocabulary.* Elgin, IL: Dome.

Dale, E., O'Rourke, J., & Bamman, H. (1971). *Techniques of teaching vocabulary.* Palo Alto, CA: Field Educational Publications.

Dalgarno, B. (2001). Interpretations of constructivism and consequences for computer assisted learning. *British Journal of Educational Technology, 32*(2), 183–194.

Dana, C., & Rodriguez, M. (1992). TOAST: A system to study vocabulary. *Reading Research and Instruction, 31*(4), 78–84.

Danielson, K. E. (1987) Readability formulas: A necessary evil? *Reading Horizons, 27*, 178–188.

Davey, B. (1983). Think aloud: Modeling the cognitive processes of reading comprehension. *Journal of Reading, 27*, 44–47.

Davey, B., & McBride, S. (1986). Effects of question-generation training on reading comprehension. *Journal of Educational Psychology, 78*, 256–262.

Davidson, J. L. (1982). The group mapping activity for instruction in reading and thinking. *Journal of Reading, 26*, 52–56.

Davis, B. (1985). *The long surrender.* New York: Random House.

Davis, F. B. (1944). Fundamental factors of comprehension in reading. *Psychometrika, 9*, 185–197.

Davis, J. (1997). *Mapping the mind: The secrets of the human brain and how it works.* Secaucus, NJ: Carol Publishing Group.

Davis, M. (1998). The Amish teachers' supper. *The Reading Professor, 21*(1), 158–164.

Davis, N. (2000). Information technology for teacher education at its first zenith: The heat is on! *Journal of Information Technology for Teacher Education, 9*(3), 277–286.

Davis, S., & Winek, J. (1989). Improving expository writing by increasing background knowledge. *Journal of Reading, 33*, 178–181.

Davis, W. C. (1985). *Touched by fire: A photographic portrait of the Civil War.* Boston: Little, Brown and Co.

Davis, W. C. (1990). *Diary of a Confederate soldier.* Columbia, SC: University of South Carolina Press.

Davison, A. (1984). Readability formulas and comprehension. In G. Duffy, L. Roehler, & J. Mason (Eds.), *Comprehension instruction* (pp. 128–143). New York: Longman.

Davison, D., & Pearce, D. (1988a). Using writing activities to reinforce mathematics instruction. *Arithmetic Teacher, 35*, 42–45.

Davison, D., & Pearce, D. (1988b). Writing activities in junior high mathematics texts. *School Science and Mathematics, 88*, 493–499.

Day, B., & Anderson, J. (1992). Assessing the challenges ahead. *Delta Kappa Gamma Bulletin, 58*(4), 5–10.

de Bono, E. (1976). *Teaching thinking.* London: Temple Smith.

Deal, D. (1998). Portfolios, learning logs, and eulogies: Using expressive writing in a science methods course. In E. G. Sturtevant, J. A. Dugan, P. Linder, & W. M. Linek (Eds.), *Literacy and community: Twentieth yearbook of the College Reading Association* (pp. 243–256). Commerce, TX: Texas A & M Press.

Dechant, E. (1970). *Improving the teaching of reading.* Englewood Cliffs, NJ: Prentice-Hall.

Deen, M. Y., Bailey, S. J., & Parker, L. (2001). *Life skills evaluation system.* Wenatchee, WA: Washington State University Cooperative Extension.

Derby, T. (1987). Reading instruction and course-related materials for vocational high school students. *Journal of Reading, 30*, 308–316.

DeSanti, R. J., & Alexander, D. H. (1986). Locus of control and reading achievement: Increasing the responsibility and performance of remedial readers. *Journal of Clinical Reading, 2*, 12–14.

Deshler, D. D., & Schumaker, J. B. (1988). An instructional model for teaching students how to learn. In J. L. Graden, J. E. Zins, & M. J. Curtis (Eds.), *Alternative educational delivery systems: Enhancing instructional options for all students* (pp. 391–411). Washington, DC: National Association of School Psychologists.

Dewey, J. (1933). *How we think.* Boston: Heath.

Diamond, M., & Hopson, J. (1998). *Magic tress of the mind: How to motivate your child's intelligence, creativity, and healthy emotions from birth through adolescence.* New York: Penguin Putnam.

Dickson, R. (2002). Creating joy: Adolescents writing poetry with young children. *Voices from the Middle, 10*(2), 38–42.

Dieu, B. (2004). BLOGs for language learning. *The Essential Teacher, 1*(4), 28–30.

Dillard, A. (1975). *Pilgrim at Tinker Creek.* New York: Harper's Magazine Press.

Dillon, J. T. (1983). *Teaching and the art of questioning.* Bloomington, IN: Phi Beta Kappa Educational Foundation. Fastback No. 194.

Dole, J. A. (2004). The changing role of the reading specialist in school reform. *The Reading Teacher, 57*(5), 462–471.

Dole, J. A., Duffy, G. C., Roehler, L. R., & Pearson, P. D. (1991). Moving from the old to the new: Research on reading comprehension instruction. *Review of Educational Research, 61,* 239–264.

Dole, J. A., Valencia, S. W., Greer, E. A., & Wardrop, J. L. (1991). Effects of two types of prereading instruction on the comprehension of narrative and expository text. *Reading Research Quarterly, 26,* 142–159.

Dole, S. (2000). The implications of the risk and resilience literature for gifted students with learning disabilities. *Roeper Review, 23*(2), 91.

Douglass, B. (1984). Variations on a theme: Writing with the LD adolescent. *Academic Therapy, 19,* 361–362.

Dove, M. K. (1998). The textbook in education. *Delta Kappa Gamma Bulletin, 64*(3), 24–30.

Downing, J. (1973). *Comparative reading.* New York: Macmillan.

Downing, J., Ollila, L., & Oliver, P. (1975). Cultural differences in children's concepts of reading and writing. *British Journal of Educational Psychology, 45,* 312–316.

Drevno, G. E., Kimball, J. W., Possi, M. K., Howard, W. L., Gardner, R., & Barbetta, P. M. (1994). Effects of active student response during error correction on the acquisition, maintenance, and generalization of science vocabulary by elementary students: A systematic replication. *Journal of Applied Behavior Analysis, 27*(1), 179–180.

Dreyer, L. G. (1984). Readability and responsibility. *Journal of Reading, 27,* 334–338.

Drum, P. (1985). Retention of text information by grade, ability, and study. *Discourse Processes, 8,* 21–51.

Drum, P., Calfee, R., & Cook, L. (1981). The effects of surface structure variables on reading comprehension tests. *Reading Research Quarterly, 16,* 486–514.

Drummond, R. J., Smith, R. K., & Pinette, C. A. (1975). Internal-external control construct and performance in an individualized community college reading course. *Reading Improvement, 12,* 34–38.

Duffelmeyer, F. A., & Baum, D. D. (1992). The extended anticipation guide revisited. *Journal of Reading, 35,* 654–656.

Duffelmeyer, F. A., Baum, D. D., & Merkley, D. J. (1987). Maximizing reader–text confrontation with an extended anticipation guide. *Journal of Reading, 31,* 146–149.

Duffy, G. G., & Hoffman, J. V. (1999). In pursuit of an illusion: The flawed search for a perfect method. *The Reading Teacher, 53,* 10–16.

Duffy, G. G., & Roehler, L. R. (1987). Teaching reading skills as strategies. *The Reading Teacher, 40,* 414–418.

Duke, N. K. (2000). 3.6 minutes per day: The scarcity of informational texts in first grade. *Reading Research Quarterly, 35,* 202–224.

Dunston, P. J. (1992). A critique of graphic organizer research. *Reading Research and Instruction, 31,* 57–65.

Durkin, D. (1979). What classroom observations reveal about reading comprehension. *Reading Research Quarterly, 14,* 481–533.

Durkin, D. (1981). Reading comprehension instruction in five basal reading series. *Reading Research Quarterly, 16,* 515–544.

Durkin, D. (1984). Is there a match between what elementary teachers do and what basal reader manuals recommend? *The Reading Teacher, 37,* 734–744.

Durst, R. K., & Newell, G. E. (1989). The uses of function: James Britton's category system and research on writing. *Review of Educational Research, 59*(4), 375–394.

Dweck, C. S. (1975). The role of expectations and attribution in the alleviation of learned helplessness. *Journal of Personality and Social Psychology, 41,* 1041–1048.

Dweck, C. S. (1985). Intrinsic motivation, perceived control, and self-evaluation maintenance: An achievement goal analysis. In C. Ames & R. Ames (Eds.), *Research on motivation in education: Vol. 2* (pp. 289–305). Orlando, FL: Academic Press.

Dwight, J. (2001). An epistemology of hypertexts. *VSTE Journal, 15*(2), 22–26.

Eanet, M., & Manzo, A. V. (1976). REAP—A strategy for improving reading/writing/study skills. *Journal of Reading, 19,* 647–652.

Earle, R., & Barron, R. F. (1973). An approach for teaching vocabulary in content subjects. In H. L. Herber & R. F. Barron (Eds.), *Research in reading in the content areas: Second year report* (pp. 84–100). Syracuse, NY: Syracuse University, Reading and Language Arts Center.

Ebbinghaus, H. (1908). *Abriss der psychologie* (M. Meyer, Trans. and Ed.). New York: Arno Press, 1973.

Egan, K. (1987). Literacy and the oral foundations of education. *Harvard Educational Review, 57,* 445–472.

Egan, M. (1999). Reflections on effective use of graphic organizers. *Journal of Adolescent & Adult Literacy, 42*(8), 641–645.

Ehlinger, J., & Pritchard, R. (1994). Using think-alongs in secondary content areas. *Reading Research and Instruction, 33*(3), 187–206.

Elley, W. B. (1992). *How in the world do students read?* The Hague, The Netherlands: International Association for the Evaluation of Educational Achievement.

Erickson, B. (1996). Read-alouds reluctant readers relish. *Journal of Adolescent & Adult Literacy, 40*(3), 217–221.

Erickson, B., Huber, M., Bea, T., Smith, C., & McKenzie, V. (1987). Increasing critical reading in junior high classes. *Journal of Reading, 30,* 430–439.

Erickson, F., & Schultz, J. (1992). Students' experience of the curriculum. In P. W. Jackson (Ed.), *Handbook of research on curriculum* (pp. 465–485). New York: Macmillan and the American Educational Research Association.

Evans, E. (2004, Spring). Comments on electronic learning. In the course Reading Instruction in the Content Areas, Virginia Commonwealth University, Spring 2004.

Ezell, H. K., Hunsicker, S. A., Quinque, M. M., & Randolph, E. (1996). Maintenance and generalization of QAR reading comprehension strategies. *Reading Research and Instruction, 36*(1), 64–81.

Facione, P. A. (1984). Toward a theory of critical thinking. *Liberal Education, 30,* 253–261.

Fader, D. (1976). *The new hooked on books.* New York: Berkley.

Farley, W. (1941). *The black stallion.* New York: Random House.

Fenwick, A. (1995). On attribution theory: Challenging behavior and staff beliefs. *Clinical Psychology Forum, 79,* 29–43.

Ferguson, D. B. (2000). Re-examining at-risk. *Curriculum Administrator, 36*(6), 79–90.

Field, M. L., & Aebersold, J. A. (1990). Cultural attitudes toward reading: Implications for teachers of ESL/bilingual readers. *Journal of Reading, 33,* 406–410.

Fielding, L. G., & Pearson, P. D. (1994). Reading comprehension: What works? *Educational Leadership, 51,* 62–68.

Fillmore, L. W. (1981). Cultural perspectives on second language learning. *TESL Reporter, 14,* 23–31.

Fink, R. P. (1996). Successful dyslexics: A constructivist study of passionate interest reading. *Journal of Adolescent & Adult Literacy, 39,* 268–280.

Fisher, C. W., & Berliner, D. (Eds.). (1985). *Perspectives on instructional time.* New York: Longman.

Fisher, D., Flood, J., Lapp, D., & Frey, N. (2004). Interactive read-alouds: Is there a common set of implementation practices? *The Reading Teacher, 58,* 1, 8–17.

Fisher, D., & Frey, N. (2003). Writing instruction for struggling adolescent writers: A gradual release model. *Journal of Adolescent & Adult Literacy, 46*(5), 395–405.

Fisher, M. (2004, October 12). Falls Church School won't teach to the test. *The Washington Post,* B1.

Fleener, C., Hager, J., Morgan, R. F., & Childress, M. (2000). *The integration of conation, cognition, affect, and social environment in literacy development.* In P. Linder, W. M. Linek, E. G. Sturtevant, & J. Dugan (Eds.), *Literacy at a new horizon: Twenty-second yearbook of the College Reading Association* (pp. 88–98). Commerce, TX: Texas A & M University–Commerce.

Fleisher, L. S., Jenkins, J. R., & Pany, D. (1979). Effects on poor readers' comprehension of training in rapid decoding. *Reading Research Quarterly, 15,* 30–48.

Fleming, C. B., Harachi, T. W., Cortes, R. C., Abbott, R D., & Catalano, R. F. (2004). Level and change in reading scores and attention problems during elementary school as predictors of problem behavior in middle school. *Journal of Emotional and Behavioral Disorders, 12*(3), 130–144.

Flesch, R. (1949). *The art of readable writing.* New York: Harper and Row.

Forgan, H. W., & Mangrum, C. T. (1985, 1997). *Teaching content area reading skills.* Columbus, OH: Merrill.

Forget, M. A., & Morgan, R. F. (1995, November). *An embedded curriculum approach to teaching metacognitive strategies.* Paper presented at the College Reading Association, Clearwater Beach, FL.

Fox, B. J. (2003). Teachers' evaluations of word identification software: Implications for literacy methods courses. In M. B. Sampson, P. E. Linder, J. R. Dugan, & B. Brancato (Eds.), *Celebrating the freedom of literacy: The twenty-fifth yearbook of the college reading association.* Commerce: Texas A & M University.

Francis, M. A., & Simpson, M. L. (2003). Using theory, our intuitions, and a research study to enhance students' vocabulary knowledge. *Journal of Adolescent & Adult Literacy, 47*(1), 66–78.

Francis-Smythe, J. A., & Robertson, I. T. (1999). On the relationship between time management and time estimation. *British Journal of Psychology, 90*(3), 333–334.

Frand, J. L. (2000). The information-age mindset. *Educause Review, 35*(5), 15–24.

Friend, R. (2001). Teaching summarization as a content area reading strategy. *Journal of Adolescent & Adult Literacy, 44*(4) 320–334.

Fromm, E. (1956). *The art of loving.* New York: Harper and Row.

Fry, E. (1968). The readability graph validated at primary levels. *The Reading Teacher, 3,* 534–538.

Fry, E. (1977). Fry's readability graph: Clarifications, validity, and extension to level 17. *Journal of Reading, 21*, 242–252.

Fry, E. (1987). The varied uses of readability measurement today. *Journal of Reading, 30*, 338–343.

Fry, E. (1989). Reading formulas—maligned but valid. *Journal of Reading, 32*, 292–297.

Fry, E. (1990). A readability formula for short passages. *Journal of Reading, 33*, 594–597.

Frymier, A. B., & Schulman, G. (1995). "What's in it for me": Increasing content relevance to enhance students' motivation. *Communication Education, 44*, 40–50.

Fulwiler, T. (1987). *Teaching with writing.* Portsmouth, NH: Boynton/Cook.

Gagne, R. (1974). Educational technology and the learning process. *Educational Researcher, 3*, 3–8.

Galeman, D. (1995). *Emotional intelligence: Why it can matter more than IQ.* New York: Bantam.

Gallagher, J. J. (1998). Accountability for gifted students. *Phi Delta Kappan, 79*(10), 739–743.

Gallagher, J. M. (1995). Pairing adolescent fiction with books from the canon. *Journal of Adolescent & Adult Literacy, 39*, 8–14.

Gambrell, L. B. (1990). Introduction: A themed issue on reading instruction for at-risk students. *Journal of Reading, 33*, 485–488.

Gambrell, L. B. (1995). Motivation matters. In *Generations of Literacy: Seventeenth Yearbook of the College Reading Association* (pp. 2–24). Commerce, TX: East Texas State University.

Gambrell, L. B. (1996). Creating classroom cultures that foster reading motivation. *The Reading Teacher, 50*(1), 14–25.

Gambrell, L. B., & Almasi, J. F. (1996). *Lively discussions: Fostering engaged reading.* Newark, DE: International Reading Association.

Gambrell, L. B., & Bales, R. J. (1986). Mental imagery and the comprehension-monitoring performance of fourth- and fifth-grade poor readers. *Reading Research Quarterly, 21*, 454–464.

Ganske, K., Monroe, J. K., & Strickland, D. S. (2003). Questions teachers ask about struggling readers and writers. *Journal of Adolescent & Adult Literacy, 57*(2), 118–128.

Gardner, J. E., & Wissick, C. A. (2002). Enhancing cooperative learning using the World Wide Web: Tools and strategies that integrate technology for students with mild disabilities. *Journal of Special Education Technology, 17*, 27–38.

Gardner, J. E., Wissick, C. A., Schweder, W., & Canter, L. S. (2003). Enhancing interdisciplinary instruction in general and special education: Thematic units and

technology. *Remedial and Special Education, 24*(3), 161–173.

Gardner, M. K., & Smith, M. M. (1987). Does perspective-taking ability contribute to reading comprehension? *Journal of Reading, 30*, 333–336.

Garner, R. (1985). Text summarization deficiencies among older students: Awareness or production ability? *American Educational Research Journal, 22*, 549–560.

Garner, R., Alexander, P., Slater, W., Hare, V. C., Smith, J., & Reis, R. (1986, April). *Children's knowledge of structural properties of text.* Paper presented at the meeting of the American Educational Research Association, San Francisco.

Garner, R., Hare, V. C., Alexander, P., Haynes, J., & Winograd, P. (1984). Inducing use of a text lookback strategy among unsuccessful readers. *American Educational Research Journal, 21*, 789–798.

Garner, R., Macready, G. B., & Wagoner, S. (1985). Reader's acquisition of the components of the text-lookback strategy. *Journal of Educational Psychology, 76*, 300–309.

Garrison, W. B. (1992). *Civil War trivia and fact book.* Nashville, TN: Rutledge Hill Press.

Gavelek, J. R. (1986). The social contexts of literacy and schooling: A developmental perspective. In T. Raphael (Ed.), *The contexts of school-based literacy* (pp. 3–26). New York: Random House.

Gebhard, A. (1983). Teaching writing in reading and the content areas. *Journal of Reading, 27*, 207–211.

Gee, J. P. (1996). *Social linguistics and literacies: Ideology in discourses* (2nd ed.). Bristol, PA: Taylor & Francis.

Gee, R. W. (1999). Encouraging ESL students to read. *TESOL Journal, 8*(1), 3–7.

Gentile, L., & McMillan, M. (1987). Stress and reading difficulties: Teaching students self-regulating skills. *The Reading Teacher, 41*, 170–178.

George, J. C. (1971). *All upon a stone.* New York: Crowell.

Gere, A. (1985). *Roots in the sawdust: Writing to learn across the disciplines.* Urbana, IL: National Council of Teachers of English.

Gersten, B. F., & Tlusty, N. (1998). Creating international contexts for cultural communication: Video exchange projects in the EFL/ESL classroom. *TESOL Journal, 7*(6), 11–16.

Gersten, R., & Baker, S. (1998). Real world use of scientific concepts: Integrating situated cognition with explicit instruction. *Exceptional Children, 65*(1), 23–36.

Gholar, C. R., Givens, S. A., McPherson, M. M., & Riggs, E. G. (1991, April). *Wellness begins when the child comes first: The relationship between the conative domain and the school achievement paradigm.* Paper presented at the meeting of the Annual Convention of the American Association for Counseling and

Development, Reno, NV. (ERIC Document Reproduction Service No. ED 329 863).

Gholar, C. R., & Riggs, E. G. (2004). *Connecting with students' will to succeed: The power of conation.* Glenview, IL: Pearson Education.

Gibbons, P. (2003). Mediating language learning: Teacher interaction with ESL students in a content-based classroom. *TESOL Quarterly, 37*(2), 247–273.

Gill, S., & Dupre, K. (1998). Constructivism in reading education. *The Reading Professor, 21*(1), 91–108.

Gillespie, C. (1993). Reading graphic displays: What teachers should know. *Journal of Reading, 36,* 350–354.

Gillett, J. W., & Temple, C. (1983). *Understanding reading problems: Assessment and instruction.* Boston: Little, Brown.

Gillies, R. M., & Ashman, A. F. (1998). Behavior and interactions of children in cooperative groups in lower and middle elementary grades. *Journal of Educational Psychology, 90*(4), 746–757.

Glasser, W. (1986). *Control theory in the classroom.* New York: Harper and Row.

Glatthaar, J. T. (1990). *Forged in battle: The Civil War alliance of black soldiers and white officers.* New York: Free Press.

Glaubman, R., Glaubman, H., & Ofir, L. (1997). Effects of self-directed learning, story comprehension, and self-questioning in kindergarten. *Journal of Educational Research, 90,* 361–374.

Glickman, C. (2004). *Letter to the next president: what we can do about the real crisis in public education.* New York: Teachers' College Press.

Godwin, K., & Sheard, W. (2001). Education reform and the politics of 2000. *Publius: The Journal of Federalism, 31*(3), 11–129.

Gold, P. C. (1981). The directed listening–language experience approach. *Journal of Reading, 25,* 138–141.

Goldberg, A., Russell, M., & Cook, A. (2003). The effect of computers on student writing: A meta-analysis of studies from 1992–2002. *Journal of Technology, Learning, and Assessment, 2*(1). Retrieved Nov. 26, 2004, from *http://www.bc.edu/research/intasc/jtla/journal/v2n1.shtml*

Goldman, S. R., Hasselbring, T. S., & the Cognition and Technology Group at Vanderbilt (1996). Achieving meaningful mathematics literacy for students with learning disabilities. *Journal of Learning Disabilities, 30*(2), 198–208.

Goodlad, J. (1984). *A place called school.* New York: McGraw-Hill.

Gottlieb, M. (2003). *Large scale assessment of English language learners.* Alexandria, VA: TESOL.

Gough, P. B. (1987, May). The key to improving schools: An interview with William Glasser. *Phi Delta Kappan,* 656–662.

Grabe, M., & Grabe, C. (1998). *Integrating technology for meaningful learning.* Boston: Houghton Mifflin.

Grady, M. P. (1990). *Whole brain education.* Bloomington, IN: Phi Delta Kappa Educational Foundation.

Graves, D. (1983). *Writing: Teachers and children at work.* Portsmouth, NH: Heinemann.

Graves, D. (1994). *A fresh look at writing.* Portsmouth, NH: Heinemann.

Graves, D. H. (2000). *A fresh look at writing.* Portsmouth, NH: Heineman.

Graves, D., Prenn, M., & Cooke, C. (1985). The coming attraction: Previewing short stories. *Journal of Reading, 28,* 594–598.

Graves, M. F. (1985). *A word is a word . . . or is it?* New York: Scholastic.

Gray, W. (1925). *Summary of investigations related to reading* (Supplementary Educational Monographs No. 28). Chicago: University of Chicago Press.

Gray, W. (1960). The major aspects of reading. In H. Robinson (Ed.), *Development of reading abilities* (Supplementary Educational Monographs No. 90). Chicago: University of Chicago Press.

Gray, W. (1984). *Reading.* Newark, DE: International Reading Association. (Originally published 1941.)

Green, F. E. (1999). Brain and learning research: Implications for meeting the needs of diverse learners. *Education, 119*(4), 682–687.

Green, J. F., & Smyser, S. O. (1996). *The teacher portfolio: A strategy for professional development and evaluation.* Lancaster, PA: Technomic Publishing.

Greenlee-Moore, M., & Smith, L. (1996). Interactive computer software: The effects on young children's reading achievement. *Reading Psychology: An International Quarterly, 17,* 43–64.

Greenough, W. T., Withers, G. S., & Anderson, B. J. (1992). Experience-dependent synaptogenesis as a plausible memory mechanism. In I. Gormezano & E. A. Wasserman (Eds.), *Learning and memory: The behavioral and biological substrates* (pp. 209–299). Hillsdale, NJ: Erlbaum.

Groff, P. (1981). Direct instruction versus incidental learning of reading vocabulary. *Reading Horizons, 21*(4), 262–265.

Gronlund, N. (1993). *How to make achievement tests and assessments.* Boston: Allyn & Bacon.

Gross, S. J. (2003). A case of American education flu. *Reading Online.* Retrieved Sept. 7, 2004, from *http://www.readingonline.org/international/inter_index.asp?HREF=gross/index.html*

Guillaume, A. M. (1998). Learning with text in the primary grades. *The Reading Teacher, 51*(6), 476–486.

Gunderson, L., & Siegel, L. S. (2001). The evils of the use of IQ tests to define learning disabilities in first and second language learners. *The Reading Teacher, 55*(1), 48–55.

Gusak, F. J. (1967). Teacher questioning and reading. *The Reading Teacher, 21*, 227–234.

Guthrie, J. (2000). Contexts for engagement and motivation in reading. In M. L. Kamil, P. B. Mosenthal, P. D. Pearson, & R. Barr (Eds.), *Handbook of reading research: Vol. III* (pp. 403–422). Retrieved Oct. 1, 2004, from *http://www.readingonline.org/articles/handbook/guthrie/index.html*

Guthrie, J. T. (2004). CORI: *Classroom practices promoting engagement and achievement in comprehension.* Keynote address PowerPoint slides. International Reading Association Annual Conference, May 1, 2004.

Guthrie, J. T., Burnam, N., Caplan, R. I., & Seifert, M. (1974). The maze technique to assess and monitor reading comprehension. *The Reading Teacher, 28*, 161–168.

Guthrie, J. T., Schafer, W. D., Von Secker, C., & Alban, T. (2000). Contributions of instructional practices to reading achievement in a statewide improvement program. *Journal of Educational Research 93*(4), 211.

Guzzetti, B. (1990). Enhancing comprehension through trade books in high school English classes. *Journal of Reading, 33*, 411–413.

Guzzetti, B., Hynd, C. R., Skeels, S. A., & Williams, W. O. (1995). Improving physics texts: Students speak out. *Journal of Reading, 38*, 656–663.

Guzzetti, B., Kowalinski, B. J., & McGowan, T. (1992). Using a literature-based approach to teaching social studies. *Journal of Reading, 36*, 114–122.

Guzzetti, B., Snyder, T., & Glass, G. (1992). Promoting conceptual change in science: Can texts be used effectively? *Journal of Reading, 35*, 642–649.

Hadaway, N., & Mundy, J. (1999). Children's informational picture books visit a secondary ESL classroom. *Journal of Adolescent & Adult Literacy, 42*(6),464–475.

Hafner, L. (1967). Using context to determine meanings in high school and college. *Journal of Reading, 10*, 491–498.

Hager, J. M., & Gable, R. A. (1993). Content reading assessment: A rethinking of methodology. *The Clearing House, 66*, 269–272.

Haggard, M. R. (1986). The vocabulary self-collection strategy: Using student interest and world knowledge to enhance vocabulary growth. *Journal of Reading, 29*, 634–642.

Haley, A. N., & Watson, D. C. (2000). In-school literacy extension: Beyond in-school suspension. *Journal of Adolescent & Adult Literacy, 43*(7), 654–661.

Halladay, M. A. K. (1994). *An introduction to functional grammar* (2nd ed.). London: Edward Arnold.

Hamachek, D. E. (1975). *Behavior dynamics in teaching, learning, and growth.* Boston: Allyn & Bacon.

Hammerberg, D. D. (2004). Comprehension instruction for socioculturally diverse classrooms: A review of what we know. *The Reading Teacher, 57*(7), 648–658.

Hancock, D. (2004). Cooperative learning and peer orientation effects on motivation and achievement. *Journal of Educational Research, 97*(3), 159–167.

Hansen, J. (1981). The effects of inference training and practice on young children's comprehension. *Reading Research Quarterly, 16*, 391–417.

Hansen, J., & Pearson, D. (1983). An instructional study: Improving the inferential comprehension of fourth grade good and poor readers. *Journal of Educational Psychology, 75*, 821–829.

Hare, V. C., & Borchardt, K. M. (1984). Direct instruction of summarization skills. *Reading Research Quarterly, 20*, 62–78.

Harris, K., & Graham, S. (1985). Improving learning disabled students' composition skills: Self-control strategy training. *Learning Disability Quarterly, 8*, 27–36.

Harris, L. A., & Smith, C. B. (1986). *Reading instruction: Diagnostic teaching in the classroom.* New York: Macmillan.

Harris, T. L., & Hodges, R. E. (1995). *The literacy dictionary: The vocabulary of reading and writing.* Newark, DE: International Reading Association.

Hart, L. (1975). *How the brain works.* New York: Basic Books.

Hart, L. (1983a). Programs, patterns, and downshifting in learning to read. *The Reading Teacher, 37*, 5–11.

Hart, L. (1983b). *Human brain and human learning.* New York: Longman.

Hartman, M., & Kretschner, R. E. (1992). Talking and writing: Deaf teenagers reading *Sarah, Plain and Tall. Journal of Reading, 36*, 174–180.

Hathaway, W. (Ed.). (1983). *Testing in the schools.* San Francisco: Jossey-Bass.

Hattie, J., Biggs, J., & Purdie, N. (1996). Effects of learning skills interventions on student learning: A meta-analysis. *Review of Educational Research, 66*, 99–136.

Haussamen, B. (1995). The passive-reading fallacy. *Journal of Reading, 38*, 378–381.

Hawkes, K. S., & Schell, L. M. (1987). Teacher-set prereading purposes and comprehension. *Reading Horizons, 27*, 164–169.

Hayes, H., Stahl, N., & Simpson, M. (1991). Language, meaning, and knowledge: Empowering developmental students to participate in the academic community. *Reading Research and Instruction, 30*(3), 89–100.

Heath, S. B. (1986). Critical factors in literacy development. In S. de Castell, A. Luke, & K. Egan (Eds.), *Literacy, society, and schooling: A reader* (pp. 209–229). New York: Cambridge University Press.

Heathington, B., & Alexander, J. (1984). Do classroom teachers emphasize attitudes toward reading? *The Reading Teacher, 37,* 484–488.

Heider, F. (1958). *The psychology of interpersonal relations.* New York: Wiley.

Heilman, A. W., Blair, T. R., & Rupley, W. H. (1986, 1994). *Principles and practices of teaching reading.* Columbus, OH: Merrill.

Heller, M. (1986). How do you know what you know? Metacognitive modeling in the content areas. *Journal of Reading, 29,* 415–422.

Henderson, M. V., & Scheffler, A. J. (2004). New literacies, standards, and teacher education. *Education, 124*(2), 390–395.

Henk, W. A., & Helfeldt, J. P. (1987). How to develop independence in following written directions. *Journal of Reading, 30,* 602–607.

Henry, G. H. (1974). *Teach reading as concept development: Emphasis on affective thinking.* Newark, DE: International Reading Association.

Herber, H. (1978). *Teaching reading in the content areas* (2nd ed.). Englewood Cliffs, NJ: Prentice-Hall.

Herber, H. (1987). Foreword. In D. Alvermann, D. Moore, & M. Conley (Eds.), *Research within reach: Secondary school reading.* Newark, DE: International Reading Association.

Herman, J. L., Aschbacher, P. R., & Winters, L. W. (1992). *A practical guide to alternative assessment.* Alexandria, VA: Association for Supervision and Curriculum Development.

Hiebert, E. H. (1999). Text matters in learning to read. *The Reading Teacher, 52*(6), 552–566.

Hill, W., & Erwin, R. (1984). The readability of content textbooks used in middle and junior high schools. *Reading Psychology, 5,* 105–117.

Hillerich, R. L. (1979). Reading comprehension. *Reporting on Reading, 5,* 1–3.

Hilliard, A. G. (1988). Public support for successful instructional practices for at-risk students. In D. W. Hornbeck (Ed.), *School success for at-risk youth: Analysis and recommendations of the Council of Chief State School Officers* (pp. 195–208). Orlando, FL: Harcourt Brace Jovanovich.

Hillocks, G., Jr. (2002). *The testing trap: How state writing assessments control learning.* New York: Teachers College Press.

Hinchman, K. A., Alvermann, D. E., Boyd, F. B., Brozo, W. G., & Vacca, R. T. (2004). Supporting older students' in-and-out-of-school literacies. *Journal of Adolescent & Adult Literacy, 47*(4), 304–310.

Hirsch, E. D. (1987). *Cultural literacy.* Boston: Houghton Mifflin.

Hittleman, D. R. (1978). Readability, readability formulas, and cloze: Selecting instructional materials. *Journal of Reading, 22,* 117–122.

Hmelo, C. E., Nagarajan, A., & Day, R. S. (2000). Effects of high and low prior knowledge on construction of a joint problem space. *The Journal of Experimental Education, 69*(1), 36.

Hoffman, J. (1992). Critical reading/thinking across the curriculum: Using I-charts to support learning. *Language Arts, 69,* 121–127.

Hoffman, S. (1983). Using student journals to teach study skills. *Journal of Reading, 26,* 344–347.

Hogan, K., Nastasi, B. K., & Pressley, M. (2000). Discourse patterns and collaborative scientific reasoning in peer and teacher-guided discussions. *Cognitive Instruction, 17,* 379–432.

Holiday, W. G. (1983). Overprompting science students using adjunct study questions. *Journal of Research in Science Teaching, 20,* 195–201.

Holmes, B., & Roser, N. (1987). Five ways to assess readers' prior knowledge. *The Reading Teacher, 40,* 646–649.

Horn, W. F., & Tynan, D. (2001). Revamping special education. *The Public Interest, 36–42.*

Hornbeck, D. W. (1988). All our children: An introduction. In D. W. Hornbeck (Ed.), *School success for at-risk youth: Analysis and recommendations of the Council of Chief State School Officers* (pp. 3–9). Orlando, FL: Harcourt Brace Jovanovich.

Hornberger, T. R., & Whitford, E. V. (1983). Students' suggestions: Teach us study skills! *Journal of Reading, 27,* 71.

Houston, G. (2004). *How writing works: Imposing organizational structure within the writing process.* Boston: Pearson Education.

Howard S., & Johnson, B. (2000). What makes the difference? Children and teachers talk about resilient outcomes for children "at risk." *Educational Studies, 26,* 321–337.

Howes, E. V., Hamilton, G. W., & Zaskoda, D. (2003). Linking science and literature through technology: Thinking about interdisciplinary inquiry in middle school. *Journal of Adolescent & Adult Literacy, 46,* 484–504.

Howland, J. (1995). Attentive reading in the age of canon clamor. *English Journal, 84,* 35–38.

Huber, J. (2004). A closer look at SQ3R. *Reading Improvement, 41*(2), 108–113.

Huck, C., Hepler. S., & Hickman, J. (1987). *Children's literature in the elementary school.* Fort Worth, TX: Holt, Rinehart and Winston.

Huey, E. (1968). *The psychology and pedagogy of reading.* Cambridge, MA: MIT Press. (Originally published 1908.)

Hurd, P. (1970). *New directions in teaching secondary school science.* Chicago: Rand-McNally.

Hwang, Y., & Levin, J. (2002). Examination of middle-school students' independent use of a complex mnemonic system. *The Journal of Experimental Education, 7*(1), 25–39.

Hynd, C. (1999). Teaching students to think critically using multiple texts in history. *Journal of Adolescent & Adult Literacy, 42*(6), 428–436.

Hynd, C., McNish, M., Lay, K., & Fowler, P. (1995). *High school physics: The role of text in learning counterintuitive information* (Reading Research Report No. 16). University of Georgia: National Reading Research Center.

Iannone, P. (1998). Just beyond the horizon: Writing-centered literacy activities for traditional and electronic texts. *The Reading Teacher, 51,*(5), 438–443.

Inspiration Software. (2000). Kidspiration (Computer Software). Portland, OR: Author.

Inspiration Software. (2002). Inspiration 7.0 (Computer Software). Portland, OR: Author.

International Reading Association. (1988). *New directions in reading instruction.* Newark, DE: Author.

International Reading Association. (1999). *High stakes testing.* Newark, DE: Author. Retrieved Sept. 7, 2004, from *http://www.reading.org/resources/issues/ positions_high_stakes.html*

International Reading Association. (2003). *Standards for reading professionals.* Newark, DE: Author, Professional Standards and Ethics Committee.

International Reading Association. (2003). *Standards for reading professionals.* Newark, DE: Author, Professional Standards and Ethics Committee.

Irvin, J. L. (1990). *Vocabulary knowledge: Guidelines for instruction. What research says to the teacher.* Washington, DC: National Education Association.

Ivey, G. (1999). Reflections on teaching struggling middle school readers. *Journal of Adolescent & Adult Literacy, 42*(5), 372–381.

Ivey, G., & Broaddus, K. (2000). Tailoring the fit: Reading instruction and middle school readers. *The Reading Teacher, 54*(1), 68–78.

Iwicki, A. L. (1992). Vocabulary connections. *The Reading Teacher, 45,* 736.

Jackson, F. R., & Cunningham, J. (1994). Investigating secondary content teachers and preservice teachers' conceptions of study strategy instruction. *Reading Research and Instruction, 34,* 11–135.

Jacobs, J., & Paris, S. (1987). Children's metacognition about reading: Issues in definition, measurement, and instruction. *Educational Psychologist, 22,* 255–278.

Jacobs, L. (1987). Reading, writing, remembering. *Teaching Pre K–8, 18,* 38.

Jacobson, J. M. (1998). *Content area reading: Integration with the language arts.* Albany, NY: Doman.

Jenkins, C., & Lawler, D. (1990). Questioning strategies in content area reading: One teacher's example. *Reading Improvement, 27,* 133–138.

Jensen, E. (1998). *Teaching with the brain in mind.* Alexandria, VA: Association for Supervision and Curriculum Development.

Jetton, T. L., & Alexander, P. A. (2000). Learning from text: A multidimensional and developmental perspective. In M. L. Kamil, P. B. Mosenthal, P. D. Pearson, & R. Barr (Eds.), *Handbook of reading research: Vol. III.* Retrieved Sept. 7, 2004, from *http://www.reading online.org/articles/handbook/jetton/index.html*

Jitendra, A. K., Edwards, L. L., Sacks, G., & Jacobson, L. A. (2004). What research says about vocabulary instruction for students with learning disabilities. *Exceptional Children, 70,* 299–322.

Johnson, D. (2002, March). Web watch: Writing resources. *Reading Online, 5*(7). Retrieved Dec. 12, 2004, from *http://www.readingonline.org/electronic/elec_index.asp ?HREF=webwatch/writing/index.html*

Johnson, D. (2002, October). Web watch: Poetry workshop. *Reading Online, 6*(3). Retrieved Dec. 12, 2004, from *http://www.readingonline.org/electronic/ elec_index.asp?HREF=webwatch/poetry/index.html*

Johnson, D., & Johnson, B. (2002, August/September). The unfairness of uniformity. *Reading Today, 20,* 18.

Johnson, D., & Pearson, P. D. (1984). *Teaching reading vocabulary.* New York: Holt, Rinehart and Winston.

Johnson, D. D. (2001). *Vocabulary in the elementary and middle school.* Boston: Allyn & Bacon.

Johnson, D. W., & Johnson, R. T. (1987). *Learning together and alone: Cooperative, conjunctive, and individualistic learning.* Englewood Cliffs, NJ: Prentice-Hall.

Johnson, D. W., & Johnson, R. T. (2003). *Joining together: Group theory and group skills.* New York: A and B Publishing.

Johnston, D. (2001). Draft Builder (Computer Software). Volo, IL: Author.

Johnston, J. (1995). Channel One: The dilemma of teaching and selling. *Phi Delta Kappan, 76,* 437–442.

Jone, H. J., Coombs, W. T., & McKinney, C. W. (1994). A themed literature unit versus a textbook: A comparison of the effects on content acquisition and attitudes in elementary social studies. *Reading Research and Instruction, 34,* 85–96.

Jones, C. H., Slate, J. R., & Marini, I. (1995). Locus of control, social interdependence, academic preparation, age, study time, and the study skills of college students. *Research in the Schools, 2,* 55–62.

Jones, F. R., Morgan, R. F., & Tonelson, S. W. (1992). *The psychology of human development* (3rd ed.). Dubuque, IA: Kendall/Hunt.

Jongsma, E. (1980). *Cloze instruction research: A second look.* Newark, DE: International Reading Association.

Juel, C., & Deffes, R. (2004). Making words stick. *Educational Leadership, 61*(6), 30–34.

Just, M. A., Carpenter, P. A., & Masson, M. E. J. (1982). *What eye fixations tell us about speed reading and skimming* (Technical Report). Pittsburgh: Carnegie-Mellon University.

Juster, N. (1961). *The phantom tollbooth.* New York: Random House.

Kaiser, Henry F. (1962). Scaling a simplex. *Psychometrika, 27*(2), 155–162.

Kane, B. (1984). *Remarks made at the regional meeting on reading across the curriculum.* Reading to Learn in Virginia, Capital Consortium.

Kapinus, B. (1986). *Ready reading readiness.* Baltimore: Maryland State Department of Education.

Karabenick, S. A. (1998). Help seeking as a strategic resource. In S. A. Karabenick (Ed.), *Strategic help seeking: Implications for learning and teaching* (pp. 1–11). Mahwah, NJ: Erlbaum.

Karchmer, R. (2001). The journey ahead: Thirteen teachers report how the Internet influences literacy and literacy instruction in their K–12 classrooms. *Reading Research Quarterly, 36*(4), 442–466.

Katayama, A. D., & Robinson, D. H. (2000). Getting students "partially" involved in note-taking using graphic organizers. *Journal of Experimental Education, 68*(2), 119.

Kauchak, D. P., & Eggen, P. D. (1998). *Learning and teaching: Research-based methods* (3rd ed.). Boston: Allyn & Bacon.

Keith, T. Z., Reimers, T. M., Fehrmann, P. G., Pottebaum, S. M., & Aubey, L. W. (1986). Parental involvement, homework, and TV time: Direct and indirect effects on high school achievement. *Journal of Educational Psychology, 78,* 373–380.

Kellogg, R. (1972). Listening. In P. Lamb (Ed.), *Guiding children's language learning* (pp. 141–170). Dubuque, IA: William C. Brown.

Kerchner, L., & Kistinger, B. (1984). Language processing/word processing: Written expression, computers, and learning disabled students. *Learning Disability Quarterly, 7,* 329–335.

Kerr, M. M., Nelson, C. M., & Lambert, D. L. (1987). *Helping adolescents with learning and behavior problems.* Columbus, OH: Merrill.

Kibby, M. W. (1995). The organization and teaching of things and the words that signify them. *Journal of Adolescent & Adult Literacy, 39,* 208–223.

Kidder, T. (1989). *Among schoolchildren.* Boston: Houghton Mifflin.

Kidder-Ashley, P., Deni, J. R., & Anderton, J. B. (2000). Learning disabilities eligibility in the 1990s: An analysis of state practices. *Education, 121*(1), 65–69.

Kinder, D., Bursuck, B., & Epstein, M. (1992). An evaluation of history textbooks. *Journal of Special Education, 25,* 472–491.

Kintch, W., & Van Dijk, T. (1978). Toward a model of text comprehension and production. *Psychological Review, 85,* 363–394.

Kirkland, N. C. (1993). *Developing a sequential relevant approach to research writing for high school juniors and seniors.* Ed.D Practicum, Nova University, Fort Lauderdale, FL. (ERIC Document Reproduction Service).

Kirsch, I. S., & Jungeblut, A. (1986). *Literacy: Profiles of America's young adults.* Princeton, NJ: National Assessment of Educational Progress.

Kleiner, A., & Lewis, L. (2003). *Internet access in U. S. public schools and classrooms: 1994–2002.* National Center for Educational Statistics 2004-011. Retrieved Dec. 14, 2004, from *http://nces.ed.gov*

Kletzein, S. B. (1991). Strategy use by good and poor comprehenders reading expository text of differing reading levels. *Reading Research Quarterly, 26,* 67–86.

Klinger, J. K., & Vaughn, S. (1999). Promoting reading comprehension, content learning, and English acquisition through collaborative strategic reading. *The Reading Teacher, 52*(7), 738–747.

Knobel, M. (2001). "I'm not a pencil man": How one student challenges our notions of literacy "failure" in school. *Journal of Adolescent & Adult Literacy, 44*(5), 404–414.

Knowles, M. S. (1980). *The modern practice of adult education: From pedagogy to andragogy.* New York: Cambridge Books.

Knowlton, D. S., & Knowlton, H. M. (2001). The context and content of online discussions: Making cyber-discussions viable for the secondary school curriculum. *American Secondary Education, 29*(4), 38–52.

Kolozow, L. V., & Lehmann, J. (1982). *College reading strategies for success.* Englewood Cliffs, NJ: Prentice-Hall.

Konopak, B. C. (1988). Using contextual information for word learning. *Journal of Reading, 31,* 334–338.

Konopak, B. C., & Williams, N. L. (1994). Elementary teachers' beliefs and decisions about vocabulary learning and instruction. *Multidimensional aspects of literacy research, theory, and practice.* National Reading Council, 43rd Yearbook, 485–493.

Koskinen, P., et al. (1999). Shared reading, books, and audiotapes: Supporting diverse students in school and at home. *The Reading Teacher, 52*(5), 430–444.

Kotulak, R. (1996). *Inside the brain: Revolutionary discoveries of how the mind works.* Kansas City, MO: Andrews and McNally.

Kowalski, T. (1995). Chasing the wolves from the schoolhouse door. *Phi Delta Kappan, 76,* 486–489.

Krashen, S. (1982). *Principles and practices in second language acquisition.* New York: Pergamon Press.

Krashen, S. (1989). *Language acquisition and language education.* Englewood Cliffs, NJ: Prentice-Hall.

Krathwohl, D. R., Bloom, B. S., & Masia, B. B. (1964). *Taxonomy of educational objectives: Handbook II: Affective domain.* New York: David McKay.

Laffey, J., & Morgan, R. (1983). *Successful interactions in reading and language: A practical handbook for subject matter teachers.* Harrisonburg, VA: Feygan.

Laing, S. P., & Kamhi, A. G. (2002). The use of think-aloud protocols to compare inferencing abilities in average and below-average readers. *Journal of Learning Disabilities, 35*(5), 436–448.

Lambiotte, J. G., & Dansereau, D. F. (1992). Effects of knowledge maps and prior knowledge on recall of science lecture content. *The Journal of Experimental Education, 60,* 189–201.

Langer, J. (1981). From theory to practice: A prereading plan. *Journal of Reading, 25,* 152–156.

Langer, J. (2001). Beating the odds: Teaching middle and high school students to read and write well. *American Educational Research Journal, 38,* 837–880.

Lankutis, T. (2001). Reaching the struggling reader. *Technology and Learning, 21*(10), 24–30.

Larson, C., & Dansereau, D. (1986). Cooperative learning in dyads. *Journal of Reading, 29,* 516–520.

Last, D., O'Donnell, A. M., & Kelly, A. E. (1998). *Using hypermedia: Effects of prior knowledge and goal strength.* Paper presented at the annual meeting of the Society for Information Technology in Teacher Education, Washington, DC.

Lauber, P. (1995). *Who eats what? Food chains and food webs.* New York: Harper Collins.

Lederer, J. M. (2000). Reciprocal teaching of social studies in inclusive elementary classrooms. *Journal of Learning Disabilities, 33*(1), 91.

Lederer, R. (1987). *Anguished English.* New York: Dell/Bantam Doubleday.

Lee, J., & Schallert, D. (1997). The relative contribution of L2 language proficiency and L1 reading ability to L2 reading performance: A test of the threshold hypothesis. *TESOL Quarterly, 31,* 713–739.

Lee, P., & Allen, G. (1981). *Training junior high LD students to use a test-taking strategy* (Eric Document No. ED 217 649).

Lee, S., Stigler, J. W., & Stevenson, H. W. (1986). Beginning reading in Chinese and English. In B. Foorman and A. W. Siegel (Eds.), *Acquisition of reading skills* (pp. 123–149). Hillsdale, NJ: Erlbaum.

Lee, V. E., & Smith, J. B. (1994). *Effects of high school restructuring and size on gains in achievement and engagement for early secondary school students.* Madison, WI: Document Service, Wisconsin Center for Education Research.

Leinhardt, G., Stainton, C., & Bausmith, J. M. (1998). Constructing maps cooperatively. *Journal of Geography, 97*(1), 19–30.

Leki, I. (1992). *Understanding ESL writers: A guide for teachers.* Portsmouth, NH: Heinemann.

Leki, I. (2001). "A narrow thinking system": Nonnative-English-speaking students in group projects across the curriculum. *TESOL Quarterly, 35*(1), 39–67.

Lemkuhl, M. (2002, May). Pen-pal letters: The cross-curricular experience. *The Reading Teacher, 55*(8), 720–722. Retrieved Dec. 12, 2004, from *http://www.readingonline.org/electronic/elec_index.asp?HREF=/electronic/RWT/lemkuhl/index.html*

Leonard, J., & McElroy, K. (2000). What one middle school teacher learned about cooperative learning. *Journal of Research in Childhood Education, 14*(2), 239.

Lester, J. H., & Cheek, E. H., Jr. (1998). The "real" experts address the textbook issues. *Journal of Adolescent & Adult Literacy, 41*(4), 282–291.

Leu, D. J., Jr. (1997). Caity's question: Literacy as deixis on the Internet. *The Reading Teacher, 51*(1), 62–67.

Leu, D. J., Jr. (2000). Literacy and technology: Deictic consequences for literacy education in an information age. In M. L. Kamil, P. B. Mosenthal, P. D. Pearson, & R. Barr (Eds.), *Handbook of reading research: Vol. III* (pp. 743–770). Mahwah, NJ: Erlbaum.

Leu, D. J., Castek, J., Henry, L. A., Coiro, J., & McMullan, M. (2004). The lessons that children teach us: Integrating children's reading and the new literacies of the Internet. *The Reading Teacher, 57*(5), 496–504.

Leu, D. J., Jr., Karchmer, R., & Leu, D. D. (1999). Exploring literacy on the Internet. *The Reading Teacher, 52*(6), 636–642.

Leu, D. J., Jr., & Leu, D. D. (1999). *Teaching with the Internet: Lesson from the classroom.* Norwood, MA: Christopher Gordon.

Levin, H. M. (1988). Accelerating elementary education for disadvantaged students. In D. W. Hornbeck (Ed.), *School success for at-risk youth: Analysis and recommendations of the Council of Chief State School Officers* (pp. 209–226). Orlando, FL: Harcourt Brace Jovanovich.

Levin, J. R. (1993). Mnemonic strategies and classroom learning: A 20-year report card. *Elementary School Journal, 94,* 235–244.

Levin, J. R., Levin, M. E., Glassman, L. D., & Nordwall, M. B. (1992). Mnemonic vocabulary instruction: Additional effectiveness evidence. *Contemporary Educational Psychology, 17,* 156–174.

Levin, J. R., Morrison, C. R., & McGivern, J. E. (1986). Mnemonic facilitation of text-embedded science facts. *American Educational Research Journal, 23,* 489–506.

Lin, L. M., Zabrucky, K., & Moore, D. (1997). The relations among interest, self-assessment comprehension, and comprehension performance in young adults. *Reading Research and Instruction, 36*(2), 127–139.

Lindfors, J. W. (1980). *Children's language and learning.* Englewood Cliffs, NJ: Prentice-Hall.

Linn, R., Baker, E., & Dunbar, S. (1991). Complex, performance-based assessment: Expectations and validation criteria. *Educational Researcher, 20*(8), 15–21.

Lipsitz, J. (1995). Why we should care about caring. *Phi Delta Kappan, 76,* 665–666.

Lipson, M. Y., & Wixson, K. K. (2003). *Assessment and instruction of reading and writing disability* (3rd ed.). New York: Longman.

Loschert, K. (2003). High-tech teaching. *Tomorrow's Teachers, 9,* 2–5.

Lovitt, T. C., Horton, S. V., & Bergerud, D. (1987). Matching students with textbooks: An alternative to readability formulas and standard tests. *British Columbia Journal of Special Education, 11,* 49–55.

Lowery, L. F. (1998). *The biological basis for thinking and learning* (monograph). Berkeley, CA: Lawrence Hall of Science.

Lowry, L. (1989). *Number the stars.* Boston: Houghton Mifflin.

Lu, M., Webb, J. M., Krus, D. J., & Fox, L. S. (1999). Using order analytic instructional hierarchies of mnemonics to facilitate learning Chinese and Japanese Kanji characters. *The Journal of Experimental Education, 67*(4), 293.

Lund, J. (1997). Authentic assessment: Its development and applications. *JOPERD—The Journal of Physical Education, Recreation, and Dance, 68*(7), 25.

Lynch-Brown, C., & Tomlinson, C. M. (1993). *Essentials of children's literature.* Boston: Allyn & Bacon.

Macan, H. T., Shahani, C., Dipboye, R. L., & Phillips, A. P. (1990). College students' time management: Correlations with academic performance and stress. *Journal of Educational Psychology, 82,* 760–768.

MacDonald, J. (1986). Self-generated questions and reading recall: Does training help? *Contemporary Educational Psychology, 11,* 290–304.

Mace, S. (1981). Minnesota's MECC educates next generation of computer users. *InfoWorld,* Dec. 7.

MacLean, P. (1978). A mind of three minds: Educating the triune brain. In J. Chall and A. Mirsley (Eds.), *Education and the brain* (pp. 308–342). Chicago: University of Chicago Press.

Magoon, A. J. (1977). Constructivist approaches in educational research. *Review of Educational Research, 47*(4), 651–693.

Mahler, W. R. (1995). Practice what you preach. *The Reading Teacher, 48,* 414–415.

Manzo, A. V. (1969). The ReQuest procedure. *Journal of Reading, 11,* 123–126.

Manzo, A. V. (1975). The guided reading procedure. *Journal of Reading, 18,* 287–291.

Marashio, P. (1995). Designing questions to help students peel back the layers of a text. *Interdisciplinary Humanities, 12*(1), 27–31.

Maria, K., & Junge, K. (1993). *A comparison of fifth graders' comprehension and retention of scientific information using a science textbook and an informal storybook.* Paper presented at the annual meeting of the National Reading Conference, Charleston, SC.

Maria, K., & MacGinitie, W. (1987). Learning from texts that refute the readers' prior knowledge. *Reading Research and Instruction, 26,* 222–238.

Maroney, S. A. (1990). Step by step. *Instructor, 110*(2), 101–102.

Martin, A. (2002). *Australian Journal of Education, 46*(16), 34.

Martin, N., D'Arcy, P., Newton, B., & Parker, R. (1976). *Writing and learning across the curriculum.* Montclair, NJ: Boynton/Cook.

Martin, S. H., & Martin, M. A. (2001). Using literature response activities to build strategic reading for students with reading difficulties. *Reading Improvement, 38*(2), 85–94.

Mason, J. M., & Au, K. H. (1990). *Reading instruction for today.* Glenview, IL: Scott, Foresman.

Massey, D. D., & Heafner, T. L. (2004). Promoting reading comprehension in social studies. *Journal of Adolescent & Adult Literacy, 48*(1), 26–40.

Mastropieri, M. A., Scruggs, T. E., & Butcher, K. (1997). How effective is inquiry learning for students with mild disabilities? *Journal of Special Education, 31*(2), 199–211.

Mathewson, G. (1976). The function of attitudes in the reading process. In H. Singer and R. Ruddell (Eds.), *Theoretical models and processes of reading* (pp. 908–919). Newark, DE: International Reading Association.

Maurer, M. M., & Davidson, G. (1999). Technology, children, and the power of the heart. *Phi Delta Kappan, 80*(6), 458–461.

Maxwell, R. (1996). *Writing across the curriculum in the middle and high schools.* Boston: Allyn & Bacon.

May, F. B. (1990). *Reading as communication: An interactive approach.* Columbus, OH: Merrill.

McAndrew, D. A. (1983). Underlining and note taking: Some suggestions from research. *Journal of Reading, 27*, 103–108.

McCombs, B. L. (1986). The role of the self-system in self-regulated learning. *Contemporary Educational Psychology, 11*, 314–332.

McConkie, G. W., & Rayner, K. (1976). Asymmetry of the perceptual span in reading. *Bulletin of the Psychometric Society, 8*, 365–368.

McCrindle, A. R., & Christensen, C. A. (1995). The impact of learning journals on metacognitive and cognitive processes and learning performance. *Learning and Instruction, 5*, 167–185.

McDonald, S., & Stevenson, R. J. (1998). Effects of text structure and prior knowledge of the learner on navigation in hypertext. *Human Factors, 40*(1), 18–28.

McGivern, J. E., & Levin, J. R. (1983). The keyword method and children's vocabulary learning: An interaction with vocabulary knowledge. *Contemporary Educational Psychology, 8*(1), 46–54.

McInnes, A., Humphries, T., Hogg-Johnson, S., & Tannock, R. (2003). Listening comprehension and working memory are impaired in attention-deficit hyperactivity disorder irrespective of language impairment. *Journal of Abnormal Child Psychology, 31*(4), 427–444.

McKeachie, W. J. (2002). *McKeachie's teaching tips: Strategies, research, and theory for college and university teachers* (11th ed.) Boston: Houghton Mifflin.

McKenna, M. C., & Kear, D. J. (1990). Measuring attitude toward reading: A new tool for teachers. *The Reading Teacher, 43*, 626–639.

McKeown, M. G., & Beck, I. L. (2003). Taking advantage of read-alouds to help children make sense of decontextualized language. In A. van Kleeck, S. A. Stahl, & E. B. Bauer (Eds.), *On reading books to children* (pp. 159–176). Mahwah, NJ: Erlbaum.

McKeown, M. G., Bede, I. L., & Worthy, J. (1992). *Engaging students with text.* Paper presented at the annual meeting of the National Reading Association Conference, San Antonio, TX.

McLaughlin, H. (1969). SMOG grading—a new readability formula. *Journal of Reading, 12*, 639–646.

McMillan, J. H., & Reed, D. F. (1994). Resilient at-risk students: Students' views about why they succeed. *Journal of At-Risk Issues, 1*, 27–33.

McMurray, M., Laffey, J., & Morgan, R. (1979). *College students' word identification strategies.* Clemson, SC: Twenty-eighth Yearbook of the National Reading Conference.

McPeck, J. (1981). *Critical thinking and education.* New York: St. Martin's Press.

McQuillan, J. (1998). *The literacy crisis: False claims, real solutions.* Portsmouth, NH: Heinemann.

McWilliams, L., & Rakes, T. (1979). *The content inventories.* Dubuque, IA: Kendall/Hunt.

Mealey, D., & Konopak, B. (1990). Content area vocabulary instruction: Is preteaching worth the effort? *Reading: Exploration and Discovery, 13*(1), 39–42.

Medo, M. A., & Ryder, R. J. (1993). The effects of vocabulary instruction on readers' ability to make causal connections. *Reading Research and Instruction, 33*(2), 119–134.

Meeks, J., & Morgan, R. (1978). New use for the cloze procedure: Interaction in imagery. *Reading Horizons, 18*, 261–264.

Meeks, J. W. (1991). Prior knowledge and metacognitive processes of reading comprehension: Applications to mildly retarded readers. *Advances in Mental Retardation and Developmental Disabilities, 4*, 121–142.

Meloth, M. S., & Deering, P. D. (1992). Effects of two cooperative conditions on peer-group discussions, reading comprehension, and metacognition. *Contemporary Educational Psychology, 17*, 175–193.

Memory, D. M. (1990). Teaching technical vocabulary: Before, during, or after reading assignment? *Journal of Reading Behavior, 22*, 39–53.

Menke, D. J., & Pressley, M. (1994). Elaborative interrogation: Using "why" questions to enhance the learning from text. *Journal of Reading, 37*(8), 642–645.

Merkley, D. J., Schmidt, D. A., & Allen, G. (2001). Addressing the English language arts technology standard in a secondary reading methodology course. *Journal of Adolescent & Adult Literacy, 45*(3), 220–231.

Metzger, M. (1989). *Voices from the Civil War.* New York: Crowell.

Mevarech, Z. R. (1999). Effects of metacognitive training embedded in cooperative settings on mathematical problem solving. *Journal of Educational Research, 92*(4), 195.

Meyer, B. J. F., Brandt, D. M., & Bluth, G. J. (1980). Use of top-level structure in text: Key for reading comprehension of ninth grade students. *Reading Research Quarterly, 16,* 72–103.

Miklos, J. (1982). A look at reading achievement in the United States. *Journal of Reading, 25,* 760–762.

Mikulecky, L., Shanklin, N., & Caverly, D. (1979). Mikulecky behavioral reading attitude measure. In *Adult reading habits, attitudes, and motivations: A cross-sectional study.* Bloomington: Indiana University, School of Education.

Minicucci, C., Berman, P., McLaughlin, B., McLeod, B., Nelson, B., & Woodworth, K. (1995). School reform and school diversity. *Phi Delta Kappan, 77,* 77–80.

Miyake, N., & Norman, D. (1979). To ask a question, one must know enough to know what is not known. *Journal of Verbal Learning and Verbal Behavior, 18,* 357–364.

Moats, L. C. (2001). When older students can't read. *Educational Leadership, 58*(6), 36–40.

Moffett, J. (1979). Integrity in the teaching of writing. *Phi Delta Kappan, 61,* 276–279.

Mohr, K. A. J. (2004). English as an accelerated language: A call to action for reading teachers. *The Reading Teacher, 58*(1), 18–26.

Mokhtari, K., & Reichard, C. A. (2002). Assessing students' metacognitive awareness of reading strategies. *Journal of Educational Psychology, 94*(2), 249–259.

Montague, M., & Applegate, B. (2000). Middle school students' perceptions, persistence, and performance in mathematical problem solving. *Learning Disabilities Quarterly, 23*(3), 215–228.

Moore, D., & Arthur, S. V. (1981). Possible sentences. In E. K. Dishner, T. W. Bean, & J. E. Readance (Eds.), *Reading in the content areas: Improving classroom instruction.* Dubuque, IA: Kendall/Hunt.

Moore, D., Moore, S. A., Cunningham, P., & Cunningham, J. (1998). *Developing readers and writers in the content areas K–12.* New York: Longman.

Moore, D., & Murphy, A. (1987). Selection of materials. In D. Alvermann, D. Moore, & M. Conley (Eds.), *Research within reach: Secondary school reading* (pp. 94–108). Newark, DE: International Reading Association.

Moore, J. C., & Surber, J. R. (1992). Effects of context and keyword methods on second language vocabulary acquisition. *Contemporary Educational Psychology, 17,* 286–292.

Moravcsik, J. E., & Kintsch, W. (1993). Writing ability, reading skills, and domain knowledge as factors in text comprehension. *Canadian Journal of Experimental Psychology, 47,* 360–374.

Morgan, R., & Culver, V. (1978). Locus of control and reading achievement: Applications for the classroom. *Journal of Reading, 21,* 403–408.

Morgan, R., Otto, A., & Thompson, G. (1976). A study of the readability and comprehension of selected eighth grade social studies textbooks. *Perceptual and Motor Skills, 43,* 594.

Morgan, R. F., Forget, M. A., & Antinarella, J. C. (1996). *Reading for success: A school to work approach.* Cincinnati, OH: South-Western.

Morgan, R. F., Meeks, J. W., Schollaert, A., & Paul, J. (1986). *Critical reading/thinking skills for the college student.* Dubuque, IA: Kendall/Hunt.

Morgan, W., & Beaumont, G. (2003). A dialogic approach to argumentation: Using a chat room to develop early adolescent students' argumentative writing. *Journal of Adolescent & Adult Literacy, 47*(2), 146–157.

Morrison, J. L. (1999). The role of technology in education today and tomorrow: An interview with Kenneth Green. *On The Horizon, 7*(1) 1–4.

Morrison, T. G., Jacobs, J. S., & Swinyard, W. R. (1999). Do teachers who read personally use recommended literacy practices in their classrooms? *Reading Research and Instruction, 38*(2), 81–100.

Mosenthal, P. B., & Kirsch, I. S. (1998). A new measure for assessing document complexity: The PMOSE/IKIRSCH document readability formula. *Journal of Adolescent & Adult Literacy, 41*(8), 638–657.

Moss, B., & Hendershot, J. (2002). Exploring sixth graders' selection of nonfiction trade books. *The Reading Teacher, 56,* 6–17.

Moss, J. (1990). *Focus units in literature: A handbook for elementary school teachers* (2nd ed.). Urbana, IL: National Council of Teachers of English.

Muller-Kalthoff, T., & Moller, J. (2003). The effects of graphical overviews, prior knowledge, and self-concept on hypertext disorientation and learning achievement. *Journal of Educational Multimedia and Hypermedia, 12*(2), 117–135.

Murray, D. (1982). *Learning by teaching.* Montclair, NJ: Boynton/Cook.

Murray, J. (2002). Creating placement tests. *ESL Magazine Online.* Retrieved Nov. 26, 2004, from *http://eslmag.com/modules.php?name=News&file=article&sid=30*

Muth, K. D. (1987). Structure strategies for comprehending expository text. *Reading Research and Instruction, 27,* 66–72.

Myers, J. W. (1984). *Writing to learn across the curriculum.* Bloomington, IN: Phi Delta Kappa.

Myers, P. (1998). Passion for poetry. *Journal of Adolescent & Adult Literacy, 41*(4), 262–271.

Myklebust, H. (1965). *Development and disorders of written language.* New York: Grune and Stratton.

Nagy, W., Herman, P., & Anderson, R. C. (1985). Learning words from context. *Reading Research Quarterly, 20,* 233–253.

Nagy, W., & Scott, J. A. (2000). Vocabulary processes. In M. Kamil, P. Mosenthal, P. D. Pearson, & R. Barr (Eds.), *Handbook of reading research: Vol. III* (pp. 269–284). Mahwah, NJ: Erlbaum.

Nagy, W., & Stahl, S. (2000). *Promoting vocabulary development.* Austin: Texas Education Agency.

Nagy, W. E. (1988). *Teaching vocabulary to improve reading comprehension.* Newark, DE: International Reading Association.

National Assessment of Educational Progress. (1998). Denver, CO: Education Commission of the States.

National Assessment of Educational Progress's (NAEP) *The Reading Report Card* (2003). Retrieved on Nov. 15, 2004, from *http://nces.ed.gov/nations reportcard/reading/*

National Center for Education Statistics. (1996). *Reading literacy in the United States: Findings from the IEA reading literacy study.* Washington, DC: U. S. Department of Education.

National Center for Education Statistics. (1999). *Digest of educational statistics, 1998.* Washington, DC: U. S. Department of Education.

National Center for Education Statistics. (2001). *Early childhood longitudinal study, kindergarten class of 1998–99.* U. S. Department of Education. Retrieved Sept. 9, 2004, from *http://www.ed.gov/programs/coe/2003/charts/chart36/asp*

National Center for Education Statistics. (2003). *The nation's report card: Reading highlights, 2003.* U.S. Department of Education, NCES 2004-452.+

National Center for Education Statistics. (2004). Learner outcomes: Academic outcomes: Indicator 10: Writing performance of students in grades 4, 8, and 12. *The condition of education.* Retrieved Nov. 27, 2004, from *http://nces.ed.gov/programs/coe/2004/section2/indicator10.asp*

National Clearinghouse for Bilingual Education. (2002). Rate of LEP growth in the United States. Retrieved Sept. 9, 2004, from *http://www.ncbe.gwu.edu*

National Commission on Excellence in Education. (1983). *A nation at risk: The imperative report to the nation and the secretary of education.* Washington, DC: U. S. Government Printing Office.

National Council of Teachers of English. (1996). *Standards for the English language arts.* Urbana, IL: National Council of Teachers of English and International Reading Association.

National Council of Teachers of Mathematics. (2000). *High-stakes testing.* Reston, VA: NCTM. Retrieved Sept. 9, 2004, from *http://www.nctm.org/position_statements/highstakes.htm*

National Reading Panel. (2000). *Teaching children to read: An evidence-based assessment of the scientific research literature on reading and its implications for reading instruction.* Washington, DC: National Institute of Child Health and Human Development.

Neckerman, K. M., & Wilson, W. J. (1988). In D. W. Hornbeck (Ed.), *School success for at-risk youth: Analysis and recommendations of the Council of Chief State School Officers* (pp. 25–44). Orlando, FL: Harcourt Brace Jovanovich.

Nessel, D. (1987). Reading comprehension: Asking the right questions. *Phi Delta Kappan, 68,* 442–445.

Nettle D., & Romaine, S. (2000). *Vanishing voices: The extinction of the world's languages.* New York: Oxford University Press.

Neuman, S. (1991). *Literacy in the television age: The myth of the TV effect.* Norwood, NJ: Ablex.

Neuman, S. B., & Celano, D. (2001). Access to print in low-income and middle income communities: An ecological study of four neighborhoods. *Reading Research Quarterly, 36*(1) 8–26.

Newman, J. M. (2000). Following the yellow brick road. *Phi Delta Kappan, 81,* 774–779.

Nodding, N. (1995). Teaching themes of caring. *Phi Delta Kappan, 76*(9), 675–679.

Noll, E., & Watkins, R. (2003). The impact of homelessness on children's literacy experiences. *The Reading Teacher, 57*(4), 362–371.

Nuthall, G. (1999). The way students learn: Acquiring knowledge from an integrated science and social studies unit. *Elementary School Journal, 99*(4), 303.

O'Brien, R. (1971). *Mrs. Frisby and the rats of NIMH.* New York: Atheneum.

O'Dell, Scott. (1987). *The serpent never sleeps.* New York: Ballantine.

O'Donnell, P., Weber, K. P., & McLaughlin, T. F. (2003). Improving correct and error rate and reading comprehension using key words and previewing: A case report with a language minority student. *Education & Treatment of Children, 26*(3) 237–255.

Ogle, D. (1986). KWL: A teaching model that develops active reading of expository text. *The Reading Teacher, 39,* 564–570.

Ogle, D. (1992). KWL in action: Secondary teachers find applications that work. In E. K. Dishner, T. W. Bean, J. E. Readance, & D. W. Moore (Eds.), *Reading in the content areas: Improving classroom instruction* (3rd ed., pp. 270–281). Dubuque, IA: Kendall/Hunt.

Olshavsky, J. (1975). Reading as problem solving: An investigation of strategies. *Reading Research Quarterly, 12,* 654–674.

Olson, M. W., & Gee, T. (1991). Content reading instruction in the primary grades: Perceptions and strategies. *The Reading Teacher, 45,* 298–307.

Opitz, M. (1992). The cooperative reading activity: An alternative to ability grouping. *The Reading Teacher, 45,* 736–738.

Oppenheimer, T. (2003). *The flickering mind: False promise of technology in the classroom and how learning can be saved.* New York: Random House.

Orfield, A. (1988). Race, income, and educational inequity. In *School success for at-risk youth: Analysis and recommendations of the Council of Chief State School Officers* (pp. 45–71). Orlando, FL: Harcourt Brace Jovanovich.

Page, B. (1987). From passive receivers to active learners in English. In J. Self (Ed.), *Plain talk about learning and writing across the curriculum* (pp. 37–50). Richmond: Virginia Department of Education.

Palincsar, A. S., & Brown, A. L. (1986). Interactive teaching to promote independent learning from text. *The Reading Teacher, 39,* 771–777.

Pallas, A. M., Natriello, G., & McDill, E. L. (1989). Changing nature of the disadvantaged population: Current dimensions and future trends. *Educational Researcher, 18,* 16–22.

Pally, M. (1998). Film studies drive literacy development for ESL university students. *Journal of Adolescent & Adult Literacy, 41*(8), 620–628.

Palmer, P. J. (1998). *The courage to teach.* San Francisco: Jossey-Bass.

Pang, V. O., Colvin, C., Tran, M. Y., & Barba, R. H. (1992). Beyond chopsticks and dragons: Selecting Asian-American literature for children. *Journal of Reading, 46,* 216–223.

Paris, S. G. (1986). Teaching children to guide their reading and learning. In T. E. Raphael and R. Reynolds (Eds.), *Context of literacy* (pp. 115–130). New York: Longman.

Paris, S. G., Cross, D. R., & Lipson, M. Y. (1984). Informal strategies for learning: A program to improve children's reading awareness and comprehension. *Journal of Educational Psychology, 76,* 1239–1252.

Paris, S. G., Lipson, M. Y., & Wixson, K. K. (1983). Becoming a strategic reader. *Contemporary Educational Psychology, 8,* 393–396.

Paris, S. G., & Oka, E. R. (1989). Strategies for comprehending text and coping with reading difficulties. *Learning Disability Quarterly, 12,* 32–42.

Paris, S. G., & Winograd, P. (1990). How metacognition can promote academic learning and instruction. In B. Jones and L. Idol (Eds.), *Dimensions of thinking and cognitive instruction* (pp. 15–52). Hillsdale, NJ: Erlbaum.

Parker, W. C. (1991). Achieving thinking and decision-making objectives in social studies. In J. P. Shaver (Ed.), *Handbook of research on social studies teaching and learning.* New York: Macmillan.

Parnes, S. J., & Noller, R. B. (1973). *Toward supersanity: Channeled freedom.* East Aurora, NY: D. O. K.

Patterson, J. H. (2001, Spring). Raising resilience in classrooms and homes. *Childhood Education, 77*(3), 180.

Pauk, W. (1997). *How to study in college* (6th ed.). Boston: Houghton Mifflin.

Paul, D. G. (2004). The train has left: The No Child Left Behind Act leaves black and Latino literacy learners waiting at the station. *Journal of Adolescent & Adult Literacy, 47*(8), 647–656.

Paulsen, G. (1990). *Canyons.* New York: Delacorte Press.

Pearce, D. (1983). Guidelines for the use and evaluation of writing in content classrooms. *Journal of Reading, 17,* 212–218.

Pearce, D. (1987). Group writing activities: A useful strategy for content teachers. *Middle School Journal, 18,* 24–25.

Pearce, D., & Bader, L. (1984). Writing in content area classrooms. *Reading World, 23,* 234–241.

Pearce, D., & Davison, D. (1988). Teacher use of writing in the junior high mathematics classroom. *School Science and Mathematics, 88,* 6–15.

Pearson, P. D. (1985). Changing the face of reading comprehension. *The Reading Teacher, 38,* 724–738.

Pearson, P. D., & Johnson, D. (1978). *Teaching reading comprehension.* New York: Holt, Rinehart and Winston.

Pearson, P. D., & Santa, C. M. (1995). Students as researchers of their own learning. *Journal of Reading, 38,* 462–469.

Pearson, P. D., & Stephens, D. (1994). Learning about literacy: A 30-year journey. In R. Ruddell, M. Ruddell, & H. Singer (Eds.), *Theoretical models and processes of reading* (pp. 22–43). Newark, DE: International Reading Association.

Pearson, P. D., & Tierney, R. (1983). In search of a model of instructional research in reading. In S. Paris, G. Okon, & H. Stevenson (Eds.), *Learning and motivation in the classroom.* Hillsdale, NJ: Erlbaum.

Pellicano, R. (1987). At-risk: A view of "social advantage." *Educational Leadership, 44,* 47–50.

Penfield, W. (1975). *The mystery of the mind: A critical study of consciousness and the human brain.* Princeton, NJ: Princeton University Press.

Peregoy, S., & Boyle, O. (1997). *Reading, writing, and learning in ESL: A resource book for K–12 teachers.* White Plains, NY: Longman.

Perez, S. A., & Strickland, D. (1987). Teaching children how to discuss what they read. *Reading Horizons, 27,* 89–94.

Peters, E. E., & Levin, J. R. (1986). Effects of a mnemonic imagery strategy on good and poor readers' prose recall. *Reading Research Quarterly, 21,* 179–192.

Peterson, S. E., & Miller, J. A. (2004). Comparing the quality of students' experiences during cooperative learning and large-group instruction. *Journal of Educational Research, 97*(3), 123–134.

Piaget, J. (1952). *The language and thought of the child.* London: Routledge and Kegan Paul.

Piaget, J. (1963). *The origin of intelligence in children.* New York: Norton.

Piaget, J., & Inhelder, B. (1969). *The psychology of the child.* New York: Basic Books.

Pinnell, G. S., & Jaggar, A. M. (1991). Oral language: Speaking and listening in the classroom. In J. Flood, J. Jensen, D. Lapp, & R. J. Squire (Eds.), *Handbook of research on teaching the English language arts.* Urbana, IL: National Council of Teachers of English; Newark, DE: International Reading Association.

Pittleman, S. D., Heimlich, J. E., Berglund, R. L., & French, M. P. (1991). *Semantic feature analysis.* Newark, DE: International Reading Association.

Pope, C., & Praeter, D. L. (1990). Writing proficiency and student use of prewriting/invention strategies. *Reading Research and Instruction, 29*(4), 64–70.

President's Information Technology Advisory Committee (2002). *Using information technology to transform the way we learn.* Retrieved on Mar. 14, 2003, from http://www.hpcc.gov/ac/

Pressley, M. (2002, September). Comprehension instruction: What makes sense now, what might make sense soon. *Reading Online, 5*(2). Retrieved Jul. 30, 2004, from http://www.readingonline.org/articles/art_index.asp?HREF=/articles/handbook/pressley/index.htm

Pressley, M., & Schneider, W. (1997). *Introduction to memory development during childhood and adolescence.* Mahwah, NJ: Erlbaum.

Pressley, M., Wharton-McDonald, R., Hampson, J., & Echevarria, M. (1998). The nature of literacy instruction in ten fourth and fifth grade classrooms in upstate New York. *Scientific Studies in Reading, 2,* 159–194.

Pulido, D. (2004, September). The effect of cultural familiarity on incidental vocabulary acquisition through reading. *The Reading Matrix, 4*(2). Retrieved Apr. 1, 2004, from http://www.readingmatrix.com/articles/pulido/article.pdf

Purcell-Gates, V., Degener, S. C., Jacobson, E., & Soler, M. (2002). Impact of adult literacy instruction on adult literacy practices. *Reading Research Quarterly, 37,* 70–92.

Purdie, N., & Hattie, J. (1999). The relationship between study skills and learning outcomes: A meta-analysis. *Australian Journal of Education, 43*(1), 72.

Purkey, W. W., & Novak, J. M. (1984). *Inviting school success: A self-concept approach to teaching and learning* (2nd ed.). Belmont, CA: Wadsworth.

Purohit, K. D. (1998). What matters most in my science class. *Voices from the middle, 6*(1), 26–29.

Purves, A. C., & Bech, R. (1972). *Literature and the reader: Research in response to literature, reading interests, and the teaching of literature.* Urbana, IL: National Council of Teachers of English.

Quirk, M. P., & Schwanenflugel, P. J. (2004). Do supplemental remedial reading programs address the motivational issues of struggling readers? An analysis of five popular programs. *Reading Research and Instruction, 43*(3), 1–19.

Radencich, M. (1985). Writing a class novel: A strategy for LD students? *Academic Therapy, 20,* 599–603.

Rakes, G. C., Rakes, T. A., & Smith, L. J. (1995). Using visuals to enhance secondary students' reading comprehension of expository texts. *Journal of Adolescent & Adult Literacy, 39,* 46–54.

Rakes, T., & Chance, L. (1990). A survey of how subjects remember what they read. *Reading Improvement, 27,* 122–128.

Ralph, J., Keller, D., & Crouse, J. (1994). How effective are American schools? *Phi Delta Kappan, 76,* 144–150.

Raphael, T. (1984). Teaching learners about sources of information for answering comprehension questions. *Journal of Reading, 27,* 303–311.

Raphael, T. (1986). Teaching question/answer relationships, revisited. *The Reading Teacher, 39,* 516–522.

Rasinski, T. V., & Padak, N. D. (1993). *Inquiries in literacy learning and instruction: Fifteenth yearbook of the College Reading Association.* Kent, OH: Kent State University.

Raths, L., Wassermann, S., Jones, A., & Rothstein, A. (1986). *Teaching for thinking: Theories, strategies, and activities for the classroom.* New York: Teachers College Press.

Raven, J. (1992). A model of competence, motivation, and behavior, and a paradigm for assessment. In H. Berlak et al. (Eds.), *Toward a new science of educational testing and assessment.* New York: State University of New York Press.

Rayner, K. (1978). Eye movements in reading and information processing. *Psychological Bulletin, 85,* 616–660.

Readance, J. E., Bean, T. W., & Baldwin, R. S. (1981). *Content area reading: An integrated approach.* Dubuque, IA: Kendall/Hunt.

Reed, D. F., McMillan, J. H., & McBee, R. H. (1995). Defying the odds: Middle schoolers in high risk circumstances who succeed. *Middle School Journal, 27,* 3–10.

Reinking, D. (1997). Me and my hypertext:) A multiple regression analysis of technology and literacy (sic). *The Reading Teacher, 50*(8), 626–643.

Reinking, D., & Pardon, D. (1995). Television and literacy. In T.V. Rasinski (Ed.), *Parents and teachers helping children learn to read and write* (pp. 137–145). Ft. Worth, TX: Harcourt Brace.

Reinking, D., & Wu, J. H. (1990). Reexamining the research on television and reading. *Reading Research and Instruction, 29,* 30–43.

Rekrut, M. D. (1997). Collaborative research. *Journal of Adolescent & Adult Literacy, 41*(1), 26–34.

Rekrut, M. D. (1999). Using the Internet in classroom instruction: A primer for teachers. *Journal of Adolescent & Adult Literacy, 42*(7), 546–557.

Restak, R. (1979). *The brain: The last frontier.* Garden City, NY: Doubleday.

Restak, R. (1982). The brain. *Wilson Quarterly, 6,* 89–115.

Restak, R. (1984). *The brain.* New York: Bantam Books.

Reutzel, D. R., & Daines, D. (1987). The text-relatedness of reading lessons in seven basal reading series. *Reading Research and Instruction, 27,* 26–35.

Reyes, D. J. (1986). Critical thinking in elementary social studies text series. *Social Studies, 77,* 151–157.

Reyhner, J., & Garcia, R. L. (1989). Helping minorities read better: Problems and promises. *Reading Research and Instruction, 28,* 84–91.

Reynolds, R. E., Sinatra, G. M., & Jetton, T. L. (1996). Views of knowledge acquisition and representation: A continuum from experience centered to mind centered. *Educational Psychologist, 21,* 93–104.

Rhodes, J. A., Robnolt, V. J., & Richardson, J. S. (2005). *Study skills in the electronic age.* College Reading Association Yearbook. In press.

Rhodes, L. K., & Shanklin, N. (1991). *Windows into literacy: Assessing learners K–8.* Portsmouth, NH: Heinemann.

Rhodes, R. (1990, October 14). Don't be a bystander. *Parade,* 4–7.

Rice, G. E. (1992, April). *The need for explanations in graphic organizer research.* Paper presented at the annual meeting of the American Educational Research Association, San Francisco.

Richardson, J. (1975). *A study of the syntactic competence of adult beginning readers.* Unpublished doctoral dissertation, University of North Carolina at Chapel Hill.

Richardson, J. (1991). Developing responsibility in English classes: Three activities. *Journal of the Virginia College Reading Educators, 11,* 8–19.

Richardson, J. (1992a). Generating inquiry-oriented projects from teachers. In A. Frager and J. Miller (Eds.), *Using inquiry in reading teacher education* (pp. 24–29). Kent, OH: Kent State University, College Reading Association.

Richardson, J. (1992b). Taking responsibility for taking tests. In N. Padak and T. Rasinski (Eds.), *Literacy research and practice: Foundations for the year 2000* (pp. 209–215). Kent, OH: Kent State University, College Reading Association.

Richardson, J. S. (1994). Great read-alouds for prospective teachers and secondary students. *Journal of reading, 38,* 98–103.

Richardson, J. S. (1995a). Three ways to keep a middle school student in the "reading habit." *Affective Reading Education, 14,* 5–7.

Richardson, J. S. (1995b). A read-aloud for cultural diversity. *Journal of Adolescent & Adult Literacy, 39,* 160–162.

Richardson, J. S. (1996). *The survival guide: Reading to learn in the English class.* Toronto, Canada: Pippin.

Richardson, J. S. (1999). *Reading is drudgery; reading is deeper meaning.* Paper presented at the 43rd conference of the College Reading Association, Hillton Head, North Carolina.

Richardson, J. S. (2000a). *Read it aloud! Using literature in secondary content classrooms.* Newark, DE: International Reading Association.

Richardson, J. S. (2000b). *Voices of adolescents and strategies for change.* Paper presented at the World Congress on Reading, Aukland, New Zealand.

Richardson, J. S. (2002). *Forum on adolescent literacy: Reading is drudgery.* Paper presented at the World Congress on Reading, Edinburgh, Scotland.

Richardson, J. S. (2004, July/August). Content area literacy lessons go high tech. *Reading Online, 8*(1). Retrieved Jul. 10, 2004, from *http://www.reading online.org/articles/art_index.asp?HREF=richardson/index.html*

Richardson, J. S., Fleener, C., & Thistlethwaite, L. (2004). Reading professionals learn online: Using threaded discussions to learn about threaded discussions. In J. R. Dugan, P. Linder, M. B. Sampson, B. Brancato, & L. Elish-Piper (Eds.). *Celebrating the power of literacy* (pp. 439–461). Commerce: Texas A&M University, College Reading Association.

Richardson, J. S., & Forget, M. A. (1995). A read-aloud for algebra and geography classrooms. *Journal of Adolescent & Adult Literacy, 39,* 322–326.

Richardson, J. S., & Morgan, R. F. (1991). Crossing bridges by connecting meaning. *Texas Affect in Reading Journal, 34*(1).

Richardson, J. S., & Morgan, R. F. (1997). *Reading to learn in the content areas.* Belmont, CA: Wadsworth ITP.

Richardson, J. S., Rhodes, J. A., & Robnolt, V. J. (2004). *Electronic study skills: What do the new study skills look like?* Paper presented at the College Reading Association, October 30, 2004, Delray Beach, FL.

Rifkin, J. (1987). *Time wars.* New York: Henry Holt.

Rifkin, J. (2002). *The hydrogen economy.* New York: Tarcher/Putnam.

Ritter, S., & Idol-Mastas, L. (1986). Teaching middle school students to use a test-taking strategy. *Journal of Educational Research, 79,* 350–357.

Robertson, J. I. (1992). *Civil War: America becomes one nation.* New York: Knopf.

Robinson, D. H. (1998). Graphic organizers as aids to text learning. *Reading Research and Instruction, 37*(2), 85–105.

Robinson, D. H., & Schraw, G. (1994). Computational efficiency through visual argument: Do graphic organizers communicate relations in text too effectively? *Contemporary Educational Psychology, 19,* 399–415.

Robinson, F. P. (1961). *Effective study* (rev. ed.). New York: Harper and Row.

Robyler, M. D., & Edwards, J. (2000). *Integrating technology into teaching.* Columbus, OH: Merrill.

Rogers, D. B. (1984). Assessing study skills. *Journal of Reading, 27,* 346–354.

Roit, M., & McKenzie, R. (1985). Disorders of written communication: An instructional priority for LD students. *Journal of Learning Disabilities, 18,* 258–260.

Romance, N. R., & Vitale, M. R. (1997). *Knowledge representation systems: Basis for the design of instruction for undergraduate course curriculum.* Paper presented at the Eighth National Conference on College Teaching and Learning, Jacksonville, FL.

Romance, N. R., & Vitale, M. R. (1999). Concept mapping as a tool for learning. *College Teaching, 47*(2), 74.

Rose, M. C. (1999). Don't stop now. *Instructor, 108*(8), 28.

Ross, J. A., Rolheiser, C., & Hoaboam-Gray, A. (1998, April). *Impact of self-evaluation training on mathematics achievement in a cooperative learning environment.* Paper presented at the annual meeting of the American Educational Research Association, San Diego, CA.

Rothstein, R. (1998). Bilingual education: The controversy. *Phi Delta Kappan, 79*(9), 672–678.

Rotter, J. B. (1966). Generalized expectancies for internal versus external control of reinforcement. *Psychological Monographs: General and Applied, 80*(1), 1–28.

Routeman, R. (2004). *Writing essentials: Raising expectations and results while simplifying teaching.* Portsmouth, NH: Heinemann.

Ruddell, M. R. (2000, July). Dot.com lessons worth learning: Student engagement, literacy, and project-based learning. *Reading Online, 4*(1). Retrieved Sept. 7, 2004, from *http://www.readingonline.org/articles/ruddell/*

Rudestam, K. E., & Schoenholtz-Read, J. (2002). Overview: The coming of age of adult online education. In K. E. Rudestam and J. Schoenholtz-Read (Eds.), *Handbook of online learning* (pp. 3–29). Thousand Oaks, CA: Sage.

Ruiz-Primo, M. A., & Shavelson, R. J. (1996). Problems and issues in the use of concepts maps in science assessment. *Journal of Research in Science Teaching, 33*(6), 569–600.

Rumelhart, D. E. (1980). Schemata: The building blocks of cognition. In R. J. Spiro, B. C. Bruce, & W. F. Brewer (Eds.), *Theoretical issues in reading comprehension* (pp. 33–58). Hillsdale, NJ: Erlbaum.

Russell, M., & Abrams, L. (2004). Instructional uses of computers for writing: The effect of state testing programs. *Teachers College Record, 196,* 1332–1357.

Russell, S. (1995). Sheltered content instruction for second language learners. *Reading Today, 13,* 30.

Ryder, R. J., & Graves, M. F. (1994). Vocabulary instruction presented prior to reading in two basal readers. *Elementary School Journal, 95*(2), 139–153.

Sagan, C. (1977). *The dragons of Eden.* New York: Random House.

Sakta, C. G. (1999). SQCR: A strategy for guiding reading and higher level thinking. *Journal of Adolescent & Adult Literacy, 42*(4), 265–269.

Salembier, G. B. (1999). SCAN and RUN: A reading comprehension strategy that works. *Journal of Adolescent & Adult Literacy, 42*(5), 386–401.

Salvia, J., & Ysseldyke, J. (1998). *Assessment* (7th ed.). Boston: Houghton Mifflin.

Sanacore, J. (1998). Promoting the lifelong love of reading. *Journal of Adolescent & Adult Literacy, 41*(5), 392–396.

Santeusanio, R. (1983). *A practical approach to content area reading.* Reading, MA: Addison-Wesley.

Scarborough, H. A. (Ed.). (2001). *Writing across the curriculum in secondary classrooms: Teaching from a diverse perspective.* Upper Saddle River, NJ: Pearson Education.

Scardamalia, M., & Bereiter, C. (1984). Development of strategies in text processing. In H. Mandl, N. L. Stein, and T. Trabasson (Eds.), *Learning and comprehension of text* (pp. 379–406). Hillsdale, NJ: Erlbaum.

Schadt, W. (1989). Literary gift exchange. *Journal of Reading, 33,* 223–224.

Schaeffer, R. K. (2003). Globalization and technology. *Phi Kappa Phi Forum, 83*(4), 30–33.

Schallert, D. L., & Kleiman, G.M. (1979). *Why the teacher is easier to understand than the textbook* (Reading Education Report No. 9). Urbana: University of Illinois, Center for the Study of Reading.

Schatz, E. K. (1984). *The influence of context clues on determining the meaning of low frequency words in naturally occurring prose.* Unpublished doctoral dissertation, University of Miami.

Schieffelin, B. B., & Cochran-Smith, M. (1984). Learning to read culturally: Literacy before schooling. In H. Goelman, A. Oberg, and F. Smith (Eds.), *Awakening to literacy* (pp. 3–23). Portsmouth, NH: Heinemann.

Schmidt, P. R. (1995). Working and playing with others: Cultural conflict in a kindergarten literacy program. *The Reading Teacher, 48,* 404–412.

Schneider, B., & Stephenson, D. (1999). *The ambitious generation: America's teenagers motivated but directionless.* New Haven, CT: Yale University Press.

Schumann, J. (1978). Second language acquisition: The pidginization hypothesis. In E. Hatch (Ed.), *Second language acquisition.* Rowley, MA: Newbury House.

Schumm, J. (1992). Content area textbooks: How tough are they? *Journal of Reading, 36,* 47.

Schumm, J., Mangrum, C., Gordon, J., & Doucette, M. (1992). The effect of topic knowledge on the predicted test questions of developmental college readers. *Reading Research and Instruction, 31,* 11–23.

Schunk, D. H., & Rice, J. M. (1992). Influence of reading comprehension strategy information on children's achievement outcomes. *Learning Disabilities Quarterly, 15*(1), 51–64.

Schwartz, D. M. (1999). *If you hopped like a frog.* New York: Scholastic Press.

Schwartz, R. M., & Raphael, T. E. (1985). Concept of definition: A key to improving students' vocabulary. *Journal of Reading, 39,* 198–205.

Scieszka, J. (1995). *The math curse.* New York: Penguin Books.

Scott, J. A., Jamieson-Noel, D., & Asselin, M. (2003). Vocabulary instruction throughout the day in twenty-three Canadian upper-elementary classrooms. *The Elementary School Journal, 103*(3), 269–288.

Scruggs, T., Mastropier, M. A., Brigham, F. J., & Sullivan, G. S. (1992). Effects of mnemonic reconstructions on the spatial learning of adolescents with learning disabilities. *Learning Disability Quarterly, 15*(3), 154–167.

Scruggs, T., White, K., & Bennion, K. (1986). Teaching test-taking skills to elementary students: A meta-analysis. *Elementary School Journal, 87,* 69–82.

Self, J. (1987). The picture of writing to learn. In J. Self (Ed.), *Plain talk about learning and writing across the curriculum* (pp. 9–20). Richmond: Virginia State Department of Education.

Shanahan, T. (1997). Reading–writing relationships, thematic units, inquiry learning . . . in pursuit of effective integrated literacy instruction. *The Reading Teacher, 51*(1), 12–19.

Shanahan, T., Mulhern, M., & Rodriguez-Brown, F. (1995). Project FLAME: Lessons learned from a family literacy program for linguistic minority families. *The Reading Teacher, 48,* 586–593.

Shanahan, T., Robinson, B., & Schneider, M. (1995). Avoiding some of the pitfalls of thematic units. *The Reading Teacher, 48,* 718–719.

Shanker, A. (1984, September 5). Where we stand: Who should evaluate the textbooks? *Education Week,* 69.

Shannon, D. (1999). *David goes to school.* New York: Blue Sky Press.

Sharan, S., & Sharan, Y. (1976). *Small-group teaching.* Englewood Cliffs, NJ: Educational Technology Publications.

Sherer, P. (1975). Skimming and scanning: De-mything the process with a college student. *Journal of Reading, 19,* 24–27.

Short, K. (1997). *Reading as a way of knowing.* York, ME: Stenhouse.

Shyer, M. F. (1988). *Welcome home, jelly bean.* New York: Macmillan.

Siedow, M. D., & Hasselbring, T. S. (1984). Adaptability of text readability to increase comprehension of reading disability students. *Reading Improvement, 21,* 276–279.

Siegle, D. (2004). The merging of literacy and technology in the twenty-first century: A bonus for gifted children. *Gifted Child Today, 27*(2), 32–36.

Silva, P. U., Meagher, M. E., Valenzuela, M., & Crenshaw, S. W. (1996). E-mail: Real-life classroom experiences with foreign languages. *Learning and Leading with Technology, 23*(5), 10–12.

Simon, K. (1993). Alternative assessment: Can real-world skills be tested? *The Link, 12,* 1–7.

Simpson, M. L. (1987). Alternative formats for evaluating content area vocabulary understanding. *Journal of Reading, 30,* 20–27.

Sinatra, R. (1986). *Visual literacy connections to thinking, reading, and writing.* Springfield, IL: Charles C. Thomas.

Singer, H., & Bean, T. (1988). Three models for helping teachers to help students learn from text. In S. J. Samuels and P. D. Pearson (Eds.), *Changing school reading programs* (pp. 161–183). Newark, DE: International Reading Association.

Singer, H., & Donlan, D. (1985). *Reading and learning from text.* Hillsdale, NJ: Erlbaum.

Singh, J. (1995). *Development of an alternative methodology for determining the readability of text.* Unpublished doctoral dissertation, Virginia Commonwealth University, Richmond.

Skinner, C. H., Cooper, L., & Cole, C. L. (1997). The effects of oral presentation rates on reading performance. *Journal of Applied Behavior Analysis, 30,* 331–334.

Slavin, R. E. (1980). Cooperative learning. *Review of Educational Research, 50,* 315–342.

Slavin, R. E. (1983). *Cooperative learning.* New York: Longman.

Slavin, R. E. (1991). Synthesis of research on cooperative learning. *Educational Leadership, 48,* 71–82.

Slavin, R. E. (1995). *Cooperative learning* (2nd ed.). Boston: Allyn & Bacon.

Slavin, R. E. (1996). Research on cooperative learning and achievement: What we know, what we need to know. *Contemporary Educational Psychology, 21,* 43–69.

Slavin, R. E. (2000). *Educational psychology: Theory and practice* (6th ed.). Boston: Allyn & Bacon.

Slavin, R. E. (2001). Cooperative learning and the cooperative school. In K. Ryan and J. M. Cooper (Eds.), *Kaleidoscope: Readings in education* (9th ed.). Boston: Houghton Mifflin.

Sloan, G. D. (1984). *The child as critic: Teaching literature in elementary and middle schools* (2nd ed.). New York: Teachers College Press.

Smith, D. (1992). Common ground: The connection between reader-response and textbook reading. *Journal of Reading, 35,* 630–635.

Smith, F. (1971). *Understanding reading.* Holt, Rinehart and Winston.

Smith, F. (1973). *Psycholinguistics and reading.* New York: Holt, Rinehart and Winston.

Smith, F. (1988). *Understanding reading: A psycholinguistic analysis of reading and learning to read* (4th ed.). Hillsdale, NJ: Erlbaum.

Smith, F. (1989). Overselling literacy. *Phi Delta Kappan, 70,* 352–359.

Smith, F. (1994). *Understanding reading: A psycholinguistic analysis of reading and learning to read* (5th ed.). Hillsdale, NJ: Erlbaum.

Smith, M. C. (1990). A longitudinal investigation of reading attitude development from childhood to adulthood. *Journal of Educational Research, 83,* 215–219.

Smith, N. B. (1965). *American reading instruction.* Newark, DE: International Reading Association.

Smith, S., & Bean, R. (1980). The guided writing procedure: Integrating content reading and writing improvement. *Reading World, 19,* 290–294.

Smuin, S. (1978). *Turn-ons.* Belmont, CA: Fearon Pitman.

Snow, C. E. (2002). *Reading for understanding. Toward an R&D program in reading comprehension.* Santa Monica, CA: RAND.

Snow, C. E., Burns, M. S., & Griffin, P. (Eds.). (1998). *Preventing reading difficulties in young children.* Washington, DC: National Academy Press.

Snow, R. (1987). Cognitive–conative–affective processes in aptitude, learning, and instruction: An introduction. In R. Snow and M. Farr (Eds.), *Conative and affective process analysis.* Hillsdale, NJ: Erlbaum.

Sommers, C. H. (2000). *The war against boys: How misguided feminism is harming our young men.* New York: Simon and Schuster.

Sosniak, L. A., & Perlman, C. L. (1990). Secondary education by the book. *Journal of Curriculum Studies, 22,* 427–442.

Spache, G. (1953). A new readability formula for primary grade reading materials. *Elementary School Journal, 53,* 410–413.

Spache, G. (1976). *Investigating the issues of reading disabilities.* Boston: Allyn & Bacon.

Sparks, D. (1995). A paradigm shift in staff development. *The ERIC Review, 3*(3), 5–7.

Speigel, D. L., & Wright, J. (1983). Biology teachers' use of readability concepts when selecting texts for students. *Journal of Reading, 27,* 28–34.

Spor, M., & Schneider, B. (1999). Content reading strategies: What teachers know, use, and want to learn. *Reading Research and Instruction, 38*(3), 221–231.

Stahl, S. (1983). Differential word knowledge and reading comprehension. *Journal of Reading Behavior, 15,* 33–50.

Stahl, S. (1986). Three principles of vocabulary instruction. *Journal of Reading, 29*(1), 662–668.

Stahl, S. A. (1999). *Vocabulary development.* Cambridge, MA: Brookline.

Stahl, S. A., & Shiel, T. G. (1999). *Teaching meaning vocabulary: Productive approaches for poor readers. Read all about it! Readings to inform the profession.* Sacramento: California State Board of Education.

Statistical abstract of the United States / 1989 prepared by the chief of the Bureau of Statistics, Treasury Department. Washington: Government Printing Office.

Stauffer, R. G. (1969a). *Directing reading maturity as a cognitive process.* New York: Harper and Row.

Stauffer, R. G. (1969b). *Teaching reading as a thinking process.* New York: Harper and Row.

Steen, P. (1991). Book diaries: Connecting free reading with instruction, home and school, and kids with books. *The Reading Teacher, 45,* 330–333.

Stefl-Mabry, J. (1998). Designing a web-based reading course. *Journal of Adolescent & Adult Education, 41*(7), 556–571.

Sternberg, R. J. (1985, November). Teaching critical thinking: 1. Are we making critical mistakes? *Phi Delta Kappan,* 194–198.

Sternberg, R. J. (1991). Are we reading too much into reading comprehension tests? *Journal of Reading, 34,* 540–545.

Sternberg, R. J. (1994). Answering questions and questioning answers. *Phi Delta Kappan, 76,* 136–138.

Sternberg, R. J., & Baron, J. B. (1985). A statewide approach to measuring critical thinking skills. *Educational Leadership, 43,* 40–43.

Stewart, M. T. (2004). Early literacy instruction in the climate of No Child Left Behind. *The Reading Teacher, 57*(8), 732–743.

Stien, D., & Beed, P. L. (2004). Bridging the gap between fiction and nonfiction in the circle setting: Reading circles can be a valuable tool for engaging students with nonfiction texts. *The Reading Teacher, 57*(6), 510–519.

Stoller, F. (1999). Time for a change: A hybrid curriculum for EAP programs. *TESOL Journal, 8*(1), 8–13.

Strahan, D. B. (1983). The emergence of formal reasoning during adolescence. *Transescence, 11,* 7–14.

Strauss, A. A., & Lehtinen, L. (1947). *Psychopathology and education in the brain-injured child: Vol. 1.* New York: Grune and Stratton.

Strauss, V. (2003). Start early with study skills instruction. *Curriculum Review, 42*(8), 3.

Streeter, B. (1986). The effects of training experienced teachers in enthusiasm on students' attitudes toward reading. *Reading Psychology, 7*(4), 249–259.

Strong, M. (1995). Socratic practice as an organizing principle. *Paideia Next Century, 4,* 5–6.

Strong, M. (2000). Students lack needed study skills. *USA Today, 128*(2659), 15.

Sturtevant, E. (1992). *Content literacy in high school social studies: Two case studies in a multicultural setting.* Unpublished doctoral dissertation, Kent State University, Kent, Ohio.

Sturtevant, E. G., & Linek, W. M. (2003). The instructional beliefs and decisions of middle and secondary teachers who successfully blend literacy and content. *Reading Research and Instruction, 4*(3), 74–90.

Swafford, J. (1995). "I wish all my groups were like this one": Facilitating peer interaction during group work. *Journal of Reading, 38,* 626–631.

Swafford, J., & Alvermann, D. E. (1989). Postsecondary research base for content strategies. *Journal of Reading, 33,* 164–169.

Swanson, H. L. (2000). Issues facing the field of learning disabilities. *Learning Disability Quarterly, 23*(1), 37–48.

Sylwester, R. (1994, October). How emotions affect learning. *Educational Leadership, 52*(2), 60–68.

Sylwester, R. (1995). *A celebration of neurons: An educator's guide to the human brain.* Alexandria, VA: Association for Supervision and Curriculum Development.

Tan, A. (1993). Two kinds. *Contemporary west coast stories.* Old Saybrook, CT: The Globe Pequot Press.

Tatum, A. W. (2004). A road map for reading specialists entering schools without exemplary reading programs: Seven quick lessons. *The Reading Teacher, 58*(1), 28–39.

Taylor, B. M., Frye, B. J., & Maruyama, G. M. (1990). Time spent reading and reading growth. *American Educational Research Journal, 72,* 351–362.

Taylor, B. M., Pressley, M., & Pearson, P. D. (2002). Research supported characteristics of teachers and schools that promote reading achievement. In B. M. Taylor & P. D. Pearson (Eds.), *Teaching reading* (pp. 361–374). Mahwah, NJ: Erlbaum.

Taylor, W. (1953). Cloze procedure: A new tool for measuring readability. *Journalism Quarterly, 30,* 415–433.

Teale, W., & Sulzby, E. (1986). *Emergent literacy: Writing and reading.* Norwood, NJ: Ablex.

Templeton, S. (1991). *Teaching integrated language arts.* Boston: Houghton Mifflin.

Thoman, E. (1999). Skills and strategies for media education. *Educational Leadership, 56,* 50–54.

Thompson, G., & Morgan, R. (1976). The use of concept-formation study guides for social studies reading materials. *Reading Horizons, 7,*132–136.

Thorndike, E. L. (1917). Reading and reasoning. *Journal of Educational Psychology, 8,* 323–332.

Thorndike, E. L. (1932). *Educational psychology.* New York: Columbia University, Teachers College Press.

Thurstone, L. L. (1946). A note on a re-analysis of Davis's reading tests. *Psychometrika, 11,* 185–188.

Tierney, R. J. (1998). Literacy assessment reform: Shifting beliefs, principled possibilities, and emerging practice. *The Reading Teacher, 51*(5), 374–390.

Toch, T. (1984, March 7). Bell calls on education to push publishers for better materials. *Education Week,* 11.

Todd, C. J. (1995). The semester project: The power and pleasures of individualized study. *English Journal, 84,* 73–76.

Tonjes, M. J., & Zintz, M. V. (1981). *Teaching reading/thinking study skills in content classrooms.* Dubuque, IA: William Brown Co.

Torgensen, J., & Licht, B. (1983). The learning disabled child as an inactive learner: Retrospect and prospects. In J. McKinney and L. Feagans (Eds.), *Current topics in learning disabilities, Vol. 1* (pp. 3–31). Norwood, NJ: Ablex.

Tse, A. (1999). Conducting electronic focus group discussions among Chinese respondents. *Journal of the Market Research Society, 41*(4), 407.

Turbill, J. (2002, February). The four ages of reading philosophy and pedagogy: A framework for examining theory and practice. *Reading Online, 5*(6). Retrieved Dec. 10, 2004, from *http://www.reading online.org/international/inter_index.asp?HREF= turbill4/index.html*

Turner, J., & Paris, S. G. (1995). How literacy tasks influence children's motivation for literacy. *The Reading Teacher, 48,* 662–673.

Twenty-fourth yearbook of the national society of the study for education. (1925). Bloomington, IN: Public School Publishing Company.

Tyner, K. (1998). *Literacy in a digital world: Teaching and learning in the age of information.* Mahwah, NJ: Erlbaum.

Unks, G. (1985). Critical thinking in the social studies classroom. *Social Education, 44,* 240–246.

Unsworth, L. (1999). Developing critical understanding of the specialized language of school science and history texts: A functional grammatical perspective. *Journal of Adolescent & Adult Education, 42*(7), 508–521.

Ur, P., & Wright, A. (1992). *Five-minute activities, a resource book of short activities.* New York: Cambridge University Press.

U. S. Department of Education. (1993). *The condition of education 1993.* Washington, DC: Author.

U. S. Department of Education. (1997). *President Clinton's call to action for American education in the 21st century: Technological literacy.* Retrieved Apr. 8, 2003, from *http://www.ed.gov/updates/PresEDPlan/part11. html*

Vacca, R. T. (2002). From efficient decoders to strategic readers. *Educational Leadership, 60*(3), 6–11.

Vacca, R. T., & Padak, N. (1990). Who's at risk in reading? *Journal of Reading, 33,* 486–488.

Valencia, S. W., & Wixson, K. K. (1999, April 1). *Policy-oriented research on literacy standards and assessment.* Ann Arbor, Ml: Center for the Improvement of Early Reading Achievement (CIERA Report No. 3-004).

Valeri-Gold, M. (1987). Previewing: A directed reading–thinking activity. *Reading Horizons, 27,* 123–126.

Van der Heuval, G. (1988). *Crowns of thorns and glory: Mary Todd Lincoln and Varina Howell Davis, the two first ladies of the Civil War.* New York: Dutton.

Vanderventer, N. (1979, Winter). RAFT: A process to structure prewriting. *Highway One: A Canadian Journal of Language Experience, 26.*

Vandiver, F. E. (1992). *Blood brothers: A short history of the Civil War.* College Station: Texas A&M Press.

Van Horn, R. (1999). The electronic classroom and video conferencing. *Phi Delta Kappan, 80*(5), 411–412.

Vann, R .J., & Fairbairn, S. B. (2003). Linking our worlds: A collaborative academic literacy project. *TESOL Journal, 12*(3), 11–16.

Van Sertima, T. (1976). *The African presence in ancient America: They came before Columbus.* New York: Random House.

Vaughan, C. L. (1990). Knitting writing: The double-entry journal. In N. Atwell (Ed.), *Coming to know: Writing to learn in the intermediate grades* (pp. 69–75). Portsmouth, NH: Heinemann.

Vaughan, J., & Estes, T. (1986). *Reading and reasoning beyond the primary grades.* Boston: Allyn & Bacon.

Veatch, J. (1968). *How to teach reading with children's books.* New York: Citation Press.

Vermette, P. (1994). The right start for cooperative learning. *High School Journal, 77,* 255–260.

Vermette, P., Harper, L., & DiMillo, S. (2004). Cooperative and collaborative learning with 4–8 year olds: How does research support teachers' practice? *Journal of Instructional Psychology, 31*(2), 130–135.

Verplaeste, L. S. (1998). How content teachers interact with English language learners. *TESOL Journal, 7*(5), 24–28.

Villaune, S. K. (2000). The necessity of uncertainty: A case study of language arts reform. *Journal of Teacher Education, 51*(1), 18.

Villaune, S. K., & Hopkins, L. (1995). A transactional and sociocultural view of response in a fourth-grade literature discussion group. *Reading Research and Instruction, 34,* 190–203.

Viorst, J. (1978). *Alexander who used to be rich last Sunday.* New York: Atheneum.

Von Glaserfeld, E. (1996). Introduction: Aspects of constructivism. In C. T. Fosnot (Ed.), *Constructivism: Theory, perspectives, and practice* (pp. 3–7). New York: Teachers College Press.

Vyas, S. (2004). Exploring bicultural identities of Asian high school students through the analytic window of a literature club. *Journal of Adolescent & Adult Literacy, 48*(1), 12–23.

Vygotsky, L. (1978a). Interaction between learning and development. In M. Cole, V. John-Steiner, S. Scribner, and E. Souberman (Eds.), *Mind in society: The development of higher psychological process* (pp. 79–91). Cambridge, MA: Harvard University Press.

Vygotsky, L. (1978b). The prehistory of written language. In M. Cole, V. John-Steiner, S. Scribner, and E. Souberman (Eds.), *Mind in society: The development of higher psychological process* (pp. 105–119). Cambridge, MA: Harvard University Press.

Vygotsky, L. S. (1962). *Thought and language.* Cambridge, MA: MIT Press.

Wade, S. E., & Adams, R. B. (1990). Effects of importance and interest on recall of biographical text. *Journal of Reading Behavior, 22,* 331–353.

Waggoner, M., Chinn, C., Yi, H., & Anderson, R. C. (1995). Collaborative reasoning about stories. *Language Arts, 72,* 582–589.

Wagner, C. L., Brock, D. R., & Agnew, A. T. (1994). Developing literacy portfolios in teacher education courses. *Journal of Reading, 37*(8), 668–674.

Wagner, J. O. (1995). Using the Internet in vocational education. *ERIC Digest No. 160* (ERIC Document Reproduction Service No. ED. 385-777).

Walberg, H. J., & Tsai, S. (1985). Correlates of reading achievement and attitude: A national assessment study. *Journal of Educational Research, 78,* 159–167.

Walker, B. (1992). *Supporting struggling readers.* Markham, Ontario: Pippin.

Walker, B. J. (1990). *Remedial reading.* Washington, DC: National Education Association.

Wallace, R. A. (1975). *Biology: The world of life.* Santa Monica, CA: Goodyear.

Walpole, P. (1987). Yes, writing in math. In J. Self (Ed.), *Plain talk about learning and writing across the curriculum* (pp. 51–59). Richmond: Virginia State Department of Education.

Walpole, S. (1999). Changing texts, changing thinking: Comprehension demands of new science textbooks. *The Reading Teacher, 52*(4), 358–369.

Wang, A. Y., & Thomas, M. H. (1995). The effects of key words on long-term retention: Help or hindrance? *Journal of Educational Psychology, 87,* 468–475.

Wang, J. H., & Guthrie, J. T. (2004). Modeling the effects of intrinsic motivation, extrinsic motivation, amount of reading, and past reading achievement on text comprehension between U. S. and Chinese students. *Reading Research Quarterly, 39*(2), 162–184.

Wassermann, S. (1987). Teaching for thinking: Louis E. Raths revisited. *Phi Delta Kappan, 68,* 460–466.

Wassermann, S. (1999). Shazam! You're a teacher. *Phi Delta Kappan, 80*(6), 464–468.

Watts-Taffe, S., Gwinn, C. B., Johnson, J. R., & Horn, M. L. (2003). Preparing preservice teachers to integrate technology with the elementary literacy program. *The Reading Teacher, 57*(2), 130–138.

Weaver, C. (1994). *Reading processes and practice.* Portsmouth, NH: Heinemann.

Wehlange, G. G., & Rutter, R. A. (1986). Dropping out: How much do schools contribute to the problem? *Teachers College Record, 87,* 374–392.

Weiner, B. (1979). A theory of motivation for some classroom experiences. *Journal of Educational Psychology, 71,* 3–25.

Weinstein, C. E. (1987). Fostering learning autonomy through the use of learning strategies. *Journal of Reading, 30,* 590–595.

Weinstein, C. E., & Mayer, R. E. (1986). The teaching of learning strategies. In M. C. Wittrock (Ed.), *Handbook of research on teaching* (pp. 315–327). New York: Macmillan.

Weir, C. (1998). Using embedded questions to jump-start metacognition in middle school readers. *Journal of Adolescent & Adult Literacy, 41*(6), 458–467.

Weiss, R. P. (2000). Brain based learning. *Training and Development, 54*(7), 21–27.

Wells, H. G. (1987). *The complete short stories of H. G. Wells.* New York: St. Martin's Press.

Wepner, S. B. (1995). Using technology for literacy instruction. In S. B. Wepner, J. T. Feeley, and D. S. Strickland (Eds.), *The administration and supervision of reading programs.* New York: Teachers College Press.

Wepner, S. B. (2004). Technology run amok: The top ten technoblunders. *Reading Online, 7*(6). Retrieved Dec. 10, 2004, from *http://www.readingonline. org/electronic/elec_index.asp?HREF=wepner2/ index.html*

Wepner, S. B., Seminoff, N. E., & Blanchard, J. (1995). Navigating learning with electronic encyclopedias. *Reading Today, 12,* 28.

White, E. B. (1951). Calculating machine. In *The second tree from the corner* (pp. 165–167). New York: Harper and Row.

Whitehead, D. (1994). Teaching literacy and learning strategies through a modified guided silent reading procedure. *Journal of Reading, 38,* 24–30.

Whittington, D. (1991). What have 17-year-olds known in the past? *American Educational Research Journal, 28,* 759–783.

Wiegel, H. G. (1998). Kindergarten students' organization of counting in joint counting tasks and the emergence of cooperation. *Journal for Research in Mathematics Education, 29*(2), 202.

Wigfield, A., & Asher, S. R. (1984). Social and motivational influences on reading. In P. D. Pearson (Ed.), *Handbook of reading research.* New York: Longman.

Wigfield, A., & Asher, S. R. (1986). Students' thought processes. In M. C. Wittrock (Ed.), *Handbook of research on teaching.* New York: Macmillan.

Wiggins, G. (1989). A true test: Toward more authentic and equitable assessment. *Phi Delta Kappan, 70,* 703–713.

Wiggins, G. (1990, August). A conversation with Grant Wiggins. *Instructor,* 51.

Wigginton, E. (1986). *Sometimes a shining moment: The Foxfire experiences.* New York: Anchor/Doubleday.

Wilcox, B. L. (1997). Writing portfolios: Active vs. passive. *English Journal, 86*(6), 34–37.

Wilkinson, L. C., & Silliman, E. R. (2001, February). Classroom language and literacy learning. *Reading Online, 4*(7). Retrieved Nov. 11, 2004, from *http://www.readingonline.org/articles/art_index.asp?HREF=/articles/handbook/wilkinson/index.html*

Will, M. (1984). *Bridges from school to working life: OSERS programming for the transition of youth with disabilities.* Washington, DC: U. S. Department of Education, Office of Special Education and Rehabilitative Services.

Willis, E. M., & Raines, P. (2001). Technology in secondary teacher education. *THE Journal, 29*(2), 54–64.

Willis, J., Stephens, E., & Matthew, K. (1996). *Technology, reading, and language arts.* Boston: Allyn & Bacon.

Wilson, M. (1988). How can we teach reading in the content areas? In C. Weaver (Ed.), *Reading process and practice: From sociopsycholinguistics to whole language.* Portsmouth, NH: Heinemann.

Wilson, M. (2004). Assessment, accountability, and the classroom: A community of judgment. In M. Wilson (Ed.), *Toward coherence between classroom assessment and accountability: 103rd yearbook of the national society for the study of education.* Chicago: University of Chicago Press.

Wilson, R. M., & Gambrell, L. B. (1988). *Reading comprehension in the elementary school.* Boston: Allyn & Bacon.

Window on the classroom: A look at teachers' tests. (1984). *Captrends, 10,* 1–3.

Winograd, P. (1984). Strategic difficulties in summarizing texts. *Reading Research Quarterly, 19,* 404–425.

Winograd, P., & Paris, S. (1988). A cognitive and motivational agenda for reading instruction. *Educational Leadership, 46,* 30–36.

Wise, H. A. (1939). *Motion pictures as an aid in teaching American history.* New Haven, CT: Yale University Press.

Wolf, G. (1996, February). "Steve Jobs: the next great thing." *Wired,* 102–163.

Wolfe, D., & Reising, R. (1983). *Writing for learning in the content areas.* Portland, ME: J. Weston Walch.

Wolfe, D., & Antinarella, J. (1997). *Deciding to lead: The English teacher as reformer.* Portsmouth, NH: Heinemann.

Wolfe, P. (2001). *Brain matters: Translating research into classroom practice.* Alexandria, VA: Association for Supervision and Curriculum Development.

Wolfe, P., & Brandt, R. (1998). What do we know from brain research? *Educational Leadership, 56*(3), 8–13.

Wollman-Bonilla, J. (1991). *Response journals.* New York: Scholastic.

Wood, K. D. (1987). Fostering cooperative learning in middle and secondary level classrooms. *Journal of Reading, 31,* 10–18.

Wood, K. D. (1992). Fostering collaborative reading and writing experiences in mathematics. *Journal of Reading, 36,* 96–103.

Wood, K. D., Lapp, D., & Flood, J. (1992). *Guiding readers through text: A review of study guides.* Newark, DE: International Reading Association.

Wood, T. M. (1996). Evaluation and testing: The road less traveled. In S. J. Silverman and C. D. Ennis (Eds.), *Student learning in physical education: Applying research to enhance instruction* (pp. 199–219). Champaign, IL: Human Kinetics.

Woodward, A., Elliott, D. L., & Nagel, K. C. (1986). Beyond textbooks in elementary social studies. *Social Education, 50,* 50–53.

Woolf, V. (1967; c 1966). *Collected essays.* New York: Harcourt, Brace and World.

Worthen, B. (1993). Critical decisions that will determine the future of alternative assessment. *Phi Delta Kappan, 74,* 444–456.

Worthy, J., & Hoffman, J. V. (2000). Critical questions—the press to test. *The Reading Teacher, 53*(7), 596–598.

Wray, D. (1994). Text and authorship. *The Reading Teacher* *48*(1), 52–57.

Wray, D., & Lewis, M. (1998). An approach to factual writing. *Reading Online*. Retrieved Dec. 12, 2004, from *http://www.readingonline.org/articles/art_index. asp?HREF=writing/index.html*

The writing report card: Writing achievement in American schools. (1987). Princeton, NJ: National Assessment of Educational Progress and the Educational Testing Center.

Yeager, D. (1991). *The whole language companion.* Glenview, IL: Goodyear.

Yell, M. M. (2002). Putting gel pen to paper. *Educational Leadership, 60*(3), 63–66.

Yochum, N. (1991). Children's learning from informational text: The relationship between prior knowledge and text structure. *Journal of Reading Behavior, 23,* 87–108.

Yolen, J. (Ed.). (1986). *Favorite folktales from around the world.* New York: Pantheon Books.

Young, J. P., & Brozo, W. G. (2001). Boys will be boys, or will they? Literacy and masculinities. *Reading Research Quarterly, 36*(3), 316–325.

Young, J. P., Mathews, S. R., Kietzmann, A. M., & Westerfield, D. T. (1997). Getting disenchanted adolescents to participate in school literacy activities: Portfolio conferences. *Journal of Adolescent & Adult Literacy, 40*(5), 348–360.

Young, T. A., & Daines, D. (1992). Students' predictive questions and teachers' prequestions about expository text in grades K–5. *Reading Psychology, 13*(4), 291–308.

Zakaluk, B., & Klassen, M. (1992). Enhancing the performance of a high school student labeled learning disabled. *Journal of Reading, 36,* 4–9.

Zaragoza, N. (1987). Process writing for high-risk learning disabled students. *Reading Research and Instruction, 26,* 290–301.

Zeilik, M., Schau, C., Mattern, N., Hall, S., Teague, K. W., & Bisard, W. (1997). Conceptual astronomy: A novel model for teaching postsecondary science courses. *American Journal of Physics, 66*(10), 987–996.

Zhang, Z., & Schumm, J. S. (2000). Exploring effects of the keyword method on limited English proficient students' vocabulary recall and comprehension. *Reading Research and Instruction 39*(3), 202–221.

Activity Contributors

Dawn Watson and Walter Richards: PAR Diagram, p. 6.

Alex Seely, Richmond, VA: Examples for primary social studies lesson and Activity 1.1

Elisabeth Groninger, Richmond, VA: Example for fourth grade science and Activity 1.2

Michael Tewksbury, Richmond, VA: Examples for middle school mathematics and Activity 1.3

James DiNardo III and Yogi Hightower Boothe: Examples for ninth grade health and physical education and Activity 1.4

Karen Curling: Activity 2.2

Beverly Marshall: Activity 2.4

Megan K. Houston: Activity 2.5

Kerry Blum: math analogy

Diana Freeman: biology analogy

Charles Carroll: Activity 3.2

Bessie Haskins: Activity 3.3

Frances Reid: Activity 3.4

Sandra Zeller and Brenda Winston: Activity 3.5

Marvette Darby: Activity 5.5

Stephen Rudlin: Activity 5.6

Sherry Gott: Activity 5.7

Mary L. Seward: Activity 5.11

Jeannette Rosenberg: Activity 6.1

Grace Hamlin: Prior Knowledge Telegram

Etta Malcolm: Activity 6.3

Laurie A. Schofield: Activity 6.5

Kathy Feltus: Activity 6.10

Jacqueline T. McDonnough: Activity 7.2

Mark A. Forget: Activity 7.4

Sandra Harlan: Activity 7. 5

Brian Alexander: Activity 7.7

Laura Clevinger: Activity 7.8

Vicki Douglas: Activity 7.9

Mendy Mathena: Activity 7.11

Serena Marshall: Activity 7.12

Susan Protich and her students: Charity Causer, Trevor Grimm, Kasalboth Soum, and Sharmaine Robinson: Activity 7.13

Jennifer Haczewski: Activity 7.14

Nancy S. Smith: Activity 7.15

Gail Perrer: Activity 7.17

Laura Allin: Activity 7.19

Ronda Clancy: Activity 7.21

Scot M. Paterson: Activity 7.22

Judy Richardson, Joan Rhodes, and Valerie Robnolt: Activity 8.1

Cornelia Hill: Activity 8.2

Jody Irvin: Activity 8.6

Stephanie Hunter: Activity 8.10

Terry Bryce: Activity 9.2

Brian Littman: Activity 9.4

Tara Furges: Activity 9.5

Ashile Wasik and Auda Jones: Activity 9.6

Suzanne McDaniel: Activity 9.8

Heather Hemstreet: Activity 9.10

Wendy Barcroft: Activity 9.12

Laurie Smith: Activity 9.13

Jackie Meccariello and Rachel Curry: Activity 9.14

Kim Blowe: Activity 9.15

Colleen Kean: Activity 9.16

William Cathrell: Activity 9.17

Laurie Smith: Activity 9.20

Ed Toscano: Activity 9.21

Barbara Woods: Activity 9.24

Mary Fagerland: Activity 9.25

Bessie Haskins: Activity 9.26

Barbara Inger: capsule vocabulary

Andrew Pettit: Figure 10.2

Kathryn Davis: Activity 10.1

Mark A. Forget: Activity 10.2 and 10.4

Dave N. Aznar: Activity 10.3

Susan Hamlin: Activity 10.5

M. J. Weatherford: Activity 10.8

Terry Bryce: Activity 10.9

Jon Morgan: Activity 10.12

Frances Lively: Activity 10.13

Betty Henderson: Activity 10.15

Dianne Duncan: Activity 10.18

Polly Gilbert: Activity 10.19

Sheryl Lam: Chapter 10 Learning Logs

Beth Pallister: Activity 11.1

Teachers at Norview High School, Norfolk, VA: Activity 11.2

Christine Rauth: Activity 11.3

Dana S. Jubilee: Activity 11.6

Cheryl Keeton: Activity 11.12

Shawn Nunnally: Activity 11.14

Jim McLeskey Jr.: Activity 11.15

Chris Birdsong White: Activity 12.6

Author Index

Shyer, M. F., 294
Siedow, M. D., 176
Siegel, L. S., 52
Silva, P. U., 334
Simmons, D. C., 280, 287
Simpson, M. L., 7, 280, 282–285
Sinatra, G. M., 166
Sinatra, R., 8, 369, 418
Singer, H., 12, 14, 218, 219
Singh, J., 142
Skinner, C. H., 249, 250
Slate, J. R., 242
Slavin, R. E., 376, 377, 396, 399
Sloan, G. O., 131
Smiley, S. S., 394
Smith, C. B., 39, 44
Smith, D., 136
Smith, F., 169, 263, 410
Smith, J. B., 428
Smith, L., 112
Smith, L. J., 179
Smith, M. C., 410
Smith, M. M., 217
Smith, N. B., 7
Smith, R. K., 432
Smith, S., 359
Smuin, S., 208
Smyser, S. O., 96
Snow, C. E., 44, 47, 280, 286
Snow, R., 412
Snyder, T., 187
Sommers, C. H., 431
Sozniak, L. A., 135
Spache, G., 139, 263
Sparks, D., 428
Speck, B. W., 105
Speigel, D. L., 161
Spor, M. W., 271
Stahl, N., 7
Stahl, S., 283, 299, 300
Stahl, S. A., 280, 281
Stainton, C., 376
Stanovich, K. E., 280, 284, 287
Stauffer, R. G., 197, 270, 433
Steen, P., 359
Steenwyk, F. L., 362
Stefl-Mabry, J., 116
Stephens, D., 193
Stephens, E., 112, 171, 330, 340, 369
Stephenson, D., 245
Sternberg, R. J., 215, 225, 226, 256
Stevenson, H. W., 45

Stevenson, R. J., 165, 166
Stewart, M., 6, 71
Stigler, J. W., 45
Stoller, F., 43
Strahan, D. B., 227
Strang, R., 236
Strauss, A. A., 366
Streeter, B., 421
Strickland, D. S., 56, 218
Strong, M., 429
Sturtevant, E., 10, 215
Sulzby, E., 332
Surber, J. R., 294
Swafford, J., 288, 379
Swanson, H. L., 51
Swinyard, W. R., 8, 9, 132
Sylwester, R., 417

Tan, A., 178
Tatum, A. W., 56
Taylor, B. M., 8, 215
Taylor, W., 146, 147
Teale, W., 332
Temple, C., 310
Templeton, S., 43, 383
Tesser, A., 386, 387
Thoman, E., 124
Thomas, M. H., 258
Thompson, G., 62
Thorndike, E. L., 193, 242, 243
Thurstone, L. L., 280
Tierney, R., 26, 95, 244
Tlusty, N., 109
Toch, T., 137
Todd, C. J., 395
Tomlinson, C. M., 384
Tonelson, S. W., 434
Tonjes, M. J., 366
Torgenson, J., 366
Tsai, S., 410
Turbill, J., 105
Turner, J., 126
Twain, M., 252, 254
Tynan, D., 51, 52
Tyner, K., 124

Unks, G., 225
Unsworth, L., 136
Ur, P., 323

Vacca, R. T., 54, 330
Valencia, S., 6, 71

Vanderventer, M., 358
Van Dijk, T., 362, 367
Van Horn, R., 114
Vann, R. J., 48
Vaughan, J., 14, 340, 386
Vaughn, S., 66
Von Glaserfeld, E., 334
Veatch, J., 138
Vermette, P., 377
Verplaeste, L. S., 46
Villaune, S. K., 131, 223, 283
Vitale, M. R., 194
Vyas, S., 48
Vygotsky, L., 332, 350

Wade, S. E., 174
Wagner, C. L., 96
Wagner, J. O., 334
Waggoner, M., 208
Wagoner, S., 236
Walberg, H. J., 410
Walker, B. J., 41, 55
Walpole, S., 137
Wang, A. Y., 258, 412
Wasserman, S., 10, 31, 217
Watkins, R., 36, 37
Watson, D. C., 66
Watts-Taffe, S., 106
Weaver, C., 193
Weber, R. P., 249
Wehlange, G. G., 40
Weiner, B., 433
Weinstein, C. E., 331, 378, 393
Weir, C., 63
Weiss, R. P., 417
Wells, H. G., 305
Wepner, S. B., 108, 109, 113
Weyhing, R. S., 243
White, K., 92
Whitehead, D., 340
Whittington, D., 5, 74
Wiegel, H. G., 376
Wigfield, A., 33, 39
Wiggins, G., 94, 96
Wigginton, E., 345
Will, M., 53
Williams, N. L., 285
Willis, E. M., 106
Willis, J., 112
Willow, D., 433
Wilson, M., 131, 135
Wilson, R. M., 55

Subject Index

Inclusion, 51
Incomplete thinking, 13
Inconsiderate discourse, 136
Incorrect prior knowledge, 173
Independent-level score, 147
Individuals with Disabilities
    Education Act (IDEA), 51, 52
Inference, 299, 300
Informed assessment, 71, 72
Information literacy, 105
Informative communication, 224
Instant message, 115, 119
Instructional cloze, 150
Instructional-level score, 147
Intention annotation, 351
Interactive cloze procedure, 153, 305
Interactive guide, 399
Internal-external journal, 433
Internal locus of control, 415, 432,
    436
Internet, 47, 65, 105, 107, 108,
    112–114, 117–119. 124, 254, 256,
    325, 370, 381, 385
Internet Relay Chat (IRC), 334

Jigsaw, 67, 378, 395, 396
Jot chart, 97, 210, 211–213, 303, 345,
    361
Jungle, The, 391, 392

Key-word strategy, 286, 313
KWL, 91, 156, 157, 197, 385

L2, 42
L & H Kurweil 3000, 54
Language Experience Approach
    (LEA), 62
Learnable knowledge, 261
Learned helplessness, 54, 434
Learning disabilities, 432
Learning log, 95, 130, 348,372, 434
LEP, 45
Levels of comprehension, 87, 93
Lexile Framework, 139
Limbic system (of brain), 418, 419
Limit testing, 41
Limited English proficiency (LEP), 45
Listen-read-discuss (LRD), 249
Listening, 249, 250
Listening guides, 249
Listservs, 116–119
Literary context, 126

Literal reading, 10
Literary gift exchange, 235, 239
Literature-based classrooms, 132–134
Literature-rich environment, 134
Local coherence, 137
Locating information, 276
Locus of control, 409, 433
Low self-esteem, 35, 38, 40, 41, 43, 66
Low socioeconomic environment,
    35–37, 66
LRD, 249

MAD (Mnemonic-A-Day) technique,
    262, 263
Magic square activity, 313–318
Mainstreaming, 51
Maps, 111, 196, 251, 254–257, 286,
    340
Mapping, 194, 195, 266, 288, 289,
    394
Marginal gloss, 218–221
Massed study, 256
Maze, 153, 154, 162
MBRAM, 422–424, 444–449
Melodrama, 360
Memory-enhancing techniques,
    256–263
Mental push-ups, 264
Metacognition, 217, 434
Metacognitive Awareness of Reading
    Strategies Inventory (MARSI), 79
Metacognitive strategies, 63, 331, 434
Metacognitive thinking, 48
Method of loci, 259, 261
Mikulecky Behavioral Reading
    Attitude Measure (MBRAM),
    422–424, 444–449
Mnemonic-A-Day (MAD), 262, 263
Mnemonic associations, 263
Mnemonic devices, 286, 294, 301, 313
Mnemonic learning techniques,
    256–263
Mnemonics, 256–259, 262, 263, 302,
    313
Modeling, 8, 9, 54, 396, 415
Modified cloze procedure, 288, 293
Morpheme, 300
Motivation, 39, 62, 377, 412, 427
Motivation annotation, 352
Mrs. Frisby and the Rats of NIMH,
    129, 222
Multicultural literature, 130

Multimedia, 113
Multitext activities, 50, 235, 239
Multitext strategy, 126, 175, 188
Mystery clue game, 59, 60, 208–210

National Assessment of Educational
    Progress (NAEP), 5, 32, 72, 74, 75
National Center for Educational
    Statistics (NCES), 5, 36, 74, 106
National Educational Technology
    standards (NETS), 106
Neocortex, 419
Networking systems, 357
New mammalian brain, 92, 419
No Child Left Behind Act (NCLB), 6,
    74–77, 99, 100, 101
Nontraditional tests, 87
Norm-referenced tests, 72, 73
Note taking, 267–269, 402

Odd word out, 313, 323
Old mammalian brain, 92, 418
Open books, 86
Open notes, 86
Open word sort, 301, 311
Organizational chart, 97, 210,
    211–213, 303
Outlining, 111, 265, 266

Paideia schools, 429
Paired reading, 378, 392, 393
Paired word sentence, 283
PAR Lesson Framework, 12, 14,
    16–18, 26, 36, 46, 65, 77, 83, 86,
    124, 133, 134, 157, 176, 180, 182,
    188, 192, 194, 200, 203, 220, 224,
    235, 238, 242, 287, 325, 327, 371,
    379, 420
Paradigm, 244, 305
Passive failure, 434
Pattern guides, 209
Patterns of organization, 205, 210
Peg word system, 260, 261
Personal computer (PC), 334
Personal inquiry, 385, 386, 404
Perspective cubing, 340
Pictures, 255
Plagiarism, 108, 119
PLEASE, 56
Poetry, 352, 360
Pop quizzes, 80–82
Portfolio, 96, 98

Text lookback, 236, 238, 239
Textual coherence, 137, 162
Thematic-unit instruction, 380, 404
Thematic units, 380–382, 385, 429
Theme, 380, 381
Thesis annotation, 351
Think-aloud, 378, 396, 397
Think/Reflect in Pairs (TRIP), 234, 235, 402, 403
Threaded discussion, 116, 119, 372, 428
Time management, 386, 387, 390, 404
Time Wars, 378
TOAST study system, 311, 312
To Kill a Mockingbird, 171
Trade books, 125, 131
Traditional test, 83, 84, 94
Triangle truths, 356
TRIP, 234, 235, 402, 403
TRIP cards, 234, 239
Triune brain, 418, 419, 436

Two-column note taking, 97, 269, 270, 273, 277, 402
Two-finger thinking, 13

Underlining, 265, 266
U.S. Department of Education, 105

Validity, 73, 442, 446
Venn diagram, 111, 214
Virginia Standards of Learning (SOLs), 17, 18, 22
Visual discrimination, 62
Visual literacy, 7, 8, 179, 195
Visual representations, 252
Vocab-lit strategy, 312
Vocabulary bingo, 313, 318, 321–323
Vocabulary connections, 288, 294
Vocabulary illustrations, 272
Vocabulary list, 297, 303
Vocabulary self-collection strategy (VSS), 312
Vocabulary study system, 312

Washback effect, 76
Webbing approach, 384
WebQuest, 114, 118, 384, 385, 414
Website, 67, 114, 118, 325
What I Know Activity (WIKA), 21, 22, 91, 133, 157, 197
Word analogies, 313
Word attack paradigm, 297, 302, 303
Word bubble, 313, 323, 324
Word inquiry, 313, 324
Word inventories, 154, 288
Word knowledge, 280, 283, 285, 303
Word map, 291, 292
Word processing, 110–112, 119, 334, 369
Word puzzles, 307
Word sort, 301, 310
World Wide Web, 111, 113, 229
Writing, 330–332, 334, 339, 342, 345, 350, 358, 359, 366, 370, 371
Written preview, 178, 188
Writing process, 366

PAR Cross-Reference Guide

	SCIENCE	MATH
Primary	Activity 2.5, p. 60 Activity 3.6, p. 97 Activity 5.4, p. 154 Activity 6.7, p. 184 Activity 9.2, p. 302 Activity 9.25, p. 321 Figure 10.2, p. 335 Activity 10.15, p. 364 Activity 11.7, p. 393	Activity 3.3, p. 85 Activity 9.27, p. 324
Intermediate	Activity 1.2, p. 21 Activity 7.2, p. 197 Activity 8.6, p. 256 Activity 9.8, p. 295 Activity 10.5, p. 346 Activity 10.11, p. 355	Activity 2.1, p. 47 Activity 2.3, p. 58 "Free rides," p. 223 Activity 10.11, p. 355
Middle	Activity 5.8, p. 157 Activity 6.5, p. 181 Activity 7.10, p. 212 Activity 7.19, p. 232 Activity 8.6, p. 256 Activity 9.10, p. 303 Activity 10.8, p. 353	Activity 1.3, p. 23 Activity 2.4, p. 59 Activity 5.7, p. 156 Activity 9.26, p. 322 Activity 11.13, p. 400
Secondary	Activity 1.4, p. 24 Activity 5.4, p. 152 Activity 5.9, p. 158 Activity 6.6, p. 183 Activity 7.7, p. 205 Activity 7.15, p. 221 Activity 7.22, p. 237 Activity 8.3, p. 249 Activity 8.11, p. 272 Activity 9.33, p. 306 Activity 10.7, p. 349	Activity 3.4, p. 88 Activity 7.2, p. 213 Activity 7.21, p. 235 Activity 10.2, p. 341 Activity 11.8, p. 393 Activity 11.12, p. 398 Activity 11.14, p. 401 Activity 11.16, p. 404